OXFORD DATA PROTECTION AND PRIVACY LAW

Series Editors
CHRISTOPHER KUNER
Professor of Law, VUB Brussel

GRAHAM GREENLEAF
Professor of Law and Information Systems, University of New South Wales

European Data Protection Regulation, Journalism, and Traditional Publishers

Balancing on a Tightrope?

OXFORD DATA PROTECTION AND PRIVACY LAW

Series Editors

Christopher Kuner, Professor of Law, VUB Brussel
Graham Greenleaf, Professor of Law and Information Systems,
University of New South Wales

The aim of this series is to publish important and original books on legal issues of data protection and privacy. This includes many different areas of law, including comparative law, EU law, human rights law, international law, privacy on the Internet, and others.

Prospective authors are welcome to submit proposals for the series, as outlined on the series website: global.oup.com/academic/content/series/o/ oxford-data-protection-and-privacy-law-odppl/

European Data Protection Regulation, Journalism, and Traditional Publishers

Balancing on a Tightrope?

DAVID ERDOS

University of Cambridge

OXFORD

UNIVERSITY PRESS

OXFORD

UNIVERSITY PRESS

Great Clarendon Street, Oxford, OX2 6DP,
United Kingdom

Oxford University Press is a department of the University of Oxford.
It furthers the University's objective of excellence in research, scholarship,
and education by publishing worldwide. Oxford is a registered trade mark of
Oxford University Press in the UK and in certain other countries

First Edition published in 2019

Impression: 2

Published in the United States of America by Oxford University Press
198 Madison Avenue, New York, NY 10016, United States of America

British Library Cataloguing in Publication Data
Data available

Library of Congress Control Number: 2019946506

ISBN 978–0–19–884198–2

Printed and bound by
CPI Group (UK) Ltd, Croydon, CR0 4YY

To my parents

Series Editors' Preface

Who controls our personal data has become one of the defining political, economic and philosophical questions of this century's first two decades, and will continue to be for some time to come. As all aspects of our lives, from our movements to our emotions, become subject to 'datafication', the distinctions between 'data protection' and 'privacy' diminish, and the scope of 'data privacy' expands.

The aim of the *Oxford Data Protection & Privacy Law* series is to publish significant and original contributions to scholarship on legal issues of data protection, privacy, and data privacy. As it develops, the series will include scholarly monographs, by sole or joint authors, dealing with legal issues stemming from many different areas, including comparative law, human rights, international and EU law, Internet regulation, and many other more specific subject areas. The series will develop a broad approach and will include also multidisciplinary works. It will be a series of global scope, welcoming national or regional studies from all parts of the world.

European Data Protection Regulation, Journalism, and Traditional Publishers: Balancing on a Tightrope? by Dr David Erdos of the University of Cambridge is an ideal volume to commence the series. It deals with the relationship between two issues that have a high value in democratic systems, but that often stand in tension with each other, namely freedom of speech and data protection. Globalised processing of personal data, particularly online processing, has brought both great benefits and an increase in misinformation and the misuse of personal data. However, until now, there has been a lack of detailed scholarly analyses of the relationship between the regulation of media and publishers and European data protection law.

The law concerning journalism and publishers has always grappled with sensitive issues of the balance between privacy and freedom of speech and publication, but now also has to deal with the apparently different demands of statutory data protection laws. This requires a high level of scholarship in both data protection and media law, a challenge that Erdos' book meets. While its specific focus is on Europe, and the European instruments that shape the relationship between these two areas of law, this is a topic with which each of the more than 130 countries around the world which has a data protection law must grapple, and so is of global relevance. It is also a study based on empirical information about practices in 31 European countries, complementing its analysis of the legal frameworks within which professional journalism and traditional publishers must work. We are thus pleased to publish it as the inaugural book in our series.

Christopher Kuner and Graham Greenleaf

Preface

This book had its intellectual origins during my work on an earlier Oxford University Press book, *Delegating Rights Protection* (2010), which explored the development of bills of human rights. In the process of completing that monograph I became firmly convinced that the importance of European data protection had been radically underestimated in both the empirical and normative literature, most especially as regards its role in reconciling the competing claims of individual personality rights and freedom of expression. Whilst such a view is quite widely accepted now, this was not the case even as recently as a decade ago. I would therefore very much like to thank the Leverhulme Trust for supporting my initial work here through an Early Career Fellowship (2010–2013) and also my former institutional home of the University of Oxford including, in particular, the Centre for Socio-Legal Studies, the Faculty of Law, and Balliol College. My move to the University of Cambridge in 2013 has provided me with a wonderful opportunity to develop my research further in this area. I am very appreciative of the support provided by the University including, in particular, the Centre for Intellectual Property and Information Law, the Faculty of Law, and Trinity Hall. The British Academy also provided me with a much-needed small grant in 2013 [grant number SG112737] which enabled me to carry out the Data Protection Authority (DPA) questionnaire and make a start on the DPA website review.

Given the length of time during which I have completed this project, it would be invidious to try to list all the individuals who have helped on the way. Indeed, reflecting the range of jurisdictions (and language texts) which I studied, I relied upon at least forty research assistants, often for only small amounts of work each due to budget constraints. I would, however, like to especially thank Michélè Finck, Ann Kristin Glenster, Marcus Carlsen Häggrot, Laura Hannan, and Eero Wahlstadt for particularly valuable assistance here. I have also benefited from conversations with a large number of friends and colleagues in academia and beyond. Again, most will have to remain nameless but I would like to record my particular appreciation to Jef Ausloos, Lionel Bently, Frederik Borgesius, Cristina Pauner Chulvi, Niko Härting, Artemi Rallo Lombarte, Juan Martinez Otero, Christopher Millard, Gillian Phillips, Giovanni Sartor, Olivia Tambou, and Hugh Tomlinson. I also thank all those within Europe's DPAs who gave up their time to provide a response to my questionnaire.

Oxford University Press have been tremendously supportive of this project throughout and I am particularly appreciative for the help of Natalie Patey and Emma Stone. I also acknowledge the reproduction of material, albeit in a significantly modified form, which was previously published in three articles of mine from 2016, namely, 'European Data Protection and Media Expression: Fundamentally Off Balance' which was published in International and Comparative Law Quarterly; 'European Regulatory Interpretation of the Interface between Data Protection and Traditional Journalism: An Incomplete and Imperfect Balancing Act?', which appeared in Public Law; and 'Statutory Regulation of Professional Journalism Under European Data Protection: Down But Not Out?', published in the Journal of Media Law.

Finally, and on a more personal level, I would like to thank my family for all their continuing support. My father, who spent his working life as an academic, has taken a special interest in this project and I am very grateful for this.

This book draws empirically on the statutory and regulatory experience over a number of decades of thirty-one European States, as well as the European Union, Council of Europe, and other transnational institutions. Inevitably, given such a wide-ranging study, there will be some omissions and mistakes. I, of course, remain responsible for these. Drawing on this extensive empirical survey, I also looked at how DPAs might best interpret and enforce European data protection *vis-à-vis* professional journalists and other traditional publishers, whilst also protecting these actors' vital role and rights as regards freedom of expression. The model of structured and strategic co-regulation which I developed is intended to have an immanent normative validity. This will hopefully prove particularly valuable to all those who need to navigate within the legal, resource, and other constraints of currently existing European data protection, including DPAs, media professionals, lawyers, and civil society activists. I am conscious, however, that a much more radical normative analysis of European data protection here would also have been of great value. That, however, has not been my project. Nevertheless, I am confident that, as the acknowledged significance of European data protection continues to grow, researchers will carry out these kinds of studies. Whatever perspective they develop, I hope that they will also find the groundwork laid down in this book of some assistance.

David Erdos
Cambridge
July 2019

Contents

PART II EUROPEAN DATA PROTECTION AND PROFESSIONAL JOURNALISM

PART III EUROPEAN DATA PROTECTION AND 'NON-JOURNALISTIC' TRADITIONAL PUBLISHERS

APPENDICES

Table of Cases

Note: For the benefit of digital users, indexed terms that span two pages (e.g., 52-53) may, on occasion, appear on only one of those pages.
Note: Where a chapter page number is cited in this Table, the specific citation of the relevant case may be provided for in a linked endnote. Direct references to endnotes are limited to those which include substantive discussion.

EUROPEAN COURT OF HUMAN RIGHTS

COURT OF JUSTICE OF THE EUROPEAN UNION
AND GENERAL COURT

EFTA COURT

NATIONAL

Table of Legislation

Note: Most of the national legislation cited are first-generation, second-generation and third-generation data protection statutes Full citation and sources for this legislation are set out in Appendices One, Two and Three respectively. The table below, therefore, uses a shortened title for these texts alongside a reference to Appendix One (A1), Two (A2) and Three (A3) as applicable.

Note: Where a chapter page number is cited in this Table, the specific citation of the relevant case may be provided for in a linked endnote. Direct references to endnotes are limited to those which include substantive discussion.

Note: For the benefit of digital users, indexed terms that span two pages (e.g., 52-53) may, on occasion, appear on only one of those pages.

NATIONAL

Austria

Belgium

Bulgaria

Croatia

Cyprus

Czechia

Denmark

List of Abbreviations

CJEU	Court of Justice of the European Union
CJ-PD	Committee of Experts on Data Protection
DPAs	Data Protection Authorities
DPD	Data Protection Directive
ECHR	European Convention on Human Rights
ECtHR	European Court of Human Rights
EDPB	European Data Protection Board
EEA	European Economic Area
EFTA	European Free Trade Association
EU	European Union
GDPR	General Data Protection Regulation
ICTs	Information and Communication Technologies
INSEE	National Institute for Statistics and Economic Studies (French)
SMS	Special Messaging Service
SNS	Social Networking Sites

PART I
EUROPEAN DATA PROTECTION AND FREEDOM OF EXPRESSION FOUNDATIONS

1

Introduction

'Reconciling the right to privacy and the protection of personal data with the right to information and freedom of expression in the age of the Internet is one of the main challenges of our time.'[1] This challenge is particularly acute in relation to professional journalism. Notwithstanding the growth of new online media, professional journalists remain pre-eminent in the 'systematic, independent attempt to establish the truth of events and issues that matter to society',[2] playing, on occasion, a vital role as a 'watchdog'[3] and even a 'bloodhound'[4] for the public. Beyond this, they also perform a critical function in 'distil[ling], put[ting] into context and explain[ing]'[5] such information. Indeed, such is their centrality that they have been called a 'fourth estate' operating alongside and monitoring 'the other estates in society—political, economic and social'.[6] However, alongside and strongly related to this role, professional journalists not only handle 'huge amounts'[7] of often highly intimate forms of personal data but, especially as a result of their ready ability to disseminate information to a large and indeterminate number of people, they also retain an ability to inflict grave and potentially unwarranted 'damage on an individual'.[8]

The professional journalistic media are not the only type of traditional actor whose central task involves collating, analysing, and disseminating information, opinions, and ideas to an indeterminate number on at least the purported basis that there is 'a public value and importance' to the production and circulation of this material.[9] On the contrary, academics within the humanities and social sciences are also critical 'social observers and commentators'[10] with a strong professional commitment to 'the methodological discovery and the teaching of truths about serious and important things'[11] of relevance to society. Their close connection with the professional journalistic role can also be uncanny. Thus, it has long been argued that the characterization of sociology as 'slow journalism' and journalism as 'instant society' are 'both apt'.[12] Meanwhile, the highly esteemed contemporary historian Brian Harrison has stated that

> there is no distinction in principle between the journalist and the historian: the historians simply have more time for research and reflection, though some journalists (the late Hugo Young, for example) somehow do a better job on historical topics than do some historians.[13]

European Data Protection Regulation, Journalism, and Traditional Publishers. David Erdos, Oxford University Press (2019). © David Erdos.
DOI: 10.1093/oso/9780198841982.003.0001

Professional writers who work independently of both the journalistic media and academia are also 'professional students of the social world'[14] and impart their understandings and evaluations to the general public through a wide range of outputs. Closely linked to this group are professional artists whose public work has been held to foster 'both individual originality and creativity and the free-thinking and dynamic society that we so much value'.[15] Although the community directly interested in the output produced by traditional publishers operating outside the mainstream media is sometimes 'small or specialized',[16] these other actors also generally retain a disproportionate ability to gather and also disseminate personal information which may be highly private or stigmatic. Therefore, as a group, their informational activities can pose particular risks of unwarranted harm.

Reflecting long-standing aims within European data protection going right back to the 1970s, the new European General Data Protection Regulation 2016/ 679 ('GDPR') aims to secure a 'high'[17] and 'equivalent'[18] level of protection of the 'fundamental rights and freedoms of natural persons and in particular their right to the protection of personal data'[19] when such information is processed. However, in doing so, it must 'reconcile'[20] this protection with freedom of expression. More specifically, in relation to journalism and similarly special forms of expression, Member State law must explicitly lay down the substantive limitations necessary for achieving such a reconciliation. Ensuring a balanced approach is inevitably challenging and often raises significant national sensitivities. Indeed, given their critical role within society, these challenges are especially acute in relation to professional journalists and other traditional publishers. Serious tensions have, therefore, been present here right from the origins of data protection in the 1970s. Moreover, these tensions have increased as a result of the ever-widening scope of the law and the transition to the world of ubiquitous online computing. Developing socio-technological changes including ever more powerful digital publication archives, the growth of 'data journalism', and the use of algorithms in publisher decision-making will make balancing in this area yet more challenging. Furthermore, the fact that online technology has also spawned an entirely new media composed of both amateur individuals and novel corporate actors (including Internet search engines and social networking sites) does not make this task of reconciliation any easier. Instead, as will be touched on especially in the book's conclusion, a range of critical new questions are emerging out of the interface between the new online media and traditional publishers.

The interrelationship between European data protection and the activities of traditional publishers engages not only the law itself but also regulatory Data Protection Authorities ('DPAs'). DPAs play an 'essential'[21] role as public authority 'guardians'[22] of data protection, being endowed with multi-faceted tasks[23] and powers[24] as well as duties to cooperate and ensure consistency across Europe.[25] In addition to handling individual complaints, they must uphold the protection of personal data in the public interest, thereby defending data protection as 'an issue of general and structural importance for a modern society'.[26] In exercising this regulatory control, DPAs must also recognize that '[t]he right to protection of personal data is not an absolute right . . . [but must] be balanced against other fundamental rights, in accordance with the principle of proportionality'.[27] Moreover, in relation to journalism and other special forms of expression, not just the substantive provisions but also this supervisory system should be modified and limited in order to ensure a proper balance. These limitations or derogations add further layers of complexity to data protection and have particular significance for professional journalists and other traditional publishers.

In sum, the issues which arise from data protection's relationship with professional journalism and other traditional publishers lie at the heart of the interaction between this regime and freedom of expression, an interaction which is assuming a heightened salience in today's online environment. Therefore, without seeking to discount the importance of also addressing the role of new actors, this book focuses on the arguably prior question of how European data protection regulation both has, and should, interact with the activities of traditional publishers.

1. Aims, Scope, and Methodology

1.1 Aims

In broad terms, the aims of this monograph are twofold. First, it seeks to develop a systematic empirical map and explanation of both the historic and contemporary interaction between European data protection regulation and public expressive activity carried out by professional journalists and other traditional publishers. This required an analysis of several overlapping aspects including statutory and other legal provisions, regulatory standard-setting and regulatory enforcement, as well as both commonalities and contrasts across time, jurisdictional space, and the type of traditional publisher involved. It especially focuses on building up a picture of the regulatory status quo in the period immediately preceding the adoption of GDPR, as well as the statutory law that implements this new framework. This focus links to the book's second aim, which is to explore how regulation might best evolve in the GDPR era. In this regard, what is developed is an immanent rather than a radical critique. In other words, the analysis takes as given the core purposes of the European data protection, the legal and regulatory structure of the GDPR, and even the broad resource constraints faced by the regulators. Such a bounded analysis aims to make the book's conclusions in this regard of direct relevance to critical stakeholders including DPAs themselves, national legislators, traditional publishers, and individual data subject representatives.

1.2 Scope

Before turning to look at this study's methodology, it is important to delineate further the book's intended scope through an analysis of some of its key terms. In the first place, the limitation of this book to European matters requires specification. At its broadest conceptualization, Europe may be taken to refer to any State lying (even if only partially) within the western projection of the Eurasian landmass.[28] Slightly more narrowly, reference may be made to those jurisdictions that have become part of the Council of Europe, a loose intergovernmental body that, since its establishment in 1949, has been open to all European states who commit to human rights and the rule of law.[29] All European States other than Belarus have now joined this group.[30] However, increasingly, it has been the narrower groupings of the European Union ('EU') and the European Economic Area ('EEA') which have become the focus for 'European' legal and policy development.

The EU, which traces its origins back to the European Economic Community in 1957, has from the outset had a highly supranational character with a central executive agency in the form of the European Commission, a common Court of Justice, and a defined legislative role for a shared parliamentary body (originally the Parliamentary Assembly and now the European Parliament). Although initially largely focused on economic cooperation, its activities have increasingly involved a much wider range of social and political concerns. This considerably broader remit was formalized in 1993 when it also acquired its current name.

Also in the 1990s, the EU together with three States within the looser European Free Trade Association ('EFTA') established the EEA. As its name suggests, the EEA has remained more focused on economic matters and its decision-making continues to be largely inter-governmental. Nevertheless, the enforcement and implementation of the EEA is principally supranational, with the EFTA affiliates being subject to the EFTA Surveillance Authority in place of the European Commission and the EFTA Court in lieu of the Court of Justice of the EU ('CJEU'). Turning specifically to data protection, although the Council of Europe was the central transnational player in this area until the early 1990s, the EU and the broader EEA have clearly become predominant here from this time. Therefore, whilst also looking at transnational Council of Europe developments up until the 1990s, this book focuses on the EU/EEA and the States that now comprise it (including the United Kingdom and its dependent territory of Gibraltar which, notwithstanding the 2016 'Brexit' referendum and its aftermath, remain members of both the EU and EEA as of May 2019).

By data protection, this book refers to a legal framework which seeks to establish an essentially comprehensive safeguarding of the rights (and fundamental interests) of individual natural persons over the manipulation or use of data (or information) relating to them. These frameworks have some relationship with more long-standing aspects of personality law including, most notably, defamation law and laws protecting aspects of intimate privacy. However, data protection itself only emerged from the 1970s onwards, consequent to the growth of computerization and online technology. Not least because of its particularly comprehensive nature, this framework raises distinct questions and challenges. Therefore, without ignoring its relationship to other parts of personality law, this book firmly focuses on this new framework that, at least in the particular area under analysis, has been rather neglected in the literature to date.[31]

The predominantly regulatory nature of data protection constitutes another important and distinctive aspect of this framework. The world's first data protection law, the Swedish Data Act 1973, 'emphasised the existence of an independent control authority as a most useful, if not indispensable, condition to ensure compliance with data protection rules'.[32] Moreover, even during the first period or generation of data protection it was found that 'practically all laws have instituted an independent authority which supervises compliance'.[33] Under the EU's Data Protection Directive 95/46 ('DPD') which was finalized in 1995 these DPAs were recognized as an 'essential component'[34] of this regime, a pivotal position which has been given further emphasis in practice, in case law, and now in the GDPR. Indeed, it has been pithily stated that '[t]he credo is that without the agency, there is no data protection'.[35] In light of their centrality, this book focuses on both the legal framework governing and the work of these regulatory agencies (or, in a few cases, other specialist bodies that have been specifically allocated their tasks in the area of journalism and other types of special expression). Rather than referring to all forms of legal standard-setting and enforcement, the reference to regulation should be understood in this narrower sense. Adopting such a restricted regulatory focus also renders achievable the book's systematic empirical approach, involving as it does a truly comprehensive multi-jurisdictional analysis both in relation to standards and enforcement. Due to the fragmented and diverse nature of the justice system across Europe, this would hardly have been practicable if attempted outside this supervisory setting. Nevertheless, private civil action has sat alongside regulation within data protection for many decades. Indeed, from the time of the DPD, it has become mandatory for all European jurisdictions to provide individuals with a civil remedy in relation to any breach of their data protection rights, as well as a civil right of compensation arising from any damage suffered.[36] Notwithstanding the dominance of regulatory agencies within this space, these broader aspects should therefore be kept in mind.

Turning to the other side of the equation, Schudson defines journalism as 'the business or practice of producing and disseminating information on contemporary affairs of general public interest and importance',[37] whilst Harcup (quoting Denis McQuail) conceptualizes it as 'paid writing (and the audio-visual equivalent) for public media with reference to actual and ongoing events of public relevance'.[38] Like any definition of a complex phenomenon, both phraseologies raise many questions requiring further analysis. First, the references to 'general public interest and importance' or 'public relevance' must be explicated. In most theories of 'good' journalism, these notions would be objectively defined, and published output that did not meet the relevant standards would then fail to constitute journalism in a full sense. However, such a narrow approach would ill-suit an empirically based study such as this. At the same time, that those pursuing this activity 'assume that there is a public value and importance in circulating [the relevant] facts and views'[39] remains critical to the core concept of journalism. For the purpose of data gathering, consideration of whether such an orientation does exist is approached subjectively. This ensures that both 'quality' and 'tabloid' forms of journalism can clearly fall within this rubric.[40] Second, it is almost trite to note in today's online context that 'anyone with access to the internet can engage in journalism at no cost'.[41] Traditionally, however, individuals had to ensure a (generally paid) connection with an entity who pursued journalism as a business.[42] More importantly, these businesses retain a privileged 'access to mass audiences' [43] and, through this, a disproportionate ability to cause certain types of informational harm. Moreover, although amateur individuals have become important co-creators of public 'opinion',[44] professionals retain their central position as the primary producers of new information, as well distilled understanding and detailed analysis for the public. It, therefore, remains important to consider how such professional journalistic activity both has been and should be regulated. Such is the focus of this book. It, therefore, does not directly explore the activities of amateur online users disseminating information to an indefinite number of people (some, but not all, of which will be for 'journalistic purposes') or the platforms and other 'new' services which also function within this broader field. For the same reason, it also excludes consideration of the journalistic media's own facilitation and structuring of this kind of activity through online comment sections, discussions forums, or similar services.[45] Nevertheless, it does encompass the growing number of individuals and groups who have moved to pursue the business occupation of journalism within an entirely online context or indeed who, like Buzzfeed or HuffPost, have been a 'digital native',[46] in it from the start. In any case, this delimitation should not be read as suggesting that a regulatory analysis of the position of amateur individuals and other truly 'new' media actors is not of high and increasing importance. Indeed, it is intended to address this more complex terrain systematically in a subsequent work, after the more historically foundational position of professional journalists and other traditional publishers has been considered. In deploying the term 'professional', it is recognized both that journalism has generally been conceived as 'a trade, or a craft, rather than a "proper" profession along the lines of medicine or the law'[47] and that many engaged in this trade or craft also conceptualize it as a 'vocation'.[48] Therefore, the reference to 'professional' here should simply be read as designating entities engaged in journalism as a business or individuals whose livelihood depend significantly on income from journalistic activity.

A final issue related to the definition of journalism arises out of the references earlier to 'contemporary affairs' and 'actual and ongoing events'. This helpfully highlights the close connection between journalism and the production and dissemination of 'news'. At the same time, it is important to recognize that journalistic organizations and now even freelance journalists also perform an important 'role in maintaining and making available to the public archives containing news which has previously been reported'.[49] This archiving is not only carried out by these journalistic actors but is also fully constituted by material that was originally journalistic and indeed was produced by professional journalists. Moreover, as will be seen, the performance of this archiving role or activity has constituted a primary site of interface between the professional journalistic media and data protection over many decades. For all these reasons, this book considers the interface between data protection and journalistic archiving alongside its relationship with the creation and dissemination of journalistic news. A related but separate issue is that even the initial published output of manifestly journalistic organizations and individuals does not always fall clearly within the concept of news. Examples of output which may well fall outside this include historical programming and other investigative reports on wide-ranging or novel issues. Thus, writing on 'investigative journalism', de Burgh argues that:

> The news journalist makes his or her selection from a range of conventionally accepted sources of information, sources which are in effect the providers of the 'news agenda' and whose regular production of information is diarised; selection from them is made according to these and other criteria of 'newsworthiness' . . . Investigative stories are different in that they may not be on the same agenda. They involve a subject that the journalists has to insist is something we should know about, in effect, by saying 'look at this, isn't it shocking!': the basis of the insistence is a moral one.[50]

'Investigative journalism' is widely recognized as critically important to society and a core part of journalistic work. Its relationship to data protection can also be particularly tricky. In any case, it would be difficult to demarcate clearly the boundary between the production by professional journalists of 'news' output and wider forms of material which seek to contribute to collective public debate. Therefore, as long as it retains this 'public' nature, this latter type of activity will also be considered within the section of the book focusing on the interface between data protection and professional journalism.

That even professional journalists produce a wide range of output which is not obviously 'news' naturally segues to a recognition that a variety of more clearly 'non-journalistic'[51] professional actors have also long created and disseminated material for the benefit of the collective public, even if sometimes the community directly interested in such output has remained 'small or specialized'.[52]

As with journalism, all references to 'professional' here should be understood in the wide sense as those pursuing such activity as part of their business or live-lihood (as well as, very often, as a vocation) rather than in terms of a specially licensed cadre or grouping. Thus, professional artists play a central (although clearly not unique) role in fostering 'a creative approach to the complexity of the world',[53] often seeking through their public work to ask 'difficult questions' of society which 'when successful, advances the entire civilization's ability to see'.[54] Thus, Becker further argues that

> [i]n their role as spokespersons for multiple points of view, for critics of society, in their refusal to become specialists, bought off by any one body of knowledge, artists may be understood as public intellectuals—those who believe and take ser-iously the importance of the public sphere and who put out . . . work which they expect the world to respond.[55]

Such work may take a variety of forms including visual, audible, plastic, and mixed; moreover, and increasingly, it may not only be produced with the aid of electronic technology but the ultimate product may exist as an entirely electronic (and often online) phenomenon.

Meanwhile, many professional writers publish work on political, social, economic, and similar issues that is also orientated towards a general public. Traditionally such work took the form of books and articles, but publication has in-creasingly occurred in a variety of exclusively online formats such as blogging and even micro-blogging. In this vein, Cole argues that

> [t]he digital revolution is undermining many publication practices that have been taken for granted for two centuries. Newspapers as we know them may not survive, and many are closing, raising questions about the future of professional journalism. The academic journal article as a preserve of specialists, published in small print runs and thereafter more or less hidden away in research libraries and accessible only to other specialists is a form of expensive elitism that society may increasingly be unwilling to support. Academics have created valuable tech-niques aimed at preserving the integrity and, as a far as is possible, the objectivity of their writing. But in this new world, where barriers between the ivory tower and the public are being eroded by the internet, and where, it turns out, the public is sometimes deeply interested in the result of our researches, historians have to ask themselves if they want always to leave the popularization of their findings to journalists, generalists and (sometimes) mere rhetoricians . . . Just as a creative writer[56] might compose poetry, short stories, literary fiction and perhaps a lighter 'entertainment' (Graham Greene's term) such as a thriller, so academics produc-ing works read online may sometimes blog and sometimes write monographs.

Each kind of writing is validated in different ways, and each has its own kind of value as truth-telling.[57]

Cole's quotation highlights that one important and discrete kind of professional writer is the academic working within the humanities and social studies. As Cole hints in this extract, academic writing may be defined by its general focus on contributing to the systematic production of knowledge about what are seen as 'serious and important things'.[58] Thus, Shills argues that '[t]he academic profession receives, assimilates and discovers knowledge by methodical study, and it interprets and transmits that knowledge; it transmits knowledge about the methods of discovery and especially of the validation of knowledge'.[59]

This helpfully links the concept to related terms such as scholarship and discipline. However, it must be recognized that the extent to which a writer prioritizes methodological system over other *desiderata* such as timeliness and persuasive power is often only a matter of degree. Moreover, as Cole also suggests, academics will sometimes legitimately prioritize these other criteria in their output. Indeed, a growing emphasis on ensuring that academic work leads to a wider 'impact'[60] outside the scholarly community itself has seen the proportion of such output increase. In any case, a focus on systematic methods probably fits better with empirical knowledge production as opposed to academic work that emphasizes normative evaluation and critique. A second approach to the definition of academic writers looks at whether the relevant individuals produce their work within the context of their membership of an institution of higher learning such as a university. Such an unabashedly institutional approach can often lead to easier demarcation and is, therefore, often used as at least a presumptive starting point in practical situations. However, even here, there are clearly ambiguities. Thus, some institutions such as certain think tanks sit uneasily between prioritizing the advancement of learning and engaging in (sometimes partisan) campaigning. Moreover, even when an individual is attached to a manifestly academic institution, it may be unclear when their work is produced within this context and when it is entirely extramural. Indeed, such 'grey zones' are increasingly common in the context of blogging, micro-blogging, and other online activity.

Even more so than professional artists, professional writers have a particularly close connection with professional journalism. First, as Brock, notes, newspapers were historically merely an 'appendage' to general publishing and '[v]ery early newspapers often took the form of books; news wasn't yet disposable and was an improvised mixture of history and almanac'.[61] Second, professional writers and journalists often grapple with the same substantive societal issues in their work, such that they have even been described as engaged in 'the same enterprise'.[62] In light of the generally much greater emphasis on contemporaneity in much of professional journalism as opposed to other professional writing, that description may have within it a degree of exaggeration. Nevertheless, the strong common-alities should not be discounted. Indeed, in this context, it is notable that early thinking about the role which liberty in discourse could play in the fostering of 'civil wisdom'[63] was originally focused on a defence of the unlicensed production of books and only later morphed into a support for the work of news journalism. Finally, and relatedly, particular individuals often engage in a combination of pro-fessional journalism and both academic and non-academic writing. In this context, they may pose the same basic questions and deploy the same 'research' methodolo-gies. Focusing on undercover investigation or covert research (a particular focus of this book), Dingwall notes that

> [j]ournalists like Barbara Ehrenreich (2001; 2005) and Polly Toynbee (2003) en-gage in it, write books that sell large numbers and generate great public excite-ment about the findings. Ehrenreich's recent books, Nickel and Dimed and Bait and Switch, both made the New York Times Bestsellers list.[64]

Even though the nature of their work is undoubtedly shifting as a result of the rise of computers, professional journalists, artists, and both academic and non-academic writers have all existed as social actors since long before the digital revolution. As a group, they may therefore usefully be described as traditional publishers, thus distinguishing them from those individual and corporate actors involved in indeterminate publication that have only emerged with the rise of on-line computing. The book's focus on traditional publishers outside journalism is, in broad terms, justified on the same basis as its emphasis on professional journalism. In sum, albeit to a much lesser extent than journalistic businesses, other traditional publishers still generally possess disproportionate informational power, including power to cause harm. Even more importantly, whilst no longer occupying essen-tially monopolistic positions, these actors continue to play a dominant role in the production and dissemination of critically important 'information, opinions and ideas'[65] for the collective public realm.

Finally, it should be stressed that this book only explores the interrelationship between European data protection regulation and these traditional publishers' public expressive activity or, in other words, their production and dissemination of material that is assumed to have 'a public value and importance'.[66] As data pro-tection regulators have themselves stressed within the journalistic context, this core freedom of expression activity should be distinguished from processing of personal data which is only tangentially linked to this including the 'processing of subscribers data for billing purposes or processing for Direct Marketing pur-poses (including processing of data on media use for profiling purposes)'.[67] Although the regulation of the latter sort of processing may increasingly raise particular issues for traditional publishers, these are best analysed in discretely focused work.

1.3 Study Sources and Methods

As emphasized at the start of this section, this book has both an empirical and a normative aspect to it. Moreover, given its bounded as opposed to radical or transcendental goal, its normative analysis remains strongly linked to the empirical. As a result, both historic and more contemporary empirical analysis lies at the very heart of the study and has necessarily been particularly wide-ranging. To begin with, all the core data protection instruments agreed at either pan-European or State level have been analysed right from the time of the drafting of the first laws in the 1970s through to the laws implementing the GDPR in the late 2010s. In most cases, authoritative English translations of these laws were used, generally as produced by the national DPAs or, in the early period, through the Council of Europe. However, where these were not available or where potential problems were identified, original language versions were consulted. (All the individual EEA State legislative data protection sources which were used are specified in the first three appendices included at the end of this book.)

Alongside these texts, a wide variety of satellite material was explored including the scholarly literature on data protection, official reports, EU legislative *traveaux preparatories*, and records of parliamentary proceedings at national level. Turning to the more directly regulatory dimensions, for the period prior to the EU becoming directly involved through the DPD, an analysis was made of the annual reports of every national DPA operating in a European country that had enacted data protection law prior to 1990.[68] Through this, a systematic picture was built up of early efforts at both regulatory standard-setting and enforcement.

Meanwhile, turning to the DPD era, a centrepiece of the book's empirics was a comprehensive survey of DPAs. This was composed of both questionnaire and website review elements. First, a questionnaire was sent to national and sub-national EEA DPAs in 2013 asking general and specific questions related to both standard-setting and enforcement.[69] Responses were forthcoming from the great majority (around twenty-five authorities, or over 75 per cent) of national DPAs, as well as some six sub-national bodies. Second, a review was carried out in the same year of the websites of all the national EEA DPAs as well as the six sub-national regulators that responded to the questionnaire. This review, which involved the use of language experts, looked for any relevant information related to standard-setting and enforcement that was readily available through this online medium. The study also analysed the records of those bodies that have performed a regulatory or quasi-regulatory function at pan-European level. In the early pre-DPD period, this included the International Conference of Data Protection Commissioners (which, although officially global, was in reality dominated by European regulators until the 1990s) and the Council of Europe's Committee of Experts on Data Protection (which, although officially inter-governmental, often comprised DPA representatives and, in any case, issued a number of quasi-regulatory recommendations and reports especially during the 1980s). Meanwhile, during the DPD era, the focus of attention shifted to Article 29 Data Protection Working Party, an advisory but influential body established under that instrument and composed of national DPA representatives from across the EEA.[70] Finally, the study also drew upon certain allied datasets that brought together related comparative material. This included population statistics and data exploring divergences in cultural values between different European jurisdictions. Of most significance here, was the dataset of self-regulatory codes of journalistic ethics for each European country compiled by the EthicNet project.[71]

In exploring these sources, a mixed methods approach was adopted. In many cases, the analysis remained qualitative, thus drawing on an empirical tradition that has a rich history within legal and socio-legal studies. However, where feasible, this was combined with a quantitative coding, a process that enabled a representational mapping of data (e.g. in charts and tables) and also simple correlations and other statistical tests to be carried out.

Finally, the study's normative strand has sought to craft an approach to the regulatory implementation of the GDPR in this area. The perspective developed remains fundamentally immanent. It, therefore, takes as its starting point the basic scope and definition of European data protection, its core aims (alongside the aims of European fundamental rights law more generally), and even the basic resource and other constraints faced by regulators. As an essentially grounded analysis, it has drawn extensively on the book's empirics including its analysis of past efforts at regulatory standard-setting and enforcement and its elucidation of the GDPR and the new national laws implementing this framework. At the same time, it also required the study of a wider range of sources including literature on regulation in general, that specific to professional journalism and academic research, and additionally case law from both the CJEU and the European Court of Human Rights. Whilst some of the latter aspects are explored in the first foundational part of the book, much of this material is introduced in the later chapters that specifically seek to develop a normative argument.

2. The Book's Core Empirical and Normative Findings

The book's empirical exploration has focused on the three sequential dimensions of the formal law, regulatory standard-setting, and regulatory enforcement. Since the GDPR only came into force in mid-2018 (and, as of May 2019, has still not implemented in a few States), the empirical analysis of regulation under this instrument is limited to the first dimension. In contrast, the analysis of both pre-DPD (first-generation) and DPD (second-generation) eras cover all three dimensions.

Turing to look at the formal law, it is found that right from the origin of European data protection, outcomes have been highly divergent and apparently inconsistent.

Historically, the law has appeared to conceptualize academic work as falling only with the restrictive default provisions set down for medical, scientific, and related forms of research. These actors have therefore been subject to far-reaching restrictions which have severely limited their ability to gather personal data (especially if a resort to non-transparent or covert methodology has proved necessary), to process data free from full regulatory oversight, and to publish personal information in identified or even identifiable form. Meanwhile, the needs of non-academic writers and artists have often been entirely ignored, especially in data protection's early period. Nevertheless, the DPD did mandate that special freedom of expression derogations covering 'artistic and literary expression'[72] were set out at national level, an instruction that the majority of States followed. The GDPR has now further expanded the concept of special expression to encompass 'academic' expression too,[73] and almost all States have now adopted derogations which in principle extend to all of this area. Therefore, notwithstanding continuing problems of implementation as regards the interface with default provisions governing scientific and related research,[74] a real change is apparent here.

In the historically 'core' area of freedom of expression, namely professional journalism, pan-European instruments have over many decades expected States law to ensure sensitive balancing between the competing rights of data protection and freedom of expression, a balancing which is ultimately grounded in a contextual public interest analysis that pays close attention to the specific circumstances and needs of this special activity.[75] However, outcomes at national level have been strongly divergent and sometimes clearly at odds with this approach of contextually balancing rights. In sum, whilst some States have long enacted very wide-ranging or even absolute exemptions here, others set out only strongly circumscribed or even no formal limitations in their law at all. Moreover, since at least the late 1990s, a broad pattern has emerged of Northern European States generally adopting a relatively liberal statutory approach and Southern and Eastern European State law continuing to focus on the need to safeguard data strictly, even within this highly sensitive area. These patterns, in turn, appear to reflect deeper cultural divergences in these societies' valuations of individualism, the need to avoid uncertainty, and the acceptance of power inequalities. Whilst such patterns remain clearly discernible in the era of the GDPR, there are some signs of a degree of convergence. Thus, almost all States now set out far-reaching, but still qualified, derogations here. Almost half have also established partial statutory limits on the regulatory powers of the DPA.

Turning to look directly at the DPAs, it is clear that these regulators have been influenced by the State-level legal outcomes (and, most likely, also the related broader cultural differences) outlined earlier. At the same time, their standard-setting efforts have also been marked by some important commonalities. In the first place, the majority have, either implicitly or even explicitly, endorsed the notion that academics should comply with the default medical, scientific, and other research provisions. Meanwhile, almost all these regulators have simply refused to specify the standards applicable to non-academic writers and artists. Finally, in the critical area of professional journalism, DPAs have increasingly sought to develop an approach that is much more obviously grounded in contextually balancing rights than the statutory law of many of the individual States would suggest. Nevertheless, published guidance has not only been relatively sparse but it is clear that regulators have struggled to develop a consistent and specified criterion of strictness as regards applicable standards. Thus, the DPA questionnaire demonstrated that these authorities have generally adopted a relatively permissive understanding of the legitimacy of undercover journalism. Indeed, over a third only required that this activity conform to a permissive public interest test that didn't explicitly incorporate a necessity threshold. In contrast, a much stricter approach was taken to the articular of standards relating to the right of individual data subjects to demand access to information related to them, with over one third arguing that this right should apply in full to journalistic data (apart from information on sources which would be safeguarded from disclosure). These differences appeared linked to the divergent treatment of these two issues within media ethics codes. In sum, whilst practically all these codes established 'self-regulatory' norms that were generally applicable to undercover journalism, almost none did so as regards the data subject access right.

Turning to the final empirical dimension of regulatory enforcement, DPAs have not surprisingly almost entirely avoided engagement with the activity of non-academic writers and artists. In contrast, enforcement action relating to academics was fairly extensive in the early period of data protection and the DPA questionnaire suggested that approximately 40 per cent of regulators also took action against social scientists under the DPD. However, published examples of action in this later period remained sparse and, furthermore, these efforts appeared increasingly focused on areas of special sensitivity such as the use of confidential data obtained by academics on safeguarded terms. Enforcement in the area of professional journalism appears to have been patchy. In the early period, some regulators intervened forcefully especially in the area of media archiving whilst others (even if operating under laws which set out no or only very limited derogations for the media) appear to have engaged in little or no activity at all. Under the DPD, the results from the DPA questionnaire indicated that over 60 per cent of authorities had undertaken some enforcement action here. However, it was also clear that over half of these DPAs had only intervened in relation to one or two generally quite diffuse areas of data protection law. The DPA website review verified enforcement in relation to 40 per cent of the DPAs and confirmed that activity had usually focused on data linked either to specific privacy interests (especially where data designed as legally sensitive was involved) and/or data whose safeguarded treatment underpinned critical socio-economic relationships (e.g. national identification numbers). In general, action had been quite limited, with a notable absence of intervention even in relation to issues, such as avoiding or rectifying significant inaccuracies, which raise only limited free speech concerns. It was also clear that both the gross and per capita resources available to DPAs were extremely limited. Indeed, in 2013 national DPAs had an average gross budget of €4.2m and median per capita budget of €0.30. Moreover, data from 2017 highlighted that these resource constraints would not be markedly different in at least the early days of the GDPR. Nevertheless, the outcomes observed were not fully explicable by this resource limitation or indeed the statutory law (which remained quite stringent in many cases), the need for contextually balancing rights or the recognition of an interface with self-regulatory norms and structures.

Looking finally at the normative aspects of this work, it is argued that a focus on contextually balancing rights does have considerable appeal and promise. DPAs must therefore ensure that it is applied not only to professional journalism and media archiving but also to other traditional publishers, namely, professional artists, non-academic writers, and also academic scholars. Moreover, it is important that this paradigm is specified and developed effectively. Given both the sensitivities of the subject matter and the resource constraints of the DPAs, this should be achieved as far as possible through robust and strategic co-regulation. The GDPR's new code of conduct and monitoring body provisions[76] should be adopted as a broad guideline here. In cases where it proves possible to establish a code and body which verifiably meets the accredited criteria then DPAs should adopt a stance of strong deference, intervening directly only as regards systemic and/or particularly serious issues. Even in cases where co-regulation does not (or even cannot) meet such criteria, an interface between statutory and self-regulation should still be encouraged. Nevertheless, in those circumstances, DPAs will need to engage directly in a systematic fashion across the entire area of standard-setting and enforcement. Finally, where there is an absence of credible co-regulatory codes and bodies, then these supervisory authorities will need to take responsibility for independently and proportionately addressing all issues and complaints.

The policy implementation perspective laid out here is undoubtedly challenging, not least for DPAs themselves. It also involves clear trade-offs and compromises within what is a complex and (especially as regards the resource constraints) imperfect environment. Nevertheless, its key virtue is that it puts in place an incentive structure for ensuring that a genuine balance between data protection and special forms of expression is achieved in practice. Such a reconciliation has been the formal goal of European data protection and regulators over many decades. Therefore, DPAs should embrace this robust and strategic co-regulatory approach as the best means for securing this in reality.

3. The Plan of the Book

This book comprises thirteen chapters that are grouped into four overarching parts. Both this and the following two chapters set out relevant background. Chapter 2 explores the development of European human rights and freedom of expression law, whilst Chapter 3 introduces the rather more technical and less understood area of European data protection regulation.

Following this foundational part, the subsequent and largest part of the book explores the past, present, and future relationship between European data protection regulation and professional journalism. Chapter 4 begins by exploring the nature of this relationship in the pre-DPD era, at both European and national level. The next three chapters then provide a comprehensive analysis of the development of this interaction during the time of the DPD. Chapter 5 examines the formal law and published regulatory guidance adopted at both EU and national level, Chapter 6 delves more deeply into regulatory standard-setting, and Chapter 7 explores regulatory enforcement. The final two chapters of this second part explore this interface in the GDPR era, with Chapter 8 setting out an empirical analysis of the formal law and Chapter 9 looking normatively at the future of statutory regulation in this area.

Part III then turns to consider the even less-explored issue of how European data protection regulation both has and should relate to the activity of other traditional publishers. Chapters 10 and 11 analyse this issue empirically in relation to both the pre-DPD and the DPD era, focusing respectively on traditional publishers within a non-academic and then an academic setting. Chapter 12 turns to the era of the GDPR, providing an empirical analysis of relevant formal law and considering normatively how European data protection regulation should develop in these areas.

Alongside appendices that collate some of the rich comparative empirical data gathered in this study, the last part of this book consists of a single concluding chapter. Chapter 13 looks at the significance of the book within a dynamic and challenging online media context. It is contended that, notwithstanding the development of both individual and corporate new media, traditional publishers not only often retain disproportionate information power but, more importantly, continue to play a vital role in generating and disseminating information and ideas of collective public interest. Their appropriate and effective regulation, therefore, remains a critical societal issue in and of itself. Beyond this, it is argued that the book's focus on contextual rights balancing, co-regulation, and strategic enforcement may also help address the complex challenges that European data protection regulation faces as regards the new online media. This issue will be further investigated in future work. In the interim, these challenges serve to highlight the continuing and profound interaction between European data protection regulation and the exercise of freedom of expression and, as a result, the importance of subjecting this to close scrutiny.

2

The Development of European Human Rights and Freedom of Expression Law

Freedom of expression, along with a range of other (civil and political) human rights, has deep philosophical and jurisprudential roots within the European liberal democratic tradition. In the immediate post-Second World War period, these rights found a place within the Council of Europe's European Convention on Human Rights ('ECHR') as well as almost all the national constitutions of the European democracies. Nevertheless, it was not until the 1970s that legal interpretation and enforcement of these rights gathered pace at both national and pan-European level. Since this time, the European Court of Human Rights ('ECtHR') in particular has built up a consolidated freedom of expression case law. This jurisprudence has prioritized the protection of information, opinion, and ideas linked to matters of public interest and (to a somewhat lesser extent) artistic expression. The Court of Justice of the European Union ('CJEU') and later the European Free Trade Association ('EFTA') Court have also recognized freedom of expression as a general principle of law and in the 2000s this right was granted a defined status within the new EU Charter of Fundamental Rights. Turning to the legislative dimension, in many European countries it has not been considered necessary to codify comprehensively the parameters within which core instances of freedom of expression such as journalism may be exercised. An exception to this has been expression in the broadcasting/audio-visual media which, partly as a result, has also been subject to wide-ranging secondary EU/ EEA legislation.

This chapter explores the expansion and nature of freedom of expression law in Europe, within the broader context of the growth of civil and political human rights law more generally. Section 1 provides an admittedly truncated summary of the broad trends. Section 2 drills down into the freedom of expression case law of the ECtHR and, to a lesser extent, also that of the CJEU and EFTA Court. Section 3 then considers codification in the area of freedom of expression. Section 4 draws some conclusions.

European Data Protection Regulation, Journalism, and Traditional Publishers. David Erdos, Oxford University Press (2019). © David Erdos.
DOI: 10.1093/oso/9780198841982.003.0002

1. The General Development of European Freedom of Expression and (Civil and Political) Human Rights Law

1.1 Origins and Post-Second World War Formal Consolidation

The idea that each individual is endowed with clearly defined and inalienable civil and political rights first coalesced in Europe during the seventeenth and eighteenth centuries. Thinkers such as Milton (1644)[1] and Voltaire (1734)[2] emphasized the central importance of public freedom of expression to the liberal public realm which the emerging European Enlightenment was trying to create. Starting with the Swedish Freedom of the Press Act (1766) and the French Declaration of the Rights of Man and the Citizen (1789), these rights began to be explicitly promulgated in the constitutional texts of not only the European States which experienced a liberal revolution but also those which were subject to more indirect Enlightenment influence.[3]

Turning to the twentieth century, the traumas of the Second World War and the onset of the Cold War prompted European States operating within the liberal democratic tradition to formalize further their commitment to 'classical' civil and political rights. As a result, by the end of the 1950s, all the European democracies aside from the United Kingdom safeguarded freedom of expression in some manner within their national constitutional instruments.[4] (The UK's exceptional position arose from a general aversion to 'those declarations or definitions or rights so dear to foreign constitutionalists'[5] rather than a lack of commitment to freedom of expression itself.) Meanwhile, the ECHR, which opened for signature in 1950 as the Council of Europe's first and pre-eminent substantive treaty, also protected freedom of expression alongside a range of other classic civil and political rights.[6]

1.2 Limitations on Legal Enforcement prior to the 1970s

Despite this, up until at least the 1970s, a range of both general and specific factors often severely limited the extent to which freedom of expression protections could be legally enforced. In the first place, national constitutional frameworks were often interpreted as excluding a judicial role in the upholding of rights guarantees when confronted with contrary legislative pronouncement. This was, for example, the case in France, Denmark, and the Netherlands. Meanwhile, at the transnational level, not all Council of Europe States ratified the European Convention and, even amongst those that did, the system of individual petition and jurisdiction of the ECtHR which later became so influential remained entirely optional and was often unavailable.[7] Turning more specifically to freedom of expression, many national constitutional provisions focused narrowly on prohibiting or restricting the use of licensing or other forms of prior restraint rather than substantively controlling the limitations on expression which could be imposed *ex post*. On the other hand, Article 10(1) of the European Convention set out much broader freedom of expression protections which encompassed the right of '[e]veryone . . . to hold opinions and to receive and impart information and ideas without interference and regardless of frontiers'.[8] However, similar to most of the national constitutions which adopted a broader approach,[9] this right was heavily qualified. In particular, Article 10(2) stated:

> The exercise of these freedoms, since it carries within it duties and responsibilities, may be subject to such formalities, conditions, restrictions or penalties as are prescribed by law and are necessary in a democratic society, in the interests of national security, territorial integrity or public safety, for the protection of disorder or crime, for the protection of health or morals, for the protection of the reputation or rights of others, for preventing the disclosure of information received in confidence, or for maintaining the authority and impartiality of the judiciary.

Article 10(1) itself also stated that it did 'not prevent States from requiring the licensing of broadcasting, television or cinema enterprises', a peculiar treatment of the broadcasting and audio-visual media sector which will be returned to later in this chapter.

1.3 Development of Legal Protection from the 1970s Onwards

The 1970s onwards resulted in a strong shift towards juridical protection of freedom of expression and other classical civil and political rights, promoted principally by new interpretations of existing texts. As Bates states, the development of the jurisprudence of the ECtHR lay at the heart of these developments:

> We may say today, with the wisdom of hindsight of course, that the years 1973–1974, were *the* turning point in the life of the Convention over its first half century. This is evident from the track record of the Court. As noted, it had delivered just a handful of judgments before 1974, but in the latter half of the 1970s things changed dramatically. The years 1975 and 1979 stand out particularly. The [then] part-time Strasbourg judges found violations of the Convention in a succession of high profile cases, with the judgments of this era becoming veritable landmarks in the law of the ECHR.[10]

Departing from its earlier jurisprudence,[11] the CJEU also articulated the idea that such 'fundamental rights form[ed] an integral part of the general principles of law' which its case law would uphold. These general principles drew inspiration from the 'constitutional traditions common to the Member States' and 'international treaties for the protection of human rights on which the Member States have collaborated or of which they are signatories' including, most especially, the European Convention itself.[12] In many individual States[13] there was a similar trend towards the judiciary interpreting and enforcing rights provisions found both in national constitutional texts and in the Convention. With the establishment of the EEA in the 1990s, the EFTA Court similarly embraced the concept of fundamental rights being part of the general principles of its law, drawing inspiration in this regard directly from the CJEU.[14]

These interpretive developments dovetailed with (usually slightly later) formal changes. Southern and then Eastern and Central European States transitioning to democracy between the 1970s and 1990s generally adopted bills of rights with strong constitutional status and broad protections for freedom of expression. Meanwhile, established democracies also adopted legal provisions which enhanced the standing of those rights found in the European Convention.[15] Reform of the Convention system itself in the 1990s finally made the system of individual petition and jurisdiction of the ECtHR compulsory.[16]

Turning to the EU, building on the explicit recognition of fundamental rights as general principles of law in the Maastricht Treaty on European Union (1992),[17] in 2000 the EU promulgated a Charter of Fundamental Rights which included an article protecting both freedom of expression and its sub-right freedom of information.[18] Largely corresponding to Article 10(1) of the European Convention, Article 11 of the Charter deleted explicit mention of the permissibility of licensing the broadcasting/audio-visual media and further stated that '[t]he freedom and pluralism of the media shall be respected'.[19] A separate article also provided that '[t]he arts and scientific research shall be free of constraint' and that '[a]cademic freedom shall be respected'.[20]

A very wide range of other civil, political, social, and economic rights was also articulated within this instrument. Although the EU Charter was originally merely declaratory, it was granted the same legal status as the EU Treaties as a result of the Lisbon Treaty coming into force in 2009.[21] Separately, under the Treaty of Amsterdam, which applied from 1999, the EU established a procedure for admonishing States found responsible for serious and persistent violation of human rights and ultimately depriving them of their voting rights. Finally, building on similar domestic developments in European States,[22] in 2007 the EU established an Agency for Fundamental Rights charged with 'the collection of information, formulating opinions, highlighting good practices, networking with civil society, and publishing thematic reports'[23] across the entire area of human rights.

Notwithstanding these important developments, the legalization of even classical civil and political rights within the EU/EEA can be exaggerated. In the first place, EU procedures for holding States accountable for their overarching level of rights compliance remains entirely political rather than legal and is subject to formidable thresholds.[24] Its effectiveness in practice has also been doubted.[25] Moreover, this potential weakness has assumed a new salience in light of the rise of political forces committed to 'illiberal' forms of democracy in a number of EU Central and Eastern European States.[26] Second, wider political concern over the potentially undue encroachment of the judiciary and, even more particularly, trans-national courts in this area remains palpable. In 2012, these concerns prompted the State Parties to the European Convention to adopt the Brighton Declaration. Whilst reaffirming their 'deep and abiding commitment to the Convention' and praising the ECtHR for 'an extraordinary contribution to the protection of human rights in Europe for over 50 years', this document called on the Court to 'give great prominence to and apply consistently . . . principles such as subsidiarity and the margin of appreciation' and, furthermore, for such principles of deference ultimately to be included in the Preamble to the Convention itself.[27] Prior to this, similar concerns over the EU granting Treaty status to the EU Charter led to the United Kingdom and Poland securing an (admittedly essentially declaratory)[28] Protocol which stated that

> [t]he Charter does not extend the ability of the Court of Justice of the European of the European Union, or any court of tribunal of Poland or of the United Kingdom, to find that the laws, regulations or administrative provisions, practices or action of Poland or of the United Kingdom are inconsistent with the fundamental rights, freedoms and principles which it affirms.[29]

The Czech Republic later also adopted this Protocol.[30]

Meanwhile, the non-EU EEA States have been even more resistant to trans-national supervision. Thus, the EEA Agreement confines mention of human rights to a vague preamble,[31] the EU Charter has no formal legal status within the EEA, and there is no EEA equivalent to either the EU Fundamental Rights Agency or the procedure for assessing States' overarching level of human rights compliance.[32] Finally, the relationship between the European Convention machinery and decision-making by the EU itself (and potentially also that of the wider EEA system)[33] remains unclear and unsatisfactory. Attempts from the 1990s onwards to ensure that the EU itself acceded to the Convention have not borne fruit.[34] Moreover, in the controversial case of *Bosphoros v Ireland* (2005), the ECtHR held by a majority of eleven to six that, given the interest in promoting further international cooperation, any

> State action taken in compliance with [legal obligations arising from a treaty concluded subsequent to the entry into force of the Convention in 1950] is justified as long as the relevant organisation is considered to protect fundamental rights, as regards both the substantive guarantees offered and the mechanisms

controlling their observance, in a manner which can be considered equivalent to that for which the Convention provides.[35]

The Court further clarified that 'equivalent' only meant 'comparable'[36] and went on to find that the EU met that standard.[37] Therefore, a presumption of compliance would in principle apply which could only be rebutted 'if, in the circumstances of the particular case it is considered that the protection of Convention rights was manifestly deficient'.[38] At the same time, however, it stressed that the individual State 'would be fully responsible under the Convention for all acts falling outside its strict international legal obligations'.[39] This last caveat has particular importance for this book given the significant margin States are granted in EU (and EEA) law as regards law and regulation relating to journalism and other sensitive types of expression.

2. European Jurisprudence on Freedom of Expression

2.1 European Court of Human Rights: A Hierarchy of Protection

In building up case law in this area over the past forty-five years the ECtHR has adopted a broad construction of freedom of expression. As a result, limitations on the receipt, holding, analysis, and imparting of information and ideas in a wide range of contexts have fallen to be analysed according to the Convention's Article 10(2) requirements that these be 'prescribed by law' and justified on a number of closed grounds as being 'necessary in a democratic society'.[40] At the same time, the Court has organized these very diverse types of expression into a distinct hierarchy and, as a result, construed the standards which Article 10(2) sets out very differently in each case. In so doing, the Court has placed emphasis on its assessment of the predominant societal orientation and therefore potential societal contribution of the expression in question.[41]

Pre-eminent within this hierarchy is public interest expression, namely that which is directly connected to 'debate on matters of public interest',[42] 'an open discussion on matters of public concern'[43] or the imparting or receipt of 'information and ideas of public interest'.[44] Claims that such phrases are limited to 'political discussion'[45] have been decisively and explicitly rejected. Instead, this category has been broadly construed as safeguarding expression on any matter which a 'democratic society' committed to the values of 'progress', 'development', and 'pluralism, tolerance and broadmindedness' can legitimately consider to be its 'concern'.[46] Nevertheless, the concept retains an objective core such that it 'cannot be reduced to the public's thirst for information about the private life or others, or to an audience's wish for sensationalism or even voyeurism'.[47] Within this area, the Court has consistently stressed that there is 'little scope under art 10(2) for restrictions'.[48] Instead, it has held that it must be 'absolutely certain' that any legal interference here be both 'proportionate'[49] and necessary for one of the reasons that this sub-article sets out.

As a result, in *The Sunday Times v United Kingdom*, a plenary chamber of the Court upheld the right to publish information relating to the deleterious effects of the drug thalidomide against the claim that it could prejudice ongoing legal proceedings and, thereby, undermine the authority of the judiciary.[50] In *Thorgeirson v Iceland*, the Court held that the publication of articles compiled on an 'objective and factual basis'[51] and detailing allegations of police brutality could not be legally prohibited, even if the accuracy of these allegations could not be verified, and their contents were 'framed in particularly strong terms'.[52] Meanwhile, in *Jersild v Denmark*, a Grand Chamber of the Court held that, given the importance of free public discussion on such matters, a broadcaster could not be criminally prohibited from disseminating the content of paid interviews with persons making extreme racists statements even if the resulting content 'did not explicitly recall the immorality, dangers and unlawfulness of the promotion of racial hatred and the ideas of superiority of one race'.[53]

Finally, the Court has generally adopted a fairly flexible approach to the additional requirement that any restrictions be 'prescribed by law', holding that this should be satisfied where the interference has a legal basis which complies with certain accessibility and foreseeability requirements.[54] Nevertheless, it has applied these standards particularly strictly within the public expression context. For example, in *Sanoma Uitgevers BV v Netherlands*, another Grand Chamber of the Court unanimously found that these standards were not met by a rule granting the public prosecutor rather than an independent judge the authority to decide whether a publisher holding material of public interest needed to disclose this material to the police in the context of a criminal investigation.[55] Whilst the rule had a clear 'statutory basis',[56] it had failed to 'indicate with sufficient clarity the scope of any such discretion conferred on the competent authorities and the manner of its exercise'.[57]

The Court has also granted a particular priority to the closely allied category of artistic expression, finding both that '[t]hose who create, perform, distribute or exhibit works of art contribute to the exchange of ideas and opinions which [are] essential for a democratic society' and that such expression is integral to the 'self-fulfilment of the individual'.[58] In so doing, it has emphasized that 'the public exchange of cultural, political and social information and ideas of all kinds'[59] lies at the heart of the Convention's protection of freedom of expression. Nevertheless, the shielding granted to purely cultural expression has been less strong than that applicable to public interest expression. Thus, in the leading case of *Müller v Switzerland*, the Court argued that, in addition to being in accordance with law, an interference would be justified in this area so long as the State had not been 'unreasonable' in finding that it was 'necessary' for one of the reasons set down in Article 10(2).[60] As a result, in that case, the Court upheld the seizure of paintings (ultimately returned) and a criminal fine for the public display of art depicting sexual activity in the form of bestiality and also homosexuality.[61] Nevertheless, in cases where the artwork has a clear socio-political message, a more exacting approach been adopted. For example, in both *Karataş v Turkey* and *Alinak v Turkey*, the Court found that a criminal conviction and the seizing of publications respectively were not 'necessary' even though the artistic materials in question might if 'taken literally . . . be construed as inciting readers to hatred, revolt and the use of violence'.[62] In both cases, the artistic expression sought to highlight the position of Kurdish people in Turkey and, in the former case, the Court explicitly noted that the material had 'an obvious political dimension'.[63]

Beyond these two special areas, the Court has often not adopted a particularly exacting construction of the Convention's requirements. Most of the cases here have involved 'commercial'[64] expression or, in other words, any expression which serves little or no other purpose than to further the economic interests of one or more natural or legal persons (e.g. advertising). Thus, in the controversial[65] but leading case of *Markt Intern v Germany*, a plenary sitting of the Court found that, beyond acting in accordance with law, it was enough here for the State merely to have had 'reasonable grounds' for considering any interference 'necessary' for one of the reasons set down in Article 10(2).[66] The standard applicable to the control of other forms of expression such as self-expression and recreational conversation, as well as services which aim at facilitating these and other expressive purposes, remains rather unclear. In some cases, a similar approach to commercial expression has been adopted. For example, *Janowski v Poland* upheld the issuing of a criminal fine for calling two municipal officials 'oafs' and 'dumb' in front of a group of bystanders during a dispute about the moving on of street vendors within a public square. Since such expression did not 'form part of an open discussion on matters of public concern'[67] it was enough that 'the reasons prompting the applicant's conviction were relevant ones in terms of the legitimate interest pursued'.[68] However, more recently and in the context of discussing online expression, the Court has stressed that regard must be had 'to the specificities of the style of communication on certain Internet platforms'[69] and, in relation to the platforms themselves, also 'specific aspects of freedom of expression in terms of protagonists playing an intermediary role on [the] internet'.[70] More generally, the Court has emphasized 'that user-generated expressive activity on the Internet provides an unprecedented platform for the exercise of freedom of expression'.[71] Clearly, with the growing prominence of social networking and a whole host of other online platforms, these emerging issues will have ever greater salience. Nevertheless, in light of both the highly gestational nature of the case law and its limited direct relevance to traditional publisher activity, these controversies will not be explicated further.

2.2 European Court of Human Rights: Press Privilege?

Some aspects of the ECtHR's jurisprudence appear to grant traditional Press actors a particularly wide margin of respect. Thus, a large number of number of cases have stressed the 'vital' and even 'pre-eminent' role of 'the press' as a 'public watchdog', as well as its more general task of imparting 'information and ideas concerning matters . . . of public interest'.[72] Nevertheless, in *Jersild v Denmark*, 'these principles' were also held to 'doubtless' apply to 'audiovisual media' such as broadcasters.[73] Admittedly, the Court did hold both that 'it is commonly acknowledged that the audiovisual media have often a much more immediate and powerful effect than the print media' and it was 'important' to take any such (potentially negative) effect into account. However, this was based on the claim that the 'audiovisual media have means of conveying through images meanings which the print media are not able to impart'.[74] Such a claim has become largely otiose as a result of the trend towards all forms of mass media publishing a wide variety of content online including in audio-visual format. Indeed, in this new context, the Court has stressed that

> the risk of harm posed by content and communications on the Internet to the exercise and enjoyment of human rights and freedoms, particularly the right to respect for private life, is certainly higher than that posed by the [traditional] press [outputs].[75]

In *Times Newspapers (nos. 1 and 2) v United* Kingdom,[76] the Court took into account the new realities of the Internet when analysing large-scale online publication by the Press in the form of news archives. Whilst acknowledging the 'substantial contribution' of such archives 'to preserving and making available news and information', the Court found that

> the margin of appreciation afforded to States in striking the balance between the competing interests is likely to be greater where news archives, rather than news reporting of current events are concerned. In particular, the duty of the press to act in accordance with the principles of responsible journalism by ensuring the accuracy of historical, rather than perishable, information publishing is likely to be more stringent in the absence of any urgency in publishing the material.[77]

Beyond these nuances, it is also critical to note that the Court has recognized the special position within freedom of expression of actors well outside the media, let alone the press. For example, in *Sorguç v Turkey*, the Court emphasized 'the freedom of expression that should normally be enjoyed by an academic in a public debate' and underlined 'the importance of academic freedom'[78] which comprised *inter alia* 'freedom to distribute knowledge and truth without restriction'.[79] The following year in *Sapan v Turkey*, the Court invoked this principle of academic freedom in finding that the Convention's freedom of expression guarantees had been infringed by an interim injunction, which had remained in place for over two and a half years, prohibiting the distribution of a book analysing the stardom of Turkish singer-songwriter Tarkan Tevetoğlu. In light of the book's explicit, controversial, and contestable evaluations of Tarkan's expressions of gender and sexuality, as well as inclusion of numerous images of him, the Turkish courts had originally considered such an injunction to be necessary to protect Tarkan's image and personality rights. However, the Court placed emphasis on the fact that the book was a partial reproduction of a doctoral thesis, that it had analysed Tarkan's stardom through 'scientific tools' ('*d'outils scientifiques*'), and that the author was an academic who had analysed the societal phenomena of stardom even prior to Tarkan's arrival on the music scene.[80] In light of these weighty academic factors, which had been recognized by two expert reports during the national court proceedings, the interim injunction was held to be insufficiently motivated and, therefore, an unnecessary interference with freedom of expression.

In sum, certain parts of the Court's case law have undoubtedly exhibited considerable respect for the position of a number of professional actors engaged in freedom of expression, including not only the press but also the audio-visual media and academics. Nevertheless, an even more fundamental strand of ECtHR jurisprudence has stressed the vital importance of subjecting all actors to a common set of principles rooted in the hierarchy of expression explored above. Thus, in *Steel v United Kingdom*, which explored the permissible limits of a libel action taken against a member of London Greenpeace, a unanimous Court stressed that

> in a democratic society even small and informal campaign groups, such as London Greenpeace, must be able to carry on their activities effectively and there exists a strong public interest in enabling such groups and individuals outside the mainstream to contribute to public debate by disseminating information and ideas on matters of public interest.[81]

Contra to this, in the press case of *Von Hannover v Germany (No. 1)*, which concerned the tabloid publication of photographs taken in public but relating to the private life of Princess Caroline of Monaco, another unanimous Court emphasized that

> A fundamental distinction needs to be made between reporting factors—even controversial ones—capable of contributing to a debate in a democratic society relating to politicians in the exercise of their functions, for example, and reporting details of the private life of individuals who, moreover, as in this case, do not exercise official functions. Whilst in the former case the press exercises its vital role of 'watchdog' in a democracy contributing to 'impart[ing] information and ideas on matters of public interest' it does not do so in the latter case.[82]

Finally, central to the strong protection of freedom of expression in *Sapam v Turkey* was the Court's understanding that the academic's book on the pop star Tarkan represented a serious scholarly or scientific contribution to public debate rather an exercise of sensationalism or idle curiosity:

> [O]n ne saurait considérer ce livre comme faisant partie des publications de la presse dite 'à sensation' ou 'de la presse du cœur', laquelle a habituellement pour objet de satisfaire la curiosité d'un certain public sur les détails de la vie strictement privée d'une célébrité.[83]

2.3 Court of Justice of the European Union (CJEU) and the EFTA Court Contributions

The CJEU's case law on freedom of expression generally dates only from the 1990s and remains much more limited than that of the ECtHR. It has tended to focus on very specific (and often quite technical) areas interfacing directly either with EU secondary legislation or the EU institutions themselves. These include 'commercial speech (especially advertising)' in the 'media sector',[84] as well as the rules applicable to staff members of the EU institutions wishing to engage in expressive activities which have not been authorized by their institution. This relatively narrow focus reflects the historic reality of the EU as a 'trade-based'[85] organization. Nevertheless, the EU's competence over and engagement with matters relating to human rights has been expanding for some time. These developments, which are epitomized by genesis of the EU Charter in the 2000s, have resulted in a deepening of the CJEU's freedom of expression case law, most particularly within the area of data protection itself.

The CJEU's case law has generally adopted a broad construction of when EU standards relating to freedom of expression will apply. At a material level, the Court has found that these standards apply not only to the EU institutions[86] themselves but also when Member States implement[87] and even when they derogate from EU law.[88] Substantively, the Court has also signalled that certain freedom of expression protections apply even to purely commercial speech, including as regards both the content[89] and even the frequency[90] of advertising. At the same time, the CJEU's analysis has often remained rather limited; indeed, Woods has found that the Court's judgements do not 'always refer to the most relevant ECHR jurisprudence on the issue in question and in some instances seem only to be making general statements about the existence and importance of freedom of expression'.[91] One example of this may be C-101/01 *Lindqvist*, which concerned an individual's criminal prosecution under data protection for publishing on her personal website 'personal data on a number of people working with her on a voluntary basis in a parish of the Swedish Protestant Church'[92] without having obtained these in-dividuals' prior consent or having registered her activity with the Swedish Data Protection Authority (DPA).[93] Lindqvist argued that the European data protection framework violated freedom of expression due to both its stringency and its uncer-tainty in such contexts. In rejecting this contention, however, the CJEU confined itself to stressing that it was 'at the stage of application at national level' and 'in in-dividual cases' that a 'balance' between 'the rights and interests involved' had to be ensured and that, in that context, 'fundamental rights' including 'Mrs Lindqvist's freedom of expression' had a 'particular importance'.[94]

In yet other cases, freedom of expression, although clearly relevant, has not been 'expressly addressed, [has been] addressed only by the [advisory opinion of the] Advocate-General, or [has been] dismissed summarily'.[95] A particularly per-tinent example of this is the Grand Chamber judgment of C-131/12 *Google Spain* which considered the data protection obligations of Internet search engines when indexing and making available public domain online material containing personal data.[96] This seminal judgment and its implications will be analysed in greater depth elsewhere in this book, particularly in Chapters 9 and 13. What is critical to note here is that, in stark contrast to the Advocate-General's Opinion, the Court did not explicitly acknowledge that search engine indexing could engage either freedom of expression in general or its sub-right of freedom of information. In contrast, other recent CJEU judgments have given freedom of expression significant weight, even whilst generally avoiding definitively answering all questions posed. Take, for ex-ample, C-73/07 *Satamedia* which *inter alia* considered whether the publishing via a hard-copy catalogue and a pay-per-view Special Messaging Service (SMS) of tax income on 1.2 million Finnish residents which was already in the public domain could fall within a derogation 'solely for journalistic purposes' which was estab-lished within European data protection[97] and, if so, how this should operate. Here, another Grand Chamber of the Court stressed that. given 'importance of the right to freedom of expression in every democratic society', it was necessary 'to interpret notions relating to that freedom, such as journalism, broadly'.[98] It followed that in the concrete case the phrase 'solely for journalistic purposes' would be satisfied where 'the sole object of those activities is the disclosure to the public of infor-mation, opinions or ideas'.[99] It was left to the national court to examine whether, on the specific facts, that was the case.[100] On the other hand, in order to achieve a 'balance' between freedom of expression and the 'right to privacy', the Court also stressed that even within this context any derogations from data protection 'must apply only in so far as is strictly necessary'.[101]

Turning finally to the EFTA Court, this body's case law contains only the most cursory consideration of freedom of expression. Nevertheless, in upholding the permissibility of national restrictions on the cross-border broadcasting of porn-ography, the Court in *Sverige v Norwegian Government* did make reference to rele-vant Article 10 ECtHR jurisprudence.[102] Therefore, although the judicial analysis of this has been extremely limited, it would appear that freedom of expression, interpreted broadly in line with the ECtHR case law, does constitute a general principle of EEA law which would be upheld by the EFTA Court in appropriate cases.

3. Codifying Rights and Limits to Freedom of Expression

3.1 General Situation

A final issue to consider is to what extent Europe has considered it necessary to set out detailed codifications of the rights and limits of core instances of freedom of expression such as journalism or academic expression. At the pan-European level and in many EU/EEA States it has not generally been considered necessary or even appropriate to set out any such comprehensive codifications in the law. Instead, the juridical framework in countries such as the United Kingdom has tended to treat activities such as journalism as simply 'the exercise by occupation of the right to free expression available to every citizen'.[103] Thus, whilst journalists have certainly been 'restricted and confined by rules that apply to all who take or are afforded the opportunity to exercise the right by speaking or writing in public',[104] detailed elaboration of the framework within which they should operate have largely been confined to self-regulation or other 'soft' instruments. Indeed, journalists in almost every European country have drawn up comprehensive self-regulatory codes of 'ethics' which will be analysed, as relevant, later in this book.[105] Meanwhile, at the pan-European level, the Council of Europe institutions have drafted a number of 'soft' guidance documents in this area including, most notably, the Parliamentary Assembly's Resolution 428 (1970) on Mass Communication Media and Human Rights, its Recommendation 815 (1977) on Freedom of Expression and the Role of the Writer in Europe, and its Recommendation 1762 (2006) on Academic Freedom and University Autonomy. These instruments have also recognized the important role played by self-regulation.[106] Moreover, the detailed elaboration of norms through political processes has generally been confined to specific issues. Most notably, in 1974 the Council of Europe's Committee of Ministers passed a Resolution (74) 26 which argued that all natural and legal persons should be able to exercise a 'right of reply' against the 'periodical media' when facts had been published 'which he claims to be inaccurate'.[107] Subsequent recommendations issued by this same body in 2004[108] and by the EU in 2006[109] have sought to apply such a right of reply also to online media.

In contrast to this, several civil law countries in Europe have a strong, albeit increasingly contested, tradition of broad legal codification in this area. For example, in Italy, '[j]ournalism is a regulated profession. Exercising that profession or using the title of journalist without being registered on the Journalists' Roll is a criminal offence punishable by imprisonment up to six months and a fine'.[110]

Even those civil law countries which have eschewed comprehensive registration requirements have often adopted wide-ranging legal codes which govern the exercise of mass communicative activity. Thus, in Hungary, an 'Act on Media Services and Mass Communication (Mttv.) handles print media and online journals under the same set of rules and calls them together as ' "press products" . . . [and] the Act on Freedom of Expression and the Fundamental Rules of Media Content (Smtv.) also extends to print media and online journals, beyond audio-visual media and radio'.[111] Slovenia similarly has a Mass Media Act which 'stipulates the rights, obligations and responsibilities of legal and natural persons and the public interest in the area of mass media'.[112]

3.2 Broadcasting, Audio-visual Media, and Audio-visual Content

In marked contrast to this general situation, there has been a strong consensus that the broadcasting and the audio-visual media sector more broadly should operate in accord with a specific and detailed legal framework. Indeed, this special treatment finds reference in the Convention's explicit validation of prior restraint over this sector in the form of 'the licensing of broadcasting, television or cinema enterprises'.[113] As noted during the discussion on *Jersild v Denmark* in section 1, the most weighty justification for this 'double standard' has rested on the potentially greater impact of audio-visual material compared to traditional Press content in the form of still images and the printed text. While the convergence of formats on, and new impacts of, the Internet have rendered the distinction between broadcasting and the Press ever more debatable, some such distinction remains standard across Europe. At the same time, the growth of convergent online services has prompted audio-visual content regulation to be extended to a range of services well beyond the traditional broadcasting sector.

Reflecting both a European tradition of regulation here and the pervasively transnational character of audio-visual publication even prior to the Internet, important elements of broadcasting and audio-visual media regulation have been harmonized within the EU/EEA. The Television without Frontiers Directive,[114] agreed in 1989 and requiring transposition in the EU by 3 October 1991, established that, subject to derogation in exceptional circumstances, Member States must accept the retransmission of television broadcasts from other Member States. In return, the Directive set down certain minimum requirements regarding television broadcasts including prohibitions on the incitement to hatred on various grounds,[115] certain child protection measures, and a right of reply or equivalent remedies.[116] The Directive and all subsequent legislation in this area was included within the EEA Agreement which was finalized in 1994.[117] In 2007, a major revision of this Directive extended its scope to all on-demand audio-visual content which were under the editorial responsibility of media service providers including, for example, online content provided by newspapers.[118] Nevertheless, the substantive rules applicable to such content have remained less onerous than in relation to broadcasting, with more limited provisions relating to child protection and no right to reply. This Audiovisual Media Services Directive, which required transposition in the EU by 19 December 2009 and was consolidated in 2010, also requires the establishment under law of independent regulatory authorities governing the audio-visual sector at national level. Whilst it does not prescribe their precise form, close cooperation including with the European Commission is envisaged.[119] Such cooperation has been facilitated through the establishment in 2014 of an advisory European Regulators Group for Audiovisual Media Services (ERGA).[120] In 2018, further important reforms were agreed which *inter alia* strengthen these regulatory requirements and, even more importantly, require video-sharing platforms to take measures to protect children and to combat 'hate speech', child pornography, and public provocation to commit a terrorist offence on their services. Reflecting that such platforms lack direct editorial responsibility for the videos uploaded by users, these measures focus on the 'organisation of the content and not the content as such'[121] including terms and conditions, age verification, and reporting/flagging mechanisms. These provisions must be transposed within the EU by 19 September 2020[122] and will be referred to further in the book's conclusion.

4. Conclusions

Like other classical civil and political rights, freedom of expression came to be articulated early on within the liberal democratic political and legal tradition in Europe. The trauma of the Second World War and onset of the Cold War witnessed a further formalization of these commitments including through the drafting of the European Convention. Nevertheless, it was not until the 1970s that such rights came to be granted strong juridical protection across most European States and at the pan-European level. Since then, the ECtHR has developed a highly influential jurisprudence on freedom of expression which has centred on an examination of the predominant societal orientation and therefore potential social value of different types of expression. Public interest expression has been pre-eminently safeguarded by the Court and artistic expression has also been especially shielded from legal interference. In contrast, the Court has generally refused to grant strong protection to other types of expression such as commercial speech. Some of the Court's case law has exhibited a particular respect for the role of professional expressive actors including the media and academics. Nevertheless, an even more fundamental strand of the Court's jurisprudence has stressed the importance of ensuring that all actors are equally subject to a common set of principles which pivot around the societal contribution of the expression in question.

Since the 1990s, several CJEU cases have also addressed freedom of expression issues. Whilst many early cases only involved relatively niche areas, both the involvement of the EU in broader policy areas including data protection and the advent of the EU Charter have resulted in a deepening of this jurisprudence. Nevertheless, the CJEU's analysis in this area has often remained rather general. Meanwhile, whilst recognizing freedom of expression as a general principles of EEA law, the EFTA Court's engagement within this space has remained extremely limited. Beyond this, several important issues remain including societal concerns over the role of transnational courts and similar institutions, the difficulty of holding States accountable for their overarching level of rights compliance and ongoing ambiguity as regards the relationship between EU law (and potentially also EEA law) and the ECtHR.

Turning finally to the issue of codification, several civil law countries have a long, albeit increasingly contested, tradition of adopting legal codes to regulate the rights and limits of core instances of freedom of expression such as journalism. Such a tradition has also influenced laws relating to broadcasting and similar media across Europe including certain pan-EEA instruments. Reflecting the convergence of media online, some of this regulatory structure has been applied to audio-visual content well beyond the traditional broadcasting sector. Nevertheless, outside this discrete area, the EU/EEA collectively and most EEA States have rejected this form of legal systematization, preferring instead to leave the elaboration of any specific overarching framework to self-regulation and other forms of 'soft' guidance.

3

The Development of European Data Protection Law and Regulation

The development of data protection presents some important similarities to that of freedom of expression law, a topic which was explored in Chapter 2. Like freedom of expression, data protection is now recognized as a fundamental right within the EU and the courts are increasingly playing a central role in defining its scope and limits. Dovetailing with a growing emphasis on formalizing the rights and safeguards for the individual, data protection has also been developing strongly since the 1970s. Nevertheless, in stark contrast to freedom of expression's established place within the liberal democratic tradition from its inception, data protection only emerged as a distinct concern in the 1970s and it was not until the Data Protection Directive 95/46 ('DPD') in the 1990s that all European Economic Area ('EEA') States came to recognize it within their law. Moreover, in contrast to the focus within freedom of expression on broad and open-textured legal rights guarantees, data protection has from its inception been primarily articulated as a detailed regulatory code. Finally, ensuring a high degree of pan-European coordination has been central to the data protection regime right from the time of its genesis and such coordination has proceeded much faster and further than in relation to freedom of expression.

This chapter provides an overview of the general development of European data protection law and regulation. Its four sections follow a broadly chronological sequence. Section 3 explores early or 'first-generation' data protection, a period from the 1970s through to the 1990s which was dominated at a transnational level by the Council of Europe. Section 2 similarly explores the origins and general contours of 'second-generation' data protection, which lasted from the 1990s to the 2010s when the EU's DPD was in force. It includes an analysis not only of formal legal provisions at pan-European and national level but also the coordinating role of the Court of Justice of the European Union ('CJEU'), European Free Trade Association ('EFTA') Court, and the Data Protection Authorities ('DPAs') as assembled in the Article 29 Working Party. Section 3 then considers the genesis and general nature of 'third-generation' data protection as it has emerged in the 2010s under the General Data Protection Regulation 2016/679 ('GDPR').[1] Finally, section 4 draws some conclusions.

European Data Protection Regulation, Journalism, and Traditional Publishers. David Erdos, Oxford University Press (2019). © David Erdos.
DOI: 10.1093/oso/9780198841982.003.0003

1. First-Generation European Data Protection (1970s–1990s)

1.1 Precursors, Origins, and Transnational Developments

Legal protections against specific forms of informational harm including in relation to natural persons go back many centuries.[2] Prompted in part by the development of a new technology of information capture—namely, the portable camera—the late nineteenth century also saw many jurisdictions developing laws that controlled information and which were explicitly focused on safeguarding the 'inviolate personality'[3] including 'the right to privacy'[4] of the individual. By the beginning of the post-Second World War period, most European Constitutions as well as the European Convention on Human Rights ('ECHR') in Article 8 set out rights related to individual privacy, albeit often with a distinct emphasis on controlling public as opposed to private sector activity.[5]

Nevertheless, despite these important precursors, the idea of ensuring a comprehensive safeguarding of information or data relating to individual natural persons ('data subjects') in order to protect their rights and interests was unknown to any legal system prior to the 1970s. The genesis of data protection law *stricto senso* at that juncture was not unrelated to the growing focus on formalizing the rights and safeguards for the individual, which was discussed in Chapter 2. Nevertheless, it emerged specifically as a response to the dramatic growth in information power which the electronic computer and online networks brought in their wake. Although originally linked to more diffuse Council of Europe initiatives which aimed to enhance the position of 'privacy',[6] discussion soon came to focus on the threats posed to the individual by the 'automatic' processing of personal data. In 1973 and 1974, the Council of Europe's Committee of Ministers adopted non-binding resolutions on the protection of the 'privacy' of individuals *vis-à-vis* electronic data banks in the private[7] and public[8] sectors respectively. Focusing on the governance of information relating to individual natural persons, these resolutions mapped out much of what remains at the core of European data protection. In sum, they established as general principles that when personal data was handled in 'electronic data banks' it should be fairly obtained, accurate, up-to-date, appropriate, relevant, time-limited, and kept secure. Further provisions both set out a reactive transparency entitlement for data subjects to access such information on demand (the right of subject access) and emphasized the need for a stricter protection of sensitive types of personal data, namely those which were related either to intimate private life or whose handling might lead to unfair discrimination.

In 1976 the Council of Europe established an intergovernmental Committee of Experts on Data Protection (the CJ-PD), with the initial task of drafting a legally binding Data Protection Convention. This Convention was ultimately agreed in 1980, opened for signature in January 1981,[9] and finally came into force in 1985.[10] The Convention broadened the scope of data protection so as to focus explicitly on all 'rights and fundamental freedoms', including but not limited to the 'right of privacy',[11] which could be affected by the 'automatic processing of personal data'.[12] The reference to 'automatic processing' fixed the law's attention on a myriad of operations which were carried out 'in whole or in part' by computer[13] and it was clarified that the term 'personal data' referred to any information relating to a natural person who remained either 'identified or identifiable'.[14] The Convention also further specified and elaborated European data protection's substantive requirements. Alongside reactive subject access, data subjects were to be enabled to ascertain the existence and core attributes of any 'personal data file'.[15] Overarching requirements to process data fairly and lawfully and to ensure purpose specification and limitation were also articulated. Finally, the concept of sensitive data was defined in a categorical fashion so as to encompass 'personal data revealing racial origin, political opinions or religious or other beliefs', 'personal data concerning health or sexual life', and 'personal data relating to criminal convictions'.[16]

The Convention was not self-executing and, in contrast to the ECHR, also avoided setting up any authoritative transnational enforcement machinery. Nevertheless, as befitted a legally binding text, it was explicit both as regards the need for 'appropriate sanctions and remedies'[17] and also the possibility of derogations in particular situations. In relation to the former, it particularly stressed that data subjects must have rights to rectify or erase data that had been subject to illegal processing.[18] Turning to the latter, the Convention provided (similarly to Article 10 of the ECHR) that all but its security principle could be derogated from by State Parties so long as this was provided for in their law, was justified on specific legitimate grounds (including protecting other 'rights and freedoms'), and satisfied a test of being a 'necessary measure in a democratic society'.[19] Another clause specifically permitted a derogation from subject access as regards data used for 'statistics or scientific research purposes', but only where there was 'obviously no risk of an infringement of the privacy of the data subjects'.[20]

In addition to these substantive and remedial provisions, the Convention established a Consultative Committee[21] and set out certain minimal duties of 'mutual assistance'[22] between the Parties. Nevertheless, the Council of Europe's broader Committee of Experts on Data Protection also continued in operation and maintained its leading role in exchanging legislative and other information and specifying authoritative but non-binding data protection standards in particular areas throughout the 1980s and early 1990s. Most notably, it drafted a series of Recommendations applying data protection to particular activities (e.g. direct marketing, payment operations, and social security purposes) which were then adopted by the Council's Committee of Ministers.[23] Whilst not explicitly required by the Convention, almost all countries adopting data protection law in this period established regulatory Data Protection Authorities (DPAs) and their representatives often took part in the work of the Committee of Experts. In addition, these authorities began meeting in an annual International Conference of Data Protection

Commissioners from 1979 and this forum similarly acquired some significance in the specification of data protection standards. Although technically open to a worldwide membership, this Conference remained dominated by European actors into the 1990s, for reasons that will become apparent in section 1.2.

1.2 Legislative and Constitutional Developments at National Level

In stark contrast to its almost complete absence in other parts of the world in this early period,[24] some twelve European countries adopted data protection laws prior to the end of 1990.[25] Aside from Finland, which only enacted a law in 1987, the Nordic countries were particularly early adopters[26]—Sweden legislated in 1973, Denmark and Norway in 1978, and Iceland in 1981. These early adopters were joined by the two behemoths of Germany (in 1977) and France (in 1978), as well as Luxembourg (in 1979). Alongside Finland, the later 1980s also saw the United Kingdom (in 1984), Ireland, and the Netherlands (both in 1988) adopt a data protection statute.

All these laws were significantly influenced by the Council of Europe data protection developments detailed earlier.[27] At the same time, they included important aspects that distinguished them both from the Council's texts and from each other. In the first place, as already noted, almost all these laws[28] provided for a DPA (or, in the case of Germany, DPAs at both federal and *Länder* level). However, the precise character, functions, and powers of these bodies differed significantly. For example, subject to the possibility of being overridden by a contrary governmental decision, the Swedish DPA was allocated a wide-ranging authority to grant or refuse licenses that were generally a mandatory requirement for personal data processing.[29] Similar provisions were included in the law of other States such as Norway.[30] In contrast, although duties to register processing with a DPA were very widespread, in most others cases requirements to obtain an *ex ante* license often only applied (if at all) to quite specific processing operations.[31] As a result, the regulatory role of many other DPAs was principally of an *ex post* nature. Turning to matters of substance, although many laws explicitly set out basic principles of data protection as articulated in the Council of Europe instruments cited earlier, this was far from true in all cases. For example, the original Swedish legislation placed most emphasis on the DPA's own duty to ensure that data processing did 'not cause undue encroachment on privacy',[32] thereby leaving the regulator itself with the responsibility for setting out most of the applicable standards through specific licensing arrangements. Aside from the subject access right, which was found in almost all these laws, the detailed rules imposed on data processing exhibited an even greater divergence. Thus, although some laws established clear proactive requirements to make processing transparent to the data subject and/or person from whom information was obtained,[33] this issue was left unaddressed in many other cases. Meanwhile, although most States stipulated that various sensitive categories of data generally could not be processed (at least) without the consent of the data subject, Austrian,[34] British, [35] German,[36] and Irish[37] law set out no or only very limited additional protection for such data.

Some of these differences may have resulted from essentially random experimentation during what was clearly a gestational period for the law. However, the overarching depth of these laws also appears related to divergent rationales for adopting data protection in the first place. In broad terms, States adopting data protection prior to the 1980s were generally understood to have done so in response to intrinsic human rights concerns arising from data processing.[38] In contrast, most the of States that adopted a law after the finalization of the Data Protection Convention in 1981 were predominantly motivated by an extrinsic fear that otherwise other jurisdictions with such laws might restrict trade which depended on a flow of personal data across its borders.[39] It is therefore unsurprising that it was these later States that generally adopted laws which stuck closely to the agreed minimum 'common core' of data protection as set out in the Convention.

One means by which a State signalled its intrinsic commitment data protection was by instantiating it as a constitutional guarantee. During this early period, Portugal (1976), Austria (1978), Spain (1978), the Netherlands (1983), and Sweden (1989) included mention of data protection within their constitution.[40] However, in the case of Portugal and Spain, this was not followed up with any implementing statutory law.

2. Second-Generation European Data Protection (1990s–2010s)

2.1 Transnational Developments including the DPD and EU Charter

The formal involvement of what are now the EU institutions in the early development of European data protection was distinctly limited.[41] In September 1990, however, the European Commission changed tack and proposed that, as part of a package of measures,[42] a Data Protection Directive should be adopted on the basis of the then European Community's internal market *vires*.[43] This proposed text set out the ambitious goal of ensuring an 'equivalent' and 'high level'[44] of personal data protection through the Community and thereby (and essentially as a quid pro quo) ensuring that the 'free flow of personal data between the Member States'[45] was not restricted for reasons related to the need for such protection. Following many amendments by the European Parliament and an extensive critique in the Council, the Commission issued a revised proposal in 1992 which was more strongly rooted in the 'common core' set out within the Data Protection Convention, as well as (similarly to its initial proposal) concrete data protection laws found within individual Member States.[46] Following extensive further negotiations, a Common Position was reached in the Council in February 1995 and, after a few minor amendments, the agreement of the European Parliament was also secured.[47] The DPD was finally adopted on 21 October 1995, with EU Member States given until 24 October 1998 to ensure full transposition.[48] Turning to the wider EEA, the DPD was adopted by the EEA Joint Committee on 26 June 1999 with the non-EU EEA States of Iceland, Norway, and Liechtenstein required to ensure implementation by the following day.[49]

Whilst excluding activities falling outside of Community law and also the 'purely personal or household' activities of a natural person,[50] the DPD adopted a broad construction of data protection's material scope. Alongside 'the processing of personal data wholly or partly by automatic means', the DPD followed the lead of a number of individual Member State's laws in also including some manually processed data. Thus, in addition to all information linked to computers, the Directive was made applicable to data 'which form part of a filing system or are intended to form part of a filing system'.[51] Otherwise, the DPD dropped any hint that regulated personal data needed to be located in a structured 'data bank' or 'file' and also expanded the concept of 'processing' to include 'any operation' performed on such data up to and including their mere 'consultation' and/or 'destruction'.[52] The DPD also significantly expanded the default substantive duties which a 'controller'—broadly defined as anyone who either 'alone or jointly determine[d] the purposes and means of processing'[53]—was required to follow. Thus, alongside a set of data protection principles[54] and a right of subject access[55] that largely mirrored those already set out in Council of Europe instruments, the DPD also mandated comprehensive proactive transparency requirements to notify data subjects about processing when personal data were directly obtained from them.[56] These also applied even if data were obtained from a third party, the public domain, or otherwise came to be processed, as long as this did not constitute at least a 'disproportionate effort' and was replaced by 'appropriate safeguards'.[57]

Turning to sensitive data, the categorical definition of this concept was not only expanded to include data revealing 'trade-union membership' but the processing of such data was generally prohibited absent waiver from the data subject.[58] The DPD also required that the controller justify the processing of any personal data under one or more of a closed list of legal bases[59] and, unless it didn't pose a likely risk to the rights and freedoms of data subjects, that processing be registered either with the DPA or, where this was provided for in State law, an internal data protection officer.[60] Furthermore, the transfer of such data outside the EEA was generally prohibited absent 'adequate protection'.[61] The latter provisions highlighted an emphasis on ensuring genuine discipline in personal data processing. Nevertheless, reflecting their essentially subsidiary goal of ensuring that other elements of the regime were not unduly undermined, these provisions remained much less onerous than, for example, the sensitive data rules. In particular, one particularly broad legal basis legitimated processing

> necessary for the purposes of the legitimate interests pursued by the controller or by the third party or parties to whom the data are disclosed, except where such interests are overridden by the interests for fundamental rights and freedoms of the data subject which require protection.[62]

Meanwhile, the requirement to register processing did not generally require that the DPA or internal officer conduct an *ex ante* check of its legality (although this was required where a Member State had designed the processing as presenting specific data protection risks). Finally, the prohibition on transferring data overseas was only to be applicable as regards those countries that had not been certified as ensuring an 'adequate' level of data protection and was further lifted in a range of specific specified situations.

Turning to the supervisory system, in addition to requiring that data subjects be provided with further ability to control data by objecting to its processing on personal grounds,[63] a right to judicial remedy,[64] and a right to compensation,[65] the DPD mandated that all EEA States establish one or more DPAs according to a common regulatory template. These 'public authorities' were to be endowed with wide-ranging powers of investigation and intervention, as well as duties to monitor application of the law and deal with complaints from data subjects.[66] They were also to act with 'complete independence'[67] in relation to this and, as an 'essential component'[68] of data protection, were to be endowed with the 'necessary means to perform their duties'.[69] Finally, the DPAs were to 'cooperate with one another to the extent necessary for the performance of the duties'[70] including through a joint advisory Article 29 Working Party which was charged with promoting the 'uniform application' of the Directive across the EEA, notably through issuing common opinions and recommendations.[71]

Dovetailing with these efforts at harmonization, the DPD attempted to address knotty problems concerning applicable law. States were to apply their legislation to controllers who were based within the EEA (only) when the relevant processing was taking place 'in the context of' the activities of an 'establishment'[72] of that controller which was situated on the national territory.[73] At the same time, the DPD still left States with a significant 'margin for manoeuvre'[74] when implementing its scheme. This was particularly the case in relation to derogations. Thus, States could elect to restrict most of the Directive's substantive provisions in particular situations, usually through a legislative measure that on specified legitimate grounds (including protecting other 'rights and freedoms') was shown to be 'necessary'.[75] However, these general derogatory clauses did not authorize a limitation on the need for a legal basis for processing, the regime regulating the transfer of data outside the EEA, the duty to ensure that risky processing was subject to registration, and the overarching supervision of the DPA. In contrast, EEA States did have a right and indeed a duty to consider adopting these and other derogations in relation to processing 'carried out for journalistic purposes or the purpose of artistic or literary expression' if (but only if) they were found 'necessary to reconcile the right to privacy with the rules governing freedom of expression'.[76] The origins and precise nature of this special expression regime, as well as specific provisions in the DPD which related to knowledge generation activities such as scientific research,[77] are clearly central to this study and will be analysed in depth later in this book.

In the year 2000, the EU drafted a Charter of Fundamental Rights. Alongside a wide range of civil, political, social, and economic rights, this include a provision on data protection drafted as follows:

1. Everyone has the right to the protection of personal data concerning him or her.
2. Such data must be processed fairly for specified purposes and on the basis of the consent of the person concerned or some other legitimate basis laid down by law. Everyone has the right of access to data which have been collected concerning him or her, and the right to have this data rectified.
3. Compliance with these rules shall be subject to control by an independent authority.[78]

As with all the other new rights the Charter set out, this provision was subject to possible limitation where this was provided for by law, respected the 'essence' of the right, was justified on the basis of either the general interest or the protection of rights and freedoms, and was both necessary and proportionate.[79] As noted in Chapter 2, although originally only a 'soft law' instrument, in 2009 the Lisbon Treaty granted the EU Charter the same legal status as the EU Treaties themselves.[80] Uniquely, the reformed Treaties also separately provided not only a *sui generis vires* for adopting data protection legislation but also that '[e]veryone has the right to the protection of personal data concerning them'.[81] It has been cogently claimed that this provision has direct horizontal effect which, if true, would itself thereby fix not only public but also private actors with certain minimum duties.[82]

Finally, in 2004 the European Court of Human Rights (ECtHR) found in the case of *Von Hannover v Germany (No 1)* that Article 8 of the ECHR placed State Parties under an obligation to adopt 'measures designed to secure respect for private life even in the sphere of the relations of individuals between themselves'[83] and that this extended to ensuring an appropriate balance between this and the exercise of freedom of expression by the professional journalistic media. In this regard it further held that 'the decisive factor in balancing the protection of private life against freedom of expression' lay in an assessment of the contribution any publication made 'to a debate of general interest'.[84] On the facts, which involved the publishing of photos of Princess Caroline of Monaco that related to her private activities but that had been taken in public, the Court held that such a contribution was not present. A violation of the Convention had, therefore, occurred.[85] Although this decision was not directly concerned with data protection, the Court emphasized that one important reason why an 'increased vigilance in protecting private life' was considered necessary arose from 'new communication technologies which make it possible to store and reproduce personal data'.[86] Moreover, an obvious (and, under the DPD, arguably necessary) way in which States could discharge their newly elucidated European Convention responsibilities was through the data protection framework. As a result, *Von Hannover* came to exert a powerful influence on data protection including, most particularly, its interaction with freedom of expression.

2.2 Legislative and Constitutional Developments at National Level

In the wake of the European Commission's DPD proposal in 1990, three States within the then Community moved to enact data protection law.[87] Meanwhile, the DPD as finally agreed made data protection according to a common template a mandatory requirement across the EU by 24 October 1998[88] and within the wider EEA by 27 June 1999.[89] Nevertheless, as highlighted in the European Commission's first review of the Directive in 2003:

> [o]nly a few Member States implemented the Directive on time. Most Member States only notified implementing measures to the Commission in the years 2000 and 2001, and Ireland has still not notified its recent implementation. Important implementation legislation is still pending in some Member States.[90]

Like Ireland, almost all the jurisdictions that were particularly late in implementing the DPD had previously adopted some data protection legislation; however, this was not invariably the case.[91] The Commission's first review also highlighted what it saw as 'incorrect implementation in various instances'[92] including as regards applicable law, the need for a legal basis for processing, the definition of sensitive data, the transparency rules, the derogations, and the rules regulating the transfer of data outside the EEA.[93] It did, however, acknowledge that some divergences between the Member States could be the 'legitimate result' of a utilization of 'the margin of manoeuvre allowed for by the Directive'.[94] Finally, the Commission noted concern as regards a 'lack of resources'[95] provided to the DPAs.

By the time enlargement of the EU to Eastern Europe, Cyprus, and Malta took place in 2004 and 2007,[96] all these States had ratified the Council of Europe's Data Protection Convention and enacted local data protection laws that were broadly in line with the DPD. Despite this, issues related to incorrect transposition, general legal divergences, and DPA financial problems remained acute. It is also clear that these issues were far from fully addressed within the EEA as a whole during the rest of the DPD-era. Thus, as regards legislative divergence, in 2010 the Commission held, in a striking echo of its findings of 2003, that:

> Member States room for manoeuvre . . . together with the fact that the Directive has sometimes been incorrectly implemented by Member States, has led to divergences between the national laws implementing the Directive, which runs counter to one of its main objectives, i.e. ensuring the free flow of personal data within the internal market . . . Moreover, the divergence in the implementation of the Directive by Member States creates legal uncertainty not only for data controllers but also for data subjects, creating the risk of distorting the equivalent level of protection that the Directive is supposed to achieve and ensure.[97]

Meanwhile, mirroring an earlier report from 2010,[98] the EU Agency for Fundamental Rights found in 2013 that 'the lack of financial and human resources has a negative impact on the quality and quantity of the DPAs' work, and limits their ability to control and sanction data protection violations'.[99]

Despite these difficulties, the harmonization achieved by the DPD compared to the status quo *ante* should not be underestimated. As Newman describes it, for the first time every EEA State not only had to enact data protection laws but also had to ensure that these contained 'similar provisions concerning the collection, processing, and transfer of personal information in the public and private sectors' as well as create 'powerful national independent regulatory agencies—data privacy [or protection] authorities—that monitor and enforce these rules'.[100] Moreover, as a result of its incorporation into EU and EEA law, data protection came to fall squarely within the remit of the CJEU and the EFTA Court (including through enforcement actions brought before these bodies by either the European Commission or the EFTA Surveillance Authority). Specific to data protection, the output of the Article 29 Working Party was also of significance. The role of these three bodies will be further considered in section 3. Over the same period, data protection grew into a truly global phenomenon. Indeed, by 2017 well over 100 jurisdictions—the majority outside Europe—had adopted such a law.[101] Many, although not all, of these laws were strongly influenced by the DPD blueprint; indeed, writing in 2014, Bygrave stated that the DPD 'has constituted the most important point of departure for national data privacy initiatives [both] within and, to a large extent outside the EU'.[102]

Turning finally to look at the protection of data protection as a fundamental right within national legal systems, whilst only five European countries had granted data protection a constitutional status prior to 1990, this number grew significantly during the later period such that by 2005:

Thirteen [EU] Member States (including the newly acceding states) have the right to the protection of personal data protected in their Constitution; these are Austria, the Czech Republic, Estonia, Finland, Hungary, Lithuania, the Netherlands, Poland, Portugal, Slovakia, Spain and Sweden.[103]

2.3 The Contributions of the CJEU, the EFTA Court, and the Article 29 Working Party

Since 2001 the CJEU has issued around fifty judgments which engage significantly with the rights and duties set down in EU/EEA data protection. Whilst it is beyond the scope of this chapter to summarize this case law in detail, the most important features of this jurisprudence will be outlined. In the first place, the Court has consistently interpreted the scope of EU data protection law broadly. Thus, as regards the construction of data protection's core terms, the Court stressed right from the time of C-101/01 *Lindqvist* that, for example, 'the act of referring, on an internet page, to various persons and identifying them by name or by other means, for instance by giving their telephone number of information regarding their working conditions and hobbies, constitutes the processing of personal data wholly or partly by automatic means'.[104]

The Court also held that the DPD's exclusion of activities falling outside the scope of Community law applied only to 'activities of the State or of State authorities and unrelated to the fields of activity of individuals',[105] whilst its similar exemption for natural persons pursuing purely personal/household activities

must be interpreted as relating only to activities which are carried out in the course of private or family life of individuals, which is clearly not the case with the processing of personal data consisting in publication on the internet so that those data are made accessible to an indefinite number of people.[106]

In the later Grand Chamber judgment of C-73/07 *Satamedia*, the Court stressed that the Directive 'does not lay down any further limitation of its scope of application',[107] that any 'general derogation from the application of the directive in respect of published information would largely deprive the directive of its effect', and that it followed that the DPD must even apply to 'personal data files which contain solely, and in unaltered form, material that has already been published in the media'.[108]

Turning to matters of substance, whilst many aspects of data protection have remained unanalysed by the Court, the decisions which it did hand down often sought to couple a high level of protection with a relatively flexible interpretative approach. For example, in C-524/06 *Huber* a Grand Chamber of the Court held that the storage of personal data in a centralized population register could satisfy the requirement of 'necessity . . . if it contributes to the more effective application of . . . legislation as regards the right of residence of Union citizens who wish to reside in a Member State of which they are not nationals'.[109] On the other hand, any such storage merely for statistical purposes was deemed unnecessary on the basis that 'it is only anonymous information that requires to be processed in order for such an objective to be attained'.[110] As noted in Chapter 2, whilst often couched in rather opaque language, the Court in both C-101/01 *Lindqvist* and C-73/07 *Satamedia* also gave particular emphasis to the need for a balance between data protection and freedom of expression. Nevertheless, since 2009 when data protection was granted the status of a fundamental right in the EU Treaties, there have been signs that the Court has moved to interpreting both the substantive and supervisory aspects of data protection more severely. For example, in C-518/07 *Commission v Germany*, a Grand Chamber of the Court upheld infraction proceedings brought against Germany by finding that the Directive's requirement that DPAs act independently entailed that they 'must remain free from any external influence, including the direct or indirect influence of the State or the Länder, and not of the influence only of the supervised bodies'.[111] In this regard, it was stressed that DPAs were an 'essential component' of data protection and 'the guardians' of the 'fundamental rights and freedoms' which it instantiated.[112] Meanwhile, in C-92/09 and C 93/09 *Volker und Markus Schecke*, another Grand Chamber judgment invoked the fundamental right to data protection (as well as that of privacy) to strike down provisions in an EU Regulation which mandated that as a condition for natural persons to be granted Common Agricultural Payments, their name, municipality, and amounts received must be published on a searchable website.[113] This increased stress on data protection has remained unabated and, especially as regards the interface between data protection and freedom of expression, is epitomized by the Grand Chamber judgment of C-131/12 *Google Spain* which was also mentioned in Chapter 2.[114] Both the continuation of this trend and its full implications for freedom of expression will be analysed further later in the book including, in particular, in Chapters 9 and 13.

Despite the DPD being incorporated into EEA law since the late 1990s, there appears to have been no EFTA Court case law clearly exploring its terms. This Court's broader case law concerning data protection has also remained extremely limited and may show a more deferential approach than is found in CJEU jurisprudence. Thus, in E-013/11 *Schenker*, the Court addressed the meaning of a provision in the EFTA Surveillance Authority's Access to Documents rules which exempted any disclosure which would undermine the protection of the 'privacy and integrity of the individual, in particular in accordance with EEA legislation regarding the protection of personal data'.[115] In C-28/08 *Bavarian Lager*, a Grand Chamber of the CJEU had held that exactly cognate wording in EU law entailed that 'any undermining of privacy and the integrity of the individual must always be examined and assessed in conformity with the legislation of the Union concerning the protection of personal data'[116] including, in particular, a specific

Regulation which subjected EU institutions themselves to the same basic approach as that set out in the DPD.[117] Whilst acknowledging that the principle of 'homogenous interpretation' of common EU and EEA law was 'indispensable',[118] the EFTA Court stressed that the EEA institutions had not been made subject to the same data protection Regulation as the EU institutions. It, therefore, rejected as 'irrelevant'[119] the European Commission's contention that the EFTA Court should prioritize data protection in the same manner as laid down in C-28/ 08 *Bavarian Lager*. Meanwhile, the later case of E-23/13 *Hellenic Capital Market Commission* had to consider whether a provision in a Directive imposing an information sharing duty on EEA market abuse authorities was compatible with placing a requirement on a requesting authority to specify 'the facts that give rise to the suspicion that the prohibition on insider dealing and market manipulation has been infringed',[120] thereby enabling the potentially disclosing authority to take steps to safeguard data protection (and, more especially, bank secrecy).[121] The Court rejected this possibility, arguing that as the entire procedure relied on 'mutual trust and recognition', it was for the requesting authority alone to undertake the relevant assessments.[122]

In contrast to the relative insignificance to date of the EFTA Court, the Article 29 Working Party came to play a crucial role in developing data protection standards during the DPD era. In particular, this pan-EEA body of DPAs adopted well over 100 opinions, recommendations,[123] and similar 'soft law statements'.[124] Although ultimately only advisory, these authoritative documents had 'considerable force'[125] since both 'national regulators and courts frequently look[ed] to the opinions of the Article 29 Working Party in their national implementation decisions'.[126] Some of these documents considered highly technical aspects of the law and/or its application to areas unrelated to this book. Nevertheless, many others explored core concepts[127] and substantive aspects[128] of EU data protection, as well as data protection's relationship to activities critical to freedom of expression including media processing,[129] social networking,[130] and search engine indexing.[131] It is difficult to provide an overall characterization of these documents, not least since the Working Party had 'some 15 subgroups'[132] and therefore many of these documents had very different drafting histories. Nevertheless, whilst also recognizing the need for 'an appropriate balance in the application of the Directive's rules',[133] the Working Party did tend towards an 'expansive view of the application of the Directive'.[134] For example, its 2007 opinion on personal data stressed 'the broad concept of "personal data" and of "processing" contained in the Directive' and noted the danger of any interpretation 'that would leave individuals deprived of protection of their rights'.[135] Meanwhile, its 2008 opinion on social networking went even beyond C-101/01 *Lindqvist*'s restrictive understanding of the personal/household exemption by arguing that even where a social network user did not engage in indefinite publication '[a] high number of contacts could be an indication that the household exemption does not apply' and that, in any case, '[t]he application of the household exemption

[was] also constrained by the need to guarantee the rights of third parties, particularly with regard to sensitive data.[136] It further recommended social networking site users 'should be advised by [the] SNS [Social Networking Site] that if they wish to upload pictures or information about other individuals, this should be done with the individual's consent'.[137]

3. Third-Generation European Data Protection (2010s to present day)

3.1 Transnational Developments Leading to the General Data Protection Regulation

In 2010, the year after the Lisbon reforms established a *sui generis* Treaty *vires* for data protection, the European Commission announced its intention to bringing forward new legislation in this area.[138] In January 2012, the Commission made good on this commitment by proposing, alongside a package of measures,[139] that the DPD be replaced by a General Data Protection Regulation ('GDPR').[140] Similar to the DPD proceedings, several years of discussions followed with (in some contrast to the DPD's drafting) the European Parliament playing a particularly active role. Whilst the Parliament adopted its position on the GDPR in early 2013, it took until June 2015 for the Council to do the same. An agreement between all three institutions was forthcoming in late 2015;[141] the final GDPR text was then adopted on 27 April 2016, and the law became directly applicable across the EU from 25 May 2018.[142] The EEA Joint Committee adopted the GDPR, with some essentially procedural modifications, on 6 July 2018[143] and, following relevant notifications by non-EU EEA States, it entered into force within the wider EEA on 20 July 2018.

Whilst maintaining the essential scope and nature of European data protection as previously established, the GPDR seeks to respond to the concerns around the incorrect implementation of, and more general legislative divergence under, the DPD. Indeed, the very choice of a Regulation as opposed to a Directive points to the initiative's emphasis on ensuring a more 'consistent level of protection for natural persons' throughout Europe.[144] Reflecting both data protection's new status as a fundamental right[145] and the threats posed by '[r]apid technical developments and globalisation',[146] the reforms also seek to ensure 'a strong and more coherent data protection framework . . . backed up by strong enforcement'.[147] Reflecting this, the GDPR furthers the broad material approach articulated in the DPD, maintaining the restriction of the personal/household exemption to activities which are 'purely' of such a nature[148] and otherwise restricting exemptions to an even narrower range of State activity.[149] Nevertheless, whilst generally adopting a broad understanding of 'personal data' especially in relation to the notion of identifiability,[150] it more clearly specifies that the potential application of data protection to information relating to deceased persons remains within the prerogative of individual States.[151]

This new instrument retains the essential framework of data protection's core substance as set out in the DPD by, in particular, specifying similarly broad data protection principles,[152] detailed transparency rules,[153] restrictive rules relating to 'sensitive' data,[154] and a wide range of 'discipline' provisions.[155] However, a number of these duties are subject to significant augmentation. For example, the new iterations of the proactive transparency rules specify that a much wider range of information should be provided than previously, including, for example, the legal basis for the processing, whether any transfer of data outside the EEA is intended and, if so, the safeguards applicable in relation to this.[156] Moreover, even though the proactive transparency rules continue in principle to be rendered inapplicable where data are not collected directly from the data subject and individual notification constitutes at least a 'disproportionate effort', it is now stated that the controller itself must then 'take appropriate measures to protect the data subject's rights and freedoms and legitimate interests, including making the information publicly available'.[157] The Regulation also further elucidates the concept of 'sensitive' data by *inter alia* including 'sexual orientation' alongside the existing category of 'sex life' data and also 'genetic data' and 'biometric data for the purpose of uniquely identifying a natural person' alongside 'data concerning health'.[158]

Moving on to consider the system of supervision, the Regulation placed a renewed emphasis on data subject control rights (including by coupling the existing right to erase illegally processed data with an explicit 'right to be forgotten'[159]), adopts a wide construction of the right to compensation (especially in relation to non-material damage),[160] and sets out possibilities for representatives of data subjects to pursue actions on behalf of these individuals.[161] Of even more significance, it greatly expands and specifies the required status,[162] resourcing,[163] tasks,[164] and powers[165] of the DPAs which remain mandated in each EEA State. Most especially, these authorities are placed under an obligation to issue 'effective, proportionate and dissuasive' administrative fines of up to either €10 million or €20 million (or either 2 per cent or 4 per cent of any commercial undertaking's annual global turnover if this is higher) for infringements of most aspects of the Regulation.[166] DPAs are also granted a wide range of investigative and corrective powers including a right to 'obtain access to any premises' of a controller which extends also 'to any data processing equipment and means'.[167]

An additional pillar of the GDPR is a set of reforms designed to ensure that DPAs themselves engage in a much more '[c]onsistent and homogenous application of the [data protection] rules'.[168] Thus, uncertain and overlapping regulatory competence, vague requirements to cooperate,[169] and a purely advisory pan-European Working Party[170] are replaced with a regulatory 'one-stop shop' and 'cooperation and consistency'[171] mechanism for 'cross-border processing',[172] all overseen by a new European agency—the European Data Protection Board ('EDPB')[173]—which is granted power to direct local DPA action or restraint in this area. 'Cross-border processing' is generally defined broadly so as to include not only the processing of personal data taking place 'in the context of the activities of establishments in more than one Member State' but also processing taking place in the context of just a single establishment 'but which substantially affects or is likely to substantially affect data subjects in more than one Member State'.[174] As regards such activity, the DPA responsible for the territory within which either the single or the 'main' establishment of the controller is located is allocated a unique overarching competence as the 'lead supervisory authority'.[175] However, as a quid pro quo for this monopolistic position, 'concerned' DPAs are enabled to participate in a formal 'cooperation and consistency' mechanism. The notion of a 'concerned' DPA is also defined expansively so as to encompass not only situations where the entity concerned has an establishment on the territory of the regulator but also where data subjects resident in this territory are 'substantially affected or likely to be substantially affected' by the relevant processing and even where a data subject has simply lodged a complaint with the relevant regulator.[176] The required duties of cooperation are generally envisaged to include not only the provision of mutual assistance but also the right to engage in coordinated joint operations.[177] Finally, under the consistency provisions, any disputes can be resolved through the EDPB. This new agency, which similarly to the erstwhile Article 29 Working Party is composed of national representatives of all the DPAs, is empowered to issue decisions binding on all relevant regulators. Whilst ordinarily the Board should act by a majority of at least two-thirds,[178] a simple majority will suffice in cases of urgency[179] or where the Board has otherwise been unable to agree.[180]

Despite the heavy emphasis on harmonization in the GDPR, the reform still leaves States with significant 'margin of manoeuvre'[181] both in relation to the substance and the oversight of data protection. For example, States are empowered to limit the use of data subject consent as a legal basis for processing special/sensitive data[182] and set down further conditions for the processing of genetic data, biometric data, and/or data concerning health.[183] Subject to the GDPR's mandatory requirements, they also remain primarily responsible for ensuring the supervision of data protection including through specifying DPA resources, structure, and the 'appropriate safeguards' necessary in the exercise of their powers.[184] The GDPR continues to provide for particular flexibility in the setting down of derogations. Thus, States can elect to restrict much of the GDPR's substantive default, usually through a detailed[185] legislative measure which, on specified legitimate grounds (including protecting other 'rights and freedoms'), is shown to be 'a necessary and proportionate measure in a democratic society' and which continues to respect the 'essence' of the relevant fundamental rights and freedoms.[186] These requirements are not only more stringent than those set down in the equivalent provisions in the DPD but, for the first time, also rule out derogations not only from the discipline and supervisory regime but also from the data protection principles in and of themselves. However, notwithstanding these new and continuing general limits, States remain responsible for setting out even more flexible and wide-ranging derogations in the area of special expression which is now defined as 'processing carried out for journalistic purposes or the purpose of academic artistic or literary expression.[187] Within this special area, derogations are to be adopted if (and insofar as) 'they are necessary to reconcile the right to the protection of personal data with the freedom of expression and information.[188] For the first time, States are also made subject to a more diffuse obligation to 'by law reconcile the right to the protection of personal data pursuant to this Regulation with the right to freedom of expression and information' both within and outside the special expressive area. These provisions on freedom of expression (including its sub-right, freedom of information), as well as those which target 'archiving purposes in the public interest', 'scientific and historical research', and 'statistical purposes',[189] will be returned to at various points later in this book including, in particular, in Chapters 8, 9, 12, and 13.

3.2 Legislative Developments at National Level

Given its status as a Regulation, on 25 May 2018 most of the GDPR became directly applicable at the national level by simple operation of law.[190] However, some parts of the Regulation have intrinsically required, whilst many others permit, further implementation through national legislation. Approximately half the EEA States had adopted a law implementing the GDPR by the mid-2018 deadline.[191] Whilst a number of the remaining States have adopted such a law subsequently, such implementation remains entirely absent (as of May 2019) in Greece, Portugal, and Slovenia.

One mandated aspect of a law at national level concerns the constitution and precise modes of operation of DPA supervision. Whilst most States have adopted for a single unitary authority concerned solely with data protection regulation, some have continued to fuse this role with other regulatory functions (notably ensuring the public's access to information held by public authorities). Meanwhile, both Germany and Spain (as regards the autonomous communities of Catalonia and the Basque Country) have continued to divide regulatory responsibilities here between national and regional DPAs. Although additional substantive requirements such as potentially applying aspects of the GDPR to data concerning the deceased are also of importance, the most significant substantive provisions adopted at national level are derogatory in nature. Almost all States have adopted derogatory provisions which seek to reconcile data protection with journalism and other forms of special expression, whilst a clear majority have also adopted detailed derogations in the areas of archiving purposes in the public interest, scientific or historical research, and statistical purposes. These derogatory provisions will be returned to later in this book. Many of the other derogations adopted have been quite technical in nature and, in many cases, also peculiar to one or a few States. In a few instances, however, States have sought to adopt much more far-reaching derogations. For example, both Irish and Swedish law seek to disable the application of all the substantive provisions in the GDPR in any case where its application is held to be contrary or incompatible with (potentially nationally idiosyncratic understandings of) freedom of expression and information including, but not limited to, special expression such as journalism.[192] Meanwhile, Dutch law attempts to authorize controllers themselves to self-derogate from potentially all of the transparency rules and data subject control rights so long as this is precisely justified on widely specified grounds (including protecting 'rechten en vrijheden' ('rights and freedoms')) and the derogation is necessary and proportionate.[193] Potentially rather similarly, Danish law enables a derogation from the transparency rules wherever these are found to be overridden by 'afgørende hensyn til private interesser' ('essential considerations of private interests').[194] However, notwithstanding these sometimes important caveats, it is clear that the formal legal divergences present within the EEA during the DPD era have been significantly reduced under the GDPR.

4. Conclusions

In contrast to the central historical position of freedom of expression within European liberal democracy, the concept of data protection only emerged clearly in the 1970s. Reflecting its close relationship with core European values such as privacy and its strong link to the emerging information society, data protection has formally developed far and fast since this time. Whilst remaining centrally concerned with privacy, it aims to safeguard all individual rights and freedoms that may be impacted by the processing of information related to an identified or identifiable natural person. In contrast to freedom of expression's abstract rights guarantees, the focus throughout has been on specifying a comprehensive regulatory code of rules and principles to govern such personal data processing. Alongside this codification, data protection has also come to be considered a fundamental right, a status that was recognized by the EU as a whole in the 2000s as a result of the EU Charter. Without displacing the central position of regulatory DPAs, this later development has seen the CJEU and other courts also emerging as important articulators of applicable norms.

At a transnational level, European data protection was originally codified in two advisory Council of Europe Resolutions in the 1970s, which led to an optional but legally binding Council of Europe Convention in the 1980s, a mandatory EU/EEA Data Protection Directive in the 1990s, and a General Data Protection Regulation in the 2010s which in most respects became directly binding and effective across the EU. These changes are reflective of an ambitious push towards ever greater European harmonization which, as a result, has become far more extensive here than was apparent in Chapter 2's discussion of freedom of expression. All these instruments have specified data protection's substance in terms of broad data protection principles, detailed rules relating to transparency, strict further limits on sensitive types of data, and a range of provisions designed to ensure genuine discipline in data processing. Alongside further harmonization, each later instrument has come to specify these substantive requirements in a more granular and often more exacting fashion. These trends have only been partially tempered by the allied specification of derogatory provisions including related to special forms of expression such as journalism. This strong commitment to ensuring a 'high level'[195] of protection is also reflected in increasingly strict formal standards of regulation which centre on now mandatory and independent DPAs who are allocated a powerful role both in relation to interpretive standard-setting and enforcement.

All these developments have taken place within the context of dramatic socio-technological change and acute rights conflict. The rest of this book analyses how European data protection has responded to the resulting challenges when regulating one critically important aspect of social life, namely the expressive activity of traditional publishers. Part II of this book commences this exploration by turning to look at the interaction between data protection and the most high-profile and arguably most important type of traditional publisher, namely the professional journalist.

PART II
EUROPEAN DATA PROTECTION AND PROFESSIONAL JOURNALISM

4

First-Generation European Data Protection Regulation and Professional Journalism

The 'first generation' of European data protection began with early Council of Europe and national initiatives in the 1970s and lasted until the negotiation of the EU's Data Protection Directive 95/46 ('DPD') in the 1990s. Notwithstanding certain efforts at pan-European coordination, a highly divergent approach emerged in different States as regards the interface between data protection and professional journalism. Furthermore, in several cases, a manifest gap—normally in favour of the media—arose between law on the books and efforts at practical implementation on the ground. Early efforts at regulation almost invariably focused on responding to the development by journalists of both internal and publicly available electronic databases, as opposed to the initial publication of personal information by the media. The latter remained almost exclusively paper-based during this period. Nevertheless, whilst limited in reach, the actions of a number of Nordic Data Protection Authorities (DPAs) were both stringent and sustained. Towards the end of the period, such intervention came under pressure as a result of both political backlash and the dramatically increased use of computers and computerized networks including, in particular, the World Wide Web. At the same time, these socio-technological changes solidified a very broad conceptualization of data protection's scope which clearly encompassed even the initial gathering and dissemination of personal information by journalists within the new digital context.

This chapter explores these early developments, many of whose contours have continued to exert an influence on the later history of European data protection. Section 1 examines the interface between data protection and journalism in the legal instruments established at pan-European level and, more especially, in those European States which had adopted legislation prior to the European Commission proposing the DPD in 1990. Section 2 then shifts focus and examines efforts at practical regulatory implementation, both within individual States and transnationally. Finally, section 3 sets out some overarching conclusions, linking these to the later trajectory of European data protection in this area.

European Data Protection Regulation, Journalism, and Traditional Publishers. David Erdos, Oxford University Press (2019). © David Erdos.
DOI: 10.1093/oso/9780198841982.003.0004

1. First-Generation Legal Instruments and
Professional Journalism

1.1 Pan-European Legal Instruments

As explored in Chapter 3, European data protection had its origin in a cluster of initiatives related to the safeguarding of 'privacy'.[1] Some of these focused on the regulation of professional journalism. Most notably, in 1970 the Council of Europe's Parliamentary Assembly issued Resolution 428 (1970) on mass communication media and human rights. Whilst expounding on the fundamentality of journalistic freedom of expression, this instrument also emphasized that national law should guarantee individuals, even including public figures, a right to privacy against not only State but also private actors including the mass journalistic media. In most respects the conceptualization of privacy that was adopted remained relatively narrow, it being specifically stated that '[t]hose who, by their own actions, have encouraged indiscreet revelations about which they complain later on, cannot avail themselves of the right to privacy'.[2] Nevertheless, some other rather ambiguous parts of the resolution did emphasize the need for safeguards as regards the accumulation of information in computerized databases and also urged ongoing consideration of problems arising from 'attempts to obtain information by modern technical devices' including 'the use of computers'.[3] Finally, the instrument stressed the desirability of developing media self-regulation through professional training, a code of ethics, and press councils. In 1974 this declaratory document was complemented by Resolution (74) 26 of the Council of Europe's Committee of Ministers which, more specifically, argued that both natural and legal persons should have a right of reply when allegedly inaccurate facts were published in the periodical media.[4]

The interface between European data protection and professional journalism would become influenced by the attempt, in Resolution 428 (1970), to marry legal reform with self-regulation and, in Resolution (74) 26, to more specifically focus on issues of inaccuracy and rectification. Nevertheless, it is important to stress that Council of Europe Committee of Ministers' 1973 and 1974 Resolutions which concerned data protection itself did not specifically address professional journalism in any way. Nor were these particularities directly confronted in any associated discussions at this stage. In some contrast, the shift to agreeing a more specific and binding Data Protection Convention in 1981 did see the first explicit, albeit rather cursory, engagement with this issue. In sum, the Convention's Explanatory Report glossed the Convention's validation of legally authorized derogations which were 'a necessary measure in the interests of . . . the rights and freedoms of others'[5] by indicating that this covered 'major interests . . . of third parties' including 'freedom of the press'.[6] This statement thereby explicitly acknowledged that there could well be a need for States to adopt specific derogations here to ensure a careful balance between divergent rights and interests.

1.2 National Legal Instruments

Turning to the national level, although a fairly stringent approach was generally adopted, the extent and manner in which specifics of professional journalism were addressed by data protection statutes diverged considerably in this first-generation period. As Table 4.1 outlines, six of the twelve European States that passed data protection legislation prior to 1990 included no derogation which was directly aimed at shielding professional journalism from their law's default provisions. This group comprised Sweden (1973), Denmark (1978), Luxembourg (1979), Iceland (1981), the United Kingdom (1984), and Ireland (1988). In stark contrast, two States— Germany (1977)[7] and the Netherlands (1988)[8]—effectively granted professional journalism a complete exemption from the need to adhere to any of the specified substantive data protection norms. The other four countries adopted partial derogations which provided the media very different degrees of special leeway. Thus, France (1978) established a media derogation from the prohibition on processing sensitive personal data and from the need to obtain authorization for transborder data flows but, even then, only when their application would limit freedom of expression and they adhered to all other legal restrictions (both within and outside of statutory data protection itself).[9] Meanwhile, although Norwegian primary legislation passed in 1978 included no provision in favour of the media, secondary legislation (adopted in 1979) exempted internal databases of the periodical press that held sensitive data from the general requirement to obtain a license for this so long as they adhered to certain security guarantees. [10] A full exemption was also set

Table 4.1 First-Generation National Data Protection Laws and Professional Journalism (with amendments highlighted)

No derogation	Partial derogation	Full (substantive) derogation
Sweden—1973	France—1978	(Germany—1977)
(Denmark—1978)	Austria—1978	Netherlands—1988
Luxembourg—1979	Norway—1978/9	(Finland—1994)
Iceland—1981	(Finland—1987)	
United Kingdom—1984	(Germany—1991)	
Ireland—1988	(Denmark—1987)	
	(Denmark—1994)	

out for *'boker tidsskrifter e.l.'* ('books, journals/magazines, and the like') but only where these had been published prior to data protection legislation coming into force.[11] In contrast to these two cases of rather limited derogation, Austria (1978) generally exempted the journalistic activities of the mass media from all substantive data protection standards.[12] However, this derogation was not only expressly stated to be to be '[b]*is zum Inkrafttreten von Datenschutzbestimmungen eines Mediengesetzes*'[13] ('pending the enactment of provisions concerning data protection in future media legislation') but also left unaffected the data subject's (albeit qualified) constitutional rights[14] to keep private personal data secret, to access information relating to them which was automatically processed, and to ensure the rectification of such data.[15] Finally, Finland (1987) provided that data protection 'shall not affect the right to publish printed matter.'[16] Although absolute in its area of application, this last provision did not explicitly shield either databases containing personal data which were used internally by the media or the publication of personal data in a publicly available electronic database (or indeed in any other manner than in printed form).

As Table 4.1 also outlines, Denmark, Germany, and Finland engaged in further legislative reform during this first-generation period or, in other words, prior to the finalization of the DPD in 1995. In 1987, Danish law absolved internal media databases 'exclusively storing data publicized in a periodical paper' from all the general data protection rules other than the right of subject access. Such databases were, however, subject to a prior notification to the Data Protection Authority ('DPA') which was additionally empowered to

> lay down more detailed terms and conditions for the register [databases] in question, including on consent by any registered party [data subject], on expunction and up-dating of data, and on safeguards against the register being wrongfully used or brought to the notice of unauthorised persons.

Other than through 'publication in a periodical paper', controllers were also prohibited from passing on information included in the database unless they had data subject consent, or this was 'provided for by other enactment'.[17] Moreover, any other internal database operated by professional journalists, as well as all publicly available databases, remained fully subject to the general law. Nevertheless, in 1994 a much more extensive reform took place through enactment of the *Lov om massemediers informationsdatabaser* (Law on Mass Media Information Databases). This *sui generis* Danish law established that databases which exclusively included unaltered text, images, and sound originally published in periodical form and stored relative to that publication would, even if they were made publicly available, fall only within the scope of the Media Liability Act rather than the general Data Protection Act.[18] The former Act *inter alia* provided that published material must be in conformity with sound journalistic ethics, established a right of reply, and required registration with the co-regulatory Press Council.[19] Other publicly available mass media databases were held to additional stipulations through the Law on Mass Media Databases Act, itself including requirements relating to subject access, to the deletion, correction, or updating of inaccurate or misleading information, to a presumption that sensitive information would not be made available after a period of three years, and to additional registration with the DPA.[20] Databases solely used internally by the media were subject only to inclusion on a public register maintained by the DPA and to certain security guarantees.[21] Finally, substantive regulatory supervision of the mass media in both Acts was allocated to the co-regulatory Press Council rather than the DPA.[22] Going considerably further even than this last enactment, in 1994 Finland released both publicly available archival databases and also internal databases produced by the media from all substantive data protection provisions, subject only to compliance with certain security guarantees. Finally, a modest reverse trend was apparent in Germany with a reform to data protection law in 1991 resulting in certain broadcasters being subject to highly qualified versions of the accuracy principle and right of subject access. At the same time, this change indicated that a data protection officer internal to the broadcasting organization should take the place of the DPA in regulating compliance here.[23]

The legal approaches adopted by European States in this early period are rather difficult to orientate into an overarching pattern. Indeed, the observed differences may have been most influenced by whether, and to what extent, specific attention was given to professional journalism during parliamentary deliberation on the data protection legislation. Clearly, all the States which adopted either a full or partial derogation here gave some specific attention to these actors. In some contrast, in many of the States which adopted legislation without explicit derogation, namely Sweden (1973), Denmark (1978), Luxembourg (1979), Iceland (1981), and Ireland (1988), little or no such discussion took place. However, such a distinction cannot provide a complete explanation of even the split between 'derogation' and 'no derogation' jurisdictions. For example, the UK Parliament did debate a number of amendments designed explicitly to shield journalism from aspects of what became the Data Protection Act 1984,[24] but ultimately decided to reject these. By contrast, in Norway, there was little or no legislative debate on this topic, yet the Government did eventually adopt explicit derogations through secondary legislation.

This deliberative factor also can do little to distinguish between those States which adopted only limited derogations and those that enacted extensive or even complete derogations. Such contrasts may relate to the particular framing of the issue within the legislature which was perhaps somewhat more idiosyncratic in this early period than in later deliberations. For example, during the original German legislative proceedings, the Government from the outset conceptualized a wide derogation from data protection regulation as essential to safeguard freedom of expression as guaranteed in the German Basic Law.[25] This, in turn, may be related to a debate in the 1950s where an earlier Government proposal for statutory regulation of the press had been clearly rejected on similar grounds.[26] In contrast, in France the adoption of even a limited derogation in favour of journalism was conceptualized as opening *'une brèche énorme'* ('a huge breach') in the new data protection framework.[27]

Finally, it should be noted that in this early era of only very partially harmonized European data protection legislation, the absence of any explicit legislative derogation in the favour of professional journalism was far from a necessary indicator that the restraints placed on the media were more severe than in States with an express, but qualified, derogation. Thus, UK and Irish first-generation data protection law lacked both special protection for sensitive data and a general regime restricting the international transfer of personal data; in addition, they included an overarching exemption (i.e. not limited to cases of publication) for any operation performed only 'for the purpose of preparing the text of documents'.[28] As a result of these general provisions, both laws provided for less stringent control of the media than the initial Finnish and, even more manifestly, the French legislation, even after allowing for the effect of the specific derogations which each of the latter included.

2. Regulatory Implementation of First-Generation Data Protection in Relation to the Professional Journalistic Media

2.1 State Developments

Early DPA activity as regards the professional journalistic media was marked by an extreme diversity which can only partially be accounted for through the disparity in legislation explored above. In six States—Austria, Finland, Germany, Iceland, Ireland, and the Netherlands—no regulatory action at all can be discerned. In Germany, the Netherlands, and Austria, such action was essentially precluded by far-reaching substantive statutory derogations in favour of professional journalism or, after the reform to German data protection law, the placing of regulatory supervision in the hands of an internal data protection officer. Meanwhile, the absence of action in Luxembourg can be related to the fact that legislation here only provided for an Advisory Board rather than a true DPA.[29] These kinds of statutory features cannot, however, explain the lack of activity in Iceland, Ireland or, prior to 1994, Finland. Meanwhile, in two States—the United Kingdom and, to a much lesser extent, France—the DPA did address these actors to a very limited extent. Finally, in three States—Denmark, Sweden, and Norway—much more extensive regulatory action was forthcoming.

Turning first to explore the limited intervention in France and the United Kingdom, French action strictly focused on data protection was confined to a consideration of whether 'transborder data transmissions by the press' could result in 'information purporting to be for press purposes' being 'used for other ends'.[30] Meanwhile, in the United Kingdom, the DPA signalled early on that 'the media' was an area which demanded '[s]pecial attention'; visits were, therefore, arranged to see 'television news and programme making at first hand'.[31] Guidance issued by this DPA also indicated that those processing data for the purposes of maintaining 'information or data banks as a reference tool or general resource' such as 'free text data bases' had to register with it under the purpose of 'information and data bank administration' and, furthermore, that this requirement particularly applied to 'news media'.[32] On a number of occasions, including in formal submissions to two official inquiries set up by the UK Government in the early 1990s,[33] this DPA advocated in favour of a broad substantive role for data protection here. The head of this DPA further argued that the legislation in force gave individuals 'the right to read their own newspaper obituary if they are stored on computers' and, 'if inaccurate', enabled them to ask either the DPA or the courts for it to be rectified.[34] At the same time, the UK DPA did not formally intervene in this area prior to the DPD being agreed in 1995. Nevertheless, in 1997—one year before the DPD came in to effect—it did prosecute a 'former private investigator who used deception to obtain information from British Telecom, such as ex-directory numbers and itemised bills, relating to people in whom the media were interested'.[35] As will be seen, the UK media's use of deception to obtain personal data included within non-media databases later came to much greater prominence in the DPD era.[36]

The limited regulatory action in France and the United Kingdom contrasts markedly with the attempt at extensive supervision of the professional journalistic media by DPAs in Denmark, Sweden, and Norway. The Norwegian DPA was first to act within this area. Its 1983 annual report drew attention to what it saw as the significant data protection concerns raised by the development digital media archives, namely that that this might make it impossible for old information to be forgotten, that incorrect information might be perpetuated, and, if the archive was open to general public, that employers would be enabled to check up on prospective employees with the use of this information.[37] Based on such concerns and following consultation with both the press and the public, in 1985 this DPA set the following two conditions when granting a license for a newspaper (*Aftenposten*) to establish a digital media archive for not only internal but also external use:

1. that it would correct any inaccuracies subsequent to original publication, noting in the article's title that corrections had been made; and
2. that, as regards the external archive only, reference to an individual being suspected, accused, or judged for a criminal act would be anonymized after

seven years, unless these data subjects were named as occupiers of a professional or public position.[38]

Its 1986 annual report[39] explicitly reported that these same license terms had been
issued to two other newspapers. The Norwegian DPA retained this basic approach
until the mid-1990s.[40]

Meanwhile, the Swedish and Danish DPA adopted an even more stringent
stance, first by regulating purely internal journalistic databases and second by
entirely prohibiting publicly available media archives which contained personal
data. Nevertheless, in both jurisdictions a political reaction to this ultimately
prompted a more liberal approach. In the Swedish case, this was facilitated by
the fact that, far from being able to carry out its functions autonomously (absent
legal challenge), the DPA's decisions could be reviewed by an ombudsman (the
Chancellor of Justice) and then amended or even overturned by the Government.
Looking first at internal databases, this issue first arose in Sweden in 1987 when
Swedish Radio applied for a DPA license to record information (including likely
sensitive data) on potential contacts, as well as on past programmes. The DPA
imposed a right for data subjects to obtain the deletion of the latter records; moreover, as a result of intervention by the Chancellor of Justice and the Government,
the obligation that data subjects be somehow informed of the existence of both
types of recordings was also stipulated.[41] Nevertheless, a change of political stance
first became apparent in 1989 when the newspaper *Pressen Bilds* applied for a license to establish an internal database of past news stories. Although both the
DPA and the Chancellor of Justice sought to ensure that any sensitive data in the
database more than five years old was only searchable by date, the Government
dissolved this restriction. It nevertheless upheld requirements to indicate when
data had been found to be incomplete, incorrect, or misleading, to log all access to
the database, and to make an announcement regarding its existence at least once
a year.[42] The Danish DPA also engaged in supervising internal media databases,
although only after a legislative reform in 1987 had established that these archives fell outside general data protection stipulations but were still subject to DPA
registration and potential licensing restrictions. In two licenses issued in 1989,
this DPA established that efforts should be made to ensure that incorrect information was not recorded in an internal media database, that inaccuracies were generally corrected through annotations, and that the database was secured against
unauthorized access.[43]

Turning to publicly available electronic media archives, both the Danish and
Swedish DPAs in the later 1980s sought to prohibit these entirely, arguing that
they would have too much of an impact on personal privacy.[44] However, difficulties in holding such a line quickly emerged. In each jurisdiction, it became
apparent that the media entities which had applied for a license to make their
electronic archive publicly available (*Daglaget Poliken* in Denmark and *VLT*

Data Klipp in Sweden) had gone ahead with this in any case; criminal proceedings were therefore initiated.[45] More generally, in each case, the media intensified its challenge to the DPA's approach through political channels. In Denmark, this resulted in the Government setting up a commission on archival press registers in 1990;[46] this commission's report and the political debate resulting from it led, as noted earlier, to a 1994 legislative reform that subjected professional journalism to only minimal data protection stipulations which were to be substantively supervised not by the DPA but rather by the co-regulatory Press Council. In Sweden, despite opposition from the Chancellor of Justice, in 1990 *VLT Data Klipp* was successful in getting the Government to overturn the DPA's prohibition on making media archives publicly available, albeit with the personal data included on this service being subject to a provisional time limit of five years post initial publication.[47] In 1992, the Swedish DPA also granted two specialist newspapers[48] permission to distribute archival records on CD-ROM. Arguing that the newspapers would remain responsible for the information even when it was in the hands of the end-user, the DPA accepted that it would not be practicable to adopt its usual practice of ensuring that newspaper information shown to be misleading or inaccurate was clearly noted as such.[49] Nevertheless, as a result, permission was only granted for a strictly limited circulation of the discs and on a trial basis only. However, in 1994 the DPA granted *Affärsdata* (Business Data) permission to distribute an archive of a range of newspapers and also a database about Swedish companies and certain individuals related to those companies on CD-ROM, without apparently any restrictions being imposed.[50] Meanwhile, in 1993–94 another media entity challenged the limitation included in its electronic media archive license that only personal data published in the media in the previous five years be allowed. The Government upheld its appeal, now arguing that such databases should be considered as cognate to radio programmes which were protected by the Swedish Fundamental Law on Freedom of Expression and, it was therefore argued, best understood as falling outside the scope of data protection entirely.[51] The Swedish DPA subsequently acceded to this new understanding.[52] Thus, despite the lack of a formal legislative change, political intervention from this time effectively rendered Swedish data protection rather impotent here.

Turning back finally to Norway, subsequent to these developments, in 1995 newspapers petitioned the DPA to lift the license provisions which generally limited the availability of criminal-related data in publicly available media archives to seven years. Alongside freedom of expression concerns, these entities argued that the spread of information to servers based outside the country, on the Internet generally and also on CD-ROM, had rendered it practically impossible for information to be controlled in this fashion. The DPA in principle indicated its acceptance of this submission, whilst indicating that the precise terms of any new license remained to be agreed.[53]

2.2 Transnational Developments

Discussion of the interface between data protection regulation and professional journalism commenced early on within various transnational forums and recurred repeatedly throughout this first-generation period. However, aside from an initial cooperative initiative by the Nordic DPAs, it proved difficult to agree on a specific harmonized approach. Nevertheless, by the end of the period, regulators were increasingly coalescing around a consensus that a wide range of professional journalistic activity in principle fell within the scope of data protection but that this area should also benefit from wide-ranging, albeit not absolute, derogations.

The first transnational explorations of these issues took place at the second through to the sixth meetings of the International Conference of Data Protection Commissioners, held between 1980 and 1984. Discussion focused both on the use of new computerized networks by the professional journalistic media and the spawning of entirely novel forms of electronic media publication by amateur individuals and associated services; however, the latter aspect falls outside the scope of this book and will be addressed in later work. The 1980 meeting concluded only on the tangential issue that 'press freedom of access to information about people [held by non-journalistic controllers] should not be without suitable protection of individual rights, especially where computerized systems are involved'.[54] In contrast, the 1981 meeting looked at the '[u]se of personal details by the press' itself, and it was agreed to explore this and other more exclusively 'new' media issues through a special committee.[55] Following considerable further discussion in 1982,[56] this committee put forward a Resolution at the International Conference in 1983. The Data Protection Commissioners unanimously adopted this Resolution which argued that that '[t]he contents of information offered' through new media technology 'must not violate personal rights' and that 'what is particularly to be avoided is a situation wherein legal regulations covering the processing of personal data and the permission to access such data, existing in one country can be circumvented in other'. The Resolution further stressed that 'even if national legislation provides for exemptions from data protection for press and broadcasting authorities', the minimum standards set down *inter alia* in the Data Protection Convention should be ensured and that 'international cooperation of data protection control institutions in the supervision of new media' was required.[57] Following on from this resolution, the Nordic Committee of DPAs collectively proposed at the 1984 meeting that more specific consideration be given electronic media archives. This initiative, however, was rebuffed.[58] Nevertheless, a Nordic DPA working group continued study of this issue. Its final report of April 1985 proposed that

1. externally available electronic media archives should not contain individuals' sensitive information;

2. that, in the alternative, such disclosure should only be possible for a limited time period such as one or two years;
3. the data subject should have free access to the information stored; and
4. there should be an easy and fast mechanism for rectifying inaccurate or misleading information.[59]

As detailed in section 2.1, the Nordic committee's report clearly had an impact on DPAs in Denmark, Norway, and Sweden (although not Iceland). However, whilst these developments were reported back to the 1985 meeting of the International Conference, they exerted little wider influence.[60] Consideration of the general issue then shifted to the Council of Europe's Committee of Experts on Data Protection which had placed the issue of 'press agencies and data protection' on its agenda by March 1987.[61] Although this body was intergovernmental in nature it remained of relevance here since, as noted in Chapter 3, DPAs regularly took part in its deliberations and, in its drafting of data protection recommendations, it performed a quasi-regulatory function. An exchange of views within the Committee, which took place principally in 1988, highlighted a wide divergence of perspectives on this topic.[62] Nevertheless, it was decided that, rather than abandoning the issue or seeking to draft a specific recommendation, a study of this topic should be prepared.[63] Published in 1991, this study stressed the growing 'potential for conflict' between data protection and 'freedom of the press'[64] given 'the increasing recourse to automation by the various organs for the media'.[65] It also argued that, in light of the principle of proportionality,

> there can be no open-ended derogation from the right to privacy/data protection. Similarly, as regards the inclusion of the media within the ambit of data protection legislation, there cannot be a total disregard of the notion of press freedom.[66]

Finally, the report tentatively suggested that the principles laid down in Council of Europe Resolutions 428 (1970) and (74) 26 'could usefully inform the approach taken by national policy makers as well as the data protection authorities in the area of data protection and the media'.[67] Thus, Resolution 428 (1970) was held to stipulate that 'personal data may only be collected by the media in a fair and lawful manner',[68] whilst its reference to a 'professional code of ethics for journalists' was felt to be

> a good mechanism for making the media aware of the data quality requirements set out in Article 5 of the data protection convention, through allowing the professional bodies representing the various organs of the media to provide the necessary ethical framework, free from government involvement.[69]

It was also emphasized that this text suggested that 'freedom of press can to some extent override the privacy claimed by public personalities'.[70] As regards the interface with Resolution (74) 26, it was argued that it might be possible to consider 'the principle of the right to reply' as 'a valid reflection of the principle of subject access',[71] therefore presumably conceptualizing the latter as also encompassing rights to rectification.

The International Conference returned to a detailed discussion of these issues at its fifteenth meeting in 1993. This discussion revealed a growing consensus that, on the one hand, most professional journalistic activity did fall within the scope of data protection but, on the other, the balancing required in this area was both sensitive and fraught with difficulty. Thus, even the Norwegian Data Protection Commissioner now argued that in his opinion 'it is impossible to draw up and decide through legislation what the media should have access to, what sources they should legally be able to use, and what is supposed to be irrelevant or relevant'.[72] Meanwhile, Alex Turk, a representative of the French DPA, presented a rather nuanced analysis arguing that, whilst some data protection provisions, such as purpose limitation (or data finality), were poorly adapted to professional journalism, others including data security, accuracy, and, with the exception of information on sources, subject access were potentially apposite.[73] Finally, the Data Protection Commissioner for the German Land of Hamburg stressed what he saw as the serious data protection concerns arising from the development of 'reality TV'. According to his argument, television reports were 'only permissible if the public has a justified interest in being informed, and not for the satisfaction of curiosity or sensationalism'; further, data subjects should have a 'right to elicit information from the television stations' and also to 'demand the correction of false assertions'.[74] He finally argued that it was 'possible to protect human dignity and privacy rights in reality TV' but only through 'collaboration between the broadcasting supervision bodies and the data protection commissioners' since in Germany the former (but not the DPAs themselves) ultimately had the possibility to withdraw required licenses to broadcast 'on the grounds of programme infringement'.[75]

3. Conclusions and Broader Implications

At first glance, an exploration of the interface between first-generation European data protection regulation and professional journalism may appear to amount to little more than digital antiquarianism. It is certainly true that some of the concrete initiatives of this time, such as the complete prohibition on publicly available media archives, will prompt the incredulity of many a modern reader. Moreover, in this early period, the pattern of legal response to the tension between data protection and professional journalism appears to have been particularly haphazard. Rather than being rooted in deep cultural differences, much seems to have depended on how the issue was initially framed or indeed if any specific legislative attention was given to this interface at all. Nevertheless, as will be seen in subsequent chapters, many of the other patterns established during this early period have had a continuing salience.

From the outset, the legislative response to the interface between data protection and professional journalism differed profoundly amongst the European States. Moreover, at least in those countries which maintained stringent formal provisions, there was often a considerable gap between the law on the books and efforts at practical regulatory standard-setting and enforcement on the ground. Abstract concerns over freedom of expression were undoubtedly (and rightly) of relevance here. However, in addition, the formidable practical difficulties faced by resource-constrained DPAs operating in the context of rapid socio-technological change were an increasingly salient factor. This period also saw more specific consideration given to the interface between statutory frameworks and self-regulation, the importance of data accuracy and rights to rectification or reply, and the need to ensure that the media did not have unimpeded access to data whose safeguarding was integral to other important social and economic relationships.

Towards the end of this period, further developments in information technology prompted a growing consensus that most forms of professional journalistic activity (and not just media 'databases') in principle fell within the scope of data protection but that, partly as a result of this, wide-ranging derogations were indeed necessary. As will be seen in the following chapters, all these important strands continued to exert a strong influence on the relationship between European data protection and professional journalism during the DPD era and indeed beyond.

5

Second-Generation European Data Protection and Professional Journalism

Formal Law and Regulatory Guidance

The Data Protection Directive 95/46 ('DPD') established a framework for a second generation of European data protection that lasted from the mid-1990s through to the mid-2010s. It mandated that all States adopt a data protection law crafted according to a common default template and including compulsory Data Protection Authority ('DPA') regulation. This new default solidified an understanding that most forms of professional journalism did, in principle, fall within the scope of data protection. At the same time, the DPD explicitly allowed and even mandated States to adopt wide-ranging derogations for processing 'solely for journalistic purposes', but only where this was 'necessary to reconcile' competing rights.[1] This stipulation acquired greater legal salience in the 2000s following the EU Charter's recognition of both data protection and freedom of expression as fundamental rights,[2] together with protection of the former within the EU treaties themselves.[3] However, although a special statutory treatment of journalism became nearly ubiquitous within second-generation data protection, these laws exhibited wide divergences. Some Northern European countries granted the media a complete or near-complete exemption from data protection, whilst other countries in Southern and Eastern Europe failed to set out any significant journalistic derogations within their data protection law at all. In contrast, several European Economic Area (EEA) State legislatures approached this interface with care, often attempting in the process to articulate a co-regulatory relationship between the statutory framework and self-regulatory norms and/or structures. As regards regulatory oversight, a recital in the DPD explicitly stated that a degree of formal supervision remained necessary in relation to this 'sector'[4] and in most EEA countries the statutory DPA itself formally retained full oversight powers and overarching responsibility here.

Turning to guidance on the interface between the journalism and data protection which was forthcoming from these DPAs (or, in a few cases, specialist media regulators designated in legislation), this material generally remained limited, incomplete, or even entirely absent throughout the period. A minority of regulators did explore specific topics in some depth, with issues concerning visual/audio-visual content, children's data, and the 'right to be forgotten'/media archiving receiving particular attention. Nevertheless, in the main, DPA guidance was

European Data Protection Regulation, Journalism, and Traditional Publishers. David Erdos, Oxford University Press (2019). © David Erdos.
DOI: 10.1093/oso/9780198841982.003.0005

confined to outlining the centrality of a contextual balancing of rights in this area, often in the process also emphasizing a link with self-regulatory norms. The precise ambit of such contextual balancing and the continued relevance or otherwise of core data protection standards, therefore, often remained rather opaque. These findings highlighted the need to engage in a deeper analysis of the DPA approach to standard-setting here. This task is pursued in the following chapter through a consideration of the results which were forthcoming from the DPA questionnaire.

This chapter is divided into two main sections which examine, first, the formal legal frameworks and, second, the published regulatory guidance produced during second-generation European data protection as this related to journalism. In both cases, the role of contextual balancing and the interface between the statutory regime and self-/co-regulatory norms and systems are specifically considered. Section 2 also explores the three specific issues noted earlier which were given special prominence in DPA guidance. In each section, the pan-European and, more especially, national dimensions of these issues are considered. Finally, section 3 brings to the fore some concluding strands which act as a springboard for Chapter 6.

1. Second-Generation Legal Instruments and Professional Journalism

1.1 Pan-European Legal Instruments

In contrast to the Data Protection Convention text, Article 9 of the DPD explicitly provided that States should set out derogations in favour of processing 'solely for journalistic purposes' but only 'if they are necessary to reconcile the right to privacy with the rules governing freedom of expression'.[5] The scope within which this instruction potentially applied was very wide. It did, however, explicitly exclude the DPD's essentially procedural requirements to ensure appropriate remedies, compensation, and sanctions for data protection infractions[6] as well as the possibility of drawing up and approving co-regulatory codes of conduct in this area.[7] Recital 37 further stated that there should be no derogation from 'the measures to ensure security of processing' and, further, that 'the supervisory authority responsible for this sector should also be provided with certain ex-post powers, e.g. to publish a regular report or to refer matters to the judicial authorities'. It also reiterated the need for the derogations as a whole to establish a 'balance between fundamental rights'.

This regime for governing journalism as a special form of freedom of expression traces back to a provision in the European Commission's original draft DPD in 1990 which permitted (but did not require) Member States to derogate 'in respect of the press and the audiovisual media' from any part of the Directive 'in so far as they are necessary to reconcile the right to privacy with the rules governing freedom of information and the press'. The Commission Communication which accompanied this proposal stressed that

> [t]he approach adopted lays emphasis on the obligation to balance the interests involved . . . This balance may take into the account, among other things, the availability to the data subject of remedies or of a right to reply, the existence of a code of professional ethics, the limits laid down by the European Convention on Human Rights and the general principles of law.[8]

The Commission's revised proposal of 1992 sought to make such derogations mandatory, expanded them to cover individual 'journalists', and also permitted States to justify them not on the explicit grounds of necessity but merely '[w]ith a view to reconciling the right to privacy with the rules governing freedom of expression'.[9] Subsequent amendments, however, reinserted a requirement of necessity into the article itself and, both through the article and a linked recital, limited the ambit of the permitted derogations to those as specified earlier. The final wording was also amended so as to protect 'journalistic purposes' rather than particular actors such as the press, audio-visual media, or journalists in and of themselves. Turning to the issue of regulatory oversight, at one stage of the negotiations the European Commission, Belgium, France, Italy, Portugal, and Luxembourg proposed that the relevant article should mandate that journalistic activity remain under the general DPA supervisory system.[10] However, as a result of concerns raised by Denmark, Ireland, the Netherlands, Sweden, and the United Kingdom,[11] this was ultimately replaced by a limited reference to the need for supervisory control in the linked text of recital 37.

The need for careful contextual balancing in this area was given new emphasis in the EU Charter of 2000 which set out both data protection and freedom of expression as fundamental rights.[12] Even more importantly, in 2009 this instrument was not only given the same legal status as the EU treaties[13] but the treaties themselves were amended to explicitly set out a right to data protection.[14]

1.2 National Legal Instruments

The extent to which national statutory laws implementing the DPD adopted derogations applicable to journalism which wholly or partially disabled default substantive data protection standards is examined in detail in my article published in 2016.[15] This book will, therefore, draw upon this earlier study, not only in this chapter but also in the chapters to come. In contrast to first-generation data protection law examined in Chapter 4, a systematic comparative study proved possible as a result of the essentially common nature of the default provisions mandated under the DPD as regards (a) data protection principles such as fairness and accuracy;[16] (b) transparency rules setting out both detailed proactive and reactive duties of openness;[17] (c) sensitive data rules setting out strict requirements as regards data deemed to connect particularly to intimate private life or the potential for unfair discrimination;[18] and finally (d) discipline requirements including requirements to register data processing and to curtail the unsafeguarded export of data overseas.[19] In sum, some eighteen directly comparable substantive provisions were located across these four dimensions. These are set out in Table 5.1.

At regards each of these individual provisions, EEA State legislation could (at the extremes) either set out no derogation at all (or, in other words, mandate this standard's full application (1)) or provide for an absolute exemption (or, in other words, provide for no application at all (0)). In between, a wide variety of intermediate positions were also possible. Given this, it was possible to position these outcomes within standardized, ordered categories arrayed along a quantitative (0–1) scale. A specification of these seven categories, as well as examples of provisions which fell within them, are set out in Table 5.2. Meanwhile, the individual provision-level coding for each EEA State may be found in Appendix 4.[20] These results include the internally autonomous British

Table 5.1 Harmonized Default Data Protection Standards (as set out in the Data Protection Directive)

Data protection principles (Dimension A)	Sensitive data rules (Dimension C)
(i) Fairness and lawfulness (A. 6(1)(a))	(ix) Racial and ethnic origin data rule (A. 8)
(ii) Purpose specificity, legitimacy, and compatibility (A. 6(1)(b))	(x) Political opinions data rule (A. 8)
(iii) Adequacy, relevance, and non-excessiveness (A. 6(1)(c))	(xi) Beliefs (religious or philosophical) data rule (A. 8)
(iv) Accuracy (and as necessary up-to-date) (A. 6(1)(d))	(xii) Trade union membership data rule (A. 8)
(v) Temporal minimization of data (A. 6(1)(e))	(xiii) Health data rule (A. 8)
Transparency rules (Dimension B)	(xiv) Sex life data rule (A. 8)
(vi) Proactive where direct collection from subject (A. 10)	(xv) Criminal data rule (A. 8)
(vii) Proactive in relation to other data (A. 11)	**Discipline requirements (Dimension D)**
(viii) Reactive subject access (A. 12)	(xvi) Legal basis (A. 7)
	(xvii) Registration of processing (A. 18-19, A. 21)
	(xviii) Data export restrictions (A. 25-26)

Table 5.2 Ordered Categories Measuring the Extent of the Continued Applicability of Specific Standards *vis-à-vis* Professional Journalism under Second-Generation Statutory Data Protection

Category and scale point	Summary	Definition (with examples in italics)
(a)/1	No derogation	No derogation provided at all from the default general minimum set out in the pan-EU legislative instrument.
		Example: Spanish data protection did not include any provision which explicitly set out a derogation in favour of journalism.
		Example: Belgium law provided no explicit journalistic derogation from any of the data protection principles.[21]
(b)/0.83	Minimal derogation	*Either* (i) no journalistic exemption set out but only a special interpretative provision which provided a gloss but did not supplant the particular data protection provision in question *or* (ii) an exemption was provided but this was limited to a narrow aspect of the provision in question.
		Examples: As regards (i), Italian law did not exempt journalists from compliance with the data protection principles but certain legal provisions including a specially drafted Code of Practice did set out special interpretative provisions in the media's favour.[22] *As regards (ii), Romanian law required journalists to comply with the general rules as regards ensuring the reactive requirement of subject access (provision (viii)) except in so far as the confidentiality of journalistic sources would be affected.*[23]
(c)/0.67	Rule restricted exemption	A wide-ranging journalistic exemption was provided from the particular provision in question so long as the processing fell within specific predefined circumstances and/or complied with specific pre-determined rules.
		Example: Luxembourg law provided a journalistic exemption from the general requirement of reactive subject access (provision (viii)) but only if the media entity instead allowed for access through 'the intermediary of the Commission Nationale pour la Protection des Donneess in the presence of the Conseil de Presse or his representative, or the Chairman of the Conseil de Presse duly called upon'.[24]

Table 5.2 *Continued*

Category and scale point	Summary	Definition (with examples in italics)
(d)/0.5	Strict/objective public interest exemption	An overarching media exemption was provided but this required compliance with a test which, whilst open-textured, appeared based on a strictly objective analysis of where, from the stand-point of the public interest, the balance lies.
		Example: Bulgarian law provided the media with an exemption from certain data protection provisions but only 'to the extent to which it did not violate the right to privacy of the person to whom such data relate'.[25]
(e)/0.33	Permissive public interest exemption	An overarching journalistic exemption was provided but this required compliance with an open-textured public interest test which, whilst imposing significant duties on journalists, appeared phrased so as to be more permissive than a strictly objective test would be.
		Example: Polish law exempted journalists from compliance with the substantive data protection provisions 'unless the freedom of expression and information dissemination considerably violates *the rights and freedoms of the data subject'.*[26]
(f)/0.17	Minimal inclusion	*Either* (i) data protection law excluded much of journalistic data processing unconditionally from the provision in question but subjected some other types of media expression data processing to it only to a limited extent, *or* (ii) an overarching exemption was provided for journalists subject only to compliance with a test of minimal substantive content.
		Examples: As regards (i), Dutch law provided journalists with a complete exemption from all of the sensitive data rules (provisions (ix)–(xv)), subject only to the requirement that the processing was 'necessary' for journalistic purposes.[127] *As regards (ii), in Germany journalists were generally entirely exempted from the requirement that data be accurate and, where necessary, up-to-date (provision (iv)). Nevertheless, the German Interstate Treaty on Broadcasting and Telemedia established that, in relation to both broadcasters and telemedia/online operators (unless subject to cognate self-regulation by the German Press Council), if a person was 'negatively affected in his interests meriting protection' by inaccurate journalistic processing, they could demand either its 'correction' or the addition of their 'own statement of appropriate length'.*[28]
(g)/0	Complete exclusion	An absolute and unconditional media expression derogation was provided from the particular data protection provision in question.
		Example: Dutch law completed excluded journalists from all of the transparency rules set out in the DPD (provisions (vi)–(viii)).[29]

overseas territory of Gibraltar which (for the purposes of this book only) is treated as a separate State to the United Kingdom, thus bringing the total number of EEA States to thirty-two.

Through an averaging of these codings, it was then possible to calculate values representing the degree to which each of the four dimensions of EU data protection formally remained applicable to journalism in each EEA State's statutory code. Finally, an overarching measure was generated along the same 0–1 scale so as to represent the extent to which the overall DPD default was still rendered applicable. In calculating this final measure, the four dimension scores were weighted according to a 3:3:3:1 ratio, with the final 'discipline' dimension placed at the end. This reflected the fact that, in broad terms, the discipline requirements such as restrictions on unsafeguarded data export only have the subsidiary function of supporting the stipulations set out in the other core data protection dimensions. It should, however, be emphasized that adopting other reasonable alternatives to combining the various values (e.g. an equal weighting either to all four dimensions or to all eighteen provisions) made little different to the general pattern observed. Chart 5.1 sets out the overarching result for each State, whilst Charts 5.2–5.5 provide a summary of the spread of average codings for each of the four dimensions of data protection.

As can be seen from Chart 5.1, notwithstanding the DPD and EU Charter's instruction to ensure a careful balancing of equally fundamental rights, an extreme variety of outcomes was in evidence at national level. Indeed, a considerable number of EEA States (e.g. Czechia, Croatia, Hungarian, Slovakia, Slovenia, and Spain) granted the media little or no formal derogation, whilst others (e.g. Germany, Finland, Iceland, and Sweden) exempted journalism from either all or the vast majority of substantive data protection restrictions. In between, practically every other permutation of outcome was also present. The average formal substantive applicability score of 0.54 indicates that, in general, formal data protection restrictions were far from entirely disapplied here. Meanwhile, the standard deviation was 0.33, thus highlighting the presence of very significant variance in outcome. Looking at the more granular data, Chart 5.2 highlights that a slight majority of States (eighteen out of thirty-two or 56 per cent) held that data protection's core (and generally open-textured) principles (provisions (i) to (v)) should remain applicable even to journalism. Meanwhile, as indicated in Chart 5.3, there was evidence of a weak trend amongst States towards recognizing that the transparency rules should either be severely limited or entirely disapplied in this area. However, in relation to final two dimensions, which are represented in Charts 5.4 and 5.5, no trend or commonality was in evidence.

Turning to the regulatory oversight of these substantive stipulations, twenty-three out of the thirty-two EEA States (72 per cent) did not clearly limit the

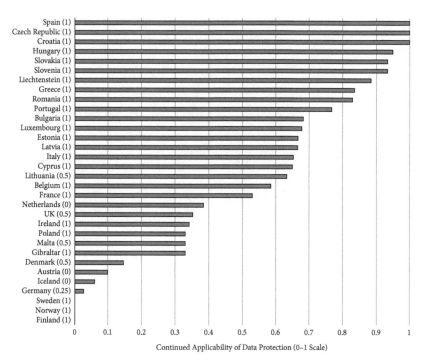

Chart 5.1 Journalism and Substantive Data Protection under the DPD (with Maximum Regulatory Supervision in Brackets)

powers of the DPA here. However, two of these States (Finland and Norway) disapplied substantive data protection duties in relation to journalism entirely, thereby effectively rendering this supervisory jurisdiction otiose. Moreover, as elucidated in section 4, in three others (France, Italy, and Luxembourg), the responsibilities of the DPA here were combined with a limited role for self-regulation. Finally, Spanish law established a federal division of responsibility across the entirety of data protection supervision, with the national DPA accorded theoretically full statutory powers over all private and most public organizations (journalistic or otherwise)[30] and the regional Basque and Catalan DPAs granted oversight only in relation to bodies established or operating under Basque or Catalan public law respectively.[31] In other words, these later regional bodies had full regulatory powers but only in relation to a very small part of the journalistic sector.

Meanwhile, five States (16 per cent) expressly provided for only very limited regulatory powers and responsibilities in this special area, allocating these either to the ordinary DPA (Malta, Sweden, and the United Kingdom[32]) or to a specialist

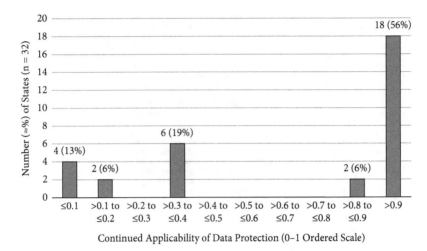

Chart 5.2 The Data Protection Principles and Journalism

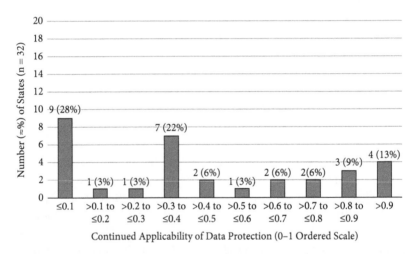

Chart 5.3 The Transparency Rules and Journalism

body with general responsibility for journalistic or media regulation (Denmark and Lithuania).[33] In the special case of Germany, not only was a federal division established through which each *Länder* DPA supervised the private sector, thus leaving the national DPA generally with oversight only as regards the federal public sector, but both the national DPA and many *Länder* DPAs were entirely denuded of all regulatory power over journalism. Nevertheless, to further complicate the picture, some *Länder* DPAs were granted limited powers and responsibilities with regard to the journalism in the broadcasting sector only.[34] Finally, in three States (Austria, Iceland, and the Netherlands) (9 per cent) formal regulatory powers and responsibility were entirely removed.[35]

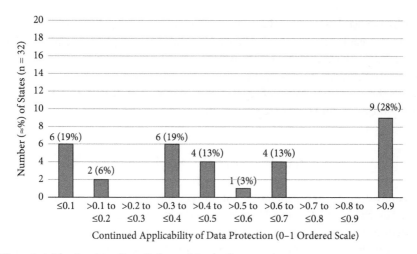

Chart 5.4 The Sensitive Data Rules and Journalism

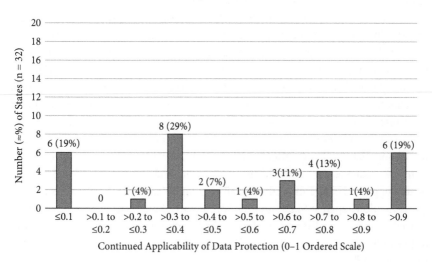

Chart 5.5 The Discipline Requirements and Journalism

These four categories of regulatory supervision can similarly be transposed on to a quantitative 0–1 scale as follows:

1. full supervisory powers over wide area (e.g. Spanish National DPA), coded as 1;
2. partial supervisory powers over wide area (e.g. UK DPA) *or* full supervisory powers over limited area (e.g. Spanish Catalan DPA), coded as 0.5;
3. partial supervisory powers only in a limited area (e.g. German Schleswig-Holstein DPA), coded as 0.25; and
4. no supervisory powers, coded as 0.

Finally, as regards any particular regulatory jurisdiction, it was also possible to represent the regulatory stringency of data protection by multiplying the substantive stringency of the law together with the extent to which any relevant regulator had powers in this area. Alongside the substantive stringency of the law, Appendix 4 details the maximum level[36] of regulatory supervision present in each State and, finally, the maximum level of regulatory stringency.

1.3 Explaining these National Divergences

In contrast to the first-generation data protection frameworks explored in the previous chapter,[37] it is much easier to orientate the statutory outcomes discussed earlier into an overarching and potentially explanatory pattern. In sum, it is clear that historically Germanic and Protestant Northern European States tended to grant journalism an extensive or even absolute derogation from default data protection norms. In contrast, Southern European States which were historically Roman Catholic or Orthodox set out little or no formal derogation even in this sensitive area. A similar outcome can be discerned as regards the post-Communist States of Eastern Europe.[38] These striking outcomes overlap significantly with Hallin and Mancini's (2005) three model typology of the media systems within Western democratic states. In sum, these two authors held that the United Kingdom and Ireland (as well as Canada and the United States) fell within a Liberal Model characterized by the dominance of the market and a non-institutionalized self-regulation of journalism. Meanwhile, the rest of Northern Europe[39] coalesced around a Democratic Corporatist model distinguished by (state-supported) institutionalized self-regulation and the legal protection of 'press freedom' against State intervention. Finally, Southern Europe was characterized by a Polarized Pluralist Model which combined strongly politicized and only weakly professionalized journalism and strong state intervention within the media sector.[40]

Hallin and Manchini's study entirely excluded the post-Communist states of Eastern Europe. However, it has been suggested elsewhere that these States align more closely to Southern (Polarized Pluralist) than Northern (Liberal or Democratic Corporatist) European patterns.[41] This hypothesis would fit with outcomes observed in relation to the DPD. However, a more serious problem with this whole literature arises from the 'rather "broad brush" character' of Hallin and Manchini's typologies and, relatedly, what has been argued to be the 'questionable validity of Hallin and Manchini's attribution of some countries to a certain model'.[42] It is, therefore, important to combine this qualitative analysis with a quantitative comparison between the outcomes presented earlier and data on the cultural divergences between the citizens of different European States.[43] In this context, Hofstede and colleagues have systematically analysed the extent to which individuals attitudes in different States diverge along the following fundamental cultural dimensions:

- Individualism: The extent to which 'the ties between individuals are loose: everyone is expected to look after him- or herself and his or her immediate family'.[44]
- Uncertainty Avoidance: '[T]he extent to which members of a culture feel threatened by ambiguous or unknown situations'.[45]
- Power distance: The extent to which 'the less powerful members [in a society] . . . expect and accept that power is distributed unequally'.[46]

The quantitative measures they computed[47] here are set out in Appendix 5. As Table 5.3 details, there are strong correlations, all significant at the 1 per cent level (one-tailed test) and in the expected direction, between the substantive stringency of the statutory law in relation to journalism during second-generation data protection and each of these measures. In sum, a more stringent statutory approach was negatively associated with individualism and positively associated with a focus on uncertainty avoidance and an acceptance of power distance. Moreover, the correlations with the regulatory stringency[48] measure were similar but even stronger, thereby demonstrating that the association between societal cultural difference and data protection outcomes here become even closer once divergence in the degree of statutory regulatory supervision of the relevant substantive norms is taken into account.

Correlation does not prove causation and any definitive findings here would, at least, require a detailed analysis of the political debates which led up to these legislative outcomes. Nevertheless, there is clear theoretical support for thesis that the

Table 5.3 Spearman Rank Correlations (and One-Tailed Significance Tests) between the Substantive and Regulatory Stringency of Default Second-Generation European Data Protection and Hofstede and colleagues' Cultural Variables ($n = 27$)

Formal law measures → Cultural measures ↓	Substantive stringency	(Maximum) regulatory stringency
Individualism	Coefficient: –0.530*** Significance: 0.002	Coefficient: –0.552*** Significance: 0.001
Uncertainty avoidance	Coefficient: 0.481*** Significance: 0.006	Coefficient: 0.526*** Significance: 0.002
Power distance	Coefficient: 0.743*** Significance: 0.000	Coefficient: 0.774*** Significance: 0.000

*** = significant at the 1 per cent level

correlations observed represent a causal relationship. Thus, a society that places a high value of the freedom of individual actors and which considers the ties between them to be relatively weak is likely to be very reluctant to impose strong restrictions on their rights to expression with a view to protecting the privacy or human dignity of others. In contrast, a society which fears uncertainty may be keen to agree to such mutual restrictions in order to guard against the unpredictability that arises from a predominantly laissez-faire approach. Finally, societies which accept the normative validity of large power divergences will presumably be more likely to feel comfortable with the State being made responsible for enforcing societal values such as personal data protection through formal and ultimately top-down and coercive legal measures, even when this is in tension with an individual actor's free expression rights.

1.4 The Relationship between the Statutory Regime and Self-Regulatory Norms and Structures

One issue which was not explicitly addressed in the 2016 study but which deserves specific attention concerns whether each State's data protection framework sought to establish a co-regulatory interface between statutory law and/or regulation on the one hand and self-regulatory norms and/or structures on the other. Article 27 of the DPD explicitly encouraged the drawing up of codes of conduct which took 'account of the specific features of the various sectors' and stated that bodies representing certain categories of controllers should be able to submit draft codes to the DPA for it to consider, 'amongst other things' whether these were in accordance with data protection requirements. Although not specific to journalism, it is notable that this co-regulatory provision was in principle excluded from the scope of derogations set out for journalism in Article 9. Meanwhile, the Commission's Communications of 1990 and 1992 both stressed that the journalistic derogations adopted under this article could legitimately take into account *inter alia* 'the existence of a code of professional ethics'.[49]

Looking at provisions at national level, ten EEA States (31 per cent) apparently failed to transpose Article 27 of the DPD into their local law at all.[50] Moreover, notwithstanding Article 27's exclusion from the ambit of Article 9, two other States (6 per cent)[51] excluded journalism from the scope of their general statutory provisions on codes of conduct and also failed to set out any comparable *sui generis* co-regulatory interface for journalism within their law. On the other hand, the law in eleven States (34 per cent) went as far as establishing a special link between statutory data protection and self-regulatory norms and/or scrutinizing structures established within journalism. As can be seen from the summaries set out in Table 5.4, whilst generally sharing key similarities, these provisions were of varying scope and weight. Thus, although some sought to ensure a strong link in relation to norms (e.g. Estonia), scrutinizing systems (e.g. Lithuania), or even both (e.g. Denmark, Italy), others merely acknowledged the presence of weak link as regards only one of these elements (e.g. the United Kingdom in relation to norms and Luxembourg as regards scrutinizing structures). Finally, although local law in two States (Gibraltar and Ireland) sought to ascribe a particular normative status to any code of practice of relevance to journalism that was approved under its Article 27 procedures, no such code was adopted in either State during the lifetime of the DPD. The *sui generis* co-regulatory media code envisaged under Maltese legislation was similarly never drawn up.

Table 5.4 Statutory Recognition of a Link between Data Protection and Self-regulatory Journalistic Norms and/or *Scrutinizing Structures*

EEA State (substantive stringency/ maximum regulatory powers— ordered by former)	Brief details of the incorporation of 'self-regulatory' norms and/or *structures*
Estonia (0.67/1)	– Journalistic processing of personal data by the media without the consent of the data subject had *inter alia* to conform with the principles of journalistic ethics.[52]
Luxembourg (0.66/1)	– *Data subject access to journalistic data (other than on sources) had to be fulfilled vicariously through the DPA after giving the Chair of the self-regulatory Press Council the opportunity to be present or send a representative.*[53]
Italy (0.65/1)	– Statutory law required the DPA and the co-regulatory[54] National Order of Journalists to attempt to draft a legally binding code of conduct for journalistic processing (but in absence required DPA alone to adopt measures and provisions).[55]
	– *Statutory law required DPA, in cooperation with the Council of the National Order, to establish measures to protect the data subject which the Council was then required to implement.*[56]
	– *The Code of Practice agreed in 1998 established a link between policing of its norms and the internal disciplinary measures of the National Order.*[57]

Continued

Table 5.4 *Continued*

EEA State (substantive stringency/ maximum regulatory powers— ordered by former)	Brief details of the incorporation of 'self-regulatory' norms and/or *structures*
Lithuania (0.63/0.5)	– *Supervision of data protection in the area of media publication was allocated to the Inspector of Journalist Ethics,[58] a State body but with a clear co-regulatory status.[59]*
France (0.53/1)	– Derogations set out for professional journalism made subject to compliance with professional ethical rules.
	– *Derogation from obligation to register processing with the DPA made subject to registered appointment of an officer within each media undertaking charged with independently ensuring application of data protection law.[60]*
United Kingdom (0.35/0.5)	– Legal assessment of the reasonableness of any belief that publication was in public interest (an integral part of the derogatory conditions) could have regard to certain specified self-regulatory (and also co-regulatory) codes of practice.[61]
Ireland (0.34/1)	– Legal assessment of the reasonableness of any belief that publication was in public interest (an integral part of the derogatory conditions) could have regard to any approved code of practice[62] (but no relevant code was ever approved).
Gibraltar (0.33/1)	– Identical to Ireland [63] (see entry above) including in that no relevant code ever approved.
Malta (0.33/0.5)	– The DPA was to encourage the drawing up of a suitable code of conduct for journalists and the media, *setting out appropriate measures and procedures to protect the data subject* (but in absence could itself establish such measures and procedures and, in any case, retained key supervisory powers).[64] No code of conduct was ever adopted.
Denmark (0.15/0.5)	– Publicly available journalistic databases could not contain information whose disclosure would be contrary to journalistic ethics.[65]
	– *Regulatory oversight of substantive standards overseen by the co-regulatory Press Council.[66]*
Germany (0.03/0.25)	– Interstate Treaty on Broadcasting and Telemedia absolved Press undertakings providing telemedia/online services from compliance with its subject access and rectification provisions when they were subject to self-regulation via the Press Code and Press Council.[67]
	– *Broadcasters subject to federal[68] and, in some cases, state[69] data protection laws required to appoint an officer to independently monitor compliance with data protection law (thus effectively taking the place of the DPA).*

2. Regulatory Guidance on the Interface between Second-Generation Data Protection and Professional Journalism

2.1 Pan-European Article 29 Working Party Guidance

Turning to guidance published by regulators the leading transnational body during the DPD era was the Article 29 Working Party, an authoritative but still merely advisory grouping made up of representatives of DPAs across the EEA. Its first formal output, which was published in 1997, was a Recommendation on 'Data Protection Law and the Media'.[70] Whilst stressing that '[d]ata protection law does in principle apply to the media', this document emphasized that as regards 'data processing for journalistic (editorial) purposes including electronic publishing'[71] there was a need to ensure a careful balance between two fundamental rights. It was, however, further elaborated that specific derogations from data protection 'might not be necessary where the flexibility of various provisions of the directive or the derogations allowed under other specific provisions . . . already allow a satisfactory balance between privacy and freedom of expression to be struck',[72] and that, in any case, any derogations needed to be 'in accordance with the law and must respect the proportionality'.[73] On the other hand, tallying the approach adopted in some national laws set out in section 1.4, the potential role of alternative remedies and safeguards including self-regulation was also acknowledged.

> The right to reply and the possibility to have false information corrected, the professional obligations of journalists and the special self-regulatory procedures attached to them, together with the law protecting honour (criminal and civil provisions concerning libel) must be taken into consideration when evaluating how privacy is protected in relation to the media.[74]

Nevertheless, in that regard the Working Party suggested that '[l]imits to the right of access and rectification prior to publication [under data protection] could be proportionate only in so far as individuals enjoy the right to reply or obtain rectification of false information after publication'.[75] This conclusion chimed with the outlook of the earlier 1991 Council of Europe report on Data Protection Law and the Media which was explored in Chapter 4. Finally, the recommendation held that

> [i]n most cases, independently of any express derogation that may exist, data protection legislation does not apply fully to the media because of the special constitutional status of the rules on freedom of expression and freedom of the press. These rules place a de facto limit on the application of substantive data protection provisions or at least their effective enforcement.[76]

Much more recently, the Working Party integrated a consideration of journalism into its more general output. For example, its 2014 opinion on the 'legitimate interests' legal base for processing personal data[77] re-emphasized that, even as regards journalistic expression, '[f]or the controller's legitimate interest to prevail, the data processing must be "necessary" and "proportionate"'[78] and, in the light of this, stressed that 'there should be no blanket permission for the media to publish any and all irrelevant details of the private life' even if this related to 'public figures'.[79] The opinion went on to set out two hypothetical journalistic case studies, one where this legitimate interest legal base was considered satisfied and one where it was considered unlikely to have been met. The former concerned the contemporaneous publication of a 'factually, accurate, well researched article' revealing that a local councillor had 'only attended one of the last eleven council meetings' and 'is unlikely to be re-elected because of a recent scandal involving the appointment of his seventeen-year-old daughter as a special assistant'.[80] In contrast, the other explored a much more tricky issue concerning the regulation of online media archives and the so-called 'right to be forgotten'. In sum, it questioned the legitimacy of a newspaper refusing to accede to the hypothetical request of former 'local celebrity, captain of a small town amateur football team' that, as regards an 'old article' which had reported on his now spent conviction for 'drunk and disorderly behaviour', it adopt 'technical measures, which would restrict . . . broad availability . . . [f]or example . . . that would aim—to the extent technology allows—limiting access to the information from external search using the individual's name as a search category'.[81] Finally, the Working Party's opinion on drones issued in 2015 stressed that, in light their capacity to collect visual, audio-visual, and related data,[82]

> Member States should be aware of the potential intrusiveness of these instruments, especially if used in an irresponsible and unethical way, and should clearly identify the duties and responsibilities carried with the exercise of freedom of expression by the use of drones. WP29 [Article 29 Working Party] attaches the utmost importance to the introduction of an appropriate framework at national level (if this is not already in place) so that the use of drones for . . . journalistic purposes does not impinge on fundamental rights to privacy and confidentiality of communications and that respect of a reasonable expectation of privacy of private life even in case of collection of personal data carried out in public life could be ensured.[83]

The somewhat more stringent approach adopted in the Working Party's 2014 Legitimate Interest and 2015 Drones opinions may be linked to broad trends within data protection explored in chapter three, namely, the legal recognition of data protection as an EU fundamental right from 2009 onwards and the concomitant growing emphasis on data protection by the Court of Justice of the European Union since that time.

2.2 State DPA Guidance: An Overview

In tandem with the DPA questionnaire (which was described in section 1.3 and will be explored as regards the media in Chapter 6 and 7), a review was undertaken in 2013 looking for guidance on journalism which was readily available on the websites of the ordinary national DPA or, where applicable, any specialist State media agency with legal authority under data protection in this area. In addition to these national bodies, the websites of the five regional DPAs which responded to the questionnaire were also analysed.

This review demonstrated that statutory guidance had been produced by the majority of DPAs. In sum, such guidance was found on the website of twenty-one out of thirty-two (66 per cent) national DPAs,[84] as well as three out of five (60 per cent)[85] of the regional DPAs which responded to the questionnaire. However, in the case of four national DPAs (13 per cent),[86] this kind of information was only found within the text of annual reports mounted on their website. Moreover, in the great majority of the other cases, the published guidance was not extensive. Indeed, it generally amounted to not more than 1,000 words. Specific guidance related specifically to data protection was also limited in the case of the two specialist media regulators which, in Denmark and Lithuania respectively, were granted explicit statutory oversight in this area. On the other hand, considerably more guidance was found on the Czechia, Greek, Italian, and Slovenian DPA websites. Indeed, in the latter two cases, substantial electronic booklets had been produced and made available on the subject.[87]

2.3 State DPA Guidance: The General Focus on Contextual Rights Balancing

The regulatory guidance which was located generally stressed a need for a contextual balancing between fundamental rights when setting standards in this area. Take, for example, that of the Cypriot DPA (0.65/1). Similar to other figures which will be placed against a DPA later in this chapter and also in Chapter 7, (0.65/1) refers in the first number to the substantive stringency of data protection which remained applicable under statute and in the second to the extent of statutory regulatory oversight powers. This DPA argued that:

> The publication of personal data is permitted for journalistic purposes, even without the consent of the subjects, so long as this does not infringe the rights to private and family life. That is why there should be a balance between the two rights, the right to privacy and the right to information and certainly the first should always be upheld. The publication of personal information that adds nothing essential to the news, simply for sensationalist purposes, is not permitted

and finally the accuracy and correctness of information should be ensured to the extent possible.[88]

Somewhat similarly, the Dutch DPA (0.38/0) stated:

> Member States may only provide exemptions [for the media] in so far as they prove necessary in order to find a balance between the protection of privacy and the protection of freedom of expression. For that reason, journalistic publications are not exempt from the general requirements in relation to due care and attention that are stipulated in [data protection] . . . nor the obligation to take measures to guarantee the security of the data processing.[89]

Finally, the UK DPA (0.35/0.5) stated that '[w]hile the Data Protection Act gives some exemptions to how data can be used by journalists, there are still expectations that the press will handle information in an appropriate way'.[90]

This focus on contextual balancing was even present in several cases where local statutory provisions appeared to be at variance with such an approach, either because of the complete absence or the extremely limited nature of any applicable derogation. Thus, the Czech DPA (1.00/1) stated that

> [p]ublication of personal . . . in [the] periodical press, as well as in other media, is undoubtedly one of those problematic areas that involve a conflict of absolutely varying interests and expectations—the justified requirement of the affected persons for the protection of privacy, on the one hand, and the no less important freedom of dissemination of information, on the other hand.[91]

Similarly, the Spanish DPA (1.00/1) argued that, whilst the Spanish Constitutional Court had determined that freedom of expression and information should take priority over the protection of privacy when public figures were involved, these two freedoms had declining value when information was private and not publicly interesting. The fundamental criterion for determining the legitimacy of an interference in an individual's privacy, therefore, rested on the public relevance of any reported fact, which should also be true.[92]

Notwithstanding this dominant approach, not every regulator suggested that a resort to contextual balancing was appropriate or even possible. In the first place, those DPAs operating in States whose local statutory law set out a near or fully complete exemption for journalism appeared reluctant to suggest that some kind of balancing was still applicable. This was notwithstanding the potential, explored in Chapter 3, for the pan-EU fundamental right to data protection to directly bind private parties (including possibly journalists) to certain minimum standards. Drawing on a 2001 case handed down by the Swedish Supreme Court,[93] the Swedish DPA sought to construe the scope of 'journalistic purposes' so that it encompassed informing, exercising criticism, and stimulating discussion on so-cial issues that were of importance to the public but which excluded publishing information of a purely personal nature about individuals.[94] However, in tension with this, it also stated that publishers could in any case obtain a certificate of re-lease from the Radio and Television Authority which would render data protec-tion law entirely inapplicable.[95] In many other cases, these issues were side-stepped through DPAs failing to set any general guidance on this issue at all.[96]

A minority of DPAs operating in States whose statutory law set out stringent data protection requirements applicable to journalism also found contextual rights balancing far from self-evident. Thus, rather than relying primarily on such an approach, the Slovenian DPA (0.93/1) sought to limit data protection's impact by construing 'personal data processing' as being restricted to 'any operation or set of operation performed in relation to personal data which is intended for its inclusion in a filing system [or is already in such a system]'.[97] Whilst lacking a clear legal foun-dation as regards the electronic manipulation of data,[98] this claim allowed the DPA to find that '[t]he publication of personal data in the media, per se, [did] not repre-sent an infringement' of this law.[99] The guidance then sought to establish when a linkage with a filing system and therefore also with data protection would be estab-lished. Thus, whilst publishing information directly derived from an identification card or an autopsy report was considered to be a form of regulated processing,[100] publishing a list of the hundred richest Slovenes was not.[101] Even more idiosyncrat-ically, it was claimed that the publication of photographs alongside further informa-tion such a person's full name would be caught by data protection, whilst other types of photography such as a crowd scene would generally be excluded.[102] Although full compliance with the default provisions was deemed necessary where data pro-tection applied, it was acknowledged that public interest considerations could be used in the interpretation of these.[103] Further complicating the picture, this guid-ance also elucidated the relationship between freedom of expression and the protec-tion of privacy and personal data outside of statutory data protection, finding this to rest more straightforwardly on contextual rights balancing.[104] Meanwhile, the Hungarian DPA (0.91/1) conceptualized data protection and freedom of the press as generally concurring rather than competing rights, the implication being that the media should usually be expected to uphold data protection rights in full.[105] The only clear exception to this that was recognized by the Hungarian regulator con-cerned public figures and, even then, it both interpreted this concept narrowly and held that certain core data protection standards were to remain unaffected.[106]

Finally, even when DPAs recognized the need for a contextual approach which looked ultimately to what was in the 'public interest', this was often also combined with an emphasis on the continued general applicability of certain peremptory norms. Most starkly, guidance produced by the Maltese DPA which focused on 'street photography'[107] but also addressed 'photojournalism' stated that 'each case should be evaluated on its merits' taking into consideration *inter alia* 'whether the publication was in the public interest'. At the same time, however, it 'strongly recommend[ed] that when the photographer intend[ed] to publish or commercially use a photograph clearly identifying a data subject' it should obtain 'the informed consent of the data subject' and further emphasized that:

> When the photographer fails to obtain the consent and forges ahead with publication, the same photographer may be subject to action (depending on the nature of the case) by this Office if a complaint is lodged or may even face a civil claim for compensation from the individual(s) concerned.[108]

Turning to a much more limited example, the Italian DPA stressed that there must be '[n]o publication of pictures of handcuffed defendants and/or convicts' in the media 'as this is in breach of human dignity'.[109]

2.4 State DPA Guidance: The Link with Self-Regulation

A focus on contextual rights balancing in DPA guidance was often connected in some way to journalistic self-regulation. As Table 5.5 elucidates, such a connection was found in guidance issued by eleven national DPAs (34 per cent), one (50 per cent) specialist media regulator which was allocated specific statutory duties in this area, and one (20 per cent) of the regional DPAs which responded to the questionnaire. In almost all instances, this guidance focused on the need to consider data protection standards and the norms articulated within self-regulation side by side. Nevertheless, the exact nature of the relationship envisaged exhibited considerable divergence. In the case of the Belgium (0.55/1), Estonian (0.67/1), and Italian (0.65/1) DPAs, the centrality of the basic standards set out in statutory data protection law itself was maintained, even whilst suggesting that the elaboration of detailed norms either required or could benefit from a collaboration with self-regulation. In some contrast, the Danish DPA (0.15/0.5) and the Lithuanian Inspector of Journalism Ethics (0.63/0.5) seemed to envisage self-regulatory journalistic norms replacing ordinary data protection standards here, albeit with the former then being enforced as a legal and not merely an ethical requirement. Meanwhile, the affiliation proposed in the guidance of the French (0.53/1), Spanish (1.00/1), and UK (0.35/0.5) DPAs remained much more inchoate, whilst the Dutch DPA (0.38/0) sought to use self-regulatory norms to restrict the meaning within data protection of the concept of 'journalism' itself. Finally, in four cases (German National DPA (0.03/0), German Rhineland-Palatinate DPA (0.03/0), Dutch DPA (0.38/0), and UK DPA (0.35/0.5)), self-regulation was seen as integral to the supervision and enforcement of norms related to data protection within professional journalism. Indeed, at least in the two German cases mentioned, these systems were understood potentially to replace the DPA or indeed any system of formal statutory regulation entirely.

This focus on self-regulation often mapped back to specific provisions found within national statutory frameworks (see section 1.4 and Table 5.4). Nevertheless, DPAs clearly retained a significant discretion here. Thus, despite this not having been specifically promoted within their national statutory law at all, the Belgium (0.55/1), Dutch (0.38/0), and Spanish (1.00/1) DPAs still

Table 5.5 Regulators Linking Journalistic Data Protection and Self-Regulatory Norms and Structures

Regulator (substantive stringency/regulatory powers—ordered by former)	Brief summary
Spanish DPA (1/1)	– 2007 annual report urged public administrations to promote self-regulation in the print and broadcast media sectors with reconciliation between freedom of information and data protection achieved through more respectful practices and a focus on the public relevance of any story.[110]
Estonian DPA (0.67/1)	– Audio-visual guidance referred to Press Code of Ethics provisions regarding publishing material concerning legal violations, court cases, accidents, children, and interviewing inexperienced persons.[111]
Italian DPA (0.65/1)	– Media guide stated that the statutory Journalism Code of Conduct arose from both cooperation and confrontation between the DPA and the National Council of the Order of Journalists. It included and endorsed a charter on children and journalism originally produced in 1990 and including updates from 2006 after input from the DPA. It mentioned other self- and co-regulatory texts including a 2008 charter concerning immigrants and asylum seekers.[112]
Lithuanian Inspector of Journalism Ethics (0.63/0.5)	– Despite remit, little focus on data protection itself. Emphasized and included the text of a Code of Ethics ratified at a meeting of journalists and publishers' organizations in 2005 and adopted under Article 44(2) of the Lithuanian Law on the Provision of Information to the Public.[113]
Belgium DPA (0.61/0)	– Justified a claim that recognizable images of those subject to criminal proceedings should be deleted on request from media archives unless the public interest overrode this by referring to the Belgium Council of Journalism's self-regulatory Code.[114] Also initiated a consultation procedure with both the Flemish and Walloon Journalism Ethics Boards in 2011 with regards to personal data published in press articles.[115]
French DPA (0.53/1)	– 2001 recommendation on jurisprudential databases on the Internet stated that news articles published on the Internet created problems of the same order when they included jurisprudential data and urged ethical reflection by the media, in consultation with the DPA, on the issue.[116]

Continued

Table 5.5 *Continued*

Regulator (substantive stringency/regulatory powers—ordered by former)	Brief summary
Dutch DPA (0.38/0)	– Drew on guidelines of the Dutch Press Council to support claim that use of the journalistic derogation required that a distinction was drawn between facts, claims, and opinions and that there was a right to reply to inaccuracies. Stated that if derogation applied, the DPA could not enforce the law but that the courts and sometimes the (self-regulatory) Press Council could.[117]
UK DPA (0.35/0.5)	– Backed 'effective self-regulation' of the Press through the (erstwhile) Press Complaints Commission. Emphasized the need for the Press to obey the law but also stated that 'the standards the press operate to and any associated guidance must have the approval of the industry', noting further that the changes to standards which it had proposed had not been adopted.[118]
Irish DPA (0.34/1)	– Held that provisions in the National Newspapers of Ireland Code of Practice and the UK Press Complaints Commission Code of Practice requiring a 'clear', or 'exceptional', 'public interest' to be present when a child (under sixteen) was identified in the media were 'a fair expression of how the principles of data protection ought to be applied in relation to children and minors'.[119]
Maltese DPA (0.33/0.5)	– 2004[120] and 2005[121] annual reports stated that DPA was bound to encourage and enforce suitable media conduct of conduct and was working with Institute of Maltese Journalists on this. In its absence, it was noted that the DPA had to establish its own measures and procedures.
Danish DPA (0.15/0.5—via Press Council)	– Stated that editorial databases must be registered with the Press Council (as well as with the DPA) and that publicly available media databases must be in conformity with press ethics.[122]
German National DPA (0.03/0)	– Argued that, given tension between press freedom and data protection, there could be no external control of press journalistic activities and so self-regulation had been created in its place.[123] In some contrast, the guidance noted the limited application of statutory data protection standards in the area of broadcasting.[124]
German Rhineland-Palatinate DPA (0.03/0)	– As above for the Press but with further detail including specifying the inclusion of data protection within the Press Code from 2001 and links to both this and Appeals Board of the Press Council.[125] Noted the (very limited) role of internal data protection officers in the area of broadcasting.[126]

emphasized the need for an interaction between the law and self-regulation in this area.

2.5 State DPA Guidance: Specific Issues Given Emphasis

As previously stated, DPA guidance on the interface between data protection and journalism during the DPD-era was, in most cases, not extensive. Nevertheless, a minority of regulators did address specific issues within this area in some detail, three of which achieved a particular prominence.[127]

2.5.1 Children's Rights and Data

First, a number of regulators emphasized the need for particular safeguards to be adopted when children's personal data was being processed. Both the Italian (0.65/1) and the Estonian (0.67/1) DPAs held that the rights of children must be considered primary and that, therefore, balancing was inapposite in this special area. As a result, they argued that, at least in the absence of parental consent, it was impermissible to identify a child in a negative manner even if they were the subject of a criminal trial. Moreover, parental consent itself would not be sufficient to justify a publication which caused serious harm to the interests of a child. At the same time, both regulators stated that, notwithstanding an absence of explicit parental consent, it was perfectly acceptable to identify a child (e.g. through an image) who was involved in a positive fashion in an event such as a sports competition or other leisure activity. The Italian DPA especially emphasized the danger of inappropriate censorship and, furthermore, held that identification could also be legitimate in a wider of range of cases, giving as an example a report on a child who had been mutilated in a car accident.[128] Other DPAs addressed this issue in somewhat similar, but generally less elaborated, terms. For example, drawing on self-regulatory norms (see Table 5.5), the Irish DPA (0.34/1) held that in cases 'involving children under 16, editors should demonstrate the existence of an exceptional public interest in order to over-ride the normally paramount interest of the child'.[129] Finally, the Hungarian DPA (0.95/1) report for 2002 (i.e. two years prior to joining the EU) went as far as arguing that a child's right to protection and care appropriate to their physical, spiritual, and moral development applied even in relation to a minor being prosecuted for homicide.[130]

2.5.2 Image Rights and Visual/Audio-Visual Content

Second, a large number of DPAs emphasized that the publication (or even gathering) of many types of visual and/or audio-visual material raised particular data protection concerns.[131] The Estonian, Italian, and Slovenia DPAs set out comprehensive guidance in this area, at least as regards rights in relation to images. In sum:

- The Slovenian DPA (0.93/1) approach was, in principle, the most restrictive. It stated that '[c]ontemporary legal practice and case law agree that photographing and/or recording a certain individual without their knowledge and consent cannot be sanctioned'.[132] However, it was also recognized that a number of exceptions had to be made to such a restrictive rule. Thus, recordings of 'absolute' public figures or, in other words, those 'who are under constant and longstanding public scrutiny, due to their role or function in society (e.g. politicians, officials, artists and athletes)' could be freely made and published so long as this did not amount to 'unmitigated or mere sensationalistic or tasteless pursuit of the individual' or involve publication 'which is either irrelevant or encroaches upon the intimate and private domain of the individual'.[133] Meanwhile, recordings of 'relative' public figures or, in other words, those 'who are only of temporary public significance most often due to their connection with a certain event' could be similarly made public but only 'when they are—due to a certain event—deemed of interest to the public and not after that period'.[134] This group included 'perpetrators of crime (kidnappers, murderers etc.)' as well as others caught up in the news such as 'winners of competitions or lotteries etc'. Finally, wider recordings of public events could also be made and published so long as no individual was a 'focal motif' of any photograph.[135] As noted earlier, this DPA also uniquely sought to restrict the general scope of data protection to information linked in some way to a filing system. However, this concept was not only interpreted extremely broadly as regards photographs/recordings,[136] but the DPA also emphasized the restrictions outlined above would in any case be legally binding as a result of other law relating to privacy (albeit, law which it judged to fall outside its regulatory jurisdiction).[137]
- The Estonian DPA (0.67/1) guidance similarly distinguished between public and non-public figures, public (as opposed to private) events, and the need in any case to avoid sensationalism, catty gossip, or the disclosure of details of private life which didn't contribute to public debate.[138]
- Finally, the Italian DPA (0.65/1) guidance stressed that the publication of individual images in public places remained legitimate so long as the image wasn't detrimental to a person's dignity and decorum, was published in an appropriate context, refrained from focusing on either an individual person or their personal details if the disclosure wasn't relevant or was excessive, and, finally, that the photographer refrained from any artifice or undue pressure. Similar principles were specified as regards the photos of suspects and arrestees, with the extra proviso that photographs such as mug shots should only be used for

their original purpose, namely the assessment, prevention, and repression of crimes.[139]

The Hungarian DPA (0.95/1) also set out relatively comprehensive guidance, albeit solely in the context of discussing certain concrete aspects of this issue in various annual reports. For example, in 2003 (just before Hungary joined the EU), the DPA condemned the highly intrusive nature of reality television shows such as Big Brother, questioning whether the processing was sufficiently defined and obtained on the basis of informed consent.[140] In 2004, the DPA additionally condemned the publication on the front page of a tabloid magazine of the images of the football player dying on the pitch, stressing that no image should violate human dignity.[141] As further explored in Chapter 7, in 2007 this DPA also held that police officers were not public figures and so publication of their images without consent was illegal, even if this was designed to and did reveal illegality or the misuse of power.[142] Nevertheless, in 2010, this DPA modified its position, clarifying that the publication of such images was permissible in the latter case, but only where the freedom of the press was obviously a more pressing concern than that of personal data protection.[143]

Meanwhile, the Belgium DPA (0.58/1) focused exclusively on the journalistic publication of recognizable images[144] within the context of reporting on criminal proceedings.[145] According to this regulator, such publication would only be permissible as regards convicts who were public figures and who either did not object to publication or where the public interest in this was overriding.[146] The Maltese DPA (0.33/05) similarly focused on a widespread but specific aspect of this issue, namely street photography. As noted earlier, this guidance strongly endorsed informed consent as a default, whilst acknowledging case-by-case deviations, taking into account not only public interest but also whether the individual was a public person and whether the photo was taken in a public place or during a public event.[147]

Finally, both the German Brandenburg (0.03/0)[148] and the German Rheinland Pfalz (0.03/0)[149] DPAs focused exclusively on the issue of reality television, criticizing how intimate details about individuals were often revealed in such programmes.[150]

2.5.3 The 'Right to be Forgotten' and (Digital) Media Archives

Finally, a considerable number of regulators explored the regulation of (digital) media archives, as well other issues linked to the so-called right to be forgotten, a notion which was generally conceptualized as granting an individual a presumptive entitlement to curtail unwelcome publicity over time.[151] These concerns dovetailed strongly with DPA intervention under first-generation data protection. However, in the intervening period, the relationship between digital archiving and the general activities of the media had changed dramatically. In particular, there had been a shift to media content being published immediately online rather than initially only through broadcasting or hardcopy print. Indeed, for much of the media, 'online' formats had become their principal interface with the public. Moreover, by default, online content was often maintained indefinitely and sometimes was even published in the form of continuous updates rather than as discretely packaged articles or programmes. Data found within that context had also generally become continuously searchable, often including through pan-Internet search engines such as Google. In sum, media archiving had shifted from being a discrete and segregated activity to being one which was increasingly integrated with the media's standard *modus operandi*. Despite this, the distinct data protection issues raised by the long-term preservation and organization of media content remained present. Indeed, the integration of archives into both the media's principal interface with the public and powerful retrieval tools such as Internet search engines rendered countervailing data protection claims such as the 'right to be forgotten' ever more pressing.[152]

Turning to the published regulatory guidance that focused specifically on the responsibilities of professional journalism itself (rather than, for example, Internet search engines),[153] in two instances DPAs highlighted the general relevance of the 'right to be forgotten' without articulating any explicit link to archiving. Thus, as has already been noted, the Slovenian DPA (0.93/1) stipulated that an identifiable image of a 'relative' public figure should only be published 'during the period when they are—due to a certain event—deemed of interest to the public and not after that period'.[154] Similarly, the Greek DPA (0.84/1) stated that repeated viewing of personal data must be in conformity with the principle of proportionality and exclusively serve the information needs of the public. It was further emphasized that the continuous and repeated viewing of personal data (especially if sensitive) might violate such principles, thereby resulting in the humiliation and shaming of individuals. However, the only medium specifically flagged up in this context was broadcast television, as opposed to (electronic) archives.[155]

In contrast, four other DPAs did primarily relate 'right to be forgotten' concerns to the operation of publicly available online media archives. Thus, as noted in Table 5.5 above, the Belgium DPA (0.58/1) drew on the Belgium Council of Journalism's self-regulatory code in order to argue that recognizable images of those subject to criminal proceedings which were included in news archives should be deleted on request unless the public interest overrode this.[156] The French DPA (0.58/1) recommendation from 2001, which urged the press to reflect ethically on its publication of jurisprudential information on the Internet,[157] was similarly motivated by an understanding that, given the presence of Internet search engines, such publication could severely threaten an individual's ability to reasonably shield themselves from their own past. On the other hand, the Dutch DPA (0.38/0) largely confined itself to arguing that the archiving of media content including on the Internet could still fall within the journalistic derogation so long as, having regard to the 'target group [i.e. audience]' for the archive and 'the period for which the publication will be available', its purpose remained 'journalistic'. Its guidance did, however, add that, even where the derogation applied, data protection stipulations 'with regards to the non-publication of incorrect or excessive data and with regards to exercising due care and attention, remain in force'.[158] Meanwhile, Danish DPA (0.15/0.5) guidance was limited to noting that those included in publicly available journalistic databases had a right in certain cases to have information corrected, deleted, or updated.[159]

Finally, the Italian DPA (0.65/1) provided by far the most comprehensive analysis of the multifaceted and complex issues which arose here. Its guidance carefully distinguished between the intentional republication of material in new journalistic output and the archiving of historical material, which might then be made available through Internet search engines. In the first case, the journalist engaging in republication was held responsible for proactively examining the public interest in such publication again, taking into account new variables including those based on the right to oblivion or to be forgotten. In contrast, the digital archiving and indexing of old stories was held to raise right to be forgotten issues not only of a quantitatively, but also of a qualitatively, different order. In addition to creating a perpetual past, such practices could result in the spread of information that was incorrect, published illegitimately *ab initio*, or was incomplete, usually due to an overemphasis on 'negative' information. The material could then be used worldwide for a great variety of purposes, including not only journalism and history but also interpersonal curiosity and conducting background checks on an individual's 'reliability'. The DPA noted that, in balancing the need for oblivion against these other interests, it had ordered newspapers to suspend making available certain news stories to Internet search engines following requests from the data subject. It also hinted that balanced solutions to the archiving of illegitimately published information *ab initio* and information that had become incomplete might be obtainable through requiring anonymization and the affixing of footnotes containing additional information respectively.[160] This DPA's annual reports also regularly touched on, and further explored, how media archives should be regulated. For example, the foreword to the 2009 annual report noted that 'large-scale availability of online media is raising unprecedented challenges' and argued that 'it is unquestionable that a wide-ranging, in-depth public discussion is necessary and that such discussion should involve both practitioners and society as a whole'. Furthermore, it explicitly questioned if such processing should be conceptualized as falling with the journalistic derogation rather than being subject to the much more restrictive rules governing processing for historical purposes,[161] stating

> One cannot help wondering whether the online reproduction of the archives of newspapers, including video archives, is to be regarded as the latter-day expression of the (by now) timeless freedom of the press, or rather equated to the dissemination of historical information—especially if the archives contain information on temporally removed events—in which case it should attract the data protection rules applying to this type of activity.[162]

As will be seen in Chapter 9, this DPA's concrete enforcement decisions in this period were even more emphatic that media archiving should be conceptualized as being for historical, as opposed to (ordinary) journalistic, purposes.[163]

3. Conclusions

In contrast to the text of the Data Protection Convention considered in Chapter 4, the DPD explicitly mandated that State law carefully balance the fundamental right to journalistic freedom of expression and those of privacy (and, by implication, also data protection itself).[164] This requirement was given added salience by the EU Charter which was drafted and given legal effect in the 2000s. However, although some special statutory treatment of journalism became nearly ubiquitous, a number of Southern and Eastern European countries failed to formalize any significant derogations for journalism at all whilst other Northern European countries granted the media a complete or near-complete exemption from their data protection frameworks. In other words, similarly to first-generation data protection law, a very strong divergence of legislative response remained present. Nevertheless, other EEA States approached this substantive interface carefully, often seeking at the same time to map out a co-regulatory relationship between the statutory standards set out and self-regulatory norms and/or structures. Finally, the vast majority of States provided that the ordinary DPA (or in a couple of cases a specialist statutory media body) should continue to exercise wide-ranging regulatory powers and responsibilities in this area.

Notwithstanding these statutory provisions, the guidance published by these statutory bodies was generally not extensive and, in many cases, appeared entirely absent. Nevertheless, most (although not all) of the material that was produced both by the pan-European Article 29 Working Party and by particular EEA State regulators stressed the need for a contextual balancing between rights grounded in a 'public interest' analysis and, relatedly, often sought to suggest a relationship between the law, statutory regulation, and journalistic self-regulation. Since statutory data protection law in several Southern and Eastern European states left little room for such a contextual paradigm, a divergence between the law on the books and regulatory interpretation thereby remained a clear feature of the landscape. A few regulators filled out their interpretative approach with detailed consideration of particular topics, notably the governance of children's rights and data, image rights and visual/audio-visual data, and finally media archiving and the 'right to be forgotten'. Nevertheless, a large majority did not provide such a specific analysis. As a result, it was not possible to drill down systematically into the detail of the approach which statutory data protection regulators adopted in relation standard-setting in this area through the analysis of published material alone. This was instead explored through discrete parts of the questionnaire which was put directly to the DPAs. The findings which thereby resulted will be addressed in the next chapter of this book.

6

Second-Generation European Data Protection and Professional Journalism

Probing Regulatory Standard-Setting

As explored in Chapter 5, most Data Protection Authorities ('DPAs')—or, in a few instances, designated specialist media regulators—were endowed with important supervisory duties and powers over professional journalism under second-generation European data protection. Given this, it is vital to explore how these regulators interpreted both the pan-European Data Protection Directive (DPD) and (often highly divergent) national data protection statutes in this period, thereby contributing to standard-setting in this area. Chapter 5's analysis of published regulatory guidance highlighted both an emphasis on a contextual balancing between rights and the promotion of an interface between legal and self-regulatory norms. However, the general absence in this published material of specific guidance on particular topics meant that it was not possible through this to build up a systematic and detailed picture of the interpretative approach adopted by the majority of regulators. As a result, the task of securing such a granular understanding was reserved to a questionnaire that was sent to European Economic Area (EEA) DPAs in 2013.[1] Some twenty-five (or 75 per cent) of the national DPAs, as well as five authorities operating at sub-national level, responded, thereby enabling a genuinely comprehensive picture to be assembled.

In light the complexity of the data protection scheme, it was recognized that it would not be feasible for the questionnaire to explore every interpretative aspect that might be relevant. Instead, four questions were formulated. The first two sought to verify a regulators' *basic substantive stance* as regards news production processing and, potentially more controversially, that which concerned the long-term publication of stories in a digital archive. Was the data protection journalistic derogation seen as engaged in both scenarios or did regulators, as suggested in Italian DPA guidance considered in Chapter 5, adopt a fundamentally different perspective in relation to one or other of these activities? Meanwhile, the latter two questions drilled down into each regulators' *detailed* approach to *standard-setting* as this related to two very different aspects of substantive data protection: first, the restrictions applicable to *undercover journalism* and second, the interface between journalistic investigation and the ability of an individual to obtain personal data under the default right of *subject access*. In relation to each question, DPAs were

European Data Protection Regulation, Journalism, and Traditional Publishers. David Erdos, Oxford University Press (2019). © David Erdos.
DOI: 10.1093/oso/9780198841982.003.0006

invited to assent to one of several alternative categorical answers, although free or supplementary text responses were also accepted. The standardized categories were designed so as to array along a comprehensive and quantifiable scale of stringency, thereby aiding comparability not only with other interpretative variables but, more particularly, with measures representing (albeit in a simplified form) the stringency of applicable statutory law and also norms set out within self-regulation.

The *basic stance* results not only confirmed the existence of a clear consensus amongst DPAs that news production should be governed under the journalistic derogation but also demonstrated that this consensus remained present, albeit in a significantly less strong form, in relation to long-term digital media archiving and publication. Meanwhile, the observed divergences on this dimension were fairly strongly correlated with differences in the formal stringency of national statutory law. Turning to the questions probing DPAs' detailed interpretative understandings, all regulators held that undercover investigative journalism was in principle legally justifiable. This often required a heavy 'reading down' of contrary provisions found in national law and, in turn, appeared to reflect the permissive adoption of norms championed within self-regulation. Nevertheless, within the narrow range within which DPA responses were clustered, the severity of statutory law remained a fairly strongly predictor of a regulator's approach. As regards the interface with *subject access*, national statutory stringency was again fairly strongly correlated with regulatory attitude. In particular, notwithstanding the protection of subject access within primary EU law,[2] any complete journalistic exemption from such a right within national statutory law was almost always accepted as peremptory. However, excepting a general recognition that information on journalistic sources should be shielded from subject access, no systematic tendency to 'read down' the law was discernible. Indeed, even though the statutory law in many of these jurisdictions appeared more permissive, some eleven DPAs (37 per cent) held that (expect in relation to sources) the media should be expected to provide individuals with their full default right to subject access. This outcome may be related to a very different self-regulatory context in this area compared to that of undercover activity. Thus, whilst the vast majority of self-regulatory codes comprehensively addressed the governance of undercover journalism, almost none did so as regards subject access.

These results confirm that DPAs in the main did seek to engage in a contextual balancing of rights when elucidating the standards applicable to professional journalism. However, they also highlight an important discrepancy. Where self-regulatory frameworks had set out relevant norms, regulators appeared drawn not only to a contextual but also a rather *laissez-faire* approach. In contrast, in situations where self-regulatory norms were absent, regulators remained focused on the norms set down within default data protection, making only minimal adjustment in this regard for the special journalistic context. In both cases, however, the stringency or otherwise of each State's statutory provisions continued to exert a

strong influence on the interpretation adopted. Moreover, irrespective of any potentially conflicting primary human rights law and ethical guidance, these statutory provisions were taken to be overriding in cases where local statute sought
to establish a complete journalistic exemption. All this suggests that it would be
helpful for third-generation data protection to delineate more carefully the relationship between the balancing imperatives of general human rights law and the
standards set down in data protection statutes, as well as that between statutory
and self-regulation. Chapter 8 will *inter alia* explore the extent to which this has
been achieved in third-generation legal statutes, whilst Chapter 9 will look further
into the evolving role of DPAs here.

The present chapter is divided into five sections. Section 1 explores the basic
interpretative stance of DPAs as regards the activities of the professional journalistic media including the relationship between this stance and national statutory law. Section 2 then presents findings relating to DPAs' detailed interpretative
standard-setting *vis-à-vis* undercover journalism and the application of subject
access rights to journalistic activity. This leads on to section 3, which explores the
interrelationship between such interpretative standard-setting, statutory law, and
self-regulatory norms. Section 4 provides a general analysis of all these findings,
and section 5 sets out some broad conclusions.

1. Exploring the Basic Interpretative Stance of the DPAs

1.1 Questions Posed

The first part of the DPA questionnaire explored the basic substantive or interpretative stance adopted by each DPA as regards the professional journalistic media.
As examined in Chapter 5, Article 9 of the Data Protection Directive 95/46 ('DPD')
clearly pointed to journalism being subject to a regime of special contextual balancing which explicitly required States to set out wide-ranging derogations as
'necessary to reconcile the right to privacy with the rules governing freedom of
expression'.[3] However, as the previous chapter also detailed, EEA State implementation of this special expression regime remained patchy and its applicability to
long-term online media archiving, in any case, contested. Moreover, at least three
other conceptualizations of the relationship between (certain types of) professional media activity and data protection could be envisaged. The most permissive, beyond even that of the special expression regime set out in Article 9, is that
this activity could be excluded from data protection's scope entirely. Considerably
less permissively than Article 9, the general scheme of protection set down in the
Directive could have been considered applicable but nevertheless interpreted with
regard for other fundamental rights such as freedom of expression. Indeed, it could
be argued that the Directive's specific clauses governing processing of data for

'historical' or related 'knowledge facilitation' purposes were, at least in part, motivated by a desire to set out a concrete articulation of just such an interpretative approach.[4] Moreover, the Court of Justice of the EU ('CJEU') has signalled, most notably in C-101/01 *Lindqvist*,[5] that such an intermediate interpretative approach may be applicable to a much wider range of expressive contexts. Finally, and clearly most restrictively, the general scheme of protection could simply have been applied in full against the media.

Following this typological schema, the questionnaire invited DPAs to indicate which of these four categorical approaches was considered applicable as regards:

1. journalistic news production ('the activities of a media entity producing a story concerning a living individual') and
2. long-term online media archiving ('[a] searchable online newspaper archive [that] publishes a newspaper story originally published a decade ago concerning a living individual').[6]

These four categorical possibilities—(a) full exclusion, (b) special expression, (c) regard for rights, and (d) full application—represent a spectrum ranging from no (0) through to complete (1) application of default data protection. As a result, it possible to transpose them on to a quantitative 0–1 scale where (a) is equal to 0, (b) to 0.33, (c) to 0.67, and (d) to 1. Finally, although such standard categorical responses were preferred in order to aid comparability, textual responses were also accepted as a supplement or even as an alternative to these.

1.2 Results Overview

Charts 6.1 and 6.2 summarize the standard categorical answers received from DPAs in relation to the two questions specified earlier. The responses of each individual DPA are also summarized in Appendix 5. Although the vast majority of DPAs provided a categorical response, four combined this with supplementary text and seven more set out entirely free text that had a certain relevance to one or more of these questions.[7]

Looking first at news production (Chart 6.1), the categorical responses received from some twenty-seven regulators confirmed a clear consensus that this activity should be governed by the special expression regime (a/0.33). Nevertheless, approximately one-quarter preferred to conceptualize this area as one in which data protection law merely had to be interpreted with regard to rights of freedom of expression (b/0.67). Neither of the other responses received significant support. This broad pattern was not affected by either the free text received from the German Rhineland-Palatinate,[8] Dutch,[9] Slovenian,[10] and UK[11] DPAs or the supplementary text that were forthcoming from the Cypriot (d/1),[12] Hungarian (b/0.33),[13]

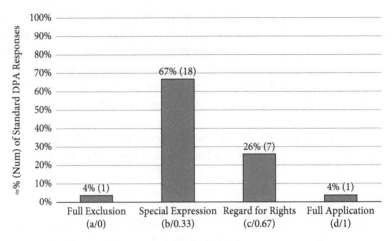

Chart 6.1 News Production—DPA Stance on Substantive Law

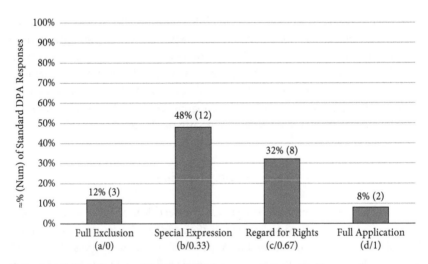

Chart 6.2 Online News Archiving—DPA Stance on Substantive Law

Swedish (d/0),[14] and Polish (b/0.33)[15] DPAs. Nevertheless, a number of these responses did highlight what was seen as the complex relationship here between data protection law on the one hand and defamation, image rights, personality, privacy, and specialist media laws on the other.[16] In general, they also pointed to a greater support for a special contextually balanced approach than the raw categorization of the standard responses alone may suggest.

Turning next to consider the long-term online archiving of journalistic content, Chart 6.2 indicates that a plurality of DPAs continued to consider that the special expression regime (b/0.33) remained applicable. However, consensus on this issue was considerably weaker than in relation to news production. Indeed, almost one-third of twenty-five regulators which provided a standard answer saw this as an area where only an interpretative gloss on data protection was necessary (c/0.67). Compared with news production, the proportion of DPAs choosing the extremes of no (a/0) and full application (d/1) of data protection law was also higher. Supplementary text from the Swedish (a/0)[17] and free text from the Austrian,[18] Slovenian,[19] and Dutch[20] DPAs addressed this activity only in a tangential fashion. Meanwhile, free text from the German Rhineland-Palatinate DPA held that only personality rights laws lying outside statutory data protection would be applicable here.[21] Finally, the Portuguese DPA's free-text response set out the most detailed perspective on this activity. It stated:

> Newspapers archives could always be searched before the Internet. The availability of online archives is a way of facilitating the public access to information. They simply reflect what was published in paper, properly dated, and the due accuracy of the moment. Though newspapers have a general duty to follow a story and provide the updates, in particular whenever it is at stake the reputation of a person, there is no legal obligation to do that. And even any updates do not replace the original information that will still be available for consultation. In this context, for example, the key principle of data quality that applies to the general personal data processing and it is an obligation of the data controllers cannot be applied the same way when it comes to media publications.
>
> Nevertheless, considering the lack of update and the lack of consent from the data subject, and having into consideration the huge negative impact that some news may have to an individual (for instance, in the case of a person that was prosecuted and then acquitted), it is our understanding that the newspapers online archives should not be indexed to the search engines, as this would be potentially damaging to a person's reputation and dignity in a larger scale. This solution is in our opinion more balanced, once history is not erased, an interested person can always make the search in an easier way, but prevents that a casual online search provides aggregate data on an individual but at the same time incomplete and erroneous.

1.3 Relationship with Statutory Law

The statutory derogations set out in EEA State law for 'journalistic purposes' were analysed in detail in Chapter 5. As will be explored in Part III the book, this special expression regime also encompassed artistic, literary, and, in a small number of States, other types of expression. In practically all cases, however, the inclusion of 'journalistic purposes' remained the designator of greatest relevance not only to news production but, albeit less compellingly, also to online news archiving. It follows that, notwithstanding certain divergences regarding the scope of special expression within national law, there is no general reason to predict a relationship between the scope of the special expression regime and differences in DPA understandings of the basic legal position of the media as regards these two activities. A relationship between these responses and the substantive depth of any statutory special expression derogation looks more credible. In sum, DPAs operating in a small minority of States which established either an absolute substantive exemption for special expression[22] or which set out no exemption/derogation at all[23] might reasonably have felt compelled to adopt stance a/0 ('full exclusion') and stance c/0.67 ('regard for rights')[24] respectively, in preference to b/0.33 ('special expression').[25] Beyond this and rather more indirectly, we might expect DPAs operating in jurisdictions whose laws provided for only a very limited substantive special expression derogation to have been more likely to collapse the governance of (some or all) media activity into a 'regard for rights' (stance c/0.67) rather than a 'special expression' (stance b/0.33) approach. The converse may also be true as regards DPAs operating under a very permissive special expression regime. Use of the substantive measure of the stringency of national data protection law presented in Chapter 5 allows us to confirm these hypotheses. In sum, a Spearman's Rank Correlation between this measure and the basic interpretative stance of each DPA as regards both news production and online news archiving produced a positive and fairly strong result (of between 0.4 and 0.5) in each case, with (one-tailed) significance at least at the 5 per cent level.[26]

2. Detailed Interpretation and Standard-Setting by the DPAs

2.1 Questions Posed

The questionnaire also sought to explore each DPA's approach to detailed interpretative standard-setting as this related to professional journalistic activity. Given data protection's breath and complexity, it was not considered possible to probe regulators on every detail of this framework. Instead, two very differently focused questions were formulated. One explored the general relationship between data protection and the widespread, albeit sometimes controversial, practice of undercover journalism. The other considered the specific relationship between journalistic investigation (of all types) and subject access, data protection's most long-standing distinctive right.

The question on *undercover journalism* presented regulators with the following concrete scenario which, although hypothetical, was deliberately based on a real-life[27] journalistic investigation.

A journalist is investigating a far-right political party following widespread claims that their true beliefs and tactics are much more extreme than their public face suggests. He intends to pose as supporter of the party and carry out undercover video recording of the party's activities.

DPAs were invited to assess the legal position of this journalist under data protection. The following five categorical possibilities[28] were presented:

(a) These journalistic methods would be legal as far as data protection is concerned.
(b) These journalistic methods would be legal so long as the public interest in freedom of expression outweighed all interferences in privacy.
(c) These journalistic methods would be legal so long as (i) it was not possible to collect this information openly and (ii) the public interest in freedom of expression outweighed all interferences in privacy.
(d) These journalistic methods would be legal so long as: (i) it was not possible to collect this information openly; (ii) the public interest in freedom of expression outweighed all interferences in privacy; and (iii) the journalistic obtained a permit from the Data Protection Authority for this activity.
(e) These journalistic methods would be illegal under data protection.

The standard answers above were based on a (necessarily simplified) representation of the restrictions set out in national statutory data protection law after any journalistic derogations had been taken into account. They were also designed to represent a spectrum ranging from no restriction (a/0) through to full restriction (e/1) of this activity under data protection, with intermediate possibilities encompassing a permissive public interest test (b/0.25), a strict/necessity-based public interest test (c/0.5), and a licensing regime (d/0.67). This typology was intended to enable comparison between the different regulatory responses and between these responses and both formal statutory law and self-regulatory norms, especially once the results had been transposed onto a 0–1 scale. Nevertheless, in recognition of the complex tangle of different legal provisions potentially engaged here, DPAs were alternatively invited to indicate that the activity had a different relationship with data protection law to any of those specified earlier and to set this out in free text.

The question on *subject access* asked DPAs whether 'an individual who is the subject of a journalistic investigation by a media entity' had a right to access the data 'held by that entity in the context of the investigation.'[29] Five standard categorical possibilities were again presented:[30]

(a) No.
(b) Yes, in principle, but in addition to the non-disclosure of journalist sources, such rights may be outweighed by the media entity's right to freedom of expression (and related rights).

(c) A modified procedure applies where the Data Protection Authority accesses the data on behalf of the data subject.

(d) Yes, the individual could have access to the data (with the exception of information relating to journalist sources, which would be protected from such disclosure).

(e) Yes, the same legal provisions apply here as in relation to other data controllers.

Again, these standard answers were based on a simplified representation of the restrictions set out in formal statutory law and were also designed to array along a quantifiable spectrum ranging from no (a/0) through to full (e/1) application of the default data protection regime. The intermediate possibilities here encompassed a human rights/public interest exemption (b/0.25), a rules-based alternative (c/0.5), and a limitation, as opposed to an exemption, from the default provision (d/0.75). Since this question only focused on the interface between journalism and one particular provision in data protection law, DPAs were not specifically invited to provide a free-text answer as an alternative to a standard one. Nevertheless, one DPA still did so and this was accepted *in lieu* of a standard response.

2.2 Results Overview

In response to question on *undercover journalism*, twenty-one standard categorical responses were received along with eight free-text answers. As can be seen from Chart 6.3, one-quarter of the standard responses held that this activity was

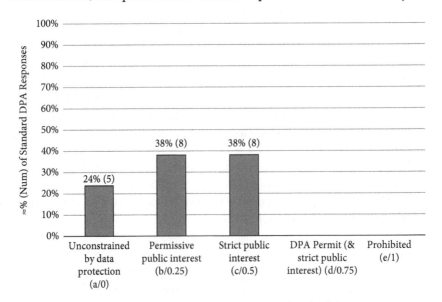

Chart 6.3 Undercover Journalism—DPA Interpretative Standard-Setting

completely unconstrained by the data protection framework (a/0). Otherwise, DPAs clustered entirely within the categories that recognized the qualified permissibility of this activity, with an equal number holding that it was necessary for a journalist undertaking undercover investigation to satisfy a permissive (b/0.25) and a strict (c/0.5) public interest test. The categorical responses of each individual DPA who provided a standard response are specified in Table 6.2 and also in Appendix 5. Turning to the eight free-text answers (which are summarized in Table 6.1), three DPAs (Germany Brandenburg-Vorpommern, Poland, and Spain Catalonia) stressed the need for a complex fact-specific inquiry here, three others (France, German Rhineland-Palatinate, Slovenia) argued that data protection law wouldn't apply but other related laws would govern this space, one (Portugal) displayed a reluctance to engage with this issue, and one (Austria) provided too little detail for further analysis.

Table 6.1 Undercover Journalism—DPA Free-Text Responses

DPA	Summary
Austrian	Translation provided of media/journalism clause in Austrian data protection law.
French	Suggested that data protection would not apply (initially/in the first place) but that processing would be illegal if collection was via methods sanctioned by criminal law.[31]
German Brandenburg-Vorpommern	Assented both to options (a/0) and (e/1).
German Rhineland-Palatinate	Stated that data protection law and control by the DPA were not applicable but that 'the fundamental rights of personality, the right to determinate about one's own images and the civil law concerning damages' applied and that action in civil court would be possible.
Polish	Stated that the rules regarding journalistic investigation are 'not precisely prescribed by law', there was no authority dealing with such questions, and so any case had to be judged 'by court, taking into account the specific circumstances of the case'.
Portuguese	Stated that the DPA did not issue permits to media companies concerning journalistic activity[32] and that the limits and legal conditions for this case would be dealt with by the media regulator and not the DPA.
Slovene	Stated that data protection law did not apply but that (as covert recording was defined as a criminal act) the provisions of the Penal Code would and that the general laws on defamation and breach of privacy might also be applicable.
Spanish Catalonian	Stated that '[i]n some cases Spanish Constitutional Court considered this kind of video recording was illegal (v. qr. STC 12/2012). Nevertheless, in other cases [it] considered that it was admissible (facts punishable).'

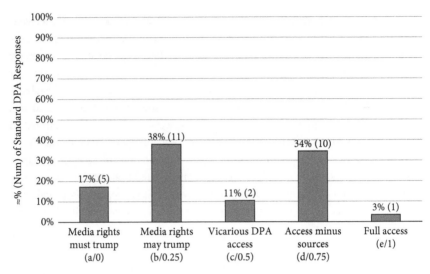

Chart 6.4 Subject Access and Journalism—DPA Legal Interpretation

Turning to the question on *subject access*, twenty-nine DPAs provided standard/categorical responses, only one of these set out further specific elaboration in supplementary text, and there was only one additional free-text answer. As can be seen from Chart 6.4, the standard responses here were much more varied and often more stringent. Almost one-fifth of the DPAs did state that there was a categorical exemption for the media here (a/0), whilst somewhat over one-third indicated that a qualified override might apply (b/0.25). On the other hand, another one-third of regulators held that subject access would apply to all but a journalist's sources (b/0.75) and one DPA even indicated (subject to some supplementary caveats[33]) that this right would apply without any special limitation (a/1). Meanwhile, only two DPAs (7 per cent) supported the rules-based alternative to direct subject access, namely through vicarious scrutiny by the regulator itself (c/0.5). The categorical responses of each individual DPA are specified in Table 6.3 below and also in Appendix 5. Finally, the free-text answer from the UK DPA appeared to sit somewhat between the qualified (b/0.25) and absolute (a/0) exemption categories.[34]

3. Exploring the Relationships between DPA Standard-Setting, Statutory Law, and Self-Regulatory Norms

3.1 Undercover Journalism, DPA Standard-Setting, and Statutory Law

The *undercover journalism* question was designed to raise issues in relation to at least three default provisions within European data protection. First, the journalist

here would clearly be collecting personal data (in the form of audio-visual recordings) from data subjects without notifying them either of their identity or of the intended purposes of the processing, both in conflict with the proactive transparency
rule which, by default, applied under the DPD when collecting information directly
from the individual data subject.[35] Second, some of this data would reveal these data
subjects' sensitive data, at the least in the form of their 'political opinions',[36] and the
journalist's activity would contradict the DPD's default prohibition on such processing[37] (at least absent waiver[38] from the relevant data subject). Finally, the non-
transparent nature of this covert investigation would sit in serious tension with the
DPD's requirement to process 'fairly'.[39] Although this principle was left completely
open within the body of the Directive, Recital 38 stated that 'if the processing of data
is to be fair, the data subject must be in a position to learn of the existence of a processing operation and, where data are collected from him, must be given accurate
and full information, bearing in mind the circumstances of the collection'.

Arraying each Member States' statutory law within the same five categories as
presented to the DPAs was complicated not only by the inevitably rather broad nature of the categories but also by the fact that, in many instances, these laws set out
different derogations for each of the three provisions cited earlier. Such a categorization was, however, achieved through the following approximations. First, given
that this undercover activity necessarily conflicted with both the proactive transparency rule and the prohibition on processing sensitive data, statutory laws were
categorized according to all of the conditions set out for a journalistic exemption
(if any) from both these provisions. Second, and as an exception to this, if the statutory law applied the fair processing requirement in full to the media then, in light
of this provision's strong steer towards transparent processing, any exemption here
was held to require compliance with at least the permissive version of the public
interest text (category d/0.25). Third, if journalism was clearly granted a derogation from the fair processing principle then, even if this was qualified by for example a public interest test, a categorization according the statute's approach to the
transparency and sensitive data rules was considered paramount. In fact, as seen in
the following, the patterns in the actual data rendered the second rule inapplicable
in all cases and the third one only potentially significant in one case.

Drawing on the more fine-grained analysis presented in my 2016 study of national statutory data protection frameworks,[40] an application of the above approximations led to a categorization of these twenty-nine DPA jurisdictions as set out
in Chart 6.5. In eight cases[41] (28 per cent of the total), statutory data protection
law provided for an unconditional journalistic exemption from both the proactive
transparency rule and the prohibition on processing political opinion data. Since
all these laws also provided for a derogation from the fairness principle (which,
aside from Austria,[42] was even unconditional in nature), they were all placed
within category a/0. In six other cases[43] (21 per cent), derogation from both the
proactive transparency and the political opinion processing prohibition depended

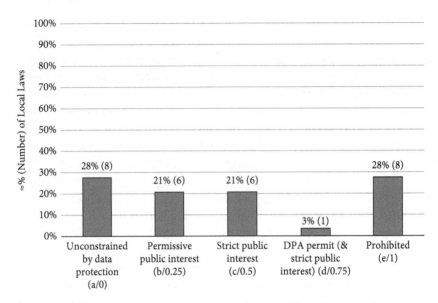

Chart 6.5 Undercover Journalism—Position in Statutory Data Protection Law

on the satisfaction of a permissive test that was nevertheless still grounded in a public interest analysis. In four of these jurisdictions the same derogation also extended to the fair processing principle, whilst in the other two the fairness stipulation continued to apply in full.[44] All these laws were, therefore, placed within category b/0.25. Laws in six further cases (21 per cent) required a strict public interest to be satisfied in order to gain, in three cases,[45] an exemption from the prohibition on processing political opinion data or, in three more,[46] also an exemption from the proactive transparency rule. Additionally, in all these cases, the fair processing principle remained applicable to journalism, although Italian law did set out an interpretative gloss here in favour of the media.[47] These laws were therefore placed within category c/0.5. Only in one case (3 per cent), namely the Greek data protection law, was it stipulated that a journalistic exemption from the prohibition on processing political opinion data not only had to satisfy a (very strictly worded) public interest test but also required a permit from the DPA. It, therefore, fell within category d/0.75.[48] In a final eight cases (28 per cent), statutory data protection law pointed to the processing of data consequent to such undercover journalism as being *ipso facto* prohibited. These cases, therefore, fell within category e/1. In four[49] jurisdictions this was due to the absence of any journalistic derogation as regards both the proactive transparency rule and the prohibition on processing data revealing political opinions. In contrast, in four others[50] only the latter provision was left fully applicable to journalism. None of these jurisdictions set out any journalistic derogation from the fairness principle.

Table 6.2 sets out a cross-tabulation of the categorization of *undercover journalism* according, on the vertical axis, to an approximation of its treatment in

Table 6.2 Undercover Journalism: Statutory Data Protection Law vs DPA Standard-Setting

DPA standards (n=21)→ / Statutory Law (n=29)↓	Violates data protection (e/1) 0 (0%)	Strict public interest and DPA permit (d/0.75) 0 (0%)	Strict public interest (c/0.5) 8 (38%)	Permissive public interest (b/0.25) 8 (38%)	Uncontrolled by data protection (a/0) 5 (24%)	*Free-text responses (outside formal calculations)*
Violates data protection (e/1) 8 (28%)			• Hungary • Liechtenstein • Lithuania	• Czechia • Slovakia		• *Portugal* • *Slovenia* • *Spanish Catalonia*
Strict public interest and DPA permit (d/0.75) 1 (3%)			• Greece			
Strict public interest (c/0.5) 6 (21%)			• Belgium • Bulgaria • Italy	• Estonia • Luxembourg	• Cyprus	
Permissive public interest (b/0.25) 6 (21%)			• Malta	• Latvia • Ireland	• Gibraltar	• *France* • *Poland*
Uncontrolled by data protection (a/0) 8 (28%)				• German Mecklenberg-Vorpommern • German Schleswig-Holstein	• Finland • German Federal • Sweden	• *Austria* • *German Brandenburg* • *German Rhineland-Palatinate*

statutory law and, on the horizontal, to the DPAs' own interpretative standard-setting. Those jurisdictions whose regulators provided an entirely free-text answers are listed *in italics* in the far right-hand column. The DPA jurisdictions falling within a darkly shaded box are those where there was a direct overlap between the approach set out in local statutory law and in the regulator's response. In general, however, a significant divergence between these two measures was apparent. Whilst jurisdictions were fairly evenly distributed vertically, they strongly clustered in the right-hand side of the table horizontally. Thus, it can be calculated from the quantified form of these results that whilst the average coded value for the statutory laws was 0.46, it was only 0.29 as regards the DPA own approach to standards. Meanwhile, greater clustering of the latter is signified by a lower standard deviation of only 0.19 compared with 0.39 as regards the statutory laws. Nevertheless, within the narrow range of categories in which they clustered, the stringency of the applicable statutory law remained a fairly good predictor of a DPA's interpretative stance. This, perhaps surprising, result is confirmed by a Spearman's Rank Correlation between these variables of 0.583, together with a one-tailed significance value of 0.003 which clearly indicated significance at the 1 per cent confidence level.

3.2 Subject Access, DPA Standard-Setting, and Statutory Law

Turning to *subject access* and again drawing on the more fine-grained 2016 study,[51] it was possible to array Member States' statutory journalistic derogation regarding subject access along the same spectrum as that presented to DPAs in the questionnaire. Indeed, since this only required a discrete analysis of the derogations made available in relation to the default subject access right itself,[52] this was generally a much simpler exercise than that which arose in relation to the undercover journalism scenario explored earlier. Thus, DPAs operating in jurisdictions whose State laws set out no journalistic derogation from subject access were coded into e/1, those only shielding journalists from the release of information on sources into d/0.75,[53] those explicitly providing for vicarious access by the DPA here into c/0.5, those with any overarching qualified derogation for journalists from subject access into b/0.25,[54] and finally those setting out an absolute exemption for the media from this right into a/0.[55] Nevertheless, a complex situation presented itself in relation to the local law applicable to the five German DPAs that responded to the questionnaire. In each of these jurisdictions, this law required certain broadcasters to adhere to an, albeit relatively media-friendly, balancing between subject access and freedom of expression (b/0.25).[56] In contrast, the print media benefited from complete legal immunity here (a/0).[57] Given the potential applicability of either

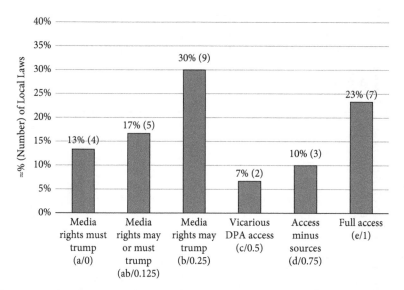

Chart 6.6 Subject Access and Journalism—Position in Statutory Data Protection Law

regime to any given professional journalist, these jurisdictions were allocated a value of 0.125 or, in other words, a coding which was midway between categories a/0 and b/0.25. This pattern produced by this analysis across all relevant EEA jurisdictions is summarized in Chart 6.6.

Table 6.3 cross-tabulates the categorization of subject access according, on the vertical access, to the position in statutory law and, on the horizontal, according to the relevant DPA's response in the questionnaire. The UK DPA uniquely provided an entirely free-text answer here and so is listed separately *in italics* in the far right-hand column. Direct overlap between these two values is signified by a darkly shaded box, whilst the two lighter shaded boxes accommodate the special situation of the German DPA jurisdictions where two different responses could each be considered to be provided for in statute. In this case, the average values between the two dimensions was very similar, namely 0.44 as regards statutory law and 0.42 in the case of the DPAs' own standards. Meanwhile, the standard deviation values were 0.37 and 0.30, reflecting only slightly more clustering in the DPA responses compared to that in statutory law. Finally, there was a moderately strong and clearly significant relationship between a DPA's own elucidation of standards here and the stipulations found in its local statutory law, with a Spearman's rank correlation between these two measures of 0.535 and a one-tailed significance value of 0.001 which thereby confirmed significance at the 1 per cent confidence level.

Table 6.3 Subject Access and Journalism—Statutory Data Protection Law vs DPA Standard-Setting

DPA standards (n = 29) → Statutory law (n = 30) ↓	Full access (e/1) 1 (3%)	Access minus sources (d/0.75) 10 (34%)	Vicarious DPA access (c/0.5) 2 (7%)	Media rights may trump (b/0.25) 11 (38%)	Media rights must trump (a/0) 5 (17%)	Free text (1 response outside formal calculations)
Full access (e/1) 7 (23%)	• Cyprus	• Greece • Slovakia • Slovenia		• Czechia • Latvia • Spanish Catalonia		
Access minus sources (d/0.75) 3 (10%)		• Italy • Bulgaria		• Hungary		
Vicarious DPA access (c/0.5) 2 (7%)			• Luxembourg • Portugal			
Media rights may trump (b/0.25) 9 (30%)		• Belgium • Estonia • Malta • Gibraltar		• Ireland • Liechtenstein • Poland	• France	• United Kingdom
Media rights may or must trump (ab/0.125) 5 (17%)		• German Schleswig-Holstein		• German Federal • German Brandenburg • German Mecklenberg-Vorpommern	• German Rhineland-Palatinate	
Media rights must trump (a/0) 4 (13%)				• Lithuania	• Austria • Finland • Sweden	

3.3 DPA Standard-Setting and Self-Regulatory Norms

Chapter 5 elucidated the significant emphasis which both DPA guidance and, to a lesser extent, State statutory law placed on promoting a co-regulatory interaction between statutory and self-regulation during the DPD era. In light of this, it is important to compare DPA interpretative standard-setting not only with the norms set out in statutory law but also with those formulated within a self-regulatory 'ethical' context. This was achieved through an analysis of the set of European codes of journalism ethics collated in English translation by the EthicNet project.[58] This included deontological instruments of direct relevance to all DPA jurisdictions other than Liechtenstein and Gibraltar.[59] These codes, as well as a summary of the analysis undertaken, are listed in Appendix 6. As will be seen shortly, this analysis revealed a pattern that was rather different from either that set out either in statutory law or in DPA interpretative standard-setting.

Turning first to *undercover journalism*, this method of journalistic investigation was addressed in some way in codes directly applicable to all but five[60] of the twenty-nine DPA jurisdictions. However, in seven of these cases, the code requirements remained too vague to be placed within the categories cited earlier.[61] Categorization was, however, possible in the remaining seventeen DPA jurisdictions. As summarized in Chart 6.7, the self-regulatory stipulations set out in eleven (65 per cent) of cases required journalists resorting to undercover techniques to satisfy a strict public interest test (c/0.5) which incorporated within it at least both a necessity and a more general public interest threshold.[62] These tests were variously phrased. For example, the code applicable to the German jurisdictions stated

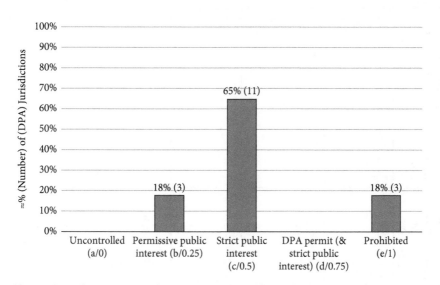

Chart 6.7 Undercover Journalism—Position in Self-Regulatory Codes

Table 6.4 Undercover Journalism—Self-Regulatory Codes vs DPA Standard-Setting

Self-regulation (Coded = 17) → / DPA standards (Coded = 21) ↓	Uncontrolled (a/0) 0 (0%)	Permissive public interest (b/0.25) 3 (18%)	Strict public interest (c/0.5) 11 (65%)	Strict public interest and DPA permit (d/0.75) 0 (0%)	Unacceptable (e/1) 3 (18%)	Not found or uncoded (outside formal calculations) (12)
Uncontrolled (a/0) 5 (24%)			• Finland • German Federal			• Cyprus • Gibraltar • Sweden
Permissive public interest (b/0.25) 8 (38%)		• Ireland[63]	• Estonia • German Mecklenberg-Vorpommern • German Schleswig-Holstein • Luxembourg			• Czechia • Latvia • Slovakia
Strict public interest (c/0.5) 8 (38%)			• Belgium • Bulgaria[64]		• Malta • Lithuania	• Greece • Hungary • Italy • Liechtenstein
Strict public interest and DPA permit (d/0.75) 0 (0%)						
Unacceptable (e/1) 0 (0%)						
Uncoded (free text) (outside formal calculations) (8)		• Poland[65] • Portugal[66]	• Germany Brandenburg • Germany Rhineland-Palatinate • Slovenia		• Austria	• France • Spanish Catalonia

that '[u]ndercover research may be justifiable in individual cases if in this way information of particular public interest is gained which cannot be procured by other means'. Meanwhile, the Finnish code stated that '[i]f matters of social signifi-cance cannot be otherwise investigated, the journalists may carry out interviews and obtain information by means that deviate from standard practice'. In only three cases (18 per cent) was it suggested that a permissive public interest test (not incorporating a necessity standard) might be acceptable (b/0.25),[67] whilst ethical norms in three further cases (18 per cent) appeared to prohibit standard investiga-tive journalistic methods entirely (e/1).

Table 6.4 cross-tabulates, on the horizontal axis, the standards set down in self-regulatory codes here with, on the vertical, the standards specified by the DPA under the legal framework. Inputs which, in either case, could not be cat-egorized are listed separately *in italics* in the last column or the bottom row as appropriate. Any direct overlap is highlighted by a darkly shaded box. As can be seen, such an overlap was only present in three cases. All the other cases which could be categorized on both dimensions clustered to the right-hand side of these boxes, thus indicating that DPA standard-setting was more permis-sive here than the ethical stipulation laid down in the relevant self-regulatory code. As a result, the average coded value of the self-regulatory provisions was 0.54, whilst it was only 0.29 in the case of the DPA standards. A Spearman's Rank test between these variables produced a correlation of 0.495 and a (one-tailed) significance value of 0.061, thus indicating a moderately strong rela-tionship between these two variables which was significant at the 10 per cent confidence level.

Turning next to the governance of *subject access*, it is striking that only of the three 'self-regulatory' codes targeted at EEA States explicitly addressed the ethical tensions arising here in an overarching manner. In sum:

- The German Press Code in principle required that in cases where a '[press] report has a negative effect on someone's personal rights' the data subject was provided on request with 'information on the data upon which the report was based and on the data on his or her person which the publication has stored'. However, this was subject to a number of very wide-ranging excep-tions including when 'imparting the data obtained by research or other means would negatively affect the publication's journalistic mission by revealing the information it possesses' or 'it otherwise proves to be necessary in order to reconcile the right to privacy with the regulations obtaining on freedom of expression'.[68]
- The Luxembourg Code of Deontology stated that '[t]he press agrees to respect the right to access personal information of any individual as defined by the law concerning the protection of information' but added that its exercise 'may never affect the protection of the sources of a journalist'.[69]

- Finally, the Italian Deontology Code (which, in fact, was the co-regulatory Code of Conduct that as noted in Chapter 5 was agreed with the DPA and had the force of law within Italian data protection law) stated that '[i]f personal data is gathered at data banks for editorial use, the editorial enterprises are obliged to make known to the public, through announcements, at least twice a year, the existence of the archives and the place in which it is possible to exercise the rights prescribed by Law no. 675/1996 [on data protection]'.[70] Aside from an oblique reference to source protection,[71] permissible limits on such rights were not addressed.

It should be recognized that one of these codes (the German Press Code) was directly applicable to all five of the German DPA jurisdictions (i.e. 17 per cent of the total) whose regulator participated in the questionnaire. However, in the other twenty-three out of thirty relevant jurisdictions (77 per cent), no such self-regulatory guidance was found at all.[72] In contrast, ethical codes targeted at twenty-five jurisdictions (83 per cent)[73] did explicitly address the ethical need (or, in a couple of cases, a journalist's ethical right) to safeguard the anonymity of journalistic sources. This protection was usually delimited to confidential sources or sources who had not given their consent to have their identity revealed. The safeguarding of such sources was extremely strong. Indeed, only four codes[74] explicitly acknowledged any permissible exceptions to it and even these set out thresholds which would be highly unlikely to be met under a subject access request.[75]

4. General Analysis

The deep probing of both the *basic stance* and *standard-setting* of DPAs as regards the professional journalistic media reinforces Chapter 5's finding that regulators have, in broad terms, based their approach on a form of contextual rights balancing which is guided principally by a public interest analysis but which also looks to norms set down within self-regulation. This is most clearly highlighted in the stance of DPAs in relation to news production, where the data confirmed a clear regulatory consensus that the special expression regime was engaged (see Chart 6.1). Moreover, whilst considerably less strong, a consensus on the need for such special accommodation remained present in relation to long-term online media archiving (see Chart 6.2). The fact that the consensus here was rather weaker is perhaps not surprising given that archiving is less unambiguously concerned with imparting a specific journalistic message to the general public[76] and, in addition, raises particularly acute conflicts with a number of data protection's core purposes. Indeed, these issues were similarly highlighted in Chapter 5 and, even more so, in Chapter 4 which focused on the situation under first-generation data protection.

At the same time, this chapter also highlighted that the stringency or otherwise of local data protection law did continue to exert a powerful effect on both a DPA's basic stance and its articulation of detailed standards. Most starkly, where journalism was granted an absolute exemption from data protection norms set down in local statute, this exemption was generally treated as conclusive. This foreclosing of contextual balancing took place notwithstanding the protection of personal data within primary law such as the EU Charter and the strong likelihood that this would have some directly effective force at least within the EU (as opposed to the wider EEA).[77] Turning to standard-setting, even in relation to activities such as undercover journalism where many DPAs heavily 'read down' their statutory provisions, the severity of this local law still clearly correlated with the regulator adopting a relatively stringent approach to the contextual balancing exercise.

It was also shown that the approach adopted by DPAs in relation to the balancing exercise appeared strongly impacted by the presence and nature of self-regulatory frameworks. In areas where clear self-regulatory norms had been established, DPAs tended towards not only a contextual but also a rather *laissez-faire* approach to standard-setting. This was most clearly highlighted by the fact that, despite the fact the great majority of self-regulatory codes mandated that a resort to undercover journalism required a strict public interest threshold (Chart 6.7), a majority of DPAs were willing to sanction this on the basis of (at most) a permissive public interest test (Chart 6.3). In contrast where, as in the case of subject access, ethical norms were poorly developed, DPAs were often only willing to sanction a minimal departure from general data protection duties. Thus, over one-third of DPAs thought that this default right would simply apply in the context of journalistic investigations (Chart 6.4), with the exception only of material on sources whose confidentiality was strongly safeguarded within self-regulatory frameworks.

5. Conclusions

Dovetailing with Chapter 5, this chapter has confirmed that the basic legal stance and interpretative standard-setting of DPAs in relation to the professional journalistic media has been dominated by contextual balancing and an emphasis on ensuring a clear link between statutory and self-regulation. At the same time, however, is has been demonstrated that such an approach has remained both imperfect and incomplete. Whilst DPAs have adopted a very *laissez-faire* approach in areas where self-regulatory norms have been articulated, they have often only been willing to validate very limited deviations from default data protection standards in the absence of this. In any case, the stringency or otherwise of local statutory law has continued to shape regulatory interpretation and, at least where journalism has been granted a complete exemption, has generally been treated as being conclusively overriding notwithstanding potentially other relevant law.

These findings highlight the need for a more coherent conceptualization of the interrelationship between competing human rights, specific local statutory provisions, DPA standard-setting, and self-regulation. Chapter 8 will look empirically at some of these issues as they relate to the new legal framework established under the General Data Protection Regulation 2016/679, whilst Chapter 9 will likewise engage in a normative analysis of how DPAs should approach their role under this new framework. However, before turning to these issues, it is important also to consider to what extent, and how, statutory regulators have deployed their considerable powers under the DPD to enforce data protection standards in this area. That will be the task of Chapter 7.

7

Second-Generation European Data Protection Regulation and Professional Journalism

Probing Enforcement

European data protection regulation does not just seek to articulate the standards applicable to personal data processing but, more concretely, aims to ensure the 'effective and complete protection of [the] fundamental rights and freedoms' of natural persons in this regard.[1] The latter goal highlights the central role of DPAs not only in 'soft' areas such as interpretative standard-setting[2] and related awareness-raising[3] but also in the area of enforcement. Indeed, it may be argued that, in emphasizing the need for 'compliance' with data protection to be 'subject to control by an independent authority',[4] the European fundamental rights *acquis* has given priority to this latter dimension. In any case, it can hardly be doubted that enforcement is 'critical to achieve deterrence and to prevent data protection violations',[5] as well as being vital to the 'successful implementation of social legislation'[6] in general.

Whilst stipulating the need to provide derogations as 'necessary to reconcile' competing fundamental rights[7] and allowing for supervisory functions to be allocated to a specialist media regulator,[8] the Data Protection Directive 95/46 ('DPD') required Member States to provide for a supervisory regime for journalistic and related forms of special expression which respected these foundational regulatory principles. Moreover, at the State level, only three Member States sought to exclude the media from statutory regulation entirely; in contrast, and as detailed in Chapter 5, the vast majority granted the ordinary DPA a potentially full supervisory role here.

This chapter, therefore, explores both the enforcement power stance and the enforcement efforts of statutory data regulators during second-generation European data protection. In so doing, it draws both on the responses to specific questions posed within the DPA questionnaire and details of enforcement activity located through the DPA website review which was carried out over the same period. It is found that, whilst being more likely than statutory law itself to conceive these as being limited, the great majority of statutory regulators accepted that they did possess enforcement powers in this area. However, enforcement activity remained

European Data Protection Regulation, Journalism, and Traditional Publishers. David Erdos, Oxford University Press (2019). © David Erdos.
DOI: 10.1093/oso/9780198841982.003.0007

very patchy, even as regards issues which are widely understood or which DPAs themselves conceived as raising only limited free speech concerns (e.g. tackling significant inaccuracy and responding to subject access requests respectively). Only around 60 per cent of regulators reported having undertaken any enforcement in relation to professional journalism and the great majority of these indicated that they had only intervened in relation to one or two aspects of the data protection scheme. The DPA website review confirmed this general picture, whilst also uncovering some problematic divergences as regards how these regulators reported their enforcement efforts.

Nevertheless, both sets of data highlighted that regulators have far from entirely ignored journalism. To the contrary, the data indicated that regulators had engaged in significant enforcement, at least in relation to the dissemination of sensitive and related categories of data that raised specific privacy concerns and also information such as national identification numbers whose safeguarded treatment was integrally linked to the ordered functioning of basic social and economic relationships. Statistical analysis further demonstrated that the stringency of local law was very strongly correlated with both the presence and extent of these regulatory enforcement efforts. Analysis run against data on the resources regulators had at their disposal was considerably more mixed. Nevertheless, the generally limited and patchy nature of enforcement did appear partially explicable by the very meagre resources which regulators as a whole had at their disposal.

The rest of this chapter is divided into five sections. Sections 1 and 2 detail the enforcement data which came out of the DPA questionnaire and the DPA website review respectively. Section 3 then seeks to explain divergences between the regulators, looking statistically at the interface between enforcement and both local law stringency and regulatory resourcing. Section 4 provides a more general and principally qualitative analysis, exploring the relationship between the enforcement patterns which were revealed and formal law, the regulatory emphasis on contextual balancing, DPA resourcing, and the interface with self-regulation respectively. Finally, section 5 sets out some conclusions which especially focus on the relevance of these findings for the future of data protection in this area.

1. The Data Protection Authority (DPA) Questionnaire

1.1 Questions Posed

Three types of question were posed to DPAs in the area of enforcement and professional journalism. The first probed the *enforcement power stance* of regulators in relation to the pursuit by the professional journalistic media of their most quintessential activity, namely news production.[9] In sum, DPAs were asked to indicate whether they considered that their 'powers to regulate' here were (a) excluded,

(b) present but limited, or (c) present (in full).[10] Given that these possibilities ranged from no (a/0) through to full powers (c/1), these responses were arrayed along a 0–1 scale. In cases where a DPA conceived its powers as present but limited (b/0.5), it was invited to specify this in supplementary text. Free-text responses were also accepted as a full alternative to a standard categorical answer.

Second, DPAs were asked to detail their *general enforcement* track record related to 'media entities' pursuit of their journalistic activities' since the transposition of the DPD. Since it was not feasible to probe regulators in relation to every potentially applicable specific provision, questions concerning action as regards three specific legal stipulations were used to highlight any focus on securing granular compliance with data protection. These potential examples of granular action were specified as: (1) 'action against media agencies for failure to register/notify' with the DPA (which directly related to article 18 of the DPD); (2) 'action to ensure individuals are afforded rights of data access' (which directly related to article 12(a)), and (3) 'action to ensure individuals are afforded the right to rectify inaccurate data' (which directly related article 6(1)(d) as regards the accuracy duty and article 12(b) in relation to rectification). Turning to more diffusely targeted efforts, DPAs were also invited to indicate whether they had taken action (4) 'to prevent the processing/publication of personal data obtained without authorization from another Data Controller' and/or (5) 'to prevent the processing/publication of personal data in contexts other than when such data was obtained without authorization from another Data Controller'. The distinction drawn between (4) and (5) was based on an understanding that enforcement in the former case would most likely be principally focused on securing the integrity of the data relationships of a range of non-journalistic organizations. The original data controller here would necessarily be processing the data for their own purposes (e.g. medical care in the case of a doctor's practice) and these purposes might be seriously undermined by an unauthorized obtaining and further processing of such material. Therefore, taking steps to protect against this may be considered as essential to maintaining the essential integrity of any data protection system. Furthermore, obtaining information without authorization often requires recourse to particularly invidious measures such as corruption or blagging.[11] In contrast, taking action in the latter case would presumptively intrude more directly on the media's own freedom of expression since it would necessarily relate to data which the media has either obtained with consent (e.g. an interview transcript) or has generated itself (e.g. a photograph). Finally, DPAs who had not signified assent to any of the five actions were invited to indicate positively that they had 'not taken any enforcement action in relation to media entities' pursuit of their journalistic activities'.

Third, in a different part of the questionnaire, DPAs were asked about their *media archive enforcement* track record. In sum, regulators were invited to indicate whether, since the transposition of the DPD, they had taken enforcement action against a 'newspaper archive' in relation to (1) 'the use of material obtained without proper authorization from another Data Controller' and/or (2) 'any other processing activity connected to publication'. This distinction between (1) and (2) was based on the same broad rationale as that of (4) and (5) in the general question above. Meanwhile, the specific focus on media archiving reflected the particular controversies over data protection regulation in this area, which have been extensively detailed in the previous chapters of Part II of this book.

Finally, it should also be noted that the questionnaire gathered responses from DPAs on various connected matters including their enforcement efforts in relation to certain 'new' online media actors as well as social scientists. This data will be referred to where relevant later in this chapter; in addition, the data on social scientists and data protection will explored in depth in Part III of this book.

1.2 Enforcement Power Stance Findings

Chart 7.1 outlines the categorical answers which were received in response to the first *power stance* question. As with all the standard results presented here, these are also specified for each individual DPA in Appendix 5. As can be seen, whilst approximately one-fifth of the regulators held that they had no powers in the area of journalistic news production (a/0), the other DPAs split evenly between conceiving their powers here as partial (b/0.5) or full (c/1). Almost all those who categorically stated that they possess partial regulatory powers also provided further specification. The three 'free-text' replies which were received from the Lithuanian, Dutch, and UK DPAs also generally indicated that they possessed regulatory powers here but that these were limited. All these textual responses are summarized in Table 7.1.

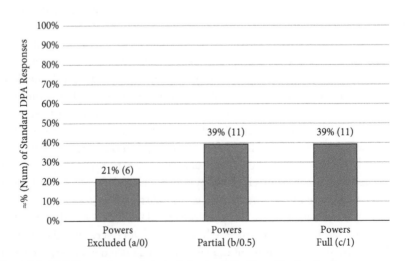

Chart 7.1 DPA Power Stance (*vis-à-vis* Journalistic News Production).

Table 7.1 DPA's Further Specification of Regulatory Powers

DPA (Statutory substantive stringency/ statutory regulatory powers)	Summary
Czechia (1/1)	Provided translation of article in the then current Czech Data Protection Act which set out general circumstances when (ordinary) personal data could be processed without consent.[12]
Finland (0/1)	Noted the procedural provisions in Finnish data protection law which continued to apply to journalism including 'general provisions and data security as well as liability in damages'.
Germany Mecklenburg-Vorpommern (0.03/0)	Stated that each public broadcasting service 'basically has its own data protection commissioner and is partially subjected to special legal regulations, such as the state treaty for broadcasting and TV'.
Germany Rhineland-Palatinate (0.03/0)	Stated that '[i]n the area of administration, without the scope of journalistic activities, we can control the media'.
Germany Schleswig-Holstein (0.03/0.25)	Stated that section 41 of the then German Federal Data Protection Act 'restricts the application of the law concerning print media'.
Greece (0.84/1)	Stated that Greek constitutional provisions assigned exclusive control and administrative sanction over radio and television to a specialist National Council (Art 15(2)) and separately prohibited prior checking such as censorship (Art 14(2)).
Ireland (0.34/1)	Stated that provisions in the then Irish law giving effect to Article 9 of the Directive provided a 'wide exemption' for data processing for these journalistic purposes.
Lithuania (0.63/0.5)	Technically ticked that 'no' it didn't have such powers but also indicated that responsibility for this area had been allocated to the Inspector of Journalistic Ethics
Luxembourg (0.68/1)	Stated that the Law of the Press and governing Freedom of Expression provided for a Press Council with a self-regulatory role for handling deontologic misconduct complaints of journalists and publishers which would include 'infringements of data protection rules unless formal enforcement by the DPA (CNPD) or action in Court'.
Netherlands (0.38/1)	Stated that it had 'no power to regulate' where data '[are] being processed for *exclusively* journalistic purposes" but also stressed that it was 'not easy to answer' if that test would be satisfied, detailing *inter alia* that it depended on the message being 'socially relevant', the processing 'structural', the activity 'an objective way of gathering the information', and their being 'an opportunity for rectification or something similar'.

Continued

Table 7.1 *Continued*

DPA (Statutory substantive stringency/ statutory regulatory powers)	Summary
Portugal (0.83/1)	Lengthy reply acknowledging that no formal regulatory exemption but that the DPA itself adopted a 'residual' approach. Variety of arguments offered including existence of media specific legislation, regulator, deontological code, conflict with other fundamental/constitutional rights, and that 'usually the cases arising from publication of a story . . . are more related to other issues than to the data protection core purposes'.[13]
United Kingdom (0.35/0.5)	Stated that it did have powers here but indicated, with reference to particular provisions set out in UK data protection law, that there were 'some restrictions'. It particularly noted that, unlike in other cases, 'the Information Commissioner may not serve an enforcement notice with respect to processing for the[se] special purposes without leave of the court'.

1.3 Enforcement Action Findings: Scope of Activity

Twenty-five DPAs submitted a standard answer in response to both the general and archive-specific enforcement track record questions. In these cases, it is possible to represent the scope of their enforcement activity through counting the number of data protection areas in which they reported having carried out some action. In total, the general enforcement track record question inquired into five such areas (three granular and two more diffuse), whilst the question on archives did likewise in two fairly diffuse areas. DPAs, therefore, could have indicated the presence of enforcement action up to seven times. As Chart 7.2 highlights, however, the enforcement actually reported was in the main far less extensive than this. Thus, although sixteen DPAs (64 per cent) reported some enforcement, half these (32 per cent) testified to action only in relation to one or two of the specified areas. Furthermore, since the different areas explored in the questionnaire at least partially overlapped, even this representation may over-represent the extent of any action which had actually been undertaken. This risk may be particularly acute in relation to the diffusely targeted areas specified in the general enforcement question (labelled as G4 and G5) and the similarly diffusely targeted areas concerning archives (labelled as A1 and A2). In this regard, it may be noted that three out of the four DPAs[14] represented as enforcing in relation to four areas obtained this result through affirming action in all four of these diffusely targeted areas. Meanwhile, only two DPAs, namely that of Slovenia (five areas) and Italy (six areas), testified to even more extensive action than this.[15]

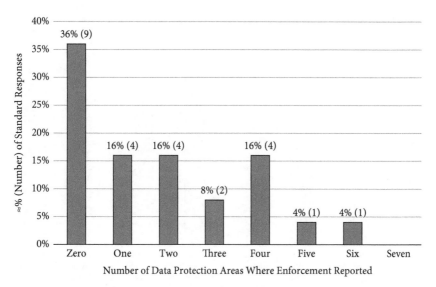

Chart 7.2 Number of Data Protection Areas where DPAs (providing a Fully Standard Questionnaire Return) Self-Reported Enforcement as Regards the Professional Journalistic Media ($n = 25$).

1.4 Enforcement Action Findings: Areas of Activity

As detailed in Chart 7.3, the standard answers received from DPAs in response to the *general enforcement* track record question suggested that the great majority of regulators had undertaken little enforcement which aimed at securing granular compliance with specific data protection provisions (see variables G1–G3). Thus, only one DPA claimed it had enforced registration/notification duties, only five (19 per cent) that they had likewise acted to ensure subject access, and only four (15 per cent) that they had enforced in relation to the rectification of inaccurate data. In some contrast, a rather larger number of DPAs indicated having at least carried out more diffusely targeted enforcement, namely ten (38 per cent) in relation the processing/publication of 'unauthorized' data (G4) and seven (27 per cent) in relation to other types of data (G5).[16] Most of the five non-standard/free-text responses which were forthcoming from the Bulgarian,[17] Czech,[18] Luxembourg,[19] Maltese,[20] and UK[21] DPAs also indicated that they had carried out some rather diffusely focused enforcement. The standard responses in relation to the cognate question on *media archive enforcement* was, as Chart 7.3 also highlights, broadly comparable to this. Nine DPAs (31 per cent)[22] indicated that they had undertaken enforcement action here in relation to 'unauthorized' personal data (A1), whilst ten (34 per cent) signified similar activity in other cases (A2).[23]

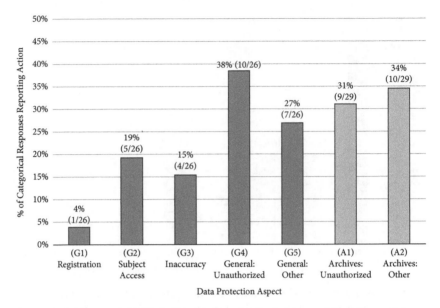

Chart 7.3 Self-Reported DPA Enforcement in Particular Areas of Data Protection as Relation to Professional Journalism in General (G1–G5) ($n = 26$) and Newspaper Archives (A1–A2) ($n = 29$).

Only one non-standard response (from the Austrian DPA[24]) was received in relation to this latter question.

2. The Data Protection Authority Website Review

In order both to add depth to, and ensure a measure of cross-checking of, the self-reported questionnaire responses, an attempt was made during 2013 to collate reports of enforcement action readily accessible on the websites of all national data protection regulators (including, in two States, the specialist media regulators with statutory data protection responsibilities)[25] and also of the five regional bodies which responded to the questionnaire. However, it became clear during this exercise that the very different ways in which regulators approached the on-line reporting, retention, and collation of information made the creation of a fully systematic and detailed dataset impossible. Notwithstanding these limitations, the data which were collated tended to confirm a picture of patchy and limited, yet also far from irrelevant, enforcement activity. Although the term 'enforcement action' wasn't explicitly defined in the questionnaire itself, for the purposes of the website review it was taken to encompass a broad range of interventions so long as these went beyond purely investigatory activity or the issuing of generic, non-binding guidance to data controllers. This spectral definition chimes with the widely endorsed 'enforcement pyramid' approach where enforcement is conceptualized as ranging from 'advisory and persuasive measures at the bottom, mild administrative sanctions in the middle, and punitive sanctions at the top'.[26]

2.1 General Enforcement Findings

Turning first to consider the website findings related to those DPAs which returned enforcement track record responses in a standard format, some evidence of enforcement was found in ten (40 per cent) of these cases. These comprised the Belgium, Cypriot, Greek, Hungarian, Irish, Italian, Latvian, Dutch, and Slovenian DPAs, as well as that of the Lithuanian DPA/Inspector of Journalist Ethics. However, in the case of Latvia the activity located took place in 2003, which was technically in the year leading up this State joining the EU and becoming fully subject to the DPD,[27] whilst in the case of Belgium the example related solely to media archiving and so will be considered in section 2.2. Although all these regulators also reported enforcement in the questionnaire, this number is clearly lower than the sixteen regulators (64 per cent) which self-reported such activity. This discrepancy may be explained not only by the fact that the review was only able to collate readily accessible website material but also by the reality that many DPA websites only provided lists of information for the past few years (as opposed to the entire period since the DPD had been in effect)[28] and, in any case, only posted public and high-profile, as opposed to all, examples of enforcement action.[29] It may also reflect an understanding on the part of some DPAs that the concept of enforcement action stretched even to specific investigations which ultimately found no legal violation or otherwise led to no further action. Finally, it should be recognized that the Polish example discussed later represents an ambiguous case. In sum, action was taken here against a prominent journalist (and freelance writer) in relation to an activity which was not directly connected to the institutional media or journalistic work per se, but nevertheless did concern the dissemination of personal information online. This DPA stated that it had not taken action in relation to media entities' journalistic activities and it was similarly coded in the website review.

Looking next at those regulators which provided a non-standard response to these questions, evidence of enforcement was found on the Bulgarian and UK but not on that of the Czech, Luxembourg, or Maltese DPA websites. Again, however, any apparent discrepancy may be explicable by the factors considered above. Turning finally to the national DPAs which did not respond to the questionnaire at all, some evidence of enforcement within the DPD period was located on the Spanish and Icelandic but not on that of the Croatia, Danish, Norwegian or Romanian DPA websites. All of these DPA website review results are reported in binary form in Appendix 5.

Moving to a detailed examination of this data, no clear support was found for the hypothesis that DPAs systematically prioritized enforcement in relation to material obtained without authorization from another controller as compared to material obtained or generated by the media in some other fashion.[30] In other respects, however, it did appear that regulators had generally adopted a targeted approach, prioritising both serious interferences with data protection rights and other infractions which had the potential to undermine the data protection system as a whole. Thus, little evidence of enforcement was found which related to very detailed and specific obligations which were set out in many second-generation data protection laws and none at all in relation to either the obligation to register data processing with the DPA or to respond to subject access requests. For reasons given above, however, one should be wary of necessarily equating this with a complete absence of activity. To the contrary, material from the UK (albeit not on the UK DPA's own website and therefore outside the website review itself) was uncovered which demonstrated that at least one photojournalist in this jurisdiction had been prosecuted for non-registration with the DPA.[31] Nevertheless, the lack of website coverage of such matters does at least indicate that this kind of activity was not considered a regulatory priority.

Meanwhile, the review did locate examples of action which related to data accuracy on the websites of the Italian (0.65/1), Icelandic (0.06/0) and Greek (0.84/1) DPAs. (As with those in chapter five and also elsewhere in this chapter the numeric designators here signify, through the first integer, the substantive stringency and, through the second, the extent of the regulatory powers set out in the statutory law of the relevant jurisdiction). The Italian DPA reported on the use by the media of photographs of individuals which had been taken off Facebook without consent in the context of reporting on the victims of accidents and violent crimes but which, in some but not all cases, related to individuals who had nothing to do with the events in question.[32] This DPA prohibited the continued publication of these images and reported the incidents to both the co-regulatory National Order of Journalists and the self-regulatory National Publishers' Federation. The Icelandic DPA admonished a newspaper in 2003 over its statement that an individual murdered some 14 years previously[33] (they were not named but, in the context, remained identifiable) had engaged in sexual activity prior to being killed, notwithstanding the fact that evidence of this was dismissed in the court case at the time.[34] Finally, the Greek DPA in case 38/2005 found that a broadcast concerning a letter the complainant had sent to a municipality asking that their brothers be allowed to purchase or rent property lawfully in the area was illegitimately misleading as it failed to include the complainant's explanation for this; any rebroadcasting of this material was specifically prohibited.[35] Nevertheless, whilst accuracy was one concern in these cases, certain other 'aggravating' circumstances were also present, including the (at least likely) illegal nature of the underlying data collection in both the Greek and Italian cases and the presence of sensitive personal data (namely, data concerning sex life) in both the Greek and Icelandic cases.

Addressing the illegitimate processing of sensitive personal data appeared central to several other Greek DPA decisions adverse to the media, some of which involved ordinary members of the public (as with case 38/2005) and others, those playing a more public role. As regards the former, case 140/2012 related to the publication of mental health information, whilst case 165/2012 arose from the publication of criminal suspicions or allegations. Turning to the latter, cases 100/2000 and 73/2005 concerned respectively the sexual data of a singer and designer (presented in the context of a journalistic inquiry into paedophilia) and the unlawful obtaining and broadcast of the erotic involvements of a bishop with an unknown person. The DPA issued fines in all these latter cases, although in case 140/2012 it did so only in relation to the newspaper rather than broadcaster. This was justified on the basis that the broadcaster had already been penalized by the Greek National Council for Radio and Television, a specialist oversight body for this sector. Meanwhile in cases 100/2000 and 165/2012 orders were variously made to destroy the data or ensure its anonymization.

A similar focus on sensitive data was found in reported actions undertaken by four other regulators (namely, the Bulgarian, Italian, Dutch, and Slovenian DPAs). The Bulgarian DPA (0.68/1) censured a newspaper for publishing the religious identity of a person who had left her family in order to join a sect, attempting at the same time to sell her father's flat in which she was living at the time. The other parts of this individual's complaint were rejected.[36] It also admonished and fined a newspaper for publishing in full an official psychiatric assessment of an individual against whom the editor of the newspaper was involved as a defendant in a criminal case.[37] The Italian DPA prohibited any further processing of sweat and urine samples which it found had been non-transparently, deceptively, and thereby illegally obtained from around fifty parliamentarians by journalists attached to a broadcaster with a view to testing them for recent drug use. This decision, made in 2006, was also sent to the co-regulatory National Order of Journalists, inviting them to consider exercising any competences which arose here.[38] Meanwhile, the Dutch DPA (0.38/0) found that a television production company (Eyeworks) had acted illegally in filming patients in a hospital without having obtained their prior, sufficiently specific, and freely given consent (which, it was further found, could not have been given due to the individuals' extraordinarily dependent position at the time). The broadcaster (together with the hospital) decided against any further broadcasting of the images which were then destroyed.[39] Finally, the Slovenian DPA (0.93/1) reported criminally fining both a newspaper and its editor in 2006 for publishing an autopsy report concerning three victims who had died at the entrance to a discotheque.[40]

A number of DPAs (the Italian, Cypriot, and Slovenian) publicized interventions arising from the dissemination of information which, although not technically sensitive, engaged with similar privacy interests as in the cases just cited. Thus, the Italian DPA 'prohibited the continued dissemination of images of the victim of a murder case that took place in Perugia, after those images had been broadcast by local TVs in utter contempt for human dignity'.[41] Drawing on the inviolability of a person's home, it also banned the publication of pictures of the interior of (the Italian Prime Minister) Silvio Berlusconi's villa taken using 'zoom lenses and intrusive, highly sophisticated systems'.[42] Similarly related to the protection of domicile, the Cypriot DPA (0.65/1) issued a fine against a media entity after it found that the inclusion of a photo showing the names of the occupants of a residential building in an article they had published concerning a lawsuit had been disproportionate.[43] More generally, the Slovenian DPA sanctioned both the newspaper and its editor for publishing unspecified personal data of a non-public figure included in a court document stressing that

> [p]ublic interest, with regard to the provision or publication of information which merely satisfies curiosity, cannot in itself be the justification for an encroachment into the information privacy and/or constitutional right to the protection of personal data of an individual who is not in the public eye.[44]

The ambiguous enforcement action by the Polish DPA (0.33/1) is best also discussed alongside these cases. In sum, in 2005 Bronisław Wildstein surreptitiously copied the index of the Polish Institute of National Remembrance archive which was 'available only to researchers and others cleared for access' and included well over 100,000 names of 'secret agents, informers, secret services employees and victims of persecution' under the former Communist regime.[45] Although this individual was a prominent journalist (and also freelance writer), information within this index was not published in the context of journalistic or media work. Instead, it was simply made available in full online. The DPA determined that this act had also been carried out by Wildstein himself (although this was disputed)[46] and, furthermore, that a criminal violation of the data protection had taken place. It notified the Polish prosecuting authorities of this but, for unclear reasons, the latter did not carry the case forward.[47]

Another important focus of enforcement highlighted in the review related to the protection of certain discrete types of information whose careful management was integrally related to the ordered conduct of basic social and economic relationships. Ensuring such integrity is, as noted earlier, central to the health of any data protection system well outside the area of journalism. Publicized actions by at least six DPAs (Bulgarian, Italian, Latvian, Lithuanian, Slovenian, and British) fell within this category, although an interaction with the two categories above was also sometimes present. Thus, the Bulgarian DPA (0.68/1) fined a newspaper for unintentionally publishing the personal identification numbers (and also the names) of individuals included in a partial list of shareholders of a company which was being discussed in one of its articles.[48] The Latvian DPA (0.67/1) censured a magazine for publishing a photograph taken from a store CCTV camera and a presenter for publishing on television an individual's identification document including its photo, identity code, and registration number.[49] Also related to maintaining the integrity of identification systems, the Lithuanian Inspector of Journalism Ethics (0.63/0.5) fined a newspaper for publishing the personal identification and social security number of the Anti-Corruption Chairman and Interim Mayor of Palanga.[50]

Similarly, the Slovenian DPA censored media organizations in three closely related cases: first, a broadcaster for including in its news coverage of a criminal complaint against three individuals not only their names and dates of birth but also their personal identification numbers; second, a newspaper reporting on a similar criminal complaint made to police for detailing, in this case, the suspect's name, date and place of birth, address, citizenship, and personal identification number; and third, for the reproduction on the websites of both a newspaper and a commercial television station of an identification card belonging to a person against whom an arrest warrant had been issued and a newspaper photo of the passport of an individual suspected of a criminal offence. In all these cases, it was stated that the action taken had secured the removal of the material.[51]

Overlapping with both the protection of core privacy interests and the basic social relationship inherent in the court system, the Italian DPA issued a general decision addressed to the entire media sector which sought to limit the publication by journalists of (often highly intimate) information contained in judicially ordered wiretap evidence obtained by the courts. This decision especially '[e]mphasised requirements for information materiality, respect for human dignity and special protection re: sex life'.[52] Demonstrating a similar overlap, the UK DPA (0.35/0.5) publicized the 2006 results of a substantial investigation which had uncovered 'an unlawful trade in confidential personal information' obtained through both corruption and deception which *inter alia* had resulted in the supply to hundreds of UK journalists a range of private personal details such as individuals' 'current address, details of car ownership, an ex-directory telephone number or records of calls made, bank account details or [even] intimate health records'.[53] Whilst not deploying any of its formal enforcement powers, the DPA called on the (erstwhile) self-regulatory Press Complaints Commission to 'take a much stronger line to tackle press involvement in this illegal trade' and stated that it would 'not hesitate to prosecute journalists identified in previous investigations who continue to commit these offences'.[54] It also called for custodial sentences to be introduced to tackle such criminality[55] and, subsequent to a freedom of information request, issued a breakdown detailing against each media publication the number of suspected transactions it had identified and the number of the publisher's journalists who had been found to be directly using these services.[56] These actions (and inactions) later came under detailed scrutiny in the report of a public Inquiry into the Culture, Practices and Ethics of the Press which was set up by the UK Government in 2011 and chaired by Lord Justice Leveson. The findings, recommendations, and impact of the resulting 2012 report[57] will be considered further later in this chapter and also in Chapter 9, which will look at the future development of the interface between European data protection regulation and professional journalism.

Tallying with a similar focus in a good deal of DPA published guidance (see discussion in Chapter 5),[58] some regulators were found to have prioritized the protection of data in the form of visual (and/or audio) recordings as opposed to text which might have provided comparable information. Indeed, a number of the enforcement actions detailed above, notably by the Italian[59] and Dutch[60] DPAs, may be conceptualized through such a prism. An even clearer case is provided by the Hungarian DPA (0.95/1) which, in 2007 and in response to specific complaints, ruled that the publication of images including the faces of police officers was prohibited without their consent, even if the image revealed the misuse of police powers or illegality.[61] However, in a new case in 2010, this DPA clarified that a photo revealing misuse, abuse, or illegality could exceptionally be published where the freedom of the press obviously carried more weight than the right to personal data protection.[62]

Meanwhile, in Spain the national DPA (1/1) issued a fine (upheld in a subsequent court challenge) against a newspaper which, without the consent of those whose images were captured, installed a webcam within its newsroom which took an image every fifteen seconds and published this on the newspaper's website.[63] Turning back to Italy, in 2007 this DPA censured Sky News for videoing and then broadcasting (without blurring) two imams who had been asked, ostensibly in private and by two individuals who purported to be husband and wife, to give their views on the wearing of the Islamic veil by women. The company was ordered to delete the data from its website and avoid any further dissemination, an instruction which also extended to RCS Quotidani which had written about the affair in the *Corriere della Sera* newspaper.[64] Another case involving photos emanated from the Irish DPA (0.34/1) which censured the now defunct *News of the World* newspaper for publishing the images of a well-known individual shopping with their child, at the same time identifying the child by name and age and referring to a third party's perception of how they were getting along.[65] Meanwhile, the Italian DPA also censured the publication of the images of the family (and in particular, the young daughters) of a doctor who had himself been the subject of legitimate public interest as a result of being the probable victim of extortion arising from his sexual behaviour and possible use of drugs. Despite the fact that the daughters' faces had been obscured here, they were still judged to be identifiable and the information published was found not to be essential to news reporting.[66]

The last two examples clearly centrally concerned children, a category of data subject which (separately from the use of recordings) also garnered some specific enforcement attention. Thus, in two actions taking place in 2009 and 2010 respectively, the Italian DPA censured and blocked the further dissemination of data indirectly revealing the identity of a child victim of sexual abuse. In the first case, the decision was sent on to the National Order of Journalists, whilst in the second the Public Prosecutor's Office was informed and asked to assess any related competence. The second (albeit still indirect) form of identification was particularly stark since some of the articles at issue had included the full name of those responsible for this abuse as well as their kinship ties to the child victim.[67]

Whilst examples of enforcement action which relate to indubitable public figures are certainly present in the data just cited, the website review as a whole suggests that DPAs generally prioritized the protection of those playing a less public role. Often this was justified by the divergent public interests in play. For example, in case 63/2010 the Greek DPA analysed a newspaper's publication of examination schedules and photographs of the daughter of a recently disgraced judge who had been found guilty of corruption. The newspaper sought to justify this on the basis that his daughter was displaying similar character traits. However, in fining the newspaper for publishing personal data relating both to this individual and also her husband, the DPA stressed that the interest of the public in knowing about a non-public figure was not comparable to that of those holding an important public position and, furthermore, that this distinction remained in place notwithstanding kinship or marriage ties to a public person.

2.2 Media Archives and Enforcement

Action manifestly involving the regulation of publicly available media archives and/or internal database records was only found on the websites of five DPAs who participated in the questionnaire (Belgium, Dutch, Greek, Italian, and Slovenian), together with one national DPA (Spanish) which did not. The approaches uncovered broadly divided into two. In Italy, Greece, the Netherlands, and Slovenia, some DPA action appeared directed at the complete removal or at least anonymization of personal data, either from published online content or even from internal records. Thus, the Slovenian DPA indicated that the action detailed earlier which it had taken against the online publication of identification records had secured its online removal, whilst the Dutch DPA appeared satisfied that its intervention against the Eyeworks documentary had resulted in the complete destruction of the relevant data. Meanwhile, the Greek DPA cases 165/2012 and 100/2000, also explored earlier, resulted in an order for the anonymization of the data in published online archives and the destruction of data held in internal records respectively. Similar to this last case and in light of the fact that processing extends even to the mere holding of data,[68] the Italian DPA's order relating to parliamentarians' sweat and urine samples would also have required that this information was deleted even from internal records.   .

Turning to the Italian DPA's regulation of publicly available archives, many of the regulator's actions explored earlier required not only that information not be disseminated anew but that it be removed from the websites of the relevant publications where it was still present. Another example of enforcement from this DPA which dated from 2004 required that the newspaper remove from its web page personal data disclosing the identification, address, state of health, and photographs of a woman who had suffered a serious attack in the past but which had been included in a new article reporting also on similar and more recent events. The DPA found that the inclusion of this old information was not necessary and so violated data protection.[69] In 2005, this DPA also mediated on a demand that an online article originally from 2002 which reported on a women's arrest and subsequent indictment for a crime from which she was ultimately acquitted be both anonymized and completed with this further information. The newspaper acceded to the request that the woman's name be replaced with a generic description of her attributes[70] and further stated that the archive was now only available internally rather than to the public generally. The DPA then closed the case.[71] Nevertheless, in a similar subsequent case from 2010, this DPA rejected the demand of a data subject that an online news article reporting on his criminal conviction be amended to reflect his later acquittal, finding that it was sufficient that the publisher had reported this elsewhere. The DPA also refused to rule on the subject's other claim, namely that the publisher ensure that the two articles be permanently electronically linked online. This failure was justified on the basis that this claim had only been raised after the proceedings had commenced.[72]

Aside from the 2005 Italian case, the active interventions from DPAs here arose after a finding that either the initial gathering or the pre-archived publication of the data in question was itself illegal.[73] Moreover, even the 2005 and 2010 cases discussed immediately above involved claims that the data in question was essentially misleading due to subsequent developments. Therefore, all these cases were very different from the actions of certain DPAs during the first generation of European data protection which were aimed at ensuring that lawfully published and still entirely accurate personal data were either never included in online media archives or were subject to anonymization after a period of time.[74]

The nature of this much more severe regulatory intervention during this earlier period was analysed in depth in Chapter 4. Its basic rationale links more clearly to a second strand of DPA action during the DPD era which was directed at applying pressure on the media not to remove or anonymize data (as some data subjects had demanded) but rather to take steps on request to shield them from the attention of Internet search engines such as Google. From 2008 onwards the Italian DPA held that individuals who 'had subsequently changed their lives for the better' should be entitled to require that the media entities responsible for the continuing online publication of 'old news reports concerning negative events in their past' take action to ensure that these were not 'indexed by the most popular external search engines using the complaints' names'.[75] For example, in 2009 it required that a publisher take steps such as utilizing the Robots Exclusion Protocol so as to ensure that a news report from thirteen years earlier, which named an individual as a victim of the crime of domestic violence, was not available in this way. Although refraining from upholding further remedies such as anonymization or restrictions on the ability to utilize search tools internal to journalistic websites, it explicitly reserved the right to take further measures in the future to protect victims of crime and similar data subjects who, it argued, were deserving of special protection.[76] Indeed, from the outset, this DPA stressed that 'we are not fully satisfied with our decisions, because we believe that they are not enough to tackle a phenomenon whose implications are difficult to fathom'.[77] Meanwhile, in its 2011 annual report, the Belgium DPA (0.61/1) stated that its mediation of a complaint against a newspaper archive for failing to prevent the indexing of a story from 2007 had similarly resulted in the editor agreeing to take steps to ensure that the article was not indexed in future. The DPA required that this action be carried out within thirty days.[78]

Finally, the Spanish DPA held that, although the continued availability in online archives of news stories containing negative information about individuals was protected by freedom of expression, the media should on request adopt technical measures to ensure that such stories were not indexed by Internet search engines whenever the legitimate interests of the individuals were considered to override the public relevance of facts disclosed. For example, such statements were included in DPA rulings in favour of deindexing a report from 1975 which named an individual arrested as part of a group for alleged terrorism[79] and even a 1989 news report which named a man who had suffocated his four-year-old son whilst suffering from paranoid schizophrenia (and where the continued circulation of this information was said by his psychiatrist to be interfering with his recovery).[80] These latter interventions link to related efforts, also spearheaded by the Spanish DPA, which sought to require Internet search engines themselves to take heed of these demands. This effort resulted in the CJEU ruling of *Google Spain*[81] which strongly endorsed the notion that Internet search engines have discrete and particular responsibilities here. Although the governance of these 'new' media actors lies outside the scope of this book, its interface with the regulation of traditional publishers will be touched on in Chapter 9 and, more directly, in the concluding analysis of Chapter 13.

Compared with the general enforcement data, the findings specific to media archives in the DPA website review exhibit an even greater gap with the questionnaire data. In sum, whilst thirteen DPAs (45 per cent) self-reported enforcement, enforcement was only verified in five (17 per cent) of these cases. Similarly to the general enforcement findings, these discrepancies are partially explained by the fact that the review only looked for readily accessible website material, the websites themselves sometimes only publicized high-profile and recent examples of enforcement action and, in contrast to the website review, some DPAs may have conceptualized 'enforcement' as encompassing investigatory activity that resulted in no further action. However, an additional and weighty issue here is that with the rise to ubiquity of online publication, the distinction between enforcement action relating only to original journalistic activity or publication and action relating to archived content has become far from clear cut. In a number of cases, DPA websites only provided rather sparse details of their enforcement actions. Some of these cases, therefore, may have had a media archives dimension even though this was not made explicit in the published data.

3. Explaining Divergences in a Regulator's Enforcement Stance and Action: Statutory Law Stringency, Resourcing, or Both?

As section 1 elucidated, DPAs' self-reported enforcement stance (see especially Chart 7.1) and their enforcement actions (see especially Chart 7.3) exhibited considerable divergence. Moreover, section 2 also elucidated variations as regards enforcement located through the website review, including via an admittedly basic binary measure of whether any action by a given DPA had been found at all. It is important to consider what might explain these differences. Two broad possibilities present themselves. First, notwithstanding the general gap between local statutory provisions and the regulatory realities, greater comparative stringency in local statutory data protection may still lead to a more assertive enforcement stance and to more enforcement activity. Second, the better resourcing of DPAs may also be expected to drive a more assertive enforcement stance and a greater range of enforcement activity. This section further specifies these various hypotheses and then tests the extent to which they are supported by the empirical evidence.

Turning first to the statutory law dimension, the DPA jurisdictions diverged here both as regards the extent to which statute sought to render *substantive* duties applicable and that the DPA's *regulatory powers* remained engaged. Given that the enforcement power stance question focused on the supervisory rights which DPAs had at their disposal, it clearly should track the powers of regulatory supervision set down in statutory law most closely. It might, however, also be affected by the substantive extent of the statutory law available to be enforced. Meanwhile, *enforcement activity* should much more clearly relate to divergences in the extent of the substance which statute indicates should be upheld but, *mutatis mutandis*, may also be influenced by the strength of the powers left to regulators when enforcing. As Chapter 5 explained (and as set out in Appendix 4), the regulatory supervision and the substantive stringency of the statutory law can both be quantified, and a combined regulatory stringency measure can also be generated by multiplying these two variables together.

Table 7.2 presents Spearman Rank correlations between these measures of local statutory law, the DPA questionnaire's power stance, its enforcement extent measure, and the enforcement binary generated from the DPA website review data. As can be seen, all the correlations are in the expected direction and all but two[82] cases are significant, at least at the 10 per cent confidence level (one-tailed test). Somewhat surprisingly, all the enforcement measures (and not just those related to enforcement action) correlated most strongly with the measure of the substantive stringency of the formal law rather than either the regulatory powers or the combined measure.[83]

Turning to look at the potential impact of divergences in resourcing, it may be hypothesized that both the willingness and the capacity of a regulator to engage in enforcement activity here may be impeded not only by a comparatively low level of gross resources but also by a similarly low level of resources as measured on a per capita basis. Thus, even if well resourced on a per capita (i.e. head of resident population) basis, a small DPA may still face unique challenges when engaging with the often complex and specialist issues which arise when engaging in enforcement against the media. Meanwhile, a comparatively large DPA but with limited per capita resources may become so overburdened by the need to respond to a myriad of routine data protection concerns that it may also find itself unable to intervene in this specialized and complex area. We might therefore expect a more active enforcement stance and more enforcement activity in the area of media processing to be positively correlated with both comparatively greater gross and greater per capita resourcing.

The means available to regulators can be measured in a variety of ways including, in particular, by looking at its financial and its human resources. In this

Table 7.2 Spearman Rank Correlations between Quantitative Measures of Statutory Law Stringency, DPA Power Stance, and DPA Enforcement Action

DPA enforcement → Formal law ↓	DPA questionnaire: power stance re: news production	DPA questionnaire: enforcement extent	DPA website review: enforcement binary
Regulatory powers	Coefficient: 0.320**	Coefficient: 0.381**	Coefficient: 0.117
	Significance: 0.048 N: 28	Significance: 0.030 N: 25	Significance: 0.245 N: 37
Substantive stringency	Coefficient: 0.447***	Coefficient: 0.757***	Coefficient: 0.264*
	Significance: 0.008 N: 28	Significance: 0.000 N: 25	Significance: 0.057 N: 37
Regulatory stringency	Coefficient: 0.408**	Coefficient: 0.660 ***	Coefficient: 0.214
	Significance: 0.016 N: 28	Significance: 0.000 N: 25	Significance: 0.102 N: 37

One-tailed significance at the 10% (*), 5% (**), and 1% (***) confidence level regard the 2013 Annual Report of the Article 29 Working Party, which was finally released in December 2016, helpfully detailed each DPA's budget and also their staffing level.[84] In light of the Report's authoritative nature and its helpful provision of two resourcing measures, it was decided to deploy these figures in preference to a measure of financial resources alone which had originally been obtained directly from DPAs through the questionnaire. Nevertheless, as with all data, these figures were not without certain drawbacks. In particular, no measures were provided for the German *Länder*, Gibraltarian or Spanish Catalan DPAs, or either the Danish Press Council or the Lithuanian Inspector of Journalist Ethics which worked alongside the regular DPAs in both these States. It was, therefore, necessary to drop from the analysis the German and Spanish, as well as the Danish, Gibraltarian, and Lithuanian, DPA jurisdictions. The Austrian DPA also failed to quantify its budget (but did provide staffing information) and so had to be dropped from the former measure.[85] Per capita measures were created using 2013 population figures for each DPA jurisdiction as available through Eurostat. In order to aid legibility this per capita staffing figure was recalculated into a measure of staffing per 100,000 head of population. These figures are all specified in Appendix 5.

Table 7.3 presents Spearman Rank correlations between these four measures of DPA resourcing and the DPA power stance and enforcement action variables. As can be seen, the results here were rather mixed. In particular, all but one of the correlations with the financial figures were negative rather than positive and, in two instances, these achieved significance at the 10 per cent confidence level. In contrast,

Table 7.3 Spearman Rank Correlations between DPA Resourcing, DPA Enforcement Stance, and DPA Enforcement Action Measures

DPA enforcement → DPA resourcing ↓	DPA questionnaire: power stance re: news production	DPA questionnaire: enforcement extent	DPA website review: enforcement binary
Gross financial	Coefficient: −0.260	Coefficient: −0.347*	Coefficient: 0.082
	Significance: 0.134 N: 20	Significance: 0.086 N: 17	Significance: 0.345 N: 26
Per capita financial	Coefficient: −0.299*	Coefficient: −0.034	Coefficient: −0.082
	Significance: 0.100 N: 20	Significance: 0.449 N: 17	Significance: 0.345 N: 26
Gross staffing	Coefficient: 0.146	Coefficient: −0.090	Coefficient: 0.201
	Significance: 0.264 N: 21	Significance: 0.366 N: 17	Significance: 0.157 N: 27
Per 100K pop. staffing	Coefficient: 0.144	Coefficient: 0.354*	Coefficient: 0.067
	Significance: 0.267 N: 21	Significance: 0.082 N: 17	Significance: 0.370 N: 27

* = one-tailed significance at 10% confidence level

all bar one of the correlations with the staffing measures were in the expected positive direction. Moreover, the correlation between the self-reported enforcement
measure and 'per capita' staffing level showed a moderate association, which was
significant at the 10 per cent level. Compared with the financial data, the staffing
figures should better reflect the potentially very significant purchasing power divergences across the DPA jurisdictions. The addition of such human resource data
therefore provides a more nuanced, reassuring, and expected indication of potential relationships here.[86] It nevertheless remains of some note that, compared with
formal law measures cited earlier, these correlations were not as strong, remained
somewhat inconsistent, and generally failed to achieve significance.[87]

4. Further Analysis

The evidence gathered in this chapter indicates that DPAs far from entirely eschewed an enforcement role in relation to professional journalism during the
DPD era. Indeed, as Chart 7.1 indicates, approximately 80 per cent (22) of DPAs
accepted that they possessed at least some enforcement powers in relation to journalistic news production, a figure which is almost identical to that set out in local
statute. Similarly, as regards concrete action (and as Chart 7.2 highlights), 64 per
cent (16) of DPAs indicated that they had engaged in some enforcement activity
against the professional media in the DPD era (although the DPA website review
only validated such action in 40 per cent (10) of the cases). Moreover, if responses
from DPAs operating in jurisdictions with local laws which seek to remove regulatory jurisdiction here[88] and/or grant journalism a complete substantive exemption[89] are excluded, then the self-reported figure rises to 74 per cent (14) and that
of the website review 47 per cent (9). In light of professional journalism's 'power to
damage citizen's lives'[90] in a sometimes clearly unwarranted fashion, it might be
considered that all DPAs with the power to do so should have enforced against the
media at some point during the DPD period. Even so, these enforcement figures
remain substantially higher than the 42 per cent (13) of DPAs' reported action in
relation to social scientists[91] or the average number (also 13, or 42 per cent) which
certified to undertaking enforcement against any one of a number of entirely 'new'
media actors, namely, individual bloggers, social networkers, social networking
sites, street mapping services, and search engines.[92]

Nevertheless, it is also clear that the vast majority of DPAs sought a bounded
enforcement role in this area. Thus, as detailed in Chart 7.1, almost 40 per cent
(11) considered that they only had limited powers. Meanwhile, turning to direct
activity and as Chart 7.2 highlighted, approximately one-third of DPAs (8) reported undertaking media-related enforcement just in relation to one or two areas
of data protection. Indeed, combined with the 36 per cent (9) which reported no
enforcement, this suggests that approximately 70 per cent of DPAs had exercised

their controlling powers here in, at most, only a very limited range of areas. Such a bounded picture of the reality during the DPA era was similarly confirmed through the DPA website review.

It may be variously argued that this bounded role is grounded in local statutory data protection provisions, a focus on the need for contextual balancing, resource constraints, and/or the interface with self-regulatory structures. However, none of these factors can provide a fully comprehensive and coherent account of the observed outcomes. Considering the relationship with statutory data protection law first, variation in DPAs' enforcement power stance was positively associated with divergences in statutory regulatory powers in this area. Nevertheless, the observed correlation was only of moderate strength (see Table 7.2) and, in any case, DPAs collectively remained far more likely to consider their to be powers limited even if not entirely eliminated than local statute suggested. Thus, as highlighted in Table 7.4, despite the fact that 40 per cent of DPAs conceived their powers as being

Table 7.4 DPA Power Stance: Statutory Data Protection (DP) Law vs DPA Interpretation (*n* = 28) (with substantive stringency of applicable statutory law in brackets)

Statutory DP law → DPA stance ↓	Powers excluded (5/18%)	Powers limited (3/11%)	Powers full (19/68%)
Powers excluded (6/21%)	• Austria *(0.1)* • Germany Brandenberg *(0.03)* • Germany Federal *(0.03)*		• Belgium *(0.59)* • Liechtenstein *(0.88)* • Sweden *(0)*
Powers limited (11/39%)	• Germany Mecklenberg-Vorpommern *(0.03)* • Germany Rhineland-Palatinate *(0.03)*	• Germany Schleswig-Holstein *(0.03)*	• Czechia *(1)* • Finland *(0)* • Greece *(0.84)* • Ireland *(0.34)* • Latvia *(0.67)* • Luxembourg *(0.68)* • Poland *(0.33)* • Portugal *(0.77)*
Powers full (11/39%)		• Malta *(0.33)* • Spain Catalonia *(1)**	• Bulgaria *(0.68)* • Cyprus *(0.65)* • Estonia *(0.67)* • France *(0.53)* • Gibraltar *(0.33)* • Hungary *(0.95)* • Italy *(0.65)* • Slovakia *(0.93)* • Slovenia *(0.93)*

* Statutory powers limited due to federalism only

limited, only approximately 10 per cent of applicable local laws explicitly set out such limits. Moreover, ultimately, there was not only a stronger positive correlation between a DPA's power stance and the *substantive* stringency of local law, but the qualitative data received from regulators indicated that those DPAs conceptualizing their powers as limited took into account a much wider range of factors than simply the statutory specification of their powers (see Table 7.1).

Turning to look at positive activity, there was a clearly significant correlation between enforcement action (especially as self-reported) and the general substantive stringency of applicable statutory provisions (see Table 7.2). Nevertheless, the detail in such local law was a very poor predictor of action by the relevant DPA, even as self-reported. Thus, whereas only one DPA (4 per cent) providing a standard response to this question reported enforcement of the requirement to provide a registration/notification of data processing (see Chart 7.3), statutory law made this provision[93] fully applicable to journalism in six of these DPA jurisdictions (23 per cent) and at least partially so in twelve (46 per cent).[94] Meanwhile, although only five DPAs (19 per cent) self-reported enforcement action in relation to subject access,[95] local jurisdictional law here made this provision fully applicable to journalism in seven (27 per cent) and at least partially so in twenty-two DPA (85 per cent) jurisdictions.[96] Finally, whilst a mere four DPAs (15 per cent) self-reported enforcement in relation to the rectification of inaccuracy, the accuracy standard remained fully applicable to journalism in fourteen (50 per cent) and at least partially applicable in twenty-four (92 per cent) of these cases.[97]

It may alternatively be argued that these enforcement patterns can be explained by DPAs' recognition of the importance of a contextual balancing of rights and, in particular, of the overriding need to ensure that data protection does not unduly interfere with freedom of expression. It is certainly true that a number of second-generation data protection laws purported to bind journalism to substantive duties which were manifestly inconsistent with freedom of expression and that, furthermore, DPAs did recognize the need to mitigate this. Thus, as elaborated in Chapter 6, no DPA held that the exercise of undercover political journalism was ipso facto illegal even though statutory data protection law in approximately 30 per cent of these jurisdictions would have pointed to this result.[98] The Greek and Portuguese DPAs also cited freedom of expression concerns as justification for considering their powers in this area to be limited (see Table 7.1). Moreover, with a few exceptions including, most notably, the Hungarian DPA's heavy (but later liberalized) restrictions on photographing police, DPAs appear to have been quite careful to ensure that their positive enforcement actions were appropriately calibrated from a freedom of expression perspective.

However, the same freedom of expression rationale cannot explain the general inaction as regards the policing of a number of key standards which often remained applicable to journalism in local statute. Some of these standards are widely recognized as presenting only a limited and generally justifiable interference with freedom of expression. Take, for example, the duty to take care to avoid the spread of significantly inaccurate personal data. Not only has a commitment to accuracy been conceptualized as 'the foundation stone on which journalism depends'[99] but (as Appendix 6 of this book specifies) practically all self-regulatory code of journalism ethics within Europe include at least one, and often many, provisions related to avoiding inaccuracy and/or taking steps to rectify this should it occur. Other poorly enforced data protection standards were similarly understood, at least by DPAs themselves, to be substantially compatible with media freedom of expression. For example, as explored in Chapter 6, the DPA questionnaire indicated that over one-third of DPAs (albeit perhaps wrongly) held that the law was best interpreted so as to require journalists to comply with subject access in full, excepting only information revealing their sources. In contrast, less than one-fifth held that journalism should be considered entirely exempt from these duties. Despite this, and as noted earlier, DPA enforcement of both accuracy and subject access requirements remained very rare.

It may also be claimed that the generally limited reality of enforcement is the result of the very sparse resources made available to DPAs. Indeed, an analysis of the figures set out in Appendix 5 from the Article 29 Working Party indicates that the gross budget of national DPAs in 2013 was only €4.2 million whilst the median per capita budget was a mere €0.30. Even the UK DPA, which reported the highest gross figure of £21m/€19.2m had an available budget which was little more than 10 per cent that of the UK Office of Communications (Ofcom), a somewhat comparable regulator which was granted £150.9m/€177.7m during the same period.[100] Moreover, whilst Ofcom has a relatively narrow range of defined responsibilities in the broadcasting and telecommunications sectors, DPAs are responsible for regulating an almost unfathomable range of data processing operations across the public and private sectors. A number, including the UK DPA, also have wider responsibilities such as policing freedom of information legislation. A lack of sufficient resources has certainly been found more widely to have resulted in DPAs having to make difficult choices within a context in which they are unable to discharge their responsibilities fully. Thus, the EU Agency for Fundamental Rights noted in 2013 that

[t]he lack of financial and human resources has a negative impact on the quantity and quality of the DPAs' work and limits their ability to control and sanction data protection violations. For example, the complainants interviewed in the Czech Republic and Portugal said that the lack of financial resources resulted in cases not being accepted or no response from the authority being received. Some of the representatives of the DPAs stated that the amount of work that the DPA currently had was at the upper limit, and they could not handle more with the resources available (e.g. DPA staff from Finland, Poland, Portugal and the United Kingdom).[101]

These factors seem capable of explaining why DPAs felt it necessary to prioritize enforcement in areas of pressing and serious concern. Thus, the DPA website review's finding that such action had focused on the illegitimate processing of sensitive data (including in relation to media archives) can find justification in the serious harms to the right to privacy which such processing often causes. Meanwhile, the emphasis on protecting other discrete data categories whose safeguarded treatment is fundamental to basic social and economic relationships helps undergird the DPAs' key role in ensuring the integrity of the data ecosystem as a whole. Nevertheless, even such a general analysis presents several apparent anomalies. Take, again, the spread through the media of seriously false personal data. Not only can this cause individuals considerable unwarranted harm and distress but, as explored further later in this chapter, evidence has been uncovered of a 'significant and reckless disregard for accuracy'[102] within parts of the media. Despite this, few DPAs undertook enforcement action in relation to this issue. Such specific anomalies dovetail with the rather mixed picture as regards the association between better resourcing and more enforcement action. This suggests that something other than a lack of resources, including potentially a DPA's own ideological orientation, may be inhibiting some regulators from engaging in what is undoubtedly often difficult and controversial territory.

A final possibility is that the limited enforcement patterns revealed in the data can be accounted for by the role of media self-regulatory structures. As elucidated in Chapter 5, not only were these structures granted some statutory recognition in around one-quarter of EEA States[103] but guidance issued by a number of DPAs also accorded such structures a significant emphasis.[104] Moreover, the norms overseen by these structures exhibited significant overlap with some of the standards which data protection law and DPAs themselves sought to uphold. Thus, the near-ubiquitous coverage of issues related to data accuracy in self-regulatory codes has already been noted in this chapter, whilst Chapter 6 highlighted how most of these codes also sought to specify when undercover journalism would and would not be acceptable.[105]

Nevertheless, even at this level, some fundamental inconsistencies are evident. Notably, whilst the statutory law and DPA interpretation in many EEA States set out strict standards for journalists to uphold in relation to the reactive transparency right of subject access,[106] this issue was left completely unaddressed in almost all the self-regulatory codes. Even more critically, the operation and efficacy of these self-regulatory instruments and associated structures have undergone strong critiques across Europe. For example, a major cross-country comparison of eleven EEA states found that even journalists themselves 'only attribute a medium or even rather weak impact to press councils'.[107] Moreover, a linked country-by-country survey was scathing about the situation in a number of jurisdictions. Thus, as regards Romania, it was found that '[t]raditional instruments of media accountability, like codes of ethics and press councils are not functional',[108] whilst in relation to Spain, it was stated that '[j]ournalists generally do not consider these instruments as valuable, and they are also hardly known among non-specialists'.[109] In addition, even though 'media accountability infrastructures in Anglo-Saxon and Northern European states' were held to be 'relatively well-developed',[110] significant problems have been highlighted even in these cases. Thus, in the survey just cited, Austria, a country traditionally categorized within media regulation as falling within northern Europe,[111] was described as 'lacking efficient media accountability instruments' and with 'hardly any internal initiatives of self-regulation within news organisations'.[112] Much more infamously, the 2012 report of Lord Leveson's Inquiry into the Culture, Practices and Ethics of the Press in the United Kingdom found that 'time and time again, there have been serious and uncorrected failures within parts of the national press that may have stretched from the criminal to the indefensibly unethical, from passing off fiction as fact to paying lip service to accuracy'.[113] Ultimately, this inquiry held that '[i]t is difficult to avoid the conclusion that the self-regulatory system was run for the benefit of the press not of the public'.[114] Meanwhile, even in Denmark, which has sought explicitly to involve the co-regulatory Press Council in the statutory supervision of data protection, the Danish Parliamentary Committee on Legal Affairs in 2012 found 'recent egregious errors in the Danish press—including a nursery manager wrongly accused of complicity in paedophile abuse, and a man wrongly branded a killer', at the same time holding that 'newspapers [were] doing their best to bury publication of Press Council decisions with as little prominence as possible'.[115]

Finally, it is important to emphasize that DPAs generally failed to articulate precisely what relationship was intended between self-regulatory control and the exercise (or non-exercise) of their own enforcement powers. It is true that the existence of self-regulatory structures was cited by a number of DPAs in justifying an understanding that their powers were limited.[116] Moreover, the DPA website review revealed that, in framing their enforcement approach, a few regulators paid heed to the overlapping role of a range of other bodies, some of which were self- or at least co-regulatory in nature. Thus, the Greek DPA took into account the responsibilities of the Greek National Council for Radio and Television, the Italian DPA that of the National Order of Journalists, the National Publishers' Federation, and the Public Prosecutor's Office, and finally, the UK DPA that of the (now defunct) Press Complaints Commission. Nevertheless, even in these cases, the linkage often remained somewhat opaque and the approach adopted may not withstand rigorous scrutiny. Indeed, the UK DPA's attempt to rely on an informal interface with the Press Complaints Commission as opposed to 'the direct exercise of its own powers and functions'[117] was strongly criticized in the 2012 report of Lord Leveson, who found that

[d]espite the abundant evidence, both patent and latent, of problems in the culture, practices and ethics of the press in handling personal information, the [UK

DPA] has not been keen to exercise the powers and functions reposed in it by Parliament in the public interest to address the matter. That is not simply a historical matter; it is perceptible in its approach today. In a context in which public concern about press standards and respect for the law has reached sufficiently acute proportions to warrant the commissioning of a judicial inquiry, that must be seen as a regulatory failure within the Terms of Reference of the Inquiry.[118]

5. Conclusions

Through an analysis of both questionnaire and public website data, this chapter has demonstrated that data protection regulators far from entirely ignored their enforcement role over the professional journalistic media during the era of the DPD. On the contrary, approximately 80 per cent accepted that they possessed some enforcement powers here and 64 per cent reported enforcement action, a claim which was verified through the DPA website review in approximately 40 per cent of these cases. Nevertheless, whilst strongly and positively correlated with the revealed patterns, local data protection statute remained systematically more stringent than suggested by either the DPA power stance or the DPA enforcement activity data. Moreover, the patchy and limited enforcement pattern which was revealed could only be partially accounted for by reference to DPAs' recognition of the need for contextual balancing, resource constraints and the interface with self-regulation.

With some important exceptions, DPA enforcement action appeared carefully calibrated so as to ensure that freedom of expression was not unduly encroached upon. Nevertheless, such a contextual focus could not explain their general inaction as regards the upholding of data protection standards in relation to accuracy and subject access, which were either widely recognized or understood by at least regulators themselves to present only a limited and generally justifiable interference with free speech. Meanwhile, the mean national DPA gross total budget of approximately €4.2m and median resources of €0.30 per capita as revealed in the Article 29 Working Party figures hardly appeared commensurate with the pursuit of anything like a comprehensive enforcement strategy in relation to the media, especially given the almost unfathomable range of areas in which DPAs have a duty to intervene.

In this context, the general regulatory focus on certain priority areas, notably safeguarding intimate sensitive data and categories of data whose protection was integral to other fundamental social and economic relationships, appeared somewhat understandable. Nevertheless, regulators remained inactive in relation to other serious problems. Moreover, the relationship between better resourcing and more enforcement action remained somewhat mixed. Alongside the other evidence, this suggests that factors such as a DPA's own ideological willingness to intervene may also play an important role in shaping outcomes within this special context. Finally, self-regulatory norms did exhibit significant overlap with relevant data protection standards, although, even here, there were significant lacunae in particular areas including subject access. However, the efficacy of self-regulatory structures has been severely questioned, its interrelationship with DPA enforcement has generally remained opaque and independent scrutiny has suggested that the emphasis placed on it in some enforcement contexts by statutory regulators may hide regulatory failure.

These findings, alongside those of the previous chapters in Part II of this book, can provide important pointers as to how DPAs can and should approach their role in this area going forward. However, this also depends on the new General Data Protection Regulation 2016/679 and its implementation in EEA State law. Chapter 8 will look at this important issue.

8

Third-Generation European Data Protection Law and Professional Journalism

As explored in Part I of this book, the agreement to move from the Data Protection Directive 95/46 ('DPD') to the General Data Protection Regulation 2016/679 ('GDPR') marked an important formal shift to a considerably more harmonized system of data protection. Nevertheless, notwithstanding contrary calls made by the European Commission's High Level Group on Media Freedom and Pluralism, its specific provisions related to professional journalism reflected a broad continuity. Similar to Article 9 of the DPD, Article 85(2) of the GDPR instructed States to provide for derogations here 'if they are necessary to reconcile the right to the protection of personal data with the freedom of expression and information'. Recital 153 admonished States to interpret 'journalism' broadly and specifically stated that the derogation should cover 'news archives and press libraries'. In most other respects, however, States were granted a considerable margin for manoeuvre in 'balancing' fundamental rights here,[1] although Article 85(3) did establish a new requirement on States to report the provisions adopted as a result to the European Commission.

Turning to the implementation of these instructions within State law, large divergences remain in evidence. As with the State law adopted in the era of the DPD, these map on to more general cultural fissures. In broad terms, Northern European countries have almost invariably granted journalism a wide derogation from much of default data protection. In contrast, the laws of many Eastern and Southern European States have continued to place journalism under much stricter data protection standards and supervision. Nevertheless, notwithstanding some clearly exceptional cases and broader ambiguities regarding the position of media archiving, there are modest but significant signs that more States have attempted to carefully balance rights than was the case under the DPD. Thus, a greater number of State laws have explicitly limited the application of not only the transparency and sensitive data rules but even the core data protection principles in this special context. At the same time, the number that essentially seeks to disable data protection entirely has also decreased. Most strikingly, although the number of States that attempt to remove statutory regulation completely remains small and has even decreased, almost half of all States have now set out partial limits Data Protection Authority (DPA) supervision in this area. The GDPR's generic clauses also provide more possibilities for a co-regulatory approach. Not

European Data Protection Regulation, Journalism, and Traditional Publishers. David Erdos, Oxford University Press (2019). © David Erdos.
DOI: 10.1093/oso/9780198841982.003.0008

only do the great majority of States maintain these within journalism but over one-third of all States set out more specific provisions promoting an interface between their statutory regime and journalistic self-regulation. Overall, the third-generation legal framework in almost all European Economic Area (EEA) States continues to allocate data protection and DPAs themselves (or, in a few instances, designated specialist media regulators) an important, yet clearly difficult, role in reconciling rights here.

This chapter explores this new legal framework within seven sections. Following an overview of the provisions in the GDPR which specifically relate to journalism in section 1, section 2 explores in detail the substantive stringency of the standards which remain statutorily applicable to this activity in each EEA State. Briefer sections then similarly elucidate the strength of the statutory regulation of journalism within these laws, compare the stringency of data protection in this area both *vis-à-vis* the DPD-era and between States and explore the formal provisions which seek to establish a co-regulatory relationship between statutory and self-regulation. Finally, section 6 turns to special complexities surrounding the position of media archiving and section 7 provides some brief conclusions that link to Chapter 9.

1. The General Data Protection Regulation (GDPR) and Professional Journalism

1.1 Overview

In contrast to its significant reforming impetus in other areas, the GDPR maintained a basic continuity of approach as regards the interface with professional journalism. Thus, similarly to Article 9 of the DPD, Article 85(2) required EEA States to set out special derogations in favour of processing carried out for 'journalistic purposes'. Unlike Article 9, this clause did not explicitly limit these derogations to processing 'solely' for such purposes, although such a limitation continued to be referenced in the accompanying recital. This recital did, however, stress that '[i]n order to take account of the importance of the right to freedom of expression in every democratic society', it was necessary to interpret notions such as 'journalism' broadly. It was also specifically stated that these derogations should apply 'in particular' not only to processing 'in the audiovisual field' but also to 'news archives and press libraries'.[2] Member States were to set out such derogations from potentially almost all of the instrument's stipulations 'if necessary to reconcile the right to the protection of personal data with the freedom of expression and information'. This necessity threshold was slightly more permissively phrased than in Article 9 of the DPD which referred to the provision of derogations 'only if necessary'. Furthermore, the accompanying recital no longer specifically stated that there should be no derogation from 'the measures to ensure security of processing' or that 'the supervisory authority responsible for this sector should also be provided with certain ex-post powers, e.g. to publish a regular report or to refer matters to the judicial authorities'.[3]

Unlike the Directive's article on codes of conduct, the GDPR's expanded co-regulatory provisions[4] were also included within a chapter that was potentially subject to a journalistic derogation. On the other hand, and also in contrast to the cognate provisions in the DPD,[5] the GDPR's chapter on 'remedies, liabilities and penalties' (which fell outside any permitted journalistic derogation) included a specific reference to a data subject's right to lodge a complaint with a DPA,[6] the obligation on the DPD to respond[7] and potentially also at least consider issuing an 'effective, proportionate and dissuasive' fine for any violations of the law,[8] and finally the data subject's right to have any response tested through judicial review.[9] Moreover, both Article 85(2) and the accompanying recital's reference to the right to data protection itself explicitly recognized the fundamental status of data protection as now laid down in Article 8(2) of the EU Charter which includes, in this regard, strong presumptions of fair and legitimate processing, data access and rectification, and independent supervisory control.[10]

Similar to Recital 37 of the DPD, Recital 153 of the GDPR emphasized that the derogations adopted should have the purpose of 'balancing' data protection on the one hand and freedom of expression and information as enshrined in Article 11 of the EU Charter on the other. Reflecting the new sensitivities arising from the move from an arms-length Directive to a directly applicable Regulation, this recital also specifically stated that '[w]here such exemptions or derogations differ from one Member State to another, the law of the Member State to which the controller is subject should apply'. In another departure, Article 85(3) also required Member States to notify the European Commission of the derogations it adopted here as well as any subsequent amendments, thereby empowering this body to perform a monitoring function.[11] Finally, complementing the more specific provisions set out in Article 85(2), Article 85(1) placed States under a general duty to 'by law reconcile the right to the protection of personal data pursuant to this Regulation with the right to freedom of expression and information' including potentially outside areas of special types of expression such as journalism.[12]

1.2 Drafting History

These provisions trace back to Article 80 and Recital 121 of the European Commission's initial draft of the GDPR as released in 2012.[13] Turning consider their intended *scope*, in each case the initial wording placed an obligation on Member

States to provide derogations 'solely for journalistic purposes'. Nevertheless, the original recital did stress that this concept should be interpreted broadly so as to include *inter alia* 'news archives and press libraries'. Drawing on a formulation proposed by the CJEU Grand Chamber in C-73/07 Satamedia,[14] this recital originally also set out a definition of journalism, stating that this should encompass activities whose object

> is the disclosure to the public of information, opinions or ideas irrespective of the medium which is used to transmit them. They should not be limited media undertakings and may be undertaken for profit-making or non-profit-making activities.

The European Parliament's draft of the Regulation, which was agreed in March 2014, proposed removing any reference to special expressive purposes such as journalism within Article 80 itself and simply requiring Member States to adopt derogations to reconcile data protection with freedom of expression.[15] Its wording of the accompanying recital, however, remained largely unchanged from that of the Commission, albeit with the reference to 'solely' being dropped. The Council's version, which was settled in June 2015, came closest to the final wording including separating out the more general instruction to reconcile data protection and freedom of expression from the specific derogatory provision for journalistic (and other special expressive) purposes. However, although the Council also proposed removing the limiting reference to 'solely', this was reintroduced into the recital in the final text.

Moving on to consider the *depth* of derogations, the Commission's initial text proposed instructing States to set out derogations 'in order to reconcile' the rights to data protection and freedom of expression.[16] However, both the European Parliament and Council texts reverted to the more exact requirement that derogations be 'necessary' to reconcile these competing rights. Nevertheless, calls from the European Commission's High Level Group on Media Freedom and Pluralism that it was 'particularly important to adopt minimum harmonisation rules covering cross-border media activities on areas such as . . . data protection'[17] went unheeded. Notwithstanding that only the Commission's version included a duty on States to notify it and keep it updated on the derogations adopted here,[18] this provision nevertheless found its way into the final instrument.[19] Finally, although the GPDR's general provision on administrative fines continued to be placed in a chapter which fell outside of the journalistic derogation, the Commission's original proposal to expressly require that States' ensure that DPAs could issue 'effective, proportionate and dissuasive' fines of up to half a million Euros or 1 per cent of annual global turnover in the area of journalistic and other special expressive processing[20] did not find its way into the final text.

2. Statutory Substantive Applicability of Data Protection *vis-à-vis* Journalism

2.1 Methodology and Difficulties

Notwithstanding the strong similarities between the GDPR and the DPD as re-gards journalism, the GDPR required States to re-legislate within this area and to notify these provisions to the European Commission. It therefore provided them with an opportunity to reassess their statutory approach. Given this, it is important to analyse the formal commonalities and contrasts at national level here in this third-generation era compared with that under the *status quo ante*. Unfortunately, however, this presents several challenges. In the first place, even as of May 2019—a year on from the GDPR's general data of application—Greece, Portugal, and Slovenia had still failed to adopt implementing legislation. A wider group also apparently failed to notify the European Commission under Article 85(3).[21] Moreover, some of the laws that had been adopted were incomplete or only provisional. For example, an Italian decree adopted in August 2018[22] dir-ectly amended a number of Italian data protection provisions concerned with journalism.[23] However, it also placed an obligation on the DPA and the National Order of Journalists to agree a new legally binding Code here.[24] For up to one year, however, the existing Codes adopted under the DPD, including that re-lated to journalism, continued in force.[25] Finally, in almost all cases, authorized translations of these laws into English had not yet been produced and inevitably imperfect attempts had to be made to translate original language versions. This posed particular difficulties given that the dividing line between the categories below—including, most notably, that between a permissive and a strict public interest derogation—is admittedly sometimes quite fine. Notwithstanding these challenges, an analysis was made of those texts which were available as of May 2019.[26] (These are listed in full in Appendix 3.) For all the reasons cited earlier, this analysis must be considered provisional.

It is logical to begin an elucidation of these findings by focusing on matters of substance or, in other words, analysing the extent to which third-generation statu-tory laws have retained data protection standards in the special area of journalism. In order to ensure comparability with outcomes under the DPD, this was explored with respect to the GDPR equivalents of the same eighteen substantive provisions that were explored in Chapter 5 in relation to DPA-era law and which, as detailed in Table 8.1, can be grouped into the four main dimensions of European data protec-tion. For the same reason, national derogations were also placed within the same seven ordered categories as those previously deployed which, as Table 8.2 indicates, range from no derogation or full application of the default provision (a/1) to a com-plete and absolute exemption or, in other words, no application (g/0). Finally, as in Chapter 5, average scores were calculated in relation to each dimension of data

Table 8.1 Specific Default Provisions across Four Harmonized Dimensions of Data Protection (as set out in the GPDR)

Data protection principles (Dimension A)	Sensitive data rules (Dimension C)
(i) Fair, lawful, and transparent (A. 5(1)(a))	(ix) Racial and ethnic origin data rule (A. 9)
(ii) Purpose specificity, legitimacy, and compatibility (A. 5(1)(b))	(x) Political opinions data rule (A. 9)
(iii) Adequate, relevant, and necessary (A. 5(1)(c))	(xi) Beliefs (religious or philosophical) data rule (A. 9)
(iv) Accurate (and as necessary up-to-date) (A. 5(1)(d))	(xii) Trade union membership data rule (A. 9)
(v) Temporal minimization of data (A. 5(1)(e))	(xiii) Health data rule (A. 9)
Transparency rules (Dimension B)	(xiv) Sex life data rule (A. 9)
(vi) Proactive where direct collection from subject (A. 13)	(xv) Criminal-related data rule (A. 10)
(vii) Proactive in relation to other data (A. 14)	**Discipline requirements (Dimension D)**
(viii) Reactive subject access (A. 15)	(xvi) Legal basis requirement (A. 6)
	(xvii) Processing registration requirement (A.30)
	(xviii) Data export restrictions (A. 44–49)

protection and then a final overarching measure, ranging along an identical 0–1 scale, was calculated according to the same 3:3:3:1 weighting as previously used.

2.2 Overview of Results

As under the DPD, States adopted a variety of approaches to the structuring of these derogations. In many cases, however, an attempt was made to craft a common harmonized scheme. Aside from those States that failed to set out any explicit derogation at all, the most uniform approach attempted was through an overarching derogation setting out one common test for application which, once triggered, potentially effected all of the substantive data protection provisions. However, whilst the scope and meaning of these overarching derogations were usually reasonably clear, in several cases their effect on particular provisions within data protection remained deeply ambiguous. A number of other jurisdictions set out a similar overarching derogation but explicitly excluded certain default data protection provisions from this. These latter substantive standards were either left in full force or were subject to their own *sui generis* derogatory scheme. A final group of States crafted legislative schemes which

Table 8.2 Ordered Categories Measuring the Extent of the Continued Applicability of Specific Standards *vis-à-vis* Professional Journalism under Third-Generation Statutory Data Protection[27]

Category and scale point	Summary	Definition
(a)/1	No derogation	No explicit derogation provided at all from the default general minimum standard set out in the GDPR.
(b)/0.83	Minimal derogation	*Either* (i) no journalistic exemption set out but only a special interpretative provision which provided a gloss but did not supplant the particular data protection provision in question *or* (ii) an exemption is provided but this is limited to a narrow aspect of the provision in question.
(c)/0.67	Rule restricted exemption	A wide-ranging journalistic exemption is provided from the particular provision in question so long as the processing falls within specific pre-defined circumstances and/or complies with specific pre-determined rules.
(d)/0.5	Strict/ objective public interest exemption	An overarching media exemption is provided but this is subject to compliance with a test which, whilst open-textured, appears based on a strictly objective analysis of where, from the standpoint of the public interest, the balance lies.
(e)/0.33	Permissive public interest exemption	An overarching journalistic exemption is provided but this requires compliance with an open-textured balancing test which, whilst imposing significant duties on journalists, appears phrased so as to be more permissive than a strictly objective public interest test would be.
(f)/0.17	Minimal Duties	*Either* (i) data protection law excludes much of journalistic data processing unconditionally from the provision in question but subjects certain other types of media expression data processing to it only to a limited extent *or* (ii) an overarching exemption is provided for journalism subject only to compliance with a test with minimal substantive content.
(g)/0	Complete exclusion	An absolute and unconditional journalistic derogation is provided from the particular data protection provision in question.

established divergent derogatory treatments for a whole range of substantive data protection provisions.

This section elucidates the general approach adopted by each EEA State but postpones detailed analysis of many of the specific provisions adopted in the last group of States to the granular discussion of the different dimensions of data protection which then follows. It begins with those States that adopted the most lenient approach and proceeds to consider those which, at least in formal statutory data protection law, have maintained the most restrictions. Chart 8.1 details the overall results for each State whilst Appendix 8 includes not only this score but also codings for each individual data protection provision and averages for all four data protection dimensions. From these statistics, it can be calculated that the average summative score was 0.49, whilst the standard deviation was 0.30.

Starting with an elucidation of the position of those States at the bottom or most lenient end of this spectrum, Sweden (0)[28] and Norway (0)[29] set out an unconditional exemption (g/0) which is applicable to all the substantive data protection provisions. (As with all similar references in this chapter, the integer in brackets after these two States provides a numerical representation of the substantive stringency of the new law.) Germany (0.03),[30] Iceland (0.06),[31] Poland (0.08),[32] and Finland (0.14)[33] also set out a very wide-ranging unconditional exemption (g/0).

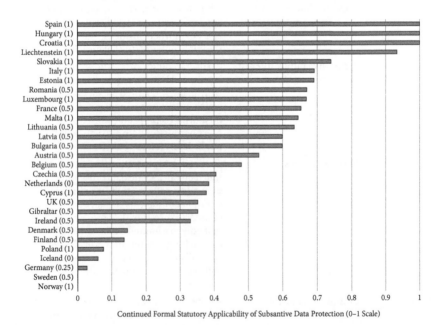

Chart 8.1 Substantive Statutory Applicability of Data Protection *vis-à-vis* the Journalism under the GDPR (with Maximum Statutory Regulatory Oversight in Brackets—see section 3.1).

However, in Poland, the criminal-related data rule (provision (xv)) and the data export restrictions (xviii) continue to apply in full, whilst in Finland there is similarly no derogation from the first two data protection principles (provisions (i) and (ii)). In addition, derogation from the data export restrictions (provisions (xviii)) in Finland uniquely depends on a strict/objective public interest threshold.[34] Meanwhile, in Iceland, exemption from the first and four data protection principles (provisions (i) and (iv)) derogations are uniquely subject to this being only '[a]ð því marki sem það er nauðsynlegt til' ('to the extent necessary') to reconcile the right of 'einkalífs annars' ('private life') and freedom of expression. In other words, an essentially objective or strict public interest test applies (d/0.5). Finally, the German approach to the fourth data protection principles (provision (iv)) and the reactive subject access right (viii) is even more casuistic and so will be explored later on within sections 2.3 and 2.4.

The next most leniently coded jurisdiction is Denmark (0.15) which, as a result of continuing with its *Lov om massemediers informationsdatabaser*, also adopts a casuistic approach which will be considered later. Meanwhile, Ireland (0.33), the UK (0.35), and Gibraltar (0.35) set out a permissive public interest derogation which is made applicable to all substantive data protection provisions in the case of Ireland but, in the case of the United Kingdom and Gibraltar, leaves the processing registration requirement (provision (xvii)) unaffected. Thus, the Irish law enables such an exemption where 'having regard to the importance of the right of freedom of expression and information in a democratic society' compliance 'would be incompatible with [journalistic] purposes'.[35] Meanwhile, both the UK and Gibraltarian derogations depend on an analysis of whether the controller 'reasonably believes' that compliance would be 'incompatible' with their journalistic purposes and similarly 'reasonably believes' that publication would be in the public interest.[36]

Next, Cypriot law (0.38) provides for an exemption from the proactive transparency where data has not been collected from the data subject themselves and also from reactive subject access (provisions (vii) and (viii)) which depends on a threshold of minimal substantive strictness (f/0.17). In sum, an exemption will apply whenever these provisions even 'επηρεάζουν' ('affect') the right to freedom of expression and information (as well as the confidentiality of journalistic sources).[37] Otherwise, the law sets out an overarching derogation whose precise relationship with the GDPR's provisions remains somewhat unclear. In sum, this derogation establishes that processing of both ordinary and sensitive personal data is 'νόμιμη' ('lawful') provided that it is 'ανάλογοι' ('analogous') to the intended objective and it respects the 'ουσία' ('essence') of the rights defined in the EU Charter, European Convention, and the national constitution.[38] The specification of 'essence' and 'analogous' only is best understood as establishing only a permissive rather than a strict public interest balance (e/0.33) between journalistic freedoms and other competing rights. Moreover, as a result of its reference to lawfulness, this balancing test clearly applies directly both to the general need for a legal basis for processing (provision (xvi)) and, in relation to sensitive data (provisions (ix)–(xv)), the rules which require a special legal basis to lift the presumptive ban which applies here. In contrast, given the more ambiguous relationship with the remaining data protection provisions,[39] this derogation was coded more conservatively as a strict or objective derogation (d/0.5) in these latter cases.

The Netherlands (0.38) achieves a broadly equivalent balance through a wide-ranging derogation which is generally unconditional in nature.[40] However, derogation from the sensitive data rules (provisions (ix)–(xv)) is subject to the minimal (f/0.17) requirement that the processing of such data is '*noodzakelijk*' ('necessary').[41] Even more significantly, application of the data protection principles (provisions (i)–(v)) and the need for legal basis for processing (provision (xvi)) remains outside any derogation (a/1). Czechia (0.41) fashions a similar approach through a number of different provisions which will be analysed later in sections 2.3 to 2.6.

Moving on to look at Belgium (0.46), the law here provides journalism with an apparently categorical exemption from both the transparency and the sensitive data rules (provisions (vi)–(xv)).[42] However, it is stated that those availing themselves of these derogations must be subject to '*des règles de déontologie journalisique*' ('journalistic ethics rules').[43] Given that these rules could intersect with these data protection provisions, the stipulations overall were coded as a case of minimal inclusion (f/0.17). Meanwhile, the data protection principles and the need for a legal basis for processing (provisions (i)–(v) and (xvi)) are left unaffected, whilst the data registration and data export requirements ((xvii) and (xviii)) are made subject to stricter derogations which will be analysed below.

Next, Austrian law (0.53) maintains the application of the data protection principles themselves but otherwise enables exemption

> [i]f it is necessary to reconcile the right to the protection of personal data with the freedom of information, in particular with regard to the processing of personal data by media undertakings, media services and their employees directly for their journalistic purposes referred to in the Media Act.[44]

Whilst not entirely clear cut, the specific reference to taking account of the particular needs of the media appears to establish a permissive derogation (e/0.33) for these actors from all but these principles (provisions (i)–(v)).

Construing the meaning of the overarching derogatory clause in Latvian (0.60) and Bulgarian (0.60) law presents even greater difficulties. In the case of Latvia, a journalism exemption is provided from all the data protection principles but only when the information published is of public interest, the interests of the data subject are not more important than the public interest, compliance would be incompatible or prevent the exercise of freedom of expression and information, and the right of private life is not violated.[45] This clearly sets out a strict or objective derogation (d/0.5) from all but provisions (i)–(v), which are expressly left unaffected. However, a separate clause sets out a general right to process data for journalistic purposes so long as this is done in order to publish information of public interest.[46] This latter clause must at least place a gloss (b/0.83) on the data protection principles themselves.

Meanwhile, Bulgarian law expressly sets out a journalistic derogation from the transparency and sensitive data rules (provisions (vi)–(xv)), as well as the legal basis (xvi), processing registration (xvii), and data export (xviii) provisions. This is subject to the processing not violating 'личния живот' ('privacy'),[47] a stipulation which in relation to any disclosure of personal data must always be assessed through a closed list of objective criteria.[48] In combination, these tests also appear to set out an objective or strict derogation (d/0.5). Moreover, whilst the data protection principles fall outside any possibility of an exemption, it stated that processing in compliance with the specified tests is 'законосъобразно' ('lawful').[49] Similar to Latvia, this must place a gloss (b/0.83) on the interpretation of the data protection principles in specific instances.

Looking next at Lithuania (0.63), the law here sets out an unconditional exemption (g/0) from the transparency rules (provisions (vi)–(viii)), registration requirement (xvii), and data export restrictions (xviii) but formally leaves the data protection principles ((i)–(v)), sensitive data rules ((ix)–(xv)), and the need for a legal basis for processing (xvi) unaffected.[50] Malta (0.65) achieves a similar overall result by setting out a derogation applicable more widely to the data protection principles (provisions (i)–(v)), the transparency rules ((vi)–(viii)), the rules applying to criminal-related data (xv), the need for a legal basis for processing (xvi), and the data registration requirement (xvii). However, in this case, any use of the derogation is subject to an ultimately strict or objective public interest test. In sum, not only (as in Ireland) must 'compliance' with a derogated provision be 'incompatible' with journalism 'having regard to the importance of the right of freedom of expression and information in a democratic society', but the journalist is specifically obliged to 'ensure that the processing is proportionate, necessary and justified for reasons of substantial public interest'.[51]

France (0.65) also sets out what in combination amounts to a strict or objective test (d/0.5) enabling a journalistic exemption from, in this case, the temporal minimization of data (provision (v)), the transparency and sensitive data rules ((vi) to (xv)), and the data export restrictions (xviii).[52] Specifically, not only must any exempted processing be in accord with 'des règles déontologiques de cette profession' ('the ethical rules of the profession') but any derogation must also be found 'necessaire pour concilier le droit à la protection des données à caractère personnel et la liberté d'expression et d'information' ('necessary to reconcile the right of the protection of personal data and freedom of expression and information').

Romania (0.67) secures a cognate formal result by providing an exemption from potentially all of substantive data protection which depends on certain predefined restrictive conditions being met (c/0.67).[53] In sum, a derogation can only apply where the personal data

> *au fost făcute publice în mod manifest de către persoana vizată sau care sunt strâns legate de calitatea de persoană publică a persoanei vizate ori de caracterul public al faptelor in care este implicată* ('were manifestly made public by the data subject themselves or related to the public nature of the data subject or of the facts in which they are involved').[54]

The law in Estonia (0.69), the next most stringently coded State, presents particularly acute interpretative difficulties. In sum, similarly to the previous law,[55] a provision establishes that data can be processed for journalistic purposes without the *'nõusolekuta'* ('consent') of the data subject.[56] Any processing must be compatible with journalistic ethics and the public interest and any disclosure of data must not cause excessive damage to the data subject. Nevertheless, in contrast to the previous law, it is no longer stated that any public interest present must be *'ülekaalukas'* ('overriding' or 'preponderant').[57] This, albeit subtle, change would appear to shift the derogation's internal threshold from a strict (d/0.5) to a permissive (e/0.33) public interest test. What is far more challenging is determining to which default data protection standards this provision is meant to apply, either fully or only partially. Under the GPDR,[58] (explicit) consent generally lifts both the restrictions on the processing of sensitive data other than those that relate to criminality (provisions (ix)–(xiv))[59] and those related to data export (provision (xviii)).[60] In these cases, therefore the derogation presumably applies in full (e/0.33). In contrast, the default data protection principles (provisions (i)–(v)), transparency rules ((vi)–(viii)), and need for a legal basis for processing (xvi) do not presume data subject consent. Consent also does not *ipso facto* lift the default prohibition on private sector processing of criminal data (xv). Nevertheless, the peremptory lack of any need to secure such consent could affect the specific interpretation of these provisions. As a result, the derogation here would (unless subject to—undoubtedly necessary—creative and far-reaching 'interpretation') only establish a legal gloss (b/0.83) on these standards. Finally, the requirement on the controller to make a registration of its processing (provision (xvii)) is not affected one way or another by the lack of a need to secure data subject consent and, therefore, would appear to remain fully applicable. Statutory provisions in Italy (0.69)[61] and Luxembourg (0.70)[62] establish a similar overall balance as in Estonia which, as a result of their casuistic structure, will be analysed in detail later in sections 2.3 to 2.6. Meanwhile, Slovakia (0.74) includes a provision that is structurally identical to Estonia's in that it authorizes processing to be carried out without *'bez súhlasu'* ('consent').[63] However, in this case, the internal threshold of the derogation requires that such processing not violate either the protection of the '*osobnosti*' ('personality') or '*právo na ochranu súkromia*' ('the right to privacy') of the data subject. It may also be excluded under a specific regulation or an international treaty binding on Slovakia. This is significantly less permissive than the phrasing in Estonia and is therefore coded as requiring a strict/objective (d/0.5) rather than a permissive (e/ 0.33) test *vis-à-vis* those parts of the law which it fully controls (namely, provisions (ix)–(xiv) and (xviii)). A gloss (b/0.83) on a wider range of other stipulations is similarly recognized.

Liechtenstein (0.93) only sets out a journalistic derogation in relation to subject access. This enables '[*m*]*edienschaffende*' ('media professionals') to limit or refuse access when the data is '*ausschliesslich als persönliches Arbeitsinstrument dient*' ('used exclusively as personal working tool') or as regards the '*redaktionellen Teil eines periodisch erscheinenden Mediums*' ('editorial part of a periodical medium'), also where the data would provide information as to its source, access to drafts of publication would have to be given or the public's freedom to form an opinion would be compromised.[64] These complex provisions are (perhaps somewhat leniently) coded as setting out a permissive public interest derogation (e/0.33) from just this one provision. However, otherwise the default GDPR is set out to apply in full. Finally, the last three States—Croatia (1), Hungary (1), and Spain (1)—fail to establish any explicit derogation in favour of journalism within their statutory data protection law at all (a/1).

2.3 The Data Protection Principles (Dimension A: Provisions (i)–(v))

Turning to explore outcomes as these relate to the data protection principles specifically, the casuistic approach adopted by four States must first be considered. Although its approach to many of the other dimensions is more complex, Luxembourg simply continues to subject journalism to the data protection principles in full (a/1).[65] Italian law also does not disapply these provisions, but the legally binding Journalism Data Protection Code does set out a gloss (b/0.83) on their interpretation.[66] Meanwhile, Czech law generally authorizes any processing that engages in journalistic purposes in a '*přiměřeným způsobem*' ('reasonable manner').[67] This authorization, which would appear to disapply the data protection principles, clearly sets out a permissive public interest test (d/0.33).

Danish law generally sets out an unconditional journalistic exemption from substantive data protection.[68] Nevertheless, its *Lov om masssmediers informationsdatabaser* establishes that publicly available mass media information databases may not hold information that cannot be legally published in the mass media,[69] that they must delete, correct, or update information which is false or misleading,[70] and that they also may not hold information whose disclosure would be contrary to journalistic ethics.[71] The first stipulation instantiates the lawfulness aspect of provision (i), the second overlaps especially with the *ex post* element of principle (iv), and finally journalistic ethics dovetails with many of the data principles, albeit with a strong emphasis on media self-regulation. However, whilst regulated databases in general comprise any electronic system disseminating news or other information, the Act specifically excludes databases that only comprise previously published and unaltered periodicals, audio or video programmes, text, and images.[72] These fall only within the Danish Media Liability Act which formally lies outside the data protection framework and, in any case, only requires a conformity with journalistic ethics.[73] Finally, information used internally by the mass media for bona fide journalistic purposes are entirely excluded from any such requirements. The restricted scope and nature of these admittedly complex provisions are best seen as an attempt to include the media within these provisions minimally (f/0.17).

Finally, Germany generally exempts the journalistic media from compliance with all of substantive data protection (g/0).[74] However, as regards the data accuracy principle (provision (iv)) it is established that if a data subject's 'Persönlichkeitsrecht' ('personal rights') are negatively affected by a broadcaster's reporting, they can demand either its 'Berichtigung' ('correction') or the addition of their 'eigenen Darstellung von angemessenem Umfang verlangen' ('own statement of appropriate length').[75] The same legal requirements are placed on the Press when providing telemedia/online services but not when these actors agree to be subject to self-regulation by the German Press Council.[76] These requirements are similarly of limited scope and applicability and also entirely *ex post* in nature. They are therefore also best classified as a case of minimal inclusion (b/0.17).

Chart 8.2 provides a summary for all States in relation to the data protection principles, with outcomes spread across ten ordered categories ranging across the 0–1 scale from not more than 0.1 to greater or equal to 0.9. Looking at the far right of the chart it can be seen that just over half establish that the principles are either essentially fully applicable (9 or 31 per cent of States) or subject to minimal derogation or gloss (6 or 21 per cent of States). Otherwise, however, no discernible overall pattern is in evidence.

2.4 Transparency Rules (Dimension B: Provisions (vi)–(viii))

Turning next to look at the applicability of the transparency provisions, the special approach adopted in five States must similarly be elucidated. Italian law sets out rule-restricted exemptions from the proactive transparency rules (c/0.67). In sum, as regards the direct collection of data (provision (vi)) the Journalism Data Protection Code requires that journalists must in all cases 'refrain from subterfuge and harassment' and more specifically 'must identify themselves, their profession

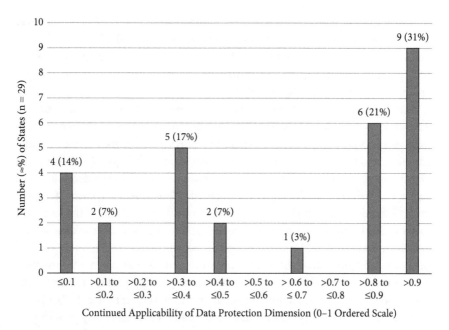

Chart 8.2 The Data Protection Principles and Journalism.

and the purposes of collection, unless this may endanger their safety or otherwise make it impossible for them to carry out their journalistic activity'.[77] Meanwhile, in cases where data are not collected from the data subject themselves, the requirement to ensure that such information is 'disclosed' renders it rather ambiguous whether (unless this would make 'it impossible for them to carry out their journalistic activity') such disclosure should still be to the data subject themselves (as would be expected by default) or simply to any third party who provided the data. In any case, more specific to provision (vii), the Code requires that '[i]f personal data collected from data banks used by editorial offices, publishing companies must inform the public at least twice a year, throughout advertisements, of the existence of such data banks' including the address at which they can apply to exercise their data protection rights.[78] Meanwhile, as regards reactive subject access (provision (viii)), Italian law continues to apply this right directly to the media, subject only to a minimal derogation (b/0.83) which protects the confidentiality of the sources of information held by journalists.[79]

Turning next to Luxembourg, derogations from the proactive transparency rules are provided which appear to be subject to requirements of only minimal substantive strictness (f/0.17). In sum, the proactive transparency rule may be dispensed with whenever its application would '*compromettrait*' ('compromise') the collection of data from the data subject (provision (vi)) or, in other cases (vii), where it would '*compromettrait*' the collection of the data, the identity of any sources or the planned publication or making available of information to the public in whatever way.[80] In contrast, only a rule-restricted derogation (c/0.67) from reactive subject access (provision (viii)) is established since, whilst journalists may protect source confidentiality, they otherwise must allow the Luxembourg DPA to vicariously access the data on any data subject's behalf.[81]

Meanwhile, as a result of numerous exemptions, Czech law also only subjects journalism to minimal duties (f/0.17) in relation to proactive transparency when personal information is directly collected from individuals (provision (vi)).[82] In sum, not only are journalists only ever expected to *'vhodným'* ('adequately') inform data subjects solely of their identity,[83] but this requirement can be excluded if it would require a *'nepřiměřené úsilí'* ('disproportionate effort') or prove *'není možné'* ('impossible').[84] Yet more sweepingly, even this test can be dispensed with if the journalist makes general information on their processing and the rights of the data subject publicly available online.[85] In contrast, given that the default rule in other cases of data processing (provision (vii)) itself permits just making transparency information publicly available if further action would constitute a 'disproportionate effort',[86] the derogation set out here only amounts to a rule-restricted exemption (c/0.67). In sum, as an alternative to complying with these provisions, a journalist may publish general information online which sets out the personal data processing which they usually perform (with the exception of information on sources which is fully exempt).[87] However, the treatment of reactive subject access (provision (viii)) returns to a minimal duties (f/0.17) approach since this right is entirely eliminated where the data have not been published by the controller and even in other cases may be excluded where justified, for example, on grounds of disproportionate effort.[88]

Finally, both Denmark and Germany categorically exclude journalism from the proactive transparency rules (provisions (vi) and (vii))) but set out certain minimal duties (f/0.17) relating to subject access (viii). Denmark grants data subjects a right at yearly intervals to be given written notice of the information related to them recorded in publicly available mass media information databases (the definition of which is, as detailed above, very heavily restricted) but, even then, not if there would be excessive difficulties in obtaining the information.[89] Germany provides that where either a broadcaster or a Press operator providing telemedia/online services negatively affects a data subject's *'Persönlichkeitsrecht'* ('personal rights'), they may make a subject access request. However, information may be denied not only if it would enable conclusions to be drawn on either the persons involved in the preparation, production or dissemination or the editorial guarantor of contributions, documentations and communications but also if enabling exploration of the information would *'beeinträchtigte'* ('prejudice') the journalistic task.[90] Finally, the Press can avoid even these limited legally enforceable duties by agreeing to be subject to self-regulation by the German Press Council.[91]

The spread of outcomes within all States along this dimension is presented in Chart 8.3. This spread indicates that the need for very significant derogations here

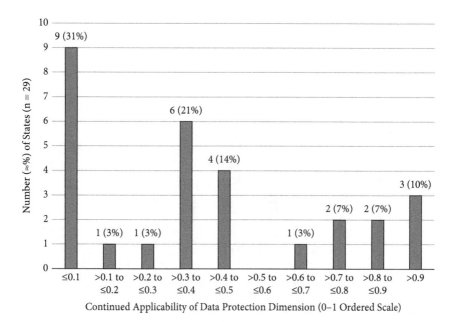

Chart 8.3 The Transparency Rules and Journalism.

have become generally recognized. In sum, countries tend to cluster either at the far left or near the middle, thus indicating either the complete exclusion of these rules or subjecting them to some kind of public interest balancing test. That said, a wide range of permutations of outcome remain present.

2.5 Sensitive Data Rules (Dimension C: Provisions (ix)–(xv))

Moving on to look at the relationship between journalism and the default restrictions on processing sensitive data, four States have adopted a specific approach here. In Luxembourg, exemption is conditional on rule-restricted criteria (d/0.67) since it can apply only to

> *des données rendues manifestement publiques par la personne concernée ou à des données qui sont en rapport direct avec la vie publique de la personne concernée ou avec le fait dans lequel elle est impliquée de façon volontaire*' ('data manifestly made public by the data subject or data which are directly related to the public life of the subject or a fact in which they are voluntarily involved').[92]

Italian data protection law provides for similar restriction on any exemption from the rules on health[93] (provision (xii)) and sex life[94] (xiv) data, whilst only requiring

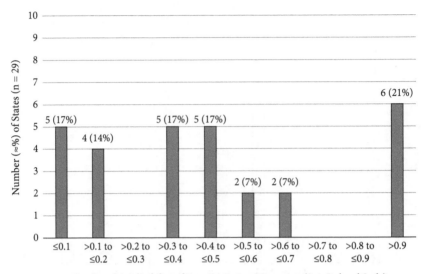

Chart 8.4 The Sensitive Data Rules and Journalism.

an objective or strict test for derogation as regards processing data in the other sensitive categories (d/0.5).[95] Czech law may best be considered to set down an objective or strict public interest test (d/0.5) from the default rules as regards all the sensitive data categories.[96] Finally, Danish law only minimally includes journalism (f/0.17) within the sensitive data restrictions since the requirements laid down here not only contain a public interest override but, more importantly, only apply to the narrow category of publicly available mass media information databases previously discussed.[97]

The outcomes in all States across this dimension are summarized in Chart 8.4. As can be seen, there is some indication of a bunching on the far left, representing near or complete disapplication, and also the middle, representing some kind of explicit public interest balancing. However, the evidence of such clustering is much weaker here than in the case of the transparency rules, not least since a significant number of States (6 or 21 per cent) group at the far right extreme of near or full formal application of this default regime.

2.6 Discipline Requirements
(Dimension D: Provisions (xvi)–(xviii))

Looking finally at the discipline requirements, this dimension ungirds the other core substantive provisions by generally requiring a legal basis for processing (provision (xvi)), a registration of processing by the controller (xvii) and restrictions on data exports (xviii). Five special cases of derogation must be detailed. Belgium statutory law provides no exemption from the need for a legal basis (a/1), a strict or objective public interest (d/0.5) exemption from the data export restrictions[98] and finally a minimal derogation or gloss (b/0.83) on the duty to register processing. Specifically on the latter, the creation and maintenance of a register of processing applies in full, but the journalist can resist making this available to the DPA where this might compromise a proposed publication or if this would constitute a measure of checking prior to the publication of an article.[99] Luxembourg law sets out no exemption from either the need for a general legal basis for processing or from the duty to register it (a/1) but, in contrast, does provide a complete exemption (g/0) from the data export restrictions.[100] Italian law provides no exemption from the duty to register processing (a/1) and merely a gloss (b/0.83) on the need for a legal basis for processing[101] but also sets out a complete exemption (g/0) from the data export restrictions.[102]

Notwithstanding its generally casuistic approach, Czech law is not clearly specified here. It, therefore, must be determined what impact section 16(1) of this this law's generally permissive authorization of journalistic processing pursued in a *'přiměřeným způsobem'* ('reasonable manner') has *vis-à-vis* these three specific provisions. Especially given that this same section of Czech law details a higher protection for processing sensitive data, this authorization is best read as fully superseding the need for a general legal basis and so the derogation here is coded as permissive (e/0.33). In contrast, a mere allowance of processing does not clearly disapply the duty to maintain a register of this and so this is found to only constitute a gloss (b/0.83) on this general duty. Finally, the relationship between such general permission and the data export provisions is yet more ambiguous since, whilst the export of data must involve processing, it is clearly processing of a special (and specifically regulated) sort. Given this uncertainty, the derogation is coded more conservatively as imposing a strict test (d/0.5) as regards this provision.

Turning finally to Denmark's regulation of journalism under data protection, the *Lov om massemediers informationsdatabaser* is not only generally limited in scope but contains no specific cognate to the idea of a legal basis for processing. Nevertheless, in light of the partial overlap between this and the Act's focus on journalistic ethics (as well ensuring that any publication is lawful aside from the data protection restrictions), this is still best seen as a case of minimal inclusion (f/0.17). Meanwhile, only a minimal derogation (b/0.83) from the duty to register processing is provided since, although journalism is excluded from the general requirements applying here,[103] the Danish law sets out a separate requirement not only to register publicly available mass media information databases with both the DPA and the Press Council but even to register internal editorial electronic information databases with the DPA (who are obliged to publish an annual list of

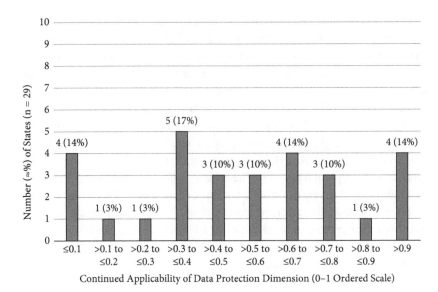

Chart 8.5 The Discipline Requirements and Journalism.

these).[104] Finally, this law sets out no restrictions at all on the export of data overseas and so the derogation is coded as absolute here (g/0).

Chart 8.5 sets out the outcomes on this final dimension for all States. As can be seen, there is no evidence of any consensus in approach. Instead, States group fairly equally across the entire spectrum.

3. Regulatory Supervision of Data Protection *vis-à-vis* Professional Journalism

3.1 State Regulatory Oversight

Turning to the supervision of data protection in relation to professional journalism, State laws can be grouped within the same four categories as deployed in Chapter 5 as regards the DPD-era. The coding of these States within these categories, which range from full (1) though to no (0) regulatory supervision, is listed in the left-hand column of Chart 8.1 and also in Appendix 7.

To begin with, some State laws do not set down any special limitation on statutory regulation here and so, in principle, a DPA's powers as set out in the GDPR itself would continue to apply in full (1). Twelve (41 per cent) out of the twenty-nine States which have so far implemented the GDPR fall within this first category. These States are Croatia, Cyprus, Estonia, Hungary, Italy, Liechtenstein, Luxembourg, Malta, Norway, Poland, Slovakia and Spain. However, similarly to the situation under the DPD, there are certain caveats to note. Thus, as elucidated in section 5 below, two of these States—Italy and Luxembourg—fuse DPA responsibilities here with a formal role for self-regulatory structures.[105] Meanwhile, Norway disapplies the substance of data protection entirely and Spain continues to divide jurisdiction between the national DPA, which remains responsible for all private and most public organizations, and regional DPAs in the Basque Country and Catalonia who are granted oversight powers in relation to bodies established under their local public law.[106]

A second group set out a partial model of statutory regulation across all forms of professional journalism (0.5). Some fourteen (48 per cent) States now fall within this category. Summaries of these provisions, which in some cases explicitly extend also to the pan-European cooperation and consistency mechanism explored later in section 3.2, are set out in Table 8.3. As can seen, the specific approaches adopted here remain quite diverse. Four States within this group—Austria, Ireland, Latvia and Romania—seek to apply the same derogatory tests here as they set out in relation to substantive data protection. However, these tests (which were explored in section 2) are not always apposite to this issue and, in particular, it generally remains unclear whether a journalist must prove that they have met the substantive data standards before they can remove themselves from regulation or, in contrast, whether the DPA is precluded from intervening unless it can prove that such standards have not been complied with. Meanwhile, Sweden simply references to the priority of its Freedom of the Press and Freedom of Expression Acts. Turning to those who adopt a more casuistic approach, a particular focus on restricting investigatory powers is generally evident. Whilst in a few cases this is limited to the protection of journalistic source confidentiality (Bulgaria, France), in many other instances it extends to the prevention or heavy restriction of regulatory prior restraint or auditing (Belgium, Czechia, Denmark, Gibraltar, UK). Danish, Gibraltarian and UK law set out further significant restrictions on the role of data protection regulation here and in Lithuania and Denmark this role continues to be allocated to a specialist media body rather than the ordinary DPA. These differences in regulatory strictness broadly map on to the more precisely measured divergences in the substantive stringency of the law which are also noted in the left-hand column of Table 8.3.

Next, as also summarized in Table 8.3, one State (3 per cent), Germany, entirely exempts the Press from statutory regulation but leaves it to each of the Länder whether to apply a partial regulatory model to its broadcasting sector only. This unusual outcome is coded 0.25 which is the mid-point between the comprehensive partial model of regulation previously detailed (0.5) and no regulation at all (0).

This final possibility of removing statutory regulation from the picture entirely (0) is adopted by only two States (7 per cent), namely, Iceland[107] and the Netherlands.[108] Even then, the Icelandic DPA retains a responsibility to promote the development of appropriate (self-regulatory) codes of conduct and monitoring bodies,[109] an aspect of the law that is returned to in section 5 below.

Table 8.3 Partial Restrictions on DPA Regulation and Limitations on Pan-European Cooperation and Consistency *vis-à-vis* Journalism within National GDPR Laws (Ordered by the Substantive Stringency of Local Statute)

EEA State (ordered by substantive stringency)	Brief details of explicit regulatory restrictions
Romania (0.67)	In order to ensure a balance between data protection, freedom of expression and the right to information, full restrictions apply but only in relation to processing concerning data manifestly made public by the data subject or which closely relates to public life of the data subject or the public character of the facts in which he or she was involved.[110]
France (0.65)	DPA prohibited from seizing data covered by journalistic source confidentiality.[111]
Lithuania (0.63)	DPA tasks and powers allocated to the specialist Inspector of Journalist Ethics with certain exclusions including the ability to carry out audits, mandate impact assessments or suspend the flow of data to recipients overseas. Inspector also lacks power to order rectification or erasure of data pursuant to specific data subject rights, but retains an ability to order a ban or modification of processing.[112] Inspector to cooperate with ordinary DPA in relation to pan-European cooperation and consistency.
Bulgaria (0.60)	Exclusion of DPA action insofar as use of powers would breach source confidentiality.[113]
Latvia (0.60)	Full exclusion insofar as processing respects the right to privacy, outweighs the interests of the data subject that require protection, is carried out with a view to publishing information of public interest and where the observance of the provisions are not compatible with or prevent the exercise of the right to freedom of expression and information.[114]
Austria (0.53)	Full restriction insofar as is necessary to reconcile data protection with freedom of expression and information.[115]
Belgium (0.48)	Restrictions on DPA insofar as this would constitute a mechanism of prior restraint or would lead to provision of information on sources.[116]
Czechia (0.41)	Exclusion of any requirement for (prior) authorization or approval. Otherwise the publisher retains the right to protect the source and content of information. Specifically stated notification of data breaches to the DPA need not disclose source or content of the data.[117]
Gibraltar (0.35)	DPA prohibited from auditing journalistic processing and engaging in any prior restraint. Otherwise, DPA enforcement restricted to action in relation to matters of substantial public importance and generally with some court oversight.[118] Derogation from pan-European cooperation and consistency depends on same permissive public interest test as applied to substantive derogations (see section 2 above).

Table 8.3 *Continued*

EEA State (ordered by substantive stringency)	Brief details of explicit regulatory restrictions
UK (0.35)	Generally identical to Gibraltar (see entry immediately above).[119] However, the DPA is also charged with drafting and keeping under review a co-regulatory code,[120] producing guidance on redress[121] and periodically reviewing journalism's compliance with data protection good practice.[122] In that regard it is granted an ability to audit journalists (so long as this excludes information which has not been verified to be already published) as well as broad information powers.[123]
Ireland (0.33)	Full exclusion insofar as incompatible with the exercise of the right to freedom of expression and information, having regard to the importance of the latter right in a democratic society.[124]
Denmark (0.15)	Ordinary DPA only granted a role in registering databases.[125] Otherwise, Press Council assigned limited tasks and power to require information already published in a publicly-available mass media database to be deleted or a reply added, as well right to demand relevant information from (but not to audit) journalists. Complete exclusion of pan-European cooperation and consistency mechanism.[126]
Finland (0.14)	DPA specifically prohibited from ordering either a temporary or permanent limitation (including a ban) on processing. Otherwise stated that DPA tasks and powers as laid down in the GDPR only apply *mutatis mutandis* given the substantive restrictions applicable here.
Germany (0.03)	Interstate Treaty on Broadcasting and Telemedia assumes no statutory regulation of the Press (and includes specific permissive provisions on self-regulation). By contrast, each Land retains some discretion as to whether and how to subject broadcasters to statutory regulation (but this is unlikely to engage with pan-European cooperation and consistency).[127]
Sweden (0)	Exclusion from DPA tasks and powers that would conflict with the Swedish Freedom of the Press Act or the Freedom of Expression Act.[128]

3.2 Pan-European Cooperation and Consistency

A related but distinct issue raised by the GDPR concerns the potential applicability of the new default mechanism which, as regards 'cross-border processing',[129] requires DPAs to ensure pan-European 'cooperation and consistency'[130] through a mechanism ultimately overseen by the European Data Protection Board. Fifteen of the twenty-nine States (52 per cent) do not set out any specific statutory derogation from this mechanism. Except for Malta, this group includes all twelve States that fail to set out a clear limitation on national DPA regulation in their statutory law (see section 3.1). It also encompasses five further States that do set out partial limits on the role of statutory regulation in general, namely: Belgium, Bulgaria, Czechia, France and Lithuania. Eight States (28 per cent) seek to qualify but not eliminate this mechanism. Other than including Malta and excluding Denmark, this group comprises all the remaining States that set out partial limits on statutory regulation over journalism in general. As can be seen from Table 8.3, the limits when specified are generally identical to those which are set out down as regards regulatory supervision confined within that State. Meanwhile, Malta applies the same derogatory tests here as are applied to limitations on substantive data protection.[131] Finally, three States (11 per cent) explicitly disapply this mechanism in full, namely, the two States that exclude all regulatory supervision (Iceland[132] and the Netherlands[133]) and also Denmark.[134]

4. Comparisons of Statutory Stringency *vis-à-vis* the DPD Era and between States

Given that this chapter deploys the same categorization of both substantive and supervisory stringency as that deployed in relation to second-generation data protection laws in Chapter 5, a ready comparison between this *status quo ante* and the new outcomes under the GDPR is possible. Looking first at applicable substantive data protection standards, there has been no dramatic change in the average extent to which these provisions are made formally applicable to journalism. Not only is the new average score of 0.49 comparable with the old average of 0.54 but, if the States which (as of May 2019) have yet to implement the GDPR locally[135] are removed from the latter dataset, the figures become even more similar. Nevertheless, there are some very slight signs of an increasing recognition of the need for a careful balancing of rights in this area. In this regard a comparison may be made of results presented in Chart 8.1 in this chapter and Chart 5.1 in Chapter 5. Whereas during the DPD-era six States (including Slovenia which has yet to implement the GDPR) were allocated a score 0.9 or above—thus indicating essentially no formal statutory derogation from the default standards—this number had fallen to four under the GDPR. The number of States allocated scores of 0.1 or below has also fallen from six to five. A comparison between this chapter's and Chapter 5's charts presenting the overall spreads across the four dimensions of data protection[136] is also instructive. Whilst no moves towards greater consistency are apparent as regards the discipline requirements, a modest shift may be detected in relation to the other three core substantive data protection dimensions. Thus, compared to the situation under the DPD, more States recognize the need to exclude or heavily qualify application of the transparency rules and (to a lesser extent) also the sensitive data rules. There is also a growing recognition that some, albeit perhaps limited, derogations from the core data protection principles may be necessary. As a result, the standard deviation in the overall results has exhibited a small decrease, moving from 0.33 under the DPD[137] to 0.30 under the GDPR.

A much clearer and more unequivocal shift can be seen in the growing consensus that partial as opposed to full regulatory supervision is warranted here. Thus, whereas some 72 per cent of States did not clearly and specifically limit DPA regulatory powers in this area during the DPD, that number has now fallen to around 41 per cent under the GDPR. Alongside this, the very small number of States that seek to completely disapply such statutory regulation has similarly fallen from three to two. Whilst some of these reforms reflect a response to the more prescriptive and exactly nature of default regulatory control under the GDPR, a change of pattern of this magnitude is clearly of significance.

Despite this, divergences in formal outcome remain marked. In relation to regulatory supervision, these differences are partially masked by large differences *within* the group of States that have now set out partial limits on this within their law (see Table 8.3). In contrast, the more granular approach to the substantive derogations enables the differences between States to be revealed more clearly. As can be seen in Chart 8.1, States cluster within the same overarching and potentially explanatory cultural groupings as that revealed during the DPD.[138] Historically Germanic and Protestant countries within Northern Europe almost invariably grant journalism very deep or even absolute formal derogations from data protection. In contrast, the historically Roman Catholic or Orthodox countries of Southern Europe generally subject this activity to significantly more statutory restrictions. A similar outcome is in evidence in the formally Communist Eastern European States. In relation to the difference between Northern and Southern Europe, these divergences map on to Hallin and Manchini's admittedly broad-brush distinction between a Polarized Pluralist Model of media systems in Southern Europe compared to either a Liberal or a Democratic Corporatist Model in Northern Europe.[139] Moreover, and also tallying with these results, literature has suggested that media systems in Eastern European generally align more closely with patterns in Southern as compared to Northern Europe.[140]

As also explored in Chapter 5, the broad cultural differences between European States have been systematically mapped by Hofstede and his colleagues along three fundamental spectra: individualism, uncertainty avoidance, and power distance. Moreover, for the reasons elucidated in Chapter 5, we may reasonably expect increased attempts at State control and regulation of journalistic activity to be associated with a less individualistic approach to social ordering, a greater desire to avoid uncertainty and also a greater acceptance of power differences. Whilst these expectations were strongly confirmed by the data collected on statutory outcomes under the DPD, it is important to see if

Table 8.4 Spearman Rank Correlations between the Substantive and Regulatory Stringency of Default Third-Generation European Data Protection, and Hofstede and Colleagues' Cultural Variables ($n = 24$)

Formal law measures → Cultural measures ↓	Substantive stringency	Regulatory stringency
Individualism	Coefficient: −0.339*	Coefficient: −0.383**
	Significance: 0.053	Significance: 0.032
Uncertainty avoidance	Coefficient: 0.503***	Coefficient: 0.538***
	Significance: 0.006	Significance: 0.003
Power distance	Coefficient: 0.632***	Coefficient: 0.628***
	Significance: 0.000	Significance: 0.001

One-tailed significance at the 10% (*), 5% (**), and 1% (***) confidence level

they have been maintained into the era of the GDPR. This was explored by correlating the values Hofstede and his colleagues computed for individual States in relation to these three fundamental cultural variables with new measures for each State as regards both the substantive stringency and the regulatory stringency of statutory data protection in the area of journalism under their third-generation laws. The values used for substantive stringency were the same as that presented in section 2. Meanwhile, a measure of overarching regulatory stringency was created by multiplying this substantive measure with the numerical representation of the extent to which a statutory regulator retained an ability to supervise these standards as presented section 3 above. The results obtained are presented in Table 8.4. As can be seen, all correlations were all in the expected direction, of moderate or greater strength and achieved (one-tailed) significance at least at the 10 per cent and generally at the 1 per cent level. Whilst considerable qualitative analysis in the individual States would be necessary to prove this conclusively, the continued presence of such strong correlations clearly suggests that fundamental cultural orientations are playing a significant role in shaping legislative outcomes in this sensitive area.

5. Formal Statutory Provisions Relating to Self-Regulation

Although not directly determinative of the stringency of a legislative scheme, professional journalism's relationship with data protection may be significantly influenced by formal provisions that establish or promote a co-regulatory relationship between the statutory regime and self-regulatory norms and/or structures. As was done in relation to second-generation data protection law in Chapter 5, it is therefore important to specifically explore this particular issue. Like the DPD before it, Article 40 of the GDPR includes general clauses requiring DPAs to encourage associations who represent certain categories of controller to propose codes of conduct for their hopeful approval. These codes should 'specif[y] the application' of the data protection regime by *inter alia* 'taking account of the specific features of the various processing sectors'.[141] Going beyond these cognate provisions, Article 41 also sets out a mechanism whereby a DPA can accredit an external body to monitor compliance with any approved code as regards processing carried out by anyone other than 'public authorities and bodies'.[142] The DPA is also generally obliged to submit the draft criteria for any such accreditation,[143] as well as any code which has a cross-border character,[144] to the pan-European 'consistency' mechanism discussed above. Nevertheless, as noted in section 1 of this chapter and in contrast to the cognate provision in the DPD, the GDPR permits these provisions (which are otherwise now self-executing) to be limited or excluded in the area of journalism (and other forms of special expression) through national law.

Notwithstanding such a possibility, relatively few States specifically curtail the potential applicability of these clauses (although more general limits, especially with regards the 'consistency' mechanism, may apply to a broader group by proxy). In sum, only two (7 per cent) States (Denmark[145] and the Netherlands[146]) completely disable these co-regulatory Articles. Meanwhile, five (17 per cent) States (Austria, Finland, Germany, Latvia and Romania) subject these provisions to the same partial restrictions that they apply to all action by the DPA here. However, aside from in Germany, these restrictions remain consistent with GDPR's code of conduct provision and should also only limit, rather than entirely prohibit, a deployment of its monitoring clause (see detail in Table 8.3). Finally, one (3 per cent) State—Lithuania—excludes only the potential for the DPA to accredit a monitoring body under article 41.[147]

Beyond the continued applicability of these default co-regulatory provisions in most States, ten (34 per cent) have adopted legislative provisions which, in the specific area of journalism, explicitly relate self-regulation to data protection in some way. These provisions, which broadly mirror those adopted in the DPD-era,[148] are summarized in Table 8.5. As can be seen, a large majority of these States have sought to connect statutory and self-regulation in the area of standard-setting, most usually through a legislative reference to journalistic ethics. Otherwise, however, the provisions are very diverse. For example, whilst Gibraltar merely acknowledges the potential for such a normative link, several other States (Denmark, Italy, and the United Kingdom) set out much more precisely the nature of such a relationship and also establish a co-regulatory approach to overseeing compliance with these and related standards.

Table 8.5 Specific Recognition of a Link between Data Protection and Journalistic Self-Regulatory Standards and/or *Scrutinizing Structures*

EEA State (substantive stringency/ maximum regulatory oversight— ordered by former)	Brief details of statutorily recognized 'self-regulatory' standards and/or *structures*
Estonia (0.74/1)	– Journalistic derogation made subject to compliance with the principles of journalism ethics.[149]
Italy (0.69/1)	– DPA and National Council of the Order of Journalists to adopt new co-regulatory code of conduct (and in interim old Code to continue for a period of up to one year). – DPA, in cooperation within the National Council, is to prescribe *measures to protect the data subject which the Council must then implement.*[150]
Luxembourg (0.66/1)	– *Data subject access to journalistic data (other than on sources) to be vicariously secured through DPA with Chair of self-regulatory Press Council (or their representative) being given opportunity to be present.*[151]
Lithuania (0.63/0.5)	– *Statutory oversight of data protection allocated to the Inspector of Journalist Ethics, a state body but with a clear co-regulatory status.*[152]
France (0.54/0.5)	– Journalistic derogation made subject to compliance with professional ethical rules.[153]
Belgium (0.47/0.5)	– Journalism defined as only encompassing those required to comply with journalistic ethical rules.[154]
Gibraltar (0.35/0.5)	– Interpretation of public interest test within this derogation must have regard to prescribed publication codes or guidelines. Currently only State-drafted audio-visual codes are prescribed but possibility left for government to include more clearly self- or co-regulatory codes at a later date.[155]
UK (0.35/0.5)	– Determination of the reasonableness of any belief that publication would be in the public interest (an integral part of the derogatory conditions) must have regard as relevant to any self-/co-regulatory media codes that are legally prescribed. – DPA must prepare a co-regulatory journalistic code of good practice which, after parliamentary assent, must then be taken into account by both DPA and courts. – DPA must evaluate media compliance with both law and good practice every four to five years. – DPA must publish guidance on redress against media organizations including *self-/co-regulatory mechanisms.* – *Government must evaluate use and effectiveness of media's alternative dispute resolution procedures every 3 years.*[156]

Table 8.5 *Continued*

EEA State (substantive stringency/ maximum regulatory oversight— ordered by former)	Brief details of statutorily recognized 'self-regulatory' standards and/or *structures*
Denmark (0.15/0.5)	– Publicly available mass media databases cannot contain information whose disclosure would be contrary to the ethics of journalism. – *Statutory oversight of substantive standards to be overseen by the co-regulatory Press Council.*[157]
Germany (0.03/0.25)	– Interstate Treaty on Broadcasting and Telemedia absolves the Press from substantive statutory data protection control if they are subject to the Press Code provisions and oversight by the *self-regulatory Press Council.*[158]

6. Formal Provisions Concerning Professional Journalism and Media Archiving

One final issue brought to the fore by the GDPR relates specifically to the data protection standards and supervisory arrangements applicable to both publicly-available media archives made up of historic journalistic output and the retention of other records which are kept by the media for internal journalistic use. The previous chapters of this book section detailed how some have disputed whether (at least) publicly available media archives should be allowed to claim the derogations generally available for 'journalistic purposes'. As noted in section 1, the GDPR has in principle clarified this controversy in the media's favour. In sum, as well as stressing that concepts such as journalism should be interpreted 'broadly', recital 153 specifically states that the journalistic derogation should apply 'in particular' to both 'press libraries' and 'news archives'. Whilst neither term is further defined, 'news archives' can reasonably be taken to refer to the practice of making previously published journalistic content permanently available to the general public including online. Meanwhile, 'press libraries' would appear to reference the internal keeping by the media of a much wider range of material for background use in their journalism.

Both recital references can be traced back to the European Commission's initial draft of the Regulation from 2012.[159] Nevertheless, at a later date, the Council of the EU proposed including within the chapter on specific data processing situations a much more restrictive default provision governing processing for archiving purposes in the public interest which was separate from the journalistic (and other special expressive purposes) derogation.[160] This suggestion was ultimately adopted in the final GDPR text.[161] Archiving in the public interest might reasonably be taken to include media archiving. Thus, not only has the European Court of Human Rights repeatedly emphasized that it is incumbent on the media 'to impart information and ideas of public interest' but it has specifically (and correctly) held that online news archives 'constitute an important source for education and historical research, particularly as they are readily accessible to the public and are generally free.'[162] A clear need, therefore, arose to explicitly ensure that the derogatory regime for journalism had priority even in this specific context. In that regard, the final GDPR text (unlike the original Commission version) adopted the suggestion (advanced by both the Council of the EU and the European Parliament) that Member States should be specifically obliged to extent the journalism derogation as necessary even to other provisions within the chapter on specific data processing situations which included archiving.[163]

Unfortunately, however, an analysis of State implementing laws indicates that only eight States (28 per cent)[164] unequivocally establish that their journalistic derogations extend to the restrictive provisions which otherwise govern processing for archiving purposes. In six other States (21 per cent), the formal position is particularly unclear. Thus, Belgian law does not reference the GDPR's provision on archiving within its journalistic derogation, but does explicitly establish that 'des fine journalistiques' ('journalistic purposes') include 'l'archivage à des fins d'informer le public, à l'aide de tout media' ('archiving for the purpose of informing the public, using any media').[165] Meanwhile, whilst Swedish law similarly fails to include the archiving provision within its otherwise extensive list of provisions from which journalism is exempt,[166] it does state that data protection is in any case not to be applied where it would conflict with the Swedish Freedom of the Press or Freedom of Expression Acts.[167] In the other four cases the lack of clarity arises from a more general ambiguity regarding the scope of the national journalistic derogation in relation to particular provisions within the GDPR.[168] Finally, the remaining fifteen States (52 per cent) clearly fail to expressly extend their journalistic derogation to the provisions set out in the GDPR (and in national law) which relate to archiving purposes.[169]

Ultimately, therefore, the relationship between media archiving and data protection's default and rather restrictive provisions governing archiving in the public interest remains ambiguous in many Member States. Whilst it may seem unlikely that this would lead to either a DPA or the courts subjecting the journalistic media to the full force of the archiving restrictions, these ambiguities may well fuel uncertainty in this area for some time to come. Moreover, as will be seen in the next section of this book, these issues dovetail with more practically pressing concerns that have arisen as a result of a similar failure in most States to establish that the derogations adopted in favour of non-journalistic forms of special expression (including, most notably, academic expression) should be granted priority over not only the archiving but also the default 'historical and scientific research' provisions.[170]

7. Conclusions

The provisional analysis of the legislative provisions relating to journalism within third-generation data protection law highlight strong commonalities, but also some important new trends, compared with the *status quo ante*. Turning first to fundamental commonalities, the GDPR continues to instruct Member States to adopt derogations as 'necessary'[171] to ensure a reconciliation between competing rights. Paralleling significant variation in fundamental cultural orientations in different parts of Europe, State implementation of that instruction has continued to exhibit wide divergence. In broad outline, Northern European States have set out very wide journalistic derogation from the default provisions set out in European data protection law. In contrast, the statutory framework established in most Eastern and Southern European States continue to subject journalistic activity to fairly exacting data protection standards. Nevertheless, notwithstanding a number of outliers and continuing broader ambiguities as regards the position of media archiving, there are some albeit small signs that a greater number of States have sought to engage in careful rights balancing here. In sum, as a result of fewer States seeking to essentially entirely disapply data protection standards and more States establishing limitations on such provisions as the transparency and sensitive data rules, slightly less divergent substantive outcomes are now in evidence.

Much more strikingly, in contrast to a small number under the DPD, almost half of the States have enacted partial limits on regulatory supervision of journalism under the GDPR. At the same time, the number seeking to entirely disable such regulation has not only remained small but has even decreased. Alongside this, the GDPR has strengthened co-regulatory possibilities within the data protection regime, complementing a pre-existing focus on codes of conduct with a new provision on the accreditation of 'self-regulatory' monitoring bodies. Although both of these provisions are potentially subject to the journalistic derogation at national level, relatively few State laws have sought to curtail their potential use. Moreover, as under the DPD, about one third of the States have set out legislative provisions that specifically relate aspects of the statutory regime to journalistic self-regulation.

In the final analysis, the new laws adopted in the vast majority of EEA States under the GDPR continue to allocate not only data protection law itself but also the DPAs (or in a few instances specialist media regulators) a significant, yet complex and delicate, role in balancing rights within this highly sensitive area. Exploring how these regulators should approach their difficult tasks here will be the focus of Chapter 9.

9

The Future Shape of European Data Protection Regulation and Professional Journalism

As explored in Chapter 8, European Data Protection Authorities (or, in a few instances, specialist statutory media regulators) ('DPAs') continue to be allocated a vital role in ensuring that professional journalism upholds appropriate data protection standards in the era of the General Data Protection Regulation 2016/679 ('GDPR'). The precise nature of this role, and the way it should be discharged, clearly depends on a range of local factors including both the specifics of State data protection law and the wider legal context. At the same time, these authorities confront a common range of core issues. Thus, whilst data protection is acknowledged throughout Europe as a fundamental harmonized and codified right, its interface with professional journalism engages the pre-eminent exercise of another right that is universally recognized, namely freedom of expression. This field is also generally characterized by an especially complex interface between self-regulatory and state regulatory norms and structures. Finally, DPAs confront very similar resourcing constraints. Given this, it is important to explore the broad stance that regulators should adopt in this vital but highly sensitive area of regulatory activity. That will be the task of this chapter. It will build on the historic experience—negative, positive, and indifferent—of the interface between data protection regulation and journalism, this having already been extensively explored in the previous chapters of Part II. It will similarly draw on the scholarly literature on regulation, both in general and specifically within the media sector.

It is important to place these issues within an evolving pan-European jurisprudential and funding context. Sections 1 and 2 will, therefore, examine respectively the case law which has emerged from both the European Court of Human Rights ('ECtHR') and the Court of Justice of the European Union ('CJEU') from around the time of the DPA questionnaire in 2013 onwards and the resources which DPAs have available to carry out their tasks today as compared also to that year. Sections 3 and 4 will look directly at how DPAs should approach their role within each European Economic Area (EEA) State, turning first to the broad area of guidance and standard-setting (including in relation to media archiving) and subsequently to monitoring and enforcement. Section 5 will then explore the potential

European Data Protection Regulation, Journalism, and Traditional Publishers. David Erdos, Oxford University Press (2019). © David Erdos.
DOI: 10.1093/oso/9780198841982.003.0009

for pan-European coordination through the new European Data Protection Board. Finally, Section 6 will conclude by drawing the various strands of the argument together.

1. The Contemporary European Jurisprudential Context

1.1 The European Court of Human Rights

As explored in Chapter 2, the European Court of Human Rights (ECtHR) has played a major role over many decades in elucidating the contours of the right to freedom of expression as set out in the European Convention on Human Rights, which remains the continent's pre-eminent rights instrument. Freedom of expression is protected, albeit in qualified terms, through Article 10 of the Convention. In contrast, data protection is not explicitly recognized, although a closely related 'right to respect for family and private life' is enunciated (also in qualified terms) through Article 8. Historically, Article 8 was widely understood to limit the activities of 'public authorities, [but] not private parties'.[1] However, again as elucidated in Chapter 2, in *Von Hannover v Germany (No 1)* the ECtHR finally held that Article 8 did require States to adopt measures that safeguarded an individual's private life also in relation to the activities of private parties. Moreover, even in the sensitive area of journalistic activity, it found that the Convention required a 'balancing [of] the protection of private life against freedom of expression' with the 'decisive factor' resting on the contribution of any resulting publication 'to a debate of general interest'.[2]

Since this seminal case, the jurisprudence of the ECtHR has continued to evolve. In *Von Hannover v Germany (No 2)* the Court reiterated that in cases where 'the right to freedom of expression is being balanced against the right for private life', an 'initial essential criterion' remained whether the publication in question contributed 'to a debate of general interest'.[3] Nevertheless, the Court went on to stress that this criterion had to be contextualized by reference to a range of other factors including:

- the public or private status of the individual being reported upon (and any nexus between this and the information's subject matter);
- the prior conduct of this person;
- the content, form, and consequences of the publication; and
- the circumstances in which the information (in the instant case, photographs) had been obtained.

It also indicated that, so long as these factors were taken properly into account, States had a significant 'margin of appreciation'[4] under the Convention when carrying out this balancing exercise. Finally, the ECtHR emphasized that the exercise of its supervisory jurisdiction 'should not, in theory, vary according to whether it has been lodged with the Court under art. 8 of the Convention, by the person who was the subject of the article, or under art. 10 by the publisher. Indeed, as a matter of principle these rights deserve equal respect'.[5] Furthermore, in contrast to the violation of Article 8 found in *Von Hannover (No 1)*, this second case refused to impugn the local German court's upholding of the right of the media to publish photos of Princess Caroline of Monaco whilst out in public but on a private holiday. In sum, these images were found not to infringe Article 8 since *inter alia* they were held to have been made in the context of reporting on the illness of Ranier III, the then ruling Prince of Monaco. It had, therefore, not been 'unreasonable' for the Germany courts to have conceptualized this as a matter of general public concern.[6] Furthermore, Princess Caroline herself had to be regarded as a 'public figure' even if she did not undertake 'official functions on behalf of the Principality of Monaco'.[7]

Compared to *Von Hannover (No 1)*, this second case has been correctly understood as liberalizing the oversight of the ECtHR in this area. Nevertheless, a public interest analysis has remained the principal lodestar for the Court when elucidating the balancing test required here. Moreover, despite the increased flexibility and deference, this test still requires very careful judgments to be made whenever information which seriously interferes with private life is to be published. The continued centrality, and weight, of this factor is well illustrated in the Grand Chamber judgment of *Satamedia v Finland*.[8] This involved an Article 10 challenge to the banning of the re-publication of public domain tax data on over 1 million Finnish citizens which had been prohibited under data protection after it was held by the Finnish courts to fall outside of the journalistic derogation as elucidated by the CJEU in *Satamedia* in 2008. In upholding this ban,[9] the ECtHR argued that

> Public interest ordinarily relates to matters which affect the public to such an extent that it may legitimately take an interest in them, which attract its attention or which concern it to a significant degree, especially in that they affect the wellbeing of citizens or the life of the community.[10]

It went on the stress that although the publication of the tax data 'might have enabled curious members of the public to categorise named individuals, who are not public figures, according to their economic status, this could be regarded as a manifestation of the public's thirst for information about the private life of others and, as such, a form of sensationalism, even voyeurism'.[11] As a result, the Court held that it could not but 'agree' with the Finnish court's finding that the activity should fall outside the journalistic derogation.[12] This case not only vividly demonstrates the continued vitality of Convention supervision but also highlights the close overlap between the kind of personal information which is often at issue in contentious data protection cases and information concerning private life as protected by Article 8 of the Convention.

1.2 Court of Justice of the European Union

Whilst ECtHR jurisprudence has become somewhat more flexible recently, the data protection jurisprudence of the Court of Justice of the European Union (CJEU) has emerged as a highly significant and increasingly independent source of authoritative norms in this same area. As already mentioned in Chapter 3, the granting in 2009 of pan-EU legal status to the EU Charter and, more particularly, the fundamental right to data protection as well as that of private life[13] has been the key catalyst for this development. It is epitomized by the Grand Chamber decisions of *Google Spain, Digital Rights Ireland*, and *Schrems*. However, the only new case to date which addresses the journalistic derogation squarely is the ordinary chamber decision of *Buivids*. Moreover, whilst all these decisions have important implications for the interpretation and application of data protection under the GDPR, they were decided on law as it existed during the Data Protection Directive 95/46 ('DPD') era.

Google Spain found that an Internet search engine providing searches 'made on the basis of a person's name'[14] had responsibilities as a data controller to ensure 'within the framework of its responsibilities, powers and capabilities'[15] that this processing met all the core default standards set down in the then DPD. Moreover, the Court stressed that in light of the 'potential seriousness' of such name-based processing it was 'clear that it cannot be justified by merely the economic interest which the operator of such an engine has in that processing' and, further, that 'the data subject's fundamental rights under Articles 7 [right to private life] and 8 [data protection] of the Charter' also 'override, as a general rule' the 'interest of internet users' in receiving information in this way.[16] Finally, the Court found that in circumstances where a search engine refused a request to cease such name-based processing, the data subject had the right to bring the matter before a DPA 'so that it carries out the necessary checks and orders the controller to take specific measures accordingly'.[17]

The logic of this albeit seminal judgment cannot be neatly carried over to the interface between the data protection and the professional journalistic media. Indeed, a critical part of its ratio was that an Internet search engine's processing could not (at least directly) benefit from the journalistic derogation.[18] In contrast, as the case of *Buivids* (see following) highlighted, most if not all the journalistic media's freedom of expression activities will fall squarely within this special framework. Nevertheless, *Google Spain* did emphasize the important role of data protection in the area of online publication and the centrality of concepts such as the 'right to be forgotten' within this context. Moreover, its core thrust links to a broader trend within CJEU Grand Chamber judgments that has seen the Court grant considerably enhanced weight to data protection rights and remedies even when these are in tension with other fundamental interests and concerns. For example, in *Digital Rights Ireland* another Grand Chamber struck down the Data Retention Directive 2006/24 on the basis that EU primary law required that 'derogations and limitations in relation to the protection of personal data must apply only in so far as is strictly necessary'.[19] This strict necessity standard was not met due *inter alia* to the Directive's failure to

> lay down clear and precise rules governing the scope and application of the measure in question and impos[e] minimum safeguards so that the persons whose data have been retained have sufficient guarantees to effectively protect their personal data against the risk of abuse.[20]

Meanwhile, in *Schrems*, a third Grand Chamber panel struck down the 'Safe Harbor' data 'adequacy' agreement with the United States that had been adopted through a European Commission secondary law Decision made under Article 28 of the DPD.[21] The *ratio* here was that, when interpreted alongside EU primary law, the DPD's transnational data 'adequacy' framework,[22] required transfers of data to be protected in a way 'essentially equivalent to that guaranteed in the EU legal order'.[23] The Court separately ruled that attempts under such Decisions to limit a DPA's supervisory powers were invalid. That part of the ruling was grounded in a finding that the State's obligation 'to set up one or more public authorities responsible for monitoring, with complete independence, compliance with EU [data protection] rules' derived 'from the primary law of the European Union, in particular Article 8(3) of the Charter and Article 16(2) TFEU'.[24]

As previously stated, the recent case of *Buivids* directly considered the meaning and regulation of journalism under data protection, albeit within the context of amateur individual rather than the professional media activity. Buivids had recorded himself 'in a station of the Latvian national police while he was making a statement in the context of administrative proceedings which had been brought against him'.[25] The resulting video, which was published on YouTube, revealed 'police officers going about their duties in the police station'.[26] After being subject to legal challenge, Buivids claimed that he sought 'to bring to the attention of society something which he considered to constitute unlawful conduct on the part of the police'.[27]

The CJEU was first asked whether Buivid's activity fell within the scope of data protection. In light of the broad meaning of 'personal data' and 'processing' and the need to interpret any exemptions from the scope of the law 'strictly',[28] the Court had no difficulty finding that it did.[29] The second, more complex question concerned whether, and if so how, the journalistic derogation should be engaged. Largely paralleling the earlier case of *Satamedia*, the Court stressed that, in order to ensure appropriate protection for freedom of expression, 'journalism' should be interpreted 'broadly'[30] and so should extent to any activity which was 'intended solely to disclose information, opinions or ideas to the public'.[31] At the same time, the Court not only reiterated *Satamedia*'s holding that derogations even within journalistic area 'must apply only in so far as is strictly necessary'[32] but emphasized that national courts (and, by implication, also initially DPAs) had a direct obligation to police this latter test. In sum:

> [i]f it should transpire that the sole objective of the recording and publication of the video in question was the disclosure to the public of information, opinions or ideas, it is for the referring court to determine whether the exemptions or derogations provided for in Article 9 of Directive 95/46 are necessary in order to reconcile the right to privacy with the rules governing freedom of expression, and whether those exemptions and derogations are applied only in so far as is strictly necessary.[33]

In cases where the processing interfered with 'the fundamental right to privacy',[34] the Court also noted the relevance of the criteria set out by the ECtHR in *Von Hannover v Germany (No 2)* and, in addition, emphasized the need to take into account 'the possibility for the controller to adopt measures to mitigate the extent of the interference'.[35] This latter stipulation echoed the focus on 'minimum safeguards' in *Digital Rights Ireland*.[36] After providing this guidance, the CJEU passed the issue back to the referring national court. The full implications of the case, therefore, remain somewhat unclear. Nevertheless, the CJEU's reasoning here opens up a new and potentially significant role for national courts and DPAs to shape the contours of legitimate journalistic (and, as will be seen later, other special expressive) processing, especially in those jurisdictions which have (on the face of it) enacted very far-reaching or even absolute exemptions in favour of such activity within their local laws. The extent and nature of this role may be further clarified in the case of *SY v Associated Newspapers*.[37]

2. The Contemporary DPA Resource Context

Although CJEU jurisprudence increasingly points to very expansive responsibilities for DPAs, the resources actually available to these regulators continue to fall well short of these ambitions. As seen in Chapter 7, although otherwise rather mixed, there is evidence that resourcing when measured on the basis of per capita staffing level positively correlates with greater (self-reported) enforcement even in the area of journalism. In any case, it is manifest that if regulation is to be effective and non-arbitrary then it must be properly resourced. Moreover, whilst it is difficult to specify precisely what resources DPAs require to carry out their many tasks, it is clear that these have been seriously deficient in the past. Thus, as Chapter 7 elucidated, the average EEA national DPA has only around €4.2m at its disposal in 2013 that had to be dedicated to regulating the myriad types of processing of personal data that take place across both the public and private sectors. Meanwhile, the total budgets all the national EEA DPAs put together came to only around €130m (which, in any case, was not exclusively allocated to data protection but also to other functions such as freedom of information which these regulators sometimes have within their remit) (see Appendix 5). In contrast, the UK Office of Communications (Ofcom) alone—a somewhat comparable regulator to a single DPA but with a circumscribed role confined to broadcasting, telecommunications, and postal services—benefited from a budget in the same period of around €177.7m (£150.9m).[38]

Unfortunately, it appears that DPA financial and staff resources have only experienced a very modest increase in the intervening period. To explore this systematically, staff[39] and financial figures as disclosed in the Article 29 Working Party's 2013 Annual Report were compared (after adjusting the latter by an average Euro inflation rate of 2 per cent over this period) with 2017 figures obtained from the European Commission (who had in turn obtained them from the Working Party). This suggested that the overall staff resources available to EEA DPAs collectively over this four-year period had increased by 20 per cent, whilst the financial resources had increased by 22 per cent. Whilst not insignificant, these increases must be placed in the context of the substantially increased demands placed on DPAs, which have arisen not only from 'ever accelerating information technology capability' but also a GDPR instrument which, as a result of its expanded obligations and scope,[40] has been described as 'the most ambitious endeavour so far to secure the rights of the individual in the digital realm for a generation'.[41] One may hope for dramatically improved resourcing of these DPAs in the future, not least since the GDPR now places a clear obligation on States to ensure these regulators are 'provided with the human, technical and financial resources, premises and infrastructure necessary for the effective performance of its tasks and exercise of its powers'.[42] Nevertheless, these basic resource constraints must be borne in mind when considering how DPAs can best perform their regulatory role here in the short to medium term.

3. State DPAs, Professional Journalism, and Standard-Setting

The regulatory role both in general and specifically in the area of data protection is complex and multifaceted. Nevertheless, in broad terms, it may be divided into two areas: (a) the interpretation, elucidation and promotion of standards ('standard-setting') and (b) monitoring and enforcing those standards ('enforcement'). These 'soft' and 'hard' sides of regulation are not only widely analysed in the literature[43] but all a DPA's default tasks as laid down in the GDPR fall within one or both these areas.[44] As Chapter 8 explored, compared with the *status quo ante*, many more States have now established special limits on the role and power of their DPA over professional journalism. Nevertheless, the vast majority continue to allocate the ordinary DPA very significant responsibilities here. Moreover, since States are likely to find it impossible to argue that it is 'strictly necessary'[45] to entirely denude DPAs of their authority as 'the guardians' of the 'fundamental rights and freedoms'[46] inherent in data protection here, it may well be that all these regulators retain some such role directly under EU primary law and/or the GDPR itself.[47] This section, therefore, turns to consider how that role should be approached in the area of standard-setting, whilst section 4 looks at the even trickier area of enforcement.

3.1 The Need for, and Dilemma of Data Protection Standard-Setting

Without some elucidation and effective promotion of appropriate standards relating to professional journalism's handling of personal data, data protection's aim to protect the privacy and related fundamental rights and freedoms of natural persons here is likely to be little more than chimerical. Indeed, such standard-setting has been correctly identified as a 'core aspect of any regulatory regime'.[48] As Chapter 5 demonstrated, a clear majority of national DPAs did publish some guidance on standards in this area under the DPD. However, aside from the few regulators who addressed particular issues such as those concerning children, visual and/or audio-visual content, and media archives in some depth, the guidance produced remained very limited. Indeed, in the great majority of cases, it amounted to no more than 1,000 words in each case. This quantitative limit was unsurprisingly associated with only vague references to notions such as ensuring a contextual balancing of rights. This type of extreme vagueness sits in tension with the regulatory literature which emphasizes that standards should have a quality of '[a]ccessibility' which is defined as 'ease of application of a rule to its intended circumstances'.[49]

An elucidation of more detailed standards is, therefore, necessary. However, such elucidation raises acute sensitivities, not least since it must grapple with a core clash of fundamental rights, namely data protection and freedom of expression. Mirroring provisions in a number of State laws passed under the DPD, some DPAs pointed to these sensitivities being best addressed through establishing a co-regulatory connection between statutory and self-regulation. However, even in relation to standard-setting, the appropriate nature of any such connection is far from straightforward. Thus, not least since media self-regulation has itself been criticized as being based on 'lists of vague prohibitions and Utopian wishes',[50] a strong and largely unconditional degree of deference will most likely simply lead to data protection being undermined. Indeed, Chapter 6's elucidation of the responses of DPAs in relation to undercover journalism indicates that an undue leniency was often forthcoming in this context. On the other hand, there is also a danger to freedom of expression if regulators adhere to an exacting approach that takes little account of the practical and philosophical concerns raised within self-regulation. Thus, many DPA questionnaire responses in relation to subject access and even some of the published guidance on specific issues (e.g. children's rights, image rights) raised precisely such problems. Empirically, the divergences in a DPA's stance in these two areas strongly correlated with the presence or absence of relevant norms within self-regulatory codes. Where, as in the case of undercover journalism, self-regulatory codes had in some way addressed the issue, strong deference from the DPA was generally evident. In contrast, as regards matters such as subject access that had been all but ignored by these codes, a rather rigid and unforgiving approach was shown.

Highlighting of these two problematic interfaces provides a useful starting point for shaping a more coherent and even-handed co-regulatory relationship in the future. DPAs should build on the strengths of both statutory and self-regulation and, through a robust interaction between these systems, ensure that concomitant weaknesses are minimized. The strengths which self-regulation can contribute here are especially self-evident. To begin with, given that any intervention in this area will necessarily interfere with these professionals' exercise of a fundamental right, is it integral to good governance that their self-perception be fully taken into account. Beyond these abstractions, those who pursue a vocation within the institutional media have concrete experience juggling 'complex intellectual, legal, commercial and ethical issues every day'[51] in order fulfil the task—central to any liberal and democratic society— of imparting information and ideas to the public at large. They will, therefore, be especially well placed to advise on how data protection checks might be built into existing editorial and other processes rather than cutting across or undermining these. They will also be able to contribute critically to the question of how data protection standards might be best interpreted so as to not unduly undermine expressive freedom.

Nevertheless, a self-regulatory perspective also brings with it a risk that the 'world vision of journalists'[52] will be given disproportionate weight, often at the expense of those whose fundamental rights are negatively and sometimes seriously impacted by journalistic activity. Beyond simple cognitive bias, those professionally engaged in journalism will often have a commercial self-interest in highly intrusive forms of personal data processing. Such self-interest can lead to a severe myopia that prevents individuals recognizing the risk that such processing could cause unwarranted harm and the need to take measures to guard against this. This kind of myopia was epitomized in the extreme sentiments expressed by Paul McMullan, an ex-journalist on the now-defunct News of the World tabloid, at the

UK's Inquiry into the Culture, Practices and Ethics of the Press chaired by Lord Leveson:

> In 21 years of invading people's privacy I've never actually come across anyone who's been doing any good. The only people I think need privacy are people who do bad things. Privacy is the space bad people need to do bad things in. Privacy is particularly good for paedophiles, and if you keep that in mind, privacy is for paedos, fundamental, no one else needs it, privacy is evil.[53]

Another issue to confront is that journalistic self-regulation has generally developed as an alternative to, rather than in direct engagement with, law. Thus, writing comparatively on the development of journalism codes of ethics, Bertrand writes that:

> the code aims at avoiding State intervention . . . When the media cause the public to distrust them, then legislators draft, and sometimes pass, repressive laws. Whenever such a danger looms, it triggers gestures of self-reform amongst professionals, the first of which is to draft a code.[54]

Whilst anything amounting to 'repress[ion]' must clearly be avoided, this quotation highlights the fact that without external pressure, self-regulatory processes will generally fail to engage with all the relevant aspects of the law. They may also simply ossify. Indeed, notwithstanding many new issues which the digital revolution has brought in its wake, Díaz-Campo and Segado-Boj found that only nine of the ninety-nine journalistic codes which they analysed from around the globe included any mention of 'the internet and ICTs' and, even when this was addressed, coverage almost invariably remained very limited.[55]

Turning to consider the strengths, weaknesses, and the role of the statutory DPAs, these bodies have a fundamental responsibility to ensure that the needs of data subjects are safeguarded. They also have specific duties in relation to 'children' and other 'vulnerable natural persons',[56] including anybody with significantly reduced capacities to defend their information interests by reason, for example, of age, learning disability, mental illness, or situational context. They should, therefore, have developed a particular interest and expertise in articulating and defending these rights and interests, as well as ensuring that they are coherently safeguarded across the whole ambit of social and economic life. As pre-eminent examples of an independent and 'quasi-judicial'[57] public authority, DPAs also have a particular duty to ensure that the legal framework is respected. In principle, this includes ensuring adherence to the statutory data protection provisions adopted in relation to journalism which were explored in Chapter 8 . Nevertheless, these provisions must at least be reasonable. In this context, it is increasingly recognized that they must be placed within the context of a more fundamental conflict of legal rights. Indeed, from this vantage point, the CJEU has stressed that DPAs themselves have a particular responsibility to ensure that the journalistic derogation is only applied 'in so far as is strictly necessary'.[58]

DPAs are, therefore, well placed to highlight the presumptive data protection rights which are in play and to require that journalists articulate a cogent justification for any departure from these. The threshold for such a justification will rightly vary greatly between the various provisions. Thus, in light of their severe and sweeping nature, a wide derogation from the sensitive data rules should be considered self-evident since otherwise, data protection would 'radically restrict the freedom of the press'.[59] In contrast, DPAs should require that any significant departure from data protection's accuracy requirements is grounded on a much more specifically justified rationale. Finally, reflecting their own origins in the digital revolution, DPAs have a particular responsibility to monitor the 'development of information and communication technologies [ICTs]'.[60] Indeed, this responsibility has led to these authorities acquiring a wide understanding not only of the development of personal data processing narrowly conceived but also allied areas such as artificial intelligence and algorithms. Especially in light of the general myopia of journalistic self-regulation here, engagement with the media on these issues has particular value.

At the same time, the limitations of DPAs within this area must also be recognized. In particular, given that these regulators are primarily established to vindicate the fundamental right to data protection, it is 'not reasonable' to expect them to be 'equally attuned' to the right of freedom of expression.[61] For example, when seeking to uphold data protection, DPAs may fail to recognize that ECtHR jurisprudence indicates that any interference with journalism (at least if conducted in the 'public interest') must itself meet a strict necessity threshold.[62] Beyond such potential normative bias, it must be recognized that DPAs are not especially responsible for supervising journalism or even freedom of expression activity more widely conceived. It is true that, as this book has demonstrated, a number of these regulators have been activity engaged in this area over many decades. Moreover, especially in the wake of *Google Spain*, many more DPAs have been acquiring valuable understanding of the broader freedom of expression ecosystem. Larger DPAs can and should also structure themselves internally so that a defined unit can acquire expertise and establish a public profile on freedom of expression issues. Indeed, the Italian DPA already has a discrete department for '*libertà di manifestazione del pensiero e cyberbullismo*' ('freedom of thought and cyber-bullying') which deals *inter alia* with the regulation of journalism, content violating the dignity of children, and the 'right to be forgotten' online.[63] Although ultimately not implemented, the Leveson Inquiry similarly recommended that the UK DPA be reconstituted

as an Information Commission, led by a Board of Commissioners with suitable expertise drawn from the worlds of regulation, public administration, law and business, and that active consideration be given in that context to the desirability of including on the Board a Commissioner from the media sector.[64]

Ultimately, however, it must remain the case that DPAs are the final supervisors of personal data processing in a whole range of public and private sector settings. They are, therefore, a quintessential example of a horizontal or cross-cutting regulator. That can result in a valuable overarching or holistic perspective. Nevertheless, it is also likely to result in DPAs lacking a deep familiarity with particular sectors, activities, and practices. The resulting risks in such epistemological weakness are particularly acute *vis-à-vis* journalism (and indeed other forms of special expression) given that supervision here raises issues for the core exercise of freedom of expression and the broader health of liberal democratic societies.

3.2 Achieving and Promoting Co-regulatory Standards

It has been argued that effective governance of professional journalism requires the elucidation and promotion of detailed standards but that, in light of this activity's special and sensitive nature, this should be achieved through a robust system of co-regulation. Such a system can best harness the strengths of both statutory regulation and self-regulation whilst also balancing and mitigating the undoubted weaknesses of both. It remains to be considered, however, how such co-regulation can be concretely actualized and developed. In a few instances, a specific mechanism for doing so is laid down in local legislation. For example, both UK and Italian law include special clauses requiring the DPA to take the lead in drafting a *sui generis* code of conduct for journalism, as well as setting out the precise legal status of the resulting instrument.[65] Nevertheless, in general, a specific modality is not established. Aside from in the few instances where this is statutorily excluded, one possibility is for DPAs to encourage the use of the GDPR's overarching code of conduct provisions as set out in Article 40.[66] Such a code can provide 'a degree of autonomy'[67] for these actors in specifying good practices and can use 'terminology that is unique and relevant' to the professional journalistic context, thereby ensuring a good fit with existing editorial checks and controls. In so far as is feasible, any organization drawing up such an instrument should 'consult relevant stakeholders, including data subjects' on its proposals and 'have regard to submissions received and views expressed in response to such consultations'.[68] Once finalized, the proposals must then be submitted to a DPA which, after providing an opinion on whether the draft code complies with data protection law, must approve it so long as it finds that it 'provides sufficient appropriate safeguards' to protect the position of the data subject.[69]

This code of conduct clause clearly provides one valuable model for actualizing co-regulation. Nevertheless, its processes imply a high degree of cooperation between all relevant actors which, in the often controversial and conflict-riven environment of professional journalism, may be overly optimistic. Not only must a representative body itself propose a code but it (rather than the DPA) must be responsible for ensuring appropriate consultation. Absent significant coordination (which potentially could be informally facilitated by the DPA), there is also a danger of many similar bodies drafting divergent, yet overlapping, codes. Such a fissiparous result would detract from the need for a coherent and legible approach. Indeed, in light of the ongoing convergence brought on by digitization, there is a need for overarching guidance encompassing not just the activity of the professional journalistic media but also the pursuit of special expression (whether journalistic, academic, artistic, or literary) by anybody including individual citizens. This is an issue that will be further considered later in the book, including in Chapters 12 and 13.

However, even if the detail within Article 40 is not considered fully apposite, it helpfully indicates the key requirements of a good co-regulatory process. These include close engagement with those subject to regulation, wider consultation including with data subjects, a presumption of a comprehensive specification of relevant standards, and a transparent process of verifying compliance with the law including the establishment of appropriate safeguards for individuals. In situations where representative bodies do not initiate the production of a code either through Article 40 or a *sui generis* national procedure, DPAs will need to be proactive. Even then, the requirements set down in Article 40 can provide the benchmarks for a process that will similarly culminate in co-regulatory guidance. Moreover, even when some representative bodies do agree to an approved code, DPAs will still need to translate its standards so that it can also speak to a wider range of actors. For example, a code drafted with reference to the institutional media may be helpfully adjusted to account for particular needs of freelance journalists (or, outside the scope of this book, even citizen journalists).

Once such guidance has been produced, it is important that DPAs prioritize its promotion. This last aspect has particular salience since studies have found that related codes are 'hardly known', at least amongst 'non-specialists',[70] and, therefore, inevitably lack impact. Again, serious thought must be given to the variety of parties to whom such guidance should have relevance. Obviously, those actively engaged in professional journalism are of primary importance. However, this group is far from homogenous. Thus, whilst the legal departments of large media organizations might reasonably be expected to digest guidance verbatim, smaller outfits as well as individual journalists are likely to require a considerably more layered approach alongside related training or other support. The need for specific engagement with the last sort of actor is highlighted by the steady growth of freelance journalists who produce material for the institutional media but 'often act outside daily newsroom routines' and therefore risk growing into a ' "journalistic underclass" lacking in ethical awareness'.[71] Another equally important and primary group is the general public. These individuals will generally be concerned to understand the nature of their rights as data subjects, although it is also important (not least from the perspective of regulatory coherence) that the position of 'citizen journalists' and those who produce related special expression material also be specifically addressed. In light of the intrinsically non-specialist nature of this group, a lay summary of the guidance should be formulated. The availability of such a summary, as well as the general role of the DPA in this area, should also be given due attention in general public awareness campaigns conducted by DPAs which flow from their general duty to 'promote public awareness and understanding of the risks, rules, safeguards and rights in relation to processing'.[72] Finally, it is important that the guidance be drawn to the attention of constituencies who lie outside professional journalism but who often deal with issues arising from their activity. The legal and judicial community are of special importance in this context given the role they play in finally interpreting the nature of data protection, as well as reviewing or even crafting remedies in concrete cases. The need for this last form of engagement is particularly highlighted by previous findings that 'legal professionals' are generally 'not aware of the applicable legal procedures and safeguards' concerning data protection and that there has been 'a lack of judges specialising in this area'.[73]

3.3 The Particular Dilemma of Media Archives

One structural issue that any co-regulatory guidance must address is the governance of media archiving. As emphasized throughout Part II of this book, media archiving has been a site of tension between data protection and the media over many decades. Profoundly impacted by the technological changes of the digital revolution, archiving has also shifted from being a relatively discrete activity to one that is fused into the wider practices of professional journalism. This development has undergirded a growing consensus that this activity falls squarely within the journalistic derogation. The media themselves have been especially insistent of the need for this. Thus, during the negotiation of the GDPR, a consortium of media groups argued that 'press freedom and journalism' would be 'seriously undermine[d]' unless the text included '[a] clear reference to "journalistic purposes"' which covered 'for example, storing of personal data in editorial archives, protection of personal data of sources, digital transmission of personal data by publishing articles and maintaining online archives'.[74] Reflecting this, the GDPR not only maintains an explicit derogation for 'journalistic purposes' but also includes a recital explicitly stating that it should apply to 'news archives and press libraries'.[75] At the same time, however, it also separately introduces specific and restrictive provisions concerning 'archiving purposes in the public interest'.[76] Moreover, although EEA States were instructed to provide a journalistic derogation even in relation to these latter provisions, many have failed to do so explicitly.

Media archiving, therefore, constitutes an important but difficult case for DPAs wishing to apply the balanced but robust co-regulatory approach mapped out earlier. As a starting point, it is vital that these regulators recognize and respect the central place of the journalistic (and indeed broader special expression) derogation within the European data protection framework. That centrality flows from the unique purpose of this derogation, which is to reconcile this framework with the core exercise of freedom of expression. It is in light of the 'importance of the right to freedom of expression in every democratic society' that the European legislator has interpreted the journalistic derogation 'broadly'.[77] That same rationale also points to the necessity of according it priority over other provisions within the law that fundamentally conflict with it. Seen from a co-regulatory context, this consideration has heightened importance when the subjects of regulation argue that their practices would otherwise be seriously undermined. Therefore, notwithstanding poor legislative drafting in many States, DPAs must ensure that *bona fide* media archiving[78] can benefit from the journalistic derogation.

At the same time, a balanced approach also points to the need for these regulators to ensure that the justification advanced by journalists for any departure from default data protection standards is duly targeted to the specific processing at issue. Thus, on the one hand, it would be unreasonable to expect the media to review the vast range and quantity of archived data proactively in the same manner as is generally expected when information is published in new journalistic material. Indeed, a 2015 judgment from the Spanish Supreme Court went as far as holding that the media could legitimately assume that its archived content remained legal unless notified otherwise by the data subject.[79] On the other hand, there is generally both an 'absence of any urgency in publishing [archived] material'[80] and the potential for such ongoing publication to have a disproportionate negative impact on individuals over many decades. This suggests that the media should be expected to design their archives so as to meet core default data standards, at least partially. Most clearly, once notified of a significant inaccuracy in an archived story, the media should be required to attach a conspicuous annotation that sets the record straight. More difficult issues arise from the fact that archived material will often fail to represent an 'up to date'[81] picture of the individual. At the least, the media should be obliged to guard against such a lack of 'timeliness' becoming fully misleading by ensuring that archived material prominently displays the date on which it was last substantively updated. Beyond this, the concept of data protection by design[82] suggests that the media should construct their archives such that stories prominently reporting on highly stigmatic events are linked (at least on demand) to later stories which complete the record. Most obviously, an individual who is subject to a report on her arrest for a criminal offence but who is ultimately acquitted might reasonably demand that the original negative story is linked in a digital archive to any later story included in the same archive that reported on the ultimate outcome. Finally, and most controversially, it may be claimed that certain old stigmatic journalistic stories will exhibit such a declining objective public interest that it will be difficult to justify the negative impact on the individual which their continued publication brings. Against this, however, must be placed the general but weighty public interest in 'preserving and making available [old] news and information' as 'an important source for education and historical research'.[83] Moreover, any ongoing disproportionate impact of the digital distribution of old media material may be better addressed through enabling individuals to obtain the deindexing of these stories from Internet search engine results in certain circumstances. Although the regulation of Internet search engines lies outside of the direct focus of this book, its interface with the journalistic media (and other traditional publishers) will be addressed further in Chapter 13.

The kind of outcomes mapped out earlier would depend on DPAs engaging in constructive, yet also challenging, interaction with the media. At times, that would undoubtedly lead to controversy and difficulty. Nevertheless, it is only through such a robust form of co-regulation that a careful and detailed balancing between journalistic freedom of expression and data protection will actually be achieved. Moreover, crafting such a result in the relatively long-standing but important area of media archiving may lay the groundwork for future interactions in novel areas such as automated and algorithmic journalism.[84]

4. State DPAs, Professional Journalism, and Enforcement

4.1 The General Context

Whilst the involvement of DPAs in the elucidation and promotion of journalistic standards certainly raises freedom of expression challenges, concrete enforcement action by these statutory regulators can easily lead to much more acute conflict. Reflective of this, it is essential that the default investigative and corrective powers set down in the European data protection are restricted here. In many instances, these limitations are now set down (at various levels of specificity and depth) within local data protection law.[85] However, even in the absence of this, limits must flow from both national and European fundamental rights law[86] including, for example, to safeguard the confidentiality of journalistic sources and internal communications concerning ongoing media investigations. The large number of DPAs who (notwithstanding the general absence of specific statutory provision in this regard) conceptualized their powers to be limited under the DPD in this area is indicative of a general awareness amongst regulators of the special normative context.[87] Even aside these specific factors, it must also be recognized that full regulatory enforcement can be very expensive. For example, albeit outside the journalistic sector, the 2018 UK DPA investigation into the use of data analytics in political campaigns (which focused on Facebook and Cambridge Analytica) required an investigatory team of over thirty and had cost £2.5m (approximately €2.8m) by October of that year.[88] Given this, and in light of their straitened resources, DPAs must find mechanisms for limiting their need to resort to such direct unmediated action.

Notwithstanding these normative and practical challenges, effective enforcement remains central to the success of data protection in journalism as in other areas. Indeed, the general literature on regulation has copiously documented 'the considerable flaws in a pure "advise and persuade" compliance strategy'.[89] Moreover, the drawbacks of such an approach have been specifically validated in the media context. Thus, Alsius and colleagues' study of the journalists' perceptions of various 'accountability instruments' found that those with the most perceived impact on behaviour, namely internal 'company guidelines' and the 'laws regulating the media', were 'precisely the two most normative instruments, which can have direct effects on the journalist in the case of transgression'.[90] In contrast, numerous specific studies of other media accountability frameworks have found them ineffective due to a lack of real teeth. Such a critique has been forthcoming not only from academics such as Fielden[91] but also official investigations including, most notably, Lord Leveson's Inquiry in the Culture, Practices and Ethics of the Press in the United Kingdom.[92]

Returning to Alsius and colleagues' study, journalists especially perceived that statutory 'regulatory authorities' had only a 'low impact', which the authors went on to hold 'can be explained by the uneven implementation of these instruments in some countries'.[93] This certainly tallies with this book's findings as regards DPAs and professional journalism. Whilst not entirely absent, regulatory enforcement here has been exceedingly patchy and often very limited. Meanwhile, although the presence of self-regulation was sometimes mentioned as a rationale for adopting a limited role here, DPAs generally failed either to articulate a clear account of the intended relationship between statutory and self-regulation or to address the myriad concerns which have been raised as to the practical efficacy of the latter. All this suggests that DPA enforcement here, whilst not entirely meaningless, has generally lacked effectiveness. It is, therefore, important that this deficiency is addressed under the GDPR.

4.2 Crafting a Strategic Enforcement Strategy

As public supervisory authorities, DPAs have a duty to deploy their very limited resources in the 'public interest'. They must therefore adopt a somewhat 'selective'[94] approach. Indeed, seen within that context, the core journalistic areas within which DPAs did prioritize an explicit use of their coercive powers under the DPD appear quite reasonable. These especially involved confronting the illegitimate publication of information which engaged specific privacy interests (particularly when this constituted 'sensitive' data) and safeguarding personal data whose careful management was integral to the activities of non-journalistic controllers who perform a central role in social and economic life (e.g. personal identification numbers). However, what appeared generally absent was evidence of DPAs adopting a strategic approach which, first, explicitly calibrated the extent of direct enforcement to the degree to which the relevant actors demonstrated a respect for applicable data protection standards and, second, systematically assessed regulatory interventions against the data protection framework's overarching requirement to achieve not only balanced but also 'effective and complete'[95] protection of data subjects. The crafting of such an approach holds the most promise for DPAs demonstrably fulfilling their core responsibilities and adding value here. Nevertheless, any such an approach must still respect the data subject's default right to lodge individual complaints with the DPA and the latter's responsibility to progress these in some way.[96] This right reflects the fundamental status of data protection in European law and the centrality of independent control through the DPA within this.[97]

In light not only of the normatively contested nature of this space but (even more so) the very limited resources available to DPAs, a strategic approach must start by seeking to establish a clear connection between statutory and self-regulation (and indeed other cognate co-regulatory or other systems which exist in particular sectors such as broadcasting). However, this connection must be much more nuanced than justifying a severe limit on statutory regulatory enforcement simply by recognizing the mere presence of a self-regulatory or other body operating within roughly the same area. Instead, any strong deference to such an external structure should be acceptable only if the latter has publicly and credibly committed to enforcing the rights and standards laid down in data protection itself. As highlighted in section 3, this could be achieved through the drafting of a code of conduct either under Article 40 of the GDPR or a cognate procedure. Moreover, and as importantly, any self-regulatory monitoring body should be expected to meet the criteria laid down in Article 41 of that instrument. In sum, the body would need to demonstrate that it has independence and expertise; robust processes to assess, monitor, and periodically review those subject to it; effective and transparent procedures and structures to handle complaints; and an absence of tasks and duties that produce a conflict of interest.

Given that those subject to self-regulation here are exercising a core fundamental right, DPAs should be ready to adopt an appropriately flexible approach to some of these criteria. For example, the mere involvement of practising journalists in adjudications should certainly not be judged as intrinsically violating the necessary independence of the process, not least since these individuals can thereby bring a wealth of understanding and experience to such a task. Such flexibility should not, however, detract from DPAs' essential responsibility to verify the integrity and impartiality of any such self-regulatory body transparently. Once any such finding is in place, DPAs should be able to defer to these bodies' handling of individual complaints unless it is shown that either the findings made, or the remedy provided, was unreasonable. Nevertheless, DPAs would still be responsible for actively monitoring these resolutions as well as undertaking a systematic reappraisal of the self-regulatory body both periodically and when and if it becomes aware of any systematic problems. Beyond this, Article 41's explicit stipulation that any such accreditation remain '[w]ithout prejudice to the task and powers'[98] of the DPA itself places an ultimate limit on the extent to which it can effectively delegate its functions here. In sum, even whilst an accredited body remains in good standing and is dealing with all complaints reasonably, a DPA must remain ready to engage in direct intervention as regards both important systematic issues of principle and particularly serious individual cases. In dealing with the latter, however, it must obviously take care to ensure that any sanctions imposed by both the DPA and the self-regulatory body do not cumulatively lead to a disproportionate outcome.

Where a self-regulatory body either cannot be fully accredited or the journalistic controller's activity sits outside this body's jurisdiction, then a DPA should be expected to intervene considerably more vigorously.[99] Several different permutations of this basic scenario must be distinguished. First, a body might meet the accreditation requirements in many but not all areas. For example, it may have appropriate standards and procedures for handling issues arising from initial news production but not as regards rectification claims relating to material that remain publicly archived online. In these cases, the DPA could strongly defer to the body in relation to the former issues but would need to examine the latter in more detail, using its formal investigation and sanctioning powers insofar as proportionate.

Second, it might be that a self-regulatory body has jurisdiction over the same issues as are regulated through data protection but that questions remain as to whether the standards that it implements and/or its procedures vindicate the law's minimum requirements. In furtherance of a general aim of developing a co-regulatory approach, a DPA should liaise and cooperate with such a body. It might even encourage data subjects to lodge complaints through this self-regulatory system and agree to consider any resulting findings when exercising its own jurisdiction. Nevertheless, the DPA's analysis of any resolution could not be confined to a mere reasonableness review and, furthermore, it must remain willing to deploy its investigatory and sanctioning powers across the board proactively.

Finally, it may be that either no other body exists at all or that the journalist falls entirely outside of any such body's jurisdiction. In these cases, the DPA will have no option but to conduct an independent assessment of any complaints and take full responsibility for ensuring that an appropriate level of data protection is achieved. Nevertheless, this should not result in the DPA applying intrinsically more stringent standards on the controller or, still less, attempting to second-guess the responsible exercise of journalistic judgment. In this regard, it must be recognized that the ECtHR has stressed that journalism 'covers possible recourse to a degree of exaggeration or even provocation' and that 'it is not for the Court, any more than it is for the national courts to substitute its own views for those of the press as to what techniques of reporting should be adopted in a particular case'.[100] These fundamental rights allowances are at least as applicable in the context of statutory regulation. More concretely, where a self-regulatory body meeting the relevant standards exists but the controller has not joined it, the DPA should be willing to take account of the approach this body has taken to cognate cases. In any case, the absence of another body exercising regulatory or quasi-regulatory functions should not inevitably result in the DPA deploying its formal powers. To the contrary, this should remain dependent on the relevant actor's broader behavioural stance. Thus, an informal 'advise and persuade' compliance strategy may remain 'valuable in encouraging and facilitating those willing to comply with the law to do so'.[101] By contrast, such a strategy 'may prove disastrous against "rational actors" who are not disposed to voluntary compliance'[102] and must, therefore, be resolutely avoided in such situations. Moreover, since no other regulator will be able to act here, it remains the case that is far more likely that a DPA will need to resort to an explicit use of its investigatory and sanctions powers than in a context where a self-regulatory system is functioning. Nevertheless, in light of their resource constraints and public interest tasks, DPAs cannot be expected to investigate and respond fully to each and every concern raised. However, as the guardians of a framework which promises individuals truly effective and complete protection, they should still actively monitor data subjects' ability to obtain tailored redress for significant violations of their rights which, in this case, would be obtainable either through the DPA itself or through the civil courts. Where such redress is not practically achievable or effective, DPAs should at least draw clear attention to this and propose concrete solutions.

5. A Role for the European Data Protection Board?

5.1 Avoiding a Coercive, Non-Deferential Approach

At least in the new era of the GDPR, an analysis of role of statutory data protection regulation within Europe cannot confine itself to individual States. To the contrary: this instrument is predicated on a dual-layered system of regulation, with DPA representatives assembled in the European Data Protection Board[103] providing guidance to the State DPAs and also overseeing a 'cooperation and consistency'[104] enforcement mechanism as regards 'cross-border processing'. This latter term is defined widely to encompass even the 'processing of personal data which takes place in the context of the activities of a single establishment' within the EEA 'but which substantially affects or is likely to substantially affect data subjects in more than one Member State'.[105] Moreover, as regards the approval of Code of Conducts under Article 40 of the GDPR, the 'cooperation' mechanism is also further engaged insofar as any Code 'relates to processing activities in several Member States'.[106] In the final analysis, the practice of journalism is intrinsically multinational (and, in fact, entirely globalized), not only in terms of the data subjects on which it reports but also as regards the locale in which processing (including, most obviously, direct news gathering) may take place. It is, therefore, easy to see how these cross-border thresholds could formally be considered to have been met. Moreover, as seen in Chapter 8, most Member States have not adopted a complete journalistic derogation from these 'cooperation and consistency' processes, although in over one-third of cases partial limits to its application have been set down in local statutory law.[107]

Notwithstanding the potential applicability of this mechanism, there are strong reasons why the Board should refrain from coercive intervention here. First and foremost, whilst it is true that the pan-European framework as a whole mandates a careful balancing between fundamental rights, its concrete application in such a sensitive area exhibits a broad legitimate variation. This explains much, although not all, of the wide divergences between the different national data protection regimes in this area. Moreover, and as we have also seen, these choices are reflective of deep cultural divergences between these States. In principle, locally situated DPAs have the legitimacy necessary to navigate this complex terrain and, at least as compared with their fellow European counterparts, the requisite understanding to do so effectively. Second, notwithstanding their undoubted transnational characteristics, journalists and the institutional media remain considerably more localized than other cognate 'cross-border' controllers. In particular, in stark contrast to many 'new media' disseminators such as Google and Facebook, the epicentre of the readership of most journalistic outlets remains national or even regional. The practical need for the formal pan-European coordination of regulation is, therefore, much reduced. Third, the decisions of the DPAs are subject to judicial review in all cases, a procedure that includes within it the possibility for interpretative disputes to be sent for preliminary reference to the CJEU (or, in the case of the non-EU EEA, the EFTA Court). Moreover, in egregious cases, enforcement action by the European Commission (or the EFTA Surveillance Authority) is also possible.[108] These more explicitly juridical mechanisms are more appropriate than those of the European Data Protection Board ('EDPB') to the resolve what will inevitably involve highly sensitive and complex conflicts of fundamental rights. Finally, at this stage of European integration, mandated regulatory harmonization in this area is likely to prove counter-productive, potentially triggering a national backlash that could ultimately undermine the development of a pan-European approach.

5.2 The Value of Guidance, Consultation, and Voluntary Cooperation

Whilst the Board should avoid coercive intervention, it can and should perform an important and supportive 'soft' role through adopting and promoting relevant (non-binding) 'guidelines'[109] and facilitating an 'exchange of information',[110] dialogue, and cooperation between the DPAs.[111] As section 3 emphasized, the elucidation of clear, digestible and well-balanced standards remains a pressing challenge. Moreover, notwithstanding key divergences, the regimes at Member State level are based on a harmonized default and a common commitment to fundamental rights balancing. The former is especially clear in the context of a directly applicable Regulation, whilst the latter has been enhanced through the developing jurisprudence of the CJEU and, at least indirectly, also the ECtHR. Smaller DPAs are particularly likely to find working through common issues within the collective setting of the Board of great practical assistance to their own development of more specific guidance. Moreover, given the increasing (even if still limited) '[m]utual interpenetration' of the institutional media and journalism between European States, it has been argued that it is 'particularly important to adopt minimum harmonisation rules covering cross-border media activities on areas such as . . . data protection'.[112] Notwithstanding its lack of binding legal status, guidance from the European Data Protection Board can go some way to achieving this.

In their former collective guise as the Article 29 Data Protection Working Party, the EEA DPAs have already collectively produced a specific recommendation on data protection law and the media and, more recently, have integrated a consideration of specific journalistic issues into a number of their general opinions. The latter has encompassed consideration of the interface between online media archives and the 'right to be forgotten' and the use of drone technology by the media.[113] However, the only specific pan-European recommendation in this area, which dates from 1997, has not only become out of date but was only ever couched in the most general and vague terms. Meanwhile, the group's more detailed coverage of particular issues has remained limited and, partly as a result of their placement in opinions primarily dealing with other issues, have failed to achieve significant visibility.

It would, therefore, be helpful for the Board to produce new and comprehensive guidance that addresses the various interfaces between data protection and freedom of expression that arise here. Such guidance should draw on DPA experience in this area, the new GDPR framework, and developing CJEU and ECtHR case law. Moreover, in furtherance of data protection's goal of ensuring the coherent development of information practices, this guidance should not be confined to the professional journalistic media but should encompass anybody pursuing journalistic purposes or, indeed, the other forms of special expression that will be examined in Part III of this book. The formulation of such special expression guidance will necessarily involve DPAs sharing concrete examples of interpretation and enforcement as well as engaging in a dialogue about good practice. Moreover, in particularly pressing cases, such generic guidance could be supplemented through the Board giving more specific advice on particular cases.[114] Finally, it should be provided that, in so far as this is consistent with their own substantive and procedural frameworks, DPAs should be willing to assist one another in concrete enforcement efforts even within the area of journalism and other forms of special expression. With such an emphasis on voluntary cooperation as opposed to coercion, the work of the Board can make a positive contribution to increasing legal and regulatory certainty in this area and ensuring the incremental development of pan-European norms.

6. Conclusions

State laws implementing the GDPR almost invariably allocate DPAs (or in a few instances specialist statutory bodies) a supervisory role over professional journalism that is important but also difficult and delicate. The detail of such a role continues to depend both on these statutory provisions and on the broader local context. Nevertheless, not only does the essential rights balancing task of DPAs remain similar but these regulators also confront a range of more specific common issues. As a result, it is valuable to look in general at how DPAs might best approach the discharge of their role here. Such an analysis must take full account not only of the GDPR itself but also both pan-European jurisprudence and the resourcing context. In this regard, developing ECtHR case law points to the need for a contextualization of the balancing between the information impacting on 'private life'[115] and freedom of expression, whilst the CJEU has increasingly emphasized an independent and potentially extensive role for data protection and DPAs across all areas of information processing. At the same time, the resources available to DPAs remain extremely modest, a limitation that inevitably constrains what contribution they can make.

Drawing on the above, past DPA experience, and the regulatory literature, it has been proposed that State DPAs should develop a co-regulatory strategic approach both in the area of standard-setting and enforcement. Turning first to standards, it has been argued that guidance will only be effective if it goes beyond vague references to such (admittedly critical) concepts as contextual balancing. At the same time, the crafting of more detailed guidance raises acute sensitivities. Past regulatory practice, the GDPR, and many local statutes all point to this being best addressed through co-regulation. This co-regulation must be finely balanced, avoiding both the granting of an unqualified strong deference to self-regulatory norms and the adoption of a rigid prescriptive stance by the DPAs. In the absence of an alternative local mechanism, the GDPR's general code of conduct clause sets out a valuable mechanism for achieving such a robust co-regulatory result. However, given that it depends on self-regulatory bodies themselves consulting on and then putting forward a code for DPA approval, its detail may imply a degree of cooperation that is unrealistic in this controversial context. Nevertheless, the clause's emphasis on ensuring a degree of autonomy for those subject to regulation, wider consultation, a transparent process of verification, and a presumption of comprehensiveness all highlight criteria that any co-regulatory process should meet. Finally, once guidance on standards is in place, it is important that it is systematically promoted, not only to large media actors but also others including individual journalists, the general public, and the legal community.

Turning to enforcement, it is clear that both fundamental rights law and the challenging resource context point to a bounded role for statutory supervision here. In this context, it is understandable that DPAs have taken note of the role of self-regulation and prioritized using their enforcement powers in particular areas, notably where publication or other journalistic processing activity affects specific privacy interests (especially in relation to 'sensitive' data) or impacts on the basic functioning of social and economic life (e.g. the misuse of personal identification numbers). Nevertheless, what must be developed alongside this is an explicitly strategic approach that systematically takes account of the extent to which relevant actors demonstrate a respect for applicable data protection standards. In particular, any strong deference to self-regulatory enforcement should be confined to situations where this body's code and monitoring mechanism have been verified either through Articles 40 and 41 of the GPDR or a cognate *sui generis* procedure. In cases where a self-regulatory body exists but has not met such verified standards, the DPA should proactively deploy its investigatory and sanctioning powers, whilst continuing to liaise and cooperate with this body. Finally, DPAs will need to adopt an even more independent and proactive stance where either no self-regulatory body exists or where the relevant professional journalist has decided to operate outside of its jurisdiction. Even here, the need for a DPA to deploy its formal powers should still depend on an analysis of the wider behavioural context. Thus, whilst a 'soft' compliance strategy may prove valuable as regards those broadly committed to meeting balanced data protection standards, a credible threat of formal investigation and sanctioning remains essential in relation to those who are resistant to this.

Alongside national action, the role of the European Data Protection Board must be considered. Notwithstanding a pan-European commitment to fundamental rights balancing, local data protection laws often continue to exhibit legitimate wide divergence and local DPAs have the particular legitimacy and understanding to navigate within the resulting complex legal terrain. Therefore, even where the GDPR's 'cooperation and consistency' mechanism may remain formally engaged, the Board should avoid adopting a coercive and non-deferential approach. Nevertheless, it can perform a valuable 'soft' role by adopting non-binding guidance, exchanging information, and promoting dialogue and cooperation. Such work would particularly aid the work of the smaller DPAs and, more generally, could increase legal and regulatory certainty and contribute to the slow development of a more pan-European approach.

The role of the Board mapped out earlier points to the emphasis that European data protection rightly places on ensuring the coherent regulation of information processing. In this context, it is important to recognize that the pursuit of professional journalism sits in a relationship of varying proximity to that of a wide variety of other controller activities. Digitization has seen the growth of 'new media' actors including, at one end of the scale, individual online publishers and, at the other, powerful corporate outfits such as Internet search engines. However, whilst sharing some important similarities with the journalistic media, these entities often do not pursue either journalism or a similarly special type of freedom of expression. Their interface with professional journalism will, therefore, be returned to in this book's conclusion. In contrast, professional artists, writers, and many academics are centrally, ubiquitously, and by vocation engaged in the same sorts of special expression as that carried out by the journalistic media. It is, therefore, important for this study to analyse in detail how they have, and should be, regulated. That will be the task of Part III of this book.

PART III

EUROPEAN DATA PROTECTION AND 'NON-JOURNALISTIC' TRADITIONAL PUBLISHERS

10

European Data Protection Regulation and 'Non-Journalistic' Traditional Publishers

First- and Second-Generation Developments Outside Academia

It is often claimed that, prior to the genesis of truly 'new' online media, professional journalists were the only actors engaged in generating and imparting information and ideas for the public at large. For example, Möller states in this vein that '[a] few years ago, only professional journalists were able to publish information', whereas 'today everybody can create content and distribute at very low cost to a global audience'.[1] Without seeking to downplay the profound significance of recent socio-technological change, this characterization of the past is overdrawn. Alongside journalists, and well before today's wide variety of digital outputs, professional writers and artists have created and disseminated material for society at large through books, pamphlets, specialist journals, and exhibitions. In fact, these 'non-journalistic'[2] forms of publisher have an historical pedigree than is even more extensive than that of the journalistic media. Brock notes that early journalism was merely an 'appendage' to a printer's business and '[v]ery early newspapers often took the form of books' being 'an improvised mixture of history and almanac'.[3] Moreover, the output of professional writers and artists has held a similar social significance to that of professional journalism,[4] being grounded in the same assumption that 'there is public value and importance' in these acts of creation and dissemination even if the number of those directly interested may remain 'small or specialized'.[5] Indeed, within the Western tradition, the free production and spread of work created by writers has been seen as the most central instance of freedom of expression. John Milton's seminal *Areopagitica* (1644) focused on this type of expression in the form of books, arguing that:

> books are not absolutely dead things, but do contain a potency of life in them to be as active as that soul whose progeny they are; nay, they do preserve as in a vial the purest efficacy and extraction of that living intellect that bred them . . . [U]nless wariness be used, as good almost kill a man as kill a good book: who kills a man

European Data Protection Regulation, Journalism, and Traditional Publishers. David Erdos, Oxford University Press (2019). © David Erdos.
DOI: 10.1093/oso/9780198841982.003.0010

kills a reasonable creature, God's image; but he who destroys a good book, kills reason itself, kills the image of God, as it were, in the eye.[6]

More concretely, like journalists, many writers are 'professional students of the social world,'[7] dedicated to imparting their acquired knowledge and understanding to society at large. It has been similarly argued that those who 'create, perform, distribute or exhibit works of art' also 'contribute to the exchange of ideas and opinions which is essential for a democratic society'.[8] All these activities may require the gathering, analysis, and dissemination of sometimes highly sensitive personal data which, on occasion, can raise many of the same data protection concerns that were addressed in relation to professional journalism in Part II. These concerns might, for example, relate to the protection of the privacy, reputation, or the dignity of individual natural persons.

In light of these factors, it is important that this book focuses not only on data protection regulation's interaction with the professional journalistic media but also with its similar interface with these other traditional publishers. That will be the task of the Part III of this book. The current chapter begins by exploring the experience of both professional artists and writers working in a non-academic context (hereinafter professional artists and writers).[9] Chapter 11 will focus on academic authors and publishers who, as will be seen, have historically been conceived within European data protection regulation as quite distinct. Finally, Chapter 12 will look to the future, exploring not only the formal changes which the General Data Protection Regulation 2016/679 and national implementing legislation introduce here but also how these might best be interpreted and applied within third-generation data protection regulation.

This chapter is divided into four sections. It starts by considering relevant aspects of the formal legal instruments established at both the pan-European and State level under first- and second-generation data protection. Sections 2 and 3 then shift the focus to look at the standard-setting and enforcement efforts of Data Protection Authorities ('DPAs') in this area during these same two periods. Finally, section 4 summarizes the main findings of the chapter, linking them back to the broader themes of the book as a whole.

1. Legal Instruments and Professional Writers and Artists

1.1 First-Generation Legal Instruments

From the outset, there had clearly been serious tension—both potential and actual—between the default norms of European data protection and the practices of writers and artists working with personal data. Practically, this tension arose initially principally in relation to textual output but, as digitization

Table 10.1 First-Generation European Data Protection Laws (with Year of Initial Adoption) and Freedom of Expression Derogations outside Journalism/Media

No specific derogations (7/58%)	Very limited derogations (3/25%)	More extensive derogations (2/17%)
Sweden—1973	Denmark—1978	Finland—1987
Germany—1977	Iceland—1981	Netherlands—1988
Austria—1978	Norway—1978/9	
France—1978		
Luxembourg—1979		
United Kingdom—1984		
Ireland—1988		

progressed, it came also to involve audio and/or visual material. Despite this, these issues were left completely unaddressed in the Council of Europe Privacy Resolutions of the 1970s, the Data Protection Convention of 1981, and in all their official explanatory material. In slight contrast, and as elucidated in Table 10.1, five out of the twelve States which adopted data protection statutes prior to 1990 grappled with certain aspects of this issue by including special derogatory provisions within their local law. Two of these derogations were of very limited scope. Thus, Denmark only excluded processing 'for use in biographical research or for publication in ordinary works of reference',[10] whilst Iceland similarly only excluded biographical writing.[11] Rather more extensively, Finland stated that the data protection provisions 'shall not affect the right to publish printed matter' and the Netherlands provided an exemption for 'books and other written publications and catalogues thereof'.[12] Finally, Norway avoided addressing this issue directly in the primary legislation which it enacted in 1978. However, secondary legislation (which was adopted in 1979) provided that internal databases used by publishers in the production of '*biografisk, konversasjonsleksikon og fagleksika*' ('biographies, conversational and subject-based works') did not need to obtain a license to hold sensitive data so long as they complied with security guarantees.[13] A separate and full exemption was set out for '*boker tidsskrifter e.l.*' ('books, journals/magazines and the like') but only in so far as such material had been published prior to the data protection legislation coming into force.[14] It bears emphasis that the scope even of these latter derogations remained quite limited. Thus, as the Council of Europe's report on *Data Protection and the Media* in 1990 stated:

> Finland's Personal Data File Act contains a provision to the effect that it shall not affect the right to publish printed matter . . . Nevertheless, it is clear from the proceedings leading to the enactment of the Personal Data File Act that the act

applies to personal data files—both automated and manual—which are kept as organised background data and are used as part of broadcasting or publishing activities.[15]

Finally, the majority of States which adopted data protection law in this period failed to address these problems explicitly within their law in any way. Nevertheless, in some cases this may partially be explained by the considerable divergence in the general stringency and even the scope of data protection in Europe in this early period. Most notably, both UK and Irish law set out a general exclusion in their law for processing performed only 'for the purpose of preparing the text of documents'.[16] Whilst not adopted with a free speech rationale in mind, these provisions had the potential to shield a good deal of activity orientated solely towards final publication in hardcopy, a format which remained the dominant means of communicating information and ideas to the general public at this time.

1.2 Second-Generation Legal Instruments

In contrast to the earlier Council of Europe instruments, the Data Protection Directive 95/46 ('DPD') proposed a specific regime applicable not only to processing solely for 'journalistic purposes' but also for 'the purpose of artistic or literary expression'. Neither its governing article nor the accompanying recitals[17] drew a fundamental distinction between the 'journalistic purposes' examined in Part II and the other special expressive purposes which concerned literature and the arts. States were therefore placed under a positive obligation to enact potentially far-reaching derogations across this space, albeit only if (and insofar) as they were 'necessary to reconcile the right to privacy with the rules governing freedom of expression'.[18]

As detailed in Chapter 5, the legislative history of this special regime traced back to a provision in the Commission's original 1990 proposal which was expressly limited to the 'press and the audiovisual media'.[19] Meanwhile, the Commission's amended draft in 1992 still sought to limit derogations here to processing 'solely for journalistic purposes by the press, audio-visual media and journalists',[20] although an accompanying explanatory memorandum did state that the latter phrase was 'intended to include photojournalists and writers such as biographers'.[21] The push to broaden Article 9 significantly came in October 1993 when the Belgian Presidency proposed adding the purpose of 'creation artistique ou littéraire' alongside that of journalistic purposes, whilst also deleting any limiting reference to specific classes of person who could benefit from the derogations.[22] No less than eight out of the then twelve EU States expressed unease at this suggestion.[23] Nevertheless, their principal concerns were not that the activities of professional writers and artists might thereby be safeguarded but rather that the wording might extend to any work of intellectual property including (potentially all) databases containing personal data.[24] To address these concerns, the English wording was changed to refer not to 'artistic or literary creation',[25] a phrase which aped that used in an intellectual property context, but rather 'artistic or literary expression'.[26] The EU Council also agreed two common Statements for the Minutes stating that 'copyright protection of artistic or literary works will not affect this Directive' and that 'literary and artistic expression is a form of expression, freedom of which is guaranteed by Article 10 of the European Convention on Human Rights'.[27]

Table 10.2 summarizes the national implementation of the special expression regime outside of journalism in the era of the Data Protection Directive 95/46 ('DPD').[28] As can be seen, twenty-one European Economic Area (EEA) States (66 per cent) safeguarded not only journalistic purposes but also literary and artistic expression[29] within their special expression regime or, in four cases,[30] even set out a freedom of expression protection which extended beyond these defined special purposes. In contrast, one (3 per cent) State (Cyprus)[31] provided for such derogations outside journalism only where the expression in question was artistic. Meanwhile, seven States (22 per cent) either limited protection to the institutional media[32] or, in one case (Greece),[33] to journalistic purposes. Finally, and as explored in Chapter 5, three (9 per cent) States[34] failed to set out any explicit freedom of expression safeguards in their law at all.

Where non-journalistic special expression was recognized, national law almost always set down derogations which were identical or comparable to that

Table 10.2 Scope of Specific Non-Journalistic/Media Freedom of Expression Derogations in Second-Generation EEA State Data Protection Law

(At least) artistic and literary (21/66%)		Artistic only (1/3%)	None (10/31%)
Belgium	Luxembourg	Cyprus	Austria
Bulgaria	Malta*		Croatia**
Denmark*	Netherlands		Czechia**
Finland	Norway		Estonia
France	Poland		Germany
Gibraltar	Portugal		Greece
Iceland*	Romania		Hungary
Ireland	Slovakia		Liechtenstein
Italy	Sweden*		Slovenia
Latvia	United Kingdom		Spain**
Lithuania			

* Set out specific freedom of expression derogations going beyond all the defined special purposes.
** Set out no specific freedom of expression derogation at all.

applicable to the journalistic media. However, Denmark and France enacted non-journalistic derogations which were clearly less stringent than those applicable to the institutional media, whilst Cyprus and Italy in contrast adopted more stringent provisions here. In Denmark, special expressive processing pursued outside of the institutional media was not subject to *Lov om massmediers informationsdatabaser* (or the Media Liability Act) but was still exempt from all the substantive and supervisory oversight provisions in general data protection law.[35] Meanwhile, in France, literary and artistic expression was granted an absolute exemption from registering processing with the DPA and, furthermore, the benefit of the other derogations was, in contrast to journalism, not made subject to the following the 'ethical rules' of any profession.[36] Conversely, in Cyprus, artistic expression was not granted an exemption from the proactive transparency rules which were made available for journalism.[37] Finally, in Italy, the minimal derogation from subject access which ensured the confidentiality of sources did not apply to non-journalistic forms of special expression.[38] If the measure of substantive stringency presented in the context of professional journalism in Chapter 5 is applied, then these differences result in the quantitative measure for Denmark and France shifting down from 0.15 to 0 and from 0.53 to 0.27 respectively, whilst the Cypriot and Italian measure variously increases from 0.65 to 0.85 and from 0.65 to 0.67. Finally, it should be noted that, in the case Denmark, the regulatory supervisory measure shifts from 0.5 (partial supervision) to 0 (no supervision) here. Appendix 8 details the minimum substantive stringency, regulatory supervision, and combined regulated stringency of data protection law as regards non-journalistic expression (however that term was defined locally) within EEA States (and DPD jurisdictions) under the DPD.

Finally, even in those jurisdictions which established special expression derogations beyond journalism, any co-regulatory features of the law which were directly laid down[39] were generally not applicable here. Thus, in Italy, the requirement placed on the DPA and the National Order of Journalists to cooperate in the production and enforcement of a code only directly instantiated co-regulation as regards professional journalism, although, in fact, the code ultimately adopted had a wider reach than this. In Luxembourg, only a representative of the Press Council was entitled to be present when and if the DPA examined special expression data vicariously on behalf of a data subject who had made a subject access request. Meanwhile, Maltese law only envisaged the DPA drawing up a code of practice in relation to journalists and the media,[40] the Lithuanian Inspector of Journalist Ethics was granted supervisory powers over literary and artistic expression as well as journalistic purposes but lacked direct co-regulatory features in this context[41] and UK law specified self-regulatory and co-regulatory codes of practice which related to journalism but did not do likewise as regards other forms of special expression.[42] Whilst these differences did not intrinsically mandate a divergence in the substantive or supervisory stringency of legal regulation here, they did provide less clear guidance to DPAs as to how they should approach their tasks outside of the professional journalistic context.

2. First-Generation DPA Standard-Setting and Enforcement

The Council of Europe's Expert Committee on Data Protection engaged with the interface between data protection and freedom of expression through its report on *Data Protection and the Media* which was published in 1991. Nevertheless, as its title suggests, this report was in principle confined to an examination of the publishing and related activities of the professional journalistic media. Moreover, the legal position of non-journalistic professional artists and writers (outside academia) was not otherwise addressed by this Committee or indeed related bodies such as the International Conference of Data Protection Commissioners. As a result, during the first generation of European data protection, no pan-European (or other transnational) guidance was forthcoming which focused on this broader field of special expression at all.

Turning to the State level, DPAs also proved reluctant to proffer guidance or set out specific standards here. Nevertheless, their generic publications often supported an expansive interpretation of the law, a reality that sometimes prompted attention from those who were at least linked to professional writers and artists. For example, the UK DPA's guidance from 1985 held that those who maintained 'information or data banks as a reference tool or a general resource' were obliged to register with the DPA even if such resources included nothing more than 'bibliographic' information.[43] Moreover, a consortium of library and associated bodies who produced more detailed notes on these issues were further advised by this DPA that 'any person or organisation downloading information from an online bibliographic database, and holding that information in a machine-readable form, must also register' under the law.[44] Clearly, this could easily have included many professional writers and perhaps even some artists. Related to this, both the UK and Irish DPAs adopted an extremely narrow understanding of the exception for document text production which, as noted previously, was set out in each of these States' first-generation laws.[45] For example, the Irish DPA stated:

> if any other operations are performed (e.g. retaining the text on disk for future reference) then the special provision will not apply. Situations in which the special provision applies in practice are very rare since in most wordprocessing systems it is usual to retain documents on disk after the text has been printed out. Such systems will come within the scope of the Act. It will be recalled that the Act applies to personal data kept or processed on every type of computer whether mainframe, minicomputer, microcomputer or wordprocessor.[46]

This kind of interpretation prompted some concern. Thus, Marcel Berlins writing in *The Times* in 1987 noted not only that 'freelance journalists who keep information on the people they are writing about on their Amstrads' came within this law and were obliged to register with the DPA, but that such requirements also extended to 'biographers of living people' and that the resulting legal responsibilities on the latter 'perhaps' had 'more serious potential consequences'.[47] Nevertheless, aside from (albeit potentially irksome and even privacy intrusive) formalities such as registration, the guidance produced by the DPAs themselves generally failed to elaborate specifically on the implications of subjecting writers and artists to data protection stipulations.

A very partial exception to this relates to the Swedish DPA's guidance produced in 1992 concerning the application of data protection to media distributed via CD-ROM. This guidance arose out of an awareness that CD-ROMs were being used to distribute large amounts of information in a wide range of products including not only directories of various sorts but also *inter alia* encyclopaedias. The DPA argued that the original producer of these materials should be held responsible under data protection for the information stored even when the discs entered the hands of a third party.[48] It then proceeded to detail a number of concrete applications of such an approach. For example, in relation to the distribution of a credit information database, the DPA stated that it had required that the company encrypt the data, guarantee that the names of natural persons were not searchable, regularly recall and reissue discs so as to enable information to be corrected and/or anonymized, and finally ensure that subscribers did not continue to hold automatically processed data which had been included on previous (but not the current) discs. In contrast, and as noted in Chapter 4, the DPA permitted two newspaper archives to be distributed without restriction on CD-ROM, albeit initially only on a limited trial basis. The guidance suggested that the production of an encyclopaedia containing personal data would also require data protection permission. However, beyond this, it failed to indicate how stringently or otherwise this kind of product or indeed any other similar literary output would be assessed and then regulated.[49]

Mirroring the general lack of standard-setting guidance, there was little evidence that DPAs engaged in the direct enforcement of first-generation data protection law here. Again, however, the Swedish DPA proved a notable exception. Following the procedure laid down in statute,[50] (and perhaps influenced by the regulatory pronouncements noted above) in 1993 a writer applied for a license to write, process, and store a book manuscript on a personal computer. It was stated that the text would contain sensitive personal data and opinions and would be stored indefinitely. The DPA refused to grant such a license, raising concerns over the length of time personal data would be stored and the absence of any particular protective measures in relation to this.[51] As was permissible under Swedish law at the time, the individual appealed against this to the Government. The latter then held that insofar as processing was a direct technical means for producing a printed publication, the Swedish Freedom of the Press Act would apply. The first section of this very long-standing and 'constitutional' statute in Sweden *inter alia* prohibited (and continues to prohibit) any prior censorship of writing. The Government's reasoning led to the conclusion that the DPA had been wrong to hold that the writer needed to obtain a license in this case at all. The latter accepted this resolution of the issue in the concrete case, whilst arguing that that the Government's approach failed to resolve the conflict between the two sets of laws in this area.[52]

3. Second-Generation DPA Standard-Setting and Enforcement

3.1 Standard-Setting Guidance

Not dissimilarly to their approach under first-generation data protection, DPAs generally avoided addressing the relationship between the DPD and the activity of professional writers and artists. Thus, as regards pan-European guidance, the Article 29 Working Party's 1997 recommendation on *Data Protection Law and the Media* baldly stated:

> Article 9 [of the DPD] provides for limitations and exemptions from the application of certain provision of the directive in relation to processing of data for journalistic purposes as well as for the purpose of artistic and literary expression. The debates of the Working Party focused on data processing by the media for journalistic purposes. The present recommendation therefore focuses on exemptions and derogations in relation to processing for journalistic purposes.[53]

The Working Party did not return to consider the position of professionals who engaged in such literary and artistic purposes in any subsequent opinion or recommendation during the time of the DPD.

Given the clear regulatory reluctance to engage in this area, it was decided not to include any questions focused specifically on this in the 2013 DPA questionnaire.[54] Nevertheless, the DPA website review,[55] which was also carried out in 2013, did seek out any readily available standard-setting guidance, as well as evidence of enforcement activity, which directly related to these non-journalistic actors.

The guidance located was (as expected) not extensive. Unsurprisingly, none of the eleven DPAs which failed even to set out guidance on the relationship between data protection and journalism provided any elucidation of the legal and regulatory position of literary and artistic expression. Meanwhile, only approximately five of the twenty-one DPAs that did address the substantive interface between data protection and journalism and/or the media[56] provided any elucidation of the position of literature and art. In the case of the Netherlands DPA, the failure to consider these latter purposes was at least explicitly acknowledged, albeit along-side a rather dubious rationale:

> The Wbp [Data Protection Act] only partially applies to the processing of per-sonal data for exclusively journalistic, artistic or literary purposes. Only the ex-emption for the purposes of journalism is discussed in further detail in these Guidelines, in view of the fact that appeals are seldom made for an exemption for artistic or literary purposes.[57]

Such a lacunae appeared particularly glaring when the relevant jurisdiction's formal law or, even more problematically, the rest of the DPA's own guidance otherwise pointed to very serious restraints on the exercise of freedom of expression. The former problem was highlighted in Czechia,[58] Hungary,[59] and Slovenia[60] since the statutory data protection law of these States did not explicitly set out any significant provision in favour of special expression at all. Meanwhile, the latter was epitom-ized in a 2001 recommendation of the French DPA which indicated that identi-fied criminal and other jurisprudential information should not be published on the open Internet, specifying a derogation in this regard only as regards the media.[61] A different part of the French website did, at least, clarify that the derogation from the obligation to register processing with the DPA applied not only in relation to journalistic purposes but also that of artistic and literary expression.[62]

In a few instances, the substantive regulation of literary and artistic expression was explicitly mentioned but the actual analysis reverted back to journalism. For example, the Belgium DPA summarized derogations in national law from the sen-sitive data restrictions, the proactive transparency rule, subject access, and the right of opposition. Whilst it was explicitly stated that these derogations applied not only as regards processing *'aux seules fins de journalisme'* ('for the sole pur-pose of journalism') but also *'d'expression artistique ou littéraire'* ('artistic and lit-erary expression'), the page went on to stress that these limits *'peut être invoquée au nom de la liberté de la presse, en particulier par un journaliste accrédité ou par toute personne remplissant un tel role'* ('may be invoked in the name of freedom of the press, in particular by an accredited journalists or by any person performing such a role'). This focus was not unsurprising given that the page as a whole was entitled *'Limitation pour des finalités journalistiques'* ('Limitation for journalistic purposes'). [63] Somewhat similarly, the Spanish national DPA's 1994 Annual Report noted that, as with the preparation of news or reports intended for the newspaper, radio, and television media, the processing of a biographical work would fall within Article 9's special expression regime being, in this case, an example of *'expresión literaria o artística'* ('literary or artistic expression').[64]

Only in the case of Italy and Malta was significant guidance located which did explicitly address literary and/or artistic expression. The Italian DPA explored these activities within a chapter of its somewhat misleadingly titled e-book *Privacy e giornalismo* ('Privacy and Journalism'). However, the principle focus of this 'non-journalistic' discussion was on the manifestation of thought by individuals on the Internet rather than the output of professional writers and artists. The guidance stressed that essentially the same derogatory regime applied here as for journalists but that certain *'punti fermi'* ('fixed points')[65] had to be adapted for what was far more varied human activity. In this regard, the DPA held that *'dell'interesse pubblico'* ('public interest')[66] could not be used as an evaluation criterion in relation to artistic expression. At the same time, however, it argued that individual rights—in particular to privacy, dignity, and personal identity—as well as principles such as information being essential in some way, relevance, and non-excessiveness still had to be respected within this broader sphere.

Meanwhile, the Maltese DPA published detailed and far-reaching guidance which focused on just one area of artistic expression, namely 'street photography'.[67] Whilst stating that it recognized 'the artistic attributes which certainly drive photographers to capture un-posed and un-staged images, predominantly when such images identify natural persons who happen to be in public places',[68] it found that any publication of identifiable images should satisfy a range of stipulations including 'providing adequate information to the data subject and seeking his consent'.[69] In cases where obtaining consent was not a realistic prospect, it held that the individual should be rendered unidentifiable by, for example, 'blurring of the face'. The guide went further by stating that, even if consent was originally obtained, a photographer should remove an image from online publication if an individual later adduced compelling legitimate grounds for this. However, in some tension with this very rigorous approach, the DPA stated that 'each case should be evaluated on its merits' and that, in this regard, it took into account whether the photograph was taken in a public place, at a public event, involved an image of a public person, and finally whether the publication was in the public interest.[70] Nevertheless, its principal note of warning remained as follows:

> Where the photographer fails to obtain the consent and forges ahead with publication, the same photographer may be subject to action (depending on the nature of the case) by this Office if a complaint is lodged or may even face a civil claim for compensation from the individual(s) concerned.[71]

Whilst this DPA signalled back in 2006 that it was in discussion with the Institute of Maltese Photographers and intended to produce guidance on photography,[72] there was no evidence that this professional body was ultimately involved in the production of the final guidance or that it had endorsed it.

3.2 Enforcement

Turning to look at enforcement, only two clear instances of action were located through the DPA website review. The Italian DPA detailed a 2008 investigation into a book *Ho vista l'uomo nero* ('I saw the black man') by Claudio Cerasa[73] which reconstructed a judicial case into alleged sexual abuse in the small municipality of Rignano Faminio. The resulting regulatory decision, which had been prompted by complaints made on behalf of a number of data subjects, accepted that the book generally constituted a legitimate exercise of the right to report and criticize facts of social or public relevance. Nevertheless, it also found that the inclusion of the full names of a number of the parents and the initials of several of the children may have rendered some of the latter identifiable. This was held to conflict with the need under data protection to give precedence to the private sphere of children through a case-by-case analysis. Such an (albeit still flexible and contextual) prioritization was found to have even greater force within the sexual sphere. However, beyond setting out this violation and urging that these issues be addressed in any re-publication of the book, the decision did not set out any remedy for the individual complainants.[74]

Meanwhile, the Slovenian DPA detailed a rather more interventionist approach that it had adopted in relation to the pursuit of photographic activity which was somewhat similar to that explored in the Maltese DPA's guidance cited earlier. In 2009, this DPA investigated a publisher of 360-degree panoramic photographs of Ljubljana and other places in Slovenia which, as a result of their high resolution, allowed for the enlargement of individual images or other details. Upon the initiation of the DPA investigation, the photographer ceased all publication of the photographs. Nevertheless, the regulator's inspection procedure continued with an examination of a sample of the material at issue. As should be recalled from discussion in Part II of this book, this DPA uniquely sought to restrict the general scope of European data protection by invoking the limiting concept of a 'filing system', even in relation to automatically processed data.[75] Nevertheless, the DPA's decision here held not only that the panoramic pictures sometimes included identifiable personal data (in the form of, for example, a person's face, specific clothing worn by an individual, or even a car plate number which could link back to an individual) but also that the digital image would constitute a 'filing system'. The DPA then divided these photographs into two categories, namely photographs of events such as marathons and festivals and photographs of geographical locations or architecture. As regards the first category, the DPA held that the legitimate interests of the photographer were overriding and so legality under data protection was established.[76] In contrast, turning to the latter group, the DPA held that the capturing of identifiable data was 'not important in any respect as regards the purpose of the photographs' and so a legal basis for this processing was absent. The photographer was therefore ordered to (a) irreversibly anonymize (e.g. via blurring) any personal data included in these (potentially publishable) images; (b) ensure further anonymization if an individual neverthe-less recognized him/herself in the images and requested this, (c) securely handle any non-anonymized photographs including ensuring that they were not com-municated to third parties without a legal basis, and finally (d) when recording in locations where 'there is exists a possibility' that sensitive personal data[77] might be captured (e.g. 'places of worship, hospitals, schools'), ensure that photographs were only taken at a time when there are 'as few visitors to such institutions as possible'.[78]

Finally, the ambiguous Polish case from 2005 which was also discussed in Chapter 7 on journalistic enforcement should be mentioned here also. In sum, the Polish DPA (unsuccessfully) sought to institute criminal proceedings against Bronisław Wildstein for his role in the surreptitious obtaining and publication of an index of the Polish Institute of National Remembrance containing the names of at least 160,000 individuals who were in some way associated with the secret service of the former Communist regime. The case is ambiguous since, although Wildstein was a freelance writer (and journalist) by profession, information within this index was not published within the context of his literary (or journalistic) work. Instead, it was simply made available in full online.[79] Moreover, Wildstein continued to claim that he had merely made the index available to 'a few trusted colleagues' and therefore was not responsible for this mass release of previously safeguarded data.[80]

Aside from these three examples, the website review located no concrete evi-dence of enforcement in this area. Whilst this must at least indicate that such ac-tion has been rare, it would be wrong to impute from it a complete absence of any such regulatory activity. As noted in Chapter 5, many DPAs only published re-cent and conspicuous examples of enforcement and, in any case, the review was only able to collate readily accessible website material. It is, therefore, highly likely that other examples of DPA action do exist. In this regard, it may be noted that wider research outside of the website review did uncover am example of at least the potential for enforcement action arising from 'Backdoored.io', a rather extreme artistic exhibition which took place in London in 2016. This exhibition featured 'images found by bots, which scanned [unsecured] webcams around the world, gather[ing] shots of unsuspecting users' including 'a family having dinner in their living room, children sleeping and a woman sitting on a sofa'. Many of these images originated from Hong Kong. Ironically, the artist, Nye Thompson, was motivated by a desire 'to demonstrate how fragile our privacy is in this bold new age of uni-versal connectivity'.[81] Following contact by the Hong Kong Privacy Commissioner, the UK DPA agreed to conduct enquiries.[82] As a result of these developments and related publicity, Thompson 'agreed to obscure the faces of people in the images, and stop selling merchandise, such as limited-edition prints, featuring uncensored pictures'.[83]

3.3 Explaining National Divergences under the DPD

The very small number of cases in which the review found evidence of regulatory intervention (whether through standard-setting guidance and/or enforcement) means that a systematic analysis of divergences between the DPAs is not possible. Nevertheless, irrespective of how this is measured, DPA engagement in this area does not appear linked either to differences in the substantive stringency of local law or to the level of resources which they had at their disposal. Instead, a wide spread of outcomes are apparent across all these measures. Thus, turning to substantive legal stringency, Slovenia did not set out any derogation for non-journalistic special expression and therefore was amongst those States with the most stringent substantive law. On the other hand, the position of Italy here was nineteenth, Malta twenty-fifth, and Poland twenty-sixth (out of thirty-two). Meanwhile, out of the twenty-seven DPAs for which full staff resourcing information was available,[84] the Polish DPA was ranked third, the Italian fourth, the Slovenian fifteenth, and the Maltese twenty-fifth when measured on a gross basis. If the financial resourcing measure is used instead, then (out of twenty-six in this case) the Italian DPA is instead ranked third, the Polish ninth, the Slovenian sixteenth, and the Maltese twenty-fifth. Turning finally to the per capita resourcing measures, if the staffing yardstick is used then the regulators array as follows: the Maltese DPA on third, the Slovenian fifth, the Poland twenty-second, and the Italian twenty-seventh. If per capita resources are measured on a financial basis, then the array changes to the Maltese DPA ranked fifth, the Slovenian sixth, the Italian twenty-fourth, and the Polish twenty-fifth. All relevant figures for these rankings are set out in Appendix 8 (as regards the substantive law under the DPD) and 5 (as regards DPA resourcing).

4. Final Analysis and Conclusion

Professional writers and artists play a crucial role in the creation and dissemination of information and ideas for society at large. However, with the spread of digitization, their expressive activities have not only come to involve the processing of personal data but also types of data processing which can seriously interfere with individuals' legally protected data protection rights. Therefore, similarly to the journalistic media, a reconciliation between default European data protection regulation and the freedom of expression of these 'non-journalistic' traditional publishers must be found. During the first generation of European data protection this need was, with certain notable exceptions, generally ignored by both formal law and the DPAs themselves. In some contrast, Article 9 of the DPD did attempt to address this issue by requiring that EEA States set out 'necessary' derogations not only in relation to 'journalistic purposes' but also 'the purpose of artistic and literary expression'. In response, a clear majority (although far from all) of the second-generation data protection laws which were adopted recognized these wider activities as forms of special expression. Nevertheless, most DPAs continued to avoid addressing the reconciliation between data protection and special expression outside of journalism. Moreover, the few DPAs that did intervene here often struggled to coalesce on applicable norms. Thus, whilst the Italian DPA crafted a rather deferential and contextual stance, both the Maltese and Slovenian DPAs adopted a considerably more peremptory and restrictive perspective. In no case was there much evidence of an attempt to develop co-regulation. Finally, the fact most DPAs failed to engage with this issue at all, even if only through standard-setting guidance as opposed to enforcement, must lead to the conclusion that the regulatory system has generally not been effective here.

Especially in light of this chapter's findings, it necessary to consider not only what difference the General Data Protection Regulation 2016/679 and its implementation in Member State law might make here but also how DPAs should orientate themselves under this new framework. However, before addressing these matters, it is important to explore the position of academic publishers. As will be seen in Chapter 11, this important subset of professional expressive actors has an experience of European data protection regulation which is both more peculiar and more troubling than that analysed here.

11

European Data Protection Regulation and Academic Publishers

First- and Second-Generation Developments

Aside from the professional journalistic media, academics within humanities and the social sciences have been the most important traditional actors producing socially relevant information and ideas for the benefit of the public at large. Not only do they function as critical 'observers and commentators' who, similarly to journalists, seek to 'describe and understand their society'[1] but, as members of the scholarly community, they also pursue the 'distinctive task' of the 'methodological discovery and the teaching of truths about serious and important things'.[2] This academic task has tended to foster certain desirable qualities including a 'concern for rigour, system, culmination and precision',[3] a 'reflexive' stance 'unconstrained by partisan passions',[4] and a 'regulative ideal of truth-telling'.[5] Paralleling this, traditional defences of the importance of public freedom of expression within the liberal legal and political tradition have often had the academic firmly in mind. For example, returning to *Areopagitica*, Milton's central example of the valuable expressive actor was essentially that of the scholarly writer:

> When a man writes to the world, he summons up all his reason and deliberation to assist him; he searches, meditates, is industrious, and likely consults and confers with his judicious friends; after all which done he takes himself to be informed in what he writes, as well as any that wrote before him.[6]

Similarly, one of his primary arguments against systems of censorship was that they constituted 'the greatest discouragement and affront that can be offered to learning and to learned men'.[7]

Given that scholars within the humanities and social sciences publish output for the benefit of the public collectively, it may be thought that their position within first- and second-generation European data protection should already have been addressed in Chapter 10. In principle, there is considerable validity in this claim. In particular, the special legal provisions adopted under the Data Protection Directive 95/46 ('DPD') to safeguard processing 'solely for . . . the purpose of artistic or literary expression' could potentially have been interpreted to encompass anyone

European Data Protection Regulation, Journalism, and Traditional Publishers. David Erdos, Oxford University Press (2019). © David Erdos.
DOI: 10.1093/oso/9780198841982.003.0011

producing published literary work, irrespective of whether these individuals had an academic or scholarly affiliation and/or orientation.[8] However, sitting alongside these provisions, European data protection has long included specific provisions focusing on what may broadly be termed 'knowledge facilitation' including, for example, statistics and historical or scientific research. Moreover, perhaps influenced by requirements in many data protection laws that processing be 'solely' for one or other of the specially accommodated purposes, Data Protection Authorities ('DPAs') have generally held that academic 'research' processing must comply with these more restrictive provisions rather than benefit from special freedom of expression derogations.

In this regard, it may also be claimed that academic 'research' processing is distinct from the purpose of publishing. Such a claim cannot, however, be sustained. First, 'processing' personal data clearly includes the direct act of publication (in addition to any other operation which results in a dissemination of that data). Moreover, as will be seen below, DPAs have been particularly emphatic on this point when examining knowledge facilitation activities. Second, and more fundamentally, similar to journalists, artists and non-academic writers, the final act of academic publication has an umbilical link to the 'research' processes which necessarily proceed it. Thus, as John Thompson cogently notes with specific reference to academic book publishing:

> The field of academic or scholarly publishing is defined by the distinctive relation between publishing organizations on the one hand, and the institutions and activities of scholarly and scientific research, on the other. Academic publishing is an integral part of the broader research process.[9]

In light of this, this chapter specifically examines the historical interrelationship between these academic actors and European data protection. Sections 1 and 2 begin by looking at the knowledge facilitation provisions which have been set out alongside the freedom of expression derogations within both pan-European and State data protection law. Section 1 will consider first-generation data protection, whilst section 2 will focus both on the DPD and the laws adopted under it. The chapter will then turn to explore how DPAs have sought to regulate the publishing and related 'research' activities of academics within the humanities and social sciences throughout these two periods. Section 3 will look at guidance produced by DPAs in this area, whilst section 4 will drill down further into regulatory standard-setting under the DPD by examining the responses to a part of the DPA questionnaire which looked at the regulation of covert methodology within social science. Section 5 will then turn to DPA enforcement activity. Finally, section 6 will conclude with a general recapitulation and analysis of the chapter's findings.

1. 'Knowledge Facilitation' Provisions in First-Generation Legal Instruments

1.1 Pan-European/Transnational Legal Instruments

In contrast to the failure of pan-European first-generation legal instruments to address the freedom of expression relationship between data protection and non-journalistic writers and artists, these instruments included a variety of provisions which were designed to both facilitate and constrain certain types of knowledge facilitation. In the Privacy Resolutions of 1973 and 1974, these latter provisions were limited to an indication that any release of information from electronic personal data banks for 'statistical' purposes should be in the form of anonymized data.[10] The regulation of electronic data banks established purely for knowledge facilitation purposes was, therefore, not specifically addressed. Furthermore, the drafters conceptualized 'release' in the broadest sense, encompassing everything from dissemination to internal executive decision-makers through to making the information directly accessible to members of the general public. At the same time, the official explanatory material recognized that the discrete release of data 'for scientific or research purposes'[11] was also common. In this indirect sense, a specific link to knowledge facilitation was in evidence.

By the time of the Council of Europe's Data Protection Convention (in 1981), this link had been deepened through direct reference in the body of that instrument to the use of personal data not only for 'statistics' but also for 'scientific research purposes'. In sum, Article 9(1) permitted State law to set out restrictions on subject access, rectification, and erasure rights in such cases but only 'when there is obviously no risk of an infringement of the privacy of the data subjects'. No clarification was provided as to how this specific provision related to Article 9(2) which enabled States to adopt much deeper derogations from the Convention's defaults standards where 'a necessary measure in a democratic society in the interests of' *inter alia* 'the rights and freedoms of others'. As explored in Chapter 4, it was this latter, much more liberal provision which played a pivotal role in the reconciliation between data protection and freedom of expression during this early period.

Two years after the finalization of the Convention, the Council of Europe's Committee of Ministers adopted Recommendation (83) 10, a much more comprehensive but non-binding instrument which sought to set out 'principles and guidelines' to 'balance' the 'need to protect the privacy of individuals in relation to the growing use of data processing in the field of scientific research and statistics' with 'the needs of the research community'. This Recommendation specifically held that any individual who directly provided data about themselves should 'be adequately informed about the nature of the project, its objectives and the name of the person or body for whom the research is carried out'.[12] A caveat excepted situations where such notification would be incompatible with the specific purpose being pursued, as might be the case 'in the field of psychology [experiments]'.[13] In these special cases, it was stated that the data subject 'should [still] be fully informed after the collection is completed, and be free to continue his co-operation or withdraw it and, in the latter case, be entitled to ask for the erasure of the data collected'.[14] The Recommendation further established that 'whenever possible', only 'anonymous data' should be used,[15] that '[p]ersonal data obtained for research should not be used for any purpose other than research',[16] that restrictions on the right of subject access would only be acceptable where any results 'do not readily identify the individual', where there were 'adequate security measures to ensure his privacy at every stage of the research project, including conservation of data for future use', and, in any case, not where 'in view of the nature of the research the individual can demonstrate a specific interest which deserves protection'.[17] Finally, and most restrictively, it was stipulated that '[p]ersonal data used for research should not be published in identifiable form unless the persons concerned have given their consent and in conformity with other safeguards laid down by domestic law'.[18]

Subject in all cases both to these limitations and to 'safeguards laid down by domestic law',[19] the Recommendation went on to validate personal data which was used for scientific research being stored indefinitely[20] and for data obtained for one project to be repurposed for another in certain restrictive circumstances[21] even in the absence of gaining the consent of, or informing, the data subject of this.

These regulatory provisions arose within a context where many academic researchers were experiencing data protection as a serious and growing impediment to accessing data sources which were important either intrinsically or as a means of obtaining contact and other details which enabled the construction of representative samples of data subjects. Thus, a conference on data access held in Cologne in 1978 expressed 'grave concern about some of the negative impact of data protection laws, regulations, and practices on the social sciences'[22] and claimed that 'there are countries where data flow for research has come nearly to a standstill'.[23] Within this troubling context, a number of academic organizations were willing to countenance both more self-regulation and greater legal control of research if this facilitated a continuation, or even an enhancement, of data access. In September 1980, the European Science Foundation adopted a Resolution along these lines[24] which strongly influenced both the Data Protection Convention[25] and Recommendation (83) 10.[26] The close connection between these various initiatives is highlighted by the inclusion within the Recommendation (83) 10 of provisions encouraging researcher access to population registers,[27] enabling safeguarded access to other data,[28] and endorsing the establishment of self-regulatory 'boards within the research community'[29] as a complement to external control.

Notwithstanding this connection, the drawing up of Recommendation (83) 10 was highly controversial and contested, not only within the academic community but also amongst policy-makers. This controversy even spilled over into the drafting process within the Council of Europe's Committee of Experts on Data Protection. Thus, the UK representative on this Committee stated the Recommendation's stipulation against publishing personal data 'would, as drafted, appear to preclude the publication of data in an identifiable form, even when that data had been drawn from published sources, and might in fact be widely known. Some sort of exception for those circumstances appears to be necessary here'.[30] Meanwhile, the Swiss representative questioned whether 'research' was intended to cover 'research into people', such as 'biographies'.[31] In the event, however, the final Recommendation made no adjustment to the prohibition on publishing personal data, whilst its Explanatory Report expressly included research which 'directly concern determined persons, for example, biographical research'.[32] Ultimately (and unusually for a non-binding instrument), four States inserted either total or partial reservations into the recommendation when it was adopted by the Committee of Ministers.[33]

1.2 National Legal Instruments

Similar to the pan-European instruments analysed earlier, many first-generation laws adopted at national level included specific provisions which were intended to enable various forms of knowledge facilitation activity, whilst also ensuring that personal data continued to be strongly protected within this context. Indeed, as Table 11.1 highlights, six out of the twelve (50 per cent) European States which enacted a data protection law prior to 1990 set out specific provisions within this area, with two further States (Germany and Iceland) joining this group later in 1991 and 1989 respectively. Although the substantive depth of these derogations varied considerably, with the exception only of Denmark (1978) they were clearly of a highly constrained nature. Thus, although all these States apart from Germany (1991)[34] provided certain limitations on subject access, Iceland (1989)[35] and Norway (1978)[36] confined their derogations to this one provision. In contrast, the Netherlands (1988) extended these special dispensations to cover a waiving of the default requirements to notify data subjects proactively of processing[37] and to permit certain special disclosures of personal data,[38] whilst Finland (1987) set out special dispensation from purpose limitation[39] and also restrictions on recording both ordinary and sensitive personal data without consent.[40] Meanwhile, Ireland (1988)[41] and the United Kingdom (1984)[42] established a derogation from the fair obtaining of data sub-principle and also enabled data to be held indefinitely. In general, the use even of these limited derogations was made subject to additional and sometimes highly restrictive requirements. Thus, in all these cases it was either expressly stated or implied[43] that the invocation of the subject access derogation would only be permissible where the results of any research would not identify any particular individual. Moreover, Irish and UK clauses derogating from the fairness provision and enabling data to be stored indefinitely only applied so long as no 'damage or distress is, or is likely to be, caused to any data subject'.[44] Finally, in 1987 Denmark joined this group when it substituted a complete exemption for processing 'solely for scientific or statistical purposes'[45] with one which prohibited the processing of any sensitive data here unless a registration was made to the DPA which was empowered to 'lay down more detailed provisions for the register in question, including provisions on the consent of the registered party, on expunction and up-dating of data, and on safeguards against the register being wrongfully used or brought to the notice of unauthorised persons'.[46]

Table 11.1 First-Generation State Data Protection Law and Specific Derogations for Statistics, Science, or Research (with amendments highlighted)

No derogations	Limited derogations	Extensive derogations
Sweden—1973	Norway—1978	(Denmark—1978)
Austria—1978	United Kingdom—1984	
France—1978	(Denmark—1987)	
Luxembourg—1979	Finland—1987	
(Germany—1977)[47]	Ireland—1988	
(Iceland—1981)	Netherlands—1988	
	(Iceland—1989)	
	(Germany—1991)	

Alongside divergences in depth, the scope of these derogations also exhibited considerable variation, often even in relation to other knowledge facilitation provisions included within the same statute. Most narrowly, the Icelandic and Norwegian provisions were limited to 'statistical extracts'[48] and 'statistical research'[49] respectively. The Finnish provisions variously related to 'opinion and market research, as well as for scientific research and statistics',[50] 'a specific scientific study',[51] and 'statistical purposes in [the] research'.[52] Meanwhile, the Dutch provisions safeguarded 'research or statistical purposes',[53] whilst both the Irish and UK provisions variously applied to 'preparing statistics or carrying out research'[54] or 'historical, statistical or research purposes'.[55]

2. 'Knowledge Facilitation' Provisions in Second-Generation Legal Instruments

2.1 The Data Protection Directive 95/46

The final text of the DPD contained a miscellany of provisions which, as regards various forms kinds of knowledge facilitation activity:

- required States to provide a derogation from the purpose limitation principle and implied that such data could be held indefinitely;[56]

- signalled that the proactive notification of data subjects other than when data was obtained directly from them might well be disproportionate;[57]
- enabled States to provide certain derogations from subject access;[58]
- indicated that it would sometimes be permissible to adopt a derogation from the prohibition on processing sensitive data here (using the DPD's general derogatory clauses);[59] and
- empowered States to provide for wider derogations as regards the storage of certain data which was already being kept before the law came into effect.[60]

These specific derogatory clauses variously applied to 'historical, statistical or scientific purposes',[61] 'statistical purposes or for the purposes of historical or scientific research',[62] 'scientific research or . . . for the sole purpose of creating statistics',[63] 'scientific research and government statistics',[64] and 'data kept for the sole purpose of historical research'.[65] Mandatory conditions applied to their use in all cases. Some of these remained relatively open-textured, such as requiring the State to 'provide appropriate safeguards'[66] or 'specific and suitable safeguards' and a justification based on 'grounds of important public interest'.[67] In many cases, however, the requirements laid down were much more precise and exacting. For example, it was suggested that the use of the purpose limitation derogation had to include safeguards which 'in particular rule out the use of the data in support of measures or decisions regarding any particular individual',[68] whilst the derogation from subject access was to apply only 'where there is clearly no risk of breaching the privacy of the data subject' and where a legislative measure in particular ensured that 'the data are not used for taking measures or decisions regarding any particular individual'.[69]

Interestingly, the European Commission's original draft Directive in 1990 had not contained any provisions specifically focused on knowledge facilitation activities, aside for a provision enabling data subjects to obtain the erasure of personal data 'held in files used for market research'[70] and a clause allowing States to derogate from subject access in relation to data held in public sector files which were 'compiled temporarily for the purpose of extracting statistical information therefrom'.[71] Moreover, its redraft of 1992 did no more than remove the former restrictive provision and amend the subject access provision so as to provide for an optional derogation applicable across both the public and private sectors for certain processing 'intended to serve statistical ends'.[72] Pressure to set out a significant number of specific derogations in favour of knowledge facilitation then arose from a number of the Member States. Their delegations were particularly concerned about the potential impact of the DPD on biomedical research, a focus highlighted by the fact that no fewer than five Member State papers during the proceedings focused exclusively on this area.[73] The *traveaux preparatoires* also reveal an awareness of the potential problems confronting statistical work, especially as undertaken by Government.[74] In contrast, the impact on wider forms of social and humanities scholarship was largely ignored. Furthermore, any such consideration was almost exclusively limited to an attempt to set out a framework within which researchers could be given safeguarded access to data originally collected for another purpose.[75] At one stage of the drafting, it was suggested that the Directive include a single derogations clause governing the '[p]rocessing of personal data for scientific and statistical purposes'.[76] Ultimately, however, this was abandoned in favour of piecemeal provisions. A number of these provisions clearly drew inspiration from earlier pan-European instruments including Recommendation (83) 10 which, at least in the area of 'scientific research',[77] technically remained in place.

2.2 National Legal Instruments

Following the DPD's steer, all European Economic Area ('EEA') States included certain derogations in their implementing laws that were specifically focused on particular types of knowledge facilitation.[78] In light not only of this study's wider focus but also the presence of a large quantity of existing analysis in this area,[79] it is not feasible to provide an exhaustive account of these provisions. Nevertheless, it is clear that they were almost universally highly constrained. The only potential exception to this arose from apparently wide-ranging derogations adopted in a minority of States in favour of certain 'historical research' processing.[80] In reality, however, these provisions only related to the retention of data (rather than any further processing) and, in any case, were only meant to apply to activity already underway before the law came into effect. As a result, their formal impact remained limited.

Aside from this unusual special case, States almost never set out a derogation from any of the data protection principles[81] other than purpose and time limitation (as has already been envisaged in the Directive itself).[82] Restrictions on the applicability of the proactive transparency rules which went beyond the DPD's general 'disproportionate effort'[83] carve-out for data not obtained directly from the data subject were also very uncommon. Indeed, in cases involving the direct collection of information, only one State (Italy) set out a (limited) derogation that was specifically focused on knowledge facilitation activities.[84] Three further States (Gibraltar, Ireland, and the United Kingdom) included a general gloss stipulating that the provision of transparency information even in the case of direct collection only applied 'as far as practicable'.[85] Finally, two further States (Liechtenstein and Luxembourg) provided a general 'disproportionate effort' derogation from the transparency rules across the board rather than (as envisaged in the DPD itself) only when data had not been obtained from the individual data subject.[86] Although derogations from the reactive subject access right and the sensitive data rules were more common, in each case between ten and fifteen States failed to legitimate processing here beyond that envisaged by the default provisions of the Directive itself.[87] In cases where no derogation was established, the processing of sensitive data was generally prohibited absent waiver from the data subject.[88] No States at all provided a derogation from the supervisory jurisdiction of the regular DPA or from the restrictive data export regime. Finally, it bears emphasis that, even when specific derogations were established, they were (as in first-generation data protection law) generally only granted based on highly restrictive conditions.[89]

3. DPA Guidance on Academic Research and Publication

3.1 First-Generation DPA Guidance

First-generation data protection lacked a pan-European body with authority to promulgate common regulatory guidance and interpretation. Nevertheless, as noted in Part I, DPAs did collaborate within an International Conference from 1979 and, in practice, this grouping was dominated by European Data Protection Commissioners until at least the mid-1990s. The Nordic regulators also met together periodically and many DPAs regularly took part in the Council of Europe's intergovernmental Expert Committee on Data Protection. Reflecting this last connection, a number of regulators thereby played a key role in the origin of Recommendation (83) 10. In particular, DPA representatives from Denmark, France, and Germany were all represented on the small sub-committee that drew up this instrument and one of them—Spirios Simitis, the German Hessen Data Protection Commissioner—penned a number of the documents that formed the backbone of the approach adopted.[90] Issues related to this area were also discussed by the International Conference[91] and the Nordic Commissioners,[92] especially over this same period but also subsequently. Whilst neither of these latter bodies promulgated a formal resolution in this area, the perspectives presented tended to endorse a heavily safeguarded and controlled paradigm for the use of data in academic research. Thus, opening the discussion on social research and statistics at the International Conference in 1981, the head of the Swedish DPA Jan Freese stated:

> Researchers do not deal well with citizens and this causes problems in ensuring informed consent exists before researchers collect or use personal data. We have found that the duty to inform is not well carried out.[93]

Similarly, at the following year's International Conference, the head of the French DPA argued that, whilst research was very important, data subjects must be informed of, and agree to the use of, personal data here.[94] Nevertheless, some highly divergent analyses to this were also occasionally given voice. Thus, at the same conference, the head of the Norwegian DPA asked the following pointed rhetorical question: 'Do we in our actual practice give the press and other media a preferential treatment compared with, for instance, research and science?'[95]

Turning to the State level, DPAs tended to endorse standards related to academic research and publication that were in line with the safeguarded approach adopted in Recommendation (83) 10. However, the extent of any such guidance varied considerably. Some DPAs, such as the United Kingdom[96] and Ireland,[97] largely confined themselves to publicizing the Recommendation itself. Other DPAs were considerably more active. For example, the French DPA set up a Research Sub-Committee which, in cooperation with the National Council of Statistics, organized a set of discussions on how to apply data protection to research and, in particular, statistical work. Ultimately, however, the Committee returned to the Council of Europe's 1982 recommendation as '*te fil directeur*' ('the guiding thread') for its analysis.[98] Meanwhile, the Swedish DPA published extensive guidance in this area based on the specificities of its local legislation. It stressed that academic researchers would need a license to process at least sensitive data and that this would only be granted if, after examining *inter alia* the nature and quantity of the data and from whom it was collected, the DPA found that it did not represent an unjustified intrusion of personal integrity. This guidance also emphasized that the DPA would require that data subjects were informed of processing not only when data was collected directly from them but also in a wide range of other situations. Finally, although the guidance did state that the DPA had established a practice of waiving a direct consideration of whether the data was needed for any stated research purpose, this was made conditional on the researcher ensuring that the identity of any particular individual was not revealed in any subsequent publication.[99]

3.2 Second-Generation Pan-European DPA Guidance

In contrast to absence of a formal pan-European structure for DPAs under first-generation data protection, the DPD set up the Article 29 Working Party and charged it with issuing authoritative (although non-binding) regulatory guidance.[100] This body was extremely productive, issuing over 100 opinions, recommendations, and similar output throughout this period. Despite this, it never issued any document which specifically focused on applying data protection to academic research and publication. Nevertheless, a few of its more generic outputs did explore aspects of this issue. By far its most extended analysis can be found in a section of its Opinion 3/2013 on 'purpose limitation' which sought to construe the DPD's stipulation that '[f]urther processing of data for historical, statistical or scientific purposes' should be considered compatible with this principle so long as any such processing was subject to 'appropriate safeguards'. The Working Party's analysis of what safeguards should be considered 'appropriate' veered rather uneasily between a peremptory rules-based and a case-by-case contextual approach. Thus, on the one hand, the DPD recital's reference to ruling out 'the use of the data in support of measures or decisions regarding any particular individual'[101] was interpreted extremely broadly so as to cover 'any relevant impact on particular individuals—either negative or positive' and 'irrespective' of whether any measures or decisions 'are taken by the controller or by anyone else'.[102] This in turn was held to require measures 'to guarantee the security of the data'[103] and led on to an extensive discussion of various means to anonymize or pseudo-anonymize information. In this context it was also argued that 'further processing of personal data concerning health, data about children, other vulnerable individuals, or other highly sensitive information should, in principle, be permitted only with the consent of the data subject', that 'any exceptions to this requirement for consent should be specified in law', and that any 'case of doubt' as regards the appropriateness of safeguards 'should be subject to prior authorisation of the competent data protection authority'.[104] On the other hand, the Opinion also held that the required safeguards only 'typically'[105] necessitated the ruling out of measures and decisions and, more specifically, that historical research 'may focus on specific individuals, such as historical figures or family history'.[106] In this latter context, it was stated that such researchers might both wish and be able 'to use historical data that pose little or no risk to persons concerned, due to the lapse of time since the data were collected', although numerous caveats to this were noted including as regards the potential for stigmatic data about the deceased to continue to impact living family members negatively.[107] Finally, it was found that these provisions in principle left 'room for professional codes of conduct',[108] although whether such codes had a role to play here would depend on local State law. Ultimately, and notwithstanding the many nuances, this guidance clearly sought to integrate academic research into the same kind of highly safeguarded framework as that set out in the knowledge facilitation legal provisions discussed in section 1.

3.3 Second-Generation State DPA Guidance

The DPA website review carried out in 2013 sought to locate readily available guidance produced by these bodies which specifically focused on academic research and/or publication. This type of guidance was discovered on eighteen out of the thirty-two (56 per cent) national DPA websites. Rather surprisingly, however, comparable guidance was not located on the websites of any of the five regional regulators which participated in the DPA questionnaire.[109] Nevertheless, the former figure is broadly comparable with that located as regards journalism in Chapter 5. Quite unlike this latter guidance, however, the great bulk of that which related to academia was predicated on a highly safeguarded model of data processing. At the same time, the focus and extent of this guidance also diverged significantly. Despite references in some cases to specific provisions in local statute, these differences were not in general the product of variation in the formal law at national level.

The Danish, Estonian, Maltese, Swedish, and, to some extent, also the Finnish and Norwegian DPAs set out comprehensive guidance which both upheld a highly protective processing model and set out far-reaching requirements for prior licensing. In sum:

- The Danish DPA stipulated not only that research projects should comply with the restrictions set down in data protection law but that, subject to limited exceptions,[110] any processing involving sensitive data would require the issuance of a prior DPA permit which would mandate additional conditions. It was also specifically stated that it was an imprisonable criminal offence not to apply for a permit or to violate its terms.[111] The standard conditions set out included that informed consent be obtained whenever data were collected through direct interaction or observation of data subjects, that only non-identifiable data was published, and that at the end of the project any personal data was deleted, anonymized, or transferred to the National Archives.[112]

- The Estonian DPA held that researchers intending to process any personal data without consent had to apply for a DPA permit which would only be granted on the basis of overwhelming public interest and where the research did not impact on the data subject (or unduly affect their rights).[113]

- The Maltese DPA set out a similar approach to the Danish DPA including specifying that in any case where 'direct one-to-one contact will be made with the participant' they 'should at least be informed on the purpose for which their personal data will be processed', 'any recipients to whom it may be disclosed', and 'the right to request access to the personal data'. However, in the Maltese case it was stated that this DPA licensing was, in practice, carried out indirectly through the University of Malta's Research Ethics Committee (including for academic work unattached to this institution), with the DPA formally endorsing projects retrospectively every six months.[114]

- The Swedish DPA specified that its local law specifically required that prior authorization for research be obtained from an ethical review board (rather than the DPA itself) and further stipulated that data subjects be provided with far-ranging information[115] about the research.[116]

- The Finnish DPA's sixteen-page research guidance was less prescriptive than the cases above but still emphasized the need for very careful management of research processing and stated that forms of sensitive data processing which had not already been authorized by the DPA had to be notified to it thirty days prior to starting any data collection.[117]

- Finally, the Norwegian DPA also published extensive guidance[118] which stated that research projects should either gain prior approval from their organization's own data protection ombudsperson (who would then notify the DPA) or, at least if using sensitive data, make a direct application to the DPA for a license.[119]

Whilst not emphasizing the need for prior licensing, the Czech DPA set out a similarly stringent approach which was stated to be generally applicable to 'scientific research'. Basing itself on a claim that the 'objective of science is to obtain a certain finding, i.e. generalization', this guidance held that 'personal data cannot be the [published] result of research'. Moreover, despite acknowledging that the freedom of scientific research was protected in the EU Charter,[120] the guidance found that when looking for a legal basis to justify any processing 'preference must be given to [the] informed consent of the data subject'. It also emphasized that derogations from the duty to inform subjects of processing were not applicable where data was directly collected from them.[121]

Another very large grouping of DPAs produced guidance that, whilst clearly furthering a highly safeguarded model of processing, explored only discrete kinds of activity. In the first place, the Greek, Slovenian, Dutch, and UK DPA guidance focused largely on the supply or use in research of personal data originally collected for another purpose. In sum:

- The Greek DPA held that any access to non-anonymous sensitive personal data held within files required prior permission from the DPA. Moreover, this would only be granted if access was necessary for scientific or historical purposes, the research findings only included anonymized data and any non-anonymous data would then be destroyed. However, as a caveat to this, it noted that it had made a formal decision in 2009 providing historical researchers with a general right to access public documents, without showing specific reasons, so long as the data did not concern the private or family life of third parties and confidentiality was not specifically prejudiced.[122]
- The Slovenian DPA held that only anonymized data could be supplied here, unless either the consent of the data subject (or their heirs if deceased) had been obtained or such supply was provided for otherwise by statute.[123]
- The Dutch DPA examined the publication of 'personal data on the Internet', stating that the derogation enabling 'personal data collected for another purpose to nevertheless be used for historical, statistical or scientific purposes' would apply only where controllers 'take the necessary measures to ensure that the data are processed only for these specific purposes'. It went on to claim that the 'exemption will therefore, in practice, only apply to strictly guarded intranets'. When sensitive data were involved it was further argued that it would be necessary to examine 'each specific research request' so as to ensure that the research was in the public interest, that the processing was necessary, that requesting express consent from the data subject would prove impossible or would require disproportionate effort, and that sufficient safeguards were in place to protect the privacy of these individuals.[124]
- Finally, the UK DPA set out a *précis* of the 'important' but 'limited' derogations[125] for research in a code of practice on anonymization which especially

focused on organizations intending 'to further research or statistical purposes by making its anonymised data available to researchers'.[126] The guide noted that it was not always possible to use truly anonymized data in research but that detailed derogations could still enable disclosure and use so long as no measures or decisions were supported in relation, and no substantial damage or distress caused, to data subjects. It was stated that a derogation from subject access would also apply if data were not published in identifiable form.[127] The guide finally argued that, amongst other data protection responsibilities, those receiving such data might have a duty to inform data subjects that they had 'obtained personal data about them'[128].

Also within this broad group, a second cluster of national DPAs from Cyprus, Germany, Ireland, and Portugal focused on medical research, an activity which whilst often carried out in an academic context generally lies at a considerable remove from the humanities and social science scholarship explored in this book. In brief summary:

- The Cypriot DPA produced guidance focused on survey work conducted in hospitals and nursing homes.[129]
- The German national DPA published brief guidance on the use of patient data in medical research.[130]
- The Irish DPA produced guidance on the use of confidential patient data in research.[131]
- The Portuguese DPA published a general deliberation applicable to scientific research in the field of health.[132]

A final group of two national DPAs—from Italy and Belgium—crafted a significantly more nuanced analysis in this area which grappled extensively with some of the core freedom of expression concerns which lie at the heart of this book. The Italian DPA, which adopted the more formalized approach, drew up two quite distinct co-regulatory codes of practices, one of which related to the processing of personal data for historical purposes and the other of which concerned processing for statistical and scientific purposes (including, but not limited to, medical research). Both built on specific provisions and regulatory duties that had already been set down in Italian data protection law.[133] Whilst recognizing 'the principle of freedom of research set forth in the [Italian] Constitution',[134] the statistical and scientific research code maintained an adherence to the safeguarded processing model which was also adopted in the DPA guidance explored earlier. In particular, researchers were admonished to secure personal data,[135] not publish such data in identified form unless the data concerned public variables,[136] proactively ensure the transparency of data processing,[137] and only process sensitive data on the basis of consent or a (general or specific) authorization issued by the DPA.[138] Meanwhile, the former code interpreted historical purposes as governing first, public and private sector archives of documents of historical interest and, second, the further processing activities of users who had been given access to such documents.[139] These two distinct types of activity were firmly distinguished and regulation of the latter was then expressly tied to the exercise of freedom of expression[140] and to the need for 'fairness and non-discrimination'[141] in respect of all types of public intellectual activity. In particular, it was both explicitly stated that '[t]he user's construction [of data from the archives] shall fall within the scope of the freedom of speech and expression as set out in the Constitution'[142] and that 'user' comprised 'any person either requesting access to or accessing documents including personal data for historical purposes, also in connection with journalistic activities and/or the occasional publication of papers, essays and other intellectual works'.[143] In so clearly tying historical purposes to journalism and cognate activity it was at least implied that, when not processing archival documents, those pursuing such historical research activities could directly benefit from the special expressive purpose derogations. Indeed, in this regard, it is notable that a recital to the (somewhat misleadingly titled) Italian Code of Conduct on the Processing of Personal Data in the Exercise of Journalistic Activities, which was substantively analysed in Chapter 5, repeated the same phraseology in stating that it also applied 'to any person who transiently processes personal data with a view to the occasional publication of papers, essays and other intellectual works'.[144]

Prompted not by local legislation but rather by the outcome of a conference on 'Privacy and Research: From Obstruction to Construction' which it organized in 2010, the Belgian DPA adopted a similar approach. In sum, it produced three *vademecums* on scientific,[145] biomedical,[146] and historical[147] research respectively. The first two adopted a strict safeguarding approach. Thus, alongside stipulating stringent security measures, both argued that projects were required to be declared in advance to the DPA and that data subjects either had to be directly notified of processing or, in cases where the data was to be indirectly obtained, a DPA recommendation sought in order to establish that this notification requirement could be waived. Finally, publication of results in identifiable form absent the explicit consent of the data subject was prohibited. In contrast, however, the historical research *vademecum* fused a similar safeguarding analysis with a strong counter-narrative based on freedom of expression. Thus, on the one hand, it outlined similar default provisions and, linked to this, also provided extensive information on how researchers could apply for access to public data banks (e.g. in health and social security) through sub-committees of the DPA. On the other hand, it also argued that historical research presented many similarities with journalistic research and, so long as the work focused on persons or events having a certain public character and the personal data closely linked to this, researchers would therefore be able to claim the 'journalistic' derogations set out in the law. In this context, it was specifically stated that historical projects might be justified in derogating from subject access and the rules against publishing non-anonymous data without consent. Finally, it was also stressed that the right to rectification did not allow the data subject to substitute their subjective opinion about historical matters for those of the researcher.

4. Second-Generation Regulatory Standard-Setting as Revealed in the DPA Questionnaire

4.1 Question Posed

The guidance gathered from the DPA website review suggested that, with a few exceptions, regulators conceptualized academic research and publication as being governed by the default data protection scheme, modified only by the strictly limited and safeguarded knowledge facilitation derogations found within these laws. Nevertheless, in many cases, these publications either remained rather general or focused on medical research, an activity which is at a considerable remove from scholarship within the social science and humanities scholarship that seeks to contribute information and ideas of direct interest to the public sphere. Given this, it was decided to include mention of one paradigm example of the latter type of activity in the DPA questionnaire. This example, which involved covert/undercover research into an issue of clear social significance, was chosen for two main reasons. First, it has been widely recognized within the academic literature that '[t]he requirement to be "up front" about your research can simply preclude valuable forms of critical inquiry', thereby curtailing 'critical scholarship that might seek to investigate high-profile, contentious issues involving powerful people or agencies'.[148] Second, such work directly dovetailed with covert/undercover journalism which was explored in the same questionnaire and elucidated in Chapter 6. Indeed, these two examples were designed to be directly comparable, subject to a few important caveats. First, the hypothetical academic example focused on police racism as opposed to the political beliefs of those involved in a political party. It was, therefore, less clearly linked to the processing of sensitive data.[149] Second, unlike the journalistic example, it was stated that the results of the study would be anonymized as far as possible. These protective techniques are commonplace within covert social science, whilst remaining much rarer in journalistic circles. Finally, the most permissive standard response set out for DPAs presumed that the academic would satisfy a strict public interest test (which incorporated a requirement of necessity) since, again, this constitutes a nearly ubiquitous practical threshold within the social science community, something that could hardly be said of at least the more salacious type of journalism.

The hypothetical example presented, which was deliberately based on real-life research,[150] read as follows:

A social scientist researching widespread claims of racism within a police force wishes [to] use covert methodology posing as a police recruit. Induction activities involving fellow recruits and police trainers would be secretly recorded, but the results of the study [would] be anonymized in so far as possible.

DPAs were asked to assess the legality of this activity under data protection law and, in this context, were presented with the following three potential categorical responses:[151]

(a) The research would be legal so long as it was (i) not possible to collect the data overtly and (ii) the benefit in terms of knowledge production outweighed the privacy invasion.

(b) Such research would only be legal if (i) it was not possible to collect the data overtly, (ii) the benefit in terms of knowledge production outweighed the privacy invasion, and (iii) the social scientist obtained a permit from the Data Protection Authority.

(c) Such research would be illegal as data would be collected directly from data subjects without their knowledge.

Subject to the caveats mentioned above, these possibilities broadly mirrored the last three options included in the cognate question on covert journalism which, as discussed in Chapter Six, also respectively set out a strict public interest test (labelled as category c/0.5), a rule-based restriction predicated on DPA licensing (category d/0.75), and the full application of data protection's default prohibition (category e/1). These options were, therefore, similarly coded as 0.5, 0.75, and 1, respectively. Finally, as an alternative to providing a standard answer, DPAs were able to indicate that the activity had a different relationship with data protection and then to indicate this in free text.

4.2   Results

The twenty-two standard DPAs responses received in response to this question are summarized in Chart 11.1 and reported at the level of each individual DPA in Appendix 8. One of these DPAs (Cyprus) provided additional text further specifying its answer and there were also seven free-text answers. These are summarized in Table 11.2. As can be seen from Chart 11.1, exactly half the standard DPA answers indicated that this kind of activity would simply be illegal (c/1). Meanwhile, nearly 20 per cent specified that it would only be allowed if a permit for it was issued by the DPA (b/0.75). However, around one-third of the standard DPA answers did find that this activity would only need to satisfy a strict public interest test (a/0.5). As Table 11.2 highlights, the free-text answers were very mixed. Two DPAs stated that prior licensing either by the DPA (Estonia) or research ethics committee (Finland) would be necessary, two appeared unsure about the legal

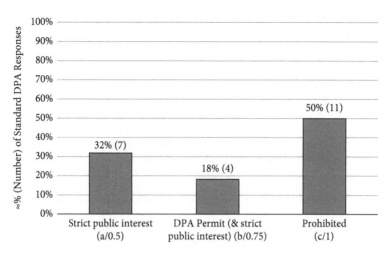

Chart 11.1 Covert Social Science—DPA Standard Legal Interpretations.

position (Gibraltar and Greece), and three (France, Slovenia, and Spain Catalonia) indicated that potentially the same legal tests as that applicable to undercover journalism would apply.

4.3 Discussion

As noted in section 2.2, almost no second-generation European data protection law set out a knowledge facilitation derogation from the essentially absolute obligation to provide proactive notice to data subjects when collecting information directly from them. Despite this, several of the DPAs' responses cited earlier adopted a more liberal approach than this highly constrained safeguarding model would allow. That would tend to indicate that at least some regulators recognized the tension with freedom of expression here. Nevertheless, the interpretations generally remained extremely restrictive and, in particular, far more so than that adopted as regards cognate journalistic activity. Thus, whereas it was seen in Chapter 6 that no regulator held that undercover journalism was either *ipso facto* illegal or was only permissible based on a DPA permit,[152] almost 70 per cent of the standard DPA responses held to one or other of these two perspectives here. Moreover, a (bare) majority even mandated a complete prohibition on this methodology. These stark divergences appeared notwithstanding the important safeguard of anonymization being explicitly adopted in this social science example, but not in the one badged as journalism. Interestingly, those DPAs operating in the few States whose local law arguably did incorporate a specific transparency derogation applicable to knowledge facilitation activity did not all coalesce on a more liberal approach or, indeed, exhibit a pattern that was markedly

Table 11.2 Covert Social Science—DPA Additional and Free Text Legal
Interpretations

DPA	Summary
Cyprus (with (c/1) response)	Derogation from the obligation to inform data subjects applies 'only to journalistic purposes' and 'does not apply to research purposes'. Also expressed serious doubts whether the proposed methodology could be considered 'scientific' which, it was argued, required *inter alia* that the researcher publish findings with a methodology that could be scrutinized and validated by the scientific community.
Estonia	In addition to security measures, processing identifiable data for scientific research without consent was permitted only if the goals would otherwise be (at least) unreasonably difficulty, there was a predominant public interest, the data subject's obligations were not changed, and their rights were not excessively damaged. Sensitive personal data processing required prior checking by DPA and in certain cases also that of an ethics committee.
Finland	Acceptance of the methodology required a statement of the ethical committee.
France	The processing would be illegal if the data had been collected by methods sanctioned by criminal law; data protection would not apply in the first place.
Gibraltar	No further specification provided.
Greece	Stated that had not dealt with such an issue and so couldn't provide an answer.
Slovenia	Data protection generally did not apply but provisions of the Penal Code would as covert recording was defined as a criminal act. The general law on defamation and breach of privacy might also apply.
Spain Catalonia	Stated that '[i]n some cases [the] Spanish Constitutional Court considered this kind of video recording was illegal (v. qr. STV 12/2012). Nevertheless, in other cases [it] considered that it was admissible (facts punishable)'.

different from that of regulators as a whole.[153] Moreover, these responses were not positively correlated with the formal stringency of legal provisions applicable to either journalism or other forms of special expression in the different jurisdictions.[154] This suggests that even those DPAs that recognized the tension with freedom of expression ultimately found themselves in an ambiguous space, stuck easily between the highly restrictive safeguarding of the knowledge facilitation regime and the much more permissive approach common to journalistic regulation.

5. DPA Enforcement in Relation to Academic Research and Publication

5.1 First-Generation DPA Enforcement

Analysis of documentary material indicates that, during the first generation of European data protection, a number of DPAs engaged in quite extensive enforcement in the area of academic research and publication. Almost invariably, this was achieved through a prior licensing system. In some cases, the interventions documented concerned medical rather than social research. Moreover, a good deal of activity in the latter field related to the access and use of especially safeguarded data sources. Nevertheless, it was also clear that several regulators sought to interfere with a much wider range of social methodologies including those, such as the gathering of information through interviews or questionnaires, which were and are routinely resorted by journalists.

The experience of the Icelandic, French, Norwegian, and Swedish DPAs provides a good indication of the variety of approaches adopted by regulators which actively intervened in this early period. The annual reports of the Icelandic DPA detail extensive enforcement managed through the licensing of research projects. However, approximately two-thirds of these concerned medical research, whilst the majority of the rest related to the use of safeguarded data. For example, as regards the latter, in 1986 two research projects were approved which involved access to data held within the Icelandic National Register on 1,000 people for a survey on religious activities and drug use respectively, whilst another project was permitted to access data on 400 married couples for research on attitudes and communication within Icelandic families.[155] At the same time, some cases of licensing were located involving the use questionnaires. Thus, also in 1986, a professor engaged in a research project within political science applied and was granted permission to conduct a social survey in various high schools and University of Iceland departments.[156] Turning to the French DPA, the annual reports here disclosed a clear intent to regulate and enforce across medical, social, and indeed all other types of academic research involving personal data. However, the social research projects detailed in the reports focused on the conditions under which safeguarded data sources could be made available in this context. For example, between 1983 and 1984, the DPA set out the formalities that it had required to be followed by each social security office in order to provide file access to a project investigating the economic efficiency of lone parent benefits.[157] Meanwhile, at the other end of this time period, in 1995 this DPA permitted an academic to obtain aggregated data from the National Institute for Statistics and Economic Studies (INSEE) that nevertheless might reveal information on identifiable individuals, so long as certain stringent safeguards were adhered to.[158] More generally, this DPA lamented that:

> [L]e secteur de la recherche, notamment de la recherche en sociologie, restait encore peu sensibilisé aux questions informatique et libertés'. En témoigne le nombre relativement faible des saisines dont elle est l'objet en provenance de ce secteur. ('[T]he research sector, notably in the case of sociological research, has remained little sensitive to the issues of "information technology and civil liberties". This is demonstrated by the relatively low number of referrals that have come from this sector.')[159]

Whilst this statement was made as early as 1982–83, it would appear that this reality did not change during the rest of the period. Meanwhile, the Norwegian DPA adopted a decentralized model for the licensing of research projects whereby data protection units within approved research bodies made 'recommendations to the Data Inspectorate [DPA]' which then 'provide[d] mandatory reports for research projects for which concession has been required'. At least as of 1988, the DPA 'had not denied any recommended concessions'.[160] However, whilst apparently relatively 'cooperative', it is clear that the breadth of this regime was far-reaching, stretching well beyond the regulation of access to safeguarded data and encompassing also the gathering of data through questionnaires. Moreover, as Øyen and Olassen pointed out in 1985, this presented acute problems for certain types of social investigation:

> The application [for a concession] must furnish information about which questions are to be used and the Data Inspectorate must decide if and when some illegal trespassing is likely to occur, in which case the concession will be denied. [But] ... data collection procedures recommended by proponents of qualitative research preclude the construction of standardized, structured questionnaires.[161]

Finally, the Swedish DPA adopted the most stringent approach to enforcement in this area. Some of the projects that it policed certainly involved access and use of especially safeguarded data. For example, in 1986 it intervened in relation to a '20-year longitudinal study by the Department of Sociology, University of Stockholm of some 15000 Stockholmers born in 1953' which had involved sourcing information from 'amongst others, the National Police Board and the Central Bureau of Statistics'.[162] Criticizing the lack of informed consent in this 'Projet Metropolit' study, it ordered that the project destroy its 'master tape of identifiers', 'thus preventing any follow-up studies'.[163] Even as regards this kind of intervention, there were protests from the academic community that 'researchers were in effect forbidden to use methods available to journalists'.[164] Beyond this, it is also clear that this DPA also sought to control the gathering of data through questionnaires, 'demand[ing] good reasons for all questions, and eliminat[ing] questions'.[165] Indeed, it was claimed that '[i]n one case of a study of political attitudes of immigrants, five more-or-less central questions about political affiliations were deleted from the questionnaire'.[166] All this prompted a sustained backlash from the academic community. Thus, Flaherty, writing in 1989, noted:

> The most significant group of nongovernmental critics [of the DPA] has been the academic research community. Researchers were surprised to discover that they require licenses for their personal registers like any other user. As in the case of Statistics Sweden, academic critics suspected that the [DPA] was attacking a weaker segment of society rather than dealing with the larger and more

sensitive data bases of the police and intelligence services. Whilst a professor at the University of Stockholm, Social Democrat Sten Johansson, now head of Statistics Sweden, publicly accused Freese [the head of the DPA] of using data protection to provide a haven for tax evaders.[167]

Due both to this resistance and a lack of awareness, the DPA struggled to secure compliance. Thus, a regulatory audit in 1988–90 of research processing in Sweden's twenty-seven universities and polytechnics resulted in no less than fourteen claiming that they did not hold any personal data research records at all. Moreover, it was found that of the other 349 records which were submitted, 99 exhibited basic problems such as retention after the DPA had been notified of deletion or the referencing of an incorrect controller as being responsible for its management, whilst a further 83 hadn't even applied for a permit which the DPA held to be necessary. Finally, no information was found to be held on some 158 records which had been issued with a (current) DPA permit. As a result of the audit a number of criminal charges were brought for *inter alia* failing to apply for permission from the DPA to process data.[168]

5.2 Second-Generation DPA Enforcement

The DPA questionnaire asked directly about any enforcement action undertaken during the DPD era against (A) a 'social scientist using archived or secondary data' and (B) any 'other social scientist'. This distinction sought to differentiate those who were likely to be using especially safeguarded data sources (i.e. A) and other cases (B).[169] Similarly to the questions focused on general journalistic activity and also newspaper archiving which were explored in Chapter 7, a further distinction was made in each case between enforcement arising from (i) 'the use of material obtained without proper authorization from another Data Controller' and (ii) 'any other processing activity connected to publication'. In total, therefore, DPAs had the opportunity to signify having undertaken enforcement action in this area in up to four types of situation. Appendix 8 details the answers forthcoming and also calculates a summative total for all enforcements combined.

As can be seen, there was no evidence of DPAs' focusing on one particular type of enforcement situation. In relation to each of the four possibilities, between six (19 per cent) and seven (23 per cent) out of the thirty-one responding DPAs reported enforcement. Overall thirteen (42 per cent) indicated that they had enforced in some way, with four (13 per cent) of these reporting intervention in just one of these situations, six (19 per cent) in two, two (6 per cent) in three, and one (3 per cent) in four. It is useful to explore statistically any possible relationship between outcomes as computed in this last figure and the same kind of variables explored in relation to journalism in Chapter 7, namely (a) regulatory and substantive measures of the stringency of local law applicable to special expression, and (b) gross and per capita measures of the resources available to the DPAs. Given that social science output may be considered to have a closer relationship with literary (and artistic expression) as opposed to journalism, the primary measures used as regards (a) were the those calculated for non-journalistic expression as presented in Chapter 10 (and also specified in Appendix 8). It should be stressed here that, as a result of wide-spread failure to provide for derogations outside journalism, no less than thirteen (42 per cent) of the thirty-one DPA jurisdictions were thereby classified as providing no derogation here at all whereas the comparable figure if the journalism stringency measure had been given priority would have been just two (6 per cent).[170] Meanwhile, as noted in Chapter 7, the resourcing measures drew on the financial and staffing figures published by the Article 29 Working Party in their 2013 Annual Report. In light of the gaps in these figures, it was not possible to include the German, Lithuanian, or Spanish DPAs in this part of the analysis or, in the case of the financial figures only, that of the Austrian DPA.

Table 11.3 presents the correlations in these seven cases. As can be seen, there was evidence of some relationship between reported enforcement and the treatment of non-journalistic special expression in statutory law. Nevertheless, the correlations remain weak (< 0.3) and achieved (at most) one-tailed significance at the 10 per cent confidence level. This is very different, therefore, to the medium-to-strong and highly significant correlations reported *vis-à-vis* journalistic enforcement in Chapter 7. Moreover, if the regular journalistic measure is substituted for the non-journalistic measure of statutory special expression stringency then even these relationships clearly disappear.[171] Meanwhile, however this is measured, there was no evidence of a relationship between enforcement here and better DPA resourcing.[172]

Turning next to look at the qualitative data gathered through the DPA website review, the material found here revealed relatively few cases of enforcement specifically focused on academic research within the humanities and social science. However, it is important to recall that the review was only able to gather readily accessible information on each site and that many DPAs only publicized details of recent and high-profile direct interventions. The latter caveat may have more relevance in an academic as opposed to a journalistic context. Thus, not only does academic research rarely attain the kind of widespread visibility as journalistic investigations, but in several cases (e.g. Malta, Norway, and Sweden[173]), the DPA had established quite strict but decentralized oversight mechanisms maintained by universities or similar research institutions themselves. Moreover, well outside of these jurisdictions, the general nature of reporting by a number of DPAs made it unclear whether their interventions related to social or, rather, purely biomedical research.[174]

Despite this, some clear cases of direct enforcement were uncovered. Many concerned access and use of specially safeguarded data sources. Amongst the most

Table 11.3 Spearman Rank Correlations (and One-Tailed Significance Tests) between Self-Reported DPA Social Science Total Enforcement and both Statutory Stringency and DPA Resourcing Measures

	Non-journalistic special expression stringency in local statute			DPA resourcing measures (computed from Article 29 Working Party 2013 Annual Report)			
	Regulatory powers	Substantive stringency	Regulatory stringency	Gross financial	Per capita financial	Gross staffing	Per 100K pop staffing
Total social science enforcement	0.240	0.232	0.262	0.175	0.160	0.067	−0.077
	Sig. 0.097*	Sig. 0.104	Sig. 0.077*	Sig. 0.219	Sig. 0.239	Sig. 0.381	Sig. 0.364
	N = 31	N = 31	N = 31	N = 22	N = 22	N = 23	N = 23

* = significant at the 10% confidence level

controversial involved action taken by both the Polish and Hungarian DPAs to regulate the use of data made available in the archives of the former Communist secret service. For example, following the surreptitious copying by Bronisław Wildstein of the name index of the Polish Institute for Historical Remembrance and its subsequent release online, the Polish DPA did not only seek Wildstein's criminal prosecution (as previously discussed)[175] but also instituted enforcement action against the latter body. Although Wildstein was not an academic by profession and nor could the form of publication be considered scholarly (or, for that matter, journalistic or literary), this latter action nevertheless impacted academic work. In sum, although the index had technically been available 'only to researchers and others cleared for access',[176] the DPA found that the Institute had been 'negligent' as regards its safeguarding. It therefore ruled that in the future, no 'reference tools' should be directly disclosed 'to persons coming outside from the Institute in the public files' reading room'. Additionally, it instructed the Institute to ensure that files including personal data were registered with the DPA and that it 'develop procedures for safeguarding personal data' including 'a procedure specifying the principles and mode of disclosure of documents to persons carrying on scientific research'.[177] This decision prompted protest from some fifteen Polish historians who argued that it prevented scientific research, disrupted the process of revealing the truth about Poland's recent history, was (as regards the reference tools) akin to preventing readers of a library accessing catalogues, and, in sum, constituted an abuse of power.[178] Interestingly, the Institute itself appealed to the courts claiming that it was exempt from both the substance of data protection law and the DPA's jurisdiction. In 2006, the Voivodeship Administrative Court rejected these contentions, whilst apparently reversing the DPA's findings 'for procedural reasons'.[179] Meanwhile, around the same period, the Hungarian DPA strongly criticized a new law on the historical archives of the former state security archives of that country, finding it a disproportionate interference with data protection. It argued that the disclosure rules ran the risk of disseminating inaccuracies (e.g. incorrectly labelling a person a former security agent) and of tarring all those mentioned in the archives as bad or immoral.[180] Moreover, the intended extent of disclosure planned by the State Security Services archives itself was held to be illegal under data protection[181] and affected individuals were urged report a criminal infringement of their rights.[182] Nevertheless, the DPA did accept that both individuals and organizations engaged in '*tudományos kutatást*' ('scientific research') were entitled to make information public if this was necessary to present research results concerning historical events.[183] Subsequent decisions, however, construed this as limited to data related to public figures or public performances.[184]

Outside this special area, in 2011 the Bulgarian DPA found that it would be illegal to supply a local historian with records of births, marriages, and deaths covering twelve families in two villages during the period 1911–1965. The DPA's decision found that the purpose and rationale of the work was insufficiently specified and so it would be illegal to provide access even with conditions such as, for example, requiring that any result of the research be anonymized.[185] Meanwhile, in 2013 the German Schleswig-Holstein DPA criticized a prison for granting a researcher constrained access to computerized prisoner records without establishing and maintaining a log of what had been in fact been accessed. This made it impossible to determine whether access had been limited only to data required in order to accomplish the relevant task.[186] Enforcement action in certain other cases concerned access and use of existing data sources that did not appear to be especially safeguarded under national law. For example, in 2011 a researcher notified the Portuguese DPA about a project on social mobility that involved using data found in the wedding registries of various cities which dated from 1860 to 1960. Despite finding that these were public documents, the DPA held that its processing would only be legitimate if the work was confined to the safeguarded processing of statistics. It, therefore stipulated that personal data should not be communicated to third parties and that no identified data should be retained.[187]

Finally, a few examples of action were located which related to the use of questionnaires and interviews. However, these were almost always in areas of very particular sensitivity. Thus, returning to the Portuguese case, in 2009 this DPA considered a social and psychological coded questionnaire involving sixteen- to eighteen-year olds, some of whom were going to be recruited from Government sources that indicated that they had been victims of maltreatment or inadequate care by their caregivers. The DPA ruled that this activity could only be justified on the basis of the express consent of the data subjects, must take account of the individual's best interests, and, furthermore, that the holder's code must be destroyed immediately after the validation of the data, thus making direct follow-up studies impossible.[188] In a related case involving interviews with some of these individuals, the DPA stipulated that the code must be deleted within a month following the defence of the individual researcher's thesis.[189]

6. Conclusions

Academics within the humanities and social sciences play a central role in publishing information and ideas of clear social significance for the benefit of the public. Moreover, similar to other studies, this published output is integrally linked to a broader research process that makes such output possible. Given this, it might be thought that this activity should have fallen centrally within the derogations for special forms of expression which have been set out in European data protection laws especially under the DPD. However, alongside these shields, European data protection has from its inception included provisions designed to regulate a range of knowledge facilitation processes. Moreover, DPAs have generally claimed that academic research can only benefit from these latter provisions. This has led to development of stringent restrictions on such activity including far-reaching transparency obligations, restrictions on the dissemination and publishing of data in identifiable form, further limitations in the case of sensitive data, and, in several instances, extensive prior licensing regimes. These kinds of restrictions were distilled by the Council of Europe in Recommendation (83) 10, within an opinion produced by the pan-European Article 29 Working Party and also in guidance issued by approximately 50 per cent of the national EEA DPAs. Moreover, the DPA questionnaire vividly highlighted that around half these regulators saw such a restrictive paradigm applying even in relation to the study of phenomena such as police racism, thus leading to the prohibition of the gathering of critically important data through necessary covert methodologies and notwithstanding that any collected personal data would have been subject to anonymization techniques prior to publication. Over 40 per cent of DPA questionnaire participants claimed to have engaged in enforcement action against social scientists under the DPD and the detailed pattern of intervention reported remained (in contrast to media enforcement) uncorrelated with divergences in the stringency statutory law applicable to journalistic processing. Public domain analysis indicated that, on occasion, a highly restrictive approach had been positively enforced by regulators during especially first- but also second-generation data protection.

At the same time, the chapter also highlighted significant features that are in tension or even contradiction with this restrictive paradigm. In the first place, it is clear that guidance produced by many DPAs was either very general or targeted at specialized forms of research, such as access and use of especially safeguarded data sources, interaction with vulnerable classes of individual or the collection of data in particularly sensitive contexts including biomedicine. Furthermore, DPA responses to the question on the much more socially engaged area of covert social science did indicate that a number were willing to countenance this activity notwithstanding that it was in clear contradiction to both the DPD's default requirements and the knowledge facilitation regime set out in most State laws. The self-reported enforcement figures from the DPA questionnaire were also, albeit weakly, correlated with the stringency of local statutory law applicable to artistic and literary expression (which compared to journalism had much more often not been subject to formal derogation). An analysis of public domain material also indicated that the enforcement of an especially restrictive approach has increasingly focused on the use of especially safeguarded data or a direct engagement with vulnerable types of data subject. Finally, an (albeit small) minority of DPAs produced guidance under the DPD which clearly distinguished between different types of academic work and, at least in the historical research context, explicitly recognized the applicability of the shields for journalism, literature, and other forms of special expression.

The picture uncovered in this chapter is therefore complex, somewhat confused, but, in certain critical respects, also clearly troubling from the perspective of freedom of expression. It is therefore important to consider how regulation should evolve here in order to reconcile effective data protection with both a clear safeguarding of the place of humanities and social science scholarship within the public realm and the imperative of non-discrimination in the exercise of free expression rights. As highlighted at the end of Chapter 10, it is also important to explore the future regulation of other professional writers and also artists under this law. However, before turning to these issues, we must also analyse what changes the General Data Protection Regulation 2016/679 and local implementing law have made in this area. All of this will be explored in Chapters 12.

12

'Non-Journalistic' Traditional Publishers and Third-Generation European Data Protection Regulation

Formal Law and the Future

As emphasized in Chapters 10 and 11, European data protection's regulation of traditional publishers outside journalism raises issues for freedom of expression and society more generally which are both profound and comparable to that which arise in relation to the traditional media. It is therefore important to consider what changes the General Data Protection Regulation 2016/679 ('GDPR') and implementing third-generation statutory data protection law makes here and, as importantly, how this new framework should be interpreted and applied by regulators in the future. Turning first to look at the formal law, the GPDR's stance *vis-à-vis* traditional publishers outside of academia remains broadly consistent with the *status quo ante*. Thus, similarly to Article 9 of the Data Protection Directive 95/46 ('DPD'), Article 85(2) of GDPR requires States to set out derogations 'necessary to reconcile the right to the protection of personal data with the freedom of expression and information' not only in the area of 'journalistic purposes' but also as regards 'artistic or literary expression'. By contrast, in the area of academic activity and publication, the GDPR importantly expands the special expression regime so as to safeguard 'academic expression'.[1] Moreover, in contrast to the more mixed picture under second-generation data protection, the new laws adopted at national level generally provide that all these special purposes are treated comparably to that of journalism. Therefore, whilst continuing to fall within the scope of data protection law and regulation, these activities in principle benefit from far-reaching derogations. Nevertheless, potentially difficult interpretative problems arise for academia as a result of the failure of most States to comply with Article 85(2)'s instruction to extend the special expression derogations explicitly to knowledge facilitation provisions which by default apply to 'scientific or historical research purposes'.[2] In theory, and as explored in Chapter 8, this mirrors similar issues which arise for media archiving as a result of a similar failure to formalize derogations to the default provisions applicable to the pursuit of 'archiving purposes in the public interest'. Nevertheless, the problems confronting academia are much more extreme, not only because such academic expression has (as seen in

European Data Protection Regulation, Journalism, and Traditional Publishers. David Erdos, Oxford University Press (2019). © David Erdos.
DOI: 10.1093/oso/9780198841982.003.0012

Chapter 11) often been treated as essentially synonymous with scientific and/or historical research purposes but also due to a general lack of awareness of the rationale for including this purpose within special expression in the first place. There is therefore a real possibility that the newly expanded scope of special expression within the GDPR could be seriously undermined.

These difficulties highlight the need for Data Protection Authorities ('DPAs') (and others) to adopt a principled understanding of the role that the special expression derogations play within the broader data protection framework. These derogations uniquely and critically seek to reconcile European data protection with the core exercise of freedom of expression, namely that which is of a journalistic, academic, artistic, or literary nature. Moreover, as the European Court of Human Rights (ECtHR) has stressed, the need for a special safeguarding of such expression cannot be denied on the basis that the expression is *'une œuvre scientifique et sociologique'* ('a scientific and sociological work').[3] To the contrary: other things being equal, these characteristics heighten the justification for such shielding. It follows that, even if the controller in question has an academic orientation or status, the scientific and historical research provisions must not be applied where they would undermine the special expression derogation's fundamental instruction. Nevertheless, these knowledge facilitation provisions could remain relevant where an expressive actor wishes to receive data from another controller on especially safeguarded terms or (more controversially and delicately) where they have assumed a clear and specific quasi-fiduciary obligation of care *vis-à-vis* the relevant data subjects. Whilst these kinds of situations are likely to be more common in an academic setting, they could also apply to those working within journalism, literature, or art.

As with the professional journalistic media, DPAs remain the ultimate guardians of a balanced system of personal information protection even as regards the special expressive activity of other traditional publishers. Moreover, not only is such activity capable of seriously impacting the privacy and other rights which data protection exists to defend, but ensuring appropriate and effective self-regulation is a greater challenge here. DPAs should, therefore, adopt a more proactive stance in this area. In particular, it is vital that they actively formulate and promote standard-setting guidance that elucidates the broad applicability of special expression regime, the relatively narrow range of expressive activity that continues to fall only within the knowledge facilitation regime, and finally the significant data protection norms which continue to apply to the pursuit of special expression. Furthermore, DPAs must engage in robust and strategic enforcement action, thereby helping to ensure the genuine effectiveness of appropriate protections for data subjects here. Whilst recognizing their limitations, regulators should constructively engage with and encourage any self-regulatory bodies that exist here whilst engaging in these twin tasks. Finally, the European Data Protection Board should support these national initiatives through 'soft' guidance and information exchange, but should avoid any 'harder' forms of intervention when processing concerns these sensitive activities.

The rest of this chapter divides into five sections. The first explores the formal legal provisions found in the GDPR and in national implementing legislation. Sections 2, 3, and 4 look at how this framework should be interpreted and applied by the regulators. Section 2 considers how State DPAs should interpret the law and set standards in this area, section 3 examines their responsibilities in relation to enforcement and section 4 explores the role of the European Data Protection Board. Finally, section 5 closes with some overarching conclusions.

1. Third-Generation Data Protection Law and 'Non-Journalistic' Traditional Publishers

1.1 The GDPR and its Drafting

The requirement Article 85(2) of the GDPR places on Member States to set out special derogations as 'necessary to reconcile the right to the protection of personal data with the freedom of expression and information' applies not only regarding 'journalistic purposes' but also 'the purpose of academic artistic or literary expression'. Recital 153 further stresses that '[i]n order to take account of the importance of the right to freedom of expression in every democratic society' it is necessary to interpret 'notions' related to freedom of expression 'broadly'. In principle, these derogations may apply to any part of the Regulation, aside from its general scope and definitions and its procedural stipulations relating to remedies, liabilities, and penalties. Under Article 85(3), States must notify the European Commission of the derogations adopted and keep such notification up to date.

Turning to legislative history, the Commission's initial draft in 2012 mirrored the previous DPD by including processing carried out 'solely' for either 'journalistic purposes' or 'artistic and literary expression' within the special expressive purposes regime.[4] All these purposes were retained in the final text and, in contrast to the period leading up to the DPD, did not prove contentious. Indeed, reflecting an emphasis on broad and generous interpretation, the requirement that any processing be 'solely' for one or other of the special expressive purposes was removed from the final article, although it was retained in the accompanying recital.[5] In marked contrast to literary and artistic expression, the relationship between the GDPR and academic scholarship gave rise to considerable controversy during the four years of negotiation leading up to the final text. In this regard, the Commission's initial draft not only failed to include mention of this activity within special expression but explicitly excluded any possibility of States using this latter regime to limit the application of the GDPR's default knowledge facilitation provisions[6] which were set out to govern 'historical, statistical and scientific research purposes'.[7] This approach prompted significant concern amongst academics working within the humanities and social science. In particular, in February 2013 the UK Economic and Social Research Council issued a position paper which argued that:

> [a] historian or social investigator working within an academic context should not be treated less favourably by the law than a historian or social investigator writing in a non-academic context. But without the protections of [the special expression regime], academic work would be subject to forms of restriction far in excess of restrictions on photos and articles which often appear in the Press. This would seriously impact on the production of valuable and informative material by academics. It is therefore essential that the work of academic social science researchers be brought within the ambit of [special expression].[8]

In March 2014 the European Parliament adopted its version of the draft GDPR which suggested that States be obliged to adopt freedom of expression derogations (which were 'necessary' and in accordance with the EU Charter) in general and not only in the area of special expression. It also included the articles on knowledge facilitation activity within the ambit of this requirement.[9] The Council of the EU, which agreed its position in June 2015, not only also similarly proposed extending the scope of the derogatory regime to these latter provisions but specifically referenced 'academic . . . expression' within a reformulated definition of special expression which remained subject to its own discrete provisions.[10] Advocacy for this clear protection of academic work continued right up to the final negotiations. In particular, later in 2015 the Wellcome Trust (supported by some ninety other research organizations) publicly backed the Council's proposals arguing that it was 'important that arts and humanities research should benefit from derogations because research in areas such as politics is unlikely to be compatible with the research model set out in Article 83 [now 89] and may not be permitted otherwise'.[11] This approach ultimately found its way into the final GDPR text that was approved in the spring of 2016.

The final text also included default provisions relating to knowledge facilitation, which was defined as encompassing 'archiving purposes in the public interest', 'scientific or historical research purposes', and 'statistical purposes'.[12] Reflecting the safeguarding model explored in Chapter 11, these provisions required that such processing 'be subject to appropriate safeguards'[13] and only set out limited derogatory possibilities. These possibilities were variously made compulsory, semi-compulsory, and entirely optional for the Member States. In sum, the Regulation stated that, subject to appropriate safeguards, the further processing of data for these purposes would not violate the principle of purpose limitation[14] and could result in data being stored for longer than otherwise would be necessary.[15] It further stipulated that the right to erasure and to be forgotten would not apply where this would 'seriously impair the achievement of the objectives of that processing'.[16]

States were also encouraged to derogate from the general prohibition on processing most sensitive categories of data absent waiver from the data subject[17] and specifically enabled to derogate from a data subject's default rights to subject access, to object to processing, and to demand its restriction.[18] In addition, the GDPR included general clauses that enabled States to adopt certain substantive limitations that, although not specifically focused on any particular processing activity, could cover knowledge facilitation activities which fell outside of special expression. Thus, Article 23 permitted derogations from all the transparency rules and data subject rights (as well as the data protections principles in so far as they had the same effect) so long as this was 'necessary' for 'important objectives of general public interest' or to protect 'the rights and freedoms of others'.[19] Meanwhile, Article 10 allowed for derogations from the requirement that the processing of data relating to criminality be 'under the control of official authority' as long as any law set out 'appropriate safeguards for the rights and freedoms of data subjects'.[20]

Both the default knowledge facilitation and the general limitation clauses drew on existing provisions within the DPD[21] and (with the exception of the provisions specifically on archiving) were found within the European Commission's initial draft text.[22] The Commission's initial text placed greatest emphasis on ensuring a harmonized approach within the knowledge facilitation area, including through setting out an unequivocal common legal basis for processing sensitive data[23] and establishing that further derogations in this area could be enacted through European Commission delegated legislation.[24] Meanwhile, the European Parliament adopted the most restrictive approach, notably by generally removing the reference to knowledge facilitation within the sensitive data derogations, eliminating the possibility for the European Commission to adopt further derogations through delegated legislation, and removing both the reference to the data protection principles and to derogations simply on the basis of the public/general interest within the principal general limitations clause. It did, however, set out provisions for certain strictly defined public interest archiving services and included their activities within the sensitive data derogations. Finally, the Council text included provisions applicable to a broader category of public interest archiving and, in general, placed the greatest emphasis on a maintenance State discretion.[25] This latter text also most closely mirrored the approach ultimately adopted although, reflecting inevitable compromises, elements from within all three perspectives may be found within the final GDPR text in this area.

1.2 National Legal Instruments[26]

Putting to one side the three States whose statutory law has failed to address the relationship between data protection and freedom of expression at all,[27] the laws implementing the GDPR have defined special expression more consistently than was the case under second-generation data protection. In sum, the great majority have adopted the definition set out in the GDPR verbatim. The clear exceptions to this are Germany, Denmark, Iceland, Liechtenstein, and Poland. Liechtenstein still provides that only '[m]*edienschaffende*' ('media professionals') may benefit from its statutory special expression derogation.[28] The framework established at a national level in Germany has a similar scope.[29] However, there are signs that more of the *Länder* have adopted broader laws at local level. For reasons of practicality, this was looked at only in relation to the four *Länder* whose DPA responded to the questionnaire in 2013. As previously noted, local statutory special expression safeguards in the Rhineland-Palatinate and Schleswig-Holstein continue only to apply to the media.[30] In contrast, in Brandenburg and Mecklenburg-Vorpommern these derogations have been widened so as to extend to all exercises of journalistic, artistic, and literary expression.[31] Nevertheless, neither of these provisions extend to the GDPR's new protection for 'academic' expression.[32] Such a restricted scope is also found in the special expression regime set out in Iceland[33] and Denmark.[34] However, the Danish law does generally state that the data protection framework should not apply where this would be contrary to the freedom of expression provisions of either the European Convention on Human Rights or the EU Charter.[35] Finally, despite mandating a far-reaching exemption for all other types of special expression, Poland has similarly granted academic expression almost no derogation from the default established in the GDPR.[36]

Minor deviations in the stringency of the law applicable to different types of special expression are apparent in at least six States. First, in Belgium, Denmark, and certain German *Länder* certain non-journalistic forms of expression are treated more leniently in data protection law than the journalistic media. Thus, returning to Denmark, Germany Brandenburg, and Germany Mecklenburg-Vorpommern, the statutory derogation set down as regards artistic and literary expression is essentially absolute in nature. This contrasts with the regulation of journalistic media which is made subject the *sui generis Lov om massemediers informationsdatabaser* in Denmark and subject to very limited accuracy and subject access requirements in German *Länder*. Meanwhile, Belgian law establishes than those engaged in all non-journalistic forms of special expression may benefit from an absolute exemption from the transparency and sensitive data rules without having to be subject to professional rules as applies in relation to journalism.[37]

Second, France presents particular complexity. On the one hand, the statutory derogation here does not require non-journalistic special expression to conform to any cognate to the professional ethical rules that it requires of the journalistic media. Although any derogation must still satisfy a 'necessity' test, this is best seen as shifting the public interest test here from a strict to a permissive one.[38] On the other hand, the prohibition on the DPA using its regulatory powers to seize data protected under confidentiality only applies to journalistic as opposed to other special expressive material.[39]

Third and finally, the law in Austria and Italy is unequivocally somewhat more stringent in relation to non-journalistic as opposed journalistic or media expression. Thus, the partial exemption which Austrian law sets out requires that special weight to be given to the processing needs of the journalistic media but does not extend this to other types of special expression.[40] A more limited divergence is apparent in Italian law which only sets out a minimal derogation from default subject access rights in order to protect source confidentiality for journalistic as opposed to other special expression content.[41]

Taking into account the divergences in all these cases and using the same schemata as that applied in relation to journalism in Chapter 8 and Appendix 7, Appendix 8 sets out a quantification of the minimum[42] level of stringency of the statutory law applicable to non-journalistic expression across all the EEA States.[43]

A broader divergence between the statutory regime applicable to journalism and other special expression arises from the fact that, whilst approximately one-third of EEA States have established specific co-regulatory provisions applicable to journalism,[44] almost none of these speak to activities outside of journalism. Thus, as explored in Chapter 8, many of the substantive derogations invoke the idea of conformity with journalistic ethics. However, this concept is not replicated in relation to academic, artistic, or literary activities. Similarly, specialist scrutinizing structures such as Press Councils (in Germany and Luxembourg), the Order of Journalists (in Italy), and the Inspector of Journalism Ethics (in Lithuania) either are not applicable or do not have a comparable self-regulatory resonance in relation to forms of special expression outside of professional journalism. Whilst these differences do not necessarily alter the stringency of the local law, they vividly highlight the greater difficulty in establishing a relationship between statutory and self-regulation within this broader area of expressive activity.

An even wider issue and potential difference arises from the confusing interface between the special expression derogations and the knowledge facilitation provisions that generally govern 'archiving purposes in the public interest', 'scientific or historical research purposes', and 'statistical purposes'.[45] This issue was considered in Chapter 8 in relation to media archiving. As explained there, notwithstanding the GDPR's clearly contrary instruction, almost two-thirds of States have failed to explicitly stipulate in their statutes that the special expression derogations apply as necessary even to these knowledge facilitation provisions. Moreover, three States that legislated for such a prioritization, namely Denmark, Germany, and Iceland, failed to include the new concept of academic expression within their definition of special expression.[46] The precarious position within which academic expression could be left is exacerbated not only by its newly minted status but also by the reality, which was explored in Chapter 11, that this activity has often been treated as falling entirely within the knowledge facilitation purpose of 'scientific or historical research'.

Turning finally to look at the default knowledge facilitation regime itself, a majority (although far from all)[47] States legislated for certain limited derogations here. However, aside from provisions in a few States that established a specific legal basis for processing criminal-related data,[48] none have utilized the general restriction clauses in order specifically liberalize the law in a way that goes beyond the default and restrictive knowledge facilitation model set out in the GDPR itself. Thus, no State provides for a specific derogation from the bulk of the data protection principles,[49] the proactive transparency rules,[50] the restrictions on transborder data flows,[51] or the entirety of the DPA supervision and pan-European cooperation and consistency apparatus.[52] Moreover, approximately one-third of the States have failed to set out a knowledge facilitation derogation from the general prohibition on the private sector processing of sensitive data absent waiver from the data subject.[53] Finally, even those States which have set out (albeit highly qualified) derogations here have sometimes combined these with restrictive and peremptory 'safeguards'[54] which even go beyond those explicitly set out in the GDPR itself. For example, UK statutory law establishes a default rule that knowledge facilitation processing should not 'cause substantial damage or substantial distress to a data subject' or (with the exception of certain specially approved medical research) be 'carried out for the purpose of measures or decisions with respect to a particular data subject'.[55]

2. State DPAs, 'Non-Journalistic' Traditional Publishers, and Standard-Setting

DPAs must discharge their tasks as the 'the guardians'[56] of data protection through interpreting, elucidating, and promoting relevant standards and then by monitoring and ensuring enforcement of the same. These twin aspects of regulation were discussed in relation to professional journalism in Chapter 9 and remain equally important, though even more fraught, as regards non-journalistic traditional publishers. This section, therefore, looks at how DPA's should approach their standard-setting role in this latter area, whilst section 3 looks similarly at enforcement.

2.1 An Initial Threshold Issue: Delimiting the Scope of Special Expression

A critical initial issue that DPAs must confront is the delineation of the scope of special expression as this relates to traditional, yet non-journalistic, publisher activity. As explored in Part II of this book, much of the historical origin of the special expression framework lies in an attempt to reconcile data protection with the freedom of expression of the journalistic media. For example, the Explanatory

Report of the Data Protection Convention in 1981 only referred to the tension between data protection and rights to expression as this concerned the 'freedom of the press'.[57] The European Commission's initial draft of the DPD's special expression clause was similarly confined to 'the press and the audiovisual media'.[58] Nevertheless, as early as the 1970s and 1980s, the law in some European States did recognize the need for special derogations to safeguard wider forms of publication. Moreover, by the time a concept of special expression had been agreed across Europe in the DPD of 1995 its definition had dropped all references to particular institutional actors and had explicitly safeguarded not only 'journalistic purposes' but also both 'artistic' and 'literary' expression.[59] Finally, the GDPR has now gone further by also including 'academic' expression within this concept[60] and stressing that '[i]n order to take account of the importance of the right to freedom of expression in every democratic society' the interpretation of 'notions' relating to freedom of expression have to be interpreted 'broadly'.[61] Not only this recital but also the expansion of the categories of special expression over time point to the need for DPAs to adopt a generous and purposive interpretation of the scope of this special regime.

Such a generous and purposive approach should lead to all activities which contribute to public knowledge, understanding, or discourse falling within these special expression safeguards, irrespective of whether the 'information, opinions or ideas'[62] at issue serve a journalistic, artistic, literary, or academic purpose and also irrespective of professional status of the actor involved.[63] It is true that the notion of 'public' in this context must be understood as a collective and, in principle, open body of persons rather simply any indeterminate number of persons.[64] However, it should not matter whether the resulting material garners wide attention or, in contrast, if those who directly engage with it remain 'small or specialized'.[65] It follows that artists, non-academic writers and also academics within the social sciences and humanities should all benefit from this regime in so far as their activities relate to this kind of publication. Such an understanding of the law is, by now, relatively uncontroversial as regards those who operate outside of an academic context. In contrast, and as elucidated in Chapter 11, many DPAs (and indeed others) have until recently held that academic processing should be governed according to data protection's restrictive default knowledge facilitation provisions. The GDPR continues with these provisions and mentions 'scientific or historical research' in this context.[66] Nevertheless, in contrast to previous instruments, it also specifically includes 'academic' expression within the definition of special expression[67] and places a clear obligation on States to enact special expression derogations even within the knowledge facilitation area.

The interpretative dilemma for DPAs (and others) arises from the reality that only a minority of State laws explicitly establish that the special expression derogations can apply to knowledge facilitation activities. That dilemma has already been confronted in Chapter 9 in the context of media archiving. It was argued there that, although media archiving might reasonably be considered to constitute 'archiving purposes in the public interest', a principled interpretation of the unique and central place of the special expression regime within the data protection framework required that the benefit of these derogations not be lost solely on that basis.[68] The need for a similar construction is even more compelling as regards academic work in the humanities and social science. It is true a good deal of work within the social sciences and humanities could be considered to be 'scientific or historical research'.[69] Nevertheless, as the ECtHR has emphasized, the fact that a publication constitutes 'une œuvre scientifique et sociologique' ('a scientific and sociological work') carried out by 'une universitaire' ('an academic') rather than material aimed (solely) at 'saisfaire la curiosité d'un certain public' ('satisfying the curiosity of a certain portion the public') as is often forthcoming from 'la presse dite "à sensation"' ('the so-called sensationalist press') should enhance rather than detract from its status as a specially safeguarded type of expression.[70] Moreover, such activity not only clearly falls within 'academic freedom'[71] but the central place of such work within special expression has now been explicitly recognized by the inclusion of 'academic' expression within the GDPR. For all these reasons, it is essential that DPA guidance makes clear that scholarly work within the humanities and social sciences both can and should benefit fully from the special expressive purpose derogations.

The damage that could be inflicted on freedom of expression in the absence of such a broad and generous interpretation can hardly be overstated. In sum, academics would be uniquely crippled in their capacity to generate socially significant information and ideas for the benefit of the public. As Chapter 11 noted, the default rules prohibiting a resort to non-transparent methodologies would 'simply preclude valuable forms of critical inquiry' including, to take one type of example, investigations into 'police racism (or corruption, sexism, excessive use of force, etc.)'.[72] Moreover, especially where sensitive data was engaged, academics would be severely hampered in their ability to publish an unvarnished analysis of the contemporary past, thereby leading to an acute risk that scholarship could become complicit in what amounts to a 'rewriting of history'.[73] Thus, as Linda Shopes has written in relation to similar restrictions which previously applied in the United States, albeit only in relation to work funded by the federal government:[74]

> [F]or historians, a deep disjunction exists between the Common Rule's concern for privacy and the canons of historical inquiry. At times information [for example] in an interview, if made public, can indeed place a person at risk of criminal or civil liability, or be damaging to his financial standing, employability, or reputation. Yet historians' deepest responsibility is to follow the evidence where it leads, to discern and make sense of the past in all its complexity; not necessarily to protect individuals from their past actions.[75]

In sum, any interpretation which led to these kind of results would fundamentally undermine the core purpose of the special expression regime which is to ensure that the generation and dissemination of 'information, opinions or ideas'[76] for the benefit of the public collectively is not unduly curtailed. It would similarly conflict with the fundamental principle that those pursuing essentially the same freedom of expression activity should be treated equally under law.[77]

2.2 A Continuing Role for the Knowledge Facilitation Regime?

Whilst academic work within both the humanities and social sciences must in principle fall within the scope of special expression, it remains important that any special contextual features of such processing are fully taken into account. Moreover, in specifically delineated circumstances, this could even result in the public interest and similar justifying tests that are generally built into the special expression regime not being fulfilled. Within these narrow circumstances, the default regime for scientific or historical research will therefore continue to apply. A particularly clear example of this arises where a 'non-expressive' actor, such as commercial organization or a Government department, agrees to share a private set of personal data with an academic for scholarly analysis but on strictly safeguarded terms. In these cases, the knowledge facilitation regime can provide an appropriate (and indeed useful) framework for this transfer and use of data, in which case a special expression justification for departing from its restrictions should also not be available. Therefore, assuming the academic in question freely consents to these restrictions then (absent an overwhelming public interest for departing from this arising subsequently) they should be compelled to abide these restrictions including directly under data protection law itself. Although the boundaries here would be much more contestable and controversial, a similar rationale may apply where academics collect data directly from individual members of the general public within a special 'relationship of power and dependence'.[78] For example, such a clearly unbalanced and dependent context would arise in 'some psychological experimentation'.[79] In this kind of situation, an academic may be taken to have assumed a quasi-fiduciary responsibility for safeguarding these individuals' interests which is akin to that which generally arises in the biomedical investigation, the paradigm example of research which clearly falls within (and only within) the knowledge facilitation regime.

Actors operating outside an academic setting also sometimes agree to process data on a strictly safeguarded basis only and/or collect data within a quasi-fiduciary care relationship. For example, a 'data journalist' may elect to receive a dataset from a non-journalistic controller on an explicitly restricted basis, whilst another journalist may commission a psychological experiment involving members of the general public. In these circumstances, the same justification for regulating the processing under the knowledge facilitation regime could arise. Moreover, although these kind of data collection contexts remain considerably more common within academia, in most cases scholars within the social sciences and humanities do not collect data within a 'carer-cared for' relationship and so owe those whom they study 'no special duty of beneficence or care beyond those owed to anyone in normal social intercourse'.[80] It therefore remains vital that the knowledge facilitation as opposed to the special expression regime only apply on an exceptional basis and in narrow and strictly delineated situations.

2.3 Crafting and Disseminating Guidance

As explored earlier, it is vital that DPA guidance in this area endorses and promulgates a broad construction of the special expressive purposes regime. At the same time, it is also important that any such guidance also supports the pan-European imperative that this regime facilitates a careful balancing between freedom of expression and the default data protection framework. In that regard, DPAs must clearly accord high respect to any reasonable balance laid down within statutory law. The need for such respect reflects not only the democratic credentials of the local legislature but also the fact that Article 85(2) of the GDPR clearly allocates this task of reconciliation primarily to that body. It also means that a wide diversity of approach between EEA States will remain in evidence.

Subject to this, DPAs (and courts) must ensure that the special expression derogations are 'necessary' and, furthermore, are applied 'only insofar as is strictly necessary'.[81] The strict necessity threshold here is particularly tricky since non-journalistic traditional publishers will often be engaged in publicly interested expression which, as the ECtHR has made clear, can itself only be restricted on satisfaction of a strict necessity threshold.[82] Courts have found that the combination of two competing, strict necessity thresholds requires a decision-making process to ensure an 'intense focus on the comparative importance of the specific rights being claimed'.[83] That must entail a careful analysis of the weight of justification for, on the one hand, the particular expression at issue and, on the other, the privacy, dignity, reputation, or other core rights concerns of the data subject. However, from the perspective of the data protection framework, it is as important that decision-making involves close scrutiny of the specific rationale for the limitation (or even full exclusion) of each of the default data protection provisions from which a derogation is being claimed. Finally, the 'essence'[84] of data protection including, for example, redress against manifestly unfair processing, must in any case remain unimpaired.

In the absence of DPAs facilitating the elucidation of clear and accessible standards to guide data controllers, this kind of careful balancing is almost certain to prove highly imperfect or even completely illusory. Unfortunately, during the previous iterations of European data protection, most regulators did not engage in such standard-setting activity. Indeed, as explored in Chapter 10, the vast majority of regulators entirely failed to address the position of non-academic artists and writers. Meanwhile, as seen in the Chapter 11, around half the DPAs crafted guidance for academics based solely on the much more restrictive knowledge facilitation regime. Reflective of this, many academics within social science and humanities found themselves subject to a 'labyrinth' of often disproportionate restrictions and controls imposed by their institutions.[85] Moreover, in the absence of clear contrary DPA guidance, these restrictions appear to be increasing within some institutions who are struggling with interpreting new GDPR provisions that, on paper and outside special expression, are much more far-reaching than the *status quo ante*. Thus, Ruben Andersson has argued that:

> just as Big Tech is swiftly taking steps to shield itself from GDPR's most onerous obligations, the regime is now trickling down to universities where it is starting to hit legitimate, qualitative and small-scale research with a range of confusing semi-prohibitions. As with last year's barrage of GDPR spam sent out by nervous companies and charities, universities are now erring on the extreme side of caution. Instead of using the GDPR exemptions for academic research to the full, they seem to be interpreting the regulation in a strict and exceedingly complex way.[86]

In contrast, non-academic artists and writers seem largely to have ignored the data protection implications of their work. Clearly, neither of these outcomes does justice to the reconciliation of rights which the data protection framework seeks to achieve.

DPAs should therefore prioritize the drafting of detailed and balanced special expression guidance addressed to all those producing and disseminating academic, artistic and literary output to the public at large. In Part II of this book exploring professional journalism, it was suggested that guidance in this kind of sensitive area would best produced through a co-regulatory fusion between statutory and self-regulation that adopted the GDPR's code of conduct provision as a guideline or benchmark.[87] Whilst normatively appealing also in the context of non-journalistic traditional publishers, the deployment of such an approach here presents formidable challenges. Thus, whilst 'ethical' reflection certainly exists within academia, 'self-regulation' within the social science and the humanities has traditionally been very informal. In sum:

> ethics were [historically] treated as matters of personal and professional integrity . . . The presumption was that individual researchers were responsible for morally interrogating their own research as an ongoing and integrated aspect of the research process. Adherence to disciplinary norms was inculcated, judged, and enforced through processes internal to the research community, such as research training, peer review, and private sanction.[88]

More recently, universities within several European States as well as many re-search funding bodies have sought to impose much more formalized and codi-fied norms on academics. These norms have largely had their origin within the biomedical sciences and are often predicted on an 'ethical standard of beneficence towards the individual research subject'.[89] However, whilst understandable within the 'carer–cared for' relationship which is normal within biomedicine (and the experimental behavioural sciences), such a standard is at 'odds with the idea of academic freedom to inquiry, public right to know, and the moral duty to expose injustice'[90] which has been central to work in the social science and the humanities. In addition, its highly formalized nature, which is often predicated on extensive *ex ante* review, may also effectively mandate a deductive 'philosophical framework for research developed for the natural sciences'[91] which is ill-suited to the messy and fluid nature of social and humanities inquiry. Such widespread 'mimicking'[92] of the biomedical governance model has been the subject of widespread and co-gent criticism from within the social science and humanities community, with many thoughtful voices decrying its effects as 'illegitimate',[93] running the risk of 'homogenizing inquiry and narrowing vision',[94] and even constituting 'a process of censorship that is disabling to the democratic values by which we seek to live'.[95] Moreover, by connecting academic processing only to data protection's knowledge facilitation derogations, DPAs have themselves played a role in entrenching this problematic model.[96] Indeed, this 'bureaucratisation of research ethics'[97] has often developed in lock-step with a 'rigid interpretation of data protection'[98] by aca-demic institutions. Thus, alongside the concerns highlighted earlier as regards the later development, Andersson notes that:

> [t]he past years have seen a sharp move away from considering ethics as an em-bedded, context-dependent process in fieldwork, replacing this with a view of ethics as protocol. This shift, in turn, is based on the application of dominant ideas around ethics in the medical and behavioural sciences, as well as on increasing demand from funders for the right boxes to be ticked. While this protocol-based model has helped protect human subjects' from powerful forms of experimental research ever since safeguards were first introduced in Cold War-era United States, it is fundamentally at odds with the aims of non-experimental research, particularly of a qualitative kind.[99]

Turning finally to consider traditional publishers outside both journalism and academia, these writers and artists generally lack any institutionalized self-regulatory structure. Moreover, the few organizations which do exist within this field—such as PEN International and writers' guilds in various countries—have almost entirely avoided addressing matters of 'ethical' controversy. Any self-regulation that does exist here has, therefore, remained entirely informal in nature.

Notwithstanding these challenges, there remains a compelling case for ensuring that guidance in this area draws upon the experience and expertise of professionals who pursue special expression as their vocation. Regulators will, however, need to be creative in working out how this might be achieved. Thus, in relation to academia, it is important that DPAs specifically engage with the social science and humanities scholarly community rather than only academic institutions such as universities who, as noted earlier, have often become dominated by the restrictive research governance model originally developed for biomedicine. This should include the many professional social science and humanities organizations that have taken an interest in this area. It could include the consortium of organizations including the Association for Social Anthropologists, the European Sociological Association, and the Royal Geographical Society which issued a joint statement in 2018 arguing that 'when universities implement the GDPR it is crucial that they make full use of the derogations designed for enabling academic research', that 'the template for the regulation of all research under current data protection legislation has been a biomedical model', but that '[t]he reference in the GDPR to academic expression is principally designed to ensure that humanities and social science scholarship is shielded within the special expression clause on an equal basis to that of journalism'.[100] It should also take note of those who have published peer-reviewed criticisms of the application of a biomedical model of research outside of this special context. The Belgium DPA's approach to crafting guidance on historical research under the DPD provides a good model here. As stated in Chapter 11, this guidance arose out of a conference which not only featured a number of academics engaged in contemporary historical scholarship but, furthermore, clearly distinguished their work from biomedicine, a field of activity which was analysed separately at the same meeting.[101] Turning to consider non-academic traditional publishers, at least the larger DPAs should consider assembling a reference panel of artists and writers whose work centrally involves the processing of personal data and to whom they can then refer drafts of guidance as these are being assembled. This may also provide regulators with an opportunity to begin reaching out to the few collective groupings that do exist here by, for example, inviting them to nominate a representative to serve within such a grouping.

Given the weaker self-organization of non-journalistic traditional publishers compared to that of the journalistic media, it seems inevitable that any initial standard-setting will need to be coordinated by the DPA itself rather than through a formalized co-regulatory process. Whilst this presents challenges from the perspective of ensuring self-regulatory involvement, it will also enable DPAs to integrate these standards into overarching guidance on the special expression regime as a whole. This guidance should ensure that the common rights conflicts faced by all traditional publishers—whether academic or non-academic, journalistic, or non-journalistic—are given proper emphasis. Although outside of this book's focus, such guidance would also provide an appropriate setting to elucidate when an amateur individual disseminating data to an indeterminate number of people can benefit from this special regime. This guidance could thereby further the coherent development of data protection regulation, a critical value integrally linked to the principle of legal equality and one of the primary rationales for the existence of DPAs in the first place. Additionally, its production would represent less of a resource burden for regulators than actively coordinating the production of multiple and overlapping sets of standards by myriad professional bodies, a factor that cannot be discounted given the straitened position of these DPAs as explored in Part II. Finally, overarching guidance would stand the greatest chance of gaining widespread visibility and thereby being noted by the many different parties to whom it relates. As emphasized also in relation to professional journalism previously, achieving such widespread dissemination is critical to the success of standard-setting efforts in these as in other areas.

Once overarching guidance is in place, it may well be that, at least within academia, various institutions and groups would seek to integrate its general approach within their internal policies and procedures. So long as these policies and procedures genuinely enable competing rights to be balanced and reconciled, DPAs should facilitate and encourage such developments. Ultimately, this could even lead to a formal co-regulatory code of conduct under Article 40 of the GDPR being agreed. However, even if does not happen, these potentialities dovetail with the need also for DPA's to develop a clear enforcement strategy, an issue which is examined immediately below.

3. State DPAs, 'Non-Journalistic' Traditional Publishers, and Enforcement

Enforcement action not only lies at the heart of a DPA's role as the ultimate guardian of data protection but is also given a renewed emphasis in the GDPR. At the same time, and as explored in Part II of this book, DPAs are faced with many increasingly pressing priorities and continue to be endowed with very limited resources. Direct enforcement can also be extremely expensive. Reflecting this, and as Chapter 11 elucidated, such action has become rare even within the academic sector, a setting which most DPAs have conceived (albeit, at least in the GDPR-era, erroneously) as falling outside of the special expression derogations. However, since the special expression regime *is* in fact generally engaged, a DPA will face significant further constraints in the form of legal restrictions on both its investigative and corrective powers. Given such a complex and sometimes less than ideal context, regulators will have to be somewhat selective in setting priorities. Nevertheless, DPAs still have a fundamental responsibility to uphold the 'effective and complete protection of data subjects'.[102] This must involve robust monitoring of the ability of individuals to obtain appropriate redress for any significant violation of their rights, whether through the DPA itself, self-regulatory bodies, or the civil courts. Where such redress is not reasonably available, regulators must at least make a clear determination of this and propose concrete change. Furthermore, they must in any case respect data subjects' default right to lodge individual complaints with them and to see that these are actively handled.[103] Finally, and most importantly given the constraints under which DPAs operate, it is vital that they adopt a strategic approach which is calibrated to the seriousness of any actual or alleged infraction and to the extent to which the relevant actor has and continues to demonstrate a commitment to comply with core data protection standards.

Turning first to look at this in relation to scholarship in the social sciences and the humanities, it is likely that many academic institutions will have established research ethics committees or similar 'self-regulatory' oversight systems which are charged with policing many of the same issues which statutory data protection also addresses.[104] Data subjects should, therefore, be encouraged to lodge any concerns with these bodies in the first instance and DPAs should be willing to liaise and co-operate with them as necessary. Indeed, far from giving data subjects short shrift, these mechanisms may (as explored earlier) often attempt to enforce a governance model that is insufficiently mindful of individual scholars' freedom of expression and the public's concomitant right to know. In these circumstances, the prime role of DPA may simply be to point decision-makers to the newly broadened scope of special expression under the GDPR. Nevertheless, even when robust internal oversight exists in theory, it cannot be assumed that its jurisdiction will precisely overlap with data protection, will always be practically operational, or that it will offer an effective redress of individual grievances. Therefore, in the absence of a code of conduct and monitoring body which is formally approved and subject to ongoing scrutiny,[105] DPAs should engage in a scrutiny of individual complaints which goes considerably beyond a mere reasonableness review of the decisions made by these other bodies. In any case, they must intervene directly where particularly serious and/or systemic *prima facie* violations of data protection come to light, not only through deployment of their investigatory powers but potentially even by formally requiring corrective action and/or imposing *ex post* sanctions.

Crafting an enforcement strategy in relation to non-academic writers and artists presents the greatest challenge. These actors are by their nature highly fissiparous and generally fall outside the jurisdiction of any self-regulatory mechanism. Even after direct investigation (which may be prompted either by an individual complaint or an own-initiative inquiry), it may prove difficult for a regulator to precisely determine the degree of culpability involved in any identified failing or, as importantly, the extent there the actor demonstrates a genuine commitment to comply with core data protection standards in the future. In many cases, these problems will be exacerbated by the relatively low likelihood of foreseeable repeat interactions between the DPA and these actors. Nevertheless, the reality to date of largely eschewing regulatory enforcement here is unsustainable. Instead, regulators should seek to adopt a robust but proportionate approach. In the first place, given the likely absence of any alternative mechanism, DPAs must remain directly responsible for assessing individual complaints. However, a form of quasi co-regulation can still be secured by taking account of cognate self-regulatory approaches in, for example, professional journalism and/or academia. The extent of such assessment and, even more so, further direct action can also take account of the priorities which DPAs as public regulators with scare resources may need to establish in the public interest. Nevertheless, in light of the central importance of 'a credible peak or tip which, if activated, will be sufficiently powerful to deter even the most egregious offender',[106] it remains necessary that all traditional publishers face a realistic prospect of formal investigation, corrective action, and sanction where serious infractions are brought to light. Meanwhile, in the case of more minor but nevertheless significant breaches, DPAs should still be ready to issue a determination that standards have not been met and, furthermore, set out the steps to be taken to ensure better compliance going forward. For example, even a sole individual might be expected to make themselves generally conversant with published guidance, whilst large organizations should be incentivized to adopt measures to promote such understanding within a wider group internally.[107] In cases where a failure to follow minimum standards is clearly wilful and/or repeated, then more formal correction action or even sanctioning will most likely be appropriate.

4. The European Data Protection Board

Both academic and non-academic traditional publishers process information about individuals who may be located anywhere in the world and also directly collect such information from within the borders of numerous jurisdictions. Moreover, they clearly publish material not only to the general public within their 'home' State, but globally. As a result, and similarly to professional journalism, they will often carry out processing 'which substantially affects or is likely to substantially affect data subjects in more than one Member State'[108] and/or is undertaken 'in the context of the activities of establishments of more than one Member State'. Their activity could, therefore, formally constitute 'cross-border processing'.[109] In many cases, Member States have not explicitly provided for a special expression derogation from the GDPR's pan-European 'cooperation and consistency' mechanism[110] that will apply here by default. Nevertheless, as with professional journalism, it remains critical that the European Data Protection Board refrain from coercive intervention in this area. In sum, the governance of special expression is the subject of wide and (generally) legitimate divergence within Europe, and local DPAs remain structurally best placed to navigate the resulting complex legal terrain. Given the sensitive nature of the governance of special expression, any formal challenge to a DPA's approach on the grounds that it conflicts with pan-European norms would be best managed through judicial review (which remains mandatory in all circumstances)[111] or, in egregious cases, enforcement action by either the European Commission or the European Free Trade Association (EFTA) Surveillance Authority. In some circumstances, elements of the processing at issue may fall only within the knowledge facilitation derogations and, as such, could become subject to full 'cooperation and consistency' scrutiny. Nevertheless, even here, the Board should defer to the local DPA in relation to any related processing where the special expression derogation is engaged.

Whilst avoiding a coercive approach, the Board can perform a very valuable role by facilitating the exchange of information, giving advice on good practice in particularly difficult cases, promoting cooperation,[112] and, perhaps most importantly, drafting 'soft' regulatory guidelines[113] that address common issues and challenges. Thus, it is manifest that the great majority of DPAs have struggled with how to interact with writers and artists operating outside both professional journalism and academia. Moreover, the majority DPA conceptualization that academic processing falls solely within the knowledge facilitation provisions clearly needs to shift in light of the GDPR's new inclusion of 'academic' expression within the special expressive purposes regime.[114] Whilst beyond the direct focus of this book, European data protection's goal of ensuring the coherent development of information governance would also be furthered by addressing the interface between the amateur individual publisher and the special expression derogations. The Board should, therefore, promote information sharing and dialogue on all these basic issues. Such a process will most likely prove particularly valuable for smaller DPAs that generally lack the capacity to engage in these kinds of complexities on their own. The ultimate aim should be the production of common and authoritative (but non-binding) guidance. Drawing on developing Court of Justice of the European Union (CJEU) and ECtHR case law, guidance should emphasize the need for a broad but internally balanced approach to special expression regulation. Moreover, whilst recognizing the continued legitimacy of divergence in State approaches here, it could also usefully draw attention to examples of good practice amongst the DPAs such as the Belgium regulator's attempt to reconcile data protection and freedom of expression rights in the context of historical inquiry.

5. Conclusions

Applying data protection to non-journalistic traditional publishers raises challenges that are similar to those which arise in the professional media context. At least beyond academia, this commonality was formally recognized by the DPD through including not only 'journalistic purposes' but also 'artistic and literary expression' within the special expression regime.[115] However, as Chapter 10 elucidated, a number of States failed to implement such a derogation within this wider context. Moreover, most DPAs continued to find this broader area perplexing and, partly as a result, generally failed to intervene in relation to it in any way. Meanwhile, the majority of DPAs conceptualized academic work as falling exclusively within the restrictive knowledge facilitation clauses. Nevertheless, by maintaining the reference to art and literature and also expressly including academic expression within the definition of special expression, the GDPR clearly and directly challenges these (in any case) problematic approaches.

Turning to the State laws that implement the GDPR, the great majority have now granted academic, artistic, and literary expression essentially the same special expression protections as applicable to journalism. However, in a potentially serious lacunae, most have failed to explicitly extend any of these derogations to the knowledge facilitation provisions. Since knowledge facilitation includes 'scientific or historical research', there is a clear risk that this academic work in the social science and humanities will be understood as still being subject to this highly restrictive framework. As Part II of this book explored, media archiving confronts a similar issue since it may be conceptualized as 'archiving in the public interest', an activity which is also specified in the knowledge facilitation framework.[116] Given that (as the ECtHR has emphasized) the scientific or scholarly qualities of work should enhance its value as a contribution to public discourse, it would be especially perverse if academic expression was denied the benefit of the special expression regime. Therefore, as with archiving, DPAs and others should adopt a purposive interpretation of the law that does not exclude expression from these shields simply on the basis that the activity could also be considered to fall within the very broadly defined knowledge facilitation purposes. This would leave the latter framework only applicable to exceptional and carefully delineated situations, such as where academics (or others) have agreed to receive a dataset on expressly safeguarded terms or have clearly assumed a special quasi-fiduciary responsibility of care over the relevant data subjects.

Although it is essential for special expression to be construed broadly, this should not result in DPAs avoiding an engagement with this space. To the contrary, given that non-journalistic traditional publishers are capable of seriously impacting the privacy and related rights which data protection exists to safeguard, these regulators retain key responsibilities here. Moreover, an emphasis on self-regulation remains even more problematic here than in the professional media context discussed earlier. In sum, at least outside academia, self-regulation remains entirely informal. Meanwhile, academics within social science and the humanities have increasingly found themselves subject to a formalized and highly safeguarded model of research governance that is understandable within the quasi-fiduciary biomedical context in which it originated but which, in this very different context, can undermine freedom of expression and the right to know. Despite this, and as with professional journalism, a genuinely co-regulatory approach remains the ideal way to approach the supervision of this complex and sensitive area. Nevertheless, in light of these heightened challenges, it is vital that DPAs adopt a proactive stance both as regards standard-setting and enforcement.

Turning to standards, DPAs should directly coordinate the drafting guidance on special expression here. In doing so, they should engage with social science and humanities scholars and their professional bodies (rather than simply generalist academic institutions) and consider assembling a reference panel composed of professional artists and writers working outside of an academic context. Such a co-regulatory production of overarching guidance would help promote the coherent development of regulation and, as a single document, could gain the greatest visibility amongst the myriad actors directly affected. In the area of enforcement, and notwithstanding their straitened resources, DPAs should craft a robust and strategic approach which is responsive both to the seriousness of any alleged infractions and to the extent to which the relevant actor demonstrates a commitment to comply with core data protection standards. In relation to academia, DPAs should engage with research ethics committees and similar mechanisms, encourage them to adopt the balancing approach inherent in the special expression regime, and ensure that they truly provide effective redress to data subjects. Outside that context, the situation remains even more challenging given the highly fissiparous nature of artists and writers and the complete absence of any formal self-regulation. Nevertheless, drawing where possible on co-regulatory perspectives developed in cognate areas, DPAs should still issue determinations where appropriate standards have clearly not been met, provide a credible peak of sanction as regards serious and intentional infractions, and, in other cases, adopt a range of graduated measures in order to ensure better compliance going forward. Finally, whilst avoiding coercive intervention, the European Data Protection Board should facilitate information exchange, advice, and cooperation amongst the DPAs and draft common 'soft' guidance in this area.

Even if DPAs adopt an approach as outlined here, it cannot be expected that this will inevitably result in an ideally reconciled environment with truly effective remedies. Instead, and especially within this kind of sensitive area, DPAs have and will continue to operate within an extremely challenging legislative, societal, and resource environment. Indeed, regulators face balancing on a thin, high tightrope in strong gales headed towards a potentially more hospitable environment but whose exact nature remains unclear. Nevertheless, the approaches mapped out here and in Chapter 9 indicate that DPAs should attempt such a traversal and can do so without fundamentally losing their balance and hurtling either towards the perils of excessive restriction or the hazards of unwarranted license. Both Chapter 9 and this chapter have focused specifically on the reconciling data protection regulation with particular actors, namely professional journalism and other traditional publishers respectively. In concluding this book, Chapter 13 will turn to a direct exploration of common themes and their relevance within an information ecosystem that is the subject of profound and unsettling change.

PART IV
CONCLUSIONS

13

Balancing on a Tightrope in an Age of New Online Media?

This book has explored the interface between European data protection regulation and traditional publishers through a systematic empirical study and, from
that base, in terms of immanent normative analysis of policy implementation
and development. It has uncovered that, even as regards the professional journalistic media, formal statutory outcomes at national level have often been
confusing and even extreme. Nevertheless, drawing on a comprehensive questionnaire of European Data Protection Authorities (DPAs) and a wide-ranging
examination of their public domain materials, it has also found that most of these
actors have sought to develop an approach based on contextual balancing. This
pan-European approach has sought through such balancing to ensure a reconciliation between two groups of fundamental rights: data protection (including
associated rights to privacy and reputation) and freedom of expression (including
the sub-right of freedom of information). Nevertheless, when implementing this
balancing approach, regulators have struggled to develop a clear and specified
benchmark of strictness regarding standards or a consistent and reliable approach
to enforcement.

In the area of standard-setting, the DPA questionnaire highlighted that many
supervisory authorities had adopted a rather permissive construction of the standards applicable to undercover journalism. In contrast, a much stricter approach
was taken to subject access, with over one third-holding that, aside from protecting
information relating to sources, journalists would be obliged to comply with the
default rules in full. These different outcomes dovetailed with a divergence of treatment within journalistic codes of ethics: whilst almost all of these established general self-regulatory norms applicable to undercover journalism, almost none did
so as regards subject access.

Turning to enforcement, although around 60 per cent of DPAs reported having
undertaken some action against professional media here, the questionnaire also
revealed that half of these had only intervened in relation to one or two areas of
the Data Protection Directive (DPD) scheme. Public domain analysis confirmed
this picture of patchy enforcement and also highlighted the severe resource constraints which these regulators confront. Outside the professional media sector, the
study highlighted even deeper confusions. In sum, whilst largely abstaining from
regulating most professional artists and writers, many regulators have attempted to

European Data Protection Regulation, Journalism, and Traditional Publishers. David Erdos, Oxford University
Press (2019). © David Erdos.
DOI: 10.1093/oso/9780198841982.003.0013

subject academic scholars to the onerous statutory restrictions set out for medical, scientific, and related research.

Building on these empirical findings, it has been argued that the contextual balancing of rights has value and should be both generalized across all types of traditional publishers and be more systematically developed. However, in light of the sensitivities involved in regulating activities that seek to contribute to public knowledge, understanding, and debate, the necessary specification and implementation of standards should be achieved as far as possible through robust and strategic co-regulation. DPAs should therefore attempt to facilitate the development of co-regulatory codes of conduct and monitoring mechanisms using the General Data Protection Regulation (GDPR) clauses in this regard as a broad guide.[1] They should adopt a deferential stance to any codes and monitoring mechanisms that verifiably meet the GDPR's standards, intervening directly only as regards particularly systematic and/or serious issues. Regulators should also facilitate co-regulatory engagement even when the GDPR's criteria have not, or cannot, be met. Nevertheless, in these cases, DPAs will need to ensure that they proactively intervene across the entire area of standard-setting and enforcement. Finally, where co-regulatory codes and bodies are entirely absent then these supervisory authorities will need to independently ensure that all issues and complaints are proportionately addressed.

Beyond this precis, this chapter does not attempt to recapitulate on the book's wide-ranging empirical and (immanent) normative findings. Readers seeking such summative detail should refer back to section 2 in Chapter 1, as well as the concluding sections of Chapters 2–12. Rather than engage in additional review, the rest of this chapter seeks to explore the significance of these findings within the contemporary information ecosystem. It begins by arguing that an analysis of the regulation of traditional publishers continues to have significance in and of itself. Notwithstanding the rise of new online corporate and individual media, traditional publishers still possess disproportionate information power and, even more clearly and importantly, continue to perform a vital role in distilling, explaining, and putting new information and ideas into the public realm. Ensuring an effective and balanced governance framework for these actors therefore has intrinsic importance to the health of liberal democracy society. The chapter then explores how the core themes of the book—contextual balancing, co-regulation, and strategic enforcement—can also speak to the regulation of the ever more salient area of new online media. It argues that, although the new media often do not orientate themselves towards a public discourse, some kind of contextual balancing of rights remains necessary, even if this only takes the form of an interpretation rather than exclusion of many default data protection norms. Co-regulation, which will need pragmatically to focus on corporate platforms but which should also include individual users, can also play some role in specifying that (albeit stricter) balance. Finally, not least given the severe resource constraints that continue to affect DPAs, strategic enforcement is likely to be necessary in this context also. The chapter closes by highlighting that, in the evolving media context, data protection is emerging as an important regulator of both traditional publishers and new online media. That holistic role vividly highlights the central importance of both this legal framework and regulatory DPAs within contemporary society.

1. The Continuing Direct Significance of Data Protection's Regulation of Traditional Publishers

The changes in the information ecosystem which the online digital revolution has brought in its wake over the past twenty-five years have been nothing short of spectacular. Most dramatically, the amateur individual has emerged as a critically important information actor in his or her own right, each armed with the potential to 'communicate his or her thoughts to the entire world'.[2] The magnitude and speed of this development can hardly be overstated. Solove provides the following figures on the early growth of personal web sites in the form of web logs (or blogs): 'There were about 50 blogs in 1999, a few thousand in 2000, more than 10 million in 2004, and more than 30 million in 2005.'[3] Meanwhile, the later growth of individual social networking has been even more startling. Indeed, Van Dijck documents that '[i]n December 2011, 1.2 billion users worldwide—82 of the world's Internet publication over the age of 15—logged on to social media sites, up from 6 percent in 2007'.[4] The growing power of the new corporate media has dovetailed such developments. These often enormous institutional actors now play a crucial role in structuring the dissemination of information worldwide. For example, social networking sites like Facebook and online platforms such as Twitter do not merely passively host material uploaded by their users but have assumed a variety of active roles including soliciting, combining, aligning, organizing, and promoting content. Meanwhile, other corporate new media actors who operate entirely independently of these users have also assumed a central position. Foremost amongst these are Internet search engines including, most notably, Google. Albeit with some hyperbole, Solove has again noted that '[w]ithout search engines, the Internet would be an endless expanse of digital babble, and finding any particular piece of information would be akin to locating a specific grain of sand in the Sahara Desert'.[5]

In this new context, it may be claimed that traditional publishers such as the journalistic media, academics, and other professional writers and artists have become so decentred that exploring how they should be regulated no longer has much direct significance. However, such an understanding would be mistaken. Notwithstanding the emergence of other important actors, traditional publishers remain critical within the information ecosystem. To begin with, although even the published output of amateur individuals can and sometimes will be widely disseminated, professional journalists and some other traditional publishers retain a ready 'access to mass audiences'[6] which most others continue to lack. They thereby exercise 'significant power' that remains capable of doing 'great harm if not exercised with responsibility'.[7] Even more significantly, traditional publishers retain a 'tremendous' and to an extent unique 'capacity to serve the public interest'.[8] Clearly, it is now possible for even an amateur individual to produce journalistic (or indeed academic, literary, or artistic) content. Moreover, whether produced by amateurs or professionals, this content is now often primarily distributed within the context of new corporate media services such as online platforms and Internet search engines. Nevertheless, the new corporate media are generally not engaged in the initial production of material but only in pulling in, organizing, combining, and pushing out such content on to users. Meanwhile, amateur individuals are often focused on contributing views and comment rather than engaging in in-depth fact-finding, research, and scrutiny. Whilst this commentary can be valuable in shaping public opinion, it cannot substitute for the investigation, analysis, and critique that has been the hallmark of both professional journalism and other traditional publishers. In sum, and as Bollinger has noted it, remains true that:

> the press cannot be composed of a multitude of isolated individuals or small organisations, however much each may be committed to high-quality journalism. At least some of the organizations that make up the press must have sufficient scale to have serious newsgathering ability to bring together multiple centres of expertise, knowledge, and capacity. The simple fact is that there are some things we want that only big organizations can provide (which is not at all to deny the benefits of a multiplicity of voices as well). All of this is important also for the development of a professional culture of journalism, which is fundamentally a collective and individual commitment to provide the public with objective and independent report and analysis. The larger whole reinforces the values for each individual member of the professional community.[9]

Considering also the special role of higher education institutions, he further states that:

> [i]t is a serious mistake to assume that a multitude or individual or small-scale Web sites would serve the same purpose as the traditional press, just as it would be a mistake to think that universities could be replaced by the many individual Web sites, each offering specialized knowledge in an atomized manner.[10]

Focusing more directly on academia, Dingwall not only argues that 'HSS [humanities and social science] research is a form of speech, and research publication is covered by the definition of "the press"'[11] but further that:

> [i]f what has traditionally been the most disinterested source of information, the universities, becomes systematically handicapped . . . then all citizens lose out.

[For example] [w]hen we give up doing participant observation with vulnerable or socially marginal groups because of the regulatory obstacles, then a society becomes less well-informed about the condition of those who it excludes and more susceptible to their explosions of discontent.[12]

Turning back to journalism, Brock has similarly stressed not only that 'difficult journalism in the public interest—either requiring large resources or resilience against attack—depends on strong institutions' but that alongside their investigative work these organizations also continue to play a crucial role in 'distil[ling], put[ting] into context and explain[ing]' the 'raw' information which comes to light.[13] The position of professional artists and writers outside academia has not been as extensively explored in this literature. Nevertheless, given their greater resources in terms of time, mental focus, community, and visibility, it is clear that this group of actors also make a special contribution to society compared to their amateur counterparts.

The combination of traditional publishers' ability to make a particularly valuable contribution to the public good and their capacity at the same time to cause serious unwarranted harm to individuals as data subjects renders an empirical and normative analysis of their regulation under data protection of continued direct social significance. Moreover, notwithstanding the inevitable and to an extent unpredictable development of the information environment, it is very unlikely that this special position will be displaced entirely by new media actors any time soon. Instead, as Brock has argued '[t]he future of journalism will be made by the combination of existing organizations that adapt and new entrants who can supply a demand better than [the] legacy' media.[14] Much the same could be said of professional academic scholarship, literature, and art.

2. The Indirect Significance of the Book's Core Themes to New Online Media

2.1 The Importance of Contextual Balancing

Aside from the book's direct significance, its focus on structured balancing, co-regulation, and a strategic approach can also provide some useful pointers as to how data protection regulation might best engage with the increasingly dominant new online media. Turning first to the role of balancing, it must be recognized that a considerable portion of new media activity is not principally orientated towards contributing to public or collective discourse. It is true that many amateur individuals publish online content that furthers such a journalistic or other special expressive purpose. For example, an amateur website or blog may seek to '*informera, utöva kritik och väcka debatt om samhällsfrågor av betydelse för allmänheten*' ('inform, exercise criticism and raise debate on social issues of importance to the public').[15] Nevertheless, even here it must be recognized that '[m]ost blogs are more akin to diaries than news articles, op-ed columns or scholarship'.[16] Such a predominant or even exclusive concern with self-expression and a general freedom to converse is even more apparent in the area of social networking. Meanwhile, the new corporate media often seeks to provide services that support a varied range of purposes, rather than being solely or even predominantly focused on publicly orientated expression. Thus, whilst Internet search engines facilitate both special expression and self-expression, many other purposes are similarly engaged including carrying out 'background check[s]'[17] on individuals for either professional or personal reasons and furthering general business needs by 'keeping current on a competitor'.[18] Moreover, as noted earlier, most of the new corporate media sit in a rather different relationship with the information they disseminate compared to core traditional publisher activity. A few services including Google's Street View system disseminate entirely self-created content. However, such direct involvement in initial publication is very much an exception. In the vast majority of cases, even highly active new media actors such as Facebook are only responsible for 'value-added operations'[19] such as soliciting, organizing, combining, aligning, and/or ensuring the retrieval of content. This has been seen to justify these actors benefiting from a special 'intermediary' shield that protects them from both initial liability and responsibility for publication. In general, these corporations draw benefit from an immunity absence notice[20] of a specific illegality or, at the least, a legal problem having arisen over a period during which they should have 'detect[ed] and prevent[ed]' it through the exercise of 'duties of care, which can reasonably be expected from them and which are specified by national law'.[21] It must also be recognized that the activities of larger new media corporate players such as Google and Facebook have a decidedly more transnational character than most if not all traditional publishers. Indeed, whilst both these entities have established subsidiaries in some European States, each is primarily based in the United States and essentially provide a single package of services that are accessed by very large numbers of users in jurisdictions worldwide.

The last factor alone may have significant implications for how much 'cooperation and consistency'[22] between DPAs is necessary under the GDPR even when these regulators are seeking to balance competing rights contextually. However, the most critical divide between traditional publisher and new media activity remains that substantively much of the latter will fall outside the immediate confines of data protection's special expressive purposes regime. Indeed, in relation to Internet search engine indexing, this point was given emphasis by the Court of Justice in its seminal *Google Spain* judgment:

> [T]he processing by a publisher of a web page consisting in the publication of information relating to individual may, in some circumstances, be carried out 'solely for journalistic purposes' . . . whereas that does not appear to be so in the

case of the processing carried out by the operator of a search engine. It cannot therefore be ruled out that in certain circumstances the data subject is capable of exercising [their default data protection rights] . . . against that operator but not against the publisher of the web page.[23]

Nevertheless, and returning to focus on commonalities between these two actors, even this fundamental divergence can be overemphasized. Thus, whilst often outside of special expression, the regulation of new media activity still requires a form of balancing between data protection and freedom of expression, including its subright of freedom of information. Indeed, the recent Advocate General Opinion on the right of Internet search engines to index sensitive personal data begins by emphasising that '[r]econciling the right to privacy and the protection of personal data with the right to information and freedom of expression in the age of the Internet is one of the main challenges of our time'.[24]

To be sure, the different weight of fundamental rights in play in the new media context should generally lead to a greater emphasis being placed on data protection. Reflecting this, the obligation place on Member States in Article 85(1) of the GDPR to reconcile data protection with freedom of expression beyond special expression points to local legislative primarily utilizing the GDPR's general derogatory[25] clauses, rather than the special expression regime,[26] in order to ensure a balance between conflicting rights in this context. In contrast to special expression, these former clauses are predicated on ensuring reconciliation within a context where the core substantive and supervisory data protection provisions are maintained. This would include the data protection principles in and of themselves,[27] the need for a legal basis for processing,[28] and relatively comprehensive oversight by the DPA.[29] Such a constrained form of balanced is also reflected in emerging Court of Justice of the European Union (CJEU) case law. Thus, albeit controversially, the CJEU in *Google Spain* found that, given the 'role play by the internet and the search engines in modern society'[30] and 'the potential seriousness'[31] of the effect of data being indexed on such a service against an individual's name, the data subject should not only have rights to request the removal of personal data from such an index but that

> those rights override, as a rule, not only the economic interest of the operator of the search engine but also the interest of the general public in finding that information upon a search relating to the data subject's name.[32]

However, although the Court unfortunately failed to recognize explicitly that freedom of expression was also engaged, it did hold that the legal outcome would be different where

> it appeared, for particular reasons, such as the role played by the data subject in public life, that the interference with his fundamental rights is justified by the

preponderant interest of the general public in having, on account of inclusion in the list of results, access to the information in question.[33]

Ultimately, therefore, a balancing between these two fundamental rights remains essential and must be ensured through legislation, case law, and regulatory approach. The focus on structured and contextual balancing as regards traditional publishers should help inspire similar efforts in relation to the new media, and vice versa. Indeed, in particular areas, the normative context will exhibit not only this general but also more specific similarities. A clear example may be found in requests to deindex journalistic news articles from that part of an Internet search engine service that focuses on the aggregation of media stories (e.g. Google News).[34] In this kind of circumstance, a DPA may particularly benefit from comparing responses to traditional publication and new media activities side by side. Similarly, turning to the potential need for certain shields from full *ex ante* liability and responsibility, the challenges faced by many traditional actors can also mirror those of new corporate media actors in several important respects. In the first place, traditional publishers have themselves taken on managing user-generated content including through 'comment sections'[35] underneath news stories and by facilitating discussions forums of various sorts. Since this kind of processing falls squarely into the same kind of 'intermediary' activity as that undertaken by the indubitably 'new' media, it has been deliberately excluded from this book. However, even beyond this, the vast archives maintained by traditional publishers of material that they originally produced themselves may present ongoing monitoring challenges that exhibit a practical similarity to that faced by the 'intermediary' media. In this context, and as noted previously in Chapter 9, the Spanish Supreme Court in 2015 sought to reconcile data protection with the expressive activity of an online newspaper archive by finding that the latter only needed to bring its continued processing of an old news story into line with standards such as adequacy and relevance after having received notice from the data subject of a potential problem. It is also notable that the final remedy ordered by the Court was not for a change to the archive itself but rather for the newspaper to take direct steps to ensure that the archived story was deindexed from Internet search engines such as Google.[36] This again highlights that a contextual balancing of rights in this area increasingly requires a combined analysis of both traditional and new media activity. As overarching regulators, DPAs should be well placed to ensure this.

2.2 The Role and Design of Co-Regulation

A second strand of this book has emphasized that effective data protection depends on the articulation and implementation of specific standards but that, given the delicate rights context of traditional publisher activity, this should be achieved through a co-regulatory fusion of statutory and self-regulation. Co-regulation has also been discussed and, to an extent, even applied within the new media context, especially as regards the large corporate actors. For example, from September 2020, Directive 2018/1808 which amended Audio-Visual Media Services Directive 2010/13/EU will require that video-sharing platforms establish 'appropriate measures' to tackle both 'hate speech' and material damaging to children's development including, for example, through setting terms and conditions and managing reporting or flagging mechanisms and age-verification systems.[37] Designated authorities will be responsible for assessing the appropriateness or otherwise of the measures adopted.[38] Alongside such arms-length regulation, video-sharing platforms will be encouraged to 'exchange best practices on co-regulatory codes of conduct'[39] and, '[w]here appropriate', the Commission '[i]n cooperation with the Member States' will also 'facilitate the development of Union codes of conduct' in this area.[40]

Turning more specifically to the data protection context, from 2013 onwards the UK DPA has held that a social networking site does have certain 'controller'[41] responsibilities for any personal data in content uploaded, maintained, and used on within their service. At the same, it suggested that such responsibilities should generally (only) extend to having policies in place that are sufficient to deal with:

- complaints from people who believe their personal data may have been processed unfairly or unlawfully because they have been the subject of derogatory, threatening, or abusive online postings by third parties;
- disputes between individuals about the factual accuracy of posts; and
- complaints about how the person or organization running the site processes any personal (such as contact details) given to it by its users or subscribers.[42]

As a result, statutory regulatory attention was to focus primarily on an analysis of whether these 'policies and [associated] procedures for dealing with complaints and disputes about the content that it allows are adequate'.[43] Indeed, focusing more specifically on enforcement, the UK DPA has subsequently stated:

[w]e sometimes work with social networking websites to help them ensure their procedures for dealing with disputes about inaccurate or derogatory posts are adequate. If their procedures are adequate then we're unlikely to consider complaints against websites about individual postings, and if we do then it's important that we recognise the right to freedom of expression guaranteed by the European Convention on Human Rights.[44]

Finally, although the CJEU in *Google Spain* emphasized that individual deindexing decisions must remain subject to individual DPA review,[45] many would see the responsibilities placed on Google and similar actors to respond to requests for deindexing material included within their general Internet search engines as also akin to a system of co-regulation. In this context, it is notable that Google alone has processed requests for the deindexing of almost 3 million website addresses since the CJEU's seminal decision.[46] Whilst approximately 56 per cent of these have been rejected,[47] perhaps only around 1 or 2 per cent of these have been subject to further individual analysis (let alone enforcement action) by a DPA.[48]

Given that the regulation of the new media often involves a balancing of competing rights, the potential value and appeal of co-regulation is clear. Nevertheless, it is important to recognize the particular challenges and limitations of any such strategy in this context. To begin with, as already noted, it is amateur individuals who are responsible for the initial generation of many forms of new media content. Corporate players such as Google and Facebook generally only facilitate and organize such content and, moreover, arguably only have an 'economic interest' in so doing.[49] Therefore, co-regulation should ideally focus at least as much on amateur individuals as on the corporate new media. However, amateur individuals are especially fissiparous, often anonymous, and have no formal self-regulatory structures at all. DPAs can and should still facilitate their participation through surveys, focus groups, and similar mechanisms. Nevertheless, it remains the case that these actors are structurally unsuited to playing a leading role within co-regulation. Realistically, therefore, the corporate new media must remain the primary interlocutors of any co-regulatory outcome. Moreover, the engagement of these actors can bring advantages as well as difficulties. Thus, whilst undoubtedly economically biased, the new corporate media have unique organizational and technical expertise at crafting user policies, locating questionable material, assessing this materially, and finally taking action to address any problems that arise. In light of the enormous reach of a number of these players, they are also in principle capable of delivering any agreed co-regulatory result at scale.

A second potential limitation of co-regulation here relates back to the divergent freedom of expression rights in play within much of the new online media compared with that of traditional publishers. It has been a central contention of this book that the later actors aim to contribute to public understanding and discourse and furthermore, have special vocational authority and expertise regarding the challenges faced within this core freedom of expression context. In contrast, large swathes of the new media do not pursue such special expression but rather self-expression, a freedom to converse, or even simply the exchange of information for essentially privatized purposes. The pursuit of these purposes lacks the strong public interest rationale that ungirds legitimate special expression. As has been recognized in case law of both the CJEU and the European Court of Human Rights,[50] greater statutory control may therefore be seen as appropriate and even necessary. Nevertheless, it must be recognized that self-expression and conversation can link strongly to an individual's 'identity and personal development'[51] and, therefore, may also engage critical aspects of human rights. Full statutory regulation of this more personal area could also easily be seen as overly intrusive. In sum, therefore, co-regulation does have some normative contribution to make in the area of new media.

Even though the appropriate role of co-regulation is somewhat reduced in the new media context compared with that of traditional publishers, the standards of good co-regulation laid out in this book remain very relevant. Thus, the adoption of any co-regulatory approach must be transparent, develop following a process of consultation, be as specific and comprehensive as possible, and be publicized widely once finalized. Moreover, any monitoring body which (even if only very partially) will stand in lieu of statutory regulation should have demonstrated independence and expertise. Since much of this new media activity will fall outside the highly sensitive context of special expression, it is also even more appropriate for the GDPR's formal code of conduct and monitoring provisions (rather than a modified procedure) to be used here.[52] In any case, both the general framework and any co-regulatory body must be subject to visible ongoing and periodic DPA review in order to ensure that it furthers the goals of the 'effective and complete protection of data subjects'[53] which is required under European data protection law itself. Whilst it is beyond the scope of this book to address this further, it would appear that many, if not all, of the co-regulatory data protection approaches adopted in the new media context to date would substantially fail to satisfy these kind of criteria.

2.3 The Need for Robust and Strategic Enforcement

One important practical challenge confronting the regulation of traditional publishers which clearly also extends to the new media concerns the extremely limited financial and human resources available to DPAs. This commonality alone provides a powerful practical rationale for a co-regulatory approach that synergizes statutory control with self-regulation and not only in the area of standard-setting but also in its supervision. Indeed, one of the principal rationales the Council of the EU gave for adopting the GDPR's code of conduct and monitoring provisions was to reduce the 'costs for public authorities responsible for enforcement'.[54] In order to add genuine value within such straightened (and imperfect) circumstances, it is also vital that the DPA's enforcement stance including in the area of co-regulation be both robust and strategic. Thus, strong deference should only be shown to self-regulatory bodies that clearly and publicly meet the standards laid down within data protection law itself. At the same time, DPAs should remain willing to liaise and cooperate with self-regulatory mechanisms that have not verifiably met these accredited standards but who nevertheless pay heed to the data protection framework and operate with some autonomy from those who are being regulated. However, this should sit alongside DPAs exercising final responsibility for the assessment and proportionality of the response to any concerns raised. Finally, where no self-regulatory mechanism exists which is separate from the ordinary managerial hierarchy of the controller itself, the DPA must continue to be fully responsible for independently assessing and responding to all complaints. Whilst this should not necessarily mean that an emphasis on advice and persuasion will be inappropriate, it should make the use of a DPA's formal investigatory and sanctioning powers considerably more likely.

As with traditional publishers, the adoption of an approach such as that mapped out here will undoubtedly be challenging. In particular, it would put more responsibilities on DPAs than at least the quotation from the UK DPA above would suggest that they have often been minded to accept themselves. Nevertheless, its key virtue is that, whilst genuinely responding to DPA resource constraints, it puts in place a clear and robust structure that incentivizes thoughtful and active compliance. Moreover, at least when their activity does not involve special expression, there would not appear to be any strong reason for DPAs to grant a generous margin of manoeuvre to corporate new media controllers who chose to operate outside of this kind of co-regulatory framework.

3. The Growing Centrality of Data Protection Regulation

As this book has demonstrated, data protection has played a strong but often unrecognized role in regulating the expressive activities of many traditional publishers right from the time of its inception in the 1970s and 1980s. Much more recently, decisions such as *Google Spain* have grabbed public attention and shifted data protection into the heart of freedom of expression debates across Europe. Whilst some have been profoundly unsettled by these developments, others have lauded them. Thus, the founder of Wikipedia, Jimmy Wales, described *Google Spain* as 'one of the most wide-sweeping internet censorship rulings I've ever seen'.[55] In contrast, the outgoing Vice-President of the European Commission, Vivienne Reding, stated that it was a 'clear victory for the protection of personal data of Europeans'.[56] Whatever one's normative view, it is clear that European data protection's central position in relation to the regulation of expressive activity is here to stay. DPAs, therefore, have a renewed task to bring regulatory coherence, balance, and effectiveness to this area. Moreover, they must do so in circumstances of acute challenge, not only regarding resources but also in terms of the unprecedented form and extent of personal data processing that comes with socio-technological change. In light of its particular focus, it has been far beyond the scope of this book to address all the issues that arise from this new and exciting interface. Nevertheless, what the book has hopefully helped to highlight is both how critical it remains to get the regulation of the journalistic media and other traditional publishers right, how this issue has been approached to date, and how it can be better developed in the future.

The continuing central position of traditional publishers within the public realm makes ensuring their appropriate regulation of significance in and of itself. Such a study can also provide important pointers for the many similar issues that are arising in relation to the new online media. That ever more critical field will be explored in detail in a subsequent monograph. What remains important to emphasize here is that the increasing overlap and interaction between the traditional and new media bolsters the centrality of data protection and DPAs as the overarching and holistic guardians and regulators of personal data. Data protection may, as the doyen of the German DPA community, Professor Spiros Simitis, suggested back in the late 1990s, ultimately be an 'impossible task',[57] not least within areas of acute rights conflict. Nevertheless, it is also becoming an ever more fundamental one within liberal democratic societies in Europe and beyond.

First-Generation European/EEA Data Protection Statutes (up to 1990)

Note: During the early period of data protection development in Europe and in furtherance of its task of ensuring the exchange of legal information, the Council of Europe's Committee of Experts on Data Protection (the CJ-PD) oversaw the production and circulation of the data protection statues adopted in its Member States, translated into the two official languages of the Council—English and French (or, in some instances, only one of these). The texts are now in the Council of Europe archives. With preference given to any English translation, these documents were used as the primary resource for analysis of the first generation data protection statutes which were enacted in twelve European States prior to the European Commission's proposal for a Data Protection Directive in 1990. In some cases, however, translations appeared incomplete or were not produced. In these instances, this resource was complemented by texts (preferably in English translation) which were found online and/or in the following texts:

- Gesellschaft für Datenschutz und Datensicherung (ed.), *Law on protection against the misuse of personal data in data processing (Federal data protection law; BDSG) of the 27th January 1977 Bilingual Edition* (Knapp, 1977).
- Norway, Datatilsynet, *Årsrapport 1980* (Universitetsforlaget, 1982).
- Austria, Bundesgesetz von 18. October 1978 uber den Schutzpersonenbezogenen (Datenschutzgesetz—DSG), *Bundesgesetzblatt für die Republik Österreich* (28. November 1978 193 Stück) (Staatsdruckeri, 1978).
- Sieghart, Paul, *Privacy and Computers* (Latimer New Dimensions, 1976).

The table below lists, against each State, the texts used, where it can be found (including the CJ-PD reference where relevant). Secondary legislation is also listed where this set out relevant special expression or knowledge facilitation provisions.

State	Law	Location (CJ-PD or Other)
Austria	Bundesgesetz von 18. October 1978 uber den Schutzpersonenbezogenen (Datenschutzgesetz – DSG)	Austria, Budesgesetzblatt
	Data Protection Act 1978	CJ-PD (88) 72
Denmark	Private Registers Act 1978 (Act No. 293, 8 June 1978)	CJ-PD (78) 7
	Public Authorities Registers' Act 1978 (Act No. 294, 8 June 1978)	CJ-PD (78) 8
	Private Registers Etc. Act (Consolidated) (as amended by Act No. 383, 10 June 1987)	CJ-PD (88) 20

State	Law	Location (CJ-PD or Other)
	Public Authorities Registers' Act (Consolidated) (as amended by Act No. 383, 10 June 1987)	CJ-PD (88) 19
	Lov om massemediers informationsdatabaser (LOV nr 430 af 01/06/1994)	https://www.retsinformation.dk/Forms/r0710.aspx?id=59461&exp=1
Finland	Personal Data File Act 30 April 1987/471	CJ-PD (88) 15
France	Act No. 78-17 of 6 January 1978 on data processing, data files and freedoms	CJ-PD (78) 1
Germany	Law on Protection against the Misuse of Personal Data in Data Processing (Federal Data Protection Law – BDSG) of the 27th January 1977	Gesellschaft für Datenschutz und Datensicherung (ed.) (1977), pp. 9-103
	Federal Data Protection Act (1991)	CJ-PD (91) 30
Iceland	Act No. 63/1981 Respecting Systematic Recording of Personal Data (Information Concerning Private Affairs)	CJ-PD (81) 3
	Act Concerning the Registration and Handling of Personal Data (1989)	CJ-PD (92) 13
Ireland	Data Protection Act 1988	http://www.irishstatutebook.ie/eli/1988/act/25/enacted/en/print
Luxembourg	Nominal Data (Automatic Processing) Act of 31 March 1979	CJ-PD (79) 3
Netherlands	Data Protection Act 1988	CJ-PD (89) 4
Norway	Act relating to personal data registers of 9 June 1978	CJ-PD (78) 5
	Kongelig resolusjon av 21. november 1979	Norway, Datatilsynet, pp. 41-3
	Kongelig resolusjon av 21. desember 1979	Norway, Datatilsynet, pp. 44-49
	Endringer av 10. mars 1981 ifr kongelig resolusjon av 21. desember 1979	Norway, Datatilsynet, pp. 51-59
Sweden	Data Act of 1 May 1973	Sieghart (1976), pp. 165-171
	Data Act as amended with effect from 1 April 1988	CJ-PD (88) 67
United Kingdom	Data Protection Act 1984	http://www.legislation.gov.uk/ukpga/1984/35/pdfs/ukpga_19840035_en.pdf

Second-Generation European/EEA Data Protection Statutes

Note: During the era of the Data Protection Directive (DPD) authoritative English versions of almost all EEA national data protection statutes were made available by the national Data Protection Authority (DPA) and/or by another government body. These texts were used as the primary sources for analysis. In the few instances where such translations were unavailable or required supplementation, official original language versions were used instead. The table provide sets out these sources and provides either an original or archived weblink of their location. Secondary legislation is also listed where this set out relevant special expression or knowledge facilitation provisions. Finally, this appendix also provides details of subnational data protection legislation applicable to each of the regional DPA jurisdictions that responded to the 2013 questionnaire.

State	Law (in authoritative English translation where possible)	Location
Austria	Federal Act concerning the Protection of Personal Data	https://web.archive.org/web/20140612133235/https://www.dsb.gv.at/DocView.axd?CobId=41936
Belgium	Act of 8 December 1992 on the protection of privacy in relation to the processing of personal data	https://web.archive.org/web/20140404142738/http://www.privacycommission.be/sites/privacycommission/files/documents/Privacy_Act_1992_0.pdf
	Royal Decree implementing the Act of 8 December 1992 on the protection of privacy in relation to the processing of personal data	https://web.archive.org/web/20130312212652/http://www.privacycommission.be/sites/privacycommission/files/documents/Royal_Decree_2001.pdf
Bulgaria	Law for the Protection of Personal Data as amended February 2013	https://web.archive.org/web/20140612133303/https://www.cpdp.bg/download.php?part=rubric_element&aid=1406
Croatia	The Act on Personal Data Protection	https://www.legislationline.org/documents/id/19201
Cyprus	Processing of Personal Data (Protection of Individuals) Law 138 (I) 200	https://web.archive.org/web/20130609071940/http://www.dataprotection.gov.cy/dataprotection/dataprotection.nsf/697e70c004f6f7759c2256e8c004a0a49/f8e24ef90a27f34fc2256eb4002854e7/$FILE/138(I)-2001_en.pdf
Czechia	Consolidated version of the Personal Data Protection Act	https://web.archive.org/web/20160805103320/https://www.uoou.cz/en/vismo/zobraz_dok.asp?id_org=200156&id_ktg=1107&archiv=0&p1=1105
Denmark	Compiled version of the Act on Processing of Personal Data	https://web.archive.org/web/20141121202340/https://www.datatilsynet.dk/english/the-act-on-processing-of-personal-data/read-the-act-on-processing-of-personal-data/compiled-version-of-the-act-on-processing-of-personal-data/
	Lov om massemediers informationsdatabaser	https://web.archive.org/web/20150423190137/https://www.retsinformation.dk/Forms/r0710.aspx?id=59461&exp=1

Estonia	Personal Data Protection Act	https://web.archive.org/web/20161024201707/https://www.riigiteataja.ee/en/eli/509072014018/consolide
Finland	Personal Data Act	https://www.finlex.fi/fi/laki/kaannokset/1999/en19990523.pdf
France	Act No 78-17 of 6 January 1978 on Information Technology, Data Files and Civil Liberties (as amended)	https://www.cnil.fr/sites/default/files/typo/document/Act78-17VA.pdf
Germany - Federal	Federal Data Protection Act (BDSG)	https://web.archive.org/web/20140612134010/http://www.bfdi.bund.de/EN/DataProtectionActs/Artikel/BDSG_idFv01092009.pdf;jsessionid=749B98C8F1B30B9AB709507F9829CEF3.1_cid329?_blob=publicationFile
	Interstate Treaty on Broadcasting and Telemedia	https://web.archive.org/web/20160119103556/http://www.die-medienanstalten.de/fileadmin/Download/Rechtsgrundlagen/Gesetze_aktuell/15_RStV_english_01-01-2013.pdf
Germany – Brandenburg	Brandenburgisches Datenshutzgesetz (BbgDSG)	http://www.ess-koeln.de/dokumente/160/15101008391 9Brandenburg.pdf
	Brandenburgisches Landespressegesetz – BbgPG	http://www.presserecht.de/index.php?option=com_content&task=view&id=16&Itemid=27
	Staatsvertrag über die Errichtung einer gemeinsamen Rundfunkanstalt der Länder Berlin und Brandenburg	https://www.rbb-online.de/unternehmen/der_rbb/struktur/grundlagen/rbb_staatsvertrag.file.html/140121-rbb_StV2013.pdf
	Staatsvertrag über die Zusammenarbeit zwischen Berlin und Brandenburg im Bereich der Medien (Medienstaatsvertrag)	https://www.rbb-online.de/unternehmen/der_rbb/struktur/grundlagen/medienstaatsvetrag.file.html/140121-medienstaatsvetrag-2013.pdf
Germany – Mecklenburg-Vorpommern	Landesdatenshutzgesetz – DSG M-V	http://www.ess-koeln.de/dokumente/160/15101008402 0Mecklenburg-Vorpommern.pdf

State	Law (in authoritative English translation where possible)	Location
	Landespressegesetz für das Land Mecklenburg-Vorpommern	http://www.presserecht.de/index.php?option=com_content&task=view&id=27&Itemid=27
	Landesrundfunkgesetz - RundfG M-V	http://www.lexsoft.de/cgi-bin/lexsoft/justizportal_nrw.cgi?xid=278667,1
Germany Rhineland-Palatinate	Landesdatenschutzgesetz (LDSG)	http://www.ess-koeln.de/dokumente/160/151010084053Rheinland-Pfalz.pdf
	Landesmediengesetz (LMG) Rheinland-Pfalz	http://www.presserecht.de/index.php?option=com_content&task=view&id=30&Itemid=27
Germany Schleswig-Holstein	Landesdatenschutzgesetz (LDSG)	http://www.ess-koeln.de/dokumente/160/151010084146Schleswig-Holstein.pdf
	Landespressegesetz Schleswig-Holstein	http://www.presserecht.de/index.php?option=com_content&task=view&id=35&Itemid=27
	Staatsvertrag über das Medienrecht in Hamburg und Schleswig-Holstein	http://www.landesrecht-hamburg.de/jportal/portal/page/bshaprod.psml?nid=5&showdoccase=1&doc.id=jlr-MedienStVtrGHAV7StVtr1&st=lr
Gibraltar	Data Protection Act 2004	https://web.archive.org/web/20140612134117/http://www.gra.gi/sites/dataprotection/downloads/104/dp_act.pdf
	Data Protection Ordinance	https://web.archive.org/web/20140612134156/http://www.gra.gi/sites/dataprotection/downloads/104/dp_commence.pdf
	Data Protection Ordinance 2004 Notice of Corrigenda	https://web.archive.org/web/20140612134213/http://www.gra.gi/sites/dataprotection/downloads/104/dp_corr.pdf
Greece	Law 2472/1997 on the Protection of Individuals with regard to the Processing of Personal Data (as amended)	http://www.dpa.gr/pls/portal/docs/PAGE/APDPX/ENGLISH_INDEX/LEGAL%20FRAMEWORK/LAW%202472-97-NOV2013-EN.PDF

Hungary	Act CXII of 2011 On Informational Self-Determination and Freedom of Information	https://www.parlament.hu/irom39/03586/03586.pdf (original language) http://www.naih.hu/files/Privacy_Act-CXII-of-2011_EN_201310.pdf (English)
Iceland	Act on the Protection of Privacy as regards the Processing of Personal Data, No 77/2000	http://www.personuvernd.is/information-in-english/greinar/nr/438
Ireland	Data Protection Act 1988 Revised	https://www.lawreform.ie/_fileupload/Restatement/First%20Programme%20of%20Restatement/EN_ACT_1988_0025.PDF
Italy	Personal Data Protection Code Legislative Decree No 196 of 30 June 2003	http://www.privacy.it/archivio/privacycode-en.html
	Code of Conduct on the Processing of Personal Data in the Exercise of Journalistic Activities	http://www.privacy.it/archivio/privacycode-en.html (Annex A1)
	Code of Conduct and Professional Practice Regarding the Processing of Personal Data for Historical Purposes	http://www.privacy.it/archivio/privacycode-en.html (Annex A2)
	Code of Conduct and Professional Practice Applying to Processing of Personal Data for Statistical and Scientific Purposes	https://web.archive.org/web/20131214074846/https://www.garanteprivacy.it/web/guest/home/docweb/-/docweb-display/docweb/1115480
Latvia	Personal Data Protection Law	https://web.archive.org/web/20140612135152/http://www.dvi.gov.lv/en/legal-acts/personal-data-protection-law/
Liechtenstein	Data Protection Act of 14 March 2002	https://web.archive.org/web/20121116112135/http://www.llv.li/pdf-llv-dss-dpa-fl_en_2009-11-30.pdf
	Ordinance of 9 July 2002 on the Data Protection Act (Data Protection Ordinance)	https://web.archive.org/web/20121116112140/http://www.llv.li/pdf-llv-dss-dpo-fl_en_2009-11-30.pdf
Lithuania	Law on the Legal Protection of Personal Data	https://wipolex.wipo.int/en/text/202094

State	Law (in authoritative English translation where possible)	Location
Luxembourg	Coordinated Text of the Law of 2 August 2002 on the Protection of Persons with regard to the Processing of Personal Data	https://cnpd.public.lu/dam-assets/fr/legislation/droit-lux/doc_loi02082002_en.pdf
Malta	Data Protection Act	https://web.archive.org/web/20180110135920/https://idpc.org.mt/en/Legislation/CAP%20440.pdf
Netherlands	Personal Data Protection Act	https://web.archive.org/web/20110626124329/http:/www.dutchdpa.nl/downloads_wetten/wbp.pdf
Norway	Act of 14 April 2000 No 31 relating to the processing of personal data (Personal Data Act)	https://web.archive.org/web/20140708042552/https://www.datatilsynet.no/Global/english/Personal_Data_Act_20120420.pdf
	Regulations on the processing of personal data (Personal Data Regulations)	https://web.archive.org/web/20140708103749/https://www.datatilsynet.no/English/Regulations/Personal-Data-Act1/
Poland	Act of 29 August 1997 on the Protection of Personal Data	https://web.archive.org/web/20150414065328/http://www.giodo.gov.pl/plik/id_p/193/j/en
	Regulation by the Minister of Internal Affairs and Administration of 11 December 2008 as regards specimen of notification of a data filing system to registration by the Inspector General for Personal Data Protection	https://web.archive.org/web/20170909100949/http://www.giodo.gov.pl/en/file/116/
Portugal	Act on the Protection of Personal Data	https://www.cnpd.pt/english/bin/legislation/Law6798EN.HTM
Romania	Law No 677/2001 on the Protection of Individuals with Regard to the Processing of Personal Data and the Free Movement of Such Data	https://web.archive.org/web/20140815095923/http://dataprotection.ro/servlet/ViewDocument?id=174 (English) https://web.archive.org/web/20180817172925/http://www.dataprotection.ro/servlet/ViewDocument?id=35 (Romanian)
	Law No 102/2005	https://www.dataprotection.ro/servlet/ViewDocument?id=172

Slovakia	Act No. 122/2013 Coll on Protection of Personal Data and on Changing and Amending of Other Acts	https://dataprotection.gov.sk/uoou/sites/default/files/kcfinder/files/Act_122-2013_84-2014_en.pdf
Slovenia	Personal Data Protection Act of the Republic of Slovenia	https://web.archive.org/web/20131109081048/https://www.ip-rs.si/fileadmin/user_upload/doc/ZVOP-1_in_ZVOP-1a__English_/Personal_Data_Protection_Act_of_Slovenia_status_2013_final_eng.doc
Spain - Federal	Organic Law 15/1999 of 13 December on the Protection of Personal Data	https://rm.coe.int/CoERMPublicCommonSearchServices/DisplayDCTMContent?documentId=09000016806af30e
Spain - Catalonia	Ley 32/2010, de 1 de octubre, de la Autoridad Catalana de Protección de Datos	http://www.apd.cat/media/2664.pdf
Sweden	Personal Data Act	https://www.wipo.int/edocs/lexdocs/laws/en/se/se097en.pdf
	Personal Data Ordinance	https://web.archive.org/web/20140612140459/http://www.government.se/content/1/c6/02/56/33/ed5aaf53.pdf
United Kingdom	Data Protection Act 1998	https://www.legislation.gov.uk/ukpga/1998/29/contents/enacted
	Data Protection (Designated Codes of Practice) (No 2) Order 2000	http://www.legislation.gov.uk/uksi/2000/1864/contents/made
	Data Protection (Processing of Sensitive Personal Data) Order 2000	http://www.legislation.gov.uk/uksi/2000/417/pdfs/uksi_20000417_en.pdf

Third-Generation European/EEA Data Protection Statutes (as of May 2019)

Note: The table below details the national laws adopted in each EEA State to implement the General Data Protection Regulation 2016/679. Given that this Regulation only applied from mid-2018, authoritative English translations of these State laws were generally unavailable. Therefore, in most cases, original language versions of the law are listed. Greece, Portugal, and Slovenia are excluded since, as of May 2019, none had enacted implementing legislation. Alongside national data protection statutes, the appendix includes secondary legislation that sets out relevant special expression or knowledge facilitation provisions. Finally, it also provides details of new sub-national data protection legislation applicable to each of the regional DPA jurisdictions that responded to the 2013 questionnaire.

State	Law (in authoritative English translation where possible)	Location
Austria	Federal Act concerning the Protection of Personal Data	https://www.ris.bka.gv.at/Dokumente/Erv/ERV_1999_1_165/ERV_1999_1_165.html
Belgium	Loi relative à la traitements de données à caractère personnel	http://www.ejustice.just.fgov.be/eli/loi/2018/07/30/2018040581/justel
Bulgaria	Закон за изменение и допълнение на Закона за защита на личните данни	http://dv.parliament.bg/DVWeb/showMaterialDV.jsp;jsessionid=17AC48BEC0100FB28FDA0294DE0C9CC0?idMat=135056
Croatia	Cro. Zakon o provedbi Opće uredbe o zaštiti podataka	https://narodne-novine.nn.hr/clanci/sluzbeni/2018_05_42_805.html
Cyprus	Ο περί Προστασίας των Φυσικών Προσώπων Έναντι της Επεξεργασίας των Δεδομένων Προσωπικού Χαρακτήρα και της Ελεύθερης Κυκλοφορίας των Δεδομένων αυτών Νόμος του 2018	http://www.dataprotection.gov.cy/dataprotection/dataprotection.nsf/BAE2F781893BC27DC225820A004B7649/$file/%CE%9D%CF%8C%CE%BC%CE%BF%CF%82%20125(%CE%99)_2018.pdf
Czechia	Zákon o zpracování osobních údajů	https://www.zakonyprolidi.cz/cs/2019-110
Denmark	Databeskyttelsesloven	https://www.retsinformation.dk/Forms/r0710.aspx?id=201319
	Lov om massemediers informationsdatabaser (with 2018 procedural amendments at Lov om ændring af lov om retshåndhævende myndigheders behandling af personoplysninger, lov om massemediers informationsdatabaser og forskellige andre love)	https://www.retsinformation.dk/forms/r0710.aspx?id=59461 (2018 procedural law at https://www.retsinformation.dk/forms/R0710.aspx?id=201317)
Estonia	Personal Data Protection Act 2018	https://www.riigiteataja.ee/en/eli/523012019001/consolide
Finland	Tietosuojalaki	https://www.finlex.fi/fi/laki/alkup/2018/20181050
France	Ordonnance n° 2018-1125	https://www.legifrance.gouv.fr/eli/ordonnance/2018/12/12/JUSC1829503R/jo/texte

State	Law (in authoritative English translation where possible)	Location
Germany – Federal	Federal Data Protection Act (BDGS)	https://www.gesetze-im-internet.de/englisch_bdsg/
	Staatsvertrag für Rundfunk und Telemedien	https://www.die-medienanstalten.de/fileadmin/user_upload/Rechtsgrundlagen/Gesetze_Staatsvertraege/Rundfunkstaatsvertrag_RStV.pdf
Germany – Brandenburg	Brandenburgisches Datenschutzgesetz (BbgDSG)	https://www.lda.brandenburg.de/media_fast/4055/BbgDSG_2018.pdf
	Brandenburgisches Landespressegesetz – BbgPG	http://bravors.brandenburg.de/gesetze/bbgPG
	Staatsvertrag über die Errichtung einer gemeinsamen Rundfunkanstalt der Länder Berlin und Brandenburg	https://www.rbb-online.de/unternehmen/der_rbb/struktur/grundlagen/rbb_staatsvertrag.file.html/140121-rbb_StV2013.pdf
	Staatsvertrag über die Zusammenarbeit zwischen Berlin und Brandenburg im Bereich der Medien (Medienstaatsvertrag)	https://www.rbb-online.de/unternehmen/der_rbb/struktur/grundlagen/medienstaatsvertrag.file.html/140121-medienstaatsvetrag-2013.pdf
Germany – Mecklenburg-Vorpommern	Landesdatenschutzgesetz – DSG M-V	https://www.datenschutz-mv.de/static/DS/Dateien/Rechtsgrundlagen/Landesdatenschutzgesetz.pdf
	Landespressegesetz für das Land Mecklenburg-Vorpommern	http://www.presserecht.de/index.php?option=com_content&task=view&id=27&Itemid=27
	Landesrundfunkgesetz - RundfG M-V	jttp://www.lexsoft.de/cgi-bin/lexsoft/justizportal_nrw.cgi?xid=278667,1
Germany Rhineland-Palatinate	Landesdatenschutzgesetz (LDSG)	http://landesrecht.rlp.de/jportal/portal/t/ud9/page/bsrlpprod.psml/action/portlets.jw.MainAction?p1=0&eventSubmit_doNavigate=searchInSubtreeTOC&showdoccase=1&doc.hl=0&doc.id=jlr-DSGRP2018rahmen&doc.part=R&toc.poskey=#focuspoint

Germany Schleswig-Holstein	Landesmediengesetz (LMG) Rheinland-Pfalz	http://landesrecht.rlp.de/jportal/portal/t/u5w/page/bsrlpprod.psml/action/portlets.jw.MainAction?p1=0&eventSubmit_doNavigate=searchInSubtree TOC&showdoccase=1&doc.hl=0&doc.id=jlr-LMGRP2018rahmen&doc.part=R&toc.poskey=#focuspoint
	Landesdatenschutzgesetz (LDSG)	http://www.gesetze-rechtsprechung.sh.juris.de/jportal/?quelle=jlink&query=D SG+SH&psml=bsshoprod.psml&max=true
	Landespressegesetz Schleswig-Holstein	http://www.presserecht.de/index.php?option=com_content&task=view&id=35 &Itemid=27
	Staatsvertrag über das Medienrecht in Hamburg und Schleswig-Holstein	http://www.landesrecht-hamburg.de/jportal/portal/page/bshaprod.psml?nid=5&showdoccase=1&doc.id=jlr-MedienStVtrGHAV7StVtr1&st=lr
Gibraltar	Data Protection 2004 (Amendment) Regulations 2018	https://www.gra.gi/data-protection-act-2004-amendment-regulations-2018
Hungary	2018 évi törvény az információs önrendelkezési jogról és az információszabadságról szóló	https://mkogy.jogtar.hu/jogszabaly?docid=A1800013.TV
Iceland	Lög um persónuvernd og vinnslu persónuupplýsinga.	https://www.althingi.is/altext/stjt/2018.090.html
Ireland	Data Protection Act 2018	http://www.irishstatutebook.ie/eli/2018/act/7/enacted/en/html
Italy	Decreto Legislativo 30 giugno 2003, n196 (with 2018 amendments at Decreto legislative 10 agosto 2018, n101)	https://www.garanteprivacy.it/documents/10160/0/Codice+in+materia+di+protezione+dei+dati+personali+%28Testo+coordinato%29.pdf/b1787d6b-6bce-07da-a38f-3742e3888c1d?version=1.6 (2018 law at https://www.gazzettaufficiale.it/eli/gu/2018/09/04/205/sg/pdf)

State	Law (in authoritative English translation where possible)	Location
	Regole deontologiche relative al trattamento di dati personali nell'esercizio dell'attività giornalistica pubblicate - 29 novembre 2018	https://www.garanteprivacy.it/web/guest/home/docweb/-/docweb-display/docweb/9067692
	Regole deontologiche per il trattamento a fini di archiviazione nel pubblico interesse o per scopi di ricerca storica pubblicate ai sensi - 19 dicembre 2018	https://www.garanteprivacy.it/web/guest/home/docweb/-/docweb-display/docweb/9069661
	Regole deontologiche per trattamenti a fini statistici o di ricerca scientifica pubblicate - 19 dicembre 2018	https://www.garanteprivacy.it/web/guest/home/docweb/-/docweb-display/docweb/9069637
Latvia	Fizisko personu datu apstrādes likums	https://likumi.lv/ta/id/300099-fizisko-personu-datu-apstrades-likums
Liechtenstein	Datenschutzgesetz (DSG)	https://www.gesetze.li/konso/pdf/2018272000?version=1
Lithuania	Asmens Duomenų Teisinės Apsaugos Įstatymo NR. I-1374 Pakeitimo Įstatymas	https://e-seimas.lrs.lt/portal/legalAct/lt/TAD/bc0837f27f9511e89188e16a6495e98c3?jfwid=9fbgs9abi
Luxembourg	Loi du 1er août 2018 portant organisation de la Commission nationale pour la protection des données et mise en oeuvre du règlement (UE) 2016/679	http://legilux.public.lu/eli/etat/leg/loi/2018/08/01/a686/jo
Malta	Data Protection Act 2018	http://www.justiceservices.gov.mt/DownloadDocument.aspx?app=lom&itemid=12839&l=1
Netherlands	Wet van 16 mei 2018 Uitvoeringswet Algemene verordening gegevensbescherming	https://zoek.officielebekendmakingen.nl/stb-2018-144.odt
Norway	Personopplysningsloven	https://lovdata.no/dokument/NL/lov/2018-06-15-38/*#*

Poland	Ustawa z dnia 10 maja 2018 r o ochronie danych osobowych	http://prawo.sejm.gov.pl/isap.nsf/download.xsp/WDU20180001000/T/D20181000L_.pdf
Romania	Legea nr. 190/2018 Regulamentul general privind protecția datelor	https://www.dataprotection.ro/servlet/ViewDocument?id=1520
Slovakia	Zákon z 29. novembra 2017 o ochrane osobných údajov a o zmene a doplnení niektorých zákonov	https://www.slov-lex.sk/pravne-predpisy/SK/ZZ/2018/18/20180525
Spain – Federal	Ley Orgánica 3/2018, de 5 de diciembre, de Protección de Datos Personales y garantía de los derechos digitales.	https://www.boe.es/buscar/doc.php?id=BOE-A-2018-16673
Spain – Catalonia	Ley 32/2010, de 1 de octubre, de la Autoridad Catalana de Protección de Datos	http://www.apd.cat/media/2664.pdf
Sweden	Lag (2018:218) med kompletterande bestämmelser till EU:s dataskyddsförordning	https://www.riksdagen.se/sv/dokument-lagar/dokument/svensk-forfattningssamling/lag-2018218-med-kompletterande-bestammelser_sfs-2018-218
Sweden	Förordning (2018:219) med kompletterande bestämmelser till EU:s dataskyddsförordning	https://www.riksdagen.se/sv/dokument-lagar/dokument/svensk-forfattningssamling/forordning-2018219-med-kompletterande_sfs-2018-219
United Kingdom	Data Protection Act 2018	http://www.legislation.gov.uk/ukpga/2018/12/pdfs/ukpga_20180012_en.pdf

Second-Generation European Data Protection Law and Professional Journalism

EEA State	Dimension A - Data Protection Principles						Dimension B - Transparency Rules				Dimension C - Sensitive Data Rules								Dimension D - Discipline Requirements				Overarching Variables		
	(1) Fair & lawful	(2) Purpose specificity etc.	(3) Adequacy, relevance etc.	(4) Accuracy etc.	(5) Temporal minimisation	Dimension A Average	(6) Proactive - Direct Collection	(7) Proactive - Other Data Collection	(8) Reactive Subject Access	Dimension B Average	(9) Racial or ethnic origin	(10) Political opinions	(11) Religious Beliefs etc.	(12) Trade Union	(13) Health	(14) Sex Life	(15) Criminal	Dimension C Average	(16) Legal Basis	(17) Registration	(18) Data Export	Dimension D Average	Combined Substantive Stringency	Maximum Regulatory Powers	Maximum Regulatory Stringency
Austria	0.33	0.33	0.33	0.33	0.33	0.33	0	0	0	0	0	0	0	0	0	0	0	0	0	0	0	0	0.10	0	0
Belgium	1	1	1	1	1	1	0.17	0.17	0.17	0.17	0.67	0.67	0.67	0.67	0.67	0.67	0.67	0.67	1	0	0	0.33	0.61	1	0.61
Bulgaria	1	1	1	1	1	1	0.5	0.5	0.83	0.61	0.5	0.5	0.5	0.5	0.5	0.5	0.5	0.5	0.5	0.83	0.5	0.61	0.68	1	0.68
Croatia	1	1	1	1	1	1	1	1	1	1	1	1	1	1	1	1	1	1	1	1	1	1	1	1	1
Cyprus	1	1	1	1	1	1	0	0	1	0.33	0.5	0.5	0.5	0.5	0.5	0.5	0.5	0.5	1	1	1	1	0.65	1	0.65
Czechia	1	1	1	1	1	1	1	1	1	1	1	1	1	1	1	1	1	1	1	1	1	1	1	1	1
Denmark	0.17	0.17	0.17	0.17	0.17	0.17	0	0	0.17	0.06	0.17	0.17	0.17	0.17	0.17	0.17	0.17	0.17	0.17	0.83	0	0.33	0.15	0.5	0.07
Estonia	1	1	1	1	1	1	0.5	0.5	0.5	0.5	0.5	0.5	0.5	0.5	0.5	0.5	0.5	0.5	0.5	1	0.5	0.67	0.67	1	0.67
Finland	0	0	0	0	0	0	0	0	0	0	0	0	0	0	0	0	0	0	0	0	0	0	0	1	0
France	1	1	1	1	0.33	0.87	0.33	0.33	0.33	0.33	0.33	0.33	0.33	0.33	0.33	0.33	0.33	0.33	1	0.83	0.33	0.72	0.53	1	0.53
Germany	0	0	0	0.17	0	0.03	0	0	0.17	0.06	0	0	0	0	0	0	0	0	0	0	0	0	0.03	0.25	0.01
Gibraltar	0.33	0.33	0.33	0.33	0.33	0.33	0.33	0.33	0.33	0.33	0.33	0.33	0.33	0.33	0.33	0.33	0.33	0.33	0.33	0.33	0.33	0.33	0.33	1	0.33
Greece	1	1	1	1	1	1	0.67	0.67	1	0.78	0.67	0.67	0.67	0.67	0.67	0.67	0.67	0.67	1	1	1	1	0.84	1	0.84
Hungary	1	1	1	1	1	1	0.83	1	0.83	0.89	1	1	1	1	1	1	1	1	1	0	1	0.67	0.93	1	0.93
Iceland	0.5	0	0	0.5	0	0.2	0	0	0	0	0	0	0	0	0	0	0	0	0	0	0	0	0.06	0	0
Ireland	0.33	0.33	0.33	0.33	0.33	0.33	0.33	0.33	0.33	0.33	0.33	0.33	0.33	0.33	0.33	0.33	0.33	0.33	0.33	0	1	0.44	0.34	1	0.34

EEA State	Dimension A - Data Protection Principles						Dimension B - Transparency Rules				Dimension C - Sensitive Data Rules								Dimension D - Discipline Requirements				Overarching Variables		
	(1) Fair & lawful	(2) Purpose specificity etc.	(3) Adequacy, relevance etc.	(4) Accuracy etc.	(5) Temporal minimisation	Dimension A Average	(6) Proactive - Direct Collection	(7) Proactive - Other Data	(8) Reactive Subject Access	Dimension B Average	(9) Racial or ethnic origin	(10) Political opinions	(11) Religious Beliefs etc.	(12) Trade Union	(13) Health	(14) Sex Life	(15) Criminal	Dimension C Average	(16) Legal Basis	(17) Registration	(18) Data Export	Dimension D Average	Combined Substantive Stringency	Maximum Regulatory Powers	Maximum Regulatory Stringency
Italy	0.83	0.83	0.83	0.83	0.83	0.83	0.67	0.67	0.83	0.72	0.5	0.5	0.5	0.5	0.67	0.67	0.5	0.55	0.67	0	0	0.22	0.65	1	0.65
Latvia	1	1	1	1	1	1	0.33	0.33	1	0.55	0.33	0.33	0.33	0.33	0.33	0.33	1	0.43	0.33	0.83	1	0.72	0.67	1	0.67
Liechtenstein	1	1	1	1	1	1	0.67	1	0.33	0.67	1	1	1	1	1	1	1	1	0.83	0.67	0.83	0.78	0.88	1	0.88
Lithuania	1	1	1	1	1	1	0	0	0	0	1	1	1	1	1	1	1	1	1	0	0	0.33	0.63	0.5	0.32
Luxembourg	1	1	1	1	1	1	0.33	0.33	0.67	0.44	0.67	0.67	0.67	0.67	0.67	0.67	0.67	0.67	1	0	0.33	0.44	0.68	0.5	0.34
Malta	0.33	0.33	0.33	0.33	0.33	0.33	0.33	0.33	0.33	0.33	0.33	0.33	0.33	0.33	0.33	0.33	0.33	0.33	0.33	0.33	0.33	0.33	0.33	1	0.33
Netherlands	1	1	1	1	1	1	0	0	0	0	0.17	0.17	0.17	0.17	0.17	0.17	0.17	0.17	1	0	0	0.33	0.38	0	0
Norway	0	0	0	0	0	0	0	0	0	0	0	0	0	0	0	0	0	0	0	0	0	0	0	1	0
Poland	0.33	0.33	0.33	0.33	0.33	0.33	0.33	0.33	0.33	0.33	0.33	0.33	0.33	0.33	0.33	0.33	0.33	0.33	0.33	0.33	0.33	0.33	0.33	1	0.33
Portugal	1	1	1	1	1	1	0	0	0.67	0.22	1	1	1	1	1	1	1	1	1	1	1	1	0.77	1	0.77
Romania	1	1	1	1	1	1	1	0.67	0.83	0.83	0.67	0.67	0.67	0.67	0.67	0.67	0.67	0.67	0.67	1	0.67	0.78	0.83	1	0.83
Slovakia	1	1	1	1	1	1	1	0.5	1	0.83	1	1	1	1	1	1	1	1	0.5	1	1	0.83	0.93	1	0.93
Slovenia	1	1	1	1	1	1	1	1	1	1	1	1	1	1	1	1	1	1	1	0	0	0.33	0.93	1	0.93
Spain	1	1	1	1	1	1	1	1	1	1	1	1	1	1	1	1	1	1	1	1	1	1	1	1	1
Sweden	0	0	0	0	0	0	0	0	0	0	0	0	0	0	0	0	0	0	0	0	0	0	0	0.5	0
UK	0.33	0.33	0.33	0.33	0.33	0.33	0.33	0.33	0.33	0.33	0.33	0.33	0.33	0.33	0.33	0.33	0.33	0.33	0.33	1	0.33	0.55	0.35	0.5	0.18

Second-Generation European Data Protection Regulation, Professional Journalism and Hofstede et al. Cultural Variables

DPA Questionnaire Data and Allied Data Concerning Professional Journalistic Media / Allied Data (Based on Public Domain)

DPA Jurisdiction	Cultural Variables — Hofstede et al. (2010)			A. DPA Standard-Setting					B. DPA Enforcement								A. Standard-Setting			B. Enforcement		C. DPA Resources (A29 WP 2013 Report)			
	(1) Individualism	(2) Uncertainty Avoidance	(3) Power Distance	(1) News Production Stance	(2) Online News Archiving Stance	(3) Undercover Journalism Detail	(4) Subject Access Detail	DPA Power Stance	(G1) Action on Registration	(G2) Action on Subject Access	(G3) Action on Inaccuracy	(G4) General Action re: Unauthorized Data	(G5) General Action re: Other Data	(A1) News Archives Action re: Unauthorized Data	(A2) News Archives Action re: Other Data	(G1 to A2) Total Reported Action	(1) Undercover Journalism: Simplified Coding of Statute (DPA Question A.3 Participants Only)	(2) Undercover Journalism: Codings of Self-Regulatory Codes (DPA Question A.3 Participants Only)	(3) Subject Access: Simplified Coding of Statute (DPA Question A.4 Participants Only)	(1) Regulatory Supervision in Statute	(2) DPA Website Review: Enforcement Binary	(1) Gross Financial Budget (€)	(2) Gross Staffing Resources	(3) Per Capita Financial Budget (€)	(4) Per 100K Capita Staffing Resources
Austria	55	70	11	0.33	Text	Text	0	0	0	0	0	0	0	Text	Text	Uncoded	0	1	0	0	0	–	21.85	–	0.26
Belgium	–	–	–	0.33	0.67	0.5	0.75	0	0	0	1	0	0	0	1	2	0.5	1	0.25	1	1	6840000	53	0.61	0.47
Bulgaria	30	85	70	0.33	0.33	0.5	0.75	1	Text	Text	Text	Text	Text	0	0	Uncoded	0.5	0.5	0.75	1	1	1378856	67	0.19	0.92
Croatia	33	80	73	–	–	–	–	–	–	–	–	Text	Text	–	–	–	–	–	1	1	0	731046	28	0.17	0.66
Cyprus	–	–	–	1	1	0	1	1	0	0	0	1	1	0	1	3	0.5	Uncoded	1	1	1	241236	17	0.28	1.96
Czechia	58	74	57	0.67	0.67	0.25	0.25	0.5	Text	Text	Text	Text	Text	0	0	Uncoded	1	Uncoded	1	0	0	4694785	100	0.45	0.95
Denmark (incl. Press Council)	74	23	18	–	–	–	–	–	–	–	–	–	–	–	–	–	–	–	–	0.5	0	(3016935)	(35)	(0.54)	(0.62)
Estonia	60	60	40	0.33	0.33	0.25	0.75	1	1	1	0	0	0	1	1	3	0.5	0.5	0.25	1	0	631329	18	0.48	1.36
Finland	63	59	33	0.33	0	0	0	0.5	Text	0	0	0	0	1	0	1	0	0.5	0	1	0	1708000	20	0.31	0.37
France	71	86	68	0.33	0.33	Text	0	1	0	0	0	0	0	1	0	1	0.25	Uncoded	0.25	1	0	16900000	178	0.26	0.27
Germany:	67	65	35																						
German Federal				0.33	0.33	0	0.25	0	0	0	0	0	0	0	0	0	0	0.5	0.125	0	0	(9090000)	(85)	(0.11)	(0.11)
Germany Brandenburg				0.33	0.33	Text	0.25	0	0	0	0	0	0	0	0	0	0	0.5	0.125	0	0	–	–	–	–

Country																						
Germany Mecklenburg-Vorpommern	–	–	0.33	0.33	0.25	0.25	0.5	0	0	0	0	0	0	0	0	0.5	0.125	0	0	–	–	–
German Rhineland-Palatinate	–	–	Text	Text	Text	0.5	0.5	0	0	0	0	0	0	0	0	0.5	0.125	0	0	–	–	–
Germany Schleswig-Holstein	–	–	0.67	0.33	0.75	0.75	0.5	0	0	0	0	0	0	0	0	0.5	0.125	0.25	0	–	–	–
Gibraltar	35	60	0.33	1	0	0.75	1	0	0	0	0	0	0	0	0.25	*No code*	0.25	1	0	–	–	–
Greece	112	60	0.67	0.67	0.5	0.75	0.5	0	0	1	1	1	4	0.75	*Uncoded*	1	1	1816500	46	0.17	0.42
Hungary	80	82	0.33	0.33	0.5	0.25	1	1	1	1	0	1	4	1	*Uncoded*	0.75	1	1	1575008	56	0.16	0.57
Iceland	–	–	–	–	–	–	–	–	–	–	–	–	–	–	–	–	0	1	415800	4	1.29	1.24
Ireland	70	28	0.67	0	0.25	0.25	0.5	1	0	0	0	1	1	0.25	0.25	0.25	1	1	1844000	30	0.4	0.65
Italy	76	50	0.33	0.67	0.5	0.75	1	1	1	1	1	1	6	0.5	*Uncoded*	0.75	1	1	8400000	122	0.14	0.2
Latvia	70	44	0.33	0.33	0.25	0.25	0.5	0	0	1	0	0	2	0.25	*Uncoded*	1	1	1	377512	19	0.19	0.94
Liechtenstein	–	–	0.67	0.67	0.5	0.25	0	1	0	0	0	1	2	1	*No Code*	0.25	1	0	596000	4.1	16.18	11.13
Lithuania (incl. Inspector)	60	42	0.33	0.67	0.5	0.25	Text	0	0	1	1	1	4	1	1	0	0.5	1	(555781)	(31)	(0.19)	(1.04)
Luxembourg	60	40	0.33	0.67	0.25	0.5	0.5	Text	Text	Text	Text	0	*Uncoded*	0.5	0.5	0.5	0.5	0	1152000	14	2.15	2.61
Malta	59	56	0.33	0.33	0.5	0.75	1	Text	Text	Text	Text	0	*Uncoded*	0.25	1	0.25	1	0	280000	9	0.66	2.14
Netherlands	80	38	Text	Text	–	–	Text	0	1	0	0	0	1	–	–	–	0	1	7706500	74.9	0.46	0.45
Norway	69	31	–	–	–	–	–	–	–	–	–	–	–	–	–	–	1	0	4747100	41	0.94	0.81
Poland	60	68	0.33	0.33	0.33	0.25	0.5	0	0	0	0	0	0	0.25	0.25	0.25	1	0	3588798	135	0.09	0.35
Portugal	27	63	0.67	0.67	0.5	0.5	0.5	0	0	0	0	0	0	1	0.25	0.5	1	0	2356436	21.5	0.22	0.21
Romania	30	90	–	–	–	–	–	–	–	–	–	–	–	–	–	–	1	0	772321	45	0.04	0.22
Slovakia	52	51	0.33	0.33	0.25	0.25	1	0	0	1	0	1	2	1	*Uncoded*	*Uncoded*	1	0	876324	33	0.16	0.61
Slovenia	27	71	Text	Text	Text	0.75	1	1	1	1	1	1	5	1	0.5	1	1	1	1291010	32	0.63	1.55

DPA Questionnaire Data and Allied Data Concerning Professional Journalistic Media / Allied Data (Based on Public Domain)

DPA Jurisdiction	Cultural Variables — Hofstede et al. (2010)			A. DPA Standard-Setting					B. DPA Enforcement								Allied Data — A. Standard-Setting			B. Enforcement		C. DPA Resources (A29 WP 2013 Report)			
	(1) Individualism	(2) Uncertainty Avoidance	(3) Power Distance	(1) News Production Stance	(2) Online News Archiving Stance	(3) Undercover Journalism Detail	(4) Subject Access Detail	DPA Power Stance	(G1) Action on Registration	(G2) Action on Subject Access	(G3) Action on Inaccuracy	(G4) General Action re: Unauthorized Data	(G5) General Action re: Other Data	(A1) News Archives Action re: Unauthorized Data	(A2) News Archives Action re: Other Data	(G1 to A2) Total Reported Action	(1) Undercover Journalism: Simplified Coding of Statute (DPA Question A.3 Participants Only)	(2) Undercover Journalism: Codings of Self-Regulatory Codes (DPA Question A.3 Participants Only)	(3) Subject Access: Simplified Coding of Statute (DPA Question A.4 Participants Only)	(1) Regulatory Supervision in Statute	(2) DPA Website Review: Enforcement Binary	(1) Gross Financial Budget (€)	(2) Gross Staffing Resources	(3) Per Capita Financial Budget (€)	(4) Per 100K Capita Staffing Resources
Spain:	51	86	57	—	—	—	—	—	—	—	—	—	—	—	—	—	—	—	—	—	—	—	—	—	—
Spain Federal	—	—	—	0.67	0.67	Text	0.25	1	0	0	0	1	1	1	1	4	1	Uncoded	1	1	1	(13524070)	(158)	(0.29)	(0.33)
Spain Catalonia	—	—	—	Text	Text	Text	Text	Text	Text	Text	Text	Text	Text	—	—	—	—	—	—	0.5	0	—	—	—	—
Sweden	71	29	31	0	0	0	0	0	0	0	0	0	0	0	0	0	0	Uncoded	0	0.5	0	4288750	41	0.45	0.43
UK	89	35	35	Text	Text	—	Text	Text	Text	Text	Text	Text	Text	0	0	cc	—	—	0.25	0.5	1	24731700	370	0.39	0.58

N.B. DPA resource figures in brackets exclude interface with, in the case of Germany and Spain, the interface with the fed

European/EEA Self-Regulatory Journalism Codes

This table lists the self-regulatory journalism codes in the European Economic Area (EEA) States. It also details the analysis of any provisions in these codes that specifically relate to undercover journalism, subject access, source protection and accuracy. The codes analysed are those included in the collation made by EthicNet (http://ethicnet.uta.fi/). It should be noted that the Italian *Deontology Code regarding the handling of personal data in the practice of journalism* is actually the same as the *Code of Conduct on the Processing of Personal Data in the Exercise of Journalistic Activities* which was granted formal legal status during second generation European data protection law in Italy (and so is also listed in Appendix 2).

EEA State	Undercover Journalism Provision (and Stringency)	Subject Access Provisions	Source Protection Provisions	Accuracy Provisions
Austria				
Code of Ethics for the Austrian Press	✓ Art. 7.2 (e/1)	✗	✗	✓ Art. 2
Belgium				
Code of Journalistic Principles including	See below	✗	✓ Art. 8	✓ Art. 7
Guidelines for Undercover Journalism	✓ All (c/0.5)			
Bulgaria				
Ethical Code of the Bulgarian Media	✓ Art. 2.1.2 (c/0.5)	✗	✓ Art. 1.3.3	✓ Art. 1.1 (& 1.2)
Croatia				
Honour Codex of Croatian Journalists	✓ Para. 14 (Vague)	✗	✗	✓ Art. 4

EEA State	Undercover Journalism Provision (and Stringency)	Subject Access Provisions	Source Protection Provisions	Accuracy Provisions
Cyprus				
Journalists' Code of Practice	✓ Art. 6 (Vague)	✗	✓ Art. 14	✓ Art. 1
Czechia				
Journalists' Code of Ethics	✓ Para. 1(j) (Vague)	✗	✓ Art. 3(c)	✓ Arts. 3 (a)-(b)
Denmark				
The National Code of Conduct	✗	✗	✗	✓ Section A
Estonia				
Code of Ethics for the Estonian Press	✓ Art. 3(7) (c/0.5)	✗	✗ (But see Art. 3.3)	✓ Art. 3.5 & 4.1
Finland				
Guidelines for Journalists	✓ Art. 9 (c/0.5)	✗	✓ Art. 14	✓ Arts. 8, 10, 11 & 20
France				
Charter of the Professional Duties of French Journalists	✓ Para. 6 (Vague)	✗	✓ Para. 10	✓ Para. 2
Germany				
German Press Code	✓ Art. 4 & Guideline 4.1 (c/0.5)	✓ Art. 8 & Guideline 8.8	✓ Guideline 8.8	✓ Arts. 1-3
Gibraltar				
No Code Found	(Not applicable)	(Not applicable)	(Not applicable)	(Not applicable)
Greece				
Code of Ethics for Professional Journalists	✓ Art. 2(h) (Vague)	✗	✓ Art. 2(i)	✓ Art 1(a),(c) & (f)
Hungary				
Ethical Code of the National Association of Hungarian Journalists	✓ Art. 3(2)(4) (Vague)	✗	✓ Art. 8(2)	✓ Art. 3.1.1., 4.1 & 5.1

EEA State	Undercover Journalism Provision (and Stringency)	Subject Access Provisions	Source Protection Provisions	Accuracy Provisions
Iceland				
Rules of Ethics in Journalism	✗	✗	✓ Clause 2	✗ (But see Clause 3)
Ireland				
National Union of Journalists' Code of Conduct	✓ Art. 5 (c/0.5)	✗	✓ Art. 7	✓ Arts. 2 & 3
Code of Practice for Newspapers and Periodicals	✓ Art. 3(2) (b/0.25)	✗	✓ Principle 6	✓ Principles 1, 2 and 4
Italy				
Charter of Duties of Journalists	✓ Duty 5 (Vague)	✗	✓ Principle 7	✓ Principle 5
Deontology Code regarding the handling of personal data in the practice of journalism	✓ Art 2.(1) (Vague)	✓ Art 2.(1)	✓ Art. 2(4)	✓ Art. 4
Latvia				
Code of Ethics	✗	✗	✓ Art. 4.1	✓ Arts. 2(1)-(2), 5(1) & 5(3)
Liechtenstein				
No Code Found	(Not applicable)	(Not applicable)	(Not applicable)	(Not applicable)
Lithuania				
Code of Ethics of Lithuanian Journalists and Publishers	✓ Art. 9 (e/1)	✗	✓ Art. 15	✓ Arts. 3, 4, 6, 7, 19 & 20
Luxembourg				
Code of Deontology	✓ Art. 7(c) & Directive addition 2006 (c/0.5)	✓ Art. 12 & Directive addition 2006	✓ Art. 7 (c) & 12	✓ Arts. 4 & 8(a)

EEA State	Undercover Journalism Provision (and Stringency)	Subject Access Provisions	Source Protection Provisions	Accuracy Provisions
Malta				
Code of Journalistic Ethics	✓ Art. 4(k) (& also 4(j)) (e/1)	✗	✓ Art. 4(a)-(b)	✓ Art. 4(d), (m) & (n)
Netherlands				
Guidelines from the Netherlands Press Council	✓ Arts. 2.1.5-7 (c/0.5)	✗	✓ Art. 2.2.2	✓ Arts. 1.1, 1.4, 1.5, 2.2.4, 6(1)
Norway				
Code of Ethics of the Norwegian Press	✓ Art. 3.10 (c/0.5)	✗	✓ Art. 3.4-3.5	✓ Arts. 4(2), 4(5) & 4(13)
Poland				
The Code of Journalistic Ethics	✓ Art. 5 (d/0.75)	✗	✓ Art. 7	✓ Arts. 1, 2 & 4
Code of Ethics	✗	✗	✓ Art. II	✓ Art. I
Media Ethics Charter	✗	✗	✗	✓ Principles 1 & 3
Portugal				
Journalists' Code of Ethics	✓ Art. 4 (b/0.25)	✗	✓ Art. 6	✓ Art. 1
Romania				
The Journalists' Code of Ethics	✓ Art. 2.4.1	✗	✓ Art. 2.3	✓ Arts. 2.2.1, 2.2.2 & 2.7
Slovakia				
The Code of Ethics of the Slovak Syndicate of Journalists	✗ (But see Art. III)	✗	✓ Art. III	✓ Art. I
Slovene				
Code of Ethics of Slovene Journalists	✓ Art. 10 (c/0.5)	✗	✗/Unclear (see Art. 4)	✓ Arts. 1, 3, 8 & 11
Spain				
Deontological Code for the Journalistic Profession	✗ (but see Art. 4)	✗	✓ Art. 10	✓ Arts. 2, 13 & 17

EEA State	Undercover Journalism Provision (and Stringency)	Subject Access Provisions	Source Protection Provisions	Accuracy Provisions
Catalonia Deontological Code	✓ Art. 4 (Vague)	✗	✗	✓ Arts. 1-3
Sweden				
Code of Ethics for the Press, Radio & Television	✗	✗	✗	✓ Arts. 1-5 & 14
UK				
National Union of Journalists' Code of Conduct	✓ Art. 5 (c/0.5)	✗	✓ Art. 7	✓ Arts. 2-4
Editors' Code of Practice	✓ Art. 10 (c/0.5)	✗	✓ Art. 14	✓ Art. 1

Third-Generation European Data Protection Law and Professional Journalism (as of May 2019)

EEA State	Dimension A - Data Protection Principles						Dimension B - Transparency Rules				Dimension C - Sensitive Data Rules								Dimension D - Discipline Requirements				Overarching Variables		
	(1) Fair, lawful & transparent	(2) Purpose specificity etc.	(3) Adequacy, relevance etc.	(4) Accuracy etc.	(5) Temporal minimisation	Dimension A Average	(6) Proactive - Direct Collection	(7) Proactive - Other Data	(8) Reactive Subject Access	Dimension B Average	(9) Racial or ethnic origin	(10) Political opinions	(11) Religious Beliefs etc.	(12) Trade Union	(13) Health	(14) Sex Life	(15) Criminal	Dimension C Average	(16) Legal Basis	(17) Registration	(18) Data Export	Dimension D Average	Combined Substantive Stringency	Maximum Regulatory Powers	Maximum Regulatory Stringency
Austria	1	1	1	1	1	1	0.33	0.33	0.33	0.33	0.33	0.33	0.33	0.33	0.33	0.33	0.33	0.33	0.33	0.33	0.33	0.33	0.53	0.5	0.27
Belgium	1	1	1	1	1	1	0.17	0.17	0.17	0.17	0.17	0.17	0.17	0.17	0.17	0.17	0.17	0.17	1	0.83	0.5	0.78	0.48	0.5	0.24
Bulgaria	0.83	0.83	0.83	0.83	0.83	0.83	0.5	0.5	0.5	0.5	0.5	0.5	0.5	0.5	0.5	0.5	0.5	0.5	0.5	0.5	0.5	0.5	0.60	0.5	0.30
Croatia	1	1	1	1	1	1	1	1	1	1	1	1	1	1	1	1	1	1	1	1	1	1	1	1	1
Cyprus	0.5	0.5	0.5	0.5	0.5	0.5	0.5	0.17	0.17	0.28	0.33	0.33	0.33	0.33	0.33	0.33	0.33	0.33	0.33	0.5	0.5	0.44	0.38	1	0.38
Czechia	0.33	0.33	0.33	0.33	0.33	0.33	0.17	0.67	0.17	0.34	0.5	0.5	0.5	0.5	0.5	0.5	0.5	0.5	0.33	0.83	0.5	0.55	0.41	0.5	0.20
Denmark	0.17	0.17	0.17	0.17	0.17	0.17	0	0	0.17	0.06	0.17	0.17	0.17	0.17	0.17	0.17	0.17	0.17	0	0.83	0	0.28	0.15	0.5	0.07
Estonia	0.83	0.83	0.83	0.83	0.83	0.83	0.83	0.83	0.83	0.83	0.33	0.33	0.33	0.33	0.33	0.33	0.83	0.4	0.83	1	0.33	0.72	0.69	1	0.69
Finland	1	1	0	0	0	0.4	0	0	0	0	0	0	0	0	0	0	0	0	0	0	0.5	0.17	0.14	0.5	0.07
France	1	1	1	1	0.5	0.9	0.5	0.5	0.5	0.5	0.5	0.5	0.5	0.5	0.5	0.5	0.5	0.5	1	1	0.5	0.83	0.65	0.5	0.33
Germany	0	0	0	0.17	0	0.03	0	0	0.17	0.06	0	0	0	0	0	0	0	0	0	0	0	0	0.03	0.25	0.01
Gibraltar	0.33	0.33	0.33	0.33	0.33	0.33	0.33	0.33	0.33	0.33	0.33	0.33	0.33	0.33	0.33	0.33	0.33	0.33	0.33	1	0.33	0.55	0.35	0.5	0.18
Hungary	1	1	1	1	1	1	1	1	1	1	1	1	1	1	1	1	1	1	1	1	1	1	1	1	1
Iceland	0.5	0	0	0.5	0	0.2	0	0	0	0	0	0	0	0	0	0	0	0	0	0	0	0	0.06	0	0
Ireland	0.33	0.33	0.33	0.33	0.33	0.33	0.33	0.33	0.33	0.33	0.33	0.33	0.33	0.33	0.33	0.33	0.33	0.33	0.33	0.33	0.33	0.33	0.33	0.5	0.17

EEA State	Dimension A - Data Protection Principles						Dimension B - Transparency Rules				Dimension C - Sensitive Data Rules								Dimension D - Discipline Requirements				Overarching Variables		
	(1) Fair, lawful & transparent	(2) Purpose specificity etc.	(3) Adequacy, relevance etc.	(4) Accuracy etc.	(5) Temporal minimisation	Dimension A Average	(6) Proactive - Direct Collection	(7) Proactive - Other Data	(8) Reactive Subject Access	Dimension B Average	(9) Racial or ethnic origin	(10) Political opinions	(11) Religious Beliefs etc.	(12) Trade Union	(13) Health	(14) Sex Life	(15) Criminal	Dimension C Average	(16) Legal Basis	(17) Registration	(18) Data Export	Dimension D Average	Combined Substantive Stringency	Maximum Regulatory Powers	Maximum Regulatory Stringency
Italy	0.83	0.83	0.83	0.83	0.83	0.83	0.67	0.67	0.83	0.72	0.5	0.5	0.5	0.5	0.67	0.67	0.5	0.55	0.83	1	0	0.61	0.69	1	0.69
Latvia	0.83	0.83	0.83	0.83	0.83	0.83	0.5	0.5	0.5	0.5	0.5	0.5	0.5	0.5	0.5	0.5	0.5	0.5	0.5	0.5	0.5	0.5	0.60	0.5	0.30
Liechtenstein	1	1	1	1	1	1	1	1	0.33	0.78	1	1	1	1	1	1	1	1	1	1	1	1	0.93	1	0.93
Lithuania	1	1	1	1	1	1	0	0	0	0	1	1	1	1	1	1	1	1	0	0	1	0.33	0.63	0.5	0.32
Luxembourg	1	1	1	1	1	1	0.17	0.17	0.67	0.34	0.67	0.67	0.67	0.67	0.67	0.67	0.67	0.67	1	1	0	0.67	0.67	1	0.67
Malta	0.5	0.5	0.5	0.5	0.5	0.5	0.5	0.5	0.5	0.5	1	1	1	1	1	1	0.5	0.93	0.5	0.5	1	0.67	0.65	1	0.65
Netherlands	1	1	1	1	1	1	0	0	0	0	0.17	0.17	0.17	0.17	0.17	0.17	0.17	0.17	1	0	0	0.33	0.38	0	0
Norway	0	0	0	0	0	0	0	0	0	0	0	0	0	0	0	0	0	0	0	0	0	0	0	1	0
Poland	0	0	0	0	0	0	0	0	0	0	0	0	0	0	0	0	1	0.14	0	0	1	0.33	0.08	1	0.08
Romania	0.67	0.67	0.67	0.67	0.67	0.67	0.67	0.67	0.67	0.67	0.67	0.67	0.67	0.67	0.67	0.67	0.67	0.67	0.67	0.67	0.67	0.67	0.67	0.5	0.34
Slovakia	0.83	0.83	0.83	0.83	0.83	0.83	0.83	0.83	0.83	0.83	0.5	0.5	0.5	0.5	0.5	0.5	0.83	0.55	0.83	1	0.5	0.78	0.74	1	0.74
Spain	1	1	1	1	1	1	1	1	1	1	1	1	1	1	1	1	1	1	1	1	1	1	1	1	1
Sweden	0	0	0	0	0	0	0	0	0	0	0	0	0	0	0	0	0	0	0	0	0	0	0	0.5	0
UK	0.33	0.33	0.33	0.33	0.33	0.33	0.33	0.33	0.33	0.33	0.33	0.33	0.33	0.33	0.33	0.33	0.33	0.33	0.33	1	0.33	0.55	0.35	0.5	0.18

European Data Protection, 'Non-Journalistic' Special Expression, Social Science and 2017 DPA Resources

| DPA Jurisdiction | DPA Resources (2017 - A29WP/Commission) | | | | Non-Journalistic Special Expression Statutory Provisions | | | | | | | DPA Questionnaire: Social Science | | | | |
| | Gross | | Per Capita | | DPD Era | | | GDPR Era | | | Interpretation | Enforcement | | | | |
	Financial (€)	Staff	Financial (€)	Staff per 100K pop.	Minimum Statutory Stringency	Minimum Regulatory Supervision	Minimum Regulatory Stringency	Minimum Statutory Stringency	Minimum Regulatory Supervision	Minimum Regulatory Stringency	Covert Social Science	Action on Secondary Data Obtained Without Authorization	Action on Other Secondary Data	Action on Non-Secondary Data Obtained Without Authorization	Action on Other Non-Secondary Data	Total Action on Social Science
Austria	1582105	28	0.18	0.32	1	1	1	0.65	0.5	0.33	0.75	0	0	0	1	2
Belgium	8472000	57	0.07	0.50	0.61	1	0.61	0.38	0.5	0.19	0.75	1	0	1	0	2
Bulgaria	–	–	–	–	0.68	1	0.68	0.60	0.5	0.30	1	0	0	0	0	0
Croatia	740073	26	0.18	0.63	1	1	1	1	1	1	–	–	–	–	–	–
Cyprus	270675	15	0.32	1.75	0.85	1	0.85	0.38	1	0.38	1	0	0	0	0	0
Czechia	6067398	101	0.57	0.95	1	1	1	0.41	0.5	0.20	0.5	1	1	0	1	3
Denmark	(3065876)	(35)	(0.53)	(0.61)	0.15	0.5	0.07	0	0	0.00	–	–	–	–	–	–
Estonia	699482	19	0.53	1.44	1	1	1	0.69	1	0.69	Text	0	0	0	0	0
Finland	2000000	23	0.36	0.42	0	1	0	0.14	0.5	0.07	Text	1	1	1	0	2
France	16908456	197	0.25	0.29	0.27	1	0.27	0.54	1	0.54	Text	0	0	0	0	0
Germany																
Germany Federal	15395000	160.5	0.19	0.19	1	1	1	1	1	1	1	0	0	0	0	0
Germany Brandenburg	2454500	30	–	–	1	1	1	0.03	0	0	1	0	0	0	0	0

Germany Mecklenburg Vorpommern	1515900	16	–	–	1	1	1	0.03	0	0	0.5	0	0	0	0
Germany Rhineland	1735000	25	–	–	1	1	1	1	1	1	0.5	0	1	0	1
Germany Schlewsig-Holstein	–	–	–	–	1	1	1	1	1	1	1	1	1	1	1
Gibraltar	–	–	–	–	0.33	1	0.33	0.35	0.5	0.18	*Text*	0	0	0	0
Greece	2380000	46	0.22	0.43	0.84	1	0.84	–	–	–	*Text*	0	1	0	0
Hungary	2072604	73	0.21	0.75	1	1	1	1	1	1	0.5	0	1	0	1
Iceland	–	–	–	–	0.06	0	0	0.06	0	0	–	–	–	–	–
Ireland	7526000	90	1.57	1.88	0.34	1	0.34	0.33	0.5	0.17	1	0	0	0	0
Italy	–	–	–	–	0.65	1	0.65	0.71	1	0.71	1	1	0	0	1
Latvia	639262	25	0.33	1.28	0.67	1	0.67	0.60	0.5	0.30	0.5	0	0	0	0
Liechtenstein	770000	4.55	20.36	12.03	1	1	1	–	–	–	0.5	0	0	0	0
Lithuania	(729200)	(30)	(0.26)	(1.05)	1	0.5	0.50	0.63	0.5	0.32	0.75	0	0	1	0
Luxembourg	2517926	23	4.26	3.89	0.68	1	0.68	0.67	1	0.67	0.5	1	1	0	1
Malta	400000	10	0.87	2.17	0.33	0.5	0.17	0.65	1	0.65	0.75	0	0	0	0
Netherlands	8987000	94	0.53	0.55	0.38	0	0	0.38	0	0	–	0	0	0	0
Norway	–	–	–	–	0	1	0	0	1	0	–	–	–	–	–
Poland	4980000	155	0.13	0.41	0.33	1	0.33	0.08	1	0.08	1	0	0	0	0
Portugal	2785468	25	0.27	0.24	0.77	1	0.77	–	–	–	1	0	0	0	0
Romania	1005527	34	0.05	0.17	0.83	1	0.83	0.67	0.5	0.34	–	–	–	–	–
Slovakia	1166279	37	0.21	0.68	0.93	1	0.93	0.74	1	0.74	1	0	0	0	0

Table: DPA Jurisdiction / DPA Resources (2017 – A29WP/Commission) / Non-Journalistic Special Expression Statutory Provisions / DPA Questionnaire: Social Science

DPA Jurisdiction	DPA Resources (2017 – A29WP/Commission)				Non-Journalistic Special Expression Statutory Provisions							DPA Questionnaire: Social Science				
	Gross		Per Capita		DPD Era			GDPR Era			Interpretation	Enforcement				
	Financial (€)	Staff	Financial (€)	Staff per 100K pop.	Minimum Statutory Stringency	Minimum Regulatory Supervision	Minimum Regulatory Stringency	Minimum Statutory Stringency	Minimum Regulatory Supervision	Minimum Regulatory Stringency	Covert Social Science	Action on Secondary Data Obtained Without Authorization	Action on Other Secondary Data	Action on Non-Secondary Data Obtained Without Authorization	Action on Other Non-Secondary Data	Total Action on Social Science
Slovenia	1495147	33	0.72	1.6	1	1	1	1	–	–	Text	0	1	1	1	3
Spain																
Spain Federal	14100000	156	0.3	0.34	1	1	1	1	1	1	–	–	–	–	–	–
Spain Catalonia	–	–	–	–	1	0.5	0.5	1	0.5	0.5	Text	0	0	0	0	0
Sweden	6900000	56	0.69	0.56	0	1	0	0	0.5	0	1	0	0	0	1	1
UK	24700000	451	0.38	0.68	0.35	0.5	0.18	0.35	0.5	0.18	–	0	0	0	0	0

N.B. DPA resource figures in brackets exclude resources of the co-regulatory Danish Press Council and Lithuanian Inspector of Journalistic Ethics.

Notes

Chapter 1

1. Case C-136/17 *GC et al v CNIL* (10 January 2019) Opinion of AG M Maciej Szpunar, EU:C:2019:14, para 1.
2. George Brock, *Out of Print: Newspapers, Journalism and the Business of News in the Digital Age* (Kogan Page 2013) 16.
3. *Thorgeirson v Iceland* (1992) 14 EHRR 843, para 63.
4. *Reynolds v Times Newspapers* [2001] 2 AC 127, 205 (Lord Nicholls).
5. Brock (n 2) 142.
6. Mark Cooper, 'The Future of Journalism: Addressing Pervasive Market Failure with Public Policy' in Robert McChesney and Victor Pickard (eds), *Will the Last Reporter Please Turn Out the Lights* (New Press 2011) 321–22.
7. Perry Keller, *European and International Media Law: Liberal Democracy, Trade and the New Media* (OUP 2011) 331.
8. UK, House of Lords, European Communities Committee, *Protection of Personal Data* (HL Paper 75) (1993) 39. Indeed, the committee went as far as holding that, '[e]xcept for government and police agencies', the journalistic media was capable of inflicting the 'gravest damage' on the individual as a result of its handling of personal information. Whilst such a strong claim would appear incorrect today given online developments, it can hardly be doubted that the journalistic media's activities retain a very significant ability to inflict grave harms.
9. Brock (n 2) 16.
10. Robert Dingwall, 'The Ethical Case Against Ethical Regulation in Humanities and Social Science Research' (2008) 3(1) Journal of the Academy of Social Sciences 1, 6.
11. Edward Shills, 'The Academic Ethic' (1982) 1–2 Minerva 105, 107.
12. Phillip M Strong, 'The Rivals: An Essay on the Sociological Trades' in Robert Dingwall and Philip Lewis (eds), *The Sociology of the Professions: Law, Medicine and Others* (Macmillan 1983) 75; cf Robert Dingwall, 'Confronting the Anti-Democrats: The Unethical Nature of Ethical Regulation in Social Science' (2006) 1(1) Medical Sociology Online 51, 54.
13. Brian Harrison, 'Evidence Submitted to the Review of The "30-Year Rule"' (2008) quoted in David Erdos, 'Freedom of Expression Turned On Its Head? Academic Social Research and Journalism in the European Privacy Framework' (2013) 1 Public Law 52, 61.
14. Strong (n 12) 59.
15. *Campbell v MGN* [2004] UKHL 22, [2004] 2 AC 457 [148] (Lady Hale).
16. Brock (n 2) 16.
17. Council Regulation 2016/679/EU of 27 April 2016 on the protection of natural persons with regard to the processing of personal data and on the free movement of such data, and repealing Directive 95/46/EC [2016] OJ L119/1, recital 6 ('GDPR').

18. Ibid.

19. Ibid art 1(2).

20. Ibid art 85(1).

21. Ibid recital 117.

22. Case C-518/07 *Commission v Germany* [2010] ECR I-1885, para 23.

23. GDPR (n 17) art 57.

24. Ibid art 58.

25. Ibid arts 60–67.

26. Peter Hustinx, 'The Role of Data Protection Authorities' in Serge Gutwirth, Yves Poullet, Paul de Hert, Cécile de Terwangne, and Sjaak Nouwt (eds), *Reinventing Data Protection?* (Springer 2009) 133.

27. GDPR (n 17) recital 4.

28. According to the *Oxford English Dictionary*, this is defined as land north of the Mediterranean and Black Seas, north-west of the Caucasus and the Caspian Sea, and west of the Ural Mountains.

29. Statute of Council of Europe (Treaty of London) art 3.

30. In the late 1980s, Finland became the last sizeable liberal European State to become a part of the Council. Central and Eastern European States joined in the 1990s following the collapse of European communism. Turning to the European microstates, San Marino joined the Council in the late 1980s, Andorra in the mid-1990s, and finally Monaco in the mid-2000s. See: Council of Europe, '47 Member States' (*COE*, 2018) <https://www.coe.int/en/web/portal/47-members-states> accessed 11 April 2019.

31. Those interested in the relationship between traditional publishers and older parts of informational personality law should refer especially to Gert Brüggemeir, Aurelia Colombi Ciacchi, and Patrick O'Callaghan, *Personality Rights in European Tort Law* (Cambridge University Press 2010).

32. Frits W Hondius, 'The Human Rights Aspect of Data Protection' in JJP Kennedy (ed), *Data Privacy and Security* (Pergamon Infotech 1986) 91.

33. Frits W Hondius, 'A Decade of International Data Protection' (1983) 30(2) Netherlands International Law Review 103, 109–10.

34. Council Directive 95/46/EC of 24 October 1995 on the protection of individuals with regard to the processing of personal data and on the free movement of such data [1995] OJ L281/31, recital 62 ('DPD').

35. Peter Blume and Christian Wiese Svanberg, 'The Proposed Data Protection Regulation: The Illusion of Harmonisation, the Private/Public Sector Divide and the Bureaucratic Apparatus' (2013) 15 Cambridge Yearbook of European Legal Studies 27, 40.

36. DPD (n 34) arts 22–23; GDPR (n 17) arts 79 and 82.

37. Michael Schudson, *The Sociology of the News* (Norton & Company 2003) 11.

38. Tony Harcup, *Journalism: Principles and Practice* (2nd edn, Sage Publications 2015) 3

39. Brock (n 2) 8.

40. Cf Harcup (n 38) 6.

41. *Kordowski v Law Society* [2011] EWHC 3185 (QB) [99].

42. See Brock (n 2) 7–54 and *passim*.

43. Brian Leveson, *Inquiry into the Culture, Practices and Ethics of the Press* (HC 2012, 780–I) 77–78.

44. Eric Alterman, 'Out of Print: The Death and Life of the American Newspaper' in Robert W McChesney and Victor Pickard (eds), *Will the Last Reporter Please Turn out the Lights: The Collapse of Journalism and What Can be Done to Fix It* (The New Press 2011) 13.

45. Thus, as argued by Article 19 in the case of *Delfi AS v Estonia* (2016) 62 EHRR 6, '[c]omment platforms enabled and promoted public debate in its purest form and this had very little to do with the provision of news. As a matter of fact and form, comments sections on news websites were better understood as newspapers appropriating the private discussion model that was native to the Internet rather than the other way around' (para 96).

46. Frances Cairncross, 'The Cairncross Review: A Sustainable Future for Journalism' (*Gov.uk*, 2019) <https://assets.publishing.service.gov.uk/government/uploads/system/uploads/attachment_data/file/779882/021919_DCMS_Cairncross_Review_.pdf> 15 accessed 2 May 2019.

47. Harcup (n 38) 18.

48. Ibid 5 (quoting former *Times* journalist Louis Heron).

49. *Times Newspapers (Nos 1 and 2) v United Kingdom* [2009] EMLR 14, para 45.

50. Hugo de Burgh, 'Introduction' in Hugo de Burgh (ed), *Investigative Journalism* (2nd edn, Routledge 2008) 13.

51. In adopting the concept of 'non-journalistic' traditional publishers as a structuring and heuristic device, this book does not mean to downplay the very close connection between these actors and the manifestly 'journalistic' media. Indeed, a central argument presented is that both engage professionally in similarly socially important freedom of expression. Moreover, in light of the need to vindicate such a core exercise of a fundamental right and in situations where no more apposite data protection derogation is available, it may well be necessary to construe a 'journalistic' and/or 'media' derogation so that it also encompasses the activities of these other traditional publishers. As will be seen later in this book, historically a considerable number of EEA States limited freedom of expression derogations in this way and at least in Liechtenstein and some German *Länder* that *status quo ante* may remain in place. Moreover, although beyond the scope of this book, a large number of States outside Europe likewise only explicitly address the freedom of expression needs of 'journalism' and/or the 'media' within their data protection statutes.

52. Brock (n 2) 8.

53. Carol Becker, 'The Artist as Public Intellectual' (1995) 17(4) The Review of Education/Pedagogy/Cultural Studies 385, 387.

54. Ibid 389.

55. Ibid 389.

56. These types of writers would, in the terms of this book, be conceived of as 'literary artists' and, therefore, fall within the concept of professional artists explored earlier. See Strong (n 12) 66.

57. Juan Cole, 'Blogging Current Affairs History' (2011) 46(3) Journal of Contemporary History 658, 670.

58. Shills (n 11) 107.

59. Ibid 112.

60. Various attempts have been made to specify the goal of achieving such broader impact. For example, in the UK's 2014 Research Excellence Framework such a goal was defined as 'an effect on, change or benefit to the economy, society, culture, public policy or services, health, the environment or quality of life, beyond academia'. See Research England, 'REF Impact' (*UKRI*, 2014) <https://re.ukri.org/research/ref-impact/> accessed 11 April 2019.

61. Brock (n 2) 10.

62. Dingwall (n 12) 54.

63. John Milton, *Areopagitica: A Speech of Mr John Milton for the Liberty of Unlicensed Printing to the Parliament of England* (Payson & Clarke 1644) 4.

64. Dingwall (n 12) 54.

65. Case C-73/07 *Tietosuojavaltuutettu v Satakunnan Markkinapörssi Oy and Satamedia Oy* [2008] ECR I-9831, para 61.

66. Brock (n 2) 8.

67. Article 29 Working Party, 'Recommendation 1/97' (*Europa*, 25 February 1997) <https://ec.europa.eu/justice/article-29/documentation/opinion-recommendation/files/1997/wp1_en.pdf> 8 accessed 11 April 2019.

68. Although Luxembourg enacted a data protection law in 1979, it only established an Advisory Board as opposed to a true DPA. See Luxembourg, Nominal Data (Automatic Processing) Act 1979, arts 30–31. Despite efforts to locate records relating to this Board, none were found.

69. The questionnaire was not sent to the specialist media regulators allocated a data protection role in the DPD era in Lithuania and Denmark since they were not judged formally to be true DPAs and, in any case, the survey dealt with a wide range of matters related to the new media and also medical research which fell well outside the scope of these bodies. In the event, however, the Lithuanian DPA submitted a return that had, where relevant, been filled out in cooperation with the specialist media body (the Lithuanian Inspector of Journalistic Ethics). Meanwhile, the Danish DPA did not respond to the questionnaire.

70. DPD (n 34) arts 29–30.

71. Kaarle Nordenstreng and Ari Heinonen, 'EthicNet—Collection of Codes of Journalism Ethics in Europe' (*EthicNet*, June 2008) <http://ethicnet.uta.fi/> accessed 13 March 2018.

72. DPD (n 34) art 9.

73. GDPR (n 17), art 85(2).

74. Ibid (17) art 89.

75. See not only GDPR, art 85(2) and DPD, art 9 but also Council of Europe, 'Explanatory Report to the Convention for the Protection of Individuals with regard to Automatic Processing of Personal Data' (*COE*, 1981) <https://rm.coe.int/16800ca434> para 58 accessed 16 April 2019.

76. GDPR (n 17), arts 40–41.

Chapter 2

1. John Milton, *Areopagitica: A Speech of Mr John Milton for the Liberty of Unlicensed Printing to the Parliament of England* (Payson & Clarkse 1644).

2. See e.g. Voltaire, *Letters on England* (Leonard Tanock (ed), first published 1734, Penguin 1980) 101 ('In London ... anyone can print what he thinks about public affairs. So the whole nation is obliged to study. One hears nothing but talk of governments of Athens and Rome, and so willy-nilly one has to read the authors who have deal with them, and this study naturally leads to literature.')

3. The former is represented by, for example, the Belgium Constitution of 1831 and the Greek Constitution of 1827. Meanwhile, the latter is epitomised by the Austrian Empire's *State Fundamental Law on the General Rights of Citizens*. Source: World Constitutions Illustrated (Hein Online).

4. See Amos Jenkins Peaslee, *Constitutions of Nations: France to New Zealand* (M Nijhoff 1956) and (Brill Archive 1950).

5. Albert Venn Dicey, *Introduction to the Study of the Law of the Constitution* (8th edn Liberty Fund 1982) 197.

6. Convention for the Protection of Human Rights and Fundamental Freedoms (European Convention on Human Rights, as amended), art 10 ('ECHR').

7. Ed Bates, *The Evolution of the European Convention on Human Rights: From Its Inception to the Creation of a Permanent Court of Human Rights* (Oxford University Press 2010) 11.

8. ECHR (n 6) art 10(1).

9. See for example, art 6(1)(i) of the Irish Constitution (in Peaslee, 1956 (n 4) 459–95), art 21 of the Italian Constitution (ibid 496–527) and art 14 of the Greek Constitution (ibid 499–527).

10. Bates (n 7) 15.

11. Case C-1/58 *Stork v High Authority* [1959] ECR 17.

12. Case C-4/73 *Nold v Commission* [1974] ECR 491. This seminal case draws on the earlier judgments of Case C-29/69 *Stauder v City of Ulm* [1969] ECR 419 and Case C-11/70 *Internationale Handelsgellschaft v Einfuhr und Vorratstelle für Getreide und Futtermittel* [1970] ECR 1125.

13. See, for example, John Bell, *French Constitutional Law* (Clarendon Press 1994) 138–89 and Hebert Hausmaninger, *The Austrian Legal System* (2nd edn Kluwer Law International 2000) 161.

14. See Davíd Björgvinsson, 'Fundamental Rights in EEA Law' in EFTA Court (ed), *The EEA and the EFTA Court: Decentred Integration* (Hart Publishing 2014).

15. For example, such laws came into force in Malta in 1987, Denmark in 1992, Iceland in 1994, Sweden in 1995, Norway in 1999, the United Kingdom in 2000, and Ireland in 2003. See Robert Blackburn and Jörg Polakiewicz, *Fundamental Rights in Europe: The European Convention on Human Rights and its Member States* (Oxford University Press 2001).

16. Protocol No 11 of the Convention for the Protection of Human Rights and Fundamental Freedom, Reconstructing the Control Machinery Established Thereby.

17. Treaty on European Union ('TEU').

18. EU Charter of Fundamental Rights and Freedoms, art 11.

19. Ibid art 11(2).

20. Ibid art 13.

21. TEU (n 17) art 6.

22. For an indication of the type of institutions that have been established at national level see European Networking of National Human Rights Institutions, 'List of Members' (*ENNHRI*, 2017) <http://ennhri.org/List-of-members> accessed 14 April 2019.

23. Paul Craig and Gráinne De Búrca, *EU Law: Text, Cases and Materials* (6th edn Oxford University Press 2015) 392.

24. TEU (n 17) art 7. The determinations of such a violation requires unanimity within the European Council and the consent of the European Parliament (art 7(2)). Voting rights may then be suspended by the Council operating based on a qualified majority (art 7(3)). As a result of a reforms introduced by the Treaty of Nice in 2003, another procedure enables a determination that a clear risk of a serious breach of human rights exists. This requires a four-fifths majority in the Council and the support of the European Parliament (art 7(1)).

25. See Gráinne De Búrca, 'The Evolution of EU Human Rights Law' in Paul Craig and Gráinne De Búrca (eds), *EU Law: Text, Cases and Materials* (6th edn Oxford University Press 2015) 484–85.

26. See Jan-Werner Müller, 'Should the EU Protect Democracy and The Rule of Law Inside Member States?' (2015) 21(2) European Law Journal 141.

27. Council of Europe, 'High Level Conference on the Future of the European Court of Human Rights' (*COE*, 2012) <http://www.echr.coe.int/Documents/2012_Brighton_FinalDeclaration_ENG.pdf> 1 accessed 15 April 2019.

28. The Protocol's provisions on social and economic rights may arguably have more force but fall outside the scope of this book.

29. Treaty of Lisbon, Protocol 30.

30. See generally Craig and De Búrca (n 23) 394–96.

31. See the Agreement on the European Economic Area (EEA Agreement) recital 1.

32. For a general overview of EEA fundamental rights law see Bjőrgvinsson (n 14).

33. For discussion on this point see Bjőrgvinsson (n 14).

34. In the mid-1990s the CJEU ruled that the then European Community could not accede to the ECHR due to the lack of an explicit Treaty basis for this. See *Opinion 2/94 Accession of the Community to the European Convention for the Protection of Human Rights and Fundamental Freedoms* [1996] ECR I-1759. As a result of changes made under the Lisbon Treaty in 2009, the Treaties now provide that the EU 'shall accede' to the Convention (TEU (n 17) art 6(2)). A Draft Accession Agreement was finalized in 2010 but in 2013 a full sitting of the CJEU declared it to conflict with the autonomy of EU law. See *Opinion 2/13 Draft international Agreement—Accession of the European Union to the European Convention for the Protection of Human Rights and Fundamental Freedoms—Compatibility of the draft agreement with the EU and FEU Treaties*, EU:C:2014:2454 (Court of Justice of the European Union, 2014).

35. *Bosphorus Hava Yollari Turizm ve Ticaret Anonim Şirketi v Ireland* (2006) 42 EHRR 1, para 155.

36. Ibid para 155.

37. Ibid paras 159–65.

38. Ibid para 156.

39. Ibid para 157.

40. As outlined later in section 2.1, even expression which has a purely economic motive still falls to be analysed through the lens of Article 10. Only expression judged to be manifestly aimed at stirring up abject hatred and/or violence has, as a result of the Convention's anti-abuse clause (art 17), been found to fall outside this protection. See, for example, *Garaudy v France* App no 65831/01 (ECtHR, 24 June 2003) (finding that a book denying the Holocaust fell outside Article 10) and *Norwood v United Kingdom* (2005) 40 EHRR SE11 (finding likewise as regards a 'general vehement attack against a religious group, linking the group as a whole with a grave act of terrorism'). Note that in *Perinçek v Switzerland* (2016) 63 EHRR 6 the Court found that repeated remarks vehemently questioning the Armenian genocide (e.g. 'an international lie' (para 15)) not only fell within the scope of Article 10 in principle but that a criminal fine for such expression violated that right.

41. Generally, such an orientation has been analysed from an objective standpoint. However, on occasion the Court has also taken account of the subjective aim of the expressive actor themselves. See, for example, *Satakunnan Markkinapörssi Oy and Satamedia Oy v Finland* (2018) 66 EHRR 8, para 174.

42. *Gerger v Turkey* App no 249191/94 (ECtHR, 8 July 1999) para 48.

43. *Janowski v Poland* (2000) 29 EHRR 705, para 31.

44. *Jersild v Denmark* (1994) 19 EHRR 1, para 31.

45. *Thorgeirson v Iceland* (1992) 13 EHRR 843, para 64.

46. See *Handyside v United Kingdom* (1976) 1 EHRR 737, para 49.

47. *Satakunnan Markkinapörssi Oy* (n 41) para 171.

48. *Gerger v Turkey* (n 42) para 48.

49. *Sunday Times v United Kingdom* (1979) 2 EHRR 245, paras 66–67.

50. Ibid para 68. Whilst eleven judges supported this conclusion, nine dissented.

51. *Thorgeirson* (n 45) para 65. One judge dissented from this holding.

52. Ibid para 67. The Court was also critical of the fact that the newspaper was sanctioned through a criminal conviction (for defamation) (para 68).

53. *Jersild* (n 44) para 34.

54. Outside public interest expression, this criteria has even been found to be compatible with a professional body setting down its own legal rules so long as it has been given legal authorization to act in this way. See *Barthold v Germany* (1985) 7 EHRR 383, para 46.

55. [2011] EMLR 4.

56. Ibid para 74.

57. Ibid para 82.

58. *Müller v Switzerland* (1998) 13 EHRR 212, para 33.

59. Ibid para 27.

60. Ibid para 36. In contrast, in *Akdas v Turkey* App no 41056/04 (ECtHR, 16 February 2010) (no official English translation available), the Court unanimously found against attempts to prohibit the distribution of Guillaume Apollinaire's *Les onze mille verge*. Whilst this 1907 novel did depict '*des scènes de rapports sexuels crues, avec diverses pratiques telles que le sadomasochisme, le vampirisme, la pédophilie, etc.*' ('scenes of raw sex, with various practices such as sadomasochism, vampirism, pedophilia, etc.'), it was found impermissible for a State '*jusqu'à empêcher l'accès du public d'une langue donnée,*

en l'occurrence le turc, à une œuvre figurant dans le patrimoine littéraire européen' ('to prevent public access in a given language, in this case Turkish, to a work within the European literary heritage'). See paras 6 and 30.

61. *Müller* (n 58) para 44. Five judges supported this decision, one dissented in full, and one dissented solely in relation to the confiscation aspect.

62. *Karataş v Turkey* App No 23168/94 (ECtHR, 8 July 1999) para 49 and *Alinak v Turkey* App No 40287/98 (ECtHR, 29 March 2005) para 41.

63. Ibid para 50.

64. See generally Eric Barendt, *Freedom of Expression* (2nd edn Oxford University Press 2005) 392–416.

65. Whilst nine judges including the President of the Court supported this judgment, no fewer than nine others dissented.

66. *Markt Intern Verlag and Klaus Beermann v Germany* (1990) 12 EHRR 161, para 37. As a result, it was held permissible for Markt Intern to be prohibited under unfair competition law from publishing its information bulletin for chemists and beauty product retailers which criticized a rival economic actor, namely, a mail-order company.

67. *Janowski* (n 43) para 32.

68. Ibid para 34. Whilst twelve judges supported this decision, five dissented.

69. *Magyar Tartalomszolgáatatók Egyesülete & Index.hu zrt v Hungary* App no 22947/13 (ECtHR, 2 February 2016).

70. *Pihl v Sweden* (2017) 64 EHRR SE20, para 28.

71. *Delfi AS v Estonia* App (2016) 62 EHRR 6, para 110.

72. *Sunday Times* (n 49) para 65.

73. *Jersild* (n 44) para 31.

74. Ibid 31.

75. *Delfi* (n 71) para 133.

76. *Times Newspapers (Nos 1 and 2) v United Kingdom* [2009] EMLR 14, para 45.

77. Ibid para 45. The Court was clearly also influenced by its finding that the Press was not pursuing a 'public watchdog' function when publishing verbatim records of previous news stories (para 45).

78. App no 17089/03 (ECtHR, 22 June 2009) para 34.

79. Ibid para 35.

80. *Sapan v Turkey* App no 44102/04 (ECtHR, 8 June 2010) (no English translation available).

81. *Steel and another v United Kingdom* (2005) 41 EHRR 403, para 89. See also *Társaság a Szabadságjogokért v Hungary* App no 37374/05 (ECtHR, 14 April 2009) para 27 and *Vides Aizsardzības Klubs v Latvia* App no 57829/00 (ECtHR, 27 May 2004) para 42 equating the civil society groups in each case as social 'watchdogs' akin to the Press.

82. *Von Hannover v Germany* (No. 1) (2005) 40 EHRR 1, para 63.

83. *Sapan* (n 80) para 34 ('This book cannot be considered as part of the publications of the so-called "sensational press" or "press of the heart", which is usually intended to satisfy the curiosity of a certain public about the details of the strictly private life of a celebrity') (own translation).

84. Lorna Woods, 'Freedom of Expression and Information' in Steve Peers and others (eds), *The EU Charter of Fundamental Rights: A Commentary* (Hart Publishing 2014) 311–49, 320.

85. Lorna Woods, 'Freedom of Expression in the European Union' (2006) 12(3) European Public Law 371, 391.

86. See, for example, Case C-274/99P *Connolly v Commission* [2001] ECR I-1611 and Case T-82/99 *Cwik v Commission* [2000] ECR II-713.

87. Case C-101/01 *Lindqvist* [2003] ECR I-12971; Case C-73/07 *Tietosuojavaltuutettu v Satakunnan Markkinapörssi Oy and Satamedia Oy* [2007] ECR I-7075; Case C-70/10 *Scarlet Extended v SABAM* [2011] ECR I-11959; Case C-360/10 *SABAM v Netlog* [2012] 2 CMLR 18.

88. Case C-260/89 *ERT v DEB* [1991] ECR I-2925; Case C-368/95 *Vereinigte Familiapress Zeitungsverlags- und vertriebs GmbH v Heinrich Bauer Verlag* [1997] ECR I-3689; and Case C-112/00 *Schmidberger Internationale Transporte and Planzüge v Austria* [2003] ECR I-5659. Case C-159/90 *Society for the Protection of Unborn Children (Ireland) Ltd v Grogan* [1991] ECR I-04685 constitutes a clear and explicit exception to this. Here, the CJEU found the activity of Irish students distributing information about abortion providers based in the United Kingdom fell outside the scope of EU law. The Court stressed that they were not distributing this information 'on behalf of' such providers and therefore their activity constituted 'a manifestation of freedom of expression and of the freedom to impart and receive information which is independent of the economic activity carried on by clinics established in another Member State' (para 26). According to Woods ((n 84) 313) this 'may be a case limited to its facts' since it 'concerned information on the termination of pregnancies, a politically sensitive question in the Member State concerned'.

89. *Familiapress* (n 88) (freedom of expression engaged by Austrian prohibition on the inclusion of prize competitions in journals).

90. Case C-245/01 *RTL Television GmbH v Niedersächsische Landesmedienanstalt für privaten Rundfunk* [2003] ECR I-12489 (freedom of expression standards applied to rules relating to the frequency of advertising as set down in Article 11 of the Television without Frontiers Directive 89/552/EEC).

91. Woods (n 85) 390.

92. *Lindqvist* (n 87) para 2.

93. Nevertheless, as the Court also noted, this material was removed 'as soon as she became aware that they were not appreciated by some of her colleagues' (*Lindqvist* (n 87) para 14).

94. Ibid paras 86–87.

95. Woods (n 85) 392.

96. Case C-131/12 *Google Spain SL and Google Inc v Agencia Española de Protección de Datos (AEPD)* [2014] 3 CMLR 50.

97. Council Directive 95/46/EC of 24 October 1995 on the protection of individuals with regard to the processing of personal data and on the free movement of such data [1995] OJ L281/31, art 9.

98. *Satamedia* (n 87) para 56.

99. Ibid para 62. The national court later found that this definition was not satisfied here and so issued an injunction prohibiting the activity. This prompted a challenge before the ECtHR. In 2017 a Grand Chamber of the ECtHR rejected fifteen to two the contention that the prohibition of this activity violated freedom of expression. By the

same majority, the Court also found that the amount of time which had been spent addressing the case at national level had led to a breach of the right to a hearing within a reasonable time as protected in Article 6(1) of the Convention. See *Satakunnan Markkinapörssi Oy* (n 41). This case will be considered further in Chapter 9 of the book.

100. In the event, the Finnish Supreme Administrative Court found that such a connection to the collective public was not present. See generally on these points David Erdos, 'From the Syclla of Restriction to the Charybdis of Licence? Exploring the Scope of the "Special Purposes" Freedom of Expression Shield in European Data Protection' (2015) 52(1) CMLR 119.

101. *Satamedia* (n 87) para 56.

102. E-08/97 TV1000 *Sverige v Norwegian Government* [1998] 3 CMLR 318.

103. Geoffrey Robertson and Andrew Nicol, *Media Law* (5th edn, Penguin 2008) xvii.

104. Ibid xvii.

105. Kaarle Nordenstreng and Ari Heinonen, 'EthicNet—Collection of Codes of Journalism Ethics in Europe' (*EthicNet*, June 2008) <http://ethicnet.uta.fi/> accessed 13 March 2018.

106. The 1970 resolution is particularly fulsome in this regard, emphasizing the desirability of developing professional training for journalists under the responsibility of editors and journalists, a professional code of ethics, and also press councils empowered to investigate and censure instances of unprofessional conduct. Meanwhile, the 1977 recommendation notes the role of the Congress of European Writers' Organisations, whilst the 2006 recommendation took inspiration from the Magna Charta Universitatum, a declaration drawn up by universities and which had been signed by some 600 of them up until that point.

107. Council of Europe, 'Resolution 74 (26) on the Right of Reply—Position of the Individual in Relation to the Press' (*COE*, 1974) <https://rm.coe.int/16805048e1> accessed 15 April 2019.

108. Council of Europe, 'Recommendation Rec (2004) of the Committee of Ministers to members states on the right of reply in the new media environment' (*EBU*, 2004) <https://www.ebu.ch/CMSimages/en/leg_ref_coe_r2004_16_right_of_reply_151204_tcm6-36730.pdf> accessed 15 April 2019.

109. Council Recommendation 2006/952/EC of 20 December 2006 on the protection of minors and human dignity and on the right of reply in relation to the competitiveness of the European audiovisual and on-line information services industry [2006] OJ L378/72, art I(1).

110. Roberto Mastroianni and Amadeo Arena, *Media Law in Italy* (2nd edn Kluwer Law International 2014) 41.

111. Judit Bayer, *Media Law in Hungary* (2nd edn Kluwer Law International 2015) 85.

112. Rado Bohinc, *Media Law in Slovenia* (Kluwer Law International 2015) 56.

113. ECHR (n 6) art 10(1).

114. Council Directive 89/552/EEC of 3 October 1989 on the coordination of certain provisions laid down by law, regulation or administrative action in Member States concerning the pursuit of television broadcasting activities [1989] OJ L298/23.

115. Namely race, sex, religion, or nationality.

116. Other standards which the Directive specified related to advertising, programme sponsorship, and the screening of European works and also cinema films. These provisions broadly dovetailed with a Council of Europe Convention on Transfrontier Television also agreed in the same year. Although this Convention technically remains in force, it has not been updated since the early 2000s.

117. Agreement on the European Economic Area [1994] OJ L1/3.

118. Council Directive 2007/65/EC of 11 December 2007 amending Council Directive 89/552/EEC on the coordination of certain provisions laid down by law, regulation or administrative action in Member States concerning the pursuit of television broadcasting activities [2007] OJ L332/27.

119. See Council Directive 2010/13/EU of 10 March 2010 on the coordination of certain provisions laid down by law, regulation or administrative action in Member States concerning the provision of audiovisual media services (Audiovisual Media Services Directive) [2010] OJ L95/1, recitals 94 and 95, art 30.

120. Council Directive 2018/1808 of 14 November 2018 amending Directive 2010/13/EU on the coordination of certain provisions laid down by law, regulation or administrative action in Member States concerning the provision of audiovisual media services (Audiovisual Media Services Directive) in view of changing market realities [2018] OJ L 303/69, recital 56.

121. Ibid recital 48.

122. Ibid art 2.

Chapter 3

1. Council Regulation 2016/679/EU of 27 April 2016 on the protection of natural persons with regard to the processing of personal data and on the free movement of such data, and repealing Directive 95/46/EC [2016] OJ L119/1 ('GDPR').

2. For example, as Solove notes, the law's protection of the confidentiality of communication between spouses can be traced back to ancient Jewish and Roman Law (Daniel Solove, *The Future of Reputation* (Yale University Press 2007) 174). The legal protection of various reputational interests has similarly ancient roots.

3. Samuel Warren and Louis Brandeis, 'The Right to Privacy' (1890) 4(5) Harvard Law Review 193, 205.

4. Ibid 207.

5. Thus, Article 8 stated: '(1) Everyone has the right to respect for his private and family life, his home and his correspondence. (2) There shall be no interference by a public authority with the exercise of this right except such as is in accordance with the law and is necessary in a democratic society in the interests of national security, public safety or the economic well-being of the country, for the prevention of disorder or crime, for the protection of health or morals, or for the protection of the rights and freedoms of others'.

6. Thus, the 1968–69 Working Programme for the Council of Europe's Committee of Ministers mandated it to look into '[t]he right to respect for privacy as affected by (a) the press and other mass media and (b) modern scientific and technological developments' (Council of Europe, *Yearbook of the European Convention on Human Rights*

1974 (Nijhoff 1976) 116). Other strands of the Council of Europe's work fed into the 1970 Declaration on Mass Communication Media and Human Rights that was explored in Chapter 2.

7. Council of Europe, 'Resolution (73) 22 on the Protection of the Privacy of Individuals vis-à-vis Electronic Data Banks in the Private Sector' (*COE*, 26 September 1973) <https://rm.coe.int/CoERMPublicCommonSearchServices/DisplayDCTMContent?documentId=0900001680502830> accessed 22 May 2019.

8. Ibid.

9. See Council of Europe, 'Explanatory Report to the Convention for the Protection of Individuals with regard to Automatic Processing of Personal Data' (*COE*, 1981) <https://rm.coe.int/16800ca434> accessed 16 April 2019.

10. See Council of Europe, 'Chart of Signatures and Ratifications of Treaty 108' (*COE*, 16 April 2019) <https://www.coe.int/en/web/conventions/full-list/-/conventions/treaty/108/signatures> accessed 16 April 2019.

11. Convention for the Protection of Individuals with regard to Automatic Processing of Personal Data (Data Protection Convention) ETS 108, art 1.

12. Ibid art 3(1). Under art 3(2), State Parties could optionally elect not to apply the Convention in certain areas, apply it also to unautomated personal data files, and even to apply it to data relating to corporate persons.

13. Ibid art 2(c).

14. Ibid art 2(a).

15. Ibid art 8(a)–(b).

16. Ibid art 6.

17. Ibid art 10.

18. Ibid art 8(c).

19. Ibid art 9(2).

20. Ibid art 9(3).

21. Ibid arts 18–20.

22. Ibid arts 13–14.

23. See Council of Europe, 'Data Protection Legal Instruments' (*COE*, 2018) <https://www.coe.int/en/web/data-protection/legal-instruments> accessed 18 March 2019.

24. Prior to 1990 only one non-European country (Israel in 1981) adopted a comprehensive law protecting personal data. In contrast several countries—the United States (1974), Canada (1982), Australia (1988), and Japan (1988)—enacted laws which were limited to the public sector. Although falling short of data protection as defined in this book, these statutes enabled these countries to participate in certain data protection fora including (where the law provided for a regulator) the International Conference of Data Protection Commissioners.

25. For full details and sources see Appendix 1.

26. This may well have reflected the 'typically prospective and preventative' policy style of Sweden and the wider Nordic grouping. See Colin Bennett, *Regulating Privacy: Data Protection and Public Policy in Europe and the United States* (Cornell University Press 1992) 61.

27. Ibid 134.

28. The exception here was the Luxembourg law, which only established an Advisory Board on Data Protection and left the government itself responsible for exercising all registration and other regulatory functions. See Luxembourg: Nominal Data (Automatic Processing) Act of 31 March 1979, arts 29–30.

29. See Sweden: Data Act of 1 May 1973, s 2. Amendments in the late 1980s sought to significantly reduce the circumstances where DPA permission would be required. See Sweden: Data Act 1973 as amended with effect from 1 April 1988, s 2.

30. See Norway: Act relating to Personal Data Registers of 9 June 1978, para 9. In the Norwegian case, a licensing requirement applied to all automatic processing of personal and manual processing which involved 'sensitive' data. Whilst the power to grant a license was technically vested in the Government, it could and was delegated to the DPA which dealt with the vast bulk of license applications.

31. For example, in both Danish and Icelandic legislation, a license was required for the systematic collection of data by private sector entities intended for processing outside of Denmark and Iceland respectively. See Denmark: Private Registers Act 1978, s 21 and Iceland: Act No 63/1981 respecting Systematic Recording of Personal Data, art 21.

32. Sweden: Data Act 1973 (n 29) s 15.

33. See Finland: Personal Data Files Act 1987, s 18 (requiring that the data subject was at least aware of any disclosure of data from a file unless this was in accordance with other legislation and/or for scientific research or statistics); France: Act No. 78-17 of 6 January 1978 on data processing, data files and freedoms, art 27 (setting out duties only in relation to individuals from who personal information was obtained); Germany: Federal Data Protection Law 1977, s 26(1) (setting out a default overarching transparency duty vis-à-vis data subject); Iceland: Act No 63/1981 art 5 (requiring data subject to be informed as regards any registration of data other than their name, domicile, identification number, position, occupation, and information available in official records); Luxembourg: Nominal Data (Automatic Processing) Act 1979, art 18 (setting out duties only in relation to individuals from whom personal information was obtained), and The Netherlands: Data Protection Act 1988, s 28 (setting out a default overarching transparency duty vis-à-vis data subject). This Icelandic provision was later removed from the law. See Iceland: Act Concerning the Registration and Handling of Personal Data 1989.

34. Austria: Data Protection Act 1978.

35. United Kingdom: Data Protection Act 1984, s 2(3) (defining certain categories of special data and establishing the possibility of the Government issuing discrete provisions in this regard, which was never done).

36. Germany: Federal Data Protection Law 1977 (setting out no concept of sensitive data within the law at all) and Federal Data Protection Act (1991), s 28(2)(1)(b) and 35(2)(2) (establishing only that the processing of sensitive data would create a defeasible presumption that the legitimate interests of the data subject outweighted that of the controller and reverse the burden of proof when information was claimed to be inaccurate).

37. Ireland: Data Protection Act 1988, s 16(1)(c) (defining certain categories of special data but requiring only that these be subject to mandatory registration with the DPA).

38. Frits W Hondius, 'The Human Rights Aspect of Data Protection' in JJP Kennedy (ed), *Data Privacy and Security* (Pergamon Infotech 1986) 88.

39. Bennett (n 26) 143.

40. Hondius (n 38) 92 and 94; Council of Europe Committee of Experts on Data Protection, *Constitutional Provisions Which Guarantee Data Protection* Council of Europe Archives (CJ-PD (93) 32 2nd Rev) 4.

41. Whilst between 1975 and 1979 the European Parliament issued a series of resolutions calling on the European Commission to propose a Directive on data protection, these was not taken up. See Gloria González Fuster, *The Emergence of Personal Data Protection as a Fundamental Right of the EU* (Springer 2014) 115–20. The Commission did assist in the drafting of the Data Protection Convention (Council of Europe Data Protection Convention Explanatory Report (n 9) para 16) and in July 1981 adopted a Recommendation calling on all Member States to ratify it by the end of 1981: Commission Recommendation 81/679/EEC of 29 July 1981 relating to the Council of Europe Convention for the protection of individuals with regard to automatic processing of personal data [1981] OJ L246/31.

42. European Commission, 'Communication on the Protection of Individuals in Relation to the Processing of Personal Data in the Community and Information Security' COM (1990) 314 final.

43. As a result of the Single European Act 1986, this *vires* had recently been broadened in scope and the threshold for its use reduced through requiring support from only a qualified majority, rather than all, Member States. See Paul Craig and Gráinne De Búrca, *EU Law: Text, Cases and Materials* (6th edn Oxford University Press 2015) 615–17.

44. European Commission (n 42) recitals 6–7.

45. Ibid art 1(2).

46. European Commission, 'Amended Proposal for a Council Directive on the Protection of Individuals with Regard to the Processing of Personal Data and on the Free Movement of such Data' COM (1992) 422 final.

47. For a full exegesis of the legislative history of the DPD see Graham Pearce and Nicholas Platten, 'Achieving Personal Data Protection in the European Union' (1998) 36(4) Journal of Common Market Studies 529.

48. Council Directive 95/46/EC of 24 October 1995 on the protection of individuals with regard to the processing of personal data and on the free movement of such data [1995] OJ L281/31, art 32(1) ('DPD').

49. EEA Joint Committee Decision 83/1999 of 25 June 1999 amending Protocol 37 and Annex XI (Telecommunication services) to the EEA Agreement [2000] OJ L296/41. This Decision adapted the DPD in a few minor respects, notably by providing that participation of non-EU DPA representatives in the Article 29 Working Party would only be as non-voting observers.

50. DPD (n 48) art 3(2).

51. Ibid art 3(1).

52. Ibid art 2(b).

53. Ibid art 2(d).

54. Ibid art 6.

55. Ibid art 12(a).

56. Ibid art 10.

57. Ibid art 11.

58. Ibid art 9. In the case of criminal data, the default prohibition was absolute but only applicable to private sector processing. The rules as regards other categories applied also the public sector but, in addition to certain very specific limitations, were subject to a general lifting where the data subject had given 'explicit consent' to the processing or where the processing concerned 'data which are manifestly made public by the data subject'.

59. Ibid art 7.

60. Ibid arts 18–20.

61. Ibid arts 25–26.

62. Ibid art 7(f).

63. Ibid art 14(a).

64. Ibid art 22.

65. Ibid art 23.

66. Ibid art 28.

67. Ibid art 28.

68. Ibid recital 62.

69. Ibid recital 63.

70. Ibid art 28.

71. Ibid art 29.

72. This latter concept was conceptualized broadly as referring to any 'effective and real exercise of activity through stable arrangements' (recital 19).

73. Ibid art 4. In addition, where the controller did not have an establishment within the EEA, States were to apply their law whenever they used 'equipment' for processing personal data other than for the purposes of transit through the territory and also where State law applied by virtue of public international law (e.g. in embassies or consulates).

74. Ibid recital 8.

75. Ibid art 13. The tests laid down for derogation from the sensitive data rules were somewhat different. Here States could derogate from the restrictions on processing sensitive data for reasons of 'substantial public interest' and subject to the provision of 'suitable safeguards' or, in the case of criminal data, simply after providing 'suitable specific safeguards' (arts 8(4)–(5)). Finally, they could also limit the ability to object to processing on personal grounds simply be setting this restriction down in legislation (art 14(a)).

76. Ibid art 9.

77. Ibid arts 6(1)(b), 6(1)(e), 11(2), 13(2), and 32(3).

78. Charter of Fundamental Rights of the European Union, art 8.

79. Ibid art 52.

80. Treaty on European Union, art 6.

81. Treaty on the Functioning of the European Union, art 16.

82. See Orla Lynskey, 'From Market-Making Tool to Fundamental Right: The Role of the Court of Justice in Data Protection's Identity Crisis' in Serge Gutwirth, Ronald Leenes, and Paul de Hert (eds), *European Data Protection: Coming of Age* (Springer 2013) 77.

83. *Von Hannover v Germany (No. 1)* (2005) 40 EHRR 1, para 57.

84. Ibid para 76.

85. Ibid. The Court was particularly influenced by the fact that 'the photos and articles related exclusively to details of her private life' and that Princess Caroline herself exercised 'no official function' (para 76).
86. Ibid para 70.
87. Namely, Portugal in 1991 and both Spain and Belgium in 1992. See Colin Bennett and Charles Raab, *The Governance of Privacy: Policy Instruments in Global Perspective* (MIT Press 2006) 127.
88. DPD (n 48) art 32.
89. EEA Joint Committee Decision (n 49).
90. European Commission, 'First Report on the Implementation of the Data Protection Directive (95/46/EC)' COM (2003) 265 final, 7.
91. For example, Liechtenstein only adopted a Data Protection Act in 2002, whilst the British intra-EU overseas territory of Gibraltar only did so in 2004.
92. European Commission (2003) (n 90) 7.
93. Ibid 11 and 17–18 (specifically citing problems as regards the transposition of arts 4, 7, 8.1, 10, 13, and 26). Another area of manifest divergence, which will be the focus of much of this book, concerns the implementation of the special expressive purposes derogation set out in art 9.
94. Ibid 11.
95. Ibid 12.
96. Alongside Cyprus and Malta, the following eight Eastern European countries joined the EU on 1 May 2004: Czechia, Estonia, Hungary, Latvia, Lithuania, Poland, Slovakia, and Slovenia. Meanwhile, Bulgaria and Romania joined the EU on 1 January 2007. DPA representatives of these candidate countries began attending Article 29 Working Party group meetings as early as 2002. See European Commission, 'Communication on the follow-up of the Work Programme for better implementation of the Data Protection Directive' COM (2007) 87 final, 3.
97. European Commission, 'A Comprehensive Approach on Personal Data Protection in the European Union' COM (2010) 609 final, 10.
98. See European Union Agency for Fundamental Rights, 'Data Protection in the European Union: the role of National Data Protection Authorities' (*Europa*, 2010) <https://fra.europa.eu/sites/default/files/fra_uploads/815-Data-protection_en.pdf> 8 accessed 17 June 2019.
99. European Union Agency for Fundamental Rights, 'Access to Data Protection Remedies in EU Member States' (*Europa*, 2014) <https://fra.europa.eu/sites/default/files/fra-2014-access-data-protection-remedies_en_0.pdf> 46 accessed 3 May 2019.
100. Abraham L Newman, 'Building Transnational Civil Liberties: Transgovernmental Entrepreneurs and the European Data Privacy Directive' (2008) 62 International Organization 103, 104 ('This legislation required all member states to enact similar provisions concerning the collection, processing, and transfer of personal information in the public and private sectors, and it mandated the creation of powerful national independent regulatory agencies—data privacy authorities—that monitor and enforce these rules.')
101. See Graham Greenleaf, 'Global Tables of Data Privacy Law and Bills' (2017) Privacy Laws and Business International Reports 14.

102. Lee Bygrave, *Data Privacy Law: An International Perspective* (Oxford University Press 2014) 53.

103. Joseph Cannataci and Jeanne Pia Mifsud Bonnici, 'Data Protection Comes of Age: The Data Protection Clauses in the European Constitutional Treaty' (2005) 14(1) Information and Communications Technology Law 5, 8.

104. Case C-101/01 *Lindqvist* [2003] ECR I-12971, para 27.

105. Ibid para 43.

106. Ibid para 47.

107. Case C-73/07 *Tietosuojavaltuutettu v Satakunnan Markkinapörssi Oy and Satamedia Oy* [2007] ECR I-7075, para 46.

108. Ibid paras 48–49.

109. Case C-524/06 *Heinz Huber v Bundesrepublik Deutschland* [2008] ECR I-09705, para 62.

110. Ibid para 65.

111. Case C-518/07 *Commission v Germany* [2010] ECR I-1885, para 25.

112. Ibid para 23.

113. Cases C-92/08 and C-93/09 *Volker und Markus Schecke* [2010] ECR I-11063.

114. Case C-131/12 *Google Spain SL and Google Inc v Agencia Española de Protección de Datos (AEPD)* [2014] 3 CMLR 50.

115. Case E-013/11 *Schenker North AB v EFTA Surveillance Authority* [2013] 4 CMLR 17, para 44.

116. Case C-28/08 *European Commission v Bavarian Lager* [2010] ECR I-6055, para 59.

117. Council Regulation (EC) No 45/2001 of 18 December 2000 on the protection of individuals with regard to the processing of personal data by the Community institutions and bodies and on the free movement of such data [2001] OJ L008/1.

118. *Schenker* (n 115) para 121.

119. Ibid para 167.

120. Case E-23/13 *Hellenic Capital Market Commission* (2014) EFTA Ct Rep 88, para 20.

121. Ibid para 52.

122. Ibid para 76.

123. All opinions and recommendations issued up to November 2016 are available at Article 29 Working Party, 'Opinions and Recommendations' <https://ec.europa.eu/justice/article-29/documentation/opinion-recommendation/index_en.htm> accessed 22 March 2019.

124. Abraham Newman, 'Watching the Watchers: Transgovernmental Implementation of the Data Privacy Policy in Europe' (2011) 13(2) Journal of Comparative Policy Analysis 181, 186.

125. Ibid 186.

126. Ibid 187.

127. See, for example, Article 29 Working Party, 'Opinion 4/2007 on the concept of personal data (WP 136) <https://ec.europa.eu/justice/article-29/documentation/opinion-recommendation/files/2007/wp136_en.pdf> accessed 23 August 2019.

128. See, for example, Article 29 Working Party, 'Opinion 3/2013 on purpose limitation (WP 203)' (*Europa*, 2 April 2013) <https://ec.europa.eu/justice/article-29/documentation/opinion-recommendation/files/2013/wp203_en.pdf> accessed 3 May 2019;

and Article 29 Working Party, 'Opinion 6/2014 on the Notion of legitimate interests of the data controller under Article 7 of Directive 95/46/EC' (*FIA*, 9 April 2014) <https://fia.org/sites/default/files/uploaded/Excerpts%20-%20Opinion%2006-2014%20on%20the%20notion%20of%20legitimate%20interests%20of%20the%20....pdf> accessed 7 May 2019.

129. Article 29 Working Party, 'Recommendation 1/97 on Data Protection law and the media (WP 1)' (*Europa*, 25 February 1997) <https://ec.europa.eu/justice/article-29/documentation/opinion-recommendation/files/1997/wp1_en.pdf> accessed 3 May 2019.

130. Article 29 Working Party, 'Opinion 5/2009 on online social networking (WP 163)' (*Europa*, 12 June 2009) <https://ec.europa.eu/justice/article-29/documentation/opinion-recommendation/files/2009/wp163_en.pdf> accessed 3 May 2019.

131. Article 29 Working Party, 'Opinion 1/2008 on data protection issues related to search engines' (*Europa*, 4 April 2008) <https://ec.europa.eu/justice/article-29/documentation/opinion-recommendation/files/2008/wp148_en.pdf> accessed 29 May 2019; Article 29 Working Party, 'Guidelines on the Implementation of the Court of Justice of the European Union Judgment on "Google Spain and Inc v Agencia Española de Protección de Datos (AEPD) and Mario Costeja González" C-131/12' (*Europa*, 26 November 2014) <https://ec.europa.eu/justice/article-29/documentation/opinion-recommendation/files/2014/wp225_en.pdf> accessed 23 August 2019.

132. Newman (n 124) 184.

133. Article 29 Working Party, 'Opinion 4/2007' (n 127) 6.

134. Rosemary Jay, *Data Protection Law and Practice* (4th edn Sweet and Maxwell 2012) 167.

135. Article 29 Working Party, 'Opinion 4/2007' (n 127) 4.

136. Article 29 Working Party, 'Opinion 5/2009' (n 130) 6.

137. Ibid 7.

138. European Commission, 'A Comprehensive Approach on Personal Data Protection in the European Union' COM (2010) 609 final, 18.

139. Most especially, the Commission also proposed adopting a data protection directive in the area of law enforcement to replace the Council Framework Decision 2008/977/JHA of 27 November 2008 on the protection of personal data processing in the framework of police and judicial cooperation in criminal matters. This initiative, which lay outside the area of EEA coordination, led to Council Directive (EU) 2016/680 of 27 April 2016 on the protection of natural persons with regard to the processing of personal data by competent authorities for the purposes of the prevention, investigation, detection or prosecution of criminal offences or the execution of criminal penalties, and on the free movement of such data, and repealing Council Framework Decision 2008/977/JHA [2016] OJ L119/89.

140. European Commission, 'Proposal for a Regulation of the European Parliament and of the Council on the protection of individuals with regard to the processing of personal data and on the free movement of such data (General Data Protection Regulation)' COM (2012) 11 final.

141. Paul De Hert and Vagelis Papakonstantinou, 'The New General Data Protection Regulation: Still a Sound System for the Protection of Individuals?' (2015) 32(2) Computer Law and Security Review 179, 181.

142. GDPR (n 1) art 99(2).

143. EEA Joint Committee Decision 154/2018 of 6 July 2018 amending Annex XI (Electronic communication, audiovisual services and information society) and Protocol 37 (containing the list provided for in Article 101) to the EEA Agreement [2018] OJ L183/23. The most significant modification was to deprive non-EU EEA DPAs of the ability to exercise a vote in, or to stand for election to chair or deputy chair of, the European Data Protection Board. It was, however, provided that the position taken by these authorities would be recorded separately by the Board during its deliberations.

144. GDPR (n 1) recital 13.

145. Ibid recital 1.

146. Ibid recital 6.

147. Ibid recital 7.

148. Ibid art 2(2)(c).

149. Ibid art 2. The GDPR was generally made applicable to all activities that fell within the scope of Union law which is a wider concept than the reference to Community law found in the DPD. However, exclusions were specified as regards processing relating to the EU's Common Foreign and Security Policy and also processing by competent authorities for law enforcement purposes. Within the EU, the last area of processing was separately made subject to its own instrument, namely, Directive (EU) 2016/680 of the European Parliament and of the Council of 27 April 2016 on the protection of natural persons with regard to the processing of personal data by competent authorities for the purposes of the prevention, investigation, detection or prosecution of criminal offences or the execution of criminal penalties, and on the free movement of such data, and repealing Council Framework Decision 2008/977/JHA.

150. Ibid art 4(1) (referencing *inter alia* 'location data' as an 'identifier').

151. Ibid recital 27.

152. Ibid art 5.

153. Ibid arts 12–15.

154. Ibid arts 9–10.

155. Ibid arts 6, 24–50.

156. Ibid arts 13–14.

157. Ibid art 14(5)(b).

158. Ibid art 9.

159. Ibid art 17. Whilst much publicized, the additional weight of the new 'right to be forgotten' is very limited. In sum, it amounts only to placing an obligation on a controller subject to an erasure duty and who has made that data public to 'take reasonable steps, including technical measures, to inform controllers which are processing personal data that the data subject has requested the erasure by such controllers of any links to, or copy or replication of, those personal data' (art 17(2)).

160. Ibid art 82.

161. Ibid art 80.

162. Ibid arts 51–54.

163. Ibid art 52(4).

164. Ibid art 57.

165. Ibid art 58.
166. Ibid art 83.
167. Ibid art 58(1)(f).
168. Ibid recital 10.
169. Ibid art 28(6).
170. Ibid art 29.
171. Ibid arts 60–67.
172. Ibid art 56.
173. Ibid arts 68–76.
174. Ibid art 4(23).
175. Ibid art 56. The notion of 'main establishment' is to be determined by an objective assessment of where the decisions on the purpose and means of the processing of personal data were taken (see art 4(16)).
176. Ibid art 4(22).
177. Ibid arts 61–62.
178. Ibid art 65(2).
179. Ibid art 66.
180. Ibid art 65(3).
181. Ibid recital 10.
182. Ibid art 9(2)(a).
183. Ibid art 9(4).
184. Ibid art 58(4).
185. Ibid art 23(2). In so far as relevant, the measure is expected to detail the purposes of the processing or categories of processing, the categories of personal data, the scope of the restrictions introduced, the safeguards to prevent abuse or unlawful access or transfer, the specification of the controller or categories of controllers, the storage periods and the applicable safeguards, the risks to the rights and freedoms of the data subjects, and the right of data subjects to be informed about the restriction (unless that may be prejudicial to the purpose of the restriction)
186. Ibid art 23(1). The general tests laid down in relation for derogations from the sensitive data rules continue to be differ somewhat. As regards criminal data, States need only enact a law that provides data subjects with 'appropriate safeguards' (art 10). Otherwise, these derogations must be justified by reasons of 'substantial public interest' and the law must 'be proportionate to the aim pursued, respect the essence of the right to data protection and provide for suitable and specific measures to safeguard the fundamental rights and the interests of the data subject' (art 9(2)(g)).
187. Ibid art 85(2).
188. Ibid art 85(2).
189. Ibid see, in particular, art 89.
190. Ibid art 99(2). Note, however, that not only did the GDPR apply slightly later in the non-EU EEA but that in these States all Regulations including the GDPR may still need to be transposed by the national legislator in order to made part of the national legal order. See Agreement on the European Economic Area, art 7(a).

191. In the area of law enforcement processing, EU States were also required to transpose Directive 2016/680 into national law by May 2018. However, this legal requirement did not apply to the non-EU EEA States and, in any case, lies outside the scope of this book.

192. See Ireland: Data Protection Act 2018, s 43; Sweden: Lag (2018:218) med kompletterande bestämmelser till EU:s dataskyddsförordning, ch 1, s 7. Danish law contains a somewhat similar provision but expressly ties this the pan-European freedom of expression standards set down in the European Convention and the EU Charter. See Denmark: Databeskyttelsesloven, s 3(1).

193. Netherlands: Wet van 16 mei 2018 Uitvoeringswet Algemene verordening gegevensbescherming, art 41.

194. Databeskyttelsesloven (n 192) s 22(1).

195. GDPR (n 1) recital 10.

Chapter 4

1. See Council of Europe, *Yearbook of the European Convention on Human Rights 1974* (Nijhoff 1976) 116.

2. Council of Europe, 'Resolution 428 (1970) containing a declaration on mass communication media and human rights' (*COE*, 2015) <https://rm.coe.int/16806461f9> 8 accessed 3 May 2019.

3. Ibid.

4. Council of Europe, 'Resolution 74 (26) on the Right of Reply – Position of the Individual in Relation to the Press' (*COE*, 1974) <https://rm.coe.int/16805048e1> accessed 15 April 2019.

5. Convention for the Protection of Individuals with regard to Automatic Processing of Personal Data (Data Protection Convention), art 9(2).

6. Council of Europe, 'Data Protection Convention Explanatory Report' (*COE*, 1981) <https://rm.coe.int/16800ca434> accessed 16 April 2019, para 58. At one stage, it was even proposed to add 'safeguarding the freedom of the press' to the derogatory clause itself. However, in May 1979 it was decided to delete this, '[i]t being understood that this idea is covered by "the rights and freedoms of others"'. See Council of Europe Committee of Experts on Data Protection, *Report on the 4th Meeting*, Council of Europe Archives (CJ-PD (79) 7) 7.

7. Germany: Federal Data Protection Law, s 1(3) ('This Law shall not protect personal data which are processed by undertakings or auxiliary undertakings in the press, radio and film sectors, exclusively for their own journalistic purposes. Section 6(1) [on data security] shall not be affected by this provision').

8. Netherlands: Data Protection Act 1988, s 2(1) ('This Act shall not apply to . . . personal data files which are solely intended for use in the public supply for information by the press, radio or television').

9. France: Act No. 78-17 of 6 January 1978 on data processing, data files and freedoms, art 33.

10. Norway: Kongelig resolusjon av 21 Desember 1979. The conditions laid down required that the database not be connected to any other database, be kept from authorised access and that no personal data be extracted from the database without the data subject's consent. Presumably, however, any extraction which was the direct result of publication in a hardcopy Press periodical was excluded from this latter requirement. A latter amendment from 1981 made clear that only databases used for journalistic activities (as opposed to, for example, payroll) were covered by these derogations. See Endringer av 10 mars 1981 ifr kongelig resolusjon av 21 desember 1979.

11. Norway: Kongelig resolusjon av 21 November 1979.

12. Austria: Datenschutzgesetz 1978, s 54.

13. Ibid s 54 ('pending the enactment of provisions concerning data protection in future media legislation'). This wording was not, however, included within the 1988 English translation of the Act deposited within the Council of Europe archives (see Appendix 1).

14. Ibid s 1.

15. In this respect, the situation in Austria was similar to that in Portugal (1976) and Spain (1978) which, whilst not enacting data protection legislation in this period, did adopt constitutional guarantees on data protection from which there was no absolute journalistic exemption. See Frits W Hondius, 'The Human Rights Aspect of Data Protection' in JJP Kennedy (ed), *Data Privacy and Security* (Pergamon Infotech 1986).

16. Finland: Personal Data File Act (1987) s 1.

17. Denmark: Private Registers Etc Act (Consolidated) (as amended by Act No 383, 10 June 1987), part 2c (News Registers of the Press).

18. Denmark: *Lov om massemediers informationsdatabaser*, s 1.

19. Denmark: The Media Liability Act, ss 34–40 and 8.

20. Denmark: *Lov om massemediers informationsdatabaser* (n 18) ss 6–11. Under s 8(3), sensitive information was defined as '[i]nformation on individuals' purely private matters, including information on race, religion and skin colour, on political, social, sexual and criminal matters, health information, serious social problems and the abuse of stimulants and the like' (translated from Danish).

21. Ibid ss 3–5.

22. Ibid ss 12–5; Media Liability Act (n 19) ss 41–52.

23. See Council of Europe Consultative Committee of the Data Protection Convention, *Compte rendu of the 10th Meeting* (23–25 November 1994) Council of Europe Archives (T-PD (94) 7) 17 regarding the Finnish reform and, as regards the German, Germany: Federal Data Protection Act (1991), ss 41–42.

24. See, in particular, HL Deb 19 July 1983, vol 443, cols 1077–84 and HL Deb 21 July 1983, vol 443, cols 1307–10.

25. See, for example, comments of Parliamentary State Secretary Baum at Germany: Bundestage, des Innenauschussen, *Kurzprotokoll*, 24 September 1975.

26. See 'Press Council: Germany' (*Accountable Journalism*, 16 August 2017) <https://accountablejournalism.org/press-councils/Germany> accessed 3 May 2019. Given overlaps in language, as well as political and legal culture, this conceptualization may also have exerted an impact on Austria. In a similar fashion, Irish data protection legislation was clearly profoundly influenced by its UK counterpart.

27. France: Assemblée Nationale, 'Débats, 5 October 1977' (*Archives Assemblee-Nationale*) <http://archives.assemblee-nationale.fr/5/cri/1977-1978-ordinaire1/005.pdf>   5881 accessed 3 May 2019.

28. Ireland: Data Protection Act 1988, s 1(1); UK: Data Protection Act 1984, s 1(8). Under s 1(7), the UK Data Protection Act 1984 also excluded all operations not performed 'by reference to the data subject'.

29. Luxembourg: Nominal Data (Automatic Processing) Act 1979, art 30.

30. 'French Commission Explores Press Transmissions' (1979) 2(1) Transnational Data Report 9. Matters here are complicated by the fact that, uniquely, the French DPA was also charged with the broader, but related, remit of ensuring that information technology be at the service of every citizen. In this context, it did undertake an early study of the development of computerization in the Press which focused not on data protection but rather on issues such as the safeguarding the position of the journalistic profession, the financial balance of newspapers, and the quality of news. See France: Commission Nationale de L'Informatique et des Libertés, *4ème Rapport D'Activité (15 Octobre 1982– 15 Octobre 1983)* (La Documentation Française 1984) 141–45.

31. United Kingdom: Data Protection Registrar, *First Report* (HMSO, 1985) 10.

32. Those providing 'information or data banks consisting primarily of data about individuals' were advised to register as 'traders in personal information'. See United Kingdom: Data Protection Registrar, *Notes to Help You Apply for Registration* (Data Protection Registrar, 1985) 21–22.

33. See David Calcutt, *Report of the Committee on Privacy and Related Matters* (Stationary Office 1990) 80 and David Calcutt, *Review of Press Self-Regulation* (Cmd 1102, 1993) 66.

34. Peter Evans, 'Living can read their obituaries' *The Times* (London, 23 September 1985) 26.

35. 'Private Eye Guilty of Deceiving BT: Privacy Invasion Against the Data Protection Act' *Data Protection Registrar News Release* (Wimslow, 28 October 1997).

36. See section 2.1 of Chapter 7.

37. Norway: Datatilsynet, *Årsmelding* (Universitetsforlaget 1983) 26. These remarks were made in the context of reporting on discussions it was having with a news agency (NTB) which was interested in setting up such an archive.

38. Norway: Datatilsynet, *Årsmelding* (Universitetsforlaget 1985) 18–19, 47–48.

39. Norway: Datatilsynet, *Årsmelding* (Universitetsforlaget 1986) 4.

40. Norway: Datatilsynet, *Årsmelding* (Universitetsforlaget 1995) 14–15.

41. See Sweden: Datainspektionens, *Årsbok 1986/87* (Allmänna förlaget 1987) 201–06 for the final decision as regards the contact database and the initial decisions regarding the past news programmes. The latter proved controversial as, first, both the Chancellor of Justice and the Government argued for a right to deletion and, second, it was unclear how practically Swedish Radio should inform data subjects of their inclusion. Ultimately, the DPA argued that the license did not need to specify the former as data protection legislation itself set out such a right. Meanwhile, the right of information was to be secured by a yearly announcement in a national mass medium setting out the content and purpose of the database and specifying that it might contain sensitive data. See Sweden: Datainspektionens, *Årsbok 1987/88* (Allmänna förlaget 1988) 186–89.

42. Sweden: Datainspektionens, *Årsbok 1989/90* (Allmänna förlaget 1990) 173–77.

43. Denmark: Registertilsynets, *Årsberetning 1989* (Registertilsynets, c 1990) 84.

44. Denmark: Registertilsynets, *Årsberetning 1988* (Registertilsynets, c 1989) 97; Sweden: Datainspektionens, *Årsbok* 1989/90 (n 42) 179–80.

45. In the Danish case, the DPA ultimately indicated that it was content for the police to stay prosecution pending political agreement on a new settlement for the regulation of journalism under data protection. See Denmark: Registertilsynets, *Årsberetning 1989* (n 44) 85 and *Årsberetning 1990* (Registertilsynet, c 1991) 77. In the Swedish case, however, a conviction against the media organisation's managing editor was secured, albeit only with a sentence of having to repay half of the defence costs. See Sweden: Datainspektionens, *Årsbok 1990/91* (Allmänna förlaget 1991) 184–86.

46. Denmark, Registertilsynet, *Årsberetning 1990* (n 45) 77.

47. Sweden: Datainspektionens, *Årsbok 1990/91* (n 45) 181.

48. Namely, *Fabriksarbetaren* (The Factory Worker) and *Metallarbetaren* (The Metal Worker).

49. 'CD-ROM-tekniken och datalagen' *DIrekt från Datainspektionen* (December 1992) 2–3.

50. *'Tidningsartiklar får lämnas ut på CD-ROM' DIrekt från Datainspektionen* (May 1992) 6.

51. Sweden: Datainspektionens, 'Regeringsbeslut TT-Nyhetsbanken behöver inget tillstånd' *DIrekt från Datainspektionen* (October 1994) 3–4.

52. See 'Tillstånd behövdes inte för Svenska Dagbladets textarkiv' *DIrekt från Datainspektionen* (December 1994) 4–5.

53. Norway: Datatilsynet, *Årsmelding* (Universitetsforlaget 1995) 14–15.

54. 'Data Protection Implementation—Accomplishments amid Frustration' (1980) 3(7) Transnational Data Report 1–2, 8, 10, 17

55. 'Data Commissioners Discuss Interpol, Social Research, New Media' (1983) 4(8) Transnational Data Report 5–8.

56. 'Data Commissioners Meeting Spotlights Lack of UK Law' (1982) 5 Transnational Data Report 1–2, 369–75.

57. 'Preserving Data Protection in the New Media' (1983) 6 Transnational Data Report 416. The resolution also stated that the 'collection, storage and communication of personal data must be restricted to the lowest possible level of utilization' and the 'compilation of personal profiles must be prohibited'. However, it seems likely that these aspects were focused not on published personal data but rather on the collection and use of background personal data about the users of these services.

58. 'Data Commissioners Review Problems, Seek Structure' (1984) 7 Transnational Data Report 380.

59. 'Scandinavians see Press Data Dangers' (1984) 7 Transnational Data Report 395–96. Sensitive information was defined broadly to include 'for instance' data 'about race, religion and colour, about political, sexual and criminal relations, about state of health, abuse of drugs and so on'.

60. See 'New and Revised Laws' (1985) 8 Transnational Data Report 394.

61. Council of Europe Committee of Experts on Data Protection, *Press agencies and data protection—Secretariat memorandum* (1987), Council of Europe Archives (CJ-PD (87) 6).

62. See, for example, Council of Europe Committee of Experts on Data Protection, *Report of the 15th Meeting* (1988) Council of Europe Archives (CJ-PD (88) 10) 15–16

(noting *inter alia* the opinion of the German expert that 'it was not particularly useful to subject press agencies to provisions of data protection legislation' and the Swedish expert's understanding that '[p]rocessing of personal data which is carried out by the press must be declared and authorisation must be obtained from the Data Inspectorate [DPA]', 'no issue of press freedom is involved', and '[n]o problems have arisen so far in this regard'.

63. Council of Europe Committee of Experts on Data Protection, *Report of the 16th meeting* (1988) Council of Europe Archives (CJ-PD (88) 71) 8.

64. Council of Europe, Committee of Experts on Data Protection, *Data Protection Law and the Media* (Council of Europe Press 1991) 24.

65. Ibid 7.

66. Ibid 18.

67. Ibid 19.

68. Ibid 21.

69. Ibid 20.

70. Ibid 20.

71. Ibid 24.

72. Georg Apenes, 'Freedom of Expression and Privacy Protection' (International Conference of Data Protection Commissioners 15th Conference Papers, Manchester, 1993) 28.

73. Alex Turk, 'Liberté d'expression et protection de la vie privée' (International Conference of Data Protection Commissioners 15th Conference Papers, Manchester, 1993) 18–26.

74. Hans-Herman Schrader, 'Television and Data Protection—the example of Reality TV' (International Conference of Data Protection Commissioners 15th Conference Papers, Manchester, 1993) 151.

75. Ibid 152.

Chapter 5

1. Council Directive 95/46/EC of 24 October 1995 on the protection of individuals with regard to the processing personal data and on the free movement of such data [1995] OJ L281/31, art 9 ('DPD').

2. EU Charter of Fundamental Rights and Freedoms, arts 8 and 11.

3. Treaty on the Functioning of the European Union, art 16 ('TFEU').

4. DPD (n 1) recital 37.

5. Ibid art 9.

6. Ibid arts 22–24.

7. Ibid art 27.

8. European Commission, 'Commission Communication on the Protection of Individuals in Relation to the Processing of Personal Data in the Community and Information Security' COM (1990) 314 final, 39. The Commission reiterated almost precisely the same understanding when publishing its revised proposal for a Directive in 1992. See European Commission, 'Amended Proposal for a Council Directive on the Protection of Individuals with Regard to the Processing of Personal Data and on the Free Movement of Such Data' COM (1992) 422 final, 19.

9. Recital 18 of the proposal did, however, continue to state that derogations should be those 'necessary' to reconcile competing rights.

10. See European Union Council, 'Document 7500/94' (9 June 1994) <https://www.cipil.law.cam.ac.uk/sites/www.law.cam.ac.uk/files/images/www.cipil.law.cam.ac.uk/documents/83.pdf> accessed 7 May 2019.

11. See European Union Council, 'Document 9951/94' (17 November 1994) <https://www.cipil.law.cam.ac.uk/sites/www.law.cam.ac.uk/files/images/www.cipil.law.cam.ac.uk/documents/95.pdf> accessed 7 May 2019.

12. EU Charter (n 2) arts 8 and 11.

13. Treaty on European Union, art 6(1).

14. TFEU (n 3) art 16(2).

15. David Erdos, 'European Union Data Protection Law and Media Expression: Fundamentally Off-Balance' (2016) 65(1) ICLQ 139. Given its stand-alone nature, this article provides much more comprehensive detail than its possible here. Readers interested in exploring this issue further should, therefore, consult that article. A listing of the laws analysed is set out in Appendix 2.

16. DPD (n 1) art 6.

17. Ibid arts 10–12.

18. Ibid art 8.

19. Ibid arts 7, 17, and 25–6.

20. Please note that, due to a problem at the proofing stage, Chart Ten of the 2016 article (n 15) arrays outcomes in relation to sensitive data rather than (as is labelled) the control conditions and (unlike the article text itself) its Appendix lists four individual variable outcomes incorrectly which slightly alters the overall summation scores for Belgium, Estonia, and Hungary. In addition, as regards provision (xvi), the Danish *Lov om massemediers informationsdatabaser* has been recoded from a full exemption (g/0) to minimal inclusion (f/0.17) since, on reflection, its requirements related to journalistic ethics are best read as minimally instantiating (f/0.17) not only to the data protection principles but also the concept of a legal basis for processing. This change is so minor that the Danish summative score remains 0.15.

21. Belgium: Act of 8 December 1992 on the protection of privacy in relation to the processing of personal data, art 3(3).

22. Italy: Personal Data Protection Code Legislative Decree No 196 of 30 June 2003, s 163.3; Italy: Code of Conduct on the Processing of Personal Data in the Exercise of Journalistic Activities.

23. Romania: Law no 677/2001 on the Protection of Individuals with Regard to the Processing of Personal Data and the Free Movement of Such Data (as amended), art 13.6.

24. Luxembourg: Coordinated Text of the Law of 2 August 2002 on the Protection of Persons with regard to the Processing of Personal Data (as modified), s 29 (3).

25. Bulgaria: Law for the Protection of Personal Data as amended February 2013, art 5 (7).

26. Poland: Act of 29 August 1997 on the Protection of Personal Data (as amended), art 3a (2) (emphasis added).

27. Netherlands: Personal Data Protection Act, art 3 (1).

28. Germany: Interstate Treaty on Broadcasting and Telemedia, art 47 (2).

29. Personal Data Protection Act (n 27) art 3.

30. Spain: Organic Law 15/1999 of 13 December on the Protection of Personal Data.

31. Spain: Basque Country: Ley 2/2004 de 25 de febrero, de Ficheros de Datos de Carácter Personal de Titularidad Pública y de Creación de la Agencia Vasca de Protección de Datos, art 2; Spain: Catalonia: Ley 32/2010, de 1 de octubre, de la Autoridad Catalana de Protección de Datos, art 3.

32. Malta: Data Protection Act, s 6; Sweden, Personal Data Act, s 7; United Kingdom: Data Protection Act 1998, ss 44, 46, 53, and 56. Again, Swedish law disapplied all substantive data protection law here, thereby rendering any remaining supervisory jurisdiction fairly meaningless.

33. Denmark: *Lov om massmediers informationsdatabaser*, ss 12–17 (assignment to Danish Press Council); Lithuania: Law on the Legal Protection of Personal Data, art 8 (assignment to Lithuanian Inspector of Journalist Ethics).

34. As regards the *Länder* DPAs which took part in the DPA questionnaire and are, therefore, analysed in the following, such powers and responsibilities were only applicable in the case of Schleswig-Holstein. See Staatsvertrag über das Medienrecht in Hamburg und Schleswig-Holstein (Medienstaatsvertrag HSH), ss 37(5)–(11).

35. Austria: Federal Act Concerning the Protection of Personal Data, s. 48(1); Iceland, Act on the Protection of Privacy as Regards the Processing of Personal Data, art 3; Netherlands, Personal Data Protection Act, art 3(1).

36. Thus, Germany is coded as 0.25 since, although the federal DPA and many *Land* DPAs had no powers in this area, other *Land* DPAs did have partial powers in relation to the broadcasting sector only. Similarly, Spain is coded as 1 since, although regional bodies such as the Spanish Catalan DPA only had very a limited public sector jurisdiction (0.5), the national DPA had a very wide jurisdiction and powers across the private and most of the public sectors (1).

37. Cf section 1.2 of Chapter 4.

38. For some more theoretical discussion of these basic demarcations see Geert Hofstede, Gert Jan Hofstede, and Michael Minkov, *Cultures and Organizations: Software of the Mind* (3rd edn McGraw-Hill Education 2010) 80–84.

39. Hallin and Machini included within this group Austria, Belgium, Germany, the Netherlands, Scandinavia, and Switzerland.

40. Daniel Hallin and Paolo Mancini, *Comparing Media Systems: Three Models of Media and Politics* (Cambridge University Press 2005) 67 and *passim*.

41. See, in particular, Angelika Wyka, 'Berlusconization of the mass media in East Central Europe: The new danger of Italianization' (Third Annual Conference Idea Exchange: Mediums and Methods of Communication in Eastern Europe, Russia, and Central Asia, Pittsburgh, February 2006) <http://www.kakanien-revisited.at/beitr/emerg/AWyka1.pdf> accessed 3 August 2018.

42. Peter Humphreys, 'A political scientist's contribution to the comparative study of media systems in Europe: A response to Hallin and Mancini' in Natascha Just and Manuel Puppis (eds), *Trends in Communications Policy Research* (Intellect 2012) 163.

43. These cultural divergences may link to socio-economic differences as well but it beyond the scope of this book to consider this.

44. Hofstede, Hofstede, and Minkov (n 38) 92. The authors add that '[c]ollectivism as its opposite pertains to societies in which people from birth onward are integrated into

strong, cohesive in-groups, which throughout people's lifetime continue to protect in exchange for unquestioning loyalty'.

45. Ibid 191.
46. Ibid 61.
47. In each case, these measures range from around 0 to around 100. See Hofstede, Hofstede, and Minkov (n 38) 56, 94, and 195.
48. In those cases (Denmark, Germany, Lithuania, and Spain) where different regulatory stringency measures were applicable to different regulators, the highest regulatory stringency measure was deployed here.
49. COM (1990) 314 final (n 8) 39; COM (1992) 422 final (n 8) 19.
50. No such provisions were found within the local legislation of the following States: Bulgaria, Croatia, Czechia, Estonia, France, Hungary, Iceland, Poland, Slovakia, and Sweden.
51. Namely, Austria, and Norway. See Austria: Federal Act Concerning the Protection of Personal Data, s 48(1) and Norway, Act of 14 April 2000 No 31 relating to the processing of personal data (Personal Data Act), s 7. Denmark also excluded journalism from the ambit of Article 27 (Denmark: Compiled version of the Act on Processing of Personal Data, s 2(10)). However, as seen later in Table 5.4, it established in its stead a *sui generis* interface between journalistic self- and co-regulation through its *Lov om massemediers informationsdatabaser.*
52. Estonia: Personal Data Protection Act, art 11(2).
53. Luxembourg: Law of 2 August 2002 (n 24) art 29(3).
54. The National Order is composed, according to a two-thirds to one-third ratio, of representatives of professional journalists and journalistic publishers. However, it is based in the Ministry of Justice and the Minister of Justice exercises 'l'alta vigilanza' ('overarching vigilance') over its operations. See Italy: Legge n 69/1963 Ordinamento della Professione di Giornalista, Titolo I, 3, 16, and 24.
55. Italy, Personal Data Protection Code, s 139.
56. Ibid s 139.
57. Italy, Code of Practice Concerning the Processing of Personal Data in the Exercise of Journalistic Activities (1998) art 13(2).
58. Lithuania: Law Amending the Law on Legal Protection of Personal Data 2008, art 8.
59. Notably, under art 49 of the Lithuanian Law on Provision of Information to the Public, the Inspector is required to be appointed by the Parliament from a list of candidates proposed by organisations representing publishers, the audio-visual sector, and journalists.
60. France: Act No 78-17 of 6 January 1978 on Information Technology, Data Files and Civil Liberties (as amended) art 67.
61. UK: Data Protection Act (n 32) s 32(3) and Data Protection (Designated Codes of Practice) (No 2) Order 2000.
62. Gibraltar: Data Protection Act 2004 s 13(3).
63. Ibid.
64. Malta: Data Protection Act (n 32) art 6(2)–(3).
65. Denmark: *Lov om massemediers informationsdatabaser*, art 8(2).
66. Ibid arts 12–17. Under s 41 of the Danish Media Liability Act, the co-regulatory Press Council must be made up of eight members comprised as follows: a chairman and

vice-chairman who must be members of the legal profession, two members as recommended by Danish Journalists' Union, two members as recommended by the editorial managements of the press, radio, and television and two members as recommended by the Danish Council for Adult Education.

67. Interstate Treaty on Broadcasting and Telemedia (n 28) art 57(2).

68. Germany: Federal Data Protection Act (BDSG) s 42.

69. See, for example, Staatsvertrag über das Medienrecht in Hamburg und Schleswig-Holstein (Medienstaatsvertrag HSH) s 37.

70. Article 29 Working Party, 'Recommendation 1/97 on Data Protection law and the media (WP 1)' (*Europa*, 25 February 1997) <https://ec.europa.eu/justice/article-29/documentation/opinion-recommendation/files/1997/wp1_en.pdf> accessed 3 May 2019.

71. Ibid 8.

72. Ibid 8.

73. Ibid 4-5. Equally, the report added, 'limits to freedom of expression, such as the ones that might derive from the application of data protection principles, must also be in accordance with the law and respect the principle of proportionality'.

74. Article 29 Working Party (n 70) 7.

75. Ibid 8.

76. Ibid 6.

77. DPD (n 1) art 7(f). Cf Council Regulation 2016/679/EU of 27 April 2016 on the protection of natural persons with regard to the processing of personal data and on the free movement of such data, and repealing Directive 95/46/EC [2016] OJ L119/1, art 6(1)(f).

78. Article 29 Working Party, 'Opinion 6/2014 on the Notion of legitimate interests of the data controller under Article 7 of Directive 95/46/EC' (*Europa*, 9 April 2014) <https://ec.europa.eu/justice/article-29/documentation/opinion-recommendation/files/2014/wp217_en.pdf> 34 accessed 18 June 2019 .

79. Ibid 39.

80. Ibid 58.

81. Ibid 58. In its 2014 guidelines on Case C-131/12 *Google Spain SL and Google Inc v Agencia Española de Protección de Datos (AEPD)* [2014] 3 CMLR 50 the Working Party signalled that 'as a rule' the right to de-listing set down in that judgment would not apply to the internal 'search tools of websites'. Article 29 Working Party, 'Guidelines on the Implementation of the Court of Justice of the European Union Judgment on "Google Spain and Inc v Agencia Española de Protección de Datos (AEPD) and Mario Costeja González" C-131/12' (*Europa*, 26 November 2014) <https://ec.europa.eu/justice/article-29/documentation/opinion-recommendation/files/2014/wp225_en.pdf> 2 accessed 18 June 2019.

82. '[I]t is the processing of images (including images of individuals, houses, vehicles, driving license plates, etc.), sound, geolocation data or any other electromagnetic signals related to an identified or identifiable natural person carried out by the data processing equipment on-board a drone that may have an impact on privacy and data protection and therefore trigger the application of data protection legislation.' (Article 29 Working Party, 'Opinion 01/2015 on Privacy and Data Protection Issues relating to the utilisation of Drones' (*Europa*, 16 June 2015) <https://ec.europa.eu/justice/article-29/documentation/opinion-recommendation/files/2015/wp231_en.pdf> 7 accessed 18 June 2019.

83. Ibid 10.

84. No guidance was found on the website of the DPA in Austria, Bulgaria, Croatia, Finland, Gibraltar, Latvia, Liechtenstein, Lithuania, Luxembourg, Norway, Portugal, Romania, and Slovakia. Three of these DPAs did publish very specific technical material, which still did not amount to general substantive guidance. Thus, the Croatian DPA indicated that in December 2011 (two and a half years before it formally joined the EU/EEA) it had organized a workshop in collaboration with the European Commission's technical assistance arm (TAIEX) examining the interface between data protection, access to information and freedom of expression in the context of media reporting. See Agencija za zaštitu osobnih podataka, 'Taiex' (*Azop*) <https://azop.hr/projekti/detaljnije/taiex> accessed 7 May 2019. The Luxembourg DPA noted that journalism was exempted from the obligation to register processing with it and also published guidance it had provided the Government on the drafting of a new media law in 2003. See Luxembourg: Commission Nationale Pour la Protection des Données, 'Exemptions du devoir de declaration' (*CNPD*, 3 August 2013) <https://web.archive.org/web/20160803012034/http://www.cnpd.public.lu/fr/declarer/traitements-exemptes/index.html> accessed 7 May 2019 and 'Délibération n° 6 bis 1/2003 relative à l'avis sur le projet de loi n° 4910 sur la liberté d'expression dans les medias' (*CNPD*, 2003) <https://cnpd.public.lu/content/dam/cnpd/fr/decisions-avis/2003/avis-liberte-expression/doc_avis_pdl4910.pdf> accessed 7 May 2019. Finally, the Portuguese DPA produced detailed guidance on the collection of the personal data of participants of television programmes, especially in the context of reality shows, in its annual report of 2001/02 but not as regards processing directly linked to broadcast. See Portugal, Comissão Nacional de Protecção de Datos, 'Relatório de Actividades 2001–2001' (*CNPD*) <http://www.cnpd.pt/bin/relatorios/anos/relat01-02.htm> accessed 10 May 2019.

85. No guidance was found on the websites of either the Meckenberg-Vorpommern or Schleswig-Holstein DPAs. However, the 2006/2007 annual report of the Mecklenburg-Vorpommern DPA did stress that increasing surveillance could threaten journalists, thereby highlighting a potential *synergy* between data protection and journalism. See Mecklenburg-Vorpommern State Commissioner for Data Protection and Freedom of Information, '8th Report, 2006/07' (*Datenschutz-mv*, 8 February 2013) <https://web.archive.org/web/20130208040447/http://www.datenschutz-mv.de/datenschutz/publikationen/tb.html> accessed 10 May 2019. The Schleswig-Holstein DPA published its proposal for an amendment to German data protection law which would have narrowed the journalistic derogation by explicitly introducing an overarching balancing test here. See 'ULD legt Gesetzesvorschlag zur Internet-Regulierung vor' (*Datenschutzzentrum*, 27 October 2010) <https://web.archive.org/web/20131028012841/https://www.datenschutzzentrum.de/presse/20101027-gesetzesvorschlag-internet-regulierung.htm> accessed 10 May 2019.

86. Namely, the Cypriot, Hungarian, Icelandic, and Spanish DPAs.

87. See Italy: Garante per la Protezione dei Dati Personali, 'Privacy e giornalismo' (*Garante Privacy*, 2012) <http://www.garanteprivacy.it/web/guest/home/docweb/-/docweb-display/docweb/1858277> accessed 20 May 2019; and Slovenia: Information Commissioner, 'Media and the Protection of Personal Data' (*IP-RS*, 2009) <https://

www.ip-rs.si/fileadmin/user_upload/Pdf/smernice/Media_and_the_Protection_
of_Personal_Data.pdf> accessed 20 May 2019. Following a recommendation of
an official inquiry under Lord Justice Leveson in November 2012, the UK DPA also
undertook to produce comprehensive guidelines here. However, these were only published in September 2014, after the survey of DPA websites had been completed. See
UK: Information Commissioner's Office, 'Data Protection and Journalism: A Guide for
the Media' (*ICO*, 2014) <https://ico.org.uk/media/for-organisations/documents/1552/
data-protection-and-journalism-media-guidance.pdf> accessed 20 May 2019.

88. Cyprus, Επιτρόπου Προστασίας Δεδομένων, 'Annual Report 2007' <https://web.
archive.org/web/20120604033246/http://www.dataprotection.gov.cy/dataprotection/
dataprotection.nsf/All/6055401E4C62567FC2257617002553EF?OpenDocument> 8
accessed 20 May 2019 (own translation).

89. Netherlands: College Berscherming Persoonsgegevens, 'Publication of Personal
Data on the Internet' (*Dutch DPA*, December 2007) <https://web.archive.org/
web/20100216150023/http://www.dutchdpa.nl/downloads_overig/en_20071108_
richtsnoeren_internet.pdf> 43 accessed 20 May 2019.

90. UK: Information Commissioner's Office, 'The Media' (*ICO*, 13 February 2014) <https://
web.archive.org/web/20140213184714/http://www.ico.org.uk/for_the_public/topic_
specific_guides/media> accessed 20 May 2019.

91. Czechia: Office for Personal Data Protection, 'Position No. 5/2009 Publication of personal data in the media' (*UOOU*, 2009) <https://www.uoou.cz/en/vismo/zobraz_dok.
asp?id_org=200156&id_ktg=1117&p1=1117> accessed 19 May 2019.

92. Spain: Agencia Española de Protección de Datos, 'Memoria 1997' (*AGPD*, 10
August 2014) <https://web.archive.org/web/20140810083103/http://www.agpd.es/
portalwebAGPD/canaldocumentacion/memorias/common/MEMORIA_1997.pdf>
104–05 accessed 19 May 2019, .

93. Case B 293-00, Judgment of 12 June 2001.

94. Sweden: Datainspektionen, 'Vad innebär undantaget för journalistiska ändamål?'
(*Datainspektionen*, 6 January 2012) <https://web.archive.org/web/20120106073059/
https://www.datainspektionen.se/fragor-och-svar/personuppgiftslagen/vad-innebar-
undantaget-for-journalistiska-andamal/> accessed 19 May 2019.

95. Sweden: Dateninspektionen, 'Vanliga frågor' (*Krankt*) <http://www.krankt.se/vanliga-
fragor> accessed 19 May 2019.

96. Thus, as stated in endnotes 84 and 85, there was an absence of any such guidance on
Austrian (0.10/0), German Brandenburg (0.03/0), German Mecklenberg-Vorpommern
(0.03/0), German Schleswig-Holstein (0.03/0.25), Finnish (0.00/1), and Norwegian
(0.00/1) DPA websites.

97. Slovenia: Information Commissioner, 'On the Air: Media and the Protection of
Personal Data' (*IP-RS*) <https://www.ip-rs.si/fileadmin/user_upload/Pdf/smernice/
Media_and_the_Protection_of_Personal_Data.pdf> 8 accessed 19 May 2019, 8.

98. Article 3.1 of the DPD (n 1) expressly states that the limitation of scope to personal data
'which form part of a filing system or are intended to form part of a filing system' related
only to 'processing otherwise than by automatic means' (i.e. manual processing) rather
than the 'automatic' (i.e. computer-based) processing of data which was covered irrespective of whether it was structured or unstructured.

99. Slovenia: Information Commissioner (n 97) 28.
100. Ibid 32–33. Similar to many of European countries, in Slovenia data concerning the deceased remained protected under second-generation data protection.
101. Ibid 41. The argument here was that, although often derived from public record data, such a list would be based on 'estimates and calculations and conclusions which . . . are to a degree speculative and hence such data do not represent personal data'. Again, given the broad definition of personal data, this reasoning would appear incorrect. For example, in Case C-434/16 *Nowak v Data Protection Commissioner* [2018] 1 WLR 3505, the CJEU emphasized that the concept of personal data 'potentially encompasses all kinds of information, not only objective but also subjective, in the form of opinions and assessments, providing that it "relates" to the data subject' (para 34).
102. Slovenia: Information Commissioner (n 97) 37–38.
103. Thus, for example, the guidance held that a special legal basis for processing sensitive personal data could be found when processing 'is authorised by other law on the basis of public interest' (ibid 32).
104. Thus, the guidance found that '[c]onflict between the right of privacy and the right to protection of personal data on the one side, and the right to freedom of expression and information on the other, is both common and indeed frequent' (ibid 13) and further that in principle 'neither the right to privacy nor the right to information has any precedence since they are both equally important' (ibid 15).
105. The pithiest statement of this approach is contained in a section of the annual report produced for 2002, two years prior to when Hungary joined the EU. See Hungary: Adatvédelmi Biztos, 'Az Adatvédelmi Biztos beszámolója *2002*' (*Adatvédelmi Biztos Irodája*, 2003) <https://www.naih.hu/files/Adatvedelmi-biztos-beszamoloja-2002.PDF> 189 accessed 10 June 2019.
106. See, for example, Hungary: Adatvédelmi Biztos, 'Az Adatvédelmi Biztos beszámolója 2004' (*Adatvédelmi Biztos Irodája*, 2005) <https://www.naih.hu/files/Adatvedelmi-biztos-beszamoloja-2004.PDF> 118–22 accessed 10 June 2019 (defining public figures as those who exercise public authority and who decide on the use of public funds, and also finding that such figures retain protection as regards their affairs related to their private life).
107. Since street photography itself may be considered to be primarily artistic, this aspect of the guidance will be discussed in greater detail in Chapter 10.
108. Malta: Office of the Information and Data Protection Commissioner, 'Data Protection and Street Photography' (*IDPC*, 2013) <https://web.archive.org/web/20140723062415/ http://idpc.gov.mt/dbfile.aspx/Data_Prot_and_Street_Photography.pdf> accessed 20 May 2019.
109. Italy: Garante per la Protezione dei Dati Personali, 'Annual Report 2003' (*Garante Privacy*, 28 April 2004) <http://www.garanteprivacy.it/web/guest/home/docweb/-/ docweb-display/docweb/1750768> 20 accessed 20 May 2019. This decision was essentially a straightforward elucidation of art 8.3 of the Italian Italy, Code of Practice Concerning the Processing of Personal Data in the Exercise of Journalistic Activities (1998) although the provision as set out in the code itself did allow for such publication where 'necessary to report maltreatment'.

110. Spain: Agencia Española de Protección de Datos, 'Memoria 2007' (*AGPD*, 2007) <https://web.archive.org/web/20140810045226/http://www.agpd.es/portalwebAGPD/canaldocumentacion/memorias/memorias_2007/common/pdfs/memoria_AEPD_2007.pdf> 36–37 accessed 20 May 2019.

111. Estonia: Data Protection Inspectorate, 'Uut Kodulehel: Kaamerate kasutamise juhis' (*AKI*, 9 April 2013) <http://www.aki.ee/et/uudised/uudiste-arhiiv/uut-kodulehel-kaamerate-kasutamise-juhis> accessed 20 May 2019.

112. *Privacy e giornalismo* (n 87) 26–28, 312–18.

113. Lithuania: Žurnalistų Etikos Inspektoriaus Tarnyba, 'Etikos kodeksas' (*IRS*, 2015)   <https://web.archive.org/web/20150606193959/http://www.lrs.lt/intl/zeit.show?theme=694&lang=1> accessed 20 May 2019.

114. Belgium: Commission de la Protection de la Vie Privée, 'Rapport Annuel 2010' (*Privacy Commission*, 2010) <https://web.archive.org/web/20120829001447/http://www.privacycommission.be/sites/privacycommission/files/documents/rapport-annuel-2010.pdf> 42 accessed 20 May 2019.

115. Belgium: Commission de la Protection de la Vie Privée, 'Rapport Annuel 2011' (*Privacy Commission*, 2011) <https://web.archive.org/web/20120829001519/http://www.privacycommission.be/sites/privacycommission/files/documents/rapport-annuel-2011.pdf> 20 accessed 20 May 2019.

116. France: Commission Nationale de l'Informatique et des Libertés, 'Délibération n° 01-057 du 29 novembre 2001 portant recommandation sur la diffusion de données personnelles sur internet par les banques de données de jurisprudence' (*CNIL*, 29 November 2001) <https://web.archive.org/web/20150921182205/http://www.cnil.fr/documentation/deliberations/deliberation/delib/17/> accessed 20 May 2019.

117. The Netherlands: College Berscherming Persoonsgegevens, 'Publication of Personal Data on the Internet' (n 89) 43–45.

118. UK: Information Commissioner's Office, 'What Price Privacy Now?' (*ICO*, 2006) <https://web.archive.org/web/20130116150750/http://www.ico.gov.uk/~/media/documents/library/Corporate/Research_and_reports/WHAT_PRICE_PRIVACY_NOW.ashx> accessed 20 May 2019.

119. Ireland: Data Protection Commissioner, 'Case Studies' (*Dataprotection*, 2017) <https://web.archive.org/web/20171218003648/https://www.dataprotection.ie/ViewDoc.asp?fn=%2Fdocuments%2Fcasestudies%2FCategoryCS%2Ehtm&CatID=10&m=c> accessed 20 May 2019.

120. Malta: Information and Data Protection Commissioner, Data Protection Annual Report 2004 (*IDPC*) <http://idpc.gov.mt/dbfile.aspx/Annual%20Report%202004.pdf> 9–10 accessed 27 May 2014, .

121. Malta: Information and Data Protection Commissioner, Data Protection Annual Report 2005 (*IDPC*) <http://idpc.gov.mt/dbfile.aspx/Annual%20Report%202005.pdf> 7 accessed 27 May 2014.

122. Denmark: Datatilsynet, 'Behandlinger omfattet af lov om massemediers informationsdatabaser' (*Datailsynet*, 29 December 2007) <https://web.archive.org/web/20120324113456/http://www.datatilsynet.dk/erhverv/redaktionelle-informationsdatabaser/behandlinger-omfattet-af-lov-om-massemediers-informationsdatabaser/> accessed 20 May 2019.

123. Germany: Bundesbeauftragten für den Datenschutz und die Informationsfreiheit, 'Datenschutz bei der Presse' (*BFDI*, 1 August 2012) <https://web.archive.org/web/20120801230812/http://www.bfdi.bund.de:80/DE/Themen/KommunikationsdiensteMedien/PresseRundfunk/Artikel/DatenschutzBeiDerPresse.html;jsessionid=1380FB505BC9113BD0300BC1E442 18A9.1_cid136> accessed 20 May 2019.

124. Ibid.

125. Germany: Landesbeauftragte für den Datenschutz and die Informationsfreiheit Rheinland-Pfalz, 'Datenschutzkontrollinstanzen: Presse' (*Datenschutz*, 2012) <https://web.archive.org/web/20120717011434/http://www.datenschutz.rlp.de/de/kontrolle.php?submenu=presse> accessed 20 May 2019.

126. Germany: Landesbeauftragte für den Datenschutz and die Informationsfreiheit Rheinland-Pfalz, 'Datenschutzkontrollinstanzen: Rundfunk/Fernsehen' (*Datenschutz*, 2012) <https://web.archive.org/web/20120717001250/http://www.datenschutz.rlp.de/de/kontrolle.php?submenu=radio> accessed 20 May 2019.

127. It is beyond the scope of this comparative work to detail all the other myriad issues highlighted by particular regulators. Nevertheless, the Italian DPA's particularly comprehensive guidance provides a good indication of the range of concerns addressed. Alongside the three issues explored in this section, this material explored *inter alia* the protection of domicile, health data, sex life data, judicial proceedings data, data on social networking sites, and restrictions on the gathering and/or use obtained by interception. See *Privacy e giornalismo* (n 87).

128. See *Privacy e giornalismo* (n 87) 55–59 and Estonia: Data Protection Inspectorate (n 111) 15–16.

129. Ireland: Data Protection Commissioner, 'Annual Report 2005' (*Dataprotection*, 2005) <https://web.archive.org/web/20171218060730/https://www.dataprotection.ie/documents/annualreports/AnnualReport2005-EN.pdf> 20 accessed 20 May 2019; repeated at Ireland: Data Protection Commissioner (n 119).

130. Hungary: Adatvédelmi Biztos, 'Az Adatvédelmi Biztos beszámolója—2002' (*Adatvédelmi Biztos Irodája*, 2003) <http://www.naih.hu/files/Adatvedelmi-biztos-beszamoloja-2002.PDF> 189 accessed 4 June 2019.

131. Specific coverage of this issue was found in the guidance of six national-level DPAs (19 per cent), as well as two out of the five regional DPAs (40 per cent) who responded to the questionnaire.

132. Slovenia: Information Commissioner (n 97) 38. Other parts of the guidance suggested that it was not the actual recording but any subsequent publication which was suspect (18).

133. Ibid 39.

134. Ibid 39.

135. Ibid 38.

136. In sum, the guidance stated that '[p]hotographs or records would represent personal data collections . . . if they were published in such a way that the individual is identified. Such a collection could be established if, for example, an article or a feature included—besides photos or records—personal data (e.g. name or surname, data of birth or residence . . .) of the individual depicted or otherwise recorded' (38).

137. Ibid 38. The guidance also stated that unjustified clandestine visual or audio recording would constitute an offence under the general criminal law where the recording or its use would 'significantly encroach upon the privacy of an individual' (40).

138. Estonia: Data Protection Inspectorate (n 111) 14–15.

139. Ibid 80.

140. Hungary: Adatvédelmi Biztos, 'Az Adatvédelmi Biztos beszámolója 2003' (*Adatvédelmi Biztos Irodája*, 2004) <http://www.naih.hu/files/Adatvedelmi-biztos-beszamoloja-2003. PDF> 127 accessed 4 June 2019. It is noted that this opinion was issued one year before Hungary joined the EU and, therefore, became formally subject to EU data protection norms.

141. Hungary: Adatvédelmi Biztos, 'Az Adatvédelmi Biztos beszámolója 2004' (*Adatvédelmi Biztos Irodája*, 2005) <http://www.naih.hu/files/Adatvedelmi-biztos-beszamoloja-2004. PDF> 273 accessed 4 June 2019.

142. Hungary: Adatvédelmi Biztos, 'Az Adatvédelmi Biztos beszámolója 2007' (*Adatvédelmi Biztos Irodája*, 2008) <http://www.naih.hu/files/Adatvedelmi-biztos-beszamoloja-2004.PDF> 138 accessed 4 June 2019.

143. Hungary: Adatvédelmi Biztos, 'Beszámolój Az Adatvédelmi Biztos 2010' (*Adatvédelmi Biztos Irodája*, 2011) <http://www.naih.hu/files/Adatvedelmi-biztos-beszamoloja-2010. PDF> 150–51 accessed 4 June 2019.

144. Or other forms of '*identification complete*' (complete identification) of data subjects.

145. As issue also deal with, as noted earlier, by the Italian DPA.

146. Belgium: Commission de la Protection de la Vie Privée (n 114) 42.

147. Malta: Office of the Information and Data Protection Commissioner (n 108).

148. Germany: Landesbeuaftragte für den Datenschutz und Akteneinsicht, 'Tätigkeitsbericht der Landesbeauftragten für den Datenschutz und für das Recht auf Akteneinsicht zum 31 Dezember 2009' (*LDA Brandenburg*, 2009) <http://www.lda.brandenburg. de/media_fast/4055/TB_15.pdf> 178–79 accessed 20 May 2019. The 2006/2007 annual report did also note concerns amongst *inter alia* journalists regarding threats surveillance posed to the confidentiality of their communication, thereby highlighting a *synergy* between data protection and the media. See Germany: Landesbeuaftragte für den Datenschutz und Akteneinsicht, 'Tätigkeitsbericht der Landesbeauftragten für den Datenschutz und für das Recht auf Akteneinsicht zum 31 Dezember 2007' (*LDA Brandenburg*, 2007) <http://www.lda.brandenburg.de/media_fast/4055/TB_14.pdf> 12 accessed 20 May 2019. Outside of these two specific areas, however, this DPA did not produce further guidance specific to journalistic activity per se.

149. Germany: Landesbeauftragte für den Datenschutz and die Informationsfreiheit Rheinland-Pfalz, 'Datenschutzbericht 2010/2011' (*Datenschutz RLP*, 2011) https:// web.archive.org/web/20130607085512/http://www.datenschutz.rlp.de/downloads/ tb/tb23.pdf 78 accessed 20 May 2019.

150. The Portuguese DPA also addressed the issue of reality shows and contests. However, their guidance focused on gathering of questionnaire and interview data on candidates during the selection process, as well as its subsequent processing. See (n 84).

151. *Privacy e giornalismo* (n 87) 47.

152. The growing power of internet search engines prompted a debate on the place of such actors themselves within the European data protection scheme. Moreover, in Case

C-131/12 *Google Spain SL and Google Inc v Agencia Española de Protección de Datos (AEPD)* [2014] 3 CMLR 50 the CJEU upheld efforts by the Spanish DPA to place direct responsibilities on them under this law. Although regulation of the new media lies outside of the focus of this monograph, this important case will be explored in later parts of this book including Chapters 9 and 13.

153. Whilst the discrete analysis of 'new' media actors such as Internet search engines lies outside the scope of this book, the interface between the regulation of traditional publishers and the 'new' media will be further explored in this book's conclusion.

154. Slovenia: Information Commissioner (n 97) 39.

155. Greece: Hellenic Data Protection Authority, 'Πληροφορίες σχετικά με ΜΜΕ' (*Greek DPA*) <http://www.dpa.gr/portal/page?_pageid=33,23093&_dad=portal&_schema=PORTAL> accessed 20 May 2019.

156. Belgium: Commission de la Protection de la Vie Privée (n 114) 42.

157. France: Commission Nationale de l'Informatique et des Libertés (n 116). See also Table 5.5 (91-92).

158. Netherlands: College Berscherming Persoonsgegevens (n 89) 45.

159. Denmark: Datatilsynet (n 122). The Spanish Catalan DPA somewhat similarly argued that data subjects had the right to rectify inaccurate data but claimed that information which was offensive or insulting should be dealt with in court under other laws such as defamation and violation of the right to honour. However, these remarks are not included in the principal analysis of this topic since they were not specifically focused on the right to be forgotten or the archiving of content. See Spain: Catalan Data Protection Authority, 'Can my personal data be published in a news article in a newspaper or website?' (*APD*, 2016) <https://web.archive.org/web/20160420100538/http://www.apd.cat/en/llistaFAQview.php?cat_id=173&preg_id=128> accessed 20 May 2019.

160. *Privacy e giornalismo* (n 87) 47–50.

161. These and related 'knowledge facilitation' provisions will be further explored in Chapter 9 and, more particularly, in Chapters 11 and 12.

162. President of the Italian Data Protection Authority, 'Speech by The President of the Italian Data Protection Authority 2010' (*Garante Privacy*, 30 June 2010) <http://www.garanteprivacy.it/web/guest/home/docweb/-/docweb-display/docweb/1738746> accessed 20 May 2019.

163. *Privacy e giornalismo* (n 87) 226–38.

164. DPD (n 1) recital 37 and art 37.

Chapter 6

1. Given that the questionnaire as a whole addressed a whole range of matters related to data protection and openness, it was not sent to the Danish and Lithuanian specialist media bodies that *inter alia* exercised limited supervision over journalism in the area of data protection. However, the Lithuanian DPA made clear that its response had been completed in cooperation with the Lithuanian Inspector of Journalist Ethics. Meanwhile, the Danish DPA did not response to the questionnaire. Note also that, as previously stated and for the purposes of this study only, Gibraltar was treated as a separate EEA State and, therefore, the Gibraltarian DPA as a national DPA.

2. EU Charter of Fundamental Rights and Freedoms, art 8(2).

3. Council Directive 95/46/EC of 24 October 1995 on the protection of individuals with regard to the processing of personal data and on the free movement of such data [1995] OJ L281/31, art 9 ('DPD').

4. However, these provisions were more usually justified not on the basis of rights but rather on a more generic societal good of ensuring that knowledge production and preservation not be unduly impeded. Moreover, stipulations in this area were often elided with the very different activity of biomedical and similar research. These issues will be examined in Chapter 11.

5. Case C-101/01 *Lindqvist* [2003] ECR I-12971. This case, which was introduced in Chapter 2 of this book, explored the relationship between European data protection and the personal activity of an individual who posted on her personal web page information about other individuals who were undertaking voluntary church activity alongside herself. The Court expressly rejected the idea that the DPD violated freedom of expression and implicitly indicated that the journalistic/special expression derogation was not engaged. Nevertheless, it did *inter alia* state that 'Lindqvist's freedom of expression in her work preparing people for Communion and her freedom to carry out activities contributing to religion life have to be weighted against the protection of the private life of the individuals about whom Mrs Lindqvist has placed data on her internet site' (para 86).

6. These questions were placed in different parts of the questionnaire and were phrased slightly differently in each case. For further details see David Erdos, 'Data Protection Confronts Freedom of Expression on the "New Media" Internet: The Stance of European Regulatory Authorities' (2015) 40(4) EL Rev 531, 538–39.

7. Since these figures take into account text which was not expressly tied to these specific questions (but, rather, a whole section or even the entire questionnaire), the values are slightly different from that previously reported in Erdos (n 6).

8. The German Rhineland-Palatinate DPA answer was difficult to interpret. It stated that data protection applied 'but there are also media-specific laws'. However, its responses to the latter questions indicated that data protection itself was considered applicable only in 'the area of administration' and not as regards 'journalistic activities' themselves, although 'the journalist has to comply with the fundamental rights of personality, the right to determinate about one's own pictures and the civil law concerning damages (§§ 823, 826 German Civil Law).'

9. The Dutch DPA did not provide a free-text answer to this specific question but rather only to the entire section of the questionnaire that concerned the professional media (excluding media archiving). This stated *inter alia* that '[t]he Wbp [Dutch Data Protection Act] applies partially in the case where data regarding persons is being processed for *exclusively* journalistic purposes . . . The articles which still apply on the controller are the ones that concerns the obligation to process data fairly and lawfully and also the duty to take security measures.' This response would appear to broadly accept the applicability of special expression regime (b/0.33) in this context.

10. The Slovenian DPA indicated that data protection would apply in full 'if the published data is such that it would be protected under data protection law, eg if it has been acquired from a data controller and published without legal grounds. In other cases the general law on defamation and breach of privacy applies. Our

law does not include the exemption for journalism, art and literature.' This would appear to be an amalgam of full application (a/1) and full exclusion (d/0) of data protection law.

11. The UK DPA stated that 'such activities would almost certainly involve the processing of personal data for the purposes of the Data Protection Act 1998. However, the so-called special purposes exemption in section 32 of the Act is likely to be engaged and will have some impact on how the provisions of the DPA apply to the specific circumstances.' This answer would appear to accept the broad applicability of the special expression regime (b/0.33).

12. The Cypriot DPA heavily qualified its standard response with text highlighting the importance of contextual balancing 'on a case by case basis taking into account its own merits and particularities' and stressing that '[i]n every case, data published for journalistic purposes should obey the principle of proportionality. To strike the right balance between the public's right to information and the data subject's right to privacy, the following criteria should be taken into account to determinate what is proportional to publish: (i) the public's particular interest for a specific story, at the time of publication (ii) if the story involves a public figure or an average person and (iii) if the story justifies the public's overriding right to be informed of the persons' names involved in the story. For example, a newspaper publishes today an article on a well know doctor, who is named, accused for tax evasion. While the current economic situation in Cyprus and the public's sensitivity on this type of stories today seem to justify the publication, few years ago, naming the doctor would have been in breach of the proportionality principle.'

13. The Hungarian DPA justified this standard response as follows: 'In Hungary it is not the general Privacy [Data Protection] Act (Act CXII of 2011) but the Act of CIV of 2010 on Freedom of the Press and on the Basic Rules Relating to Media Content which provide a special legal protection for journalists and the sources they use in their investigation activities. Therefore the Act on the Freedom of the Press shall be applied as lex specialis compared with the Privacy Act . . . On the other side it has to be underlined that the special legal protection of the journalists is only in relation with "public data of public interest", which also covers personal data that are made public by virtue of a public interest (e.g. relevant personal information of a politician or other public figure). If the data controlled by the journalists does not qualify as data of public interest in relation with freedom of information general data protection regulation applies.'

14. The Swedish DPA stated, albeit not specifically in relation to this question, that 'Traditional Media entities (such as newspapers, radio and TV) and their publication of information on the Internet falls under the Freedom of Press and Freedom of Expression legislation and is thus exempted from the Data Protection Rules.'

15. Similarly to the Austrian DPA (n 18) but specifically related to this question, the Polish DPA included a translation of then current Polish Data Protection Act's 'Press clause' which provided for a qualified derogation from data protection for journalistic activity within the meaning of the Polish Press Law.

16. See the responses from the Austrian, German Rhineland-Palatinate, Hungarian, Polish, and Slovenian DPAs (n 18, 8, 13, 15, and 10).

17. See Swedish DPA (n 14).

18. The Austrian response simply stated that '[t]he relationship of data protection and media is regulated in section 48 of the Austrian data protection act', provided an English translation of this and further held that '[t]his regulation refers most legal questions regarding the media to the Media Act, a special law that covers media companies'.

19. The Slovenian DPA's answer here was identical to that in relation to news production (n 10) apart from the absence of the sentence '[o]ur law does not include the exemption for journalism, art and literature'.

20. The Dutch DPA stressed their strongly case-by-case approach and did not expressly answer this question. Nevertheless, they included a copy (in Dutch) of a set of their published guidelines which, as explored in section 2.5.3 of Chapter 5, held that online news archives could, in principle, benefit from the special expressive purposes regime.

21. In sum, this DPA linked its answer to that which it supplied in relation to the undercover journalism question explored in Table 6.1 later. The pertinent part stated that '[h]is journalistic activities are without the control of the data protection authority; the data protection law is not applicable. But the journalist has to comply with the fundamental rights of personality, the right to determine about one's own pictures and the civil law concerning damages (§§ 823, 826 German Civil Law).'

22. Namely, DPAs in Finland, Sweden, and (not a questionnaire participant) also Norway. In Germany DPAs faced a similar situation but only in relation to the Press (rather than the audio-visual media).

23. Namely, DPAs in the Czechia, Spain, and (not a questionnaire participant) also Croatia.

24. Or even potentially stance (d/1) ('full application').

25. Moreover, in the single case of Liechtenstein, the reference in a number of the special expression provisions to use in an 'editorially controlled section of a periodically-published media organ' or as a 'personal work aid' might have especially pointed to news archiving being regulated outside of special expression (stance (b/0.33)). See Liechtenstein: Data Protection Act, art 13; Data Protection Ordinance, art 4.

26. In sum, the correlation between local law stringency and the DPA's interpretative stance regarding news production was 0.442 with one-tailed significance of 0.011 (significant at the 5 per cent level). Meanwhile, the correlation between local law stringency at the DPA's stance regarding news archiving was 0.480, with a one-tailed significance of 0.008 (significant at the 1 per cent level).

27. Namely, BBC Panorama's 2004 'The Secret Agent' documentary where Jason Gwynne spent six months undercover as an infiltrator of the British National Party. See BBC, 'Archive 2004: The Secret Agent' (*BBC News*, 22 October 2009) <http://news.bbc.co.uk/panorama/hi/front_page/newsid_8320000/8320387.stm> accessed 19 May 2019.

28. These possibilities were presented to DPAs in the reverse order but have been rearranged for heuristic purposes.

29. The question cited in brackets in art 14 of the DPD (n 3) which, although concerned with the data subject's right to participate in processing concerning them, does not provide detail on the provisions relating to subject access. The clearly defined nature of the questions itself and the potential responses to it ensured that there was no confusion as to the focus of the inquiry.

30. These possibilities were presented to DPAs in the reverse order but have been rearranged, for heuristic purposes.

31. Strictly speaking this DPA only indicated that this explanation would apply to the activity of the covert social scientist examined in Chapter 11. However, as it seems highly likely that this DPA intended to indicate the same understanding also in relation to the undercover journalist, it is also summarized here.

32. The answer did clarify that such permits were issued for processing 'in other areas of the company, such as human resources, video surveillance systems, marketing [and] service subscriptions by clients'.

33. In sum, the Cypriot DPA stated that '[w]hen planning to publish an exposé it is a common practice for journalists to ask the persons involved to comment on it prior to publication. We have had no cases of access to media insofar [sic]. In Cyprus the Journalists Code of Ethics is not binding by virtue of Law. The Code provides *inter alia* that a journalist is not obliged to reveal his sources.'

34. In sum, it stated '[i]n principle yes, the individual has the right to make a subject access request under section 7 of the DPA [Data Protection Act]. However, in practice the organisation is likely to be able to apply the special purposes exemption in order to refuse to supply the requested information in response to the request.'

35. DPD (n 3) art 10. The only general exemption set out here applied when the data subject already has this information which clearly would not have been the case here.

36. It is perfectly possible that other types of 'sensitive' data might also have been processed, such as data concerning 'philosophical beliefs' and data relating to criminal 'offences'. See DPD (n 3) arts 8(1) and (5).

37. DPD (n 3) art 8(1).

38. Ibid art 8(2). The only default special legal *vires* lifting the prohibition here were either that the subject 'has given his explicit consent to the processing' (art 8(2)(a)) or that 'the processing relates to data which are manifestly made public by the data subject' (art 8(2) (e)). At least when private spaces are being recorded, it is clear that only the first legal basis—explicit consent—would suffice.

39. Ibid art 6(1)(a). Absent a strict public interest test being satisfied (c/0.5), such processing would probably also have failed to satisfy a general legal *vires* set out in the Directive. Thus, in the exercise of essentially private as opposed to public law functions and in the absence of the consent of, or a contract with, the data subject, any processing had not only to be 'necessary for the purposes of the legitimate interests pursued by the controller or by the third party to whom the data are disclosed' but also could be 'overridden by the interests for fundamental rights and freedoms of the data subject' (DPD (n 3) art 7(f)). In practice, however, including this default provision and derogations from it within the categorization laid out would have made no difference to the pattern presented below.

40. See David Erdos, 'European Union Data Protection Law and Media Expression: Fundamentally Off-Balance' (2016) 65(1) ICLQ 139, 161–63. See also the summary set out in Appendix 4.

41. Austria, Finland, Sweden, and the five German DPA jurisdictions.

42. In Austria, the derogation applicable to the overarching fairness principle depended on the satisfaction of a permissive test grounded ultimately in a public interest analysis.

43. France, Gibraltar, Ireland, Latvia, Malta, and Poland.

44. The two exceptional cases were France and Latvia.

45. Belgium, Cyprus, and Luxembourg.
46. Bulgaria, Estonia, and Italy. Note that in Italy, section 2(1) of the Code of Conduct on the Processing of Personal Data in the Exercise of Journalistic Activities generally permitted a journalistic departure from the proactive transparency rule so long as this proved necessary but somewhat ambiguously did outlaw 'subterfuge' entirely.
47. In sum, Section 137.3 of the Italian Personal Data Protection Code provided that when data are communicated or disseminated in the exercise, and for the sole purpose, of the journalistic profession, 'the limitations imposed on the freedom of the protection to protect the rights [instantiated by the data protection regime], in particular concerning materiality of the information with regard to facts of public interest, shall be left unprejudiced. It shall be allowed to process the data concerning circumstances or events that have been made known either directly by the data subject or on account of the latter's public conduct.'
48. See Greece: Law 2472/1997 on the Protection of Individuals with regard to the Processing of Personal Data, art 7(2)(g) which provided that a permit could be 'exceptionally' granted but only when '[p]rocessing concerns data pertaining to public figures', 'that such data are in connection with the holding of public office or the management of third parties' interests', 'processing is absolutely necessary in order to ensure the right to information on matters of public interest, as well as within the framework of literary expression', and 'provided that the right to protection of private life is not violated in any whatsoever'. For completeness, it may be noted that the fairness principle continued to apply in full here, whilst the derogation from the proactive transparency rule also only applied when the processing 'refer[red] to public figures' (art 11(5)).
49. Czechia, Slovakia, Slovenia, and Spain Catalonia.
50. Hungary, Liechtenstein, Lithuania, and Portugal.
51. See Erdos (n 40).
52. DPD (n 3) art 14. It is just arguable that the applicability of the 'fair' processing principle could also have some impact on the duties of professional journalists in relation to subject access in certain circumstances. If so, then the categorization of Austrian and Lithuanian law as entirely excluding journalism from subject access would become questionable since the media in these cases was rendered fully (Lithuania) or partially (Austria) subject to this principle.
53. In Bulgaria, such shielding was clearly restricted to sources who were natural persons. In contrast, the Hungarian and Italian provisions were more wide-ranging and would, therefore, have also protected organizational sources.
54. Such qualifications were generally based on a permissive public interest test but in the case of Estonia depended on a strict public interest test and in Belgium on a minimal 'interference' test.
55. An analysis of these legislative stipulations is provided in Erdos (n 40) 161–63. The detailed coding that were thereby generated are also set out in provision eight of Appendix 4.
56. All these provisions were modelled on the German Interstate Treaty on Broadcasting and Telemedia, art 47(2). For the details see Germany: Federal Data Protection Act, ss 41(2)–(4); Landesmediengesetz (LMG) Rheinland-Pfalz, s 12; Staatsvertrag über das Medienrecht in Hamburg und Schleswig-Holstein (Medienstaatsvertrag HSH) s 37;

Landesrundfunkgesetz—RundfG M-V, s 61 and Staatsvertrag über die Errichtung einer gemeinsamen Rundfunkanstalt der Länder Berlin und Brandenburg, ss 36–37.

57. See generally Germany, Federal Data Protection Act, s 41(1) and additionally Landesmediengesetz (LMG) Rheinland-Pfalz, s 12; Landespressegesetz für das Land Mecklenburg-Vorpommern, s 18a; Landespressegesetz Schleswig-Holstein, s 10 and Brandenburgisches Landespressegesetz, s 16a.

58. Kaarle Nordenstreng and Ari Heinonen, 'EthicNet—Collection of Codes of Journalism Ethics in Europe' (*EthicNet*, June 2008) <http://ethicnet.uta.fi/> accessed 13 March 2018.

59. However, as a UK dependent territory, Gibraltar could be considered to be vicariously covered by UK entry which included two ethical codes.

60. In addition to Gibraltar and Liechtenstein where no codes were found at all, the codes for Latvia, Slovakia, and Sweden did not clearly address undercover journalistic methods. Outside of the jurisdictions whose DPAs participated in the questionnaire, such coverage was also found to be absent in the codes for Denmark and Iceland.

61. This was the case as regards the codes applicable to Cyprus, Czechia, France, Greece, Hungary, Italy, and Spain. Vagueness arose often from the use of somewhat ambiguous concepts such as not using 'dishonest means' (France). In the case of the Hungarian Code, the coding difficulty arose from it only setting out a necessity test for a resort to covert methods rather than explicitly referring to anything akin to the public interest.

62. Outside of those jurisdictions whose DPA was a respondent to this question, a strict public interest was also found in codes applicable to the Netherlands, Norway, Romania, and the United Kingdom.

63. Note, this codification of self-regulatory norms is ground on article 5 of the National Union of Journalists' Code of Conduct. If grounded on article 3(2) of the Code of Practice for Newspapers and Periodicals then the coding becomes b/0.25.

64. Section 2(1)(2) of the Ethical Code of the Bulgarian Media also explicitly required that the undercover methods be indicated in the published story.

65. Note, however, that the Polish Code of Journalistic Ethics uniquely restricted the meaning of 'public interest' here to journalism 'revealing crime, corruption or misuse of power' (art 5).

66. Note, however, that art 4 of the Portuguese Journalists' Code of Ethics does require that the public interest be 'unquestionable'.

67. Even here, certain complexities are apparent. Thus, as regards Ireland, although a permissive test was stated in Code of Practice for Newspapers and Periodicals, a strict test was laid down in the National Union of Journalists' Code of Conduct. Meanwhile, the Polish code severely narrowed the meaning of 'public interest' to journalism 'revealing crime, corruption or the misuse of power'.

68. German Press Code, guideline 8.8.

69. Luxembourgish Code of Deontology, art 12.

70. Italian Deontology Code, art 2(2).

71. Ibid art 2(3) (referring only to 'personal archives of journalists').

72. Similarly, no ethical guidance was found in relation to any of the jurisdictions whose DPA did not participate in the questionnaire.

73. Alongside the two jurisdictions where no codes were found at all (Gibraltar and Liechtenstein), the relevant provisions in Estonia stopped short of setting this out as a journalistic right or duty and no relevant provision was located in either the Austrian or Swedish codes. A similar lacuna was found in relation codes targeted at two jurisdictions whose DPA did not participate in the questionnaire, namely Croatia and Denmark. For the full results see Appendix 6.

74. German Press Code, guideline 5.1 (confidentiality may be non-binding if 'the information concerns a crime and there is a duty to inform the police' or if 'important reasons of state predominate, particularly if the constitutional order is affected or jeopardised'); Portugal: Journalists' Code of Ethics, art 6 (waiving duty where the journalist 'has been abused by false information'); Slovakia: Code of Ethics of the Slovak Syndicate of Journalists, art 3 (providing carve-out if journalist 'is exempted from this duty . . . by the court'); Spain (including Catalonia): Deontological Code for the Journalistic Profession, art 10 (providing for a derogation where 'the source has deliberately falsified information or if revealing the source is the only way to avoid serious and instant damage to people').

75. The reference in the Portuguese and Spanish codes to the (deliberate) provision of false information by a source (e.g. relating to a third-party natural person) could, however, be relevant in some cases.

76. Somewhat tallying this, the European Court of Human Rights held, albeit in a defamation rather than data protection context, that news archiving fell outside the 'primary function of the press' which was 'to act as a "public watchdog"' but constituted a 'valuable secondary role' of the Press, serving as 'an important source for education and historical research' (*Times Newspapers (Nos 1 and 2) v United Kingdom* [2009] EMLR 14 para 45).

77. The under-engagement of the EU Charter here dovetails with findings made within a broader data protection context. Thus, Porcedda's 2018 general study found that '[i]n their day-to-day practice, NDPAs [national Data Protection Authorities] do not seem to adhere to the theory of sources, but rather than follow a pragmatic approach dictated by their restricted mandate. This seems to challenge the formal primacy of the Charter': Maria Grazia Porcedda, *Use of the Charter of Fundamental Rights by National Data Protection Authorities and the EDPS* (Centre for Judicial Cooperation 2017) 3.

Chapter 7

1. Case C-131/12 *Google Spain SL and Google Inc v Agencia Española de Protección de Datos (AEPD)* [2014] 3 CMLR 50, para 38.

2. Hielke Hijmans, *The European Union as Guardian of Internet Privacy* (Springer 2016) 336.

3. European Union Agency for Fundamental Rights, 'Annual Report 2010' (*Europa*, 2010) <https://fra.europa.eu/sites/default/files/fra_uploads/917-AR_2010-conf-edition_en.pdf> 6 accessed 3 May 2019.

4. EU Charter of Fundamental Rights and Freedoms, art 8(2). Whilst clearly setting out a multi-faceted role for regulators, the DPD similarly emphasises the need for DPAs to be generally endowed with effective powers to investigate, intervene and engage in legal proceedings. See Council Directive 95/46/EC of 24 October 1995 on the protection of individuals with regard to the processing of personal data and on the free movement of such data [1995] OJ L281/31 art 28(3) ('DPD') and for further commentary Hielke Hijmans (n 2) 334–35.

5. EU Agency for Fundamental Rights (n 3) 8.

6. Neil Gunningham, 'Enforcement and Compliance Strategies' in Robert Baldwin, Martin Cave, and Martin Lodge, *The Oxford Handbook of Regulation* (Oxford University Press 2010) 120.

7. DPD (n 4) art 9.

8. Ibid recital 37.

9. In other words, 'a media entity producing a story concerning a living individual'.

10. These possibilities were presented to DPAs in the reverse order as 'No', 'Yes, but our powers are limited in this regard', and 'Yes'. They have been reordered and re-expressed for heuristic purposes.

11. See UK: Information Commissioner's Office, *What Price Privacy?* (The Stationary Office 2006).

12. Interestingly, the cognate provision in DPD (n 4) itself (art 7) conceptualized these legal bases not as true exceptions to consent but rather as equally valid bases for processing.

13. The reply further stated that 'the DPA would only step in whenever there is a case not covered by the existing legislation, and even then, it would have to strike the balance with other fundamental rights. Indeed, it never happened. The DPA does not receive complaints regarding the publication of personal data by the professional media.'

14. Namely, the Greek, Lithuanian, and Spanish Catalonian DPAs. Similar to its responses to the interpretative questions considered in Chapter 6, the Lithuanian DPA clarified that its responses in relation to enforcement activity had been filled in jointly with the Lithuanian Inspector of Journalist Ethics.

15. As will be become manifestly clear when the DPA website review data is considered later in this chapter, the Italian DPA had clearly engaged in a greatest range, as well as the greatest amount, of enforcement in this area.

16. In answering affirmatively to both these cases, the Greek DPA slightly altered the wording provided. In sum, it replaced the phrase 'action to prevent the processing/publication' with 'action to erase the published personal data'. In light of its broad legal meaning (DPD (n 4) art 2(b)), this activity would still constitute enforcement to prevent 'processing'. As a result, it was felt a standard response could still be recorded.

17. The Bulgarian DPA stated that it had conducted 'inspections and follow-up imposition of administration penalties to paper media' in connection with both 'unlawful personal data dissemination' and 'excessive personal data processing by media by publishing bigger amount of individuals' personal data then [sic] necessary for the performance of journalistic investigations and lack of adequate technical and organisation measure for protecting the data against unlawful dissemination'.

18. The Czech DPA stated that it had 'taken an action to remove an article containing personal data from the electronic media'.

19. The Luxembourg DPA provided a seemingly inconsistent response, ticking that it had both 'taken action to prevent the processing/personal data in contexts other than when data was obtained without authorization from another Data Controller' and that it had 'not taken any enforcement action in relation to media entities' pursuit of their journalistic activities'. Whilst this can't be definitively determined, it seems quite possible that it had accidentally ticked the options immediately below the statements it meant to assent to which, if correct, would suggest that it had undertaken a variety of diffuse enforcement activities both as regards data obtained without authorisation and in other cases.

20. The Maltese DPA stated that it had 'taken action to ensure removal of contents from journalistic blogs or media related internet publications which involved the unlawful processing of personal data'.

21. The UK DPA stated that although it had not undertaken enforcement action 'in the sense of issuing enforcement notices or monetary penalties' it had carried out 'other forms of regulatory action' including 'most notably' publishing 'two reports on the use of private investigators by the media' which 'focused on the unauthorized obtaining of personal information in pursuit of journalistic activity'.

22. The responses from both the Finnish and French DPAs did indicate enforcement activity against news archives, despite stating in relation to the previous general enforcement track-record question that they 'not taken any enforcement action in relation to media entities' pursuit of their journalistic activities'. This may reflect an agreement with the suggestion made in Italian DPA guidance considered in Chapter 6 that at least some newspaper archives fell outside the scope of the media's journalistic activities.

23. Interestingly, both the Czech and Maltese DPAs indicated that they had not undertaken any such enforcement, despite stating in response to the previous *general enforcement track-record* question that they had ordered certain journalistic material to be removed online (n 18 and 20). These apparently divergent responses vividly highlight the difficulties of defining archiving in a now ubiquitous online environment.

24. Whilst stating that it had undertaken enforcement action in relation to a range of cognate actors, the Austrian DPA did not positively assert the same in relation to news archives. It nevertheless stated that its 'list is probably incomplete as we are unable to search all case files of the last decade. It is quite likely that action has been taken against any kind of actor at least once.'

25. Namely, the Danish Press Council (alongside the Danish DPA) and Lithuanian Inspector of Journalism Ethics (alongside the Lithuanian DPA).

26. Gunningham (n 6) 126.

27. Given its very close temporal proximity to when Latvia became a full EEA member, these findings were nevertheless treated as confirming relevant enforcement activity.

28. For one such example, see Estonia: Data Protection Inspectorate, 'Ettekirjutused' (*AKI*, 14 January 2019) <http://www.aki.ee/et/menetluspraktika/ettekirjutused> accessed 20 May 2019.

29. This, in part, may relate to the fact that 'processes for resolving privacy complaints are often carried out in private' (International Conference of Data Protection and Privacy Commissioners, 'Resolution on Case Reporting' (*ICDPPC*, 2009) <https://icdppc. org/wp-content/uploads/2015/02/Resolution-on-Case-Reporting.pdf> accessed 20 May 2019).

30. The review revealed a roughly equal number of examples of enforcement action which could best be characterized as involving material obtained without authorization and enforcement which appeared to relate to other issues. In sum, enforcement actions falling into the former category were found on seven DPA websites (two of which provided a non-standard response to the survey) and those falling within the latter category on eight DPA websites (one of which had provided a non-standard response to the survey). However, partly as a result of the limited information that was sometimes disclosed on the DPA website, the attempt to place examples in one or other of these categories was no easy task and, in some cases, proved impossible.

31. Paul McNally, 'Freelancers threatened with data protection fine' (*Press Gazette*, 8 August 2008) <http://www.pressgazette.co.uk/node/41852> accessed 20 May 2019.

32. Italy, Garante per la Protezione dei Dati Personali, 'Speech by Francesco Pizzetti, President of the Italian Data Protection Authority Introducing the Annual Report for 2008–2009' (*Garante Privacy*, 2 July 2009) <https://www.garanteprivacy.it/en/home/docweb/-/docweb-display/docweb/1630962> accessed 20 July 2018.

33. Unlike in a number of other EEA States, in Iceland data relating to the deceased remained protected as personal data. See Iceland, Act on the Protection of Privacy as regards the Processing of Personal Data, art 2 (1).

34. Iceland: Persónvernd, 'Ársskýrsla Persónuverndar 2003' (*Personuvernd*, 2003) <http://www.personuvernd.is/utgefid-efni/arsskyrslur/2003/> accessed 20 May 2019. Interestingly, three years later, and also in response to a complaint against the same newspaper, this DPA held that it had no authority to rule on journalistic matters. See Iceland: Persónvernd, 'Persónuvernd Ársskýrsla 2006' (*Personuvernd*, 2006) <http://www.personuvernd.is/media/frettir/arsskyrsla2006.pdf> 45-47 accessed 20 May 2019.

35. A list of, and links to, all the Greek DPA media cases referenced here can be found at Greece, Hellenic Data Protection Authority, '14) Μέσα Μαζικής Ενημέρωσης' (*DPA*, 2018) <http://www.dpa.gr/portal/page?_pageid=33%2C15453&_dad=portal&_schema=PORTAL&_piref33_15473_33_15453_15453.etos=-1&_piref33_15473_33_15453_15453.arithmosApofasis=&_piref33_15473_33_15453_15453.thematikiEnotita=187&_piref33_15473_33_15453_15453.ananeosi=%CE%91%CE%BD%CE%B1%CE%BD%CE%AD%CF%89%CF%83%CE%B7> accessed 20 May 2019.

36. Bulgaria: Комисия за защита на личните данни, 'РЕШЕНИЕ № 14/19.03.2009 г' (*CPDP*, 19 March 2009) <http://www.cpdp.bg/index.php?p=element_view&aid=145> accessed 20 May 2019.

37. Bulgaria: Комисия за защита на личните данни, 'РЕШЕНИЕ № 69/23.01.2008 г' (*CPDP*, 23 January 2008) <https://www.cpdp.bg/index.php?p=element_view&aid=105> accessed 20 May 2019.

38. Italy: Garante per la Protezione dei Dati Personali, 'Privacy e giornalismo' (*Garante Priv acy*, 2012) <http://www.garanteprivacy.it/web/guest/home/docweb/-/docweb-display/docweb/1858277> accessed 20 May 2019, 111–13. For a wide range of other such cases pursued by the Italian DPA see 135–68.

39. Netherlands: College Berscherming Persoonsgegevens, 'Jaaverslag 2012' (*Autoriteitpe rsoonsgegevens*, 2012) <https://autoriteitpersoonsgegevens.nl/sites/default/files/downloads/jaarverslagen/jv_2012.pdf> 9–10 accessed 20 May 2019.

40. Slovenia: Information Commissioner, 'Decision 0613-1/2006-22' (*IP-RS*, 6 June 2006) <https://www.ip-rs.si/index.php?id=379> accessed 20 May 2019. Similarly to Iceland (n 34) and Italy (n 41), in Slovenia data relating to the deceased continued to be regulated under data protection. See Slovenia, Personal Data Protection Act, art 23.

41. Italy: Garante per la protezione dei dati personali, 'Introduction to Annual Report 2008–09' (*Garante Privacy*, 2009) <http://www.garanteprivacy.it/web/guest/home/docweb/-/docweb-display/docweb/1630962> accessed 20 May 2019. This case would appear to relate to the death of Meredith Kercher. Similarly to Iceland (n 34) and Slovenia (n 40), data concerning the deceased fell within the scope of second generation Italian data protection. See Italy, Personal Data Protection Code, s 9(3).

42. Ibid and Italy: *Privacy e giornalismo* (n 38) 210–15. In contrast, the DPA upheld the legality under data protection of pictures taken nearby of individuals on a beach and on a pontoon.

43. Cyprus: Επιτρόπου Προστασίας Δεδομένων Προσωπικού Χαρακτήρα, 'ΑΠΟΦΑΣΗ: Δημοσίευση υπερβολικών δεδομένων στην εφημερίδα «ΠΟΛΙΤΗΣ»' <http://www.dataprotection.gov.cy/dataprotection/dataprotection.nsf/All/878B2BB3BB9C507FC2257914003A27B9?OpenDocument> accessed 20 May 2019.

44. Slovenia: Information Commissioner, 'Annual Report 2009' (*IP-RS*, 2009) <https://www.ip-rs.si/fileadmin/user_upload/Pdf/porocila/Annual-report-2009.pdf> 31 accessed 20 May 2019.

45. 'Poland in uproar over leak of spy files' *Guardian Online* (London, 5 February 2005) <https://www.theguardian.com/world/2005/feb/05/poland> accessed 20 May 2019.

46. Wildstein himself claimed that he had only send the list to a few trusted colleagues (and, therefore, that somebody else must have been responsible for the final publication).

47. Poland: Generalny Inspektor Ochrony Danych Osobowych, 'Judgment of the Voivodeship Administrative Court in the Case of the Decision of the Inspector General for Data Protection Concerning the Institute of National Remembrance' (*GIODO*, 20068) <http://www.giodo.gov.pl/259/id_art/347/j/en/> accessed 29 August 2013.

48. Bulgaria: Комисия за защита на личните данни, 'РЕШЕНИЕ № 551/11 г' (*CPDP*, 22 June 2011) <https://www.cpdp.bg/index.php?p=element_view&aid=503> accessed 21 May 2019.

49. Latvia: Datu valst inspekcija, '2003.gada darba rezultāti' (*DVI*, 2003) <http://www.dvi.gov.lv/lv/wp-content/uploads/inspekcija/gada-parskati/2003.pdf> 19–20 accessed 1 November 2016. The DPA specifically stated that a warning only had been issued in the latter case as the infraction was unintentional.

50. Lithuania: Žurnalistų etikos inspektorė, 'Surašytas administracinis nurodymas laikraščio "Palangos tiltas" redaktoriui-direktoriui' (*LRS*) <http://www.lrs.lt/intl/zeit.show?theme=781&lang=1&doc=3133> accessed 3 June 2014.

51. Slovenia: Information Commissioner, 'Annual Report 2007' (*IP-RS*, 2007) <https://www.ip-rs.si/fileadmin/user_upload/Pdf/porocila/Letno-porocilo-07-ang.pdf> 32–33 accessed 1 November 2016.

52. Italy: Garante per la protezione dei dati personali, 'Annual Report for 2006—Summary' (*Garante Privacy*, 2006) <http://www.garanteprivacy.it/web/guest/home/docweb/-/docweb-display/docweb/1750262> accessed 1 November 2016.

53. UK: Information Commissioner's Office (n 11) 5.

54. Ibid 6.

55. Ibid.

56. Ibid 9.

57. See UK: Brian Leveson, *Inquiry into the Culture, practices and Ethics of the Press* (HC 2012, 780–I).

58. See section 2.5.1 of Chapter 5.

59. See (n 32, 41, and 42). For details of these and a number of other cases see generally Italy: *Privacy e giornalismo* (n 38) 207–25.

60. See The Netherlands: College Berscherming Persoonsgegevens (n 39).

61. Hungary: Nemzeti Adatvédelmi és Információszabadság Hatóság, 'Az Adatvédelmi biztos beszámolója 2007: Case 1848/K/2007' (*NAIH*, 2007) <http://www.naih.hu/files/ Adatvedelmi-biztos-beszamoloja-2007.PDF> 137–38 accessed 6 June 2019 (arguing that in cases where illegality is alleged the information should not be published on the web but the Prosecutor's Office should be informed).

62. Hungary: Nemzeti Adatvédelmi és Információszabadság Hatóság, 'Beszámoló az adatvédelmi bistos 2010. évi tevékenységéröl' (*NAIH*, 2010) <http://www.naih.hu/files/ Adatvedelmi-biztos-beszamoloja-2010.PDF> 150–51 accessed 21 May 2019.

63. 'Sentencia De la Audiencia Nacional de 24-01.2003. Sala de lo contenciosoadministrativo. Sección primera. Tratamiento de datos de carácter personal a través de imágenes captadas por una webcam y su transmisión a través de Internet' (*AGPD*, 2003) <https://web.archive.org/web/20120706174234/https://www. agpd.es/portalwebAGPD/canaldocumentacion/sentencias/common/Sentencia-De-la-Audiencia-Nacional-de24.pdf> accessed 22 May 2019.

64. *Privacy e giornalismo* (n 38) 116–20. In a separate case, the DPA upheld the legality of a television network publishing a video of a friar sexually harassing a young male acquaintance (who had taken the undercover video himself). Although the friar still considered himself identifiable, the network had taken numerous steps to mask the identity of the individuals including blacking out the face and masking the voice (121–23).

65. The case's outcome was also integrated into the Irish DPA's general guidance. See Ireland: Data Protection Commissioner, 'Case Study 6 of 2006: News of the World: Limits of the Media Exemption' (*DPC*, 18 December 2017) <https://web. archive.org/web/20171218003648/https://www.dataprotection.ie/ViewDoc.asp?fn=% 2Fdocuments%2Fcasestudies%2FCategoryCS%2Ehtm&CatID=10&m=c> accessed 21 May 2019.

66. *Privacy e giornalismo* (n 38) 132–33.

67. *Privacy e giornalismo* (n 38) 126–31.

68. DPD (n 4) art 2(2).

69. Italy: Garante per la protezione dei dati personali, 'Relazione 2004' (*Garante Privacy*, 2004) <https://www.garanteprivacy.it/documents/10160/10704/1093820> 55–56 accessed 20 July 2018. This DPA's action against the continued publication of images taken off Facebook (see n 32) would presumably also have required their deletion from external online archives.

70. Namely, *'nota immobiliarista milanese'* ('well-known Milan real estate agent').

71. Italy: Garante per la Protezione dei Dati Personali, 'Provvedimento del 9 novembre 2005 [1200127]' (*Garante Privacy*, 2005) <https://www.garanteprivacy.it/web/guest/ home/docweb/-/docweb-display/docweb/1200127> accessed 20 July 2018.

72. *Privacy e giornalismo* (n 38) 239–41.

73. Admittedly, this DPA's 2004 intervention did involve the republication of old data but in a new article.

74. See section 2.1 of Chapter 4.

75. Italy: Garante per la Protezione dei Dati Personali, 'Annual Report for 2008—Summary' (*Garante Privacy*, 2008) <https://www.garanteprivacy.it/en/home/docweb/-/docweb-display/docweb/1750199> accessed 21 May 2019.

76. *Privacy e giornalismo* (n 38) 230–35. This book details a further case where such deindexing was ordered (ibid 226–230) as well as one (which related to 1990s news reports concerning the judicial investigation of an individual who was still a leading political figure) where it was not (235–38).

77. Italy: Garante per la Protezione dei Dati Personali, 'Speech by Francesco Pizzetti, President of the Italian Data Protection Authority Introducing the Annual Report for 2008–2009' (*Garante Privacy*, 2 July 2009) <https://www.garanteprivacy.it/web/guest/home/docweb/-/docweb-display/docweb/1630962> accessed 20 July 2018.

78. Belgium: Commission de la protection de la vie privée, 'Rapport annuel (2011)' (*Privacy Commission*, 2011) <https://web.archive.org/web/20120829001519/http://www.privacycommission.be/sites/privacycommission/files/documents/rapport-annuel-2011.pdf> 52–53 accessed 7 August 2013.

79. Spain: Agencia Española de Protección de Datos, 'Procedimento No TD/01887/2009 Resolución No R/01680/2010' (*AEPD.es*, 2009) <https://www.aepd.es/resoluciones/TD-01887-2009_REC.pdf> accessed 25 August 2013.

80. Spain: Agencia Española de Protección de Datos, 'Procedimento No TD/00030/2010 Resolución No R/00962/2010' (*AEPD*, 2010) <https://www.aepd.es/resoluciones/TD-00030-2010_REC.pdf> accessed 25 August 2013.

81. Case C-131/12 *Google Spain* (n 1).

82. Namely, the correlation between the DPA website review's enforcement binary and both the statutory law measure of regulatory powers and the measure of regulatory stringency. The last correlation came extremely close to achieving such significance.

83. It may be argued that, since this study was looking at enforcement since the transposition of DPD up until 2013, it would be appropriate to drop the enforcement activity measures for Croatia (which only joined the EEA in 2013, the same year as the survey) and augment the enforcement activity measures for the Eastern European jurisdictions as well as Cyprus and Malta which only became subject to EEA law well after 24 October 1998 when transposition of the DPD was generally required (see DPD (n 4) art 32(1)). Whilst the three non-EU EEA States only became subject to the DPD on 26 June 1999, this seven-month gap is clearly too small to exert a significant effect on the results and so no adjustment can be considered warranted. Augmentation can be achieved by adjusting both enforcement measures to reflect the fact that, whilst the study generally probed fourteen and a half years of potential enforcement, Bulgaria and Romania only joined the EU on 1 January 2007 and therefore 'lost' around eight years of potential enforcement (55 per cent of the total period), whilst the other relevant States joined on 1 May 2004 and therefore similarly 'lost' approximately five and a half years (approximately 38 per cent of the total period). Such an adjustment tended to strengthen not weaken the correlations here. In sum, the formal law correlations with the augmented

DPA questionnaire enforcement extent figure shifted to 0.398** (sig. 0.024), 0.743*** (sig. 0.000), and 0.671*** (sig. 0.000). Meanwhile, the correlations with the augmented DPA website enforcement binary shifted to 0.172 (sig. 0.158), 0.338** (sig. 0.022), and 0.301** (sig. 0.037).

84. Article 29 Working Party, 'Seventeenth Report Covering the Year 2013' (*Europa*, 2016) <https://publications.europa.eu/en/publication-detail/-/publication/675c47e0-b864-11e6-9e3c-01aa75ed71a1/language-en> accessed 21 May 2019.

85. Amongst the more technical difficulties, DPAs did not generally differentiate between either financial or staffing resources allocated to data protection as opposed (in a few cases) also to others activities, for example freedom of information. This, therefore, could not be taken into account. As regards staffing, Portugal provided figures which were averaged and otherwise data on full-time equivalents (FTEs) were preferred to other data. Turning to the budgeting figures, three DPAs only provided 'approximate' figures here which were therefore used. Three more DPAs provided two figures (e.g. budget as allocated and budget as executed) and in these cases an average of these was taken. In addition, six DPAs provided figures only in currencies other than the Euro. In these cases, a conversation was made according to the average relevant exchange rate throughout 2013 as provided by the European Central Bank.

86. For an analysis of correlations between media enforcement measures (excluding news archives) and resourcing based on financial data alone (as self-reported by DPAs in the questionnaire), see David Erdos, 'Statutory Regulation of Professional Journalism Under European Data Protection: Down But Not Out?' (2016) 8(2) Journal of Media Law 229, 255. The analysis was performed before the Article 29 Working Party made the financial and staffing figures available.

87. Use of augmented enforcement figures for Eastern Europe, Cyprus, and Malta and dropping of Croatia as specified in (n 83) slightly strengthened both the reported negative and the reported positive correlations but otherwise made little difference. In sum, the correlations with the augmented DPA questionnaire enforcement extent figure shifted to –0.445** (sig. 0.037), –0.009 (sig. 0.487), –0.174 (sig. 0.253), and 0.454** (sig. 0.034). Meanwhile, the correlations with the augmented DPA website enforcement binary shifted to –0.92 (sig. 0.331), –0.173 (sig. 0.205), 0.136 (sig. 0.254), and 0.172 (sig. 0.201).

88. Namely, the German Brandenburg, German Mecklenberg-Vorpommern, German Rhineland-Palatinate, and the Dutch DPAs.

89. Namely, the Finnish and Swedish DPAs.

90. Hugh Grant, 'Introduction' in Brian Cathcart (ed), *Everybody's Hacked Off: Why We Don't Have the Press We Deserve and What to Do About It* (Penguin 2012) viii.

91. See section 4.2 of Chapter 11.

92. See David Erdos, 'European Data Protection Regulation and Online New Media: Mind the Enforcement Gap' (2016) 43(3) Journal of Law and Society 534, 546. This value has been calculated from the figures reported in Table Two of this article excluding that of newspaper archives which are not entirely 'new' media actors.

93. DPD (n 41) art 18.

94. See Appendix 4, provision 17 noting that the substantive figures for Germany cover all the German DPA jurisdictions, whilst those for Spain cover both the Spanish federal and the Catalan DPA jurisdictions. Details of how all the granular codings were arrived at are provided in David Erdos, 'European Union Data Protection Law and Media Expression: Fundamentally Off-Balance' (2016) 65(1) ICLQ 139.

95. DPD (n 4) art 12(a).

96. See both 'Subject Access: Simplified Coding of Statute' in Appendix 5 and provision 8 in Appendix 4. Even if we exclude the German DPAs which in fact had no statutory power to enforce these provisions, this figure only reduces to 18 (69 per cent).

97. See provision 4 in Appendix 4. Again, if the German DPAs with no regulatory powers here are excluded, this figure only reduces to 20 (77 per cent).

98. See Chart 6.5 (112). Furthermore, a number of other provisions, including those requiring the universal registration of journalistic processing with a statutory regulator i.e. the DPA, could also be considered to unreasonably to interfere with freedom of expression and it may be that some DPAs held off enforcing these on that basis.

99. Leveson Inquiry (n 57) 673.

100. UK: Office of Communications, *Annual Report and Accounts for the Period 1 April 2013 to 31 March 2014* (Stationary Office 2014) 85.

101. European Union Agency for Fundamental Rights, 'Access to Data Protection Remedies in EU Member States' (*Europa*, 2013) <http://fra.europa.eu/sites/default/files/fra-2014-access-data-protection-remedies_en.pdf> 46 accessed 26 July 2018.

102. Leveson Inquiry (n 57) 11. See also the findings cited by Lara Fielden (n 115).

103. See especially Table 5.4 (83-84).

104. See section 2.4 of Chapter 5and especially Table 5.5 (91-92).

105. See section 3.3 of Chapter 6.

106. See, in particular, Table 6.3 (116).

107. Susanne Fengler and others, 'How effective is media self-regulation? Results from a comparative survey of European journalists' (2015) 30(3) European Journal of Communication 249.

108. Mihai Coman and others, 'Romania: Twenty Years of Professionalization in Journalism—still Counting' in Tobias Eberwein and others (eds), *Mapping Media Accountability—in Europe and Beyond* (Herbert von Halem Verlag 2011) 142.

109. Salvador Alsius, Marcel Mauri, and Ruth Rodríguez Martínez, 'Spain: A Diverse and Asymmetric Landscape' in Tobias Eberwein and others (eds), *Mapping Media Accountability—in Europe and Beyond* (Herbert von Halem Verlag 2011) 155.

110. Fengler and others (n 107) 252.

111. See Daniel Hallin and Paolo Mancini, *Comparing Media Systems: Three Models of Media and Politics* (Cambridge University Press 2014).

112. Matthias Karmasin and others, 'Austria: A Border-Crosser' in Tobias Eberwein and others (eds), *Mapping Media Accountability—in Europe and Beyond* (Herbert von Halem Verlag 2011) 22.

113. Leveson Inquiry (n 57) 739.

114. Ibid 1579.

115. Lara Fielden, 'Regulating the Press: A Comparative Study of International Press Councils', (*INFORRM*, 3 May 2012) <https://inforrm.org/2012/05/03/regulating-the-press-a-comparative-study-of-international-press-councils-lara-fielden/> accessed 27 July 2018. Although the Press Council's responsibilities in relation to data protection are specified in the *Lov om massemediers inofmrationsdatabaser*, its responsibilities are primarily laid out in the Media Liability Act 1998.

116. See Table 7.1 (127-128) noting the responses of the German Rhineland-Palatinate, Greek, Luxembourg, and Portuguese DPAs. Whilst the structures noted by the German Rhineland-Palatinate and Luxembourg DPAs were clearly self-regulatory, the bodies in the other cases appear co-regulatory or perhaps even examples of specialist state regulation.

117. Leveson Inquiry (n 57) 1051.

118. Ibid 1070–71.

Chapter 8

1. Council Regulation 2016/679/EU of 27 April 2016 on the protection of natural persons with regard to the processing of personal data and on the free movement of such data, and repealing Directive 95/46/EC [2016] OJ L119/1, recital 153 ('GDPR').

2. Ibid.

3. Council Directive 95/46/EC of 24 October 1995 on the protection of individuals with regard to the processing of personal data and on the free movement of such data [1995] OJ L281/31, recital 37 ('DPD').

4. GDPR (n 1) arts 40–41.

5. DPD (n 3) arts 22–24.

6. GDPR (n 1) art 77(1).

7. Ibid art 77(2).

8. Ibid art 83.

9. Ibid art 78.

10. See EU Charter of Fundamental Rights and Freedoms, art 8(2).

11. The accompanying recital also clarified that where the derogations differ 'from one Member State to another, the law of the Member State to which the controller is subject should apply'.

12. One remedial provision in the GDPR, namely the 'right to erasure ('right to be forgotten')', was directly disapplied to the extent that processing was 'necessary for exercising the right of freedom of expression and information'. See GDPR (n 1) art 17(3)(a).

13. European Commission, 'Proposal for a Regulation of the European Parliament and of the Council on the protection of individuals with regard to the processing of personal data and on the free movement of such data (General Data Protection Regulation)' COM (2012) 11 final.

14. Case C-73/07 *Tietosuojavaltuutettu v Satakunnan Markkinapörssi Oy and Satamedia Oy* [2007] ECR I-7075.

15. The original Commission, European Parliament and Council versions of the GDPR may all be found in Council of the European Union, 'Document 10391/15' (*Europa*, 8 July 2015) <http://data.consilium.europa.eu/doc/document/ST-10391-2015-INIT/en/pdf> accessed 28 April 2019.

16. Commission (n 13) art 80(1).
17. European Commission High Level Group on Media Freedom and Pluralism, 'A Free and Pluralistic Media to Sustain European Democracy' (*Europa*, 2013) <https://ec.europa.eu/digital-single-market/sites/digital-agenda/files/HLG%20Final%20Report.pdf> 3 accessed 28 April 2019.
18. Commission (n 13) art 80(2).
19. GDPR (n 1) art 85(3).
20. Ibid art 79(5)(g). Strangely, this provision was limited to cases *not* involving special/sensitive personal data. An inter-Commission version of the text leaked in late 2011 indicated that this reflected an initial proposal to include a requirement to provide for a more stringent fine (of between €100K and €1M or 5 per cent of annual global turnover) in cases involving special/sensitive personal data processing. See art 79(4)(b) at European Commission, 'Proposal for a Regulation of the European Parliament and of the Council on the protection of individuals with regard to the processing of personal data and on the free movement of such data (General Data Protection Regulation)' (29 December 2011) <http://statewatch.org/news/2011/dec/eu-com-draft-dp-reg-inter-service-consultation.pdf> accessed 28 April 2019.
21. As of the end of May 2019, such notifications were also not available for Czechia, Iceland, Italy, Malta, Liechtenstein, Norway, and Spain. Finally, the UK notification did not address the position of Gibraltar. See European Commission, 'EU Member States notifications to the European Commission under the GDPR' (*Europa*) <https://ec.europa.eu/info/law/law-topic/data-protection/data-protection-eu/eu-countries-gdpr-specific-notifications_en> accessed 26 April 2019.
22. Italy: Decreto legislativo 10 agosto 2018, n 101 ('2018 Italian Legislative Decree').
23. See Decreto Legislativo 30 giugno 2003 (as amended), n 196, arts 136–138 ('2003 Amended Italian Legislative Decree').
24. Ibid art 139.
25. 2018 Italian Legislative Decree (n 22) art 20. The continuing temporary legal effect of the journalism code has been specified in Italy: Regole deontologiche relative al trattamento di dati personali nell'esercizio dell'attività giornalistica pubblicate—29 novembre 2018.
26. For a summary of the laws consulted see Appendix 3. The analysis also looked at the notifications made to the European Commission here. However, in almost all cases, these notifications simply refer to the relevant provisions in the laws themselves. A notable exception to this was Hungary's which mentions a number of legal provisions outside of data protection which somehow related to freedom of expression. See 'IGAZSAGOGYI MINISZTERIUM KECSMAR KRISZTIAN európai uniós es nemzetkozi igazsagugyi egyuttmukodesert felelos allamtitkar' (*Europa*, 2018) <https://ec.europa.eu/info/sites/info/files/hu_notification_art_51.4_84.2_85.3_88.3_90.2_publish.pdf> accessed 26 April 2019. These provisions were not mentioned specifically in the Hungarian data protection law itself, and neither did this law formally establish that it was subordinate within the legal hierarchy to these other provisions. Therefore, for the purposes of the analysis below, these other laws have not been taken into account. Meanwhile, the German notification exhaustively details relevant laws across each of the *Länder* (as well as the federal level). See 'Notifizierungspflichtige Vorschriften Deutschlands gemäß der

Verordnung (EU) 2016/679' (*Europa*, 2018) <https://ec.europa.eu/info/sites/info/files/de_notification_articles_49.5_51.4_83.9_84.2_85.3_88.3_90.2_publish.pdf > accessed 26 April 2019. In light both of the great complexity of these provisions and the fact that only some have been specifically updated as a result of the GDPR, reliance was instead placed on the provisions in the newly redrafted inter-*Länder* agreement in this area, namely, sections 9c and 57 of the Staatsvertrag für Rundfunk und Telemedien.

27. Examples of statutory provisions which fall within each of these categories may be found the cognate table in Table 5.2 in Chapter 5 (74-75).

28. Sweden: Lag (2018:218) med kompletterande bestämmelser till EU:s dataskyddsförordning, s 7 ('Lag (2018:218)').

29. Norway: Personopplysningsloven, s 3.

30. Germany: Staatsvertrag für Rundfunk und Telemedien, s 9(c) ('German Broadcasting Treaty').

31. Iceland: Lög um persónuvernd og vinnslu persónuupplýsinga, art 6 ('Icelandic Personal Data Protection and Processing Act').

32. Poland: Ustawa z dnia 10 maja 2018 r o ochronie danych osobowych, art 2.1.

33. Finland: Tietosuojalaki, s 27.

34. In sum, derogation is only possible where it is shown that the application of the restrictions would violate the right to freedom of expression or information.

35. Ireland: Data Protection Act 2018, s 43(1).

36. See UK: Data Protection Act 2018, sch 2, pt 5, para 26 and Gibraltar: Data Protection 2004 (Amendment) Regulations 2018, sch 2, pt 5, para 22.

37. Cyprus: περί της Προστασίας των Φυσικών Προσώπων Έναντι της Επεξεργασίας των Δεδομένων Προσωπικού Χαρακτήρα και της Ελεύθερης Κυκλοφορίας των Δεδομένων αυτών Νόμος του 2018, s 29(2).

38. Ibid s 29(1).

39. Namely, the data protection principles (provisions (i)–(v)), the proactive transparency rule where data is collected directly from the data subject (vi), the processing registration requirement (xviii), and the data export restrictions (xviii). It is notable that none of these provisions refer only to the lawfulness of processing narrowly conceived.

40. Netherlands: Wet van 16 mei 2018 Uitvoeringswet Algemene verordening gegevensbescherming, arts 43(1)–(2) ('Dutch Data Protection Act 2018').

41. Ibid art 43(3).

42. Belgium: Loi relative à la traitements de données à caractère personnel, art 24(2) ('Belgian Data Protection Act').

43. Ibid art 24(1).

44. Austria: Federal Act Concerning the Protection of Personal Data, s 9.

45. Fizisko personu datu apstrādes likums, art 32(2) ('Latvian Personal Data Processing Law').

46. Ibid art 32(1).

47. Закон за изменение и допълнение на Закона за защита на личните данни, art 25h(1) ('Amended Bulgarian Law on the Protection of Personal Data').

48. Ibid art 25h(2).

49. Ibid art 25h(1).

50. Asmens Duomenų Teisinės Apsaugos Įstatymo NR I-1374 Pakeitimo Įstatymas, art 4 ('Lithuanian Amended Data Protection Law').

51. See Malta: Data Protection Act 2018, s 9 (*emphasis* added).
52. France: Ordonnance n° 2018–1125, art 80. Note that, uniquely amongst the EU States, France has 'transposed' most of the GDPR's default provisions into its domestic law. Therefore, in most cases, the derogations explicitly cite these domestic provisions. For the purposes of this coding, these references are understood to also implicitly reference the cognate GDPR provisions themselves.
53. Legea nr 190/2018 Regulamentul general privind protecția datelor, art 7 ('Legea nr 190/2018').
54. Ibid.
55. Estonia: Personal Data Protection Act 2007, s 11(2) (see Appendix 2).
56. Estonia: Personal Data Protection Act 2018, s 4.
57. The excising of this term was checked by consulting the original language version of the old legislation (*Isikuandmete kaitse seadus*) at Riigikogu, 'Isikuandmete kaitse seadus' (*Riigiteataja*, 30 June 2014) <https://www.riigiteataja.ee/akt/130122010011> accessed 9 May 2019.
58. The general role played by consent under the GDPR is different from the role it played under Estonia's erstwhile transposition of the DPD through its Personal Data Protection Act 2008 (n 55). As a result, the coding of the law is somewhat modified here compared to the *status quo ante*. For an analysis of the previous position see David Erdos, 'European Union Data Protection Law and Media Expression: Fundamentally Off Balance' (2016) 65(1) ICLQ 139, 152–53.
59. GDPR (n 1) art 9(2)(a).
60. Ibid art 49.
61. 2003 Amended Italian Legislative Decree (n 23); 2018 Italian Legislative Decree (n 22).
62. Luxembourg: Loi du 1er août 2018 portant organisation de la Commission nationale pour la protection des données et mise en oeuvre du règlement (UE) 2016/679 ('2018 Luxembourg Data Protection Act') art 62.
63. Estonia: Zákon z 29 novembra 2017 o ochrane osobných údajov a o zmene a doplnení niektorých zákonov, s 78(1).
64. Liechtenstein: Datenschutzgesetz (DSG) art 25.
65. 2018 Luxembourg Data Protection Act (n 62) art 62.
66. In particular, the first article of this code states *inter alia* that '[t]he journalistic profession is carried out without being subject to authorisation or censorship as provided for by Article 21 of the Italian Constitution. On account of its being a prerequisite for freedom of the press, the fact of collecting, recording, keeping and disseminating information on facts and occurrences concerning persons, collective entities, official bodies, custom, scientific research and intellectual movements—when carried out within the scope of journalistic activity and for the relevant purposes—is essentially different in nature from the storage and processing of personal data by databases or other entities'. See Italy: Code of Conduct on the Processing of Personal Data in the Exercise of Journalistic Activities ('Italian Data Protection Journalism Code'), art. 1(2).
67. Czechia: Zákon o zpracování osobních údajů, s 17(1).
68. Denmark: Databeskyttelsesloven, ss 3(6) and 3(8) ('Danish Data Protection Act').
69. Denmark: *Lov om massemediers informationsdatabaser*, s 3(8).
70. Ibid s 3(9).

71. Ibid s 3(8).
72. Ibid s 1(2).
73. Denmark: Media Liability Act 1998, s 34.
74. See especially in German Broadcasting Treaty (n 30) ss 9c(1) and 57(1).
75. Ibid art 9c(3).
76. Ibid art 57(2).
77. Italian Data Protection Journalism Code (n 66), art 2(1) (granted continuing temporary legal effect as specified in Italy: Regole deontologiche (n 25)). Note that the complete prohibition on 'subterfuge' is particularly far-reaching.
78. Ibid art 2(2).
79. 2018 Italian Legislative Decree (n 22) art 138.
80. 2018 Luxembourg Data Protection Act (n 62) arts 62(3)–(4).
81. Ibid art 62(5).
82. Zákon o zpracování (n 67) s 18.
83. Ibid s 18(1).
84. Ibid s 18(32.
85. Ibid s 18(1).
86. GDPR (n 1) art 14(5)(b).
87. Zákon o zpracování (n 67) s 18(2).
88. Ibid s 19(2).
89. Denmark: *Lov om massemediers informationsdatabaser,* s 11(1).
90. German Broadcasting Treaty (n 30) ss 9c(3) and 57(2).
91. Ibid s 57(2).
92. Luxembourg Data Protection Act 2018 (n 62) art 62(1).
93. Art 10 of the Italian Data Protection Journalism Code (n 66) states that journalists 'must avoid publishing analysis data of exclusively clinical interest' and further that '[i]n referring to the health of an identified or identifiable person, journalists must respect his/her dignity, right to privacy and decorum especially in cases of severe or terminal diseases'. Nevertheless, as a highly qualified, rule-based restriction to this it is stated that '[p]ublication is allowed for the purpose of ensuring that that all material information is disclosed and by respecting a person's dignity, if such person plays an especially important social or public role'.
94. Art 11 of the Italian Data Protection Journalism Code (n 66) states baldly that journalists 'must avoid reporting the sex life of any identified or identifiable person'. The same rule-based caveat is then stated to apply in relation to health data under art 10.
95. Thus, art 5 of the Code (n 66) provides that when processing any sensitive data 'journalists must ensure the right to information on facts of public interest, by having regard to the materiality of such information, and avoid any reference to relatives or other persons who are not involved in the relevant events' but adds the caveat that '[w]ith regard to data concerning circumstances or events that have been known directly by the persons concerned or on account of their public conduct, the right to subsequently provide proof of the existence of lawful justification deserving legal protection is hereby left unprejudiced'. The application of art 5 to criminal-related data is specified by art 12(2). Finally, art 9 of the Code further requires that '[i]n exercising the rights and duties related to freedom of the press, journalists must respect a person's right to non-discrimination on account of his/her race, religion, political opinions, sex, personal circumstances, bodily or mental condition'.

96. This provision was subject to a last minute amendment and it may be that the changes agreed are best considered to transform this into a permissive public interest test. See Zákon o zpracování (n 82) ss 17(1).

97. Art 8 of the Danish *Lov om massmediers informationsdatabaser* provides that, subject to a clear override where the interest in freedom of information is more weighty, information considered sensitive should not be stored in such a database after three years from the event that gave rise to the database entry or, if such a date cannot be fixed, three years after the information was entered into the database. For the purposes of this section, sensitive information is defined as information on individuals' purely private matters, including information on race, religion and skin colour, on political, social, sexual and criminal matters, health information, serious social problems and the abuse of stimulants and the like.

98. In sum, an exemption is only possible where this is found necessary to reconcile the right to the protection of personal data with freedom of expression and information. See Belgian Data Protection Act (n 42) art 24(4).

99. Ibid art 24(5).

100. 2018 Luxembourg Data Protection Act (n 62) art 62(2).

101. No express derogation is provided from the legal basis provisions set down in Article 6 of the GDPR (n 1). However, Article 137(3) of the 2018 Italian Legislative Decree (n 22) does state a journalistic right to communicate information of significant public interest and also data concerning circumstances or events that have been made known either directly by the data subject or on account of the latter's public conduct. The Italian Data Protection Code (n 66) further protects journalistic comments and opinions (art 6(3)) but, on the other hand, sets out additional restrictions including in order to safeguard a person's residence (art 3), protect children (art 7), and protect personal dignity (art 8).

102. 2003 Amended Italian Legislative Decree (n 23) art 137(2)(b).

103. See Danish Data Protection Act (n 68) ss 3(6) and 3(8).

104. Denmark: *Lov om massemediers informationsdatabaser*, ss 1(1), 3, and 6.

105. In addition, Italian law expressly states that where the Journalism Data Protection Code is violated, the DPA may ban processing under art 58 of the GDPR (n 1). See 2003 Amended Italian Legislative Decree (n 23) art 139(4). This statement might be taken to place an implicit limit on the use of other corrective powers set out in art 58.

106. See Ley Orgánica 3/2008 for references throughout both the Spanish DPA and the regional authorities. For the time being it appears that the latter remain established under pre-GDPR legislation, namely, Basque Country, Ley 2/2004, de 25 de febrero, de Ficheros de Datos de Carácter Personal de Titularidad Pública y de Creación de la Agencia Vasca de Protección de Datos, art 2 and Catalonia, Ley 32/2010, de 1 de octubre, de la Autoridad Catalana de Protección de Datos, art 3.

107. Icelandic Personal Data Protection and Processing Act (n 31) art 6.

108. 2018 Dutch Data Protection Act (n 40) art 43.

109. Icelandic Personal Data Protection and Processing Act (n 31) art 6.

110. Legea nr 190/2018 (n 53) art 7.

111. Ordonnance n° 2018-1125 (n 52) art 19(2).

112. Lithuanian Amended Data Protection Law (n 50) art 7(2).

113. Amended Bulgarian Law on the Protection of Personal Data (n 47) art 25h(4).

114. Latvian Personal Data Processing Law (n 45) art 32(2).
115. Austria: Federal Act Concerning the Protection of Personal Data, s 9.
116. Belgian Data Protection Act (n 42) art 24(5).
117. Zákon o zpracování (n 82) ss 17(2) and 19(4).
118. Gibraltar: Data Protection 2004 (Amendment) Regulations 2018, s 158(2).
119. UK: Data Protection Act 2018, sch 2, pt V, paras 25(5)–(8).
120. Ibid ss 124 and 126(3).
121. Ibid s 177. This provision only relates to 'media organisations' so would appear to exclude redress available in relation to individuals such as freelance journalists.
122. Ibid s 178.
123. Ibid sch 17.
124. Gibraltar: Data Protection Act 2018, s 43(1).
125. Denmark: *Lov om massemediers informationsdatabaser*, ss 3 and 6
126. Danish Data Protection Act (n 68) ss 3(7)–(8).
127. German Broadcasting Treaty (n 30) ss 9c(4) and 57(2).
128. Lag (2018:218) (n 28) s 6.
129. See generally GDPR (n 1) art 4(23).
130. Ibid arts 60–67.
131. Malta: Data Protection Act 2018, s 9. Note that Gibraltar and the United Kingdom also apply the derogatory tests set out in relation to substantive data protection rather than ordinary regulatory supervision in this context.
132. Icelandic Personal Data Protection and Processing Act (n 31) art 6.
133. 2018 Dutch Data Protection Act (n 40) art 43(2).
134. Danish Data Protection Act (n 68) ss 2(5)–(8).
135. Namely, Greece, Portugal, and Slovenia.
136. Namely, Charts 8.2–8.5 in this chapter and Charts 5.2–5.5 in chapter five (78-79).
137. This same standard deviation is obtained if the three States which as of May 2019 had not implemented the GDPR are excluded .
138. See section 1.3 of Chapter 5.
139. Daniel C Hallin and Paolo Mancini, *Comparing Media Systems: Three Models of Media and Politics* (Cambridge University Press 2005) 67 and *passim*.
140. See especially Angelika Wyka, 'Berlusconization of the mass media in East Central Europe: The new danger of Italianization' (Third Annual Conference Idea Exchange: Mediums and Methods of Communication in Eastern Europe, Russia, and Central Asia, Pittsburgh, February 2006) <http://www.kakanien-revisited.at/beitr/emerg/AWyka1.pdf> accessed 3 August 2018.
141. GDPR (n 1) art 40.
142. Ibid art 41. Such accreditation remains 'without prejudice' to the DPA's own tasks.
143. Ibid art 41(3).
144. Which in this context is specifically defined as relating to 'processing activities in several Member States' (art 41(7)).
145. Danish Data Protection Act (n 68) ss 3(4)–(8). Note, however, that Danish law continues to set out a *sui generis* mode of co-regulation in the area of journalism through its *Lov om massemediers informationsdatabaser*.
146. 2018 Dutch Data Protection Act (n 40) art 43(2).

147. Lithuanian Amended Data Protection Law (n 50) art 4. Note that, in addition, Finland only directly states that the code of conduct provision (GDPR (n 1) art 40) applies to journalism but does not expressly exclude application of the monitoring provision (art 41). Its position, therefore, remains rather ambiguous. See Finland: Tietosuojalaki, s 27.

148. See Table 5.4 (83-84).

149. Estonian Personal Data Protection Act (n 55) s 4.

150. 2003 Amended Italian Legislative Decree (n 23) art 139.

151. 2018 Luxembourg Data Protection Act (n 62) art 62(5).

152. Lithuanian Amended Data Protection Law (n 50) art 7(2).

153. Ordonnance n° 2018-1125 (n 52) art 80(2).

154. Belgian Data Protection Act (n 42) art 24(1).

155. Gibraltar: Data Protection Act 2018= Sch 1, Pt V, s 22(5)–(7).

156. UK: Data Protection Act 2018, s 179(2).

157. Denmark: *Lov om massemediers informationsdatabaser,* ch 4.

158. German Broadcasting Treaty (n 30) s 57(2). Note also that under § 9(c) the *Länder* are granted considerable discretion in their approach to the regulation of broadcasters which may, therefore, also result in a connection with self-regulation.

159. See European Commission (n 13) recital 121.

160. The original Commission, European Parliament and Council versions of the GDPR may all be found in Council Document 10391/15, 8 July 2015 (n 15).

161. GDPR (n 1) ch IX, art 89(1) and (3). Since these archiving provisions essentially form part of the GDPR's 'knowledge facilitation' regime, their legislative origins and general nature will be explored in depth in Chapter 12 of this book, which focuses on the relationship between the GDPR and other traditional publishers including academics.

162. *Times Newspapers (Nos 1 and 2) v United Kingdom* App [2009] EMLR 14 paras 40 and 45.

163. See reference to chapter IX in GDPR (n 1) art 85(2).

164. These States were Austria, Denmark, Germany, Iceland, Latvia, Lithuania, Norway, and Romania. For references to the relevant laws, see section 2.2 earlier in this chapter.

165. Belgian Data Protection Act (n 42) art 24(1).

166. Strangely, this provision did reference the chapters within this statute itself that established further provisions on archiving.

167. Lag (2018:218) (n 28) s 7.

168. Namely, Cyprus, Estonia, Finland, and Slovakia. Excepting Finland, these ambiguities have already been outlined in section 2.2 earlier in this chapter. In Finnish legislation, the issue arises from establishing a list of GDPR provisions which to which journalism is not subject and a list of provisions to which it was. Similarly to the situation as regards the clause on monitoring bodies (see n 147 including for legislative reference), art 89 of the GDPR (n 1) concerning archiving is not included on either list.

169. In the case of Croatia, Hungary, and Spain, this problem arises from the total absence of a journalistic derogation within their law. In all the other cases, the journalistic derogation sets out precisely the provisions which it is intended to affect but these do not expressly include either the GDPR's specific provision on archiving in the public interest (art 89) or any national provision providing further specification in this area. For details of all these laws see section 2.2 earlier in this chapter.

170. GDPR (n 1) arts 85(1)–(2).
171. Ibid art 85(2).

Chapter 9

1. Council of Europe, 'Resolution (73) 22 on the Protection of the Privacy of Individuals vis-à-vis Electronic Data Banks in the Private Sector Explanatory Report' (*COE*, 1973) <https://rm.coe.int/CoERMPublicCommonSearchServices/DisplayDCTMContent? documentId=0900001680502830> accessed 15 April 2019, para 2.
2. *Von Hannover v Germany (No. 1)* (2005) 40 EHRR 1 para 76.
3. *Von Hannover v Germany (No 2)* (2012) 55 EHRR 15 para 109.
4. Ibid para 126.
5. Ibid 106.
6. Or, in the phraseology of the German courts, 'an event of contemporary society' (para 118).
7. Ibid para 120.
8. *Satakunnan Markkinapörssi Oy and Satamedia Oy v Finland* (2018) 66 EHRR 8.
9. Two out of the fifteen judges penned a dissent holding *inter alia* that they did not 'believe that domestic courts should be in the business of passing judgment on what counts as "journalistic activity"'. Thirteen of the fifteen judges did find that there had been a violation of the right to a fair trial (under Article 6 of the Convention) on account of how long the proceedings had taken (even after discounting—following the ruling in *Bosporus v Ireland* (2005) 42 EHRR 1—the delay caused by the Court of Justice of the European Union (CJEU) proceedings).
10. *Satamedia* (n 8) para 171.
11. Ibid para 177.
12. Ibid para 178.
13. See EU Charter of Fundamental Rights and Freedoms, arts 7 and 8 and, in relation to right to data protection, also Treaty on the Functioning of the European Union (TFEU), art 16 (1).
14. Case C-131/12 *Google Spain SL and Google Inc v Agencia Española de Protección de Datos (AEPD)* [2014] 3 CMLR 50 para 82. More generally, the court found that such obligations would apply whenever 'data processing carried out the context of the activity of a search engine can be distinguished from and is additional to that carried out by publishers of websites and affects the data subject's fundamental rights additionally' (para 83).
15. Ibid para 84.
16. Ibid para 81.
17. Ibid para 77.
18. Ibid para 85.
19. Cases C-293/12 and C-594/12 *Digital Rights Ireland and Seitlinger v Minister for Communications, Marine and Natural Resources* [2014] ECR I-238, para 52.
20. Ibid para 54.

21. Council Directive 95/46/EC of 24 October 1995 on the protection of individuals with regard to the processing of personal data and on the free movement of such data [1995] OJ L281/31, art 28 ('DPD') and Decision 2000/520/EC on the adequacy of the protection provided by the safe harbour privacy principles and related frequently asked questions issued by the US Department of Commerce.
22. DPD (n 21) art 26.
23. Case C-362/14 *Maximillian Schrems v Irish Data Protection Commissioner* [2015] ECR I-650 para 96.
24. Ibid para 40.
25. Case C-345/17 *Buivids* EU: C: 2019: 122, para 15.
26. Ibid para 16.
27. Ibid para 18.
28. Ibid para 41.
29. Confirming an understanding going back to Case C-101/01 *Lindqvist* [2003] ECR I-12971, the Court held that the exemption for personal or household purposes (DPD (n 21) art 3(2)) was inapplicable since in posting the video online, Buivids had taken no steps to restrict access and so he had thereby permitted 'access to personal data to an indefinite number of people' (*Buivids* (n 25) para 43).
30. *Buivids* (n 25) para 51.
31. Ibid para 62.
32. Ibid para 64.
33. Ibid para 69.
34. Ibid para 66.
35. Ibid para 66.
36. *Digital Rights Ireland* (n 19) para 54.
37. Case C-687/18 *SY v Associated Newspapers Ltd*. This case involves a direct challenge to UK data protection law's prohibition on prepublication injunctive relief under data protection in the area of journalistic (and other special expressive) processing. For the initial reference to the CJEU see *Stunt v Associated Newspapers* [2018] EWCA Civ 1780, [2018] 1 WLR 6060.
38. UK: Office of Communications, *Annual Report and Accounts for the Period 1 April 2013 to 31 March 2014* (Stationary Office 2014) 85.
39. Measured by full-time equivalents (FTEs) where disclosed.
40. Bert-Jaap Koops, 'The Trouble with European Data Protection Law' (2014) 4(4) IDPL 250, 256.
41. Giovanni Buttarelli, 'The EU GDPR as a Clarion Call for a New Global Digital Gold Standard' (2016) 6(2) IDPL 77, 77.
42. Council Regulation 2016/679/EU of 27 April 2016 on the protection of natural persons with regard to the processing of personal data and on the free movement of such data, and repealing Directive 95/46/EC [2016] OJ L119/1, art 52(5) ('GDPR').
43. See, for example, the chapters by Colin Scott ('Standard-Setting in Regulatory Regimes') and Neil Gunningham ('Enforcement and Compliance Strategies') in Robert Baldwin, Martin Cave, and Martin Lodge, *The Oxford Handbook of Regulation* (Oxford University Press 2010).

44. GDPR (n 42) art 57. For example, its first task to 'monitor and enforce the application of this Regulation' clearly falls within enforcement (art 57(1)(a)), whilst the second and third tasks, which relate to 'promoting public awareness and understanding' (art 57(1) (b)) and 'advis[ing], in accordance with national law, the national parliament, the government and other institutions and bodies on legislative and administrative measures relating to the protection of natural persons' rights and freedoms with regard to processing' (art 57(1)(c)), clearly relate to standard-setting.

45. *Buivids* (n 25) para 68.

46. Case C-518/07 *Commission v Federal Republic of Germany* [2010] ECR I-1885 para 23.

47. However, in relation to the non-EU EEA such primary law would not apply and even the GDPR may lack the general applicability (absent State implementation) that it clearly enjoys within the Union.

48. Scott (n 43) 117.

49. Ibid 108.

50. Claude-Jean Bertrand, *Media Ethics and Accountability Systems* (Routledge 2018) 138. Rowbottom similarly notes that the requirements set out within self-regulatory texts are 'often vague in nature'. See Jacob Rowbottom, *Media Law* (Hart Publishing 2018) 261.

51. Tony Harcup, *Journalism: Principles and Practice* (2nd edn Sage Publications 2015) 5.

52. Bertrand (n 50) 138.

53. 'Leveson Inquiry: Day 9' (*National Archives*, 29 November 2011) <https://webarchive. nationalarchives.gov.uk/20140122201803/http://www.levesoninquiry.org.uk/ wp-content/uploads/2011/11/Transcript-of-Afternoon-Hearing-29-November-2011. pdf> accessed 22 May 2019, 90–91.

54. See Bertrand (n 50) 42.

55. Jesus Díaz-Campo and Francisco Seado-Boj, 'Journalism ethics in a digital environment' (2015) 32(4) Telematics and Informatics 735, 737. Admittedly seven of these codes originated from within an EEA State. However, not only does this still constitute less than a quarter of the total number of EEA States but in three of these cases the reference was confined simply to stating that the general principles of the code applied online and in only one was there a specific section on journalism and digital media.

56. GDPR (n 42) recital 75.

57. UK: Brian Leveson, *Inquiry into the Culture, Practices and Ethics of the Press* (HC 2012, 780–8I) 1109.

58. *Buivids* (n 25) para 68.

59. *Campbell v Mirror Group Newspapers* [2002] EWCA Civ 1373, [2003] QB 663 [123] (Lord Phillips).

60. GPDR (n 42) art 57(i).

61. Daphne Keller, 'The Right Tools: Europe's Intermediary Liability Laws and the EU 2016 General Data Protection Regulation' (2017) 33(1) Berkeley Technology Law Journal 287, 345.

62. See Chapter 2, section 2.1 and *Sunday Times v United Kingdom* (1979) 2 EHRR 245.

63. Garante per la Protezione dei Dati Personali, 'L'ufficio' (*Garante Privacy*) <https://www. garanteprivacy.it/web/guest/home/autorita/ufficio> accessed 14 May 2019.

64. Leveson Inquiry (n 57) 1109–10.

65. See Table 8.4 (172-173).

66. GDPR (n 42) art 40.
67. European Data Protection Board, 'Guidelines 1/2019 on Codes of Conduct and Monitoring Bodies Under Regulation 2016/679 (Version 2.0)' (Europa, 2019) <https://edpb.europa.eu/sites/edpb/files/files/file1/edpb_guidelines_201901_v2.0_codesofconduct_en.pdf> accessed 15 June 2019, 9
68. GDPR (n 42) recital 99.
69. Ibid art 40(5).
70. Salvador Alsius, Marcel Mauri, and Ruth Rodríguez Martínez, 'Spain: A Diverse and Asymmetric Landscape' in Tobias Eberwein and others (eds), *Mapping Media Accountability—in Europe and Beyond* (Herbert von Halem Verlag 2011) 155.
71. Susanne Fengler and others, 'How effective is media self-regulation? Results from a comparative survey of European journalists' (2015) 30(3) European Journal of Communication 249, 260.
72. GDPR (n 42) art 57(1)(b).
73. EU Agency for Fundamental Rights, *Access to Data Protection Remedies in EU Member States* (Publications Office of the European Union 2013) 9.
74. European Federation of Journalists and others, 'EFJ, EMMA, ENPA and EPC statement on the need to preserve press freedom and journalism in the EU draft General Data Protection Regulation' (*EPC*, 2013) <http://epceurope.eu/wp-content/uploads/2013/12/Joint-publishers-and-journalists-statement-EU-draft-Regulation-on-Data-Protection-comments-final.pdf> accessed 21 May 2019.
75. GDPR (n 42) recital 153.
76. Ibid arts 89(1) and (3).
77. Ibid recital 153.
78. In sum, any such archive must remain orientated towards 'the disclosure to the public of information, opinions or ideas' (*Buivids* (n 25) para 54). That would rule out the use of the derogation in relation to services which do not seek to make such a collective contribution but rather to provide a discrete benefit to an albeit perhaps indeterminate number of self-interested legal or natural persons. One example of the latter type of archival service is the Know Your Candidate's Adverse Media Check, which 'enables employers to search a vast array of media sources quickly for articles linking their candidate to crime or terrorism'. See Know Your Candidate, 'Adverse Media Check' (Know Your Candidate) <https://www.knowyourcandidate.co.uk/adverse-media-check> accessed 22 May 2019.
79. Spain: Sentencia del Tribunal Supremo (Sala de lo Civil) 15 October 2015, ES:TS:2015:4132.
80. *Times Newspapers (Nos 1 and 2) v United Kingdom* [2009] EMLR 14 para 45.
81. GDPR (n 42) art 5(1)(d).
82. As set out specifically in GDPR (n 42) art 25.
83. *Times Newspapers (Nos 1 and 2)* (n 80) para 45.
84. For an overview of some of the issues already arising here see Konstantin Dörr and Katharina Hollnbuchner, 'Ethical Challenges of Algorithmic Journalism' (2017) 5(4) Digital Journalism 404.
85. These statutory limitations have been explored in depth in Chapter 8. In addition to the partial limitations, the DPAs in Iceland, the Netherlands, and in certain instances also Germany have been deprived of all potential for such statutory intervention (and

no attempt has been made to allocate such powers to an alternative regulator either). Putting aside the case of Iceland (which is not subject to EU primary law), such a radical limitation is clearly inconsistent with the requirement set out in art 8(3) of the EU Charter (n 13) that compliance with data protection be 'shall be subject to control by an independent authority' and would unlikely to be justifiable under the limitation conditions set out in art 52 either (especially as such independent control is likely to be judged an 'essence' of data protection).

86. Another more doubtful possibility is that such limits may be established in other statutory instruments and apply by implication also in the data protection context. The Hungarian Government's notification to the European Commission of its 'implementation' of the journalistic/special expression derogation (required under GDPR (n 42) art 85(3)) appears based on such a potentiality. See 'Hungarian Notification' (*Europa*, 2018) <https://ec.europa.eu/info/sites/info/files/hu_notification_art_51.4_84.2_85.3_88.3_90.2_publish.pdf> accessed 22 May 2019.

87. See Chart 7.1 (126).

88. Rebecca Hill, 'ICO has pumped almost £2.5m and 36 staff into its political data probe—but only 2 are techies' *The Register* (London, 20 December 2018) <https://www.theregister.co.uk/2018/12/20/ico_foi_facebook_probe/> accessed 22 May 2019.

89. Gunningham (n 43) 122.

90. Alsius and others (n 70) 103.

91. Lara Fielden, 'Regulating the Press: A Comparative Study of International Press Councils' (*INFORRM*, 3 May 2012) <https://inforrm.org/2012/05/03/regulating-the-press-a-comparative-study-of-international-press-councils-lara-fielden/> accessed 27 July 2018.

92. See UK: Leveson Inquiry (n 57) 1070 (finding that inaction on part on the part of UK DPA constituted 'regulatory failure within the Terms of Reference of the Inquiry') and 1579 (finding that, as regards the self-regulatory UK Press Complaints Commission, '[i]t is difficult to avoid the conclusion that the self-regulatory system was run for the benefit of the press not of the public').

93. Alsius and others (n 70) 104.

94. Hielke Hijmans, *The European Union as Guardian of Internet Privacy* (Springer 2016) 373.

95. *Google Spain* (n 14) para 58.

96. GDPR (n 42) art 57(1)(f).

97. EU Charter (n 13) art 8(3).

98. GDPR (n 42) art 41(1).

99. As regards public broadcasters, it may even be argued that Article 41 cannot be invoked since Article 41(4) states that it 'shall not apply to processing carried out by public authorities and bodies'. However, given that these bodies will be pursuing similar freedom of expression activity to that of a purely private media company, the better argument is that they should be treated as falling within the private as opposed to the public sector here.

100. *Axel Springer v Germany* [2012] ECHR 227 para 81.

101. Gunningham (n 43) 139.

102. Ibid 139.

103. The European Commission, as guardian of the EU Treaties, and the European Data Protection Supervisor, as the DPA responsible for pan-EU processing, also participate in the Board's activities. However, the former lacks voting rights in all cases, whilst the latter only has such rights 'on decisions which concern principles and rules applicable to the Union institutions, bodies, offices and agencies which correspond in substance to those of this regulation' (GDPR (n 42) art 68). Finally, under art 1 of the EEA Joint Committee's Decision 154/2018 the EFTA Surveillance Authority is allocated the same participation role within the Board as the European Commission.

104. GDPR (n 42) chapter VII.

105. Ibid art 4(23)(a). The clause separately covers 'processing of personal data which takes place in the context of the activities of establishments of more than one Member State' (art 4(23)(b)).

106. Ibid art 40(7).

107. See Chapter 8, section 3.2.

108. TFEU (n 13) art 258; Agreement between the EFTA States on the Establishment of a Surveillance Authority and a Court of Justice [1994] OJ L344/1, art 31.

109. Ibid art 70(1)(e).

110. Ibid art 70(1)(u).

111. In a few States, local law (Denmark, Iceland, the Netherlands, and potentially also Germany) has sought deploy the journalistic derogation in order to disable not only the 'cooperation and consistency' mechanism but all the activities of the Board here. It is difficult, however, to claim that preventing the Board engaging in mere guidance and information-sharing functions could be seen as 'necessary' to reconcile these two fundamental rights (GDPR (n 42) art 85(2)). Moreover, these kinds of activities could be seen as permitted as a result of the general oversight role allocated to DPAs. Indeed, these regulators have already produced guidance on journalism throughout the era of the DPD (despite similar derogations in these local laws during this period). In the case of the EU jurisdictions, these tasks could also be seen to arise directly from article 8(3) of the EU Charter (n 13). Finally, even if these few regulators felt that they needed to recuse themselves from pan-European deliberations, this should not inhibit the other DPAs from pursuing the tasks duly allocated to the Board here.

112. European Union High Level Group on Media Freedom and Pluralism, 'A Free and Pluralistic Media to Sustain European Democracy' (*Europa*, 2013) <https://ec.europa. eu/digital-single-market/sites/digital-agenda/files/HLG%20Final%20Report.pdf>   3 accessed 22 May 2019.

113. See Chapter 5, section 2.1.

114. Indeed, the EDPB has already discussed in this context the Romanian DPA's probe into the RISE, an investigative journalism project concerned with exploring and exposing organised crime and corruption (including amongst politicians), after concerns were raised about this including in the European Parliament. See Andrea Jelinek 'Letter from 12 November 2018 on Romanian DPA Investigation' (*Europa*, 23 January 2018) <https://edpb.europa.eu/sites/edpb/files/files/file1/edpb_letter_on_romanian_dpa_ investigation_en.pdf> accessed 19 February 2019.

115. European Convention on Human Rights, art 8(1).

Chapter 10

1. Christian Möller, 'Media convergence' in Dunja Mijatović (ed), *The Online Media Self-Regulation Guidebook* (OSCE Representative on Freedom of the Media 2013) 13.

2. As emphasized in the introduction to this book, in using the term 'non-journalistic' I am certainly not seeking to downplay the close connection between journalism and these other publishers' activities. I also recognize that in State data protection laws (both within and outside Europe) which confine their freedom of expression derogation to 'journalism' or the 'media', it will be necessary to interpret such terms creatively so that they also protect other forms of expression directed to the collective public. Indeed, the Court of Justice of European Union (CJEU) appeared to have just such a potential need in mind when they emphasised in C-73/07 *Satamedia* that the concept of 'journalistic activities' could not be limited to 'media undertakings' and (at least in the concrete case) should cover any activity whose 'object is the disclosure to the public of information, opinions or ideas, irrespective of the medium which is used to transmit them'. See *Tietosuojavatuutettu v Satakunnan Markkinapörssi Oy and Satamedia Oy* [2008] ECR I-9831 at [61]. Nevertheless, as is in fact recognized within the special expression provisions set out within pan-European data protection, it is conceptually clearer to attempt to distinguish journalistic expression from other forms of public expression such as that which is artistic, literary, or indeed academic in nature.

3. George Brock, *Out of Print: Newspapers, Journalism and the Business of News in the Digital Age* (Kogan Page 2013) 9.

4. Moreover, if 'journalism' is strictly construed as being limited not just to 'the occupation or writing for a public journal' but at least 'primarily' to the production of 'output on news and current affairs' (*BBC v Sugar (No 2)* [2012] UKSC 4, [2012] 1 WLR 439 [70]), then a good deal of the output of even the professional journalistic media may need to be justified on this wider rationale. Examples include output that is principally concerned to 'entertain' or 'educate' ([70]) including 'historical programmes dealing with analysis of the past' (UK: HC Deb 2 February 1998, vol 585, col 443 (Minister of State Geoff Hoon, MP)).

5. Brock (n 3) 8.

6. John Milton, *Areopagitica: A Speech of Mr John Milton for the Liberty of Unlicensed Printing to the Parliament of England* (Payson & Clarke 1644) 6–7.

7. Phillip M Strong, 'The Rivals: An Essay on the Sociological Trades' in Robert Dingwall and Philip Lewis (eds), *The Sociology of the Professions: Law, Medicine and Others* (Macmillan 1983) 59.

8. *Vereinigung Bildender Kunstler v Austria* (2008) 47 EHRR 5, para 26

9. These writers often produce material for 'trade publishing' which may be defined as 'the sector of the publishing industry that is concerned with publishing books, both fiction and non-fiction, that are intended for general readers and sold primarily through bookstores and other retail outlets' (John B Thompson, *Merchants of Culture: The Publishing Business in the Twenty-First Century* (Polity Press 2010) 12).

10. Denmark: Private Registers Act 1978, s 1(2) and repeated in Denmark: Private Registers Act 1987, s 2(2). Full references to all these historic laws are set out in Appendix 1.

11. Iceland: Act No 63/1981 Respecting Systematic Recording of Personal Data (Information concerning Private Affairs) (1981) art 2 and repeated in Iceland: Act Concerning the Registration and Handling of Personal Data (1989) art 2.

12. Finland: Personal Data File Act 1987 s 1; Netherlands, Data Protection Act 1998 s 2(1)(c).

13. Norway: Kongelig resolusjon av 21 Desember 1979. The conditions laid down required that the database not be connected to any other database, be kept from unauthorized access and that no personal data be extracted from the database without the data subject's consent. Presumably, however, any extraction which was the direct result of hardcopy publication of a biography, conversational, or subject-based work was excluded from this latter requirement.

14. Norway: Kongelig resolusjon av 21 November 1979.

15. Council of Europe, *Data Protection and the Media* (Council of Europe, 1991) 13.

16. Ireland: Data Protection Act 1988, s 1(1); UK: Data Protection Act 1984, s 1(8). Under s 1(7), the UK Act also excluded any processing not performed 'by reference to the data subject'.

17. Council Directive 95/46/EC of 24 October 1995 on the protection of individuals with regard to the processing of personal data and on the free movement of such data [1995] OJ L281/31, recitals 17 and 37.

18. Ibid art 9.

19. European Commission, 'Proposal for a Council Directive Concerning the Protection of Individuals in Relation to the Processing of Personal Data' COM (1990) 314 final, art 19.

20. European Commission, 'Amended proposal for a Council Directive on the protection of individuals with regard to the processing of personal data and on the free movement of such data' COM (1992) 422 final, art 9.

21. Ibid, Explanatory Memorandum, 19.

22. European Union Council, 'Document 7693/93' (7 October 1993) (no English version available) Council of the EU Archives.

23. European Union Council, 'Document 7500/94' (9 June 1994) <https://www.cipil.law.cam.ac.uk/sites/www.law.cam.ac.uk/files/images/www.cipil.law.cam.ac.uk/documents/83.pdf> accessed 7 May 2019 (noting reservations of Germany, Spain, France, Greece, Italy, Portugal, and to a certain extent Luxembourg, as well as the suggestions of Spain).

24. Ibid (noting specific comments from Spain on this point). The strength of these concerns was clearly related to the discussion on another Directive underway at the same time which was aimed at granting databases protection under intellectual property law. These later negotiations eventually spawned Directive 96/9/EC of 11 March 1996 on the legal protection of databases [1996] OJ L27/03.

25. Ibid.

26. European Union Council, 'Document 9951/94' (17 November 1994) <https://www.cipil.law.cam.ac.uk/sites/www.law.cam.ac.uk/files/images/www.cipil.law.cam.ac.uk/documents/95.pdf> accessed 7 May 2019.

27. European Union Council, 'Document 12148/94 (Annex)' (16 December 1994) <https://www.cipil.law.cam.ac.uk/sites/www.law.cam.ac.uk/files/images/www.cipil.law.cam.ac.uk/documents/95.pdf> accessed 7 May 2019.

28. Full references to all these laws are set out in Appendix 2.

29. Belgium, Bulgaria, Finland, France, Gibraltar, Ireland, Italy, Latvia, Lithuania, Luxembourg, Netherlands, Norway, Poland, Portugal, Romania, Slovakia, and the United Kingdom. The provision in the Italian Personal Data Protection Code (s 136(1)) was originally categorized as being restricted to artistic expression. However, its phraseology 'articles, essays, and other intellectual works in terms of artistic expression' is better construed as covering both literary expression ('articles' and 'essays') and also artistic expression ('other intellectual works in terms of artistic expression').

30. Denmark, Iceland, Malta, and Sweden.

31. Cyprus: Processing of Personal Data (Protection of Individuals) Law, s 6(1)(i).

32. Austria, Estonia, Germany, Hungary, Liechtenstein, and Slovenia. In the German case, the federal Data Protection Act and the Interstate Treaty on Broadcasting and Telemedia only addressed the interface between data protection and the media. Nevertheless, it is possible, that some *Länder* enacted broader freedom of expression derogations at local level. However, such broader provisions were not found in the local jurisdictional law of any of the four German Land DPAs which responded to the Questionnaire. For full details of the legislation consulted see Appendix 2.

33. Greece: Data Protection Act, art 7(2)(g) and art 11(5). Art 7(2)(g) did appear to link 'journalistic purposes' not only to the provision of 'information on matters of public interest' but also to engaging in 'literary expression'. However, this suggestive language cannot detract from the fact that the gateway for any exemption remained being engaged in 'journalistic purposes'.

34. Croatia, Czechia, and Spain.

35. Denmark: Data Protection Act, s 2(10).

36. France: Act no 78-17 of 6 January 1978 on Information Technology, Data Files and Civil Liberties (as amended) art 67.

37. Cyprus: Processing of Personal Data (Protection of Individuals) Law, s 11(5).

38. Italy: Personal Data Protection Code, s 138.

39. See Table 5.4 (83-84).

40. Malta: Data Protection Act as of 2012, arts 6(2)–(3).

41. Lithuania: Law on Legal Protection of Personal Data, art 8.

42. See UK: Data Protection Act 1998, s 32(3) and Data Protection (Designated Codes of Practice) (No 2) Order 2000. The statute provided that these codes could be used one factor in ascertaining whether the controller had a reasonable belief in the public interest of any publication at issue.

43. UK: Data Protection Registrar, *Data Protection Act 1984: Notes to help you apply for Registration* (Data Protection Registrar, 1985) 21.

44. Data Protection Working Party, *Data Protection Guidelines for Library, Information and Related Services* (Aslib 1985) 3–1. The regulator also encouraged this group to interpret the various terms in data protection very widely. Thus, the final guidance held that '[t]itles with a living individual, such as the Queen, the Archbishop of Canterbury, the Dalai Lama or the Duke of Wellington are also considered to be identification data within the meaning of the Act' and '[t]he question of whether the data are "public" or "private", however these terms are defined, has no bearing on the requirement to Register' (2-1 to 3-1).

45. See (n 16).

46. Ireland: Data Protection Commissioner, *Annual Report* (Office of the Data Protection Commissioner1990) 22. Similarly, the UK DPA stated that data protection law would apply 'if, although perhaps first entered only to prepare the text of documents, the information is kept in the computer with a view to having a store of personal data which can be added to, amended or used when required' (see UK: Data Protection Registrar, *Data Protection Act 1984: The Definitions* (Data Protection Registrar, 1989) 17).

47. Marcel Berlins, 'Safety Means a Notebook' *The Times* (London, 11 November 1987). Amstrad were the makers of a range of popular personal computers at the time.

48. On the other hand, it held that if information was copied on to this individual's computer or transferred in some other way, then the third party would become responsible for this.

49. 'CD-ROM-tekniken och datalagen', *DIrekt från Datainspektionen* (No 3/92) (December 1992) 2–3.

50. Sweden: Data Act 1973 (as amended in 1988) s 2.

51. 'Ingen tillstånd för datoriserat bokmanus', *DIrekt från Datainspektionen* (No 3/93) (December 1993) 3.

52. 'Tillstånd behövs inte för datoriserat bokmanus', *DIrekt från Datainspektionen* (No 1/94) (May 1994) 3.

53. Article 29 Working Party, 'Recommendation 1/97 on Data Protection law and the media (WP 1)' (*Europa*, 25 February 1997) <https://ec.europa.eu/justice/article-29/documentation/opinion-recommendation/files/1997/wp1_en.pdf> accessed 3 May 2019, 4.

54. In retrospect, this may well have been unfortunate as the answers received could have provided valuable data. Certainly, future work could fruitfully focus on exploring this under-explored area in more detail including through direct interaction with the DPAs.

55. As previously stated, this review encompassed the websites of all national DPAs within the EEA and also those of the regional DPAs which had responded to the questionnaire.

56. See Chapter 5, section 2.2.

57. Netherlands: College Bescherming Persoonsgegevens, 'Publication of Personal Data on the Internet' (*Autoriteitpersoonsgegevens*, 2007) <https://autoriteitpersoonsgegevens.nl/sites/default/files/downloads/mijn_privacy/en_20071108_richtsnoeren_internet.pdf> accessed 22 May 2019, 43.

58. Czechia: The Office for Personal Data Protection, 'Opinion No 5/2009 Publication of personal data in the media' (*UOOU*, February 2014) <https://www.uoou.cz/stanovisko-c-5-2009-zverejnovani-osobnich-udaju-v-nbsp-mediich/d-1517/p1=2515> accessed 22 May 2019.

59. Hungary: Adatvédelmi Biztos, 'Az Adatvédelmi Biztos beszámolója 2004' (*Adatvédelmi Biztos Irodája*, 2005) <https://www.naih.hu/files/Adatvedelmi-biztos-beszamoloja-2004.PDF> 118–22 accessed 10 June 2019.

60. Slovenia: Information Commissioner, 'Media and the Protection of Personal Data' (*IP-RS*, 2009) <https://www.ip-rs.si/fileadmin/user_upload/Pdf/smernice/Media_and_the_Protection_of_Personal_Data.pdf> accessed 22 May 2019.

61. See France: Commission Nationale de l'Informatique et des Libertés, 'Délibération n° 01-057 du 29 novembre 2001 portant recommandation sur la diffusion de données personnelles sur internet par les banques de données de jurisprudence' (*CNIL*, 29 November 2001) <https://web.archive.org/web/20140302122654/http://www.cnil.fr/documentation/deliberations/deliberation/delib/17/> accessed 22 May 2019.

62. France: Commission Nationale de l'Informatique et des Libertés, 'Journalisme, expression littéraire ou artistique' (*CNIL*) <https://web.archive.org/web/20140521074659/http://www.cnil.fr/vos-obligations/declarer-a-la-cnil/dispense/mon-secteur-dactivite/mon-theme/mon-fichier/dispense-selectionnee/dec-mode/DISPLAYSINGLEFICHEDISP/dis-uid/25/> accessed 22 May 2019. This page also clarified that the artistic derogation only covered the creation of artistic works themselves as opposed to the commercialization of these works or personnel files created within the framework of artistic activities.

63. Belgium: Commission de la protection de la vie privée, 'Limitation pour des finalités journalistiques (*Privacy Commission*) <https://web.archive.org/web/20140130082338/http://www.privacycommission.be/fr/droit-image/droits/limitation-finalites-journalistiques> accessed 22 May 2019.

64. Spain: *Agencia Española de Protección de Datos*, 'Memoria 1994' (*AGPD*, 1994) <http://www.agpd.es/portalwebAGPD/canaldocumentacion/memorias/common/MEMORIA_1994.pdf> 60 accessed 2 July 2014.

65. Italy: Garante per la Protezione dei Dati Personali, 'Privacy e giornalismo' (*Garante Privacy*, 2012) http://www.garanteprivacy.it/web/guest/home/docweb/-/docweb-display/docweb/1858277 45; accessed 20 May 2019.

66. Ibid 46.

67. Malta: Office of the Information and Data Protection Commissioner, 'Data Protection and Street Photography' (*IDPC*, 2013) <https://web.archive.org/web/20140723062415/http://idpc.gov.mt/dbfile.aspx/Data_Prot_and_Street_Photography.pdf> 1 accessed 20 May 2019.

68. Ibid 1.

69. Ibid 2.

70. Ibid 1–2.

71. Ibid 4. The guidance also argued that privacy rights distinct from data protection might also result in unlawfulness but that consideration of these fell outside the remit of the DPA.

72. See Malta: Information and Data Protection Commissioner, 'Annual Report 2006' (*IDPC*, 2006) <http://idpc.gov.mt/dbfile.aspx/AR2006.pdf> 6–7 accessed 27 May 2014.

73. Although this author was also a journalist with *Il Foglio* newspaper, the fact that this work was published separately as a book would, in this study's schemata, render this work an instance of literary expression rather than that of journalism. Nevertheless, as also detailed by the DPA, an extract of this book was also reproduced in a weekly a magazine (*Privacy e giornalismo* (n 65) 125). This illustrates the extensive blurring of boundaries and convergence between categories in this area.

74. *Privacy e giornalismo* (n 65) 124–25. This e-book also detailed two further cases (both from 2010) where the DPA had investigated book publication but where no violation had been found. In the first, an individual had complained about religious references to them and also a photograph included in an (apparently autobiographical) book published by their sister. However, the DPA found that the references were justified not only by the emphasis in the book on the religious journey of the family but by the fact that the complainant had taken on a community role as a Rabbi and had given published interviews relating to this. Meanwhile, to the extent that the photograph enabled

identification of the individual, it was found not to be harmful to their image or dignity (193–94). Meanwhile, in the second case a judge objected to references to him in the book *Le due guerre* edited by Giancarlo Caseilli. However, these references were held to be justified in light of the individual's significant judicial role in countering terrorism in the 1970s. It was also noted that the facts referred to were already well-known and had been referred to in some of the judge's own publications.

75. For further details see Chapter 5, section 2.3.

76. The DPA nevertheless added a rider that, severable from data protection, individuals might have broader privacy and images rights in law which could result in the successful application for an injunction or damages in court.

77. DPD (n 17) art 8.

78. Slovenia: Information Commissioner, 'Decision Number 0613-128/2011' (*IP-RS*, 29 September 2011) <https://www.ip-rs.si/fileadmin/user_upload/Pdf/mnenja/Fotografije__Sklep_o_ustavitvi__ANG.pdf> 10 August 2018.

79. Poland: Generlny Inspektor Ochrony Danych Osobowych, 'Judgment of the Voivodeship Administrative Court in the Case of the Decision of the Inspector General for Personal Data Protection Concerning the Institute of National Remembrance' (*GIODO*, 2006) <http://www.giodo.gov.pl/259/id_art/347/j/en/> accessed 10 June 2019.

80. AP in Poland, 'Poland in uproar over leak of spy files' *Guardian Online* (London, 5 February 2005) <https://www.theguardian.com/world/2005/feb/05/poland> accessed 20 May 2019.

81. Harminder Singh, 'Prying webcams used by artist to capture unsuspecting Hongkongers in controversial UK exhibition' (*South China Morning Post*, 16 August 2016) <https://www.scmp.com/news/hong-kong/law-crime/article/2004219/prying-webcams-used-artist-capture-unsuspecting-hongkongers> accessed 10 August 2018. Although this exhibition was being hosted in a gallery owned by London Metropolitan University, the artist in question was neither an academic nor engaged in systematic knowledge production. The potential regulation of her work, therefore, lies clearly within the scope of this chapter rather than Chapter 11.

82. 'UK artist asked to remove webcam images of HK people from show' (*Ejinsight*, 17 August 2016) <http://www.ejinsight.com/20160817-uk-artist-asked-to-remove-webcam-images-of-hk-people-from-show/> accessed 10 August 2018.

83. Ben Pang, 'Images from unsecured HK webcams end up in London Backdoored.io art exhibition' *Young Post* (10 August 2019) <https://yp.scmp.com/news/hong-kong/article/104170/images-unsecured-hk-webcams-end-london-backdooredio-art-exhibition> accessed 22 May 2019.

84. As in Chapter 7 and in light of the unclear overlap with sub-national bodies, the Danish Press Council and the Lithuanian Inspector of Journalistic Ethics (for which comparative information was not available), these computations exclude the German, Danish, Lithuanian, and Spanish DPAs.

Chapter 11

1. Robert Dingwall, 'The Ethical Case Against Ethical Regulation in Humanities and Social Science Research' (2008) 1(3) Journal of the Academy of Social Sciences 1, 6.

2. Edward Shills, 'The Academic Ethic' (1982) 1–2 Minerva 105, 107.

3. Robert Dingwall, 'Confronting the Anti-Democrats: The Unethical Nature of Ethical Regulation in Social Science' (2006) 1(1) Medical Sociology Online 51, 54.

4. Ibid 54.

5. Dingwall (2008) (n 1) 6.

6. John Milton, *Areopagitica: A Speech of Mr John Milton for the Liberty of Unlicensed Printing to the Parliament of England* (Payson & Clarke 1644) 34.

7. Ibid 33.

8. See David Erdos, 'Freedom of Expression Turned on Its Head? Academic Social Research and Journalism in the European Privacy Framework' (2013) 1 PL 52.

9. John Thompson, *Books in the Digital Age: The Transformation of Academic and Higher Education Publishing in Britain and the United States* (Polity Press 2005) 81. Similarly in relation to journalism, the ECtHR has stated, for example, that 'it is well-established that the gathering of information is an essential preparatory step in journalism and an inherent, protected part of press freedom' (*Satakunnan Markkinapörssi Oy and Satamedia Oy v Finland* (2018) 66 EHRR 8, para 128).

10. See Council of Europe, 'Resolution (73) 22 on the Protection of the Privacy of Individuals vis-à-vis Electronic Data Banks in the Private Sector' (*COE*, 26 September 1973) <https://rm.coe.int/CoERMPublicCommonSearchServices/DisplayDCTMContent?documentId=0900001680502830> principle 10 accessed 22 May 2019; Council of Europe, 'Resolution (74) 29 on the Protection of the Privacy of Individuals vis-à-vis Electronic Data Banks in the Private Sector' (*COE*, 20 September 1974) <https://rm.coe.int/16804d1c51> principle 8 accessed 22 May 2019.

11. See Resolution (74) 29 (n 10) Explanatory Report, para 32. As noted in para 32 of the Explanatory Report of Council of Europe Resolution (73) 22 (n 10), an advisory opinion was also obtained from the International Statistical Institute, the professional body for statisticians.

12. Council of Europe, 'Resolution (83) 10 on the Protection of Personal Data Used for Scientific Research and Statistics' (*COE*, 1983) <https://rm.coe.int/CoERMPublicCommonSearchServices/DisplayDCTMContent?documentId=09000016804bc647> Annex, para 3.1 accessed 25 March 2019.

13. Ibid Explanatory Memorandum, para 28.

14. Ibid Annex, para 3.3.

15. Ibid Annex, para 2.2.

16. Ibid Annex, para 4.1.

17. Ibid Annex, para 6.

18. Ibid Annex, para 8.

19. Ibid Annex, paras 4.2 and 9.2.

20. Ibid Annex, para 9.2.

21. Ibid Annex, para 4.2 (providing that any new project should not be 'substantially different in its nature or objects from the first' except where it would be 'impracticable' to obtain new data subject consent 'by reason of the lapse of time or because of the large number of persons concerned').

22. Ekkehard Mochmann and Paul J Müller, *Report of the Cologne Conference on Emerging Data Protection and the Social Sciences' Need for Access to Data* (University of Cologne 1978) 5.

23. Ibid 6.

24. *The Protection of Privacy and the use of Personal Data for Research: Information Document submitted by the European Science Foundation (ESF)* (Council of Europe Archives, CJ-PD-GT4 (80) 3 revised).

25. Council of Europe, 'Data Protection Convention Explanatory Report' (*COE*, 1981) <https://rm.coe.int/16800ca434> para 59 accessed 16 April 2019.

26. Recommendation R (83) 10 (n 12) Explanatory Memorandum, paras 11–12 (detailing also that representatives of the European Science Foundation participated in the drafting of the Recommendation as observers).

27. Ibid Annex, para 5.1 (providing that access to 'public population registers' should be facilitated to enable researchers 'to obtain the samples required for making surveys' and that '[s]ubject to any limitations which may be imposed by national authorities in certain cases, such samples may reveal name, address, date of birth, sex and occupation').

28. Ibid para 4.4 (establishing that personal data may be released by public or private bodies for the purposes of research not only 'with the consent of the person concerned' but also 'in accordance with other safeguards laid down by domestic law').

29. Ibid para 10.1.

30. *Draft recommendation on the protection of personal data used for scientific research and statistics: Observations submitted by the British expert* (Council of Europe Archives, CJ-PD (82) 16) 3.

31. *Draft recommendation on the protection of personal data used for scientific research and statistics: Summary of observations by the committee's experts* (Council of Europe Archives, CJ-PD (82) 26) 2.

32. Recommendation R (83) 10 (n 12) Explanatory Memorandum, para 40. The reference to such work was made in the context of indicating that an exemption from subject access might not be appropriate here. Meanwhile, the memorandum's direct reference to the definition of 'scientific research' was confined to stating that it 'may be taken to cover both the exact sciences and the social sciences' (para 20).

33. Ibid fn 1 (indicating that Ireland explicitly reserved the right not to comply with the recommendation in its entirety, that the United Kingdom and Germany reserved the right not to comply the recommendation's stipulation that manual as well as automatically processed data should be covered, that Germany in addition reserved the right not to comply with the provisions on informing and obtaining the consent of data subjects (para 3), and encouraging (self-regulatory) boards within the research community (para 10(1)), and finally that Norway reserved the right not to comply with the stipulation that only anonymous data be used where possible (para 2.2)).

34. Full references to all national first-generation data protection laws are set out in Appendix 1.

35. Iceland: Act Concerning the Registration and Handling of Personal Data 1989, art 11.

36. Norway: Act relating to Personal Data Registers (1978), para 7.

37. Netherlands: Data Protection Act 1988, s 33. Given that rectification and objection rights were effectively tied to subject access, these control rights were also effectively disabled in this context.

38. Ibid s 11(2).

39. Finland: Personal Data File Act 30 April 1987/471, s 16.

40. Ibid ss 5 and 7(7).
41. For all the relevant provisions see Ireland: Data Protection Act 1988, ss 2(5) and 5(1)(h).
42. For all the relevant provisions see UK: Data Protection Act 1984, s 33(6) and Sch 1, Pt II, para 7.
43. For example, by referring to the permitted output as being of a statistical nature.
44. See Ireland: Data Protection Act 1988, s 2(5) and UK: Data Protection Act (n 44) Sch 1, Pt II, para 7.
45. Denmark: Private Registers Act 1978, s 1(2).
46. Denmark: Private Registers Act 1987, s 2(3). Analysis of the Danish DPA's Annual Reports suggests that this change was principally prompted by a backlash against a Danish study parallel to the Swedish Projet Metropolit research detailed in section 5.1 of this chapter. See Denmark: Registersynet, årsbok (Registersynet, 1986) 46–67.
47. German data protection law did state that data did not need to be blocked 'where they are indispensable for scientific research' and that identifying data could be stored along-side 'anonymous' data if necessary for scientific purposes. However, neither were true derogations since the first limitation was merely given as an example where 'the over-riding interests of the storage unit or a third person' trumped data protection, whilst the second simply specified allowance for storage when 'necessary to achieve the aims for which the data were stored'. See Germany: Law on Protection against the Misuse of Personal Data in Data Processing (Federal Data Protection Law—BDSG) of the 27 January 1977, ss 14(2) and 36(1).
48. Iceland: Act Concerning the Registration and Handling of Personal Data (1989), art 11.
49. Norway: Act relating to personal data registers of 9 June 1978, para 7.
50. Personal Data File Act (n 39) s 5.
51. Ibid s 7(7).
52. Ibid ss 12(3) and 16.
53. Data Protection Act 1988 (n 37) s 11.
54. Ireland: Data Protection Act (n 44) s 5(1)(h); United Kingdom: Data Protection Act (n 44) s 33(6).
55. Ireland: Data Protection Act (n 44) s (2)(5); United Kingdom: Data Protection Act (n 44) para 7, Pt II, Sch 1.
56. Council Directive 95/46/EC of 24 October 1995 on the protection of individuals with regard to the processing of personal data and on the free movement of such data [1995] OJ L281/31 ('DPD'), arts 6(1)(b) and 6(1)(e).
57. Ibid art 11(2).
58. Ibid art 13(2).
59. Ibid recital 34.
60. Ibid art 32(3).
61. Ibid arts 6(1)(b) and 6(1)(e).
62. Ibid art 11(2).
63. Ibid art 13(2).
64. Ibid recital 34 and arts 8(4) and 8(5).
65. Ibid art 32(3).
66. Ibid art 11(2). See similarly the reference only to providing 'suitable safeguards' as re-gards the transitional saving for data kept solely for historical research detailed earlier (art 32(3)).

67. Ibid recital 34.
68. Ibid recital 29.
69. Ibid art 13(2).
70. European Commission, 'Communication on the Protection of Individuals in Relation to the Processing of Personal Data in the Community and Information Security' COM (1990) 314 final, art 14(6).
71. Ibid art 15(3).
72. European Commission, 'Amended Proposal for a Council Directive on the Protection of Individuals with Regard to the Processing of Personal Data and on the Free Movement of such Data' COM (1992) 422 final, art 14(4) (stating further that such ends must be 'of such a type that the persons concerned can no longer be reasonably identified').
73. Namely Presidency, 'Use of Personal-Data Files in Medical Research (Personal-Record Research) 6454/93' (14 May 1993) <https://resources.law.cam.ac.uk/cipil/travaux/data_protection/38%2014%20May%201993%20Note.pdf> accessed 27 May 2019 (Danish Presidency); AP Holt, 'Research Council: Data Protection/Health Research 574061' (2 December 1993) <https://resources.law.cam.ac.uk/cipil/travaux/data_protection/62%202%20December%201993%20Note.pd> accessed 27 May 2019 (UK); Spanish Delegation, 'Proposal for a Directive on the Protection of Individuals with Regard to the Processing of Personal Data 4859/94' (15 February 1994) <https://resources.law.cam.ac.uk/cipil/travaux/data_protection/69%2015%20February%201994%20Note.pd> accessed 27 May 2019 (Spain), Netherlands Delegation, 'Note de la délégation néerlandaise sur la protection des données médicales SN 2463/94 (SAN)' (26 April 1994) and UK Delegation, 'Draft Directive on the Protection of Individuals with Regard to the Processing of Personal Data 9415/94' (21 September 1994) <https://resources.law.cam.ac.uk/cipil/travaux/data_protection/89%2021%20September%201994%20Note.pdf> accessed 27 May 2019.
74. Thus, the national Statistical Offices of the European Union submitted official evidence during the legislative proceeding outlining the various issues which it saw as arising. See Presidency, 'Amended Proposal for a Council Directive on the Protection of Individuals with Regard to the Processing of Personal Data and the Question of the Processing of Such Data for Statistical Purposes, Particularly in the Area of Scientific Research 8525/94' (20 July 1994) <https://resources.law.cam.ac.uk/cipil/travaux/data_protection/86%2020%20July%201994%20Document.pdf> accessed 28 May 2019.
75. See, for example, the focus on providing safeguarded derogations from purpose limitation in Council Document 8525/94 (n 74). The only somewhat broader mention of this kind of work was located in a paper submitted by Denmark, very late in the legislative proceedings (General Secretariat of the Council, 'Research Related Issues 10934/94' (14 November 1994) <https://resources.law.cam.ac.uk/cipil/travaux/data_protection/94%2014%20November%201994%20Cover%20note.pdf> accessed 28 May 2019), which *inter alia* stated: 'Denmark has stressed strongly during the negotiations that the present wording [as regards research and statistics] is too restrictive. Basic research today is to a large extent based on the establishing and running of registers (databases), especially within medical research, and the directive as proposed may hinder important sociological, historical and medical research as well as statistical work.'

76. As originally proposed by Denmark (Danish Delegation, 'Transmission Note 8217/93 (ANNEX)' (28 July 1993) <https://resources.law.cam.ac.uk/cipil/travaux/data_protection/46%2028%20July%201993%20Note.pdf> accessed 28 May 2019) this provision would have had potential scope comparable to the special expressive purposes regime in art 9. However, its use would have been subject in all case to 'prior notification to the supervisory authorities' who in order to obtain 'adequate guarantees' would have been able to 'lay down detailed provisions for the processing in question'. In practice, therefore, only limited derogations from data protection control were envisaged.

77. In 1997 the Council of Europe Committee of Ministers agreed a new and more detailed recommendation related to statistical purposes. See Council of Europe, 'Recommendation R (97) 18 concerning the protection of personal data collected and processed for statistical purposes' (COE, 1997) <https://rm.coe.int/CoERMPublicCommonSearchServices/DisplayDCTMContent?documentId=090000 1680508d7e> accessed 25 March 2019.

78. Full references to the second-generation data protection laws enacted at national level are set out in Appendix 2.

79. Notably, David Matthew Townend and others, *Implementation of the Data Protection Directive in relation to medical research in Europe* (Ashgate 2004) which provides an exhaustive account of the law in each of then then fifteen EEA States. Although focused on medical research, in most instances the same provisions would have also applied to scientific (and often other) types of research.

80. See e.g. Ireland: Data Protection Act (n 44) s 3(c).

81. The only slight caveats to this were found in Irish and Gibraltarian law which stipulated that data used for 'statistical or research or other scientific purposes' (and also historical purposes in Gibraltar) would not be regarded as having be 'obtained unfairly by reason only' that such purpose was 'not disclosed when it was obtained' so long as 'no damage or distress is, or is likely to be, caused to any data subject'. Gibraltarian law further stipulated that the data not be kept in a form which permits identification of the data subjects. See Ireland: Data Protection Act (n 44) s 2(5) and Gibraltar: Data Protection Act 2004, s 6(1)(3).

82. Even here, whilst a clear majority did set out an almost always qualified derogation from the purpose limitation principle (DPD (n 56) art 6(1)(b)), only a minority expressly did so in relation to temporal minimization (art 6(1)(e)).

83. DPD (n 56) art 11(2).

84. See Italy: Code of Conduct and Professional Practice Applying to Processing of Personal Data for Statistical and Scientific Purposes art 6(2) (providing that so long as the processing does not involve sensitive (special or judicial/criminal data) then provision of information directly to data subjects could be deferred so long as this was necessary for the study). The code of practice for historical purposes contained no such provision. See Italy: Code of Conduct and Professional Practice Regarding the Processing of Personal Data for Historical Purposes.

85. Gibraltar: Data Protection Act (n 81) s 10(4)(a); Ireland: Data Protection Act (n 44), s 2(d)(1)(a); UK: Data Protection Act (n 44), Sch 1, Pt II, para 2(1)(a). Note that as regards

the fairness principle's application to the obtaining of data, Gibraltar and Ireland also set out a derogation that was directly linked to knowledge production. See (n 81).

86. Liechtenstein: Data Protection Act of 14 March 2002, art 5; Luxembourg: Coordinated Text of the Law of 2 August 2002 on the Protection of Persons with regard to the Processing of Personal Data, art 27.

87. In the case of reactive subject access, no such derogation was located in the case of Austria, Belgium, Bulgaria, Croatia, Cyprus, Czechia, Denmark, Germany, Gibraltar, Hungary, Iceland, Lithuania, Romania, Slovakia, Slovenia, or Spain. Meanwhile, as regards sensitive data, such a derogation also appeared generally absent in the case of Bulgaria, Croatia, Czechia, Hungary, Latvia, Liechtenstein, Lithuania, Romania, Slovakia, Slovenia, or Spain. Meanwhile, Ireland did set out such a knowledge facilitation derogation but limited this to 'medical research' (see Ireland: Data Protection Act (n 44), s 2B(1)(viii)). Similarly, French law also only provided a derogation in the case of 'medical research' (as well as statistical research by the National Institute of Statistics and Economic Studies). See France: Act No 78-17 of 6 January 1978 on Information Technology, Data Files and Civil Liberties (as amended), art 8(2)(7) and art 8(2)(8).

88. See DPD (n 56) arts 8(2)(a)–(e).

89. For example, in Belgium, a derogation from the sensitive personal data rules in the interests of 'scientific research' required a permit to be issued by the DPA unless the data in question was pseudonymized. See Belgium: Act of 8 December 1992 on the protection of privacy in relation to the processing of personal data, arts 6(2)(g), 7(2)(k), and 8(1)(e). Meanwhile, in the United Kingdom, a research derogation here required that any processing outside the medical context was in the substantial public interest, was necessary for research purposes, did not support measures or decisions with respect to any particular data subjects other than with explicit consent, and did not cause (and nor was likely to cause) substantial damage or substantial distress to the data subject or to any other person. See UK: Data Protection (Processing of Sensitive Personal Data) Order 2000, para 9.

90. See Council of Europe, *Expert Committee on Data Protection, Interim Report by Working Group No 4* (Council of Europe Archives, CJ-PD (81) 2, 23 June 1981). This report not only detailed the representation noted earlier but also outlined the important role played by Spiro Simitis' memorandum 'Data for Research and Statistics' and his paper 'Data Protection and Research: A Case Study on the Impact of a Control System'. The later was published in volume 29(4) of The American Journal of Comparative Law in 1981. See also Spiro Simitis, 'Impact of Data Protection Laws on Social Science' (1981) 4 Transnational Data Report 13–14.

91. See 'Data Commissioners Discuss Interpol, Social Research, New Media' (1983) 4(8) Transnational Data Report 5–8, 6 (detailing general discussion at meeting); 'Data Commissioners Meeting Spotlights Lack of UK Law' (1982) 5 Transnational Data Report 1–2, (detailing general discussion at meeting); Iceland: Tölvunefndar, *Ársskýrsla* (Ríkisprentsmijðan Gutenberg, 1986) 30 (detailing that treatment of scientific research was discussed) and 'Data Commissions Consider Wider Horizons' (1988) Transnational Data Report 10–16, 15 (detailing discussion of research specific to AIDS).

92. See 'Data Protection Implementation—Accomplishments amid Frustration' (1980) 3(7) Transnational Data Report 1–2, 2 (detailing that the Nordic Commissioners were scheduled to discuss the common treatment of social science research activities at their next meeting); Iceland: Tölvunefndar, *Ársskýrsla* (Ríkisprentsmijðan Gutenberg,1987) 28 (discussion on the gathering of data for scientific research); Iceland: Tölvunefndar, *Ársskýrsla* (Prentvinnsla, 1989) 32 (detailing that Nordic DPAs at their meeting had addressed how approval will be attained in the case of data collection for research purposes).

93. 'Data Commissioners Discuss Interpol, Social Research, New Media, TDF' (n 91) 6.

94. 'Data Commissioners Meeting Spotlights Lack of UK Law' (n 91) 371.

95. Ibid. This stance may have been influenced by the fact that the freedom of expression provisions included in Norwegian data protection law at this time unusually explicitly protected '*fagleksika*' ('subject-based' or even 'discipline-based' work). See Norway: Kongelig resolusjon av 21 Desember 1979.

96. United Kingdom: Data Protection Registrar, *Third Report of the Data Protection Registrar* (Stationary Office 1987) 22. The UK DPA also worked with the peak body of UK universities to produce a data protection code of practice for these entities (9). However, although aware that research processing fell within its scope, this document did not focus on such work beyond robustly upholding a subject access exemption here (so long as any disclosures remained non-identifiable). It did, however, stress the breadth of the meaning of personal data and the need to ensure a comprehensive registering of it and that disciplinary sanctions were possible as regards any infringements committed by either staff or students. The Code also recommended that the latter should only have access to personal data where essential to their work and, even then, only under the supervision of their tutor. See Committee of Vice-Chancellors and Principals, *Data Protection Act 1984: Code of Practice for Universities* (CVCP 1987).

97. Ireland: Data Protection Commissioner, *Annual Report* (Office of the Data Protection Commissioner 1989), Appendix E.

98. France: Commission Nationale de L'Informatique et des Libertés, *4ème Rapport D'Activité (15 Octobre 1982–15 Octobre 1983)* (La Documentation Française 1984) 156.

99. Sweden: Datainspektionen, *Personregister i forskningen* (Allmänna förlaget 1987–88).

100. DPD (n 56) arts 29–30.

101. DPD (n 56) recital 29.

102. Article 29 Working Party, 'Opinion 3/2013 on purpose limitation (WP 203)' (*Europa*, 2 April 2013) <https://ec.europa.eu/justice/article-29/documentation/opinion-recommendation/files/2013/wp203_en.pdf> accessed 3 May 2019, 28.

103. Ibid 30.

104. Ibid 32.

105. Ibid 28.

106. Ibid 29.

107. Ibid 29. As regards the latter, possible examples given included 'information that a deceased individual has been a secret agent or a collaborator of an oppressive regime, a paedophile, perpetrator of crimes, suffered from a mental illness giving rise to stigma, or suffered from a hereditary disease'.

108. Ibid 28.

109. Whilst not constituting guidance as such, the annual reports of the Spanish Catalan DPA did include discussion of medical and historical research. This argued that medical research projects should only use medical record data with the consent of the data subject or where the data had been anonymized (Spain: Agència Catalana de Protecció de Dades, 'Memòria 2007' (*APD*, 2007) <http://www.apd.cat/media/536.pdf> accessed 29 May 2019, 252). Turning to historical research, the DPA suggested that those providing access to data for historical research had to comply with a number of safeguards to protect privacy. They also noted that they had taken part in the 2010 conference 'Privacy and Research: From Obstruction to Construction' organized by the Belgium DPA (see section 3.3) which, according to them, had demonstrated that considerable discrepancies remained between different European countries as regards the level of protection for personal data (ibid 195 and 214–15).

110. Namely, certain medical studies and also undergraduate student projects (and the like) where all processing was consented to by the relevant data subjects.

111. Denmark: Datatilsynet, 'Private forsknings—og statistikprojekter' (*Datatilsynet*, 11 October 2011) <https://web.archive.org/web/20120321131637/http://www.datatilsynet.dk/erhverv/forskere-og-medicinalfirmaer/private-forsknings-og-statistikprojekter/> accessed 29 May 2019.

112. Denmark: Datatilsynet, 'Standard terms for research projects' (*Datatilsynet*, 10 March 2008) <https://web.archive.org/web/20140928095246/http://www.datatilsynet.dk/erhverv/forskere-og-medicinalfirmaer/standard-terms-for-research-projects/> accessed 29 May 2019.

113. Estonia: Data Protection Inspectorate, 'Isikuandmete töötlemine teadusuuringus' (*AKI*, 2013), <http://www.aki.ee/sites/www.aki.ee/files/elfinder/article_files/teadusUuringute_juhis_veebr2013.rtf> accessed 19 June 2019.

114. Malta: Data Protection Commissioner, 'Processing of personal data for research and statistics' (*IDPC*), <https://web.archive.org/web/20140723102726/http://www.idpc.gov.mt/dbfile.aspx/DPCresearchguidelines.pdf> accessed 11 June 2019.

115. Generally it was held that such information should include who is responsible for the research, the purpose of research, what kinds of personal data are involved, from where the data are obtained, the recipients of the data (if any), how long the data will be stored, rights to subject access and rectification, information about IT security, and a statement that participation is voluntary.

116. Sweden: Datainspektionen, 'Personuppgifter i forskningen—vilka regler gäller?' (*Datainspektionen*, 2011) <https://web.archive.org/web/20150316150211/http://www.datainspektionen.se/Documents/faktabroschyr-pul-forskning.pdf> 7–8 accessed 29 May 2019.

117. Finland: Titosuojavaltuutetun Toimisto, 'Teitosuoja ja tieteellinen tutkimus henkilötietolain kannalta' (*Tietosuoja*, 2010) <https://web.archive.org/web/20130809161539/http://tietosuoja.fi/uploads/8evlt8qrbsw3ud.pdf> accessed 29 May 2019.

118. Norway: Datatilsynet, 'Veileder: Bruk av personopplysninger i forskning DEL II Hvilke regler gjelder for forskning?' (*Datatilsynet*, 2005) <https://web.archive.org/web/20140712133322/http://datatilsynet.no/Global/04_veiledere/forskningsinfo_del_II_1_0.pdf> accessed 29 May 2019.

119. Norway: Datatilsynet, 'Veileder: Bruk av personopplysninger i forskning DEL I Meldeplikt eller konsesjonsplikt?' (*Datatilsynet*, 2005) <https://web.archive. org/web/20150426134058/http://www.datatilsynet.no/Global/04_veiledere/ forskningsinfo_del_i_1_0.pdf> accessed 29 May 2019.

120. EU Charter of Fundamental Rights and Freedoms, art 15.

121. Czechia: Office for Personal Data Protection, 'Position No 2/2006 Personal Data Processing in Science' (*UOOU*, 2006) <https://www.uoou.cz/en/vismo/zobraz_dok. asp?id_ktg=1129&p1=1129> accessed 2 August 2013.

122. Greece: Hellenic Data Protection Authority, 'Πληροφορίες για υπεύθυνους επεξεργασίας' (*DPA*, 28 June 2015) <https://web.archive.org/web/20150628180848/ http://www.dpa.gr/portal/page?_pageid=33,131872&_dad=portal&_ schema=PORTAL> accessed 29 May 2019.

123. Slovenia: Information Commissioner, 'Personal data protection' (*IP-RS*) https://www. ip-rs.si/index.php?id=488 21 accessed 1 August 2018.

124. Netherlands: College Bercherming Persoonsgegevens, Publication of Personal Data on the Internet (*Dutch DPA*, 2007) <http://www.dutchdpa.nl/downloads_overig/ en_20071108_richtsnoeren_internet.pdf> 13–14 accessed 8 August 2013.

125. UK: Information Commissioner's Office, Anonymisation: Managing Data Protection Risk Code of Practice (*ICO*, 2012) <http://www.ico.org.uk:80/for_organisations/guid- ance_index/~/media/documents/library/Data_Protection/Practical_application/ anonymisation-codev2.pdf> 45 accessed 13 August 2013.

126. Ibid 8.

127. Ibid 45–47. The guide stated that the other derogations would apply even if data was published in identified form but noted that it was arguably a breach of data protection 'to publish or disclose data for research purposes in a form which identifies individuals where there is an alternative to this'. It further stated that it was good practice to accede to a subject access request even if the derogation did apply.

128. Ibid 47.

129. Cyprus: Γραφείο Επιτρόπου Προστασίας Δεδομένων Προσωπικού Χαρακτήρα, 'ΕΡΩΤΗΜΑ: Συλλογή δεδομένων για ερευνητικούς σκοπούς' (*Dataprotection*, 20 December 2010) <https://web.archive.org/web/20130627085922/http://www.dataprotection.gov.cy/ dataprotection/dataprotection.nsf/All/8F9D97AAAAA55483C22579170030E8F0> ac- cessed 29 May 2019. This guidance mandated DPA notification, the securing of data subject consent after providing him or her with extensive information, ensuring personal data confi- dentiality, and destroying the data after the competition of the research.

130. Germany: Der Bundesbeauftragte für den Datenschutz under die Informtationsfrieheit, 'Medizinische Forschung' (*BFDI*) <http://www.bfdi.bund.de/DE/Datenschutz/ Themen/Gesundheit_Soziales/ForschungArtikel/MedizinischeForschung.html> accessed 11 November 2013. This guidance provided that if the research could not be achieved in another way and was in the interests of patients then it could proceed without data subject consent.

131. Ireland: Data Protection Commissioner, 'Data Protection Guidelines on research in the Health Sector' (*Dataprotection*, November 2007) <https://web.archive. org/web/20171218010531/https://www.dataprotection.ie/documents/guidance/

Health_research.pdf> accessed 27 November 2013. This stipulated that such work be based on consent or use either pseudo-anonymized or fully anonymized data.

132. Portugal: Commissão Nacional de Protecção de Dados, 'Deliberação N° 227 /2007 Aplicável aos tratamentos de dados pessoais efectuados no âmbito de estudos de investigação científica na área da saúde' (*CNPD*, 2007) <https://www.cnpd.pt/bin/orientacoes/DEL227-2007-ESTUDOS-CLINICOS.pdf> accessed 25 August 2013. This Deliberation stated that research projects involving sensitive data required prior licensing from the DPA and set out the conditions under which this would be granted in the field of health research.

133. See Italy: Italian Personal Data Protection Code Legislative Decree No 196 of 30 June 2003, ss 101–03 (processing for historical purposes) and ss 104–10 (processing for statistical or scientific purposes).

134. Italy: Code of Conduct and Professional Practice Applying to Processing of Personal Data for Statistical and Scientific Purposes (2004) recital 1.

135. Ibid arts 15 and 17.

136. Ibid art 8.

137. Ibid art 6. This was to be done through direct contact with the data subject or, where data had been collected for other purposes or from a third party, adopted alternative suitable publicity mechanisms after notifying the DPA in advance of these.

138. Ibid arts 9–10.

139. Italy: Code of Conduct and Professional Practice Regarding the Processing of Personal Data for Historical Purposes (2001) art 1.

140. Ibid recitals 7(a) and (c), art 9(1).

141. Ibid recital 6.

142. Ibid art 11(1). It was, however, added that this was 'without prejudice to the data subjects' right to privacy, personal identity and dignity'.

143. Ibid art 2(b).

144. Italy: Code of Practice Concerning the Processing of Personal Data in the Exercise of Journalistic Activities, recital 2.

145. Belgium: Commission de la Protection de la Vie Privée, 'Le Vade-mecum du Chercheur' (*Privacy Commission*, n.d.) <https://web.archive.org/web/20141109030024/http://www.privacycommission.be/fr/node/7156> accessed 29 May 2019.

146. Belgium: Commission de la Protection de la Vie Privée, 'Vade-mecum Recherche Biomédicale' (*Privacy Commission*, n.d.) <https://web.archive.org/web/20141109030024/http://www.privacycommission.be/fr/node/7156> accessed 29 May 2019.

147. Belgium: Commission de la Protection de la Vie Privée, 'Vade-mecum Recherché Historique' (*Privacy Commission*, n.d.) <https://web.archive.org/web/20141109030024/http://www.privacycommission.be/fr/node/7156> accessed 29 May 2019.

148. Kevin Haggerty, 'Ethics Creep: Governing Social Science Research in the Name of Ethics' (2004) 27(4) Qualitative Sociology 391, 406.

149. Admittedly, it is still quite possible that the hypothetical covert academic would end up recording sensitive data. Indeed, it could plausibly be argued that racism itself could constitute a 'philosophical belief', albeit a highly repugnant one.

150. Namely, Simon Holdaway's seminal covert study which, by posing as police recruit, uncovered 'very negative and suspicious attitudes towards Black youths' within a specific British police force. Whilst reporting these finding in general terms Holdaway ensured that all his publications 'rendered the names and places of officers and locations of incidents to anonymity' and adopted '[s]uitable safeguards' to protect the raw personal data itself. See Simon Holdaway, *Inside the British Police: A Force at Work* (Blackwell 1983) 81, 77.

151. These possibilities were presented to DPAs in the reverse order but have been rearranged for heuristic purposes.

152. See Chart 6.3 (108) and Table 6.1 (109).

153. In sum, both the Italian and Irish DPAs indicated that the activity would be illegal (category (c)), whilst the Liechtenstein and Luxembourg DPAs stated that it would only need to satisfy a strict public interest test (category (a)). The Gibraltarian DPA stated that the legal treatment would be different from the categorical options here but failed to specify what this would be. Finally, the UK DPA did not participate in this part of the questionnaire.

154. Spearman's rank correlations were performed between these responses and (a) the minimum level of substantive statutory data protection stringency applicable to non-journalistic expression (presented in Chapter 10 and listed in Appendix 8); (b) the general stringency of such law as regards journalism (presented in Chapter 5 and listed in Appendix 4); and (c) the simplified measure of the stringency of statutory data protection law as regards covert journalism (presented in Chapter 6 and also listed in Appendix 4). In each case the results were moderately negative rather than positive, although only in the first case was (one-tailed) significance achieved. In sum correlations were −0.300, −0.245, and −0.167 and the (one-tailed) confidence values 0.088, 0.136, and 0.228.

155. Iceland: Tölvunefndar, *Ársskýrsla* (Ríkisprentsmijðan Gutenberg, 1986) 21–22.

156. Ibid 13–14.

157. France: Commission Nationale de L'Informatique et des Libertés, *5e Rapport D'Activité (15 Octobre 1983–31 Décembre 1984)* (La Documentation Française 1984) 117–18. In this same year, the CNIL rejected an application to use the electoral register to generate a sample for a project on the consumption of medicine by the elderly, arguing that this database should only be used for electoral purposes.

158. France: Commission Nationale de L'Informatique et des Libertés, *16e Rapport D'Activité* (La Documentation Française 1995) 373–80. In sum, the researcher had to sign a contract with INSEE, agree not to pass the data on to any third party and ensure that only findings concerning groups above 5,000 inhabitants were published.

159. Commission Nationale de L'Informatique et des Libertés (n 98) 156 (own translation).

160. Anne Akeroyd, 'Ethnology, Personal Data and Computers: The Implications of Data Protection Legislation for Qualitative Social Research' (1988) 1 Studies in Qualitative Methodology 179, 212.

161. Quoted ibid 191. Citing the same authors, Akeroyd also noted with concern the requirement that 'at the end of a project, data registered by electronic aids or other media must be destroyed unless they are transferred to the social science data archive; and even then identifiers will be deleted unless the research can establish an acceptable likelihood that the data will be useful for future research' (197).

162. Ibid 210.
163. Ibid 190–91.
164. Ibid 211.
165. Ibid 190.
166. Ibid.
167. David Flaherty, *Protecting Privacy in Surveillance Societies* (University of North Carolina Press 1989) 111.
168. Sweden: Datainspektionens, *Årsbok 1989/90* (Allmänna förlaget 1990) 202–203.
169. Moreover, the former category was kept firmly separate from another research area which was probed, namely 'epidemiological medical research', which lies at a considerable remove from the themes pursued in this book and so it is not explored here. The three research areas included covered much of the field of academic work which interface strongly with data protection. Nevertheless, although the dividing line between social science and the humanities is highly contested, it would in retrospect to have been worthwhile asking also about enforcement specifically in relation the latter type of activity (e.g. contemporary historical research).
170. Namely, the Czechia and Spanish Catalonian DPA jurisdictions.
171. In sum, the three measures from left to right become 0.047 (sig.: 0.401), 0.010 (sig.: 0.478), and 0.085 (sig.: 0.324).
172. Similar to the journalistic enforcement results presented in Chapter 7, it could be argued that the enforcement totals for the Cypriot, Maltese, and Eastern European DPAs should be augmented to account of the years when they were not members of the EU/EEA and therefore 'missed' an opportunity engage in enforcement. If this is done, however, then all the patterns presented remain essentially stable. In sum, the seven results from left to right become 0.223 (sig. 0.114), 0.254 (sig. 0.084*), 0.272 (sig. 0.069*), 0.170 (sig. 224), 0.133 (sig. 0.277), 0.083 (sig. 0.353), –0.075 (sig. 0.367).
173. See n 114, 118, and 116.
174. For example, the 2010 annual report of the Belgium DPA simply stated that 18/0.64 per cent of its cases that year concerning scientific research, whilst one concerned historical research. See Belgium: Commission de la Protection de la Vie Privée, 'Rapport Annuel 2010' (*Privacy Commission*, 2010) <https://web.archive.org/web/20120829001447/http://www.privacycommission.be/sites/privacycommission/files/documents/rapport-annuel-2010.pdf> accessed 20 May 2019, 80. Meanwhile, its 2011 report similarly stated that 24/0.84 per cent of its cases concerned scientific research. See Belgium: Commission de la Protection de la Vie Privée, 'Rapport Annuel 2011' (*Privacy Commission*, 2011) <https://web.archive.org/web/20120829001519/http://www.privacycommission.be/sites/privacycommission/files/documents/rapport-annuel-2011.pdf> accessed 20 May 2019, 92.
175. See Chapter 7, section 2.1 and Chapter 10, section 3.2.
176. 'Poland in uproar over leak of spy files' *Guardian Online* (London, 5 February 2005) <https://www.theguardian.com/world/2005/feb/05/poland> accessed 20 May 2019.
177. Poland: Generalny Inspektor Ochrony Danych Osobowych, 'Judgment of the Voivodeship Administrative Court in the Case of the Decision of the Inspector General for Data Protection Concerning the Institute of National Remembrance' (*GIODO*, 20060) <http://www.giodo.gov.pl/259/id_art/347/j/en/> accessed 29 August 2013.

178. 'Historycy IPN kontra GIODO' *Gazeta.pl Wiadomości* (Warsaw, 2 September 2005) <http://wiadomosci.gazeta.pl/wiadomosci/1,114873,2897035.html#ixzz2ZljNfTEn> accessed 12 June 2019.

179. Generalny Inspektor Ochrony Danych Osobowych (n 177).

180. Az Adatvédelmi Biztos, 'Beszámolója 2005' (*NAIH*, 2005) <http://www.naih.hu/files/Adatvedelmi-biztos-beszamoloja-2005.PDF> 301–04 accessed 29 May 2019. For action on this issue prior to when Hungary joined the EU/EEA see Az Adatvédelmi Biztos, 'Beszámolója 2003' (*NAIH*, 2003) <http://www.naih.hu/files/Adatvedelmi-biztos-beszamoloja-2003.PDF> 118–19 accessed 29 May 2019.

181. Az Adatvédelmi Biztos 2005 (n 180) 438.

182. Ibid 277.

183. Ibid 438.

184. Az Adatvédelmi Biztos, 'Beszámolója 2006' (*NAIH*, 2006) <http://www.naih.hu/files/Adatvedelmi-biztos-beszamoloja-2006.PDF> 122 accessed 29 May 2019.

185. Bulgaria: Комичията За Защита На Личните Данни, 'Становище по искане с рег.№ 2640/10.06.2011г' (*CPDP*, 26 June 2011) <https://www.cpdp.bg/?p=element_view&aid=542> accessed 12 June 2019. Although this historian appears to have been attempting to engage in academic inquiry, it seems unlikely that he or she had an academic affiliation.

186. Germany: Unabhängige Landeszentrum für Datenschutz Schleswig-Holstein, 'Tätigkeitsbericht 2013' (*Datenschutzzentrum*, 2013) <https://www.datenschutzzentrum.de/tb/tb34/uld-34-taetigkeitsbericht-2013.pdf> 53 accessed 12 June 2019. Considerably more interventionist actions were located in this broad area, but it is likely that these related to biomedical rather than social research. For example, in 2012 the Norwegian DPA fined the University of Bergen 250,000 kroner (approximately €25,000) after a research project used survey data (which included sensitive information) on some 13,000 people held by the Public Health Institute without requisite permission. See Norway: Datatilsynet, 'Universitetet i Bergen ilagt overtredelsesgebyr' (*Datatilsynet*, 2012) <https://web.archive.org/web/20140710133206/http://www.datatilsynet.no/Regelverk/Tilsynsrapporter/2012/Helseopplysinger-om-13-000-personer-brukt-uten-tillatelse/> accessed 29 May 2019.

187. Portugal: Commissão Nacional de Protecção de Dados, 'Autorização N°12464/2011' (*CNPD*, 2011) <http://www.cnpd.pt/bin/decisoes/aut/10_12464_2011.pdf> accessed 1 August 2013. The DPA argued that since the data collected included that related to illegitimacy it could result in a data subject being subject to negative discrimination in the absence of such safeguards.

188. Portugal: Commissão Nacional de Protecção de Dados, 'Autorização N°1853/2009' (*CNPD*, 2009) <https://www.cnpd.pt/bin/decisoes/Aut/10_1853_2009.pdf> accessed 29 May 2019.

189. Portugal: Commissão Nacional de Protecção de Dados, 'Autorização N°6622/2011' (*CNPD*, 2011) <http://www.cnpd.pt/bin/decisoes/aut/10_6622_2011.pdf> accessed 29 May 2019.

Chapter 12

1. Council Regulation 2016/679/EU of 27 April 2016 on the protection of natural persons with regard to the processing of personal data and on the free movement of such data, and repealing Directive 95/46/EC [2016] OJ L119/1, recital 153; cf art 85(2) ('GDPR').

2. Ibid arts 89(1) and (2)

3. *Sapan v Turkey* App no 44102/04 (ECtHR, 8 June 2010) para 31.

4. European Commission, 'Proposal for a Regulation of the European Parliament and of the Council on the protection of individuals with regard to the processing of personal data and on the free movement of such data (General Data Protection Regulation)' COM (2012) 11 final, art 80 and recital 121.

5. See GDPR (n 1) art 85(2) and recital 153.

6. See European Commission (n 4) art 80 (note that it does not mention Chapter IX on 'special data processing situations' which included the provisions set out for historical, statistical, and scientific research purposes).

7. Ibid art 83.

8. UK: Economic and Social Research Council, 'Response to the European Commission's proposed European Data Protection Regulation (COM(2012) 11 final)' (*ESRC*, 21 February 2013) <https://esrc.ukri.org/files/about-us/policies-and-standards/esrc-response-to-the-european-commission-s-proposed-european-data-protection-regulation-2013/ accessed 29 May 2019, 2. I was involved not only in drafting this paper but I have also been involved in other initiatives (including as cited elsewhere in this chapter) which were designed to ensure that academic scholarship was protected as a type of special expression within European data protection law.

9. See Council of the European Union, 'Document 10391/15' (*Europa*, 8 July 2015) <http://data.consilium.europa.eu/doc/document/ST-10391-2015-INIT/en/pdf> art 80 accessed 28 April 2019 .

10. Ibid art 80(2).

11. Wellcome Trust, 'Academic Research Perspective on the European Commission, Parliament and Council Texts of the Proposal for a General Data Protection Regulation—2012/0011(COD)' (*Wellcome*, July 2015) <https://wellcome.ac.uk/sites/default/files/research-perspective-data-protecton-regulation-proposal-wellcome-jul15.pdf> 10 accessed 29 May 2019. This document also noted that the European Parliament's text similarly created 'scope for such derogations but is less clear since it does not include the word "academic".

12. GDPR (n 1) art 89.

13. Ibid art 89(1). At a minimum the GDPR itself specified that the safeguards 'shall ensure that technical and organisational measures are in place in particular in order to ensure respect for the principle of data minimisation'.

14. Ibid art 5(b).

15. Ibid art 5(e).

16. Ibid art 17(3)(d). The GDPR text included various other interpretative glosses within this area that, in general, were designed to facilitate such processing within heavily safeguarded and qualified parameters. See recitals 33, 50, 62, 65, 73, 113, 156–162, and art 14(5)(b).

17. Ibid art 9(2)(j). In sum, such a provision was to be 'proportionate to the aim pursued, respect the essence of the right to data protection and provide for suitable and specific measures to safeguard the fundamental rights and the interests of the data subject'. This provision was not directly replicated in art 10, which set down rules applicable to data relating to criminality.

18. Ibid art 89(2). In relation to 'archiving purposes in the public interest' only, derogations were also specifically enabled as regards the right to data portability and the right following a *bona fide* request for the rectification, erasure, or restriction of data to obtain information on which recipients had received this data and, unless this proved constituted a disproportionate effort or proved impossible, to have information on the rectification, erasure or restriction communicated by the controller to each recipient. See art 89(3).

19. Ibid art 23.

20. Ibid art 10. This article did however state that a 'comprehensive register of criminal convictions shall be kept only under the control of official authority'.

21. The DPD's main provisions specific to knowledge facilitation were discussed at length in Chapter 11. Meanwhile, its principal general limitation provisions were set out in arts 8(4)–(5) as regards the sensitive data rules and art 13(1) in other cases: Council Directive 95/46/EC of 24 October 1995 on the protection of individuals with regard to the processing of personal data and on the free movement of such data [1995] OJ L281/31 ('DPD').

22. See European Commission (n 4) art 9(2)(g) (general restrictions possibility as regards the sensitive data rules), art 9(2)(i) (knowledge facilitation legal basis to process sensitive data), art 21 (overarching general restrictions clause), and art 83 (overarching knowledge facilitation clause).

23. Ibid art 9(1)(i).

24. Ibid art 83(3).

25. All three texts may be found in Council of the European Union Document (n 9). The most relevant provisions are art 9 (special/sensitive data), 9a (criminal data), 21 (general restrictions), 83 (an overarching knowledge facilitation clause), and 83a (a specific derogatory provision for archive services).

26. References to all State laws implementing the GDPR are set out in Appendix 3.

27. Namely, Croatia, Hungary, and Spain.

28. As set out in Chapter 8, this provision in any case only provides for a qualified derogation from one provision in the GDPR, namely subject access. In contrast, albeit subject to certain restrictive conditions, Liechtenstein law does set out knowledge facilitation derogations from the sensitive personal data rules, subject access, and various data subject rights. Therefore, uniquely amongst those States that have legislated in both areas, Liechtenstein appears to treat special expression such as journalism less favourably that ordinary knowledge facilitation purposes such as scientific research. See Liechtenstein: Datenschutzgesetz, arts 25 and 27.

29. Thus, ss 9c and 57 of the Staatsvertrag für Rundfunk und Telemedien only sets out a derogatory scheme for broadcasters and the Press. Meanwhile, the federal German Data Protection Act (BDGS) currently makes no mention of special expression.

30. See Rhineland-Palatinate: Landesmediengesetz (LMG) Rheinland-Pfalz, s 13; Schleswig-Holstein: Landespressegesetz Schleswig-Holstein, s 10; and Staatsvertrag über das Medienrecht in Hamburg und Schleswig-Holstein, s 37.

31. See Brandenburg: Brandenburgisches Datenshutzgesetz (BbgDSG) s 29 and Mecklenburg-Vorpommern: Landesdatenshutzgesetz—DSG M-V, s 12.

32. Through Germany's notification to the European Commission under art 85(3), Brandenburg has lodged its derogation for scientific and historical research performed by public authorities under the special expression regime. However, although notable for addressing the need for historical research to publish identified data in certain circumstances, this derogatory scheme essentially falls largely within the safeguarded knowledge facilitation scheme established under art 89 rather than art 85 of the GDPR. See Germany: 'Notifizierungspflichtige Vorschriften Deutschlands gemäß der Verordnung (EU) 2016/679' (*Europa*, 27 September 2018) <https://ec.europa.eu/info/sites/info/files/de_notification_articles_49.5_51.4_83.9_84.2_85.3_88.3_90.2_publish.pdf> 10 accessed 29 May 2019

33. Iceland: Lög um persónuvernd og vinnslu persónuupplýsinga, art 6.

34. Denmark: Databeskyttelsesloven, art 3(8).

35. Ibid art 3(1).

36. Within the typology presented in Chapter 8, the only derogation it has set out here is an absolute exemption from proactive transparency when data is being collected directly from the subject themselves (provision (vi)) and the duty to register processing (xvii), as well as a minimal derogation just from the obligation to provide not access to, but rather a copy of, the data in response to a subject access request (viii). See Poland: Ustawa z dnia 10 maja 2018 r o ochronie danych osobowych, art 2(2). In other contexts, the same derogations apply as those elucidated in Chapter 8. These, in sum, subject special expression only to the data export regime (xviii) and restrictions on criminal-related data (xv)—the latter almost certainly only as a result of a drafting error.

37. The Estonian statutory derogation applicable to non-journalistic special expression is also different from that applicable to the media in that it only explicitly requires consideration of whether the processing causes 'kahjusta ülemäära' ('excessive damage') to the rights of the data subject. See Estonia: Personal Data Protection Act 2018, s 5. However, this continues to constitute a permissive public interest test and so the overall stringency measures remain the same.

38. France: Ordonnance n° 2018-1125, art 80

39. Ibid art 19(III)

40. Austria: Federal Act concerning the Protection of Personal Data, art 9.

41. Italy: Decreto Legislativo 30 giugno 2003, n196 (as amended) art 138.

42. The qualification 'minimum' is used advisedly since, as per previous discussion within this section, the law applicable to academic (as opposed to literary and artistic) expression remains much more stringent in Denmark, Germany Rhineland-Palatinate, and Germany Mecklenburg-Vorpommern.

43. Comparing the two data sources, it can be seen that the minimum substantive stringency of the law shifts in Austria from 0.53 to 0.65, in Belgium from 0.48 to 0.38, in Denmark from 0.15 to 0, in France from 0.65 to 0.54, in the two specified German *Länder* from 0.03 to 0, and in Italy from 0.69 to 0.71. Meanwhile, the minimum regulatory supervision shifts in Denmark from 0.5 to 0 and in France from 0.5 to 1. The combined regulatory stringency variable which take into account both of these primary measures also shifts in these cases.

44. See Chapter 8, section 5 and especially Table 8.4 (176).

45. GDPR (n 1) art 89.

46. The complex position of Germany in this respect has already been noted. Only the journalistic media are safeguarded at national level and, although some local *Länder* have gone further, it seems that most have still not included reference to academic expression.

47. No mention of this kind of processing by the private sector was found within implementing law in Croatia, Hungary, Lithuania, Poland, or Slovakia. Meanwhile, such a provision was found within Cypriot law but this was confined to setting out additional safeguards for such processing. See Cyprus: Ο περί της Προστασίας των Φυσικών Προσώπων Έναντι της Επεξεργασίας των Δεδομένων Προσωπικού Χαρακτήρα και της Ελεύθερης Κυκλοφορίας των Δεδομένων αυτών Νόμος του 2018, s 31.

48. See, for example, Gibraltar: Data Protection 2004 (Amendment) Regulations 2018, sch 1, pt 3; Netherlands: Wet van 16 mei 2018 Uitvoeringswet Algemene verordening gegevensbescherming, s 3.2; and UK: Data Protection Act 2018, sch 1, pt 3.

49. GDPR (n 1) art 5.

50. Ibid arts 13–14.

51. Ibid arts 44–49.

52. Ibid arts 51–84.

53. In addition to the six States which have failed to set out any additional derogations (see n 47), France (outside of medical research), Latvia, Malta, and Romania have all failed to set out a knowledge generation vires for processing sensitive data.

54. GDPR (n 1) art 89(1).

55. UK: Data Protection Act (n 48) s 19.

56. Case C-518/07 *Commission v Germany* [2010] ECR I-1885, para 23.

57. Council of Europe, 'Data Protection Convention Explanatory Report' (*COE*, 1981) <https://rm.coe.int/16800ca434> accessed 16 April 2019, para 58.

58. European Commission, 'Communication on the Protection of Individuals in Relation to the Processing of Personal Data in the Community and Information Security' COM (1990) 314 final, art 19.

59. DPD (n 21) art 9.

60. GDPR (n 1) art 85(2).

61. Ibid recital 151.

62. Case C-345/17 *Buivids* EU:C:2019:122, para 53.

63. It follows that, at least in principle, non-professional individuals (e.g. some bloggers) and also some 'new' media actors (e.g. certain discussion forums) may often fall within special expression (paras 55–56). Detailed consideration of this question, as well as how the 'new' media should be regulated under data protection, fall outside the scope of this study. However, the interface between this and the regulation of traditional publishers will be explored in the book's conclusion.

64. cf *Buivids* (n 62) para 58.

65. George Brock, *Out of Print: Newspapers, Journalism and the Business of News in the Digital Age* (Kogan Page 2013) 16.

66. GDPR (n 1) art 83.

67. Ibid art 85(2).

68. See especially Chapter 9, section 3.3.

69. Some work in the social science and humanities might also be considered to constitute 'archiving purposes in the public interest'. However, as with the institutional media, the special expression derogation must still apply at least when either a publicly available archive only includes content that has already been published as special purposes expression or a restricted archive or library of records is only used as a direct resource for future publications.

70. *Sapan v Turkey* App no 44102/04 (ECtHR, 8 June 2010) para 34.

71. *Sorguç v Turkey* App no 17089/03 (ECtHR, 23 June 2009) para 34. The Council of Europe's Recommendation 1762 (2006) on Academic Freedom and University Autonomy (which was noted in Chapter 3) also states that 'academic freedom in research and in training should guarantee freedom of expression and of action, freedom to disseminate information and freedom to conduct research and distribute knowledge and truth without restriction'. See Council of Europe, Parliamentary Assembly, 'Recommendation 1762 (2006) Academic Freedom and University Autonomy' (*COE*, 2006) <http://assembly. coe.int/nw/xml/XRef/Xref-XML2HTML-en.asp?fileid=17469&lang=en> accessed 15 June 2019.

72. Kevin Haggerty, 'Ethics Creep: Governing Social Science Research in the Name of Ethics' (2004) 27(4) Qualitative Sociology 391, 406.

73. Antoon De Baets, 'A Historian's View on the Right to be Forgotten' (2016) 30(1–2) International Review of Law, Computers and Technology 57, 64.

74. 45 CFR pt 45 (2009). Note that the revised Regulations issued in 2018 have addressed a number of these concerns by excluding from their ambit '[s]cholarly and journalistic activities (e.g. oral history, journalism, biography, literary research, and historical scholarship), including the collection and use of information, that focus directly on the specific individuals about whom the information is collected'. See 45 CFR pt 46 (2018) s 102(l)(1).

75. Linda Shopes, 'Oral History, Human Subjects, and Institutional Review Boards' (*Oral History*, 2009) <https://www.oralhistory.org/about/do-oral-history/oral-history-and-irb-review/> accessed 29 May 2019.

76. Case C-73/07 *Tietosuojavaltuutettu v Satakunnan Markkinapörssi Oy and Satamedia Oy* [2007] ECR I-7075 para 61.

77. This principle of non-discrimination when exercising a fundamental right or freedom is explicitly laid down in article 14 of the European Convention on Human Rights.

78. Robert Dingwall, 'Confronting the Anti-Democrats: The Unethical Nature of Ethical Regulation in Social Science' (2006) 1(1) Medical Sociology Online 51, 52.

79. Ibid 52.

80. Sarah Dyer and David Demeritt, 'Un-ethical Review? Why it is Wrong to Apply the Medical Model of Research Governance to Human Geography' (2009) 33(1) Progress in Human Geography 46, 54.

81. *Buivids* (n 62) para 68.

82. See, in particular, *Sunday Times v United Kingdom* (1979) 2 EHRR 245.

83. *Re S (a child)* [2004] UKHL 47, [2005] 1 AC 593 [17] (Lord Bingham) (addressing the need for a similar balance between freedom of expression under Article 10 and the right to respect for private life under Article 8 of the European Convention on Human Rights).

84. EU Charter of Fundamental Rights and Freedoms, art 51(2).

85. See David Erdos, 'Constructing the Labyrinth: The Impact of Data Protection on the Development of "Ethical" Regulation in Social Science' (2011) 15(1) Information, Communication and Society 104.

86. Ruben Andersson, 'The Need for a New Research Ethics Regime' (2019) 407 Oxford Magazine 13, 14.

87. GDPR (n 1) art 40

88. Dyer and Demeritt (n 80) 47–48.

89. Ibid 54.

90. Ibid 55.

91. Ibid 57.

92. Dingwall (n 78) 53.

93. Martyn Hammersley, 'Against the Ethicists: On the Evils of Ethical Regulation' (2011) 12(3) International Journal of Social Research Methodology 211, 220.

94. Haggerty (n 72) 412.

95. Dingwall (n 78) 57.

96. See Erdos (n 85).

97. Andersson (n 86) 13.

98. Ibid 14.

99. Ibid 13.

100. Association for Social Anthropologists and others, 'Joint Statement on the Implementation of GDPR in UK Universities' (RGS, 2018) <https://www.rgs.org/geography/news/joint-statement-on-the-implementation-of-gdpr-in-u/> accessed 29 May 2019.

101. See 'Tutorials' (Privacy and Research, 22 November 2010) <https://web.archive.org/web/20120120230427/http://www.privacyandresearch.be/programme> accessed 29 May 2019.

102. Case C-131/12 Google Spain SL and Google Inc v Agencia Española de Protección de Datos (AEPD) [2014] 3 CMLR 50, para 38.

103. GPDR (n 1) art 77.

104. I am currently a member of the University of Cambridge Research Ethics Committee, the University of Cambridge Humanities and Social Science Research Ethics Committee, and I am also an independent ethics advisor of a Horizon 2020 project at the University of Cambridge. However, all views expressed here reflect my personal perspective only rather than that of any of these groupings or institutions.

105. For example, via arts 40–41 of the GDPR (n 1). Similarly to public broadcasters pursuing professional journalism, it may even be argued that the monitoring body clause (Article 41) cannot include public universities and other similar institutions since Article 41(4) states that it shall not apply to processing carried out by public authorities and bodies. However, given that these bodies will be pursuing similar freedom of expression activity to that of a purely private academic institution, the better argument is that they should be treated as falling within the private as opposed to the public sector here.

106. Neil Gunningham, 'Enforcement and Compliance Strategies' in Robert Baldwin, Martin Cave and Martin Lodge, The Oxford Handbook of Regulation (Oxford University Press 2010) 126.

107. However, in light of the fact that DPA guidance is rightly challengeable in court, it would be illegitimate for a DPA to require that these actors necessarily commit to following such guidance in the future.
108. GDPR (n 1) art 4(23).
109. Ibid art 4(23).
110. Ibid arts 60–76.
111. Ibid art 78.
112. Ibid art 70(1)(u).
113. Ibid art 70(1)(e).
114. Ibid art 85(2).
115. DPD (n 21) art 9.
116. GDPR (n 1) art 89.

Chapter 13

1. Council Regulation 2016/679/EU of 27 April 2016 on the protection of natural persons with regard to the processing of personal data and on the free movement on such data, and repealing Directive 95/46/EC [2006] OJ L199/1 ('GDPR'), arts 40–41.
2. Daniel Solove, *The Future of Reputation* (Yale University Press 2007) 21.
3. Ibid 21.
4. José Van Dijck, *The Culture of Connectivity: A Critical History of Social Media* (Oxford University Press 2013) 4.
5. Solove (n 2) 9.
6. Brian Leveson, *Inquiry into the Culture, Practices and Ethics of the Press* (HC 2012, 780–I).
7. Ibid 78.
8. Ibid 76.
9. Lee C Bollinger, *Uninhibited, Robust, and Wide-Open: A Free Press for New Century* (Oxford University 2010) 109–10.
10. Ibid 110.
11. Robert Dingwall, 'The Ethical Case Against Ethical Regulation in Humanities and Social Science Research' (2008) 1(3) Journal of the Academy of Social Sciences 1, 8.
12. Ibid 10.
13. George Brock, *Out of Print: Newspapers, Journalism and the Business of News in the Digital Age* (Kogan Page 2013) 141–42.
14. Ibid 16.
15. 'Ramsbo v Public Prosecutor in Stockholm (PUL-B 293-00) (B 293-00)' (*Bankrattsforeningen*, 12 June 2011) <http://www.bankrattsforeningen.org.se/hddomslut.html> accessed 4 January 2019, 10.
16. Solove (n 2) 24.
17. Ibid 41.
18. 'Google Alerts - Monitor the Web for Interesting New Content' (*Google*, 2011) <http://www.google.com/alerts> accessed 27 July 2012.

19. Joris Van Hoboken, 'The Proposed Right to be Forgotten Seen from the Perspective of Our Right to Remember' (*NYU*, 2013) <http://www.law.nyu.edu/sites/default/files/up-load_documents/VanHoboken_RightTo%20Be%20Forgotten_Manuscript_2013.pdf> 28 accessed 4 January 2018.

20. Council Directive 2000/31/EC of 8 June 2000 on certain legal aspects of information society services, in particular electronic commerce, in the Internal Market ('Directive on electronic commerce') [2000] OJ L178/1, art 14.

21. Ibid recital 48. See generally Council of Europe, 'Council Recommendation CM/Rec(2018)2 of the Committee of Ministers to Member States on the Role and Responsibilities of Internet Intermediaries' (*COE*, 7 March 2018) <https://search.coe.int/cm/Pages/result_details.aspx?ObjectID=0900001680790e14> accessed 29 May 2019

22. GDPR (n 1) art 60–76.

23. Case C-131/12 *Google Spain SL and Google Inc v Agencia Española de Protección de Datos (AEPD)* [2014] 3 CMLR 50, para 85. Whilst the English translation only stated that this derogation 'does not appear' to be engaged here, the authoritative Spanish version used the much more definitive phrase that it was '*no es el caso*' ('not the case') that this derogation was engaged.

24. Case C-136/17 *GC et al v CNIL* (10 January 2019) Opinion of AG M Maciej Szpunar, EU:C:2019:14 para 1.

25. GDPR (n 1) arts 23, 9(2)(g) and 10.

26. Ibid art 85(2).

27. Ibid art 5.

28. Ibid art 6.

29. Ibid arts 51–76. Note, however, that the exercise of DPA powers may still be subject to 'appropriate safeguards, including effective judicial remedy and due process' as set out in Member State law (art 58(4)).

30. *Google Spain* (n 23) para 80.

31. Ibid para 81.

32. Ibid para 97.

33. Ibid para 97.

34. As stated by Brock (n 13) 138, Google News is an aggregating service which (as of early 2010s) 'scan[ned] 50,000 sources in 30 languages and claim[ed] to connect one billion users per week to news stories'.

35. *Delfi AS v Estonia* (2014) 58 EHRR 29, para 96.

36. Spain: Sentencia del Tribunal Supremo (Sala de lo Civil) 15 October 2015, ES:TS:2015:4132. Note, however, that in C-291/13 *Papasavvas v O Filelefheros Dimosia Etairia Ltd* [2014] 9 WLUK 273 the CJEU clearly ruled that the specific 'intermediary' liability shields set out in Directive 2010/31/EC (n 20) could not apply to an online newspaper archive since the company 'has, in principle, knowledge about the information which it posts and exercises control over that information' (para 45).

37. Council Directive (EU) 2018/1808 of 14 November 2018 amending Directive 2010/13/EU on the coordination of certain provisions laid down by law, regulation or administrative action in Member States concerning the provision of audiovisual media services (Audiovisual Media Services Directive) in view of changing market realities [2018] OJ L303/69, recital 23. The date for implementation is set down in art 2.

38. Ibid recital 25.

39. Ibid recital 23.

40. Ibid recital 6.

41. UK: Information Commissioner's Office, 'Social Networking and Online Forums – When Does the DPA Apply?' (*ICO*, 2013) <https://ico.org.uk/media/for-organisations/documents/1600/social-networking-and-online-forums-dpa-guidance.pdf> 10 accessed 29 May 2019.

42. Ibid 10.

43. Ibid 15.

44. UK, Information Commissioner's Office, 'Online Safety' (*ICO*) <https://ico.org.uk/your-data-matters/online/social-networking/> accessed 29 May 2019.

45. *Google Spain* (n 23) para 77.

46. 'Transparency Report: Search Removals Under European Privacy Law' (*Google*) <https://transparencyreport.google.com/eu-privacy/overview> accessed 29 May 2019.

47. Ibid.

48. For example, based on figures obtained which related to the first three years of the implementation of *Google Spain* (n 23), Google received 108,000 deindexing claims relating to around 267,000 URLs from UK residents (or who otherwise lodged their claims in the United Kingdom). It would appear that 61 per cent of these were rejected. However, only around 800 of these claims (or 1.2 per cent) were further considered by the UK DPA and formal enforcement action was taken in only one case. See David Erdos, 'Unlikely to be Forgotten: Assessing the Implementation of Google Spain in the UK Three Years On' (*Blog Droit Européean*, 2017) <https://blogdroiteuropeen.com/2017/05/29/unlikely-to-be-forgotten-assessing-the-implementation-of-google-spain-in-the-uk-three-years-on-by-david-erdos/> accessed 29 May 2019.

49. *Google Spain* (n 23) para 97.

50. See *Google Spain* (n 23) and *Delphi AS v Estonia* (2016) 62 EHRR 6 para 147 (which appeared to endorse the understanding of the CJEU in *Google Spain* on this crucial point).

51. *F. G. and J. H. v United Kingdom* no. 44787/98 (2001) 46 EHRR 51, para 56.

52. GDPR (n 1) arts 40–1.

53. *Google Spain* (n 23) para 34.

54. Statement of the Council's reasons: Council Position (EU) No 6/2016 at first reading with a view to the adoption of a Regulation of the European Parliament and of the Council on the protection of natural persons with regard to the processing of personal data and on the free movement of such data, and repealing Directive 95/46/EC (General Data Protection Regulation) [2016] OJ C159/1, 5.6.

55. Dave Lee, 'Google ruling "astonishing", says Wikipedia founder Wales' (*BBC News*, 14 May 2014) <https://www.bbc.co.uk/news/technology-27407017> accessed 29 May 2019.

56. BBC, 'EU court backs "right to be forgotten" in Google case' (*BBC News*, 13 May 2014) <https://www.bbc.co.uk/news/world-europe-27388289> accessed 29 May 2019.

57. Spiros Simitis, 'Legal and Political Context of the Protection of Personal Data and Privacy' (Speech in Montreal, September 1997) Council of Europe Archives (T-PD (97) 17).

Index